The House Where My Soul Lives

Walker signing a copy of *Jubilee*

The House Where My Soul Lives

The Life of Margaret Walker

MARYEMMA GRAHAM

OXFORD
UNIVERSITY PRESS

UNIVERSITY PRESS

Oxford University Press is a department of the University of Oxford. It furthers
the University's objective of excellence in research, scholarship, and education
by publishing worldwide. Oxford is a registered trade mark of Oxford University
Press in the UK and certain other countries.

Published in the United States of America by Oxford University Press
198 Madison Avenue, New York, NY 10016, United States of America.

CIP data is on file at the Library of Congress

ISBN 978–0–19–534123–2

DOI: 10.1093/oso/9780195341232.001.0001

Printed by Sheridan Books, Inc., United States of America

To Mom and Marona

In Memoriam:
Norma Grice Alexander 1953–2021
Margaret Alexander Williams 1954–2022
Sigismund Alexander 1952–2022
Marion Alexander Coleman 1944–2022

Contents

Acknowledgements and Sources ix

Timeline xv

Introduction: The Woman We Thought We Knew xxiii

Acronyms and Abbreviations xli

PART I. SOUTHERN SONG, 1915–1932 (BIRMINGHAM AND NEW ORLEANS)

1. In This Place Where I Was Born 3

2. A Preacher's Daughter 24

3. The Fire Burning Within 39

4. Get Her Out of the South 65

5. Goodbye New Orleans 82

PART II. GROWING OUT OF SHADOW, 1933–1938 (CHICAGO)

6. The House Where My Soul Lives 93

7. Brave New World 109

8. Colleagues and Comrades: South Side Writers 130

9. Marriage Is a Green Apple 155

10. The Author of "For My People" 164

PART III. NO ENEMIES SAVE MYSELF, 1938–1943 (IOWA; NEW ORLEANS; NEW YORK)

11. Dear Dick 185

12. As Low Down as the Blues Will Let You Be 201

13. Time Is a Mighty Healer 214

14. A Year of New Beginnings 230

15. October Journey 249

PART IV. THE POET AS WOMAN, 1944–1962
(NORTH CAROLINA; JACKSON, MS)

16. Find Somebody to Love   267

17. Every Child Is a Book I Didn't Write   286

18. The Walls of My Prison House   301

19. All My Roots Are Gathered in One Place   312

20. Turn Loose and Sink or Swim   327

PART V. A NOT SO QUIET RADICAL, 1962–1974
(IOWA; JACKSON, MS)

21. *Jubilee*: A Community of Memory   343

22. A Woman of Ideas   367

23. To Teach, to Lead, to Change the World   384

24. The Institute: Race, Region, and a Mission Possible   405

25. Midwife to a Movement   422

PART VI. UNHOLY WARS, 1974–1986 (MISSISSIPPI)

26. On Being Female, Black, and Free   441

27. Fame and Infamy   468

28. Making Peace with My Soul   498

29. The Outlaw Spirit Prevails   521

PART VII. THIS IS MY CENTURY, 1986–1998
(MISSISSIPPI)

30. Politics and Possibilities   549

31. Reaping the Whirlwind   580

32. Call Me Cassandra   594

Afterword   611
Notes   615
Recommended Reading   645
Index   647

Acknowledgements and Sources

Without Margaret Walker Alexander this book would not exist. Her gifts to me I fully acknowledge—unlimited time to talk and ponder the significance of her full life, what she had accomplished and what she had not, and most of all, the opportunity to watch her in action for nearly two decades. Walker welcomed me—a young, quite uncertain student, far from a scholar I hoped I could become. It was her extraordinary patience that gave us the time that made trust possible. Walker's voice and mine often merge in this book as I became her interpreter. I am grateful for this partnership that continued through the archive as I prepared to tell the story of her life after her death.

I consider it a special blessing that I was able to interview and rely on scores of people to gain a comprehensive view of Walker. I acknowledge at the outset the members of Walker's birth family who would not live to share the joy of this book's completion. Mercedes, Gwendolyn, and "Brother," (Sigismund Jr.) saw their older sister in revealing ways as did Antoinette Handy, a childhood friend in New Orleans. Others who are no longer with us helped me to understand the critical periods in Walker's life when no one else could. For a clearer picture of Walker's life in Chicago and Iowa, I had the rare privilege of meeting and interviewing Walker's close friends, Fern Gayden, Margaret Burroughs, Russell Marshall, Lerone Bennet, and Elizabeth Catlett. I was able to witness a conversation between Walker and Dorothy West who did not meet until they were much older. My talks with Val Gray Ward, the lone survivor of this group, allowed me to see a similar resilience that evoked Walker's spirit and commitment to push through any ordeal. The interviews with Walker's in-laws in High Point, North Carolina, Josephine Rogers and Dorothy Williams, provided a point of view on the woman after Chicago and Iowa. They recalled Walker's early days as a wife and mother who was wholly unprepared for the life she had been immediately thrust into, a life that became absorbed into the writing of *Jubilee*.

I wish to thank the Alexander family, Marion, James, Sigismund, and Margaret for their patience and generosity. While I met each of them at separate moments of my life, starting with the two Margarets at Northwestern, each in turn offered a unique perspective that this book needed. My family and I met Sigis and his wife Norma on our first visit to Jackson after arriving at the University of Mississippi in the 1980s. Norma was a kindred spirit: characterizing herself as an insider/ outsider, she gave me the benefit of her double vision. My conversations became more intentional and expansive when Marion and her husband Emmett, their twin daughters along with Margaret with her two children, made routine visits from Chicago to Jackson. We bonded over a common goal: to tell a story that was as complete and accurate as possible. Seeing Walker as a woman and a mother through their memories combined with the Walker I saw in real time. She was simply "Grandma" to the three children with whom she shared the home she would live in for nearly fifty years. Far more than the writer I had come to know, I saw a woman who could be many things at once.

I am indebted to the Margaret Walker Center at Jackson State University for the near flawless record tracing Walker's steps from the moment she arrived at Jackson State in 1949. The files and documents from the Institute for the Study of Life, History, and Culture of Black People, including the twenty programs she directed between January 1969 and January 1979, the year she retired, are a major part of the collection. This book is based largely on the abundant primary material in that archive: the unfinished autobiographies and journals; manuscripts of creative materials and personal correspondence; brochures, press reports, periodicals, and assorted memorabilia, all acknowledged in my endnotes. The Center's staff honored Walker's request to grant me full access, even before the collection was fully processed. The detailed journal entries between 1929 and 1996 helped to identify key themes and solidified my desire to understand the source of Walker's persistence that guided every stage of her life. My sincere appreciation to Alferdteen Harrison, Robert Luckett, Angela Stewart, and Trina Toles; Christina Wolf, Rico Chapman, and Patricia Gallion, the first to organize the archive and tolerate my badgering; and to Darlita Ballard, University and Digital Archivist at the H. T. Sampson Library Archives. I remain grateful to Carolyn Brown, author of *Song of My Life*, who published a first biography of Walker in 2014. Encouraged by the University Press of Mississippi, the book was an important moment for Walker's centennial just a year later. Carolyn left many doors open for me to enter and gave willingly of her time to problem solve. I, in turn, benefitted from the energy generated by her book's appearance.

The two edited essay collections that Walker and I published and the single volume of criticism on her work between 1990 and 2001 helped to lay the foundation for many of the ideas that the biography would flesh out. *On Being Female, Black and Free: Essays by Margaret Walker, 1932-1992* had begun to circulate among a post 1970s generation stimulating new interest in Walker as a public intellectual and an unnamed feminist. I was not surprised by how much Walker had published that had not been compiled or fully recognized, and yet essential for any biography of a writer. I acknowledge the painstaking work of Walker's friend and colleague, the late Bernice L. Bell, JSU librarian, and Robert A. Harris, a University of Kansas graduate student at the time, who completed the extensive "Selected Bibliography of Works by and About Margaret Walker." Its appearance in *Fields Watered With Blood: Critical Essays on Margaret Walker* (2001) has made it singularly important as a treasure map for anyone doing work on Walker.

Many of the personal and professional networks that had been so crucial to Walker were beginning to disappear by the time my project began. To make sense of Walker's life meant that I had to recreate if not unpack a dynamic world where ideas and cultural practices emerged from the same source, one that was Black, primarily southern, and nurtured by historically Black institutions. I welcomed and grew dependent upon the interviews and debates with those who had one or both feet in that world. The critical core who led me to new discoveries and connections include Jerry W. Ward, Bettye Parker Smith, Luana Jean Clayton, Ruth Campbell, Charlotte Momon, and Dr. Robert Smith, all of whom knew Walker longer and far better than I did. To Parker Smith and Ward, I express heartfelt thanks for my initial introduction to Mississippi, an encounter that altered the course of my life. I also wish to thank Walker's professional colleagues in the College Language Association (CLA), especially Ruthe T. Sheffey, Eugenia Collier, Eleanor Traylor, and the late Marianna White Davis, who understood and operated with an understanding of intersectionality before the term became common parlance. The annual meetings for CLA as well as the regular gatherings of Wintergreen Women Writers Collective would continue to be the place where friends and colleagues sustained me in various ways throughout this book's journey.

Individual and collective conversations with poets, critics, scholars, publishers, journalists, university administrators, biographers and many others encouraged me to see Walker through a variety of filters. I thank the following for offering me special guidance in interpreting Walker's career trajectory and critical reception and freely sharing with me their personal and professional encounters with her: Mari Evans, Doris Saunders, Charles Harris, Sonia Sanchez, Nikki Giovanni, Rita Dove, Nikky Finney, Eugene Redmond, C. Liegh McInnis, Doris O. Ginn; Natasha Tretheway, Ann and Dale Abadie, John A. Peoples, Florence Howe, Paula Giddings, Charlotte Sheedy, Claudia Tate, Jacqueline Miller Carmichael, and Ronald Bailey. Louise Knight, who was working on her third biography by the time we met, quickly accepted me as a peer, taking time away from her pressing deadlines to help me get unstuck and move forward in a deliberate manner.

While Walker was a proud member of Alpha Kappa Alpha Sorority, she was also very involved in a range of social networks of long standing, like the Jackson chapter of Mary Church Terrell Literary Club. Opportunities to speak and meet with their members deepened my appreciation for Walker's educational philosophy as it intersected with other ideas about Black womanhood more generally. I am also grateful for the unplanned encounters with those who came to Walker exclusively through her work, like Katharina King, whose research uncovered new information on Black women in the WPA that I would otherwise not have had. Randy Klein became an instant Walker fan who could translate Walker's work in new ways which stimulated fresh ideas as I was writing the biography.

I realized quite early how aware Walker was of documenting her work and her foresight regarding the use of media. I am thankful that I came to know Roy Lewis and Robert Townsend Jones, the two photographers on whom Walker often relied to document her events. Although Jones would pass before I could interview him, his photographs waited for me. His along with those from the Roy Lewis Collection make this book far richer than I could have imagined, especially for those years when Walker was Director of the Institute. Energetic conversations about Walker came with the permission to use photographs by Roland Freeman, William R. Ferris, and C. B. Claiborne, all of whom took special interest in capturing Walker either during her life and/or in numerous related events after her passing in 1998. I am indebted to Earl Richardson, whose mastery of restoration photography gave new life to many of the photos that were otherwise unusable.

Participating in seminars, workshops, and special events allowed me to test ideas and share advance versions of chapters in return for thoughtful commentary. I wish to thank the following for their professional generosity in extending these invitations: Carolyn Vance Smith and the Natchez Literary and Cinema Celebration; Louise Maynor and The Mason Sekora Lectures Series, North Carolina Central University; Hui Meng and Harbin Engineering University, China; Seretha Williams and the African American Read-In, Augusta State University; and Pearl McHaney, Georgia State University, where an extended stay as the Provost Visiting Scholar presented opportunities for a wide range of conversations with vastly different and fully engaged audiences. I am grateful to all of those who shared ideas in meaningful encounters, both formal and informal.

I acknowledge the following archives and collections that served as important sources of verification and documentation, and from whom I received permission to use copyrighted materials: Beinecke Library, Yale University, Richard Wright Papers; Bethune-Cookman University Archives, Bethune-Cookman University; Black Women's Oral History Project, Schlesinger Library/Collections, Harvard Radcliffe Institute; Corporation of Yaddo; Ernest Withers Collection; Estate of Elizabeth Catlett; Iowa Digital Library, University of Iowa; Limited Editions Club; Mississippi Department of Archives and History; Mississippi Educational Television; Schomburg Center for Research in Black Culture, New York Public Library; Southern Historical Collection, University of North Carolina at Chapel Hill; Stuart A. Rose Manuscript, Archives and Rare Book Library, Emory University: Mari Evans Papers; Vivian Harsh Research Collection, Chicago Public Library: Marion Perkins Papers and Sue Woodson

Papers; Special Collections, Deering Library, Northwestern University; and especially Dr. Walter O. Evans for sharing his private collection.

The completion of this book would not have been possible without the uninterrupted time to write supported with fellowships from the following: The Schomburg Center for Research in Black Culture, The National Humanities Center, The American Council of Learned Societies, and a sabbatical from the University of Kansas. A critical period in the writing process was facilitated first by the six-month stay under the auspices of Northwestern University's African American Studies Department, with the support of Darlene Clarke Hine and the department staff. My thanks also to Dwight McBride, who made his Northwestern office available to me, an ideal 24-7 workspace close to Deering Library and the Evanston home where the Walker sisters lived during their time at Northwestern. Secondly, I thank Malinda Maynor Lowery and Terri Lorant for their support which allowed for an enormously productive period at the Center for the Study of the American South at the University of North Carolina at Chapel Hill, even as the Covid-19 pandemic redefined the world as we had come to know it. At a crucial moment, the various parts of the book project came together and moved forward in an intentional way when Faith Childs stepped in with a steady agent's hand. Her advice and counsel took me to the finish line. Barbara Watkins and Vicki Julian, my sincere appreciation for your thorough editorial support and commitment to a book that we could work on together.

This book begins and ends with family. As many have pointed out, it may have been fortuitous that two of my children, Malika and Robeson, were born in Chicago, while the last two, Marona and Rance, were born in Mississippi. Having my life retrace Walker's steps in the two places where her professional career had its deepest roots seemed to be a blessing in disguise. What unfolded for us as a family during the writing of this book is hard to describe. The ups and downs were important moments of transference. Walker had already become a household name in our family when our Mississippi years found my children in and out of Walker's home, where they spent time with the Walker grandchildren, who were similar in age. This book's journey was therefore a journey for my family as well. As my children were becoming the various versions of their adult selves, and as each of them also moved to Chicago, I had a parallel experience. I grew dependent upon them as they had earlier been dependent upon me. The reversal was an invaluable experience as each of us experienced growing pains. I grew more and more comfortable taking their advice as the book progressed, seeing them as the ideal readers. I am not certain if the benefits to them were as great as those I received. What I do know is that this book would not have been possible without them. Malika, the oldest, whose memories of Mississippi are the clearest, became a partner who understood the flow of the narrative intuitively so that she easily stepped in, especially in the months leading up to and during the production process. This book made us a family of a new type, and I gladly share any successes that may derive from it with them. More than anything, I know that I have gained in them—as well as in my final reader, longtime family friend Gladys Nealous Sanders—my most incisive critics.

The other family is the one I gained over the last two decades—colleagues, friends, and supporters—who eagerly exchanged ideas, listened to my complaints, and pushed me farther than I thought I could go. They believed that this book needed to be done and were committed to seeing that I did it. They are far too many in number to be listed here. I will be eternally grateful to the vision we shared. An inveterate talker, I remember their dictum: "Shut up and write!" As I did, I found my greatest pleasure came from the realization that I was not only responsible for "safe keeping" another's life, but that I would be educated and inspired by all I learned during the process.

Timeline

1841   Margaret Duggans Ware Brown, maternal great-grandmother, born

1856   Edward Lane Dozier, maternal grandfather, born Butler, AL

1858   Elvira E. Ware Dozier, maternal grandmother, daughter of Margaret Duggans Ware Brown, born

1884(?)   Sigismund Constantine Walker Sr., father, born, Buff Bay, Portland Parish, Jamaica

1896   Marion Dozier Walker, mother, born, Pensacola, FL

1910   Firnist James Alexander born, Morrisville, NC

1915   Margaret Abigail Walker, born July 7 in Birmingham, AL; Margaret Duggans Brown dies; Elvira Ware Dozier moves in with family

1917   Mercedes Elvira Walker, sister, born

1920   Parents go to teach at Haven Institute for Negroes, to Meridian, MS; Walker begins school

1921   Gwendolyn Stewart Walker, sister, born

1922   Sigismund Constantine Walker Jr., "Brother," born

1925   Family moves to New Orleans; Randall Ware dies in Georgia; Walker family eventually purchase a home at 5524 Perrier Street, which remains the family residence; receives daybook for tenth birthday and begins recording poems

1926   Enters Gilbert Academy for high school

1930   Graduates from Gilbert Academy (age fourteen); enters New Orleans University (present-day Dillard University) for college

1931   Wins College Freshman Writing Prize

1932   Publishes first essay, "What Is to Become of Us?," in *Our Youth,* a New Orleans magazine; meets James Weldon Johnson, Marian Anderson, Langston Hughes; enrolls in Northwestern University in Chicago as a junior, sister Mercedes as a Freshman; meets W. E. B. Du Bois, editor of *The Crisis,* official magazine of the NAACP

1933   Sisters return home to New Orleans to save money

1934   Returns to Northwestern for senior year; meets Harriet Monroe, editor of *Poetry* at Northwestern lecture series; publishes first poem, "Daydream," in *The Crisis*

1935   Drafts first 300 pages of *Jubilee* for Creative Writing class; graduates from Northwestern University with a BA degree in English in August (age twenty)

1936   Joins Federal Writers' Project as junior writer; meets George Dillon and Muriel Rukeyser through *Poetry* magazine events; meets Richard Wright and joins the South Side Writers Group (SSWG)

1937   Publishes "For My People" in *Poetry* in November issue; SSWG disbands

1938   Publishes poems in *Poetry*, *Opportunity*, and *New Challenge*

1939   Makes first trip to New York to attend American Writers Congress; breaks off friendship with Richard Wright; enters University of Iowa for graduate school; meets Elizabeth Catlett and forms lifelong friendship

1940   Graduates from University of Iowa with MA degree and a complete manuscript of poems; publishes short stories in *Anvil* and *Creative Writing*; returns to New Orleans, suffering from depression and burnout

1941   Publishes "For My People" in *Negro Caravan*

1942   Joins faculty of Livingstone College, Salisbury, NC, for spring semester; joins English Department at West Virginia State College beginning fall semester; attends first meeting of the College Language Association; wins Yale Series of Younger Poets award; *For My People* published in October; inducted into Alpha Kappa Alpha Sorority

1943   Signs with the National Artists and Concert Corporation and begins first national paid tour of Negro Colleges in Georgia, Alabama, Tennessee; spends a week at Yaddo with writers, including Langston Hughes; publishes "Growing Out of Shadow" in *Common Ground*; meets Firnist James "Alex" Alexander on train during break from tour

1944   First child and daughter, Marion Elizabeth, born July 19; receives Rosenwald Fellowship to do research on *Jubilee*; Elvira Ware Dozier dies

1945   Marries "Alex" on June 13 in High Point, NC; returns to Livingstone College to teach

1946   Second child, Firnist James Alexander Jr., born May 3

1949   Third child, Sigismund "Sigis," born July 26; joins English Department of Jackson State College, Jackson, MS

1951   Publishes "How I Told My Child about Race" in *Negro Digest*

1952   Organizes 75th Anniversary of founding of Jackson State College (October 19–24); invites fellow poets, including Sterling Brown, Arna Bontemps, and Langston Hughes

1953   Rev. Sigismund Constantine Walker dies; receives Ford Fellowship to continue research on *Jubilee*; spends a semester at Yale; conducts research in Georgia, Alabama, and the University of North Carolina's Southern Historical Collection

1954   Fourth child, Margaret Elvira, born June 17

1955   Moves to permanent home, 2205 Guynes Street; in 1957 becomes the neighbor of Medgar and Myrlie Evers

1961   Returns to University of Iowa for summer school and enters doctoral program

1962   Begins two-year leave from Jackson State to work on PhD; welcomes the support of retired Iowa English professor Alma Hovey, whose home she shares

1963   Neighbor, Medgar Evers, shot at his home, which inspires the beginning of *Prophets for a New Day*

1965   Earns PhD from University of Iowa with *Jubilee* as her dissertation; returns to Jackson State with book contract from Houghton Mifflin

1966   *Jubilee* published in September; wins Houghton Mifflin Literary Award, Mable Carney Student National Education Association Plaque for Scholar-Teacher of the Year, and Alpha Kappa Alpha Sorority Citation for Advancement of Knowledge; celebrates in New York with friends Ruby Dee, Ossie Davis, Cicely Tyson, Moses Gunn, Roscoe Brown, James Earl Jones, Gloria Foster, and Langston Hughes

1967   Paperback rights to *Jubilee* sold to Bantam; teaches Creative Writing workshop on Cape Cod

1968   Publishes "Religion, Poetry, History: Foundations for a New Educational System," important essay for establishment of the Institute for the Study of the History, Life, and Culture of Black People at Jackson State (later the Margaret Walker Alexander Research Center); receives key to city from New Orleans mayor Victor Schiro; speaks at national convention of the NAACP; begins long working relationship with Alleane Currie; identifies with the Black Aesthetic/ Black Arts Movement sweeping the nation

1969   Returns to Northwestern to teach for spring semester during height of student protests

1970   *Prophets for a New Day* published by Third World Press; police killing of James Earl Green and Philip Gibbs at Jackson State; serves as witness before President's Commission on Campus Unrest

1971   Turns down Fulbright Hayes Fellowship opportunity to teach at the University of Trondheim, Norway, for personal reasons; publishes essay on Richard Wright after returning to the University of Iowa to give a lecture; takes two-year sabbatical to write

1972   *How I Wrote "Jubilee"* published by Third World Press; receives National Endowment for the Humanities Senior Fellowship; attends centennial celebration of Paul Lawrence Dunbar at the University of Dayton and conceives of Phillis Wheatley Festival; delivers key speeches, "Agenda for Action: Black Arts and Letters" at the Black Academy Conference sponsored by Johnson Publishing Company" and "Humanities with a Black Focus: A Black Paradigm," reflecting her alignment with the cultural and ideological shift

1973   Hosts Phillis Wheatley (bicentennial) Poetry Festival at Jackson State in November 4-7; *October Journey* published by Broadside Press; appears before Federal Communications Commission regarding racial discrimination in the media; participates in the Library of Congress conference, giving talk, "The Writer and Her Craft"

1974   *A Poetic Equation: Conversations between Nikki Giovanni and Margaret Walker* published by Howard University Press; receives honorary degrees from Denison University, Northwestern University, and Rust College

1975   First two grandchildren born: Joy Dale Alexander, born to James and Patricia, Khari Kamau Alexander to Sigis and Norma; publishes "Chief Worshippers at All World Altars" in *Encore*; records *Margaret Walker Reads Margaret Walker and Langston Hughes, Poetry of Margaret Walker Read by Margaret Walker,* and *Margaret Walker Reads Langston Hughes, Paul Laurence Dunbar, and James Weldon Johnson*; appears as witness in Mississippi book censorship/adoption case; participates in Bicentennial Symposium on American Slavery with Carl Degler, James Blassingame, and Benjamin Quarles; takes trip to visit Elizabeth Catlett and husband Francisco Mora in Cuernavaca

1976   Publishes "Some Aspects of the Black Aesthetic" in *Freedomways*; premiere of Ulysses Kay's adaptation of *Jubilee* by OperaSouth, celebrating the novel's tenth anniversary

1977   Files suit against Alex Haley, author of *Roots*, for plagiarism; twin granddaughters Karen and Katherine Coleman born to Marion and Emmet

1978   Jackson State University sponsors "Margaret Walker: A Woman for All Seasons" retirement tribute

1979   Awarded emerita status by Jackson State University; receives "Living Legacy Award" from President Jimmy Carter in absentia; begins work on Richard Wright book; husband Alex diagnosed with cancer; JSU approves the appointment of Alferdeen Harrison as Walker's successor as the Center director

1980   Gives speech "Mississippi and the Nation" for inauguration of William Winter; July 12 proclaimed "Margaret Walker Alexander Day" by Governor Winter; husband, Alex, dies (November);

publishes "On Being Female, Black, and Free" in *The Writer and Her Work,* edited by Janet Sternburg

1981   Two grandsons born: Sigismund Walker Alexander to Sigismund and Norma and Jarrett Jamal Williams to Margaret and Vernon; Guynes Street renamed Margaret Walker Alexander Drive

1982   Receives W. E. B. Du Bois Award from Association of Social and Behavioral Scientists

1983   Marion Dozier Walker dies; delivers "Moral Education: Who's Responsible" at conference for the Mississippi Committee for the Humanities

1984   Elected delegate to Democratic National Convention and serves as chairperson, Mississippi National Rainbow Coalition supporting Jesse Jackson for president; Daughters of Margaret Walker Alexander, a professional arts ensemble founded

1985   Gives keynote address at "Mississippi's Native Son: An International Symposium on Richard Wright" at Ole Miss; attends fiftieth class reunion at Northwestern University; serves as writer-in-residence at Randolph Macon Woman's College; honored by the Mary Church Terrell Literary Club Diamond Jubilee

1986   Grandaughter Gwendolyn Gail Williams born to Margaret and Vernon; Commissioned volume *For Farish Street* published by Jackson Arts Alliance; gives readings at Medgar Evers College, National Conference of Black Artists, Medgar Evers College; honored at Langston Hughes Festival at City College of New York, meeting James Baldwin and Toni Morrison

1987   Grandson Jamian Alexander born to Norma and Sigismund

1988   Branch of Hinds County library renamed Margaret Walker Alexander Library under the auspices of Director Charlotte Momon, including public exhibit of Walker's life and work; *Richard Wright: Daemonic Genius* published by Amistad Press; celebration held at Old Capitol Museum, Jackson

1989   *This Is My Century: New and Collected Poems* published by University of Georgia Press, followed by East and West Coast book promotion tour; the Institute for the Study of the History, Life, and Culture of Black People at Jackson State renamed the Margaret Walker Alexander National Research Center for the Study of the Twentieth-Century African American; receives three-year fellowship from the Lyndhurst Foundation; attends Federal Writers Project reunion in Chicago; featured in opening of *I Dream a World* exhibition; appears on *Nightwatch* with Charlie Rose.

1990   *How I Wrote "Jubilee" and Other Essays on Life and Literature* published by Feminist Press; receives Living Legend Award for Literature from Atlanta National Black Arts Festival; unveils historic marker at Richard Wright's home in Roxie, MS, inaugurating the Natchez Literary Festival

1991   Receives senior fellowship from the National Endowment for the Humanities for Lifetime Achievement and Contributions to American Literature; publishes "Natchez and Richard Wright" in *Southern Quarterly*

1992   International Conference on "Black Women Writers of Magic Realism" held at Jackson States to commemorate the fiftieth anniversary of *For My People*; receives Lifetime Achievement Award from the College Language Association, Governor's Award for Excellence in the Arts (Mississippi), Golden Soror Award from Alpha Kapa Alpha Sorority, and a tribute, together with Ralph Ellison, from the Modern Language Association; *For My People*, five multicolored lithographs created by artist Elizabeth Catlett in an oversize volume (18½″ × 22½″) published by the Limited Editions Club; Roland Freeman publishes *Margaret Walker's "For My People": A Tribute*, University Press of Mississippi

1993   Receives American Book Award for Lifetime Achievement, The Before Columbus Foundation

1994   Receives honorary degree from Spelman College, by Dr. Johnnetta B. Cole; delivers keynote address "Discovering Our Connections: Race, Gender, and the Law" at American University Washington College of Law

1995   "Margaret Walker Alexander Week" (November 27–December 2) hosted by the Margaret Walker Alexander National Research Center; named by *Ebony* magazine as one of the "Fifty Most Important Women in the Past Fifty Years"; "Whose Boy Is This," a critique of Clarence Thomas appears in *African American Women Speak Out on Anita Hill-Clarence Thomas*, edited by Geneva Smitherman, published by Wayne State University Press

1996   Donates private papers, including 135 private journals, to the Margaret Walker Alexander National Research Center; honors include John Hurt Fisher Award from South Atlantic Association of Departments of English and Agnes Scott College; monograph *Setting the Record Straight*, privately printed by Dr. Walker O. Evans, Detroit surgeon

1997   Final collection *On Being Female, Black, and Free: Essays by Margaret Walker, 1932–1992*, published by University of Tennessee Press;

	Margaret Walker Alexander National Research Center moves into newly renovated Ayer Hall
1998	Diagnosed with cancer (June); receives Arts Achievement Award, Jackson, MS; honored by the Zora! Festival of Arts and Humanities in Eatonville, FL; final reading at the George Moses Horton Society at University of North Carolina, Chapel Hill; inducted into the African American Literary Hall of Fame at the Gwendolyn Brooks Center at Chicago State University; dies in Chicago, November 30; funeral in Jackson on December 4
2009	Premiere of *Lineage: A Margaret Walker Song Cycle* musical performance/adaptation of "For My People" by composer Randy Klein, University of Kansas; ten performances between 2010 and 2015, throughout Mississippi and the United States, including Jackson State University, Plainfield, NJ, James Madison University, and San Diego State University
2010	Mercedes Elvira Walker dies
2013	*This Is My Century: New and Collected Poems* reissued by University of Georgia Press, foreword by Nikky Finney; Sigismund Constantine Walker Jr. ("Brother") and Gwendolyn Stewart Walker die
2014	*Song of My Life: A Biography of Margaret Walker* by Carolyn J. Brown published by University Press of Mississippi
2015	"100 Years of Margaret Walker Alexander, 1915–1998," Centennial Celebration events January–July, hosted by the Margaret Walker Center
2016	Fiftieth-anniversary edition of *Jubilee* published by Houghton Mifflin (Mariner Books); foreword by Nikki Giovanni
2017	Margaret Walker Center receives a two-year planning grant from the National Endowment for the Humanities to support "This Is My Century: The Life and Legacy of Margaret Walker," a traveling, digital and permanent exhibit
2019	Mississippi Writers Trail Marker in honor of Margaret Walker dedication at Ayer Hall
2020	Margaret Walker inducted in the Hall of Fame, The Mississippi Arts and Entertainment Center (The MAXX)
2022	"Truth & Flame: Margaret Walker's poetry in song," Mississippi Symphony Orchestra; "Black Synthesis of Time," centerpiece of permanent exhibition, Mississippi Museum of Art (poem taken from *This Is My Century: New and Collected Poems*)

Introduction: The Woman We Thought We Knew

I have come through the doors of hell because I am black,
because I am poor, because I live in America, and because
I am determined to be both a creative artist and maintain
my inner integrity and my instinctive need to be free.

—Margaret Walker, 1980

I don't know when I first heard the name Margaret Walker, but I am pretty sure it was associated with the poetry reading contests I had entered frequently in a city claimed by de facto segregation. Augusta, Georgia, was certainly not rare, just as the recitation—which implied much more than simply reading—of widely circulating Black poetry was not. Walker had written "For My People" in 1937, her signature poem as she would later call it, giving generations of young Black women the opportunity to speak in a voice that made others take notice of them. There must have been boys among us who read the poem well, but I can only recall the girls who were masters of the oratory that gave the poem a unique purpose. "For My People," like "Negro Mother" by Langston Hughes and "The Creation" by James Weldon Johnson, earned us a regular space on many a church program or other public gatherings in those communities that honored this form of excellence. Although my closest girlfriend, a born actor before she knew the word, earned more accolades for her rendering of such poems, like those before and after me, I knew the rhetorical flourishes that brought an appreciative audience. Such readings became a communal experience as much as they generated a sense of obligation, if not an understanding that excellence was not simply an individual achievement. It symbolized that unique history of denial and sustained oppression that made such an achievement an act of collective resistance.

I did not meet Walker until years later, and it was not in the South. A sign posted on a bulletin board shortly after my arrival at Northwestern University referred to a welcome reception for Margaret Walker, *visiting writer in residence*, a then unfamiliar term. In those years, when the picture of an African American appeared on a bulletin board of a predominantly white university, it caught your attention. I inquired about the classes she might be teaching, only to learn that I had to get permission to register for this advanced class, presumably

The House Where My Soul Lives. Maryemma Graham, Oxford University Press. © Oxford University Press 2022.
DOI: 10.1093/oso/9780195341232.001.0001

for creative writers. Although "creative writer" was an equally new term for me, I decided to take my chances. In the days before email, you presented yourself before a professor whose approval you wanted. Her office had not yet been set up and classes were soon to begin, making the only choice a visit to the Orrington Avenue apartment where she was staying.

My childhood memories of the Walker I imagined, whose poem I had read, came back to me when I walked timidly to her apartment. Timid not in antic-ipation of meeting a famous writer or uncertain of what I would say, but be-cause of the context of the times. I had been in Evanston a few days and felt a sense of isolation that was new to me. Northwestern would have a volatile situ-ation on its hands well into the 1970s: Black student protests had shaken up the campus, making demands to which the administration was forced to comply. One of those was an insistence on hiring more Black faculty; I don't remember any being at Northwestern, or any other historically white university at that time. Northwestern's administrators first turned to Lerone Bennett, the well-known Black historian who lived in nearby Chicago; and then to Walker, one of its own alums, who had been in Mississippi since the late 1940s. Walker would be re-turning to her alma mater for the first time since she'd graduated in 1935. Having these "visiting" faculty would be among Northwestern's early attempts to appease the protesting students. Her return necessarily brought mixed feelings especially when she remembered the letter that she and a group of her classmates had sent to President Walter Dill Scott about the conditions that Negro students faced in 1934. He responded by reminding them that their presence at the elite private institution was a *privilege*, not a *right*. Thirty-five years later, Walker had nothing but praise for the bold actions that the Northwestern students had taken, seeing them as a younger version of herself.

The Margaret Walker I was about to meet had earned a reputation for her un-compromising nature, outspokenness, and her intellect—three qualities that almost everyone cites about Walker. That was the Margaret Walker who would sharply criticize the media for their silence after a horde of police shot into a crowd of unarmed protesting students at Jackson State University where she was teaching. Less than two weeks after the widely publicized Kent State Massacre, as it was called, which triggered a national outcry, the murder of two Black stu-dents and the twelve who were injured, drew little notice outside the region. Those who were responsible were neither charged nor held accountable. In char-acteristic fashion, Walker memorialized the Jackson State incident in a poignant elegy: "Death came and took our frozen young, our finest flowers, our black-eyed-susan boys and men and wounded dozens more: women crouching in vain behind the broken window pane, lying along stairs, faces caricatured into spasms of despair."[1] I would not have known that it was this Walker I was about to meet, a woman who would provide a certain kind of map, who would become the guide that National Book Award–winning poet Nikky Finney believes Margaret Walker served for her and a generation of developing young poets.

With my palms pressing together and turning, then slowly releasing, I tapped on the door of a second-floor apartment. It suddenly occurred to me that she might think me too presumptuous. Should I have sent a note in advance? The door opened to reveal a teenage girl. "Oh, sorry," I apologized quickly, thinking that I had the wrong apartment. As I turned to go away, she said, "Oh, you must be looking for Mother." And then from a distance came a crackling, high-pitched voice, "Margaret, who is it?"

Before I knew it, I was in, lulled to a table by the smell of collard greens, sweet potatoes, and baked ham covered by a layer of slighted browned pineapple rings. I remember talking incessantly to a woman I felt I had known all of my life. She pulled every story out of me with a stream of questions in rapid fire: Who was I again? Where had I come from, and who were "my people"? What church had I attended, and most important, why had I come to Northwestern?

My response to this last question drew an odd look from her. I felt as if I was taking my first test and waiting to hear whether I had failed or not. Since my arrival in Evanston, I had questioned my fate in this new environment, what some called that "larger education," which for me meant "outside the South." I also thought I could relate to Chicago, the only city I had laid eyes on that could qualify as "up North." A decade earlier I accompanied my mother to the funeral of my Uncle Charlie, a man I had never seen. As I quickly learned, however, Evanston was *not* Chicago.

In exchange for my stories, I learned that Walker had left the South at seventeen, when her parents drove her and her sister Mercedes to Evanston in the family's first car. She was hell-bent on being a writer, her sister on preparing to be a world-class pianist, neither of which, they were convinced, could happen in the South. Then suddenly she offered up the gem, asserting, "I'm black, a woman, and Southern." We both laughed, knowing exactly what she meant. Yet the pride that I sensed in her words suddenly struck me as also an indictment, although about what, I did not know. Whatever entered my mind I kept there, content to enjoy the full dinner she had prepared. The tension between those two feelings wasn't about to let me go.

For the next several months, I became a regular fixture in Walker's apartment, showing up conveniently at dinner time to join the two Margarets—one, the doting mother and teacher whose culinary skills coexisted comfortably beside her vast knowledge she eagerly shared; the other, her namesake, often referred to as "little Margaret," an attentive teenager who was clearly used to sharing her mother with others, and who never seemed bored by what she must have heard many times. My real education began at Walker's dinner table. Whenever I look back at the many occasions we spent time together after that, the most important conversations took place when she was routinely preparing a meal, interjecting useful chef-like instructions into one of her off-the-cuff lectures.

Looking back, it felt like I was entering the eye of a storm, getting too close to a particular history that claimed Walker by association, as much as by her own actions. I quickly read all I could about her over those months, so that I could ask an intelligent question that I knew would tell me something I didn't know—like when she knew it was time, or even safe, to go back south, in no way disguising my selfish interests. Or, after learning that we were both from a family of teachers, I asked if she felt her identity as a poet had been compromised by a teaching career. This one drew a slightly dismissive "Hmph," from her, as she explained how women balanced multiple priorities all the time; it was second nature. It was only later when I collected, edited, and published a group of her essays that Walker's views on the "feminine principle" seemed to be rather conservative.

Since her reputation as a novelist was still something she was getting used to—*Jubilee* had been published, but most of the world still saw her as a poet. It was clear that she saw herself that way as well, taking delight in talking about her early adventures with poetry. I was listening, but not always understanding the connections she was making. That a child should be seen and not heard was a mantra we both knew, and one that our parents tried to enforce. I had gone to a school located across from the local library, the Wallace Branch, serving the Black community, and it became an instant babysitter. I learned to cherish the silence the library required, giving me uninterrupted reading time, and a great deal of practice with patience as I waited for my parents to pick me up from school. My frequent visits turned into a job, helping to put books back on the shelves. My passion had been for reading books, about which I always wanted to talk. Writing for me would come much later. In contrast, Walker had been given a daybook, into which she was encouraged to write her thoughts, once her family discovered she had more to say than they or anybody else they believed wanted to hear. An early reader, however, she also liked the way words sounded and looked on the page, and she quickly began to imitate what she was told was poetry. My impressions from those visits to her Evanston apartment provided the elements of literary biography: how a writer comes to language and what one does with that language.

Most of our early conversations alternated between what she thought about herself as a writer, sometimes playing a familiar script, and what was happening in Mississippi, a state that had become her adopted home, a place she never expected to leave. I knew that Northwestern was wooing her, hoping she would consider staying as a permanent faculty member, as many of the students wished. One of her former professors had retired and was also pushing the idea. Walker was steadfast—Mississippi was home, and she believed that it had a role to play in the nation's future. That was where she needed to be. Everyone she talked about was from Mississippi or had been born there, and they were the characters in our conversations. There was Fannie Lou Hamer, a fellow Mississippian she knew and greatly admired, who stood up to every indignity there was as a civil rights activist and community organizer. Walker lived down the street from Medgar Evers and was away when he was assassinated, but she believed his life and death served as one of the many examples for why Mississippi could only move forward. After the murders of civil rights workers added to their history of Klan violence and other oppressive practices, Medgar Evers's death seemed to be the low point for the state. Walker believed that reaching rock bottom meant it could only go up. I found this optimism remarkable. Without denying what others said about the state, Walker's descriptions of its future were always bright.

I did not see Margaret Walker again until she was back on her home turf. Another fellow Mississippian, Bettye Parker Smith, had urged me to attend the Phillis Wheatley Poetry Festival, one of the many unforgettable events that Walker would host in her lifetime. I was still uncertain about my professional goals, thinking that a career in journalism would satisfy my sense of adventure and my love of stories. But my first visit to Mississippi put me in Margaret Walker's orbit. Perhaps I had yet to shed the traditional bias that other Southerners have about Mississippi. No matter where you were from in the South, it could never be as bad as Mississippi, people would say. But once in Jackson at a conference—the Phillis Wheatley Festival—marking the bicentennial of the first known Black person in America to publish a book of poetry, I found myself surrounded by other Black women, "sister-poets" as Walker called them, who had begun to carve out a new space for themselves in a world. They believed that students like me, who had come to the festival, were the new initiates. I had never before seen that many professional Black women, all associated with writing or some form of expressive art, in one place at one time in my life. They had all heeded Walker's call to celebrate the beginning of their tradition and to take ownership of it. Thus, in 1973, as she correctly pointed out, while you could count the number of Black women writers who had gained much attention on one hand, Walker had seen the writing on the wall. Walker and Gwendolyn Brooks were the "foremothers" to a new generation, since even today's best-known writers like Toni Morrison were just beginning their careers with a first novel. Morrison may have claimed the title of writer for herself, but the world was still trying to figure out the meaning of *The Bluest Eye*. A first collection of poetry by Alice Walker, who was living in Mississippi at the time, had preceded her first novel, *The Third Life of Grange Copeland*. The only person in attendance who was older than Walker was Dorothy Porter Wesley, the powerhouse at Howard University. Walker's assessment at the time, now a proven fact, was that Black women's writing "would go on to unprecedented heights" and that a continuing tradition of Black women's literary excellence was undeniable.

I was probably hooked by the time I left the Phillis Wheatley Festival. The Margaret Walker I saw was in her element. Bringing writers and publishers together with visual and performing artists, all Black women, was a reckoning as much as a celebration. It was easy to miss what seemed hidden behind Walker's Southern charm and genteel manner. The evidence of her power became clear as local television stations, state government officials, and the national media made their way to the Jackson State campus over the course of the weekend. The same Mississippi known for William Faulkner, Eudora Welty, and Richard Wright became a newly opened society. Walker, who had crossed paths not only with several generations of Black writers by that time, but also with the likes of Muriel Rukeyser, Carson McCullers, Katherine Anne Porter, Agnes Smedley, and Eudora Welty, never doubted what was possible. She was intent on rewriting history. It was no longer the place "where the Klan ran wild and you were brutalized and afraid,"[2] as one of the festival participants said. In contrast, the reimagining of Mississippi and its history of violence as a place of creative, constructive engagement gave Walker the confidence she needed to continue her work. Part of that work was to provide the spiritual nurturing for a new movement.

I did not know what witnessing meant and the responsibility that it thrust upon a person. But I learned quickly that Walker kept that as her secret weapon. My opportunity to learn more about her and about Mississippi came years later after I had married, completed my doctorate, and begun a teaching career. With two young children in tow, my husband and I had accepted teaching positions at the University of Mississippi. "Mississippi needs you," she had told me in a phone call. Despite some trepidation, we made the trek from the Midwest to the Deep South—to the state that had produced more Black writers, musicians, and artists than any other, the same state that led the nation in infant mortality, unemployment, and poverty, at the time running only slightly behind California in illiteracy. I was indeed in the eye of a continuing storm.

Still, the words "I am black, a woman, and Southern" kept haunting me as I became more curious about who Walker really was, and what it meant to live such a provincial life on the surface, only to step completely outside of that provincialism when it did not accomplish her particular goal. Whether it was providing an incubator for a new movement among Black women or building a new structure for questioning the basic premises of Western thought, Walker knew what kind of scaffold to provide. Every new idea or new practice needed a place to grow. Whenever she was in that creative space, a book didn't necessarily emerge. Instead, creativity became that fearless, relentless, push against the grain for a woman who willed a project into being.

My path to writing this biography, however, was anything but even, and it was longer than most, now nearly two decades. I had access to more material than any biographer could imagine since Walker left hundreds of journals to serve as my guide. The silence to which she was subjected as a child, and the vehicle that she had been given, became complementary forces in her life. She wrote every thought down, rehearsing it time and time again before it emerged fully formed. The safe space where she could be her most intimate unfiltered self remained the journal. One of her reasons for founding the Institute for the Study of the Life History and Culture of Black People in 1968 was to share her vision of what American education could be if it took its lessons from the social and political movement of the 1960s. The academic term "Black Studies" was the shorthand for her reimaginings. But she added a critical component, a repository that might house all that she left behind, the said and the unsaid, launching a new era of cultural preservation. The Institute became the project that consumed the last decade of her working life.

I suspected that Walker understood the reasons for my curiosity from the very beginning. I kept asking questions but held in just as many. When I began the research for the biography in earnest, the public perceptions about Walker became one of the first forks in the road. Even as the person who ushered in a renaissance in Black women's writing, Walker remained in the background. One reason seemed to be that she was openly critical of the new directions in which she saw Black women's writing going. Her criticisms and concerns about the movement's connection to changing gender expectations, which challenged her fixed views of men and women, were sufficient to cancel her right to claim any relationship with it or with many of the women who became its major force. Was this unbridled jealousy, owing to the difficulty of finding an audience for her work in a new era, when Black women's writing was flourishing? That she did not or could not keep up with the pace of younger writers made her a "has been," as one writer said to me, too old-fashioned.

Yet Walker was the release valve for generations of Black women writers, which her 1966 novel *Jubilee* provided. The novel's continued popularity inside and outside of the United States in translation brought her new audiences. Beyond that, it was the first contemporary novel to consider the subject of slavery with a Black woman as the central character. A new term was later coined for this type of fiction, the "neo-slave narrative," which retrospectively included her. For Walker, however, *Jubilee* was a folk novel that brought the past into the present to demonstrate the power of human agency at a pivotal moment in American history. She did not need critics to tell her why or for whom it mattered since she had her own reasons. Nevertheless, an era of Black women writers brought a new vision that caught up with her at the same time it seemed to leave her behind, an ever-present contradiction in Walker's life. She could be ahead of her time with a list of significant firsts and yet slow in coming to important realizations. Both made it difficult for Walker to sustain a critical following for her new poetry and fiction.

While it is usually understood that Walker's work ushered in a flourishing novel writing market in late twentieth- and twenty-first-century fiction, when we think of slavery as it figures into the contemporary novel, we think immediately of Morrison's *Beloved*, published more than two decades after *Jubilee*. Although *Jubilee* continued to be widely read and translated, accessible, and transparent, it depicted an enslaved woman whose loyalty to her white mistress did not fit the new profile for Black women characters in late twentieth-century Black fiction. As successful as it was, among Black and white readers, *Jubilee* did not seem radical or psychologically complex enough. The division between a "literary" and "popular" novel made it easier for Walker to recede into the background. Her name joined the list of other significant writers, who did not have sufficient cultural capital for inclusion in those conversations about Black women writers and thinkers after the 1980s.

As I began to dig deeper into the various components of Walker's life—writer, wife, mother of four, Sunday School teacher, entrepreneur, and other facets that were constantly surfacing—the story I saw unfolding produced more questions than answers. Did Walker see her life in terms of contradictions? Were they of her own choosing? What did it mean to step into a career at age twenty-seven with high expectations of what would follow? Then to make a tactical retreat for personal reasons, expecting to step back into that place a quarter of a century later? I had to investigate the truth of Nikki Giovanni's 1998 words when I told her I was thinking about a biography. "Margaret Walker . . . singlehandedly turned poetry upside down with her declaration of love and her challenge to the future of her people," she said. "Margaret is the most famous person nobody knows."[3] She was a person we thought we knew, but in fact did not.

I made regular visits to Walker over the next two decades, the most frequent during the years I was at the University of Mississippi. Each time, I looked for signs that she was aware of being at odds with changing ideas of the times. I know that she enjoyed my company, and because my own children were close in age to her grandchildren who shared her Jackson residence, it was easy to form a close working relationship. I cannot say whether I chose Walker or she chose me, but I do know that every visit generated new questions that I found myself unable to answer easily. We would spend hours talking, and some of the stories she'd repeat many times about the New Negro connections she had made in her youth: for example, her meeting Langston Hughes or meeting Zora Neale Hurston at her mother's childhood home. The writer and anthropologist would disappear from history until Alice Walker's discovery of her grave in the 1970s. Yet Marion Dozier [Walker] and Hurston had known each other as children growing up in Florida; both had fathers who were ministers. I knew that Walker was guiding me to the version of her story she wanted others to hear. But I also knew a much bigger story needed fleshing out.

In the few years leading up to Walker's final illness, I saw several versions of her unfinished autobiography in typescript, which Mrs. Alleane Currie was instructed to share with me. I had begun filling in the detailed outline that I received, for which there were alternate titles, suggesting a level of uncertainly about its focus. Mrs. Currie had worked with Walker since before the *Jubilee* days and had seen if not typed every word Walker had written, serving as a reliable assistant during the Institute. The two women grew even closer after their respective retirements and saw eye to eye on almost everything. Walker would send me to Mrs. Currie to answer questions or find a document in her files. I began to recognize the silent partner I had in Mrs. Currie in those early days of my research. She knew when and where to speak and when her opinions mattered. With Mrs. Currie's help, I could begin to identify the major gaps in Walker's life, especially some very complicated years leading up to and following her retirement. Two projects would take over Walker's life in those immediate years after retirement: her lawsuit against Alex Haley and the publication of her biography of Richard Wright, both of which brought Walker the kind of notoriety that outstripped her earlier fame. Mrs. Currie's memory, together with the documents that provided corroborating evidence, enabled me to see sides of Walker that no one else did.

After Walker's death in 1998, as I began to settle on an approach to her life, I would tell people I was interested in writing a biography of Margaret Walker. Invariably I got only two questions: "Wasn't she in love with Richard Wright?" *Richard Wright: Daemonic Genius* was her biography that took a decade to appear. The reviews, including some by those scholars who had great praise for Walker's earlier work, considered the book to be the musings of a vindictive, jealous woman whose career paled in comparison to Wright's. The second question was, "Why would she sue Alex Haley?" This was before Haley's *Roots* research was proven to be a hoax and Haley discredited. In 1979, however, Walker would lose her lawsuit against Haley for copyright infringement. Her claim, supported by extensive evidence that he had lifted entire sections of *Jubilee* for his 1976 novel *Roots*, fell on deaf ears. Perhaps blinded by the commercial success, no judge would entertain the thought that Haley could get anything from an unknown like Walker. But Walker was discovering the under workings of corporate greed. What was required to ensure the success of the bestselling novel and blockbuster television miniseries could not be exposed. Many sued Haley, but Walker was the most vulnerable, whose role could easily be switched: she suddenly became the person accused, not someone who had a right to accuse another. Isolated and bitter, Walker was forced to become a one-woman campaign in her own defense, unable to contain herself whenever the issue came up in public. Truth indeed became a set of alternative facts that an entire industry needed to protect. Walker had little power to fight what she realized was a powerful machine.

When asked these questions, I responded with what I knew. Regarding the first, I argued that we should not judge someone's entire life by a few years (in this case, fewer than three), which is the amount of time Walker and Wright were in Chicago working for the Federal Writers Project. They formed a working relationship that turned into a close friendship during their time together as members of the South Side Writers Group. To the second, evidence of others who had won their lawsuits against Haley made it easier to believe that Walker simply did not have sufficient legal representation to go against the major corporate backers who defended Haley. That my answers were valid and made sense was not the point. The dismissive attitude deeply concerned me. Until I could countercharge that Walker was jealous of other writers' success, or shatter the image of her as a "woman scorned," I feared that any story I would tell, no matter how much evidence backed it up, would never be convincing. Walker's reputation would always be judged in the court of public opinion.

My decision in the end was to tell the story I knew, grounded in the abundant archival evidence that existed. Margaret Walker left more books in various stages of completion than those she had published during her lifetime. For most writers, these might be sketches or outlines. And while Walker relied heavily on outlines for all of her work, she preferred to write in long hand full versions of anything she was drafting, whether it was a book, an essay, a speech, or a letter. Always a perfectionist, she never hesitated to write as completely as possible, knowing that she would revise. Regular references in interviews and annual self-assessments that appear in her journals are to "a book I am working on." Speaking about her various projects with a degree of certainty was proof that Walker lived inside her head in many ways, in order to balance much of what she confronted on a daily basis throughout her life.

When Walker retired from teaching at Jackson State University in 1978, where she had spent three decades, she was still young enough to finish the several books she had drafted and/or outlined. But her commitment to the Richard Wright biography was unfailing, even in the face of orders to cease and desist, and refusals by two publishers (Howard University and Dodd Mead) that feared the backlash from the Wright estate. Neither felt they could provide the necessary legal protection. Nevertheless, Walker finished the book, *Richard Wright: Daemonic Genius,* which finally appeared in 1988 as a publication from a new imprint, Amistad, which Charles Harris negotiated with HarperCollins. Harris had proven his loyalty by following the book through to its publication. Without interruption, Walker began to compile her published and unpublished poems for a final volume, *This Is My Century*. I worked closely with Walker, and with the help of then University of Mississippi student Nadene Dunlap, the manuscript went to the University of Georgia Press, which published it in 1989. Poetry was a necessary return for Walker as she began to close the circle of her life.

During my final years at the University of Mississippi, Walker, Mrs. Currie, and I compiled some of her essays into two separate volumes. *How I Wrote "Jubilee"* and *Other Essays on Life and Literature* brought Walker back into the fold of women writers in 1990 with the help of Florence Howe, at the Feminist Press. Her new wave of popularity continued when Special Editions published the mammoth fiftieth-anniversary edition of *For My People*, with lithographs by her longtime friend Elizabeth Catlett. She was in New York for the celebration, but her health was in decline by the time *On Being Female, Black, and Free*, a second collection of her essays, appeared in 1997, the year before she died. It is through these conversations and essays that one sees a more definitive evolution of a woman on whom nothing was ever lost. She had something to say about everything, not because she was opinionated, which she was, but because she had actually studied the topic, feeling duty-bound to examine every angle in order to understand its historical perspectives and global implications. When she issued her opinion, she rarely did so until after she had weighed all others available to her, which usually meant a consideration of prehistoric times, through African, Indigenous, Eastern and Western thought, European and North American migration, and the formation of our modern and postmodern worlds. This extended to her political thinking just as it did to her social and cultural observations. Her reflections are never muted, and they were cultivated by a lifetime of journal writing. As a popular speaker who could tackle any subject, Walker was able to pull from a wide range of scholarship. When she did elect to share her thoughts in a more accessible format, on topics like the essays "Money, Race, and Politics," "Revolution and the University," or "On Being Female, Black, and Free," she was often highly personal, revealing those parts of her life that would fit each topic. Her intention was always to write to and for her people. At the conclusion of *This Is My Century*, Walker summarized her life for her readers in one paragraph, beginning with a self-inscribed epitaph. Although she admitted to "going out of the South only to study, teach or lecture," she claimed the South as home "real or imagined, violent and nonviolent . . . the subject and source of . . . my life."[4]

* * *

What we know about Walker is that she was born into an African American and Jamaican family who knew hardship and despair, but who had risen above both, which made for her somewhat unusual childhood. She was more than familiar with a generation we refer to as "New Negroes," was barely twenty by the time the Harlem Renaissance began to peak, and was among those who would accept the education that the North would provide, but who ultimately also saw little else that the North had to offer. Her birth in 1915, near the Ishkooda Mines area outside of Birmingham, Alabama, coincided with the death of Booker T. Washington in Tuskegee, 135 miles away—a death that signaled the end of the so-called era of Black accommodation. But as much as Walker claimed the South, it was a relatively different South, namely New Orleans, that shaped most of her early years. Much of what had been associated with the South—doggedness and determination, respect for traditional values, the refusal to accept failure, love of home and family—she embraced as values to live by, always pushing through those boundaries that might have otherwise restrained her. In fact, she could claim a mixed heritage, the rural and urban South and the Northern United States, just as she knew about the two critical historical periods of slavery and freedom. African, Native, and white parts of her family tree came together and often split to take root elsewhere. What she did not lose were her maternal grandmother's memories of enslavement that were readily absorbed into her child's mind. The freedom she identified with the imagination that memories can conjure had no limits. The balance between the fixed history and her boundless imagination translated into the alternately precocious and deeply troubled child whose emotional distress during her later teens was difficult to shed. In time, she learned to manage and adjust, almost always through her writing and daydreaming. Her sensibility was cerebral, artistic, and embedded in a deep spiritual faith, as much inherited as it was original to her. She was accustomed to a high level of productivity that fed recurring periods of self-reinvention. A sixty-year career gave birth to extraordinary ideas and projects in the twentieth century that became sustained practices in the twenty-first century.

Buried within the facts above is a life lived on and off the page, where contradictions abound, and where well-thought-out plans gave birth to new decisions and expression. Walker appreciated structure where she could examine and define her writing and subsequent actions. Through this structure you can trace the evolution of her ideas, some of which were too big to execute, so she'd push them as far as she could and wait until she had matured enough and found the inspiration or the ability necessary to bring them to fruition. To that end, Chicago was a site of enormous convergence, where subsidized work like those programs associated with the Works Progress Administration integrated with radical ideas, Marxist thought, and the energy of a distinct group of young artists and intellectuals. Chicago helped to hone her skills, expanding those literary networks that led her to become an early literary star. The intensely political period in post-Depression Chicago offered her seven years of active writing, working, and involvement in Communist-affiliated groups before she began graduate study at the University of Iowa. Having turned her Iowa thesis into her first book, *For My People* (1942), she was ready to move on to another goal: to marry and have children. Over the course of her tenure at Jackson State College [University] in Mississippi, she became a powerful force in the state, especially in her later years. Those who sought her advice came from universities within the United States and included scholars from abroad. Statesmen and politicians from the governor on down came calling on her for support in winning elections. Through it all, Walker wrote as a witness to a world divided by race and region and as a harbinger of things to come. She seemed to have direct access to the prophets of old, seeing through a contemporary lens. And she recorded it in her journal in order to make sense of it. At the time of her death in 1998, few scholars were unaware of her writing life that lasted nearly seventy decades.

Most people who remember Walker today met her during the last two decades of her life, just as she was about to retire, well past her most productive literary period. Her primary focus was on completing *Daemonic Genius*, which brought undue critical attention for the second time in her life. But she was always intentional. Her impulsivity was planned, and her creative energies were continually restorative. The characters in her early unpublished work like "Goose Island" were as important as a meeting of the National Negro Congress; or later in her life, an international conference of Black politicians and intellectuals she had convened for an important discussion on the future of Africa. Her interests and abilities were varied. After decades of work as an institution builder, Walker could bring to closure more quickly collaborative-based efforts, no matter how large or costly. She could easily turn an event into a modern-day think tank with high people involved. She rarely had downtime because of a complicated and structured home life, and often used hospital stays as "official" rest and relaxation.

She cooked all the meals for her family, doted on her husband, and gave full attention to all the stages of growth for her four children, and in her later years her grandchildren, living in an intergenerational household. Family mattered above all else, and she had been the primary breadwinner. Her friends could become enemies, but food was the great unifier. She made up for somewhat uneven periods of productivity with volumes of unpublished work and the pleasure she derived from having a full life, not only as a writer and educator, but as a daughter, sister, wife, mother, and grandmother. As a result, even with tactical departures from her deep religious upbringing, her faith provided the bookends for a life that followed the mandate of Luke 12:48: "to whom much is given, much will be required."

What is clear is that Walker's absences from the public literary scene and her unwillingness to pursue what would become conventional pathways to publishing success and recognition corresponded with the moment when writers had less control over their audiences than publishers did, and the reviewing media and the advertising industry had mastered the art of predicting if not determining public reading tastes. By the time she returned to active publishing, the world had changed, and as a dedicated-race woman, who respected the system's approach that Marxism provided while holding firmly to her Christian ideals and provincialism, critics did not know where to place her. Through her speeches and essays, she offered penetrating critiques that rupture the categories we have so often relied upon for interpretations of twentieth-century literature. Publishers more often than not distinguish between literary and popular fiction, just as they cater to specialized or other target audiences. Having established her writing career as a poet with the support of male mentors, she liked the directness of communicating with those publishers they identified for her, and more importantly with the readers of her work, believing that agents were both wasteful and unnecessary. She remained devoted to the people she found to be wholly dependable until the end of her life, her listening and reading audiences.

Walker did not like labels, but if anyone ever asked, she would describe herself as a humanist, the subject about which she had a lot to say, which made it into her numerous essays and speeches. She was insistent that the literature of Black people emerged in Egypt more than 3,500 years ago. If Toni Morrison claimed that African Americans were the first modernists, Margaret Walker called humanism the necessary reality in the lives of Black people, especially in America. It meant that despite the history of oppression, Black people refused total suppression, refused to be made into machines, or to give up their ancient inheritance of secular play, warmth, and gaiety of love and joy. It provided a sustained awareness of the strength that comes from continuous suffering and a search for freedom, peace, and human dignity. Humanism was everywhere visible within Black life.

The critical appraisal that Walker wrote one good novel, now and again great poetry, and a poor biography of Richard Wright, hides much truth. Whether we consider decades or specific literary periods, from the second wave of the New Negro Renaissance in 1930s Chicago to the Black Women's literary renaissance in the 1980s, her influence is there. Because she strove to both preserve and create history, Walker fashioned herself into an institution builder leaving a blueprint. She gave as much to her public as she demanded of them, refusing to allow her voice to be co-opted.

I have approached Walker's life as the individual subject she saw herself to be, shaped by an intense intellectual and social environment during her early years. I read her psychological development against a larger dialogue about gender, race, and modernity. Walker, a fearful, prepubescent, and highly imaginative young girl, who fed what she called "the fire burning within" with romantic excursions, matured into an intellectual whose political education tempered those early romantic inclinations and expanded her creative possibilities. I watch her art evolve as her imagination confronted her moral sensibility. What struck me most about Walker was her early understanding of a complex dynamic—being an artist, a woman, and Black. She necessarily found her social, literary, and familial relationships and responsibilities were often in conflict with one another, a central thread that is the story of her life. There are important ruptures that occurred from her expanding political awareness, spurred by radical politics and a personal and political relationship with Richard Wright. But Walker's ability to put that period of her life in perspective presents her with the opportunity for self-renewal during the height of the Civil Rights Era. Her publications between 1966 and 1989 underscore her significance as a precursor and visionary in shaping and transforming both the Black Arts Movement and the Women's Movement.

In contrast to the way Walker read her own life, one that shows evidence of fabrication now and again, and her need to control her own narrative, Walker's self-presentation as a race woman was part of refashioning and self-censoring that defined middle-class Black women of her era. Beneath the cloak of respectability politics and Southern womanhood, which brought protection to the generation of Black women to which Walker belonged, was a vibrant cosmopolitanism. From a strong background reading philosophy, she became a student of ancient and modern cultures that combined with the political education of her Chicago years. The result was a global sensibility and inclusiveness that remained the foundation of her thinking. These qualities help to explain why Walker, whose only international travel was to her father's Jamaica, welcomed to her home a constant stream of writers and scholars from outside of the United States where she was well known.

How does one bridge the interminable contradictions of growing up as a precocious African American girl in the Jim Crow South, born to well-educated parents, who learned to read at four, and who filled the 365-page daybook with her poems at age fifteen, all before she had any formal instruction in poetry? How did her passion for history and poetry find common ground? How did the culture of high expectations, which privileged spiritual values over material wealth, prepare her for the inevitable setbacks that did not unsettle her? Believing that she had no boundaries, except those she set for herself, how did she transform her confrontations with racism and sexism into meaningful lessons? How did self-confidence and idealism confront her need for love and emotional security, the things she believed only came through marriage? Walker's way of being in the world was asking questions and then working out her own answers and rationale, which she then tested in real time. If the questions were often private, the answers were public. "What Is to Become of Us?," her first publication in 1932, became her model for life. The question doubled as a pronouncement about who she was and what her life must be. It was that sign that Walker's "I" had to become "We"; her "Me," "Us."

The questions about Wright and Haley persist, and they explain in part the degree to which an unfairly earned infamy replaced the critical attention that she deserved. The naked facts matter, but more important to this story is Walker's resistance to such violations. From the time she began to write as a child, she knew that she would have to make a creative space for herself. The legacy of the talented tenth bequeathed to her a kind of radicalism that was most visible in the doggedness of her mission as an artist and innovator, and in her forthrightness against racism and gender bias, even when it invited public controversies and her dismissal by others. If she is "the spiritual if not designated godmother" [to] "her younger contemporaries"[5] despite their reluctance to praise her, as Southern writer and critic Trudier Harris believes, Walker was the epitome of the private woman and professional writer who was her best and worse critic.

Walker's friends and peers, including Langston Hughes, Richard Wright, Ralph Ellison, and Gwendolyn Brooks, achieved greater prominence and lasting fame. She was, on the other hand, the last surviving member of a distinct literary cohort, one she would not let us forget: Robert Hayden, Melvin Tolson, Margaret Danner, Owen Dodson, and John Oliver Killens. Her academic community was an even larger cohort of Black intellectuals who spent, if not all, the majority of their careers at historically Black institutions, with primary responsibility for shaping the next several generations of Black students trying to understand the relationship between a legacy inherited from the past and an uncertain future. Those who had hoped and worked for progressive social change would face a deepening racial divide, an entrenched caste system, and our endangered ecological order.

When at sixteen in 1930, Margaret Walker asked the question, "What is to become of us?" by the end of her life, most would have asked "what became of her?" Both questions are exploratory and demand an answer. One answer to is to look at the end of her life. By then, Walker was far better known through her relationships with those she dared to criticize publicly. She believed, as she told me, that no one should have had her fate. In telling her story nearly a quarter century after her death, levels of disclosure offer a clearer perspective on what made her *who she was* and *what* she was not.

This biography is intended to open up new dialogues about the artist as woman, engaged in the complexities of life, who must learn to build an arsenal of weapons to confront each necessary battle. Walker's version of her story, the typescripts she left behind, gives us the template of her life but nothing of the passion that drives the autobiographical impulse. Many of her personal essays provide more compelling sketches of selected memories. The autobiography was the thing Walker believed she needed to do in order to exercise some control over the way people would remember her, and to give order and meaning to her life. We find important revelations in her decisions to produce one kind of art or another, and to live one kind of life or another. The kind of examination necessary to capture the texture of the life she was given and her efforts to make it coherent would have taken more time than she had left and more psychological mining than her abilities allowed. That search for coherence was grounded in her sense of womanhood, a crucial source for self-examination, even when the feminist urges found no place for acknowledgment. Yet she never saw the need to advocate for women's liberation as it was understood by the larger social movement for, "in my mind," Walker said, "I am absolutely free."[6]

The mental and emotional freedom Walker employs occurs through language. She achieved her greatest satisfaction in her ability to remake words, giving them power to resound in a particular way without being lost, in the same way that "For My People" renews itself for every generation. Her poetry, fiction, essays, speeches, and most importantly her unpublished manuscripts, journals, and notebooks, are the workable materials, if we take the time to read them, that get us the closest that we will ever be to the Margaret Walker we did not know. This biography is the beginning of that process. Each chapter title is a direct quote from Walker that refuses to allow her voice to be silenced.

Acronyms and Abbreviations

ABC	American Broadcasting Corporation
ACP	American Communist Party
Alex	Firnist James Alexander, husband of Margaret Walker
AME (Church)	African Methodist Episcopal
A&T	North Carolina Agricultural and Technical State University (Greensboro, NC)
AWC	American Writers Congress
BAM	Black Arts Movement
Blueprint	"Blueprint for Negro Writing"
Brother	Refers to Charlie Walker (Margaret Walker's brother)
CAAA	Conference on Africa and African Affairs
Calvinism/Calvinist	Reference to 16th century religious reformist John Calvin
Catlett	Elizabeth Catlett (also in footnote)
CLA	College Language Association
CP-USA	Communist Party–United States of America
Croppers	share croppers
Daemonic Genius	References Richard Wright
Dies	Martin Dies
Dodd, Mead	Dodd, Mead and Company (publishing)
Duboisian (thought)	Reference to Du Bois
DW	Refers to Richard Wright in Margaret Walker's journals
FESTAC	Festival of African Culture
FIPSE	Fund for the Improvement of Post-Secondary Education (in footnote)
Fisk	Fisk University (Nashville, TN)
FAMU	Florida Agricultural and Mechanical University
FWP	Federal Writers Project
Gilbert	Gilbert Academy for Girls
HBCU	Historically Black Colleges and Universities
HIWJ	How I Wrote Jubilee and Other Essays on Life and Literature
Howard	Howard University (when citing institution of higher learning)
HUAC	House Committee on UnAmerican Activities
JRB	James Russell Brown, Walker's suitor in Chicago who proposed marriage
JSU	Jackson State University (Jackson, MS)
KKK	Ku Klux Klan
Litany	Litany for a Dark People
LSU	Louisiana State University

Marxism/Marxist	References Karl Marx belief system
MFA	Master of Fine Arts
Monkey-chaser	Derogatory West Indies term
ms	manuscript
MWA	Margaret Walker Alexander
MWC	Margaret Walker Center
MWP	Margaret Walker Papers (used in a footnote)
NAACP	National Association for the Advancement of Colored People
NCAC	National Concert and Artists Corporation
NCC	North Carolina College (North Carolina Central University)
NCBS	National Council for Black Studies
NCWA	National Conference on Women and the Arts
np	non published
Northwestern	Northwestern University (Chicago, IL)
NOU	New Orleans University (New Orleans, LA
OBFBF	*On Being Female Black and Free*
Ole MISS	University of Mississippi
PWI	Predominately white institutions
Rosenwald	References Rosenwald Fellowship
R.S.M.	Religious Sisters of Mercy
RWP	Richard Wright Papers
Shelley	Percy Bysshe Shelley
Sigis	Sigismund Alexander, Walker's youngest son
SSCAC	South Side Community Art Center
SSWG	South Side Writers Group
SNYC	Southern Negro Youth Congress
Talladega	Talladega College (Talladega, AL)
The Institute	Institute for the Study of Life History and Culture of Black People
The Symposium	reference to People's Inaugural Symposium
TIMC	This is My Century
UA	Unpublished Autobiography
UCLA	University of California Los Angeles
UNC	University of North Carolina
Voltaire, Rousseau, Emerson	Reference to François-Marie Arouet Voltaire, Jean-Jacques Rosseau, Ralph Waldo Emerson
YWCA	Young Womens Christian Association
WPA	Works Progress Administration

PART I

SOUTHERN SONG

1915–1932

(Birmingham and New Orleans)

1

In This Place Where I Was Born

There were more than the usual records of Margaret Walker's birth. The family Bible recorded July 7, 1915, as a day destined to bring good luck to a firstborn—the seventh day of the seventh month. Both her parents and her grandmother had their own accounts. When she was old enough, Walker recorded this in her first journal: "They tell me I was born July 7, 1915 at 5 AM in the house of one Mrs. Boulware in Mason City community in the west end area of Birmingham, Jefferson County, Alabama." With tongue in cheek she added, "Unfortunately I do not remember the incident."[1]

She was aware of a proper birthright. "Being born into a good family, a clean house," she boasted, "with healthy and intelligent parents with little if any significance attached to being poor and black in the deep South."[2] There was the doting grandmother who provided the explanation of a child born with good luck. As Walker remembered it, "Both my parents were the seventh and youngest of their mother's children and I was born on the seventh day of the seventh month in the year. My parents' birthdays were seven days apart and I was born seven days before my mother's birthday."[3] Walker took from this observation two important things: seven was a lucky number and introduced her belief in life cycles of seven; and the universe had its own order, which would eventually take her to astrology, a belief system that provided a fitting complement to the religious faith that she inherited from her family. Being born for "good luck" according to the traditional Southern thinking, was the forecast of a bright future that made one fearless in the face of adversity. She could remind herself that she was expected to embrace the "*sturm and drang*,"—the pattern that teaches you "not to get too excited or happy over good fortune and not to be too disturbed over the bad."[4] Walker's birth in a family that spanned two centuries privileged her identity and gave her life purpose:

> I am a child of the twentieth century, a century of War and Revolution. Born early in the century like my mother, during the Spanish-American War and my grandmother, during the Civil War, I was a child of War and dislocation and a generation later my own children would be born in another World War.[5]

Written from the perspective of her adult, older self, these words suggested a kind of determinism with a predilection for the symbolic and reverential. The

The House Where My Soul Lives. Maryemma Graham, Oxford University Press. © Oxford University Press 2022.
DOI: 10.1093/oso/9780195341232.003.0001

Walker's birth home in Mason City, Alabama, outside of Birmingham

common thread is family, both immediate and extended, which she grew up surrounded by, and which was the central element in every stage of her life thereafter.
Her father, Sigismund Constantine Walker Sr., was a well-educated minister who
pastored churches before pursuing a better-paying job as a college teacher. Her
mother, Marion Dozier Walker, was a well-bred young woman headed toward a
successful career in music when she fell in love with the persuasive young minister just out of seminary.

Walker came to know the world through her father, to whom she felt the
stronger connection. It was to her father that she turned to explain her inaugural racial encounter. "When I was five," she wrote in 1943, her earliest personal
memoir; "I was busy discovering my world, and it was a place of happiness and
delight. Then, one day, a white child shouted in my ears 'nigger' . . . and I was
startled. I had never heard the word before, and I went home and asked what it
meant."[6] Sigismund Walker was often silent when his firstborn raised such questions, and they came steadily, since she had never learned to hold her tongue.
She saw her father as the man who knew everything, who was brilliant beyond
belief, and whose gentle spirit pervaded the house where the family resided—
first in Birmingham, Alabama, and then New Orleans. When he couldn't answer

her questions to her complete satisfaction, he would pull a book from his library and begin reading to her, or give her a sheet of loose paper and tell her to draw. She could always tell when the discussions were serious. On these occasions, the family would kneel to pray, asking for God's mercy and guidance in a troubled world. Growing up in the Alabama Black Belt, thinking of herself only as a member of a family and a community would offer little opportunity for exposure to racial difference. Sigismund Walker knew how to translate such encounters into a social value that she would understand. From her father she learned that people who used such words did not have an education, were not Christian at heart, and were certainly not fortunate enough to have the parents that she did. It was a gesture intended to remove any hurt, countering the negative with positive reinforcement.

It was Sigismund Walker who fed his daughter's belief about the perfect family. As a child, Walker felt she had the most remarkable parents in the world; she had no cause to complain about them since they provided her with an extraordinarily rich education and the most important ideals to live by. She knew that her father's formal education in theology set him apart from ordinary men, and her mother's love of classical music made their home different from others. On Sundays, Rev. Walker preached to congregations from the words of the biblical scriptures but during the week, he read British history, studied philosophy and the classics, and shared them with his eager-to-please daughter. He brought none of his public voice home. There, he was a quiet man that she found easy to love. He prayed, preached, and read, and looked for answers that she needed in books that sometimes had none. He had the same questions, but had learned to contain them.

Sigismund Walker was the last child born to Margaret Corby Carter, who already had four daughters when she married her second husband Richard Stuart Walker. Richard became very successful as a wine merchant and banana farmer in Port Antonio, Jamaica, and the three sons from this marriage were as ambitious as he was. One son went to McGill University to study medicine, a second to Cambridge to study law. The elder Walker expected his youngest, Sigismund, to join his older brother in Cambridge, where he would prepare himself for the Anglican priesthood. Richard Walker may have seen himself establishing a dynasty. With a lawyer, a doctor, and a priest, together with his own commercial success, he practically guaranteed a place for himself, if not his sons, in Jamaica's colonial government. But what came to pass was this: Sigismund was headed for Cambridge, but after an epiphany at a Wesleyan revival meeting, he abandoned his Anglican faith forever. The spirited young evangelists impressed him more than the solemn orthodoxy of the Anglican Church of his childhood. His conversion to Methodism drew the ire of his father, who refused to provide any further support. He was his mother's favorite child—she had given birth to him in a difficult labor when she was forty-seven—but her death, just as he was approaching adulthood, took away any buffer zone there might have been between father and son. Finding himself in a difficult situation, Sigismund left to seek his fortune elsewhere.

After taking several jobs in an effort to raise funds for his education, Sigismund learned a great deal about the world of work and exploitation, but earned little money. He was not only quick and efficient as a bookkeeper, but he also spoke all the local languages—Spanish, French, Hindustani, the Jamaican patois—and he easily picked up new ones. Thus, he was an ideal employee for seasonal projects in Jamaica, the other islands, and beyond. But his sensibilities worked against him in all of the jobs, for he was a supervisor over the Black workers, having to carry out the orders of the colonial administrators. When the projects failed, he was glad. His luck changed when a group of Quaker benefactors agreed to finance his trip to the United States.

In 1908, Sigismund Walker boarded a ship bound for the United States, entering at the Port of Mobile and headed for the only place he knew, Tuskegee Institute. He did poorly in the fields and in the kitchen at this agricultural and vocational training school, but because of his skills in shorthand, bookkeeping, and typing, Emmett Jay Scott, Booker T. Washington's right-hand man, employed him in the office.[7] However, as he became increasingly aware that the course of study at Tuskegee was not advancing him in the Methodist ministry, Sigismund soon followed a friend to Atlanta, where he enrolled in Gammon Theological Seminary. His three-year tenure there was highly successful since his facility

Tuskegee Institute Leaders, 1906. Bottom row middle; Emmett J. Scott, Booker T. Washington. Top row far right, George Washington Carver. Courtesy of Tuskegee University Archives, Photograph Collection, 1906

with languages and the thoroughness of his previous formal education gave him a decided advantage over those who were both older and less well trained. More important, Gammon and Atlanta brought lifelong friendships that helped Sigismund put the differences with his father behind him. They served effectively to cancel out any desire to return to his native land. He never did.

When Walker's father spoke about Jamaica, something he did not do very often, it was not his family that he remembered, but the land, its palm trees, blue waters, and pink sand, or the times he spent as a checker on the banana wharves of Port Antonio. What happened to his four sisters, he never said. Neither was Walker ever aware of any communication from his family in Jamaica, or his two older brothers. She did recognize Jamaica as a place, if not its people. The images evoked scenes of unparalleled beauty, serenity, and peace. Her father's silence, like his retreat into his books, told her that he had resigned himself to the America that had given him what he wanted. His heavy Jamaican accent did not make him exotic as much as it distinguished him as someone from another time, another place. And so he kept his silence for the most part, except when he preached his Sunday sermons. It helped to keep him firmly on American soil, covering any unpleasant memories.

Growing up, Walker might not have been aware that the Atlanta to which her father retreated had been a "growing mecca for black intellectuals,"[8] as she would later write, realizing that he had shared his time there with W. E. B. Du Bois and J. W. E. Bowen, who were the first African Americans to earn PhDs in the late nineteenth century from Harvard and Boston University respectively. Sigismund would certainly have been drawn to Atlanta for another reason as well: a fellow West Indian, William H. Crogman, was president of Clark University. While Sigismund trained for the ministry at Gammon he had Crogman as a model, a man with a similar history. An orphan who had left home for the sea, Crogman came to America and was educated first at a New England preparatory school, and then at Atlanta University, where his exceptional abilities led to a successful career in higher education.

It was not the young Sigismund Walker's preaching that attracted Marion Dozier when they first met in Pensacola, Florida, in the second decade of the twentieth century. She was in the process of completing the college preparatory curriculum at the Nannie Helen Burroughs Training School for Girls in Washington, DC. Like Sigismund, she was the last of seven children in her family, but unlike him, Marion was the daughter of Elvira Ware and Edward Lane Dozier, born in 1858 and 1856 respectively, which meant that they were born into slavery.

Edward taught himself to read the Bible and heard the calling to preach while still a young man. He quickly earned a reputation for two things: "outstanding preaching and a wandering eye for the ladies." He had learned to deliver

Grandmother Elvira Dozier

his sermons in the best of "the King's English, and strutted around in a prince Albert coat."[9] A tall, Black, and handsome man, Elder Dozier, as he was called, founded in 1875 the original Union Baptist Church in Pensacola, Florida. After seventeen years he moved to Jacksonville, where according to family legend, he took not only another church, but another woman. Elvira would not be humiliated and refused to leave Pensacola. Marion, born in 1895 when her mother was nearly thirty-seven, knew her father most by reputation. What she knew also, however, was that she would not be like her mother, tied to a man whom the women loved and who rarely honored his word. With such obvious contradictions, Elder Dozier visited his Pensacola family only occasionally. His death, "in another woman's house," as his wife reported,[10] meant little, and Marion did not shed a tear when her mother sent her two older daughters to bring their father's body home for a "proper burial" because "Grandma knew her duty," as Margaret reported it.[11] Marion was twelve and still in grade school when her father died. She was seven years younger than her next closest sibling Bedo, and seventeen years younger than her sister Abigail (Abbie) to whom she was the closest.[12]

Grandfather Rev. Edward Lane Dozier

Marion's mother, Elvira Ware Dozier, never learned to read or write. She took in laundry but refused to work in white people's kitchens, as was the custom of the day. Typical for a minister's wife, she could sing and play without the benefit of any training, and she was also a skilled seamstress. Both talents she passed on, with her dreams, to her children. Giving them a sense of empowerment was ultimately more important than having a devoted father, she had concluded. From Elvira, Marion inherited her strong sense of independence and, like her sisters and brothers, she was talented musically. She had watched her mother endure a difficult marriage and successfully raise her children, but Marion decided quite early to follow a different path. Her brothers had left home early in pursuit of their dreams and had challenged the conventional roles for Black men in the days following slavery. Charlie and Bedo became traveling blues and jazzmen who died young, and a third brother earned respect as an enlisted man in the US Navy. Abbie was a seamstress, but was equally as talented as a pianist and organist, which gained her a reputation in the town's churches and musical programs.

By the time of Elder Dozier's death, only Abbie, now the family's bread-winner, remained at home. It was this last child Marion, therefore, who not only absorbed the family's hopes and aspirations, but also the possibility of their achievement. She would be the one who would represent the best in all of them, who would make it, going far beyond the others. Elvira was especially determined that this last daughter would have the benefit of a full formal education; she, too, did not want her daughter's life to repeat her pattern. It was Marion, whose talent was already judged exceptional; Marion, whose education had to continue at all costs. Education, they all believed, was necessary to "be a lady."[13]

It was not a minor point for that place and time. Black women born into slavery were intent upon enhancing their self-respect and overcoming the legacy of slavery. They often did so by transmuting an image of abuse and suffering to self-possession, and the ideal of true womanhood. Abbie had similar aspirations, and because she had gained a degree of independence from her sewing and her musical ability, she served as a model for Marion. Though Abbie could only achieve a measure of local success, Marion, they believed, could go all the way. Elvira's resourcefulness and natural talent would inspire all of them, including her unborn granddaughter.

"They were all of one accord," Walker wrote, "that [Marion] should go away to school and finish college," three years after Elder Dozier's death.[14] She had gone as far as the educational system in Pensacola, Florida, would allow a Black child to go in 1910 when she finished grade school. Luckier than most, she had access to a rural school that had taken her through the rudiments of learning, and she had her sister Abbie as her tutor.

"On September 1, 1910," Walker remembered her mother saying, "her family and Church members put her on the train for Washington, D.C. bound for the Nannie Burroughs School for Girls."[15] That Walker would recall with such precision this date in the life of her mother is significant for a number of reasons. First, it suggests the value placed on Black education in an era when the majority of African Americans remained illiterate. It also reflects a long-standing tradition when the first child in a family goes away to school. It is a source of pride not only for the family, but also for the entire community, and becomes a collective endeavor. This event and any associated stories would be frequently repeated, just as Walker herself reported this one:

> The local Baptist Church took up collections and raised the money to send her away. Her sister, Abbie, and her mother made a wardrobe of beautiful clothes including the high-waisted long sleeve white blouses worn with long black and navy blue skirts. Her hair was puffed above her ears—fur hat and three puffs and that was the uniform.[16]

A photo would have accompanied this departure of a fifteen-year-old girl, leaving home for the first time alone, knowing that she would not see her mother or any of her family for a full three years. Marion Dozier was her family's pride and joy, and her sadness could not be acknowledged as a factor on this occasion. It was she who was given the ultimate opportunity, one so few would have.

The Nannie Burroughs School was one of the most influential boarding schools for young Black women in the nation in the first decade of the twentieth century. The young women who were enrolled there experienced a complete transformation. If she were born to the Black middle class, she would expect the very structured life there, a first-class education and the necessary training to be exemplary in every way, as a wife or a future race leader. But as the examples of Mary McCleod Bethune and Nannie Burroughs indicated, these were the young women being primed to become the nation's new race leaders in their own right. The philosophy of education as racial uplift was synonymous with proper manners and decorum. For those young women born to more humble status, attending Miss Burroughs's school was the chance of a lifetime to realize the dreams of those they left behind, to accept the mantle of service to a race of people whose struggles they shared, and to whose uplift they were committed.

Marion expressed her gratitude, writing home often, reporting on all the opportunities that came her way. She quickly associated herself with one of the influential Baptist churches in the Washington, DC, area that served as a site for the activities of newly created organizations, predecessors to the soon-to-be-formed NAACP. As the accompanist for the women's glee club, she got to travel throughout the region, and her musical abilities frequently put her in contact with those individuals associated with the work of the Women's Temperance Society and the Women's Club movement. She had less money than the other girls, but she stood out among her more middle-class colleagues because of her extensive and fashionable wardrobe made possible by the experienced seamstresses in her family who could "make anything they saw in a book or on a store mannequin."[17] She was mature, alert, accustomed to meeting new people and found Washington a thrilling place to live in 1910. She progressed quickly in her studies, completing the four-year college preparatory curriculum, and her courses in piano and vocal music curriculum, in three years. Walker noted that this included the requisite courses in "beauty culture, learning how to use Madam C. J. Walker's straightening comb, and typing according to the touch system."[18]

As a child, Walker remembered conversations between her parents about the peculiar caste system in both Atlanta and Washington, the "blue-veined" society that drew her comment that "during this time, no one in our immediate family could qualify for this strange select group, nor did they wish to."[19] It may well have been this that made Marion weary from the long hours that turning oneself into a lady required. Like all the students, the days went from six to four, and she was assigned a work duty—the most hated one for Marion, "scrubbing on her knees the long dining hall."[20] In any case, although she graduated in the top ten of her class and was offered an opportunity to continue her studies with a scholarship to pursue music at Howard University, Marion hesitated. She needed a break from school. She wanted to continue in college, but she wanted and needed to go home to her family whom she had not seen in three years. Elvira consented for Marion, now a proper and educated lady, to return to Pensacola. What Marion feared had already happened. Upon her return, she learned that one of her brothers who had left home had died.

Before Marion arrived, the newly ordained Sigismund Walker, divinity degree in hand, had met Elvira Dozier and one of her grandsons on the train. They were returning to Pensacola from Greenville, Alabama. He was coming to accept his new appointment as pastor of St. Paul Methodist Church in the city. Knowing that Abbie, her older and as yet unmarried daughter played for St. Paul, it would have been strange for Elvira, now a prominent widow, *not* to introduce herself in a most gracious and hospitable manner and invite the young minister to dinner. That the chance meeting would allow for an introduction to Abbie goes without saying. The young Rev. Walker visited the Dozier home on the summer of Marion's return "ostensibly to see Abbie, his organist [when he] saw Marion for the first time."[21]

The story of the meeting, courtship, and marriage between Sigismund Walker and Marion Dozier was Walker's favorite. It took only one look for Sigismund Walker to make up his mind about his future wife. "Reverend Walker was smitten for life. My mother was a very pretty girl—clear pretty brown skin and laughing eyes and long black hair in two hanging plaits, and she was only eighteen years old."[22] The attraction went unnoticed for a while, and Rev. Walker continued to visit and meet with Abbie. When he came to ask for her daughter's hand, Elvira assumed that the choice was Abigail; and pleased that her daughter was finally getting married, happily shared the news with the community. When she learned of her mistake, Elvira was understandably upset, and Abbie despondent. Although she tried to persuade Sigismund that Marion was too young, still in school with a brilliant career ahead of her, and that Abbie was clearly a better mate as a pastor's wife, Sigismund was not interested. He wanted to and would marry Marion; that he made absolutely clear. Walker remained convinced that Elvira and Abbie had always wished otherwise.

Marion Dozier did not return to school the following fall. She was no less committed to her music, but equally committed to marrying the young minister with the thick Jamaican accent. Elvira's matchmaking had gone awry. Remembering her own experience as a minister's wife, she feared that her youngest daughter might have a similar fate. By now, however, Marion's training at the Burroughs school and her exposure to a world much larger than Pensacola, had taken root.

She had begun to accept the contemporary view that young women could and should seek to uplift themselves and their race through marriage to the right man. Sigismund Walker had such impressive credentials and obvious potential that it would have been difficult for them *not* to fall in love. Sigismund was thirteen years older than she was, not an uncommon age difference between men and women who were couples at the time. Abbie, by contrast, was four years his senior.

Marion saw the possibility of her own ambitions being realized in Sigismund Walker and followed her heart. On September 14, 1914, after promising Elvira Dozier that he would make sure her daughter finished her education, Sigismund Constantine Walker married Marion Dozier. He was thirty-two; she was nineteen. Both had had the experience of living on their own and away from their immediate families. Religion was a crucial factor in both of their lives, and they knew from the beginning that theirs would be a deeply religious household.

Their honeymoon was spent on the train to Birmingham where Rev. Walker would begin an assignment in the largest city in Alabama in 1914. A major, and rapidly growing, iron and steel production center, it attracted migrants from throughout the Southern region in search of jobs, no matter that they received the lowest of wages for working in the mills, factories, and furnaces that would produce a new era of Southern white wealth and gentility. Itinerant workers with no formal education came, newly freed from slaving in the soil and eager to sell their labor for money they could call their own. They settled in communities at the northern and western edges of the city, unwelcome as they were in the downtown centers. When they found more or less stable employment, they became active participants in the life of these small communities, in accordance with the routine patterns of social segregation. They sent their children to nearby schools and churches, and maintained no contact with whites, other than those for whom they worked. For most of them, the choices were limited. Either they had been enslaved or they were sharecroppers, and those who had gotten any education had done so through stealth. Yet they lived within communities that took care of their own and had ambitions that they sought to realize. In every case, there were a few Blacks who had received more than the usual amount of training and whose job it was to serve in the capacity of ministers, teachers, and doctors. If a town was lucky, there would be both a segregated public school and another school run by one or more of the Black denominations such as Miles College, founded by the Colored Methodist Episcopal Church, which began as a secondary school for the city's Black residents in 1898. Sigismund Walker, however, was a member of the Methodist Episcopal Church South, the segregated unit of Methodist Episcopal Church that had also developed a strong base in rural areas of the South.

By the time the Walkers arrived, Birmingham was considered the model for industrialization in the New South, a modern-day boom town. It had the basis for producing great wealth, made possible by the unusual proximity of mineral deposits that provided the essential ingredients for making steel and cast iron pipes, which also contributed to its image as a melting pot of society as well as of metals. During the early decades of the twentieth century, there were several large Black enclaves where the more enterprising among them went into business, opening up establishments such as barbershops, beauty parlors, dance halls, an occasional restaurant, and funeral parlors. The nearby normal, or training school, offered opportunities for greater cultural enrichment. Rarely were there Black-owned shops that sold clothes, dry goods, or groceries. Most Black towns could not get the capital to open such businesses. Given the preponderance of skilled Black seamstresses and tailors, store-bought clothes were an unaffordable, if unnecessary luxury.

Because Birmingham was characteristically divided along racial and class lines, the city's growth was uneven at best. This does not suggest that the undeveloped areas were without their own livelihood or their own culture. Amid the orderly patterns of streets and avenues that constituted the city were significant outposts. These were strategically located where crops of cotton, corn, and potatoes grew easily, feeding the families of farmers and mill workers alike. There was poverty, judging by today's standards, yet mill workers could afford to buy what they didn't grow in their gardens. They also went into town to market on the weekends. Their deprivation was relative in terms of where they had come from and what they had achieved since then, not in terms of what they saw in others of a different complexion. Ever conscious of the racial codes of Southern life, the city's Black population was self-contained and self-sustaining . . . as long as these people met the demands for labor in the steel mills and factories.

The strength of Birmingham's private sector hardly bolstered the public economy. As a result, Birmingham in the years that the Walkers lived there might be described as a potentially progressive city with a rural-dominated political leadership and a business community that championed traditional Southern values—in short, a model Southern city in the 1920s. Its wealth was guarded, not shared, its tax base too low to support routine municipal services. If Alabama ranked last among the states in expenditures for public schools, then Birmingham ranked last in the list of cities in this same category.

Birmingham's signs of increasing economic prosperity were visible in the Black areas. The exodus to the North, the Great Migration, would eclipse any positive effects of that economic boom in only a few years. But in 1915, both Enon Ridge in the north end, and Mason City in the west end, with the city's Black residents sandwiched in between, extended the city's boundaries up the slopes of the Red and Ishkooka Mountains. Both would become familiar to

Walker in her childhood since they were two major areas that continued to absorb Birmingham's growing Black population. The growth of the Black community had other dimensions as well. Industrial High School became the largest accredited Negro industrial high school in the country. Likewise, the community established several newspapers so that Birmingham was well represented in the national Black media.

Rev. Walker and his bride had gone to Enon Ridge first, but he was soon assigned to the church in Mason City. The city's patriarch was Dr. M. C. B. Mason, a local physician, whose years of selfless service had been rewarded when the community was named after him. The church had neither money nor a parsonage, but the status of the Mason City Methodist Episcopal mattered little. The Walkers were glad to feel somewhat settled when Marion was ready to give birth, almost ten months after she and Sigismund were married.

They named their firstborn Margaret, the name of both Sigismund's mother and Marion's grandmother, both of whom were deceased. But they also wanted to honor Marion's oldest sister. They were both aware that Abbie had been visibly crushed when the two of them had married. She had lost her last chance, for at thirty-five, spinsterhood was now her only option. The resentment took little time to reveal itself, however much she tried to hide it beneath the excitement of gaining a new niece as her namesake. The newborn, Margaret Abigail, quickly gave Abbie her new place as a proud sister, sister-in-law, and doting aunt who must have received some vicarious satisfaction from seeing her youngest sister wear the well-designed creations that were the products of Abbie's skillful hands.

When a second child was born a year later, she was given the name Mercedes Elvira, honoring two more of the family's women, including Marion's mother. Walker recalled seeing a stillborn child in a basket when she was four and who was never spoken about. Two other siblings followed—Gwendolyn, and finally a boy named Sigismund after his father, who, as the only male sibling, was known for the remainder of his life as "Brother."

Marion and Abbie never spoke openly about what had transpired between the two of them, although Abbie came from Pensacola to Birmingham to visit after Walker was born. Her Aunt Abbie and her father would argue about the smallest things. Abbie eventually left Pensacola, moved to Boston, and ironically, was a major source of support when Walker's own daughter Marion was born some twenty-five years later.

That Sigismund Walker was a source of conflict between her two daughters, who had been the closest, must have also made it easier for Elvira to find her new son-in-law lacking in many ways as a husband and father. As a West Indian, Sigismund was naturally suspect among some family members who saw a "conceited foreigner . . . who would treat a woman like a slave."[23] Walker had her own opinion of this, confirmed by her experience growing up as the oldest daughter.

"Maybe in Jamaica it would have been different, but if anybody was dominated it was Daddy. . . . I think my father worshipped the ground my mother walked on and from the day he saw her until the day he died he loved and adored her."[24]

Elvira also traveled from Pensacola to Mason City to meet her new grand-daughter. She was "Grandma Dozier," there to care for the bright-eyed, pink-faced infant; she took full responsibility for the firstborn, leaving little for Marion to do. Though tiny, the child seemed to have no lack of energy at first, but she soon grew weak when she couldn't keep anything in her stomach. She was losing the little weight she had, and death seemed a very likely prospect during her first year. For Elvira, who had lost two of her sons before they barely reached adult-hood, death was not an option. She refused to leave Margaret's side and even elected not to return home for her mother's funeral. Once she had nursed her granddaughter back to health, she remained a permanent fixture in the Walker household until her death in 1944. One suspects that her discomfort about the marriage might have been a key motivation for the guardian role that she readily accepted.

Marion grew into the marriage slowly. She wanted children but not the day-to-day responsibilities for a family. Mason City was a mill town unable to offer much to a talented nineteen-year-old whose constant companion had been music. She could hardly stand being confined to home with a new baby. Grandma Dozier's presence gave Marion the freedom to accept her lack of aptitude for mother-hood and the domestic sphere. By the time her daughter was barely six weeks old, Marion accepted a job outside the home. She gave as her reason the need to supplement her husband's meager income from the church. When Marion began teaching music at Central Alabama Institute, the Methodist school in Mason City, she was making a declaration: she would never become just a housewife, and she never did.

Marion's absence mattered little. The young Walker thrived under Grandma Dozier's tutelage; she learned to cook, to sew and embroider, and to keep a house while serving as her grandmother's constant companion. The cooking skills she fully embraced, but the rest she did only because she had to. If Sigismund had objected to the replacement of his mother-in-law for his wife in certain domestic matters, it wouldn't have made any difference.

Because Elvira was primarily responsible for her granddaughter, she was able to provide an important link to an era with which Walker would become increasingly more fascinated as she grew older. She also provided the neces-sary balance against the senior Walkers' aspirations toward a solid middle-class life, one implied by their education and status, if not their income. Elvira was a natural storyteller who never forgot having been born in slavery and reared in its shadow. She was fifty-seven when Walker was born, and from all indications, had a perfect memory. Her rich archive of oral lore made her eager to transmit to her granddaughter a strong maternal legacy, if only to assure its survival in this marriage between two very different strains of Black culture. She did not want her son-in-law's Jamaican background, his British-style education (which he seemed to prefer to his American one), and his aristocratic manner to overshadow *her* side of the family. Whether it was self-defense or sheer enjoyment at having her granddaughter all to herself, Elvira Dozier initiated a ritual of storytelling that captivated her granddaughter. There were endless rounds of tales about slavery days and about the three generations on the maternal side of the family in the South who lived in Georgia, Alabama, and Florida—people who had survived and endured, had raised large families, and who had unique gifts and talents to pass on. For Elvira, who had never seen the inside of a school, these stories were as important as what her granddaughter would learn when she left home to begin her formal education.

As a child, Walker was "enthralled in . . . grandmother's stories."[25] Even when her parents chastised Grandma Dozier for telling "all those harrowing tales" of slavery rather than more acceptable bedtime stories, with indignation rising in her voice, Elvira would announce, "I'm not telling her tales; I'm telling her the naked truth."[26] Learning to make no distinction between the "naked truth" and its fictional equivalent was one of the first lessons Walker learned in childhood. Grandma Dozier's stories were the truth as she remembered it, and it was the truth that would form the basis of her own later narrative. During those times when her parents were in school or working, their narrative exchanges had few interruptions.

Generally the stories began with the women in the family, the first of whom was always Walker's great-grandmother and Elvira's mother Margaret Duggans Ware Brown. So too had Margaret Brown's mother died when she was a small child. Duggans was married first to Randall Ware, gave birth to three children, and had nine more with her second marriage to Henry Brown, a freed slave. Walker's grandmother, Elvira Ware Dozier, was one of the first three of the second set of children. The awareness of her own mother's musical background began to make more sense to Walker, who knew early that that music was never far from her mother's mind. The stories seemed even more remarkable when she later realized what her grandmother's life as a minister's wife had been like. She learned of Elder Dozier's indiscretions and Elvira's refusal to move to Jacksonville, sparing both her children and herself further embarrassment. It was then that she first learned the concept of the "devil's music," which had been the attraction for her uncles, whose short lives on the riverboats playing in New Orleans, Mobile, Memphis, and St. Louis left the family many stories of living hard and dying young. Elvira was proud that her girls—both Abbie and Marion—used their gifts wisely, stayed in church, and far removed from the devil's music.

Great-grandmother Margaret Duggans Ware Brown

Walker was not a passive listener. "As I grew older and realized the importance of the story my grandmother was telling, I prodded her with more questions. . . . I was already conceiving the story of *Jubilee* vaguely, and early on in
my adolescence while I was still hearing my grandmother tell old slavery-time
stories and incidents from my mother's life, I promised my grandmother that
when I grew up I would write her mother's story."[27] Elvira, for her part, watched
her son-in-law grow increasingly self-centered, determined to strain the family
finances with his unending desire to go "way up North to get all that education
that didn't make him preach any better."[28] He had promised that Marion could
finish school, and knowing something of her own daughter's dreams and hopes,
Elvira had seen nothing she considered positive after eight years of their marriage and the birth of four children. She was afraid for her daughter and for her
grandchildren, but never allowed her dissatisfaction to show. She kept telling the
stories and making sure she kept the house in order, something that no one else,
especially Marion Walker, ever had an inclination to do.

Walker's parents were highly conscious that the environment they were
creating for their children defied the norm for most Black and white families

of the period. It was, moreover, well suited for the making of an artist. No one tried to contain Walker's imagination, her natural youthful curiosity was not repressed, and she had access to multiple ways of knowing and understanding the world. This somewhat unusual Black family, a little more than half a century removed from the era of slavery, personified the phrase "up from slavery." The family's powerful work ethic was linked directly to breaking down the barriers of caste and class prejudice as they maintained a reverence for Southern folkways. Hearing her grandmother's stories and joining with her in singing the old-time spirituals affirmed for Walker the value of an oral, vernacular tradition. Her parents represented the talented tenth; she and her siblings were the logical extension of this ideal in an emerging generation. It was up to Walker to learn to negotiate both of these traditions and to find a way to synthesize them in her own vision of the world.

Marion had to do a great deal more growing up and adjusting than her husband. She had chosen to be a minister's wife, but it is likely that she also imagined a career trajectory for her husband that would move him beyond the pastoring of small rural Black churches. His opportunities for advancement would have been far better in the African Methodist Episcopal, or Baptist churches with traditional, Black-controlled denominations where the racial ceiling did not apply. His choice to remain with the Central Jurisdiction of the Methodist Episcopal Church meant that he was confined to small churches or those slightly larger until he finally accepted a full-time teaching appointment in order to support his family. The ambitions that Marion could not realize in herself or her husband, she transferred to her children. What she did recognize early on was the need to take charge, something she had learned from Elvira, and what had been exhibited in her sister Abbie. She came to represent this for her children. Despite the thirteen-year age difference between her husband and herself, Marion was clearly the boss. What she lacked in years, she more than made up for in her controlling style.

Rev. Walker found it difficult, or elected not to object to his wife's approach to managing their lives, and in time, withdrew more and more from discussions, allowing Marion to have her way. Walker remembered never having conflicts with her father, and always having conflicts with her mother. "Mother wanted to dictate everything we did, and even after I was married, she continued to tell me what I should and shouldn't do."[29] But Marion Walker was never able to break her oldest daughter's rambunctious spirit, no matter how hard she tried. She found her daughter stubborn and spiteful, as strong-willed children were often described at the time. Walker, who never seemed to see herself in her mother, made up her mind about those things she wanted, and did those things she was told she could not.

Though Marion disliked keeping house or cooking, she was firmly committed to cultivating the artistic talents in her offspring early. While music education experts have cited the optimal age to introduce a child to music to be five, especially in anticipation of a professional career, Marion began musical instruction for her children as soon as they could walk. The piano's foreboding presence in the living room gave it a central place in their lives, perhaps even more than their Bible reading and daily prayers. Marion played and sang, while all of the children were always encouraged to perform for each other. Though all four children exhibited musical aptitude, Mercedes was by far the most talented. She had a magnificent singing voice, played the piano with gusto, and never had to be forced to practice. Brother was next, although he preferred to pick out the tunes to popular songs rather than practice his assigned lessons. But Walker learned to play moderately well, often seeing herself in competition with Mercedes, whose talents were frequently the subject of conversation in the household.

Walker soon accepted the limits of her ability. She eventually learned to play well enough to accompany a soloist and play routine church hymns. Although Marion thought that a shift to the violin might work better for her oldest daughter, they ultimately concluded that her talents lay elsewhere. Marion's passion for music, nevertheless, drove much of the family's social activity. She leaped at the chance to attend an opera or a concert, even if it meant having to sit upstairs in the Jim Crow section of the concert hall in downtown Birmingham. If Marion had given up her chance at a professional music career, she would make sure that the Ware-Brown-Dozier musical legacy was not lost. She intended for it to flourish in her own children. By the time the children had started school, Marion had planned their futures: Margaret was expected to be a writer; Mercedes was expected to be a musician; Gwendolyn and Brother were expected to be teachers.

Having a home situation that did not conform to what their schoolbooks said about "negroes"—the word was yet to be capitalized—was the first obstacle the Walker children had to overcome. Having a determined mother gave them high expectations, even though she was the source of tremendous conflict. These expectations never altered, a fact that would help account for much of Walker's drive as well as her adaptability as she confronted momentous crises over the course of her life. The words Walker used most frequently for her parents were "gentle and intelligent."[30] She was likely referring to the traditional religious values that the family observed and a somewhat unusual parental practice: corporal punishment was not used as a means for correcting misbehavior. The children were expected to observe the strictest standards of social behavior. From their parents, they learned that morality was directly tied to virtue and required a visible demonstration as the measure of one's spiritual faith. This method of enforcing good behavior was based on (1) a clear set of standards for what was right and wrong, what was good and bad, what was moral and immoral; and (2) the knowledge that one did the "right," "good," and "morally correct" thing because of the felt presence of the Holy Spirit in one's soul.

Even with an acceptable and somewhat liberal range for childhood misbehavior, Walker tested all the existing boundaries. She interpreted this as the temptation from the devil, who was always present, and whose influence could only be countered with sustained and persistent Christian faith. The formula she discerned was simple: a weak faith made one easy prey to wrongdoing. In the presence of weak faith, then, the application of corporal punishment was meaningless. The problem was much more deeply spiritual and had to be addressed at this most basic level. These were rather mature lessons to be learned at such a young age, but they were part of the parental training that characterized the Walker method. Her confrontation with the presence or absence of faith in her life came so early and with such intensity that it formed the major subject of her journal entries from the very beginning, before she finished elementary school. As a precocious, sensitive child, she observed the families around her and learned of the practices of her school friends, only to conclude that hers was an extraordinary life, the cause of which must have been her extraordinary parents. Having them as a model made her more firmly committed to achieving the expectations that they had established for her.

In the Walkers' worldview, the importance of education and racial uplift came second only to one's spiritual faith. For the New Negro generation, racial progress was signified by educational advancement and achievement, and while a necessary and worthy goal itself, more importantly, education was directly linked to social and economic mobility with an important byproduct—political advancement. Marion and Sigismund Walker were their own best examples. Although he was one of a select few formally trained ministers of his time, Sigismund continued to pursue advanced education. Likewise, Marion remained determined to finish college over the course of ten years and went for advanced studies in music at Northwestern with her husband. Thus, a competitive spirit, persistence, and a desire for high achievement were the principal ingredients of the Walker formula for success.

When Walker was five, the family moved to Meridian, Mississippi. Because she had already begun to read, Marion took her along to the school where she taught. A year later, they were back in a Birmingham elementary school where the teachers marveled at Walker's ability to read and write at such a young age. The bevy of compliments may have encouraged her acting out, since by the time she turned six, she was already currying her mother's disfavor for her disobedient manner, mostly having to do with her refusal to pay attention when she was preoccupied with a book. Yet, her most consistent and unforgivable childhood crime was an inability to keep her silence when she had something to say or was told not to do so. She was a child who "talked back" without fear of consequences in an era that held no tolerance for such behavior. Mother and daughter were in a constant battle, while Marion was the source of Sigismund's unexpressed frustration. They were two strong-willed personalities, but Marion, exercising her right as a mother, was determined to be the winner. The daughter eventually came to see it as her mother's need for control, derived from a sense of inadequacy. Likely it had a great deal to do with Marion having gone from childhood to adulthood quickly, since at eighteen she had married, and within less than a year, had become a mother. As she grew up, Walker grew increasingly critical of her mother while simultaneously adopting a negative self-image. The more she acted out, the more her mother enforced behavioral sanctions, believing that her daughter was indeed headed straight to hell. Walker intuited from these conversations that she was no different from those whom she read about who had "fallen by the wayside of sin."[31] A physical whipping might well have been better, for what she took away from these early experiences was a sense of her own sinfulness and utter depravity.

The crucial transformative moment came at age eight when Walker decided she was not going to be scolded by her mother ever again. If she wasn't going to be allowed to speak her mind, then she would write, she declared in a rage. The thought of being a writer suddenly became immensely attractive since this was the one thing that she could control. After that point, going to school became synonymous with the idea of not having to be silent, of having the freedom to speak when and about whatever she wanted. Becoming a writer would not only be a way to express herself, but also a way to fight with force and conviction. It made going to school even more important. If her grandmother had given her a birthright, one that she could never abandon, going to school would help to establish the goal of also finding the voice that would make her a writer. The birthright gave her the authority and mandate to speak. The only question was how.

A contributing factor to Walker's identity as a woman was the woman-centered household in which she grew up. The experience would figure prominently in her developing ideas about womanhood that would mature in the novel *Jubilee* and become the subject of later essays. While her future social status as a Black woman was being cultivated at home and at school, she became aware of tensions having to do with class and gender distinctions uniquely tied to place and the particular dynamics within her own family. She learned to operate best in an environment that replicated, rather than resolved, these tensions. Her family stood inside and outside of mainstream folk and urban communities as these pertained to Blacks in the South, and she remained psychically and historically connected to those communities as well. To her way of thinking, there was no conflict in her internalization of the values inherent in both. Moreover, coming to know different worlds—a Black one, a woman-centered one, and one privileged by her class status—gave her a certain sense of power; her writing would in fact become the point of convergence for all three. She saw Black women working, they were heads of households, and they were professionally employed, but they were not all the same. Her family had taught her that difference was not a means of negating her relationship to others, but rather an opportunity to affirm her own individuality and human connection. Not only did this difference invite a dialogue with others, but it also confirmed her complex cultural conditioning as a Black woman in the first half of the twentieth century.

2

A Preacher's Daughter

Even if Walker's tension with Marion grew, it did not stop her from seeing Mason City, the Birmingham Black enclave where her parents had made a family, as magical. She was surrounded by the most important sources that give a young child psychic comfort. Life was filled with the discovery of the sights and sounds that fed her vivid imagination. As a child, Walker was known to carry on conversations with imaginary playmates, replacing her sister whose interest in the piano precluded such activities. Her keen powers of observation stored images of "red miners dressed raggedly and wearing carbide lamps / . . . the swing of dinner buckets." She saw "croppers' rotting shacks" and met people who knew "famine, terror, flood, and plague."[1] Her first ten years were her freest, and the life she discovered was her own. She had no commitments, other than emotional ones, and absorbed a certain knowledge of the functions of this self-contained, closely knit community. Moreover, living in Mason City, Enon Ridge, Meridian, and Birmingham allowed her to experience the continuum between slavery and the era of legal segregation.

Going to elementary school in Birmingham gave Walker a grasp of the South in terms of its symbols, myths, and rituals. Once she began to understand that she was going to school to learn to be a writer, she absorbed the poetic elements that she thought would be useful. She began to trust her imagination and record the world that it embraced. Birmingham became the most frequent city referenced in her early poetry. It was the place of yearning for "the last whippoorwill call of evening / settling over mountains / . . . When memories of my fancy ridden life / Come home again,"[2] even as she boldly denounced the South's oppression and violence. Although this contrasting vision—the South as a place to love and hate—offered Walker the emotional basis for a relationship with the South that would find fuller expression in Chicago, Birmingham provided her the fragments that her imagination devoured, storing them for her later use.

Rev. Walker continued to serve as the key to his daughter's intellectual development. While Walker remembered her mother as a talker, she knew her father as stern, but loving, and above all, a thinker. She was clear that even as he continued to serve as a pastor, what he enjoyed the most was teaching, alternating between positions at Central Alabama Institute, Parker Industrial High School, and a short stint at Miles Memorial College in Birmingham. Spending these years in the Alabama Black Belt under her father's watchful eye, seeing herself as

The House Where My Soul Lives. Maryemma Graham, Oxford University Press. © Oxford University Press 2022.
DOI: 10.1093/oso/9780195341232.003.0002

Rev. Sigismund Walker, upon completion of his graduate degree
from Garrett Biblical Institute, Northwestern University, 1929

her father's child, and seeking his deliberate approval made it easier to accept her
mother's constant reminder that she was a preacher's daughter. More important,
perhaps, she shared her father's lyrical imagination. With his oldest daughter,
Rev. Walker shared the books from which he taught, treating her as if she were
as old as his high school students. Walker had the feeling that her father was
teaching *her* what he taught *them*, something he would not have done had she
not been such an apt pupil.

Many of her early teachers were women who encouraged the development of
oratorical skills in particular. She was featured at many events and enjoyed the

attention she received, but she felt most in control when she wrote. Writing allowed her to bring everything into a world that she occupied in her mind. When
she was puzzled about the contradictions she saw in the world around her—
segregated hospitals, churches, and schools—she began to imagine a time when
the world would be another way. "Then I began to daydream: It will not always
be this way. This injustice will also end; this internal suffering will cease; this ache
inside for understanding will exist no longer. Someday, I said, when I am fully
grown, I will understand, and I will be able to do something about it. I will write
books that will prove the history texts were distorted. I will write books about
colored people who have colored faces, books that will not make me ashamed
when I read them."[3]

If her experiences growing up in the Deep South fueled Walker's imagination, they also challenged her intellect, forcing more questions about the world
that surrounded her childhood. Because of her family's class position, she was
shielded from the more brutal effects of racism, although the Walkers were never
entirely outside of racism's orbit. Memories of the South's Jim Crow culture remained with her. "One year when my father's schoolwork took him out of town
constantly, my mother lived in fear of our lives because there was no man in the
house to protect us against the possibility of some attack. Once we climbed the
fire escape to see a movie, because there was no Negro entrance, and after that
we saw no movies. Another time my mother stood for hours upstairs in a dark-
ened theatre to hear a recital by Rachmaninoff, because there were no seats for
colored. My father was chased home one night at the point of a gun by a drunken
policeman who resented seeing a fountain pen in a 'nigger's' pocket."[4]

Like many middle-class Black families, the Walkers depended on their domestic stability and community insularity to counter an otherwise repressive racial environment that demanded two separate worlds. Frequent references to the
contrast between home, school, and the world around her in her writings suggest
that Walker not only derived a great deal of inspiration from the domestic arrangement she found at home, but that she also had identified the elements for
constructing her own form of domestic feminism.

In fall 1923, Walker began attending Slater Elementary School in Birmingham,
ten miles from Mason City. She was excited to meet new friends, but the girls she
met at Slater were "fast," as her mother often referred to them. She ignored her
mother's repeated orders to keep to herself, but with four children to manage,
Marion's decision to follow her longtime dream of starting her own music studio
left little time to remind her daughter of what she should and should not do.
Marion's outbursts became less frequent for a while, and Walker suspected that
her mother was finally doing something that she enjoyed.

Slater's one large room with a pot-bellied stove provided fond memories for
the inquisitive fourth grader. What she liked most about Slater was being away

from her mother, with whom she had gone to school most of her life. Slater was the first school she could claim as her own. The ten miles on the trolley daily to and from downtown Birmingham gave her ample opportunity to do what she was told she could not.

After Slater School, Walker would have gone to Birmingham's Parker Industrial High School. Here she would have met other children her age from all over the city and state. But this was not to be. Margaret's mother may well have seen this as another reason to think about moving. Leaving Birmingham around the time her oldest daughter was ready for high school would eliminate the need to argue against her going to Industrial High. Seeing her daughter's eagerness to meet other children and to talk to boys prompted Marion's desire to redirect her daughter's newly found interests. That Sigismund had taught at Industrial High offered little endorsement for the school. Walker soon stopped talking about it; it only made her mother mad, and with her father frequently away, she dared not send Marion into a rage.

On a page in her composition book, which was already beginning to double as a journal, beside the lines from songs that she wanted to be sure to remember, she wrote what was troubling her most. "God expects me to be good only one day at a time. What am I doing now?"[5] What did being good mean? She was already beginning to think that she wanted to be the writer her mother had proclaimed; writing had become the way she could think through things that troubled her, things that she could not talk to anyone about. Writing things down always cleared her mind, steadied her, making her more peaceful. She began to wonder if writing was that important to her, would she be able to become a writer *and* get married and have a family? She also wrote to calm her anxieties about the move. She knew the move was inevitable and began to organize how she wanted it to happen, as if she had total control over her future. She took this mapping of her life very seriously, predicting those things she expected and wanted to happen to her. The exercise gave her some sense of security and introduced a practice that she followed for the remainder of her life.

Walker wrote about an incident that happened during the year at Slater School. One day she was walking home from the trolley with a friend. Suddenly, she found herself surrounded by white boys who teased and beat her.[6] There is no explanation or detail about this incident, other than her sense that it was racially motivated. She escaped, glad that she only had a few scrapes to show for it. But nothing could replace the embarrassment and fear she felt at what might have happened. Only years later, in New Orleans, when she and her sister saw the initials "KKK" carved into the wood of a mantelpiece, did she realize just how much danger she had been in. Walker was afraid of telling her parents since she would have to admit much more than she was willing to share. Telling her parents would only have furthered Marion's resolve to remove her daughter from the school where she was finally out of her mother's reach, at least, for a part of the day. However, she could not deny this first wake-up call—a recognition of her own vulnerability. She carried this feeling with her as she began to seek some assurance for protection in her life. The only place she knew to go was church, to pray for guidance, and to confirm her faith. The other source of protection was her father. She soon discovered, however, that she would have to put those feelings on hold.

Marion Walker had endured the early years as a small-town preacher's wife, and she was pleased when her husband elected to follow an educational path within the church. The pride and ambition her mother exhibited for her husband and children Walker sometimes interpreted as scorn, especially when Marion compared her own family with others. Understandably, Marion's desire to curb her daughter's enthusiasm for her new friendships with dreaded cautionary tales made her daughter uneasy. Walker especially feared that her mother would drive a wedge between the friendships she was beginning to form. More important, in just a few years she would be the age of those students her father taught, an age when she imagined having the kind of bond with her father that allowed them to share almost anything. He would understand her need for these new companions who could teach her things that girls needed to know.

Even if Walker thought that her father's seminary education was being put to good use, his aspirations were far more visible in what he did next—returning to school for an advanced degree. He had never spoken publicly about such ambitions, leading Walker to conclude that it was her mother who organized, planned, and decided what was going to happen. Her father was typically silent, reading his Bible and preparing his lessons or sermons.

Antoinette Handy, whose sisters and brothers grew up with the Walker family after they'd moved to New Orleans, suggests that there may have been other factors that explain Rev. Walker's career shift away from the ministry and toward higher education. Handy remembered that Rev. Walker became a district superintendent, a rank slightly higher than a minister, but couldn't seem to move up any higher. "Margaret's father was very brilliant, but he just didn't have what it took for leadership. His wife was the power. She was domineering and people didn't like her."[7]

If Marion Walker was the reason her husband didn't make it to the top leadership of the Methodist Church, she certainly would not allow him to miss an important opportunity that might present itself. It appears that Robert Nathaniel Brooks, the president of Central Alabama Institute, who had hired Rev. Walker to teach, had taken an active interest in him, seeing the young clergyman as a rising star in the hierarchy of the Central Jurisdiction of the Methodist Church. Brooks's ministry itself had been limited, and he may have seen Rev. Walker's trajectory as similar, someone whose contribution would go beyond his pastoral responsibilities. He advised Sigismund of an opening at New Orleans University at the same time the presiding Methodist bishop for the region had hoped to transfer him to another church. Sigismund preferred to follow the advice offered by Brooks, the man he considered his mentor, who also explained what he needed to do to secure the position: complete a graduate program. Teaching at New Orleans University, then considered one of the best undergraduate schools in the South for Negroes, would afford Rev. Walker a solid income, one that could not only support the family, but also educate his children for free or a fraction of the regular cost.

We do not know what actually transpired as the family made what must have been a difficult decision. There was no money coming in, and there were four children to support. Walker concluded that the decision must have been a sudden one for her parents. She was unaware of any discussion about changing careers or moving the family away from Birmingham. However, the matter of an advanced degree presented a problem, at least in 1924. There was no university in the South that Rev. Walker could attend for graduate study, and he had already gone as far as he could at the Gammon Theological Seminary in Atlanta. His interest in pursuing an advanced degree in theology gave him few options.

Marion was not one to think of what was *not* possible, a trait that her daughter would take from her mother. In fact, Marion seemed to want the job more than her husband and took it upon herself to ensure that nothing got in the way of his getting the job *and* the degree. Brooks had gone to Garrett Biblical Institute in Evanston, Illinois, a Northwestern-affiliated institution, that offered a reduced tuition rate for ministers and their children. When Marion learned this, her mind was made up. "It was the summer of 1924, and my mother bought a steamer trunk, packed it with some new and old clothing for my father, borrowed his fare and insisted he take the train for Evanston, Illinois. Daddy cried,"[8] Walker wrote, and it was the first time she'd seen her father display such emotion. But she knew it would do nothing to change her mother's mind. She saw in her father's relationship with her mother what she would later see in her own relationship with her husband: a conflict between one's duty and one's desire. When her father argued that they had no money, Marion dismissed it. She *knew* he wanted this, if not for himself, then for his family, and she insisted. Walker remembered the first words in her father's letter to them after he arrived in Chicago: "In Chicago there are only two kinds of people, the quick and the dead. If you are not quick, you will be dead."[9] The nine-year-old wondered which of these categories would describe her if ever she went to Chicago.

That summer Aunt Abbie joined her sister, her mother, and the four Walker children. She brought them a surprise—their new cousin Samuel, her son. Abbie had finally married, and although Walker knew few details, Abbie and Marion had been in regular touch and the anger between them seemed to subside. The house was filled with activity, taking her mind away from her absent father. If Marion missed her husband when he went off to summer school at Northwestern, there was no indication of it. She stayed busy with her new studio, the Johnson Walker School of Music, thus assuring her family of necessary income as she became one of the most sought-after accompanists in the community. She gave private music lessons, organized recitals, and performed at assorted functions. The Dozier sisters were together again, and Abbie and Marion had many opportunities to perform concerts for their appreciative local audiences. Abbie's melodious voice, accompanied by Marion's expert piano playing, struck at the very core of Walker's being. The rhythms and sounds were like nothing she had experienced before. She had wanted to sing, but her voice seldom cooperated. Whenever she tried, her friends always laughed at her. But rhythm and sound could be put to other uses. She was sure of that.

It would be their last summer in Birmingham, and she wanted it to be special. She flung herself into the summer activities sponsored by the Daily Vacation Bible School and made her mother proud by winning the prize for reciting the Ten Commandments from memory. She also felt that she had to counter her mother's generally negative reports to her father: she wouldn't do her household chores, was easily distracted, daydreamed a lot; and when chastised, Marion reported, there was more talking back than usual. The devil had gotten into her, and it certainly must have been because of the fast girls, those new acquaintances she'd made at Slater School, her mother concluded. In their nightly prayers, Marion insisted that her daughter ask for the Lord's forgiveness and His help in getting her back on the right path.

Soon after her ninth birthday, Walker received permission from her mother to attend a revival meeting with a school friend. Marion viewed this as a good opportunity for her daughter to develop more appropriate and safer friendships. Walker easily identified with the kinetic energy that came from the music and the people in attendance, which was unlike anything she'd ever seen. When the minister called for the children to come forward and take the hand of God, she could hardly contain herself, wanting desperately to join the throng of children who rushed forward. Unaccustomed to being away from the watchful eye of her parents, Walker hesitated even though she was experiencing something she had ever felt before. The fire-and-brimstone sermon forced her to consider the truth of Marion's assessment that a life in a secular, godless world awaited her daughter's future. Most of what she cared about, what she wanted in life, seemed to be outside of what the people about whom she cared the most considered acceptable. None of these anxieties was she able to articulate yet. Conflicting feelings of fear and ecstasy came rushing forth; an urgent need to respond battled with the desire for confirmation, especially from her parents. She could feel her "soul crying out in desperate need for the love of Christ . . . and the presence of his holy spirit. . . . I want to feel that life is sweet," she wrote, "[to] know I am doing thy will."[10]

At a very practical level, in her nine-year-old mind, Walker believed that the call to join the church would please her mother. She rushed home, quickly and boldly announced her decision, only to be stunned by Marion's sudden and intense disapproval. She found herself confronted with another layer of complexity. It was not only important to *join* the church, but it had to be the *right* church. How could her mother know how she felt inside? Wasn't God the only person who could tell a person what to do with her spiritual life and when to do it?

What Walker did not understand until later was that her family's connection to the Methodist Episcopal Church set them apart from other Black Methodist denominations, which were far more popular and visible in the Birmingham area. Though all Methodist churches may have looked to John Wesley for their early history and were not autonomous like the Baptists, African American Methodism emphasized its role in building the institutional church after the end of slavery. Because religious worship among slaves was feared to be a site for organizing resistance and rebellion, Blacks in the South had conducted their services in secret, which allowed for the preservation of African-derived rituals and new forms of musical expression to emerge, especially in places with concentrated Black populations. As a result, African Americans developed a religious culture significantly different from those directly connected to white denominations. Alabama, where the African Methodist Episcopal Church (AME) was particularly strong, bore the powerful legacy of bishops such as Henry McNeal Turner and Daniel Payne, both of whom were assigned to the North Alabama Conference. For these men—Turner, who would make his mark next on Africa, and Payne—and those who followed them, their spirit of enthusiasm was matched only by their zeal and sanctified energy.

Marion Walker had probably not considered that the AME outdoor tent revival, which is what her daughter had been given permission to attend, would have the effect it did. Although her father Rev. Dozier was as charismatic as the minister at the revival, Marion hardly knew him. He had left the family to pastor a church in a city her mother never visited, coming home only to be buried. Her religious experience and practice as wife of a professionally trained minister-turned-educator precluded any thoughts about her daughter's response to the experience. The incident shows how little Marion actually knew about her daughter—and how little her daughter understood the class and cultural differences that were intended to set her apart from others.

Walker was, therefore, receiving a lesson framed in a spiritual encounter that connected her more to a folk-derived culture that she could store for later. These routine revivals allowed a visiting minister, selected because of his preaching ability, to build on his reputation by also attracting converts. Although she was accustomed to going to Sunday School and youth fellowship meetings, this was Walker's first experience at a revival, which most churches found to be effective strategies for recruitment and growing smaller churches into bigger ones. She would not forget the experience, one entirely different from any previous ones and a likely source for the images and her preference for the cadence in much of her poetry. The rejection that she received from her mother only made these moments stand out as something to hold on to precisely because she was expected to disregard them. Walker knew that differences based on color existed within families, but the depth of meaning that race and class differences could impart in other aspects of their lives was a revelation. That this difference extended itself to and affected decisions one made about religion and faith would have appeared to her as hypocritical. The Methodist church services her family attended, especially those where her father served as the pastor or guest minister, did not adapt easily to the musical and other preferences of more traditional Black congregations. The Walkers' perceived status—symbolized by their education and Marion's classically trained musical background—set them apart. Whatever the difference was, it would invite the attention of a child with Walker's curiosity. Her parents' resistance to her exuberance and desire to join the choice left troubling questions about the separations and distinctions that she would only be able to explain to her satisfaction later in her life.

The experience was another example of her mother's practice of pushing her own ideas of what she wanted her children to become, interpreted by her daughter as a threat to Walker's desire for control over her own choices. Not until later, when she had four children of her own, was Walker able to realize that her mother was a determined woman who wanted (1) to feed and clothe her children well; (2) to give them a good education in a religious environment suitable for developing their God-given talents; and (3) to provide musical opportunities through recitals, shows, live theater, and always books.[11] She was forced to give her mother some credit for her success and that of her siblings. Marion had prepared Mercedes especially well; she eventually completed her training at a musical conservatory, would go on to play at Carnegie Hall, and have a successful career as a music educator. She did what Marion was never able to do in making the family, especially her mother, proud. Brother, who kept his passion for New Orleans jazz a secret while Marion was alive, nevertheless earned her approval because he played so well. He became a highly respected music teacher, but had another life playing at nightclubs, which he only pursued actively after he retired and Marion was long dead. Walker lived for the day she was finally free of the forced instruction. In the meantime, she had to live with the constant reminder of her failure to accomplish what her sister and brother did so easily.

Despite any minor adjustments that she believed she was making, her relationship with her mother grew more distant. She was convinced that her mother disapproved of everything about her, and that she wanted to break Walker's will and change her personality. Marion finally resorted to corporal punishment, breaking with the standard practice in the family. It probably began after Rev. Walker left for graduate school, which kept him away for extended periods of time. The whippings apparently were so severe they often left welts on her back. "I turned inside more and more to books and journals and writing," not that it always kept her mother at bay.[12] But she was aware of the strategies that her father adopted in negotiating with such a strong-willed wife when he was home. She always had the feeling that her father had much to say, but finding it impossible to do so with a determined, implacable, and unrelenting wife, preferred to leave most things unsaid. Her father's absences, therefore, made his daughter more willful and defiant since without his intervention, Marion was free to give what she considered an appropriate response to her daughter's misbehavior.

Marion did recognize that her daughter had talents other than those she had wanted to cultivate. She also realized that while the extensive musical instruction she gave produced accuracy in her performance, Walker played only when she was required to and never with feeling. Later, Walker would discover the real lessons she gained from music: superior listening skills and an ability to quickly recognize differences in tone and pitch, all of which were invaluable for creating sound sequences with words. She also acquired a fuller appreciation for formal musical concerts like those she would later attend. The elements of music held fascination for her in another way as well—they enhanced her ability to capture and intensify emotion. Understanding the effect sounds had on the listening ear provided a model for achieving a similar effect with words on a page.

Guiding her daughter's development did exact a price. "You haven't got long golden hair, you'd better get some sense in your head," Marion told her daughter.[13] But her efforts to please her mother were never enough, Walker thought. During these preteen years, she was nervous and miserable most of the time. Fighting against her mother sapped her energy, but if she were going to be her own person, she thought she had no choice. Always small for her age, she complained of stomachaches and began to feel sorry for herself, but the battles went on.

Mothers and daughters find this a familiar story: a daughter's need to be released from the image and expectations of a mother who, unconsciously or not, shapes a child into the image she is unable to fulfill for herself. Although this can be true between fathers and daughters, gender similarity can make the mother-daughter struggle more intense. For Marion and her oldest daughter, the struggle was extreme, and the accompanying rebellion was sometimes self-destructive. But Walker's bad behavior had some value. Her constant back talk allowed her to hone her language skills; she demonstrated quick wit and a sharp tongue that became especially useful as she grew older. The fighting with

Marion ceased only when she left home to go away to school. And even then, it simply took a break.

Talking back, however, could also be a sign of assertiveness in a child, and it was in this case. If on the one hand she angered her mother with too much mouth, she did find ways, on the other hand, to gain her mother's much-needed attention and approval. Having grown accustomed to her mother's many recitals, and participating in countless school operettas, she also decided to write and produce one of her own. On one occasion, she gathered her playmates, sisters Mercedes and Gwen, and directed them in a play she had written herself. The production was complete with costumes, a set they created, and the front porch of their house was used for a stage.

She did not take the debut of "The Golden Whistle" lightly. It was a first public creative effort during the summer before they left Birmingham. Walker learned several things from this experience. First, she could write an extended work that told a story. Second, in order for her work to have meaning, she needed an audience. It became clear that she would have to write for others as much as for herself. The audience for "The Golden Whistle"—Brother, Aunt Abbie, Cousin Samuel, Grandma Dozier, her mother, and a host of neighborhood children as well—witnessed her growing confidence in directing the play and gaining the cooperation of others. Having an outlet for her love of language was an important discovery.

If Walker did not see her mother in herself, neither did Marion see how much like her this daughter was. She wanted to write and direct others; she liked being in charge. She recalled Walker's first Easter speech when they lived in Meridian, Mississippi. She was pleased with the creative spark she saw in the five-year-old. She had learned the entire speech, one that ordinarily would have been given to a much older girl had Walker not demanded it for herself. Now, four years later, Marion began to understand that spark, that self-confidence, and what it might lead to. She liked what she saw in her oldest daughter—a fierce spirit that was willing to get what she wanted, no matter what it took. Marion thus had to make adjustments of her own if she were going to meet her daughter's needs.

In Birmingham, Walker had made new friends, but having learned that the family would be moving, she was certain she would never see them again. She hated the thought of starting over in a new place and longed to talk to her father about the impending move. Why did they need reminding how special they were, how different they were from other children, and how important it was for them to set a good example for others?

When Sigismund returned from Northwestern at the end of summer in 1924, he immediately moved to New Orleans to accept a teaching assignment at Gilbert Academy, associated with New Orleans University. Named after William L. Gilbert, a Connecticut businessman and philanthropist who contributed financially to the education and well-being of African Americans in the South, Gilbert Academy had been founded by the Freedmen's Bureau on the original Bayou Teche Plantation after the Civil War as the Colored Orphans' Home. Before the end of the nineteenth century it had moved, changed its name, and had become the preparatory school for New Orleans University. Like many of the private high schools operated by African American denominations, Gilbert Academy would survive until the mid-twentieth century. When the move toward integrated public education made its existence less urgent, other educational opportunities began to open up for Blacks in New Orleans.[14]

Their decision to move to New Orleans made explicit the nature of the family's class aspirations. In practical terms, it meant less insularity, more opportunity, and greater access to a New Negro world. Artists like Roland Hayes and Marian Anderson—names Marion praised—made regular appearances in New Orleans. Walker only came to realize later what all of this would mean for her. As an adult, she acknowledged her birthplace in Birmingham, but New Orleans she always called home . . . "the place that furnished a wonderful environment and made me want to write. I thought New Orleans must be the most beautiful city in the world."[15]

The only person who was opposed in principle to the move from the very beginning was Elvira Dozier. She bore her widowhood proudly, holding firm to her beliefs in the communal culture of the post-slavery South. New Orleans was for her an evil city, and she remembered how two of her sons had met their deaths following the riverboats that left from the New Orleans port. She dared not go to a place where the devil incarnate claimed too many converts. She could not understand why her son-in-law seemed to be abandoning his call to the ministry, and was convinced that the family was headed straight to hell. But for the Walker family, it was the right move.

Preparations for the family's move to New Orleans were gradual. Even though she was not especially happy about the move at first, Walker's imagination began to entertain exciting thoughts of life in the big city. She could tell the difference immediately after her father returned. He began receiving invitations to speak as soon as he got home, invitations he accepted in order to replace some of the family's income. Margaret sensed that the family was already more secure. The truth was that they would have to make it through the next five summers when her father returned to Northwestern annually for the long summer-school quarter. The family would have to survive on Marion's income alone. When Sigismund finally received his master's degree in biblical literature, he proudly brought his diploma home to Marion, who, he said, "had really earned it."[16]

Rev. Walker assumed his new appointment at New Orleans University and began looking for a house where they could join him. The transition would not go as smoothly as they had hoped, but not for the reasons they anticipated.

Just a year earlier, the Louisiana legislature had passed permissive legislation that granted cities with a population of twenty-five thousand or more the power to mandate residential segregation. One week after the legislature voted, the New Orleans City Council passed unanimously a segregation ordinance, appointing a special attorney to prosecute cases where violations of the new law occurred. Although the law would be repealed in 1927, between 1924 and 1926, successive waves of racial unrest with angry politicians on both sides of the political fence claimed the city's attention. People took to the streets, and the actions of a vibrant young NAACP chapter in New Orleans infuriated a white-controlled city seeking to keep Negroes in their place. Negroes fought back, fearing the loss of the few victories they had worked so hard to achieve.

Sigismund Walker entered this tension-filled city beginning to second-guess his decision. When he talked about New Orleans, he painted pictures of tree-lined boulevards, describing New Orleans University as bigger than anything they had ever seen. As if to appease his wife, he described the city's social and cultural life, the new season at the downtown opera house, and of course, the Negro artists and performers who had appeared at the university the year before along with the list of those scheduled for the coming year.

Walker wanted to be near her father. He had already spent the first summer without them, but it was too much for her. She began to feel sadness unlike any she had known. During the school day and afterwards, she began to write more short rhymes in her composition book, looking for a way to fill the loneliness in anticipation of her move. Her experiences from then on would be regularly recorded in those books, and later, in her journals.

Although there was no guiding hand for her writing, Walker loved to read poetry she found in her father's library. In his absence, she had the full freedom to browse. There she found easy-to-recite poems by the English Romantics, especially William Wordsworth and the English Victorian writers. But she was especially fond of the poems by American writers Edgar Allen Poe, Edgar Guest, and Paul Laurence Dunbar, which she easily memorized and added to her repertoire. She loved the affirmation that a grateful audience provided, and she read and recited before others whenever and wherever she could. Probably the influence of Dunbar's poetry made that of Langston Hughes, whom she would meet in just a few years, so appealing. She modeled many of her verses after the more popular writers, those more frequently anthologized like Alfred Lord Tennyson and Henry Wadsworth Longfellow. Marion was encouraging, especially when she and her daughter could share a common interest in the performance of classical pieces. Marion was known to be an exacting teacher, who welcomed opportunities to show her children excellence in not only music, but in all the other arts as well.

Grandma Dozier was not the only person who saw New Orleans as a dangerous city for unsuspecting youth. Marion's major concerns were those of a protective parent. Girls had to be carefully guarded, and while New Orleans had far more to offer than Birmingham for the making of a young lady, the spurious reputation of the Red Light District was widely discussed. Although the Walkers would join a community of educators, making them part of an intellectual elite, they constituted a very small portion of the city's colorful landscape. Her parents could only hope that the speakeasies, the cabarets, and the brothels—all the activity in the French Quarter and on Rampart and Bourbon Streets—would not deter their children from the higher purposes that motivated their move to this city in the first place.

None of these thoughts entered her mind as Walker imagined her future. For her, the city meant only that the family would be reunited with their father. It had taken him longer than expected to find a house, and as the summer dragged on, Marion had made herself sick with worry. August passed and then September, and Sigismund had made little progress. School had already started, and if they waited any longer, the children would have to sit out the term. Finally, Marion purchased their train tickets and began the long process of packing and crating all their goods and furnishings. The piano would need to be packed very carefully, for this was Marion's most important possession. No matter if nothing else made it, the piano would have to get there.

Early in October, they said goodbye to Grandma Dozier, who would wait for her other daughters to come get her. She had made plans to return to Florida to live with them. The sadness of leaving her closest family member was overshadowed by thoughts of her first train ride. They headed to downtown Birmingham to the station, found the New Orleans track, and walked along the side of the train until they found the coach assigned for "Colored." A neighbor had packed lunches for them—generous portions of homemade veal loaf, caramel cake, nuts, and fruit—knowing that the dining car was off-limits to Negroes. The ride took all day, but the children were rarely bored. It was their custom to sing when they traveled, and the favorite song on this trip was "I Shall Not, I Shall Not Be Moved." While a popular song from the period, neither Walker nor her family could have known what would come to pass as they sang on the train that day, seated in the "Colored section." Just thirty years later, those words would stand firm for Rosa Parks in Montgomery, Alabama, just as they did for the students at North Carolina A&T College in Greensboro as the Civil Rights Movement experienced some of its most painful and uncertain years.

In spite of their excitement and playfulness, however, they knew that this was the beginning of a new life, one their parents had worked hard to make happen. Indeed, they would not be moved from this place to which they now came. She watched out the window as the landscape shifted away from the rows of low cotton. When the train drew nearer to their destination, she could see small streams flowing into one great river running through what seemed like little towns and swamps and marshes. She looked with intense curiosity on the endless rows of tract houses with nothing but tiny windows through which she could see the occupants clustered around a barrel in makeshift chairs. Their laughter seemed contagious, undisturbed by the muddy water flowing past the doorless shanties. There were children, too, playing with sticks and stones, and running past each other with gleeful chatter. As the train pulled into the station at nightfall, it seemed as if a thousand red lamps welcomed them.

She hardly noticed when the train stopped, so immersed was she in daydreaming. At least that's what her parents called it—the way she looked directly at something, her small body sometimes trembling as she focused her gaze. Then she would freeze, closing her eyes, totally absorbed by what seemed like a power beyond her control. The experience she knew well and eventually tried to describe it in a poem she published in 1934. "Daydream" would appear in *The Crisis* after she had heard an inspiring lecture by W. E. B. Du Bois. The poem made clear what she wanted to do with her life: to find a way to order the scattered words and phrases which she had grown accustomed to recording in her composition books, and in her memory. Poetry, she soon discovered, came through as daydreams in their directness and intimacy, like a force driving her from the intense self-consciousness that she had practiced as a child; her poetry would have to find its way outward. When she learned how to release and "frame [the] dreams into words," they could become "a mirrored pool of brilliance in the dawn."[17]

3

The Fire Burning Within

Margaret did not see her father standing on the platform when Marion ushered them from the train. They had been traveling all day and were arriving weeks later than they had anticipated. Going to bed in a strange place, they needed to get started early the next day to register for school, which had already started for the year. With the household items arriving in two weeks and no place as yet to stay, Marion was anxious, something that her seeming self-confidence did little to mask. As always, Rev. Walker was calm and showed little emotion, except he greeted each of them warmly, with a slightly longer embrace for his wife. Walker, who saw him looking back, seemed surprised that he was expecting Grandma Dozier. The dismissive tone that her mother adopted led Walker to believe that Marion was terribly upset about all of this, but didn't want anybody to know. Grandma Dozier had lived with them all of their lives and left precisely at the moment when they seemed to need her the most. Marion had nothing more to say on the matter, suggesting that it had to be kept from the children.

Elvira's decision had taken its toll on Marion who became so ill she had to close her music studio. Walker assumed that it was due to their imminent departure from Birmingham. But during the months before they left, Marion seemed to lose total control of the household and was forced to leave the packing to others. The illness—some unnamed psychological disorder —and her slow recovery made her more determined to go. That had been the *real* reason she bought the train tickets and announced to her husband that they would wait no longer, even though they had initially agreed to time their arrival with the move into the house Sigismund had found for them. Instead, Sigismund shuttled them into a car, whose driver dropped them at a friend's home, where they would spend the first two weeks.

The first order of business the next day was to get everyone enrolled in school, except for Brother. Since they were a month late, Walker feared that she would be way behind the other children. Luckily, her father had made the school enrollment plans without Marion's help, although this did little to allay his daughter's fears and embarrassment about being seen as a dummy. She wanted to make a most favorable first impression, which now seemed impossible.

Marion was more temperamental than usual during the first few days of their arrival, and it gave the entire family a deeper understanding of how her father managed difficult situations with his wife. Her outbursts seemed

The House Where My Soul Lives. Maryemma Graham, Oxford University Press. © Oxford University Press 2022.
DOI: 10.1093/oso/9780195341232.003.0003

Gilbert Academy/New Orleans University faculty in 1925. Sigismund Walker is back row, left. Courtesy of Dillard University Archives

to come without any prompting. Their origins, though undetermined, were deeply psychological. She had been handling too much, but had let go of the things that helped her to keep her balance, like the music studio. She had practically forced her husband to return to school and to accept the new teaching job before his family could join him, but she was unprepared for the life that now defined her: four children, a husband starting a new career, the departure of her mother, and moving her family to a new city. Her older and more-settled husband was restrained and detached, while she was passionate, almost obsessive. Despite his quiet manner, Sigismund knew when to make certain kinds of

The Walkers' faculty yearbook picture. Sigismund and Marion Walker bottom row. Courtesy of Dillard University Archives

interventions. This was one of those times. He would wait for the right moment to give her the most important announcement: Marion had been promised a position in the music department at Gilbert Academy. Since she had given up her music studio, they had all seen the change in Marion. The mood swings that had all but vanished were returning, and she no longer seemed normal. They all knew her cycles: the restlessness would surface, making her utterly unpredictable. When she heard the news, Marion felt a calm. It was more than she could ever hope for, especially without a college degree. She saw opportunity as affirmation.

For Walker, this episode confirmed that the relationship between her mother and father was not just "love at first sight." At moments like these, she saw the inner workings of a relationship between two people whose differences were profound. Marion had thought that coming to New Orleans was important to her husband. But it was her husband who would have to help her see how important it would also be for her, whose talents could flourish in new ways. Sigismund was intent on giving Marion renewed hope; he had found a way to work through the unresolved issues that had been at the center of their marriage from the very beginning. She was too young to marry a man his age, and yet she had accepted his love unconditionally, turned down a college scholarship, given up her plans for a musical career, bore him children, and resigned herself (though not always happily) to the lackluster life among people who offered food more than money as payment for his services.

Whatever her psychological condition, Sigismund felt partially to blame for its existence and was most eager and prepared to be the harbinger of relief. Music was indeed Marion's passion, and if she couldn't perform professionally, then teaching music to others would be a suitable alternative. The success she had already with her own children, especially Mercedes and Brother, which had been the inspiration behind the founding of the studio in Birmingham, could be repeated in New Orleans. In contemplating his destiny, then, Sigismund acknowledged the vibrancy of his wife's identity without subordinating herself to him. New Orleans is where Marion would complete her college education at the newly founded Xavier University, and assume the leadership of both the New Orleans University Orchestra and its Choral Club. The institution could not have found a better match for what became one of the strongest and most widely recognized music departments in Negro schools.

New Orleans University (NOU) had two preparatory programs: the Model Grade School and Gilbert Academy. Margaret and Mercedes were both enrolled in the Model Grade School, where Margaret expected to spend her seventh- and eighth-grade years before moving on to Gilbert Academy. NOU was affiliated with five feeder schools throughout the state, but Gilbert Academy was at the top of that list.

Early in January 1927, Walker moved from the Model Grade School directly to Gilbert Academy's freshman class. She weighed sixty pounds, and at eleven and a half, was two full years younger than most of her classmates. Thin and frail, she looked even younger as she walked around the wooden frame building for the first time. She was enrolled as a day student since their home on Perrier Street was only a few blocks away from the Pitt and Atlantis Streets entrance to the Gilbert campus. She sometimes wished that she could board at Peck Hall, where girls who lived too far to commute resided. Mrs. Neal, the matron of Peck Hall who doubled as one of the Bible teachers, liked her. Walker would see her in class, but also when she took home economics required for all of Gilbert's female students. To Mrs. Neal, Walker was one of her most capable students, already familiar with fine arts such as embroidery and crocheting. Thus, Walker could quickly advance in Mrs. Neal's sewing classes where one learned to do feather stitching, blanket stitching, and French seams. They would remain close friends until she graduated. In Walker's senior Missionary Book, Mrs. Neal wrote the encouraging words, "I shall always expect to hear great things of you. Achieve! Achieve!"[1]

Walker enjoyed walking from the main classroom building to Peck Hall, for it was one of the few times that the students could mingle together without supervision. The school kept the grounds immaculate. Carefully manicured lawns and geometrically cropped hedges lined every walkway while playful squirrels shot between the laurel and spruce trees that were arranged neatly throughout the campus. Students knew to use the paved walkways that connected the buildings to one another, staying clear of the dedicated yard crew of men scurrying around picking up leaves and discarded refuse, always taking pride in their jobs. In the spring, the flowers offered a magnificent display of colors that invited admiring visitors and donors who found great satisfaction in these signs of the school's self-pride. If the girls walked slowly on their way to the Pitt Street end of campus, they could catch the desired glimpse of the boys practicing for sports on the football field before some attentive teacher shooed them off to their afternoon dining-hall assignments.

With the weight of her parents' and her own high expectations, Walker had a sense of urgency about everything—what she had to learn and how well she needed to learn it, keeping a careful account of what she did. This only increased during the years in high school. She was enrolled in a traditional college-prep curriculum, which meant taking four years of languages, specifically Latin and French; a core of science subjects, including biology, botany, and chemistry; yearly courses in history, literature, and English composition; and the Bible. Even though she was not particularly competent in math, and in fact failed algebra at one point, everything else excited her. She could easily relive moments of the French Revolution and talk incessantly about the characters. Intent on mastering the French language as a part of her fascination with New Orleans' French culture, she would practice at home, rolling her tongue to get the right effect with the letter "r." She threw herself into the dramatic world of Greek and Roman history, having already mastered their myths in grade school. The required memorization of speeches by Caesar, Hamlet, and Othello fueled her love of oratory.

Her characteristic nervousness and adolescent clumsiness always gave way to newfound self-confidence whenever she stood before her classmates. She could see herself as some other person then, and practically begged the teacher to call on her for recitations. Many evening hours found her translating Homer's *Iliad* from the original Latin, hoping for the opportunity to recite in class. Her family encouraged her to enter oratorical contests, where she competed with the best students throughout the city and the state. She never seemed to get stage fright and relished the dress-up occasions that invited a new outfit made by her mother, grandmother, or Aunt Abbie. She loved the attention, the authority her voice claimed, and those places and moments that sustained her mind's pleasure. She won her first oratorical contest in her second year in high school with an essay she had written, "The American Negro to Africa: The Vision and the Task." The essay has not survived, but the impact of the award did. The school's dean presented her the first-prize gifts: a gold chain and her first personally inscribed Bible. She took literally the dean's words: "If you will read this Bible and let it be a guide to your life, your life will not only be a good one; it will be a great one."[2] The gift came at a critical moment in her adolescent development. She believed what she had been taught: that evil is not only in one's actions, but in one's thoughts as well. Because she had yet to join a church in New Orleans, she could not be sure of the extent of evil attributed to her thoughts, actions, or deeds. From the moment Walker received the Bible, she believed that somewhere in that great book, which reported on the faithful and the faithless from ages ago, she would find a way out of her discomfort.

Despite or perhaps because of her precociousness, her willfulness and outspokenness continued to draw the ire of her mother. Although her father confirmed his disapproval of whipping his children, Marion had come to understand it as a necessary evil, the only way she could hopefully redirect the energy of a difficult child. "Bad" had several degrees of meaning, and though the Walkers considered themselves progressive, Marion was the primary disciplinarian, was exasperated with her rambunctious daughter, and accepted conventional wisdom: "spare the rod, spoil the child." An attentive, well-behaved student by day, at home Walker routinely challenged her mother saying whatever she thought, and caring little for the consequences of these actions. Even after their move to New Orleans, Walker admitted that "I wasn't especially happy because almost daily for seven years I was doing or saying the wrong thing and getting slapped, whipped, or beaten by adults. I was not afraid of the whippings. In fact

I was defiant. I stiffened my back to a miserably monotonous life. Sunday was a bright spot because the only thing we had to look forward to was Church."[3]

Walker's youngest sister Gwendolyn suggests that this might have been an exaggeration, confirming that her oldest sister was obstinate and always insisted on having her own way.[4] Of the two things, among others, that parents need are money and time, and the Walkers had little of either. Marion and Sigismund were working full time, and Marion had gone back to school, but they still managed to provide a comfortable life for their four children. And yet busy, working parents can often give rise to unruly, demanding children who need more attention. If Walker dreamed of doing things and going places that were simply not affordable, it is easy to see how she might begin to act out. Even when she was older, Gwen remembered her sister having what most saw as temper tantrums, making everybody's life miserable. While it is true that Walker was neither submissive nor easily satisfied as a teenager, she was also exposed to a world that promised more than it could deliver, leaving her justifiably bewildered and restless.

The Bible was where Walker could turn inward, finding stories and explanations that helped to diffuse her anger and calm her restlessness. She was captivated by the evocative nature of this ancient oral literature. Even before any formal training in poetry, she was attracted to the biblical cadence and typology that would become so important in her work. The Bible as a spoken text gave further confirmation of her later preference for narrative poetry. Reading the Bible aloud was not far removed from reading poetry aloud. The parallelism, repetition, the musical texture, and elevated rhetoric recalled the sermons embellished by her father's Jamaican accent that she was so accustomed to hearing. Walker so strongly identified with the biblical form of poetry that her first attempts had a strong prayer-like quality to them, like this poem found in an early scrapbook:

> Morning
> Dear God, the morning comes from Thee,
> Just as my life and breath
> The breeze that stirs in every tree
>   Is sweet, and cool and health.
> The grass is green and damp with dew;
>   The sky is clear and bright.
> The south wind bears a message too,
>   That calms all fears of night.
> And so this bright and sunny morn,
>   I fill my lungs with air;
> And trust my soul anew is born
>   Within Thy loving care.[5]

The poem resembles others that appear throughout her school composition notebooks, poems Walker usually considered doggerel. "Morning" lacks the maturity and sophistication of her later poems, and the end rhyme here is forced with little or no originality. However, it marks her concern with process. She knows that what happens in poetry is a connection through language between two things that are different in kind. As the outer world of nature—the sky, the wind, the grass, day and night—show certainty and order, so too, does the inner world of the soul. Learning poetry through the Bible as she did, it is not surprising that Walker returned again and again to poetry that had a strong biblical connection, the best examples of which are found in her 1970 volume, *Prophets for a New Day*. The spiritual and literary model that the Bible provided was as powerful as any instruction she would later receive.

Having busy parents also proved advantageous for the development of early writing habits. Recalling those early years, she wrote: "Many mornings I would rise early and sit on the side steps writing. At school I scribbled poetry in my composition book and at home in the night when I was not reading to myself or my grandmother, I was trying to write."[6]

About the New Orleans years in particular, Walker was clear: "I was learning my craft, finding my voice, seeking discipline as life imposes and superimposes the discipline upon the artist."[7] Instruction and encouragement at Gilbert were reinforced by what had now become common practice at home: "hearing my mother's music, my sister and brother playing the piano, reading my father's books and the trees that I watched through the bedroom windows, hearing his sermons, and trying every day to write a poem."[8] As she said later, "writing must come out of living." What she learned in New Orleans was that nothing could be taken for granted. It was all "invaluable stimuli."[9]

When Walker was later asked to explain how the poet creates, she could look back at her early experiences as having all the necessary ingredients. "There was something mysterious about this process," she believed, "a poet thinks in figurative language and symbolic terms, at least one sees these initially. Ideas come later, but concepts are first and we conceive in pictures and feel the rhythms intuitively. . . . I mastered things unconsciously and automatically before I became conscious and self-conscious."[10] But she was certain that a central element in this equation was something she called "the feminine principle."[11] Influenced by conventional nineteenth-century ideas of womanhood and femininity, from which she never wavered, gender divisions did not negatively represent her artistic vision. "I am sure God is not merely male or female but He-She—our Father-Mother-God. All nature reflects this rhythmic and creative principle of feminism and femininity: the sea, the earth, the air, fire, and all life whether plant or animal."[12] She resolved any potential conflict by giving a gendered and specifically feminist decoding of the creative process.

During the four years she spent at Gilbert Academy, her favorite classes were literature and English composition. Her teachers tried to keep her focused on reading the Masters, as they called it, English writers, but Walker preferred her own reading and writing, filling her notebooks with ideas and lines for poems that waited to be fleshed out later. She took each composition assignment as an opportunity to explore a new topic of interest. It was difficult to be detached from all that was going on around her. This kind of attentiveness was not new. Once, when she lived in Birmingham, she had watched President Warren G. Harding in a parade; she found herself wondering why the white people were waving flags on one side while the Black people waved on the other. Her alertness to these cultural signs seemed to come natural to her.

She observed her father's activities at various churches and began to read more about the foundations of Judaism. Because New Orleans was a Catholic city, Walker was struck by the sight of Black nuns in their habits, many of whom taught at Black Catholic schools, which were more numerous in New Orleans than in any other Southern city. Because her father had already gotten a library card for each of them for the Dryades Street Library, the Colored branch of the New Orleans Public Library, every new experience demanded a visit to the library. The library card soon became her most prized possession; it was the key that unlocked the secret door to world knowledge. She would enter and be carried along by the book-lined shelves, daring herself to stop anywhere, anytime to pull down a mountain of words. She devoured the books and received instant gratification.

DRYADES BRANCH (COLORED)

Dryades Library, the Colored Branch of New Orleans Public Library

As often as she could, she would exchange the austere, restrained environment of Gilbert Academy for the freedom she found at the Dryades Library. Although she was expected to remain in the juvenile section, she quickly outgrew it. She would go right to the adult section, where the shelves were high enough to conceal her tiny frame. She felt a certain power in the knowledge that no one could see or bother her. What she learned there was hers and hers alone. She intended to keep it that way. She revealed important secrets allowed only in her journals, where she made a practice of storing them. She loved to talk, but knew the risk of sharing some things to be too great, soon finding security in her "mental castle." "I like to think of my mind as being a door step," she said, "leading through a door with a chamber and it in turn leads into another chamber. I do not know how many rooms there are but I like to think there are many, like a labyrinth . . . that in the last room of the house in my mind—my mental castle—my soul lives."[13] Margaret felt protected in and by her mind, the one thing she could trust. Emerging from the library hours later, usually when her mother came to claim her, she felt victorious in her deceit. She cherished these days of stolen knowledge, feeding her passion for learning.

Her second year at Gilbert, the Walkers finally gave consent for their daughter to join Trinity Methodist Episcopal Church, where the family regularly attended Sunday school and where her father sometimes served as a guest minister. The event itself passed somewhat unnoticed for the most part, but for Walker, it provided another moment of deep reflection and spiritual yearning. She sensed the devil bargaining for her soul, and in order for him not to win, she needed to strengthen her resolve through immediate religious affiliation. In her journal entries from 1929 and continuing through 1932, she is obsessed with trying to explain and respond to a set of recurring psychic experiences, those visions she had during her high school and early college years. She numbered these visions that caused her great consternation dating back to 1926. Vision I occurred in her eleventh year when she saw a "blazing white cross in the sky." As she described the incident, she was standing on a neighbor's porch, looking up at a blue and white sky when suddenly the snowy white cross flung itself in the middle. Finding that she alone has seen this vision, she suffers a near collapse from a "tangle of emotions and desires and dreams that shelter themselves in my bosom and head." Vision 2, not soon after, found her "lying in my grave and seeing my mother or my father dead or seeing my bed drop through the floor into a cellar and lifted up again after a short period of awful suspense." These experiences become the "fire burning within," from which she cannot escape.[14]

It is evident from the journals that Walker was not prepared for what was happening to her emotionally or physiologically as she entered puberty. There was no sex education in the Walker household. Her parents believed that one should and would get through any crisis on the strength of one's religious conviction, faith, and prayer. "A little brother was the only explanation we had for sexual difference,"[15] Walker wrote. Although her father seemed to think that the early poetry writing was a "puberty urge,"[16] neither he nor her mother understood the intensity of their daughter's distress, at least as she reported it in her journals. Marion Walker was keen on keeping her girls safe from any harm that lurked everywhere in a city like New Orleans. She cautiously monitored their playmates and prohibited them from any friendships with the opposite sex.

How significant was this failure to address the important developmental issues for their children, one cannot say. Walker was the only one of her siblings who married. Her parents routinely disapproved of any suitors she had; neither would they accept Firnist James Alexander, the man their daughter married and a constant source of conflict within her family. Rev. Walker is reported to have said to Firnist when they met, "Margaret was raised to have a career and be an independent person; she was not brought up to marry."[17] It is very likely that the issue had more to do with whom she was marrying rather than whether she should get married at all. That the Walkers were aware of certain class implications of educating their children is clear. During the era of racial uplift and social progress, it was common for upwardly mobile parents, just as it is today, to be explicit about their expectations for their children and to express the strongest desires for their unparalleled success. The Walkers were not unusual in this regard and would have seen no contradiction between their choices and those they saw possible for their children. Above all, they did not want their children to be limited in their opportunities to achieve the success that would be commensurate with their training. The possibility existed, they understood, that preparing for a successful professional career and future would require sacrifices up to and including marriage. Such values became in time a source of conflict for Walker, who decided early that she wanted to have a career, to marry, and to have a family.

It was the innocence and uncomplicated nature of her younger years to which she referred when Walker wrote, "My childhood ended when I was ten."[18] The specific incident was the onset of puberty, signaled by the beginning of menstruation. Her physical discomfort from severe cramps and emotional discomfort appear to have been more than typical growing pains. Throughout her life, she suffered bouts of ill health and was frequently confined to her bed when she was not in the hospital for an extended stay. These illnesses ranged from nervous conditions, diabetes, appendicitis, high blood pressure, and finally to cancer. Dr. Robert Smith, the physician and close friend who attended Walker for more than thirty years remarked that she was a woman with enormous willpower and psychic control, and that, based on her medical history, her life span could easily have been much shorter.[19]

Although the source of her illness during childhood and adolescence was never clear, it was probably related to her chronic depression, a condition that went undiagnosed until her early twenties, and one that she would continue to struggle desperately to combat with prayer, astrology, and other self-help and homeopathic remedies. Today, Walker would probably be diagnosed as having had one of several conditions affecting prepubescent girls, such as hormonal imbalance, which might have been treatable early with proper diet and better access to medical care. The frequent illnesses kept her from gaining any weight as her body tried to find a way to balance the psychological and emotional extremes that characterized her existence. She alternated between going to bed without food or water, and stuffing herself during episodes of ravenous hunger. Given Marion's difficulties and sensitivities, her oldest daughter may also have unconsciously imitated certain nervous behaviors and anxieties exhibited by her mother.

What she did learn to do well, however, was to compensate for her anxieties and recurring health crises with a lively imagination. While she suffered from malnutrition because of her early digestive difficulties, chronic fatigue because of her fear of sleeping, and was anemic, she also exhibited an exuberant spirit. She would read about other places and put herself there; she would write stories and create characters who were the kinds of people she wanted to be. Throughout it all, she was planning methodically for her future.

The recurring dream episodes now became morbid, reaching a climax at the end of her thirteenth year. In Vision 3, she was "grappling with an evil spirit, who was dark and slender, in my own likeness, but stronger and more pernicious."[20] In her dreams there was no one to help her—all rescue efforts fail. Since in her dreams, her mother and father are dead, she is left to confront her own sins, descending into the pit of hell. This is the state of eternal damnation, with no expectation that the torture will or can end. During her waking hours, and to help ward off the nightly death dream, Walker prayed constantly, hoping for relief. Then one day, without warning, her prayers were answered. "My sisters noticed my radiant and enraptured face and demanded [to know] what was the matter with me . . . was I crazy? I was dazed with the power of His presence and my fingers trembled as I sought to transfer my experience onto paper."[21]

These initial efforts at writing corresponded with, or perhaps more accurately were driven by, this desperate need to capture and express those experiences that alternately frightened and captivated her. When the experience itself was followed by moments of such ecstasy, Walker wanted to be able to comprehend and, no doubt, share the experience as best she could. Having gained greater confidence in her own ability to write, and surrounded by biblical literature, she felt a responsibility to add her voice to those who had gone before her. This sense of equality in the world was rarely disturbed, not even when she and her sisters were caught in nearby Audubon Park by a policeman who reminded them of the racial codes: Negroes were not allowed to sit on the park benches. These psychic experiences and dreams could always replace real-world events as they prepared her for spiritual independence.

She understood the dreams to mean that her parents could no longer protect her, and that she must learn to define her own relationship to the world in intellectual and spiritual terms. She had taken her first steps in this process by professing her faith and joining a church, signifying her surrender to God. She came to understand the battle in her soul to be between good and evil, and she believed it was her responsibility, and hers alone, to choose the right path.

What gave structure to Walker's life during these years was the home that the family moved into a few weeks after their arrival in New Orleans. The family boasted that it had been built by a Black man, and the house at 5424 Perrier Street was the largest home they had seen. She thought of it as a mansion with its twelve-foot-high ceilings and green-shuttered windows. The house sat rather high off the ground, in keeping with the architecture in a city below sea level, and the front porch was longer than most of the houses on the street. Initially the kitchen was at the rear, and Grandma Dozier—who had finally consented to rejoin them—returned to her habit of structuring all of their lives around the meals she prepared. For a short while during their residency, the Walkers supplemented their income by renting rooms to male students from the college. The young men who lived there were rarely in a hurry to leave since their meals were part of their boarding arrangement.

Perrier Street accommodated Walker's rebellious spirit. On its side steps, the tree limbs formed an archway shielding the sun's brightness. These steps opened to a large space that would later be their driveway. Until she was fifteen, when her father bought their first car, Walker found her nesting place on those steps. When she wanted to escape her kitchen duties, she could sit on the first step hidden from view writing peacefully in her journal, or losing herself as she watched the tall grass and blooming clover. The rear of the house, near the kitchen and the backyard, belonged to her grandmother. She had her own room to do the washing in three tin tubs: one was for washing on a scrub board; two were for rinsing.

Walker frequently avoided unwanted tasks, but she always joined her sister in pinning the clothes on the double clotheslines that stretched across the backyard. Her grandmother washed the family linens every Saturday when they weren't in school. On those days, they could stay outside most of the morning, playing between the carefully hung muslin sheets billowing in the wind as they absorbed the sun's brightness. Later she would find herself being wooed by a splashing brook or a pond where she imagined ducks and frogs counting the clouds. Sometimes early in the morning, especially in the summer, she got up quietly, put on her clothes, and ran outside to see what colors were bursting from the sky. When it rained, she could watch the winds part the trees just slightly, enough for her eyes and then her body to catch their rhythms. She liked nothing better than to run her hands through the dew or rain-soaked earth, only to come back later in the afternoon to see that same earth baked by the Southern sun. *Her* sun, *her* earth—they belonged to her as surely as the words she searched for to describe her experiences.

New Orleans presented much that piqued Walker's adolescent curiosity. There were more types of Black people than she'd ever seen before, since the part of Birmingham they had lived in afforded limited contact with a more stratified Black community. From the side steps of their home, she could hear sounds of various voices as people walked past on the sidewalk in front of their house. They would sometimes stop for a moment and comment on the roses and azaleas in full bloom in their front yard, another one of her Grandma Dozier's domains.

In the summer of 1928, her parents arranged for her to take German lessons from the Sisters of the Blessed Sacrament. Although she learned some German, she was more interested in the stories about the nuns' native countries. When one of the nuns began to speak disparagingly of Martin Luther, Walker became immersed in the history of Martin Luther and the Protestant Reformation. What could be so awful about a man who had changed the course of religious history? Like many of her questions, the answers were neither immediate nor simple.

On her walks to class or to music lessons, which Marion insisted that she continue, Walker observed people making the sign of the cross as they passed a Catholic church. When she met children who were Catholic, she couldn't stop asking them questions about what she saw as strange practices. She became more and more aware of the complexities of religion, class, color, and family background and drew some troubling conclusions about who was and was not appropriate to befriend. In the presence of adults, she never learned to "speak only when spoken to." In the presence of children in general, she was always curious, if somewhat detached, allowing her to expand her powers of observation.

As fascinating as New Orleans was—or at least the part they were allowed to visit—much of her time was spent at programs and events featuring speakers her parents were intent on exposing their children to, like Clarence Darrow who came to speak at the New Orleans City Auditorium. But what stayed with her even more was the sense of being a part of history as it was being written before her eyes. She later remembered meeting George Washington Carver and noted the "tall man with a wrinkled forehead, a pip squeak high pitched voice, wearing unpressed clothes and old worn-out shoes."[22] But when she saw the flower in Carver's lapel, and all of the products and inventions he had made or that were developed based on his work on exhibit in the school gymnasium, she realized that every school that bore the name "Carver" was a tribute to this great man.

When Zora Neale Hurston came to New Orleans, she stopped by their home to see Marion, whom she knew from Florida. In Walker's vague recollection years later, there was mention of something exciting happening in New York, and a new book that had just been published by James Weldon Johnson, *God's Trombones*. The Johnsons, James Weldon and J. Rosamond, were also from Florida and musicians, whose careers Marion followed closely. When James Weldon Johnson came to the campus to speak, Walker was pleased to discover the book was poetry that they had been referring to, not music as she had thought. Marion's delight in taking her children to see Marian Anderson at the First Baptist Church and Roland Hayes at the Jerusalem Temple was contagious. It made Walker realize how much music had been bred into their lives and how much she appreciated it. In that instant, she felt more grateful for her mother than ever. To be able to have such moving experiences through music heightened its effect whenever she heard it—the sacred songs at church, the piano and violin practices her sister and brother performed as their daily ritual, or the "devil's music" she had heard in the streets. Despite their differences, music was the one thing she shared with her mother and her siblings.

The passion that claimed her most during these years was poetry. The first step in her parents' acceptance of this fact came on the occasion of her twelfth birthday. Her father had seen her writing in her school composition books and would find scattered pieces of loose paper throughout the room she shared with her sister. Her mother encouraged her to keep writing and suggested that she date and title her poems. She also began to submit poems to Gilbert Academy's yearbook, *The Tiger*. Yet she received mixed signals at times. Although Sigismund Walker told his wife not to get excited about having a poet in the family, he gave his daughter her first poetry lesson: "Poetry should have three things," he said, "rhythm, pictures, and meaning."[23] Whatever her father's intentions were with this gesture, he had succeeded in giving her license to write and provided her with the tools to do so.

Several factors may have precipitated her parents' interest. Marion and Sigismund had both gone away to Northwestern's summer school in 1928. When they returned, they began to plan the lyceum programs for NOU, drawing on some of the contacts they had made in Chicago. In her third year of high school, thinking ahead to graduation, Walker was already talking about going away to school. She was desperately hoping that her parents would see the importance of her leaving home for Fisk University in Nashville or Talladega College in Alabama. She was just turning fourteen, but the Walkers knew they faced a recalcitrant, if not angry, daughter who needed their attention and needed to be taken seriously. Her parents contacted Professor Richard Kirk in the English department at Tulane University, to whom they showed their daughter's poetry. Kirk was the first to make her aware of the need to pay closer attention to craft. He was encouraging, but did not agree to a tutorial arrangement, stating that she could discipline herself to write daily and continue recording her poems. When she began her senior year at Gilbert Academy, she was already thinking of herself as a poet.

Whatever her talents were, Walker believed they were a gift from God, that is, she had had no control over what she had been given, although it *was* her job to enhance the gift. She affirms this belief in all of her writings, whether framed as a secular or religious discourse. She would have taken literally the examples and lessons she received from Sunday school, her daily readings of the Bible, and the religious conversations among her family members. Those things that she was not allowed to talk about loomed large in her mind and were a great source of fear. She developed an elaborate system for replicating that fear as she grew older in order to exercise control over it. "Realizing I am weak ... my flesh hesitates ... I am too sensuous to be willing to sacrifice bodily comfort. I like rich food and good living too well. I desire much social contact and these dull my spiritual sense much to my dismay."[24] She also saw that too many earthly desires "dull [the] spiritual sense," compromising one's ability to stay on the true Christian path, concluding that, because human weakness is inevitable, the only solution is "greater renunciation of myself and a fuller communion or union with God."[25]

If she approached religion with a degree of certainty, there was little carryover into her relationship with her family during her high school years. She wanted to prove that her superior school achievements were not deserving of the constant whippings she received. Lurking in the back of her mind was her belief that, despite her enormous interest in poetry, her parents assumed she would be a failure, so convinced were they of the long-term impact of her defiant behavior. They had reason, of course, to think so. The Walkers knew too well that the America in which they lived would not take kindly to a Negro child who would willingly speak her mind, show utter disregard for authority, and dare to exhibit her intelligence. They carefully monitored their own activities in New Orleans and shielded their children from the intensity of racial prejudice. They would not share their attitudes about what to do when faced with racial encounters since they made it their business to keep their distance from them. Instead, they concentrated on advancing themselves and their children. Their own attitudes were necessarily shaped by the conventional ideas about racial progress, achievement, mobility, and the relationship between literacy and freedom. These were the same ideas that led to the founding of independent Black schools and churches, in which the Walkers were fully invested. It was the responsibility of those Black people who excelled to help those who could not because of poor abilities or circumstances.

The possibility exists that the frequency of whippings she received was intended to build up a certain immunity against future hurt. If her parents called her wild dreams of being a professional writer foolish, they were responding to concerns as any Black parents would in America in the 1920s. The Walkers believed that being a teacher, preacher, or doctor was one of the most influential and meaningful professions a member of their race could have. Moreover, these professions could lay the foundation for other work they could and would do.

The disparaging comments that Walker remembered hearing from Marion must be seen in this context. Her mother constantly reminded her to "pull your lips up."[26] The concern about "nappy" or "kinky" hair or thick lips and other African-derived features, or light skin in particular, is a by-product, and certainly not a cause of, the internalized racism stemming from the legacy of slavery. That it would plague Margaret Walker's generation, and has hardly disappeared, is not surprising. Many people still react to it, knowing the damage that it has caused. Walker's parents were as affected by this view as anyone else. They believed, on the other hand, that nothing should dictate what their children could or could not do or become. This is evident from all that they did as parents, educators, and community leaders throughout their lives. This is not to deny that the intense drive for excellence, coupled by what she perceived as scarce praise, lack of emotional support, and a repressed sexual development, was derived from her parents' well-grounded fears. In their eagerness to protect their children, they sometimes dealt crushing blows to their ebullient and gifted fourteen-year-old, who would suffer the crippling effects of low self-esteem for years to come. Such instances of low esteem could have a reverse effect as well. When prevented from playing with boys or attending coed parties, for example, she considered it appropriate to be scornful of those from whom she desired attention.

The troubled relationship with her parents carried over into her relationship with her siblings. She always believed that greater demands and restrictions were placed on her than on the other children, and that her brother had total freedom as a child. Her two sisters learned how to avoid punishment and parental censure far better than she did, no doubt seeing their older sibling as the model for what *not* to do. As a result of her extreme self-consciousness, she complained of being teased, insulted, and treated unfairly. Such obsessive behaviors would certainly have appeared odd to the younger children, who may not have caused their parents the same amount of concern as their daughter who had such uncontrollable tendencies. Normal sibling rivalry was perhaps most exaggerated during her teen years, when she believed that as the oldest, she should have been permitted more freedom. What she got instead were reprimands and chastisement that fed her bewilderment, which bordered on neurosis. When she turned twenty, she would look back at the years of her tortured adolescence. Her notes show how conscious she was of having evolved out of a creative sensibility:

Have always lived in a world of imagination. Played with dolls into teens. Mental and intellectual side emphasized above everything else. I.Q. always superior and generally mental age has been four years ahead of chronological age. Mathematics and reasoning power poor. Lack of humour. Memory and imagination powers very good. Excel in English, Composition and correct speech—very good speller and reader. Fair penmanship—good student of history and geography. Able to read and write foreign languages, but lacked the power to retain rules or memorize rules. Early susceptibility and love of poetry and good literature as a whole. Admirer or worshipper of music and art in all forms.[27]

In later years, while she still believed that her physical life was warped and stunted and her mental life crippled under the strain despite her superior IQ, she no longer saw her parents as the enemy. She simply saw them as neurotic, suggesting that what happened was not intentional, but inevitable, given the circumstances.

The hostility and beatings she received from Marion finally generated visible responses from Sigismund. At some point she was no longer just a preacher's daughter, but Sigismund Walker's daughter. Because she exhibited his sensibility and many of his inner qualities, if he consented to her persecution by his silence, he was not only denying her the right to be her own person, but he was also denying himself.

During Christmas break 1929, Walker was in her usual frenzied state, lashing out at everyone, provoking Marion's explicit disdain. She closed herself off in her room, and when she came to the dinner table, she refused to speak. When she woke up on Christmas morning, however, she was determined to be more pleasant to everyone. As she walked out of her room, there on the side table where they celebrated Christmas was a bound leather daybook. She opened it up and read the inscription: "To Margaret, from her Daddy, December 25, 1929."[28] He believed he had done the best he could in a difficult situation, and he may well have been thinking that it would help to curb her outspokenness that had been so irksome for Marion. For Margaret, it was the confirmation she needed to begin her writing life in earnest. The gift could also have been a somewhat delayed compensation for her father's absences. The summers he had spent away between 1924 and 1929, she remembered as being among the most difficult. That final summer, when he had officially graduated, he brought the photograph of himself in his commencement attire, since none of the family could afford to attend the graduation. The daybook and the photograph were both an end and a beginning for the daughter who needed his approval more than anything else.

She began recording her poems in the daybook immediately, copying poems that she had written much earlier. The first titles to appear—"The Two Ways," "Consecration," and "Lord Guide My Hand"—joined a host of new ones she composed immediately after the first of the new year. In her journal, she is quick to blame herself and praise her parents for rewarding her unworthiness. "My fingers trembled as I sought to transfer my experience onto paper. . . . This quiet peace surges anew within my soul and I can only exclaim over and over to myself how happy I am."[29] This is a poignant moment when her complaints must cease and a spiritual renewal must begin.

The excitement about the daybook was, however, bittersweet. One suspects that the timing of the gift had a more hidden purpose all along. As much as it offered a reprieve from a rough period, it was the prelude of another, connected to the earlier discussion the family had been having about Walker's desire to go away to college. The closer she came to graduation, the more desperate she became to get away from home. Her parents were generally in agreement and consented to her application to and acceptance of Talladega College. In the end, however, the Walkers took the advice of the two people they trusted the most, their minister, Rev. J. W. E. Bowen Jr., and later, the president of NOU Dr. Otto E. Kriege. Bowen fed into their prevailing fears about their daughter: "Are you thinking about letting Margaret go away from home as young as she is? You have a nice young girl and when she comes back she'll be smoking and drinking and everything else."[30] Kriege was understandably self-serving. He questioned the wisdom of sending the Walker's firstborn to "another Negro college in the South, unless NOU wasn't so good as any other college."[31] If she were going away, he contended, they should send her to a white school. In the end, even after they'd sent the deposit and transcripts to Talladega, their daughter knew that she'd be remaining at home and entering NOU following graduation from Gilbert Academy.

Gilbert Academy graduation card

High school graduation photo, 1930

She had a powerful sense that her fate was changing, and she now realized that it had begun with her father's gift that Christmas. A week later, for her New Year's resolution, she made a promise to her father to fill every page. In the writing frenzy that followed, she produced more than 400 poems, all of which survive, dated from 1929. Strangely, her disappointment with her family's decision that she remain home did not elicit the expected anger. The gift had bought her silence just as the frenzy of written words had absorbed any bitterness. There were no more conversations about her going away to college as she had found an inner peace: "I am so happy . . . that God's spirit has come to me . . . and [I] have felt God's wonderful and blessed enlightenment."[32] Some of the poems would appear later in print, but only a few she considered serious or noteworthy enough to select for publication. Their importance is that she was putting words on a page and learning her craft.

By framing her concerns as religious and spiritual, Walker could rationalize the unfamiliar, now especially as she confronted a new set of feelings that extended beyond puberty. They were more than likely driven by a need to repress certain sexual urges, which she interpreted as a crisis of faith. In her own mind, she felt prompted to recommit herself to God, concluding that that she must "love God and his people." The mental debates with her own soul are continuous and expressed through poems, catalogues, and repeated declarations of faith. She began to have visions again, at least two more, that caused her to ask, "What if following Jesus should mean that this must be given up—my poetry become a secondary thing or even of third importance? Suppose it should mean burying myself among my people and ministering to their needs?"[33] Just a few lines later she adds, "My father is afraid I shall marry directly after I am finished. Such is strongly not my intention."[34] While some of these burning questions, especially about her religious convictions, might have been the subject of family discussions, Walker continued to find solace in her silence.

We can assume that Walker, exceedingly bright, the daughter of Methodist parents who had excelled as educators, would have been under observation by those charged with identifying the best possible talent who could help the Methodist Church brand its Christian Education model, especially in the South. Under the "Department of Education for Negroes," Southern Methodists continued to build schools and a growing network of educators that had begun with the Freedmen's Aid Society, co-founded with the American Missionary Society after slavery. Both of her parents were beneficiaries of Methodist funding, Sigismund Walker for his entire education at Northwestern's Garrett Biblical Institute, and Marion who joined her husband there for one summer school term. Their accomplishments would have been enough to plant a small seed of desire for a life in Christian service as either a missionary or a deaconess, a Methodist laywoman called by God. More important, for ten years at NOU— from fifth grade through two years of college—Walker was under the tutelage of unmarried Methodist women whose encouragement and support bolstered her. Their dedication to the uplift of Black youth would have made them models to emulate. Following such a career path was not only promising, but would also satisfy her parents. Walker, who wanted to be like her father, also wanted to please her mother, who saw her daughter's talent compromised by her perpetual obstinance. Their refusal to allow her to go away to college made a religious option something that allowed Walker to take control of her life. Finally, because her parents had forbidden any contact with boys and she had difficulty containing her excitement about new experiences, a life committed to Christian service offered the necessary balance, if not protection when she was away from them.

In any case, for the remainder of the two years at NOU, Walker was left to her own devices, becoming more and more dependent on her journal as her confidante. When she needed to talk about love, marriage, and family, which could not be a public discussion, she acquired a whole series of dicta about these subjects based on perceived notions of female respectability and desire. In an extended commentary over several journal pages, she combined the ideal of true womanhood with the prevailing ideology of racial uplift, which came easy because she had her mother's example from the Burroughs boarding school days. Because her parents believed that she had never learned to observe the proper social boundaries, they would have been concerned about her inability to adhere to the appropriate sexual boundaries. In fact, however, Walker internalized her parents' fears, especially her mother's, by expressing a zealous desire to set high standards for herself, standards she knew they would approve, and to create from them a catechism for her life. The habit of planning out her life in stages was now firmly in place. Maps and outlines presented specific goals as she rehearsed various scenarios, and believing fervently that if she remained faithful to God, even without the support of others, she'd meet with success.

Shortly after her NOU graduation, when many of her friends may have been making plans to get married, Walker established a new agenda. On June 12, 1932, she recorded the principles that would guide her search for the right mate:

1. I shall keep myself fit for a man who has love for a pure girl, who is willing to keep his body in every way clean and normal but his mind and soul as pure as possible as well.
2. The ideal man will refrain from foul words and will allow nothing foul to enter or come from his mouth.
3. He must be considerate at all times to older people to children and women.
4. He must be self-respecting but neither a snob nor vain.
5. He must feel it his sole obligation to feed, clothe, and shelter his wife and any children she may bear him.
6. He must be sufficiently ambitious and anxious to advance himself.
7. He must be a fit companion intellectually and spiritually.
8. He should not stop to ask of a girl more than he is willing to pay for, more than he should like his mother or sister to give or have given.
9. He should not take advantage of ignorance or poverty.

With renewed dedication to finding the right partner in life, Walker reconsecrates herself to God.

While the search for certainty that accompanied this major life change did not seem unusual, in comparison to most young women her age, white or Black, Margaret Walker's early life experiences defied the norm. She operated in a context that not only respected her intelligence but nurtured it. She was given the tool of language and quickly learned its power to negotiate her way in the world. Most of all, she inherited a female identity that brought with it a silent woman's story, one imprinted in her memory. Because Walker was privileged to have a voice, in her mind she felt mandated to let others speak through her. Learning to live inside and outside the different worlds of the Black and white South was training for her future. What she had learned in her fifteen years in the South was to listen to its various voices, and it didn't matter whether they were in competition or agreement.

Walker came to see her life in New Orleans, and completing her education at Gilbert Academy and NOU, as an important apprenticeship period for her development as a poet. She was only beginning to write free verse, after having had grown accustomed to the system of end rhyme. An early untitled poem demonstrated that style: "There is blue in the sky / And buds on the trees / The days swiftly fly / And there's life in the breeze / For spring's in the air."[35] These predictable patterns of versification she would continue to rely upon for many of the poems in her canon. Their frequent appearance in her published collections were certainly a choice. New Orleans had helped her to find a public voice, and Walker knew from her audience's responses that accessibility is the gift of rhymed verse. At the same time, she was becoming keenly aware of the incongruity between the African American experience and the language available for articulating that experience. What she saw as her strength was an ability to tease out those interior spaces with a language of feeling, which validated the culture. Later, she coined the phrase *feeling tone*, as the African American's gift to our national culture. It was this that any writer who wished to write about the African American experience would need to understand. She did not accept the idea of a natural-born poet. One could only call oneself a poet after thorough rigorous study and training.

What she had also begun to recognize was her acceptance of the contradictory impulses she felt about her experiences living in the South. In her most personal poems, these impulses become an opportunity for self-reflection. A classic example is a poem that appeared in *October Journey*, her most personal volume, one that did not gain a nod from the critics. The poem harkens back to her time in New Orleans and a moment of self-acceptance.

> Dear are the names that charmed me in my youth:
> the dark bronze faces I rejoiced to see.
> One taught me love, another taught me truth

and one of them brought bitterness and ruth.
But all of them inspired my life to be
a charging promise ringed with rhapsody.[36]

The important nurturers in her life appear in the poem. Her grandmother is associated with "love." Marion "brought bitterness and ruth," no doubt a reference
to their strained relationship. Even if Marion could not fill all the duties of a genteel Southern lady, she presided over her middle-class family imposing her ideas
and expectations, ensuring that everyone fulfilled the destiny that she had imagined for them. If her husband had to leave home in order for that to happen, so
be it. It was up to her that her children model the excellence that she saw as their
birthright. Because of the tensions with her mother, Walker claimed at least part
of her feminine identity in opposition to her mother, an identity that she saw
Marion display only on the surface, that of woman as nurturer. At the same time,
Walker absorbed those strong-willed attributes that she despised in her mother.

Although her parents shared many of the same values, Walker acknowledged
certain preferred values from her father. Despite his seeming detachment and
lack of affection, Sigismund Walker instilled in his daughter a strong desire to
seek the truth—moral and aesthetic. Whatever he lacked in assertiveness, his
daughter more than made up for in her stubbornness, most often seen in a refusal to surrender to silence when she had something to say. Bold and forthright
in her actions, Walker practiced standing her ground early in life. The practice
would follow her into adulthood, and if anything, grow stronger as the stakes
grew higher. Ultimately, it was Sigismund, her intellectual and spiritual guide,
and her grandmother, a psychological and emotional tether, who established for
her a distinct set of moral values that privileged family and a conventional home
life, the two things she would eventually realize she could not do without.

And where was poetry in all of this? More important than the content of her
father's instruction was the method he introduced her to. He taught her how to
outline as she worked with him in preparing his sermons and speeches. His basic
advice on the nature of poetry was never replaced by any of the formal teachers
she had throughout her years at NOU, Northwestern, and later at Iowa. And although there was a division of labor for domestic chores, the Walkers had no
gender-imposed restrictions on any of the children's intellectual and academic
development. Following her grandmother's instructions for maintaining a
proper home and pursuing the highest level of academic excellence, on the face
of things, never presented themselves as a conflict. In this sense, Walker was not
only a New Negro, but a New Woman as well.

As for her "fire burning within," Walker had found a coping mechanism unlike
any other. The daybook not only contained her poems, but it also became the personal companion. Gilbert Academy and NOU had a strong writing curriculum,

and writing stories, just like the recording of her daily activities, grew naturally from her love of reading. While those earliest entries were exclusively associated with school and experiences in New Orleans, the transition to more public writing other than poetry came quickly. Her first effort was a prose composition for a seventh-grade English assignment. Ten years old at the time, Walker chose a Thanksgiving theme. That story, "A Band of Pilgrims," no doubt finding some inspiration from the family's journey from Alabama to New Orleans that summer, gave her early practice with formal narrative, even if she found greater satisfaction in the writing and reciting of her poetry.

A source of Walker's drivenness was her desire to excel in an area where her siblings did not. Reading and writing became the things she did best, but they were also appropriate pastimes for keeping a precocious child out of trouble. As she developed the foundation for the lyrical elements in her poetry and prose, she was drawn to African and African American oral traditions that included the spirituals, which her mother regularly performed, along with the idioms she became accustomed to listening to her Grandma Dozier's Southern Black speech. What she saw and heard at home, church, and school provided her with cultural capital that she could put to good use.

What Walker slowly came to realize was that the South was not only home, but an unwritten book that saw its beginning with her life. The South was the place from which she could imagine herself to be anything, a place that allowed her to go anywhere because it always embraced her return. And it was out of her desire to comprehend the South, to explore and explode its tensions, to confront her own conflicting impulses, that the possibility of a literary career emerged. Her New Orleans imaginings combined her Alabama roots with memories of people and natural landscapes where the imposition of strict segregation laws was seen as an outside force. Any imposed violence was not sufficient to replace customs of long standing. In a poem like "Southern Song," nature and history come together: "I want . . . no fiend to stand between my body's southern song . . . the fusion of the South, my body's song and me."[37] The "fusion of the South" was Walker's way of expressing her characteristic synthesis of the disparate elements she had been confronted with for as long as she could remember.

Through this synthesis of natural, religious, historical, and moral elements, Walker could make meaning of her environment, one that was at once hostile to African American existence and deeply indebted to it. Walker's weighted paragraphs in poems such as "For My People," "We Have Been Believers," "Delta," and "Prophets for a New Day" convey the depth of the undeniable connection between African Americans and Southern soil. For Walker, the South was an ancestral homeland. Her poetry therefore became a way of creating the space where the symbols of that homeland could be reimagined and understood and its spirituality protected.

During most of Walker's growing-up years, the South was still the land of Booker T. Washington, but W. E. B. Du Bois's theory of the talented tenth had gained ascendancy as a means toward racial progress. Walker was not privy to the debates that existed within the African American community at the time. It was enough that she learned to articulate the South's heritage in creative ways, owing to her immersion in African American culture. What started as conflicting elements, taken from so many parts of her early life, became synthesized into an organic philosophy that became her trademark. As she began to imagine a journey out of the South, she stored those memories that could sustain her. She had the foundational elements, but would continue to find ways to tease out the complex relationship between those historical experiences, what they felt like, and how to archive them into a repository of collective memory. Poetry became her medium of negotiating that relationship.

4

Get Her Out of the South

While Walker transferred from one building to another during the two years she spent at New Orleans University, she remained confined to the narrow world she'd known since she was nine. In her worst moments she saw her parents' change of heart, their refusal to allow her to leave home, as a cruel punishment. It made it worse that she had to see them at home and at school. The more visible they were, the smaller and more insignificant she felt. Their success as faculty members carried over into their leadership of major campus programs and invitations for the students to attend some of the events in the city where racial restrictions were temporarily lifted.

Because she always believed that Marion had been the principal force behind the decision that kept her at home for two additional years, she turned to her father for comfort. But he had none to give, since he found it extremely difficult to take any side against his wife, who was now probably more well-known than he was with her frequent appearances with the school's orchestra. Her anger at them both, but especially her father's silence, caused outbursts that were immediately followed by bouts of depression. Rather than remain sullen and withdrawn, however, the anger would fuel her defiance, which had an effect opposite of what she wanted. Each exhibition of this disposition was confirmation for Marion that they had done the right thing. How could they even think about allowing such an immature daughter to leave home? Walker's emotional instability made it difficult for her to live reliably on her own, and even if her father wanted to come to her defense, he knew it to be a huge risk that he could not take. When one of the girls in the church they attended became pregnant, "fallen by the wayside in sin," people said, it set off an alarm within the family's group of friends. Increased vigilance was essential. As the mother of two teenaged girls and a third one not far behind, Marion became more determined that none of her girls would suffer such a fate. That they were all preacher's kids simply imposed even greater demands on the Walker children.

Journal entries from the period show self-doubt as well: what if she were unable to resist certain evil forces in the world? What her mother believed about her she came to believe about herself: it was easy for her to go astray because she had not developed the strength to fight off the temptations that confronted young women daily. Falling victim to her own moral weakness was so real that Margaret routinely recorded a prayer at the conclusion of her journal entries: "God

The House Where My Soul Lives. Maryemma Graham, Oxford University Press. © Oxford University Press 2022.
DOI: 10.1093/oso/9780195341232.003.0004

Bus station, Memphis, 1961. Courtesy of the Ernest Withers Collection. "These photographs Ernest Withers put before us [are] the same kinds of images I wanted to capture in my poetry" (Margaret Walker, 1992)

strengthen me in thy holy will and keep me from the hollow of thy hand . . . lest the devil bargain for my soul and win it!"[1] While these self-admonitions were not without the encouragement of her family, they also contributed to her anxiety, fear, and emotional distress. The most obvious physiological manifestation was her nervous stomach.

When Walker summed up her years at Gilbert Academy and NOU, she believed they had been generally good. The focus on the spiritual foundation of all learning, however, gave just cause for her to be somewhat less than the model academic student by the standards of the day. She studied her lessons dutifully and was extremely diligent in completing the assignments, but she was also prone to ask too many questions that she believed brought less-than-satis-fying answers. Because she was the youngest in all of her classes, and certainly brighter than most of her classmates, others perceived her eagerness for know-ledge to be less than genuine—she was a smart aleck. The inability to control her tongue at home extended itself into school, which her peers rarely appreci-ated. What may have been a sign of keen intelligence nevertheless made people uncomfortable.

For Walker, writing poetry was something she *did*, but the idea of writing poetry *as a career* evolved slowly. The need to define her career became magnified
whenever it was compared to her sister's plans to become a concert pianist, which
Marion naturally supported. While opportunities to play the piano and perform
in front of audiences seemed to expand for Mercedes, few people saw poets or
understood what they actually did. Marion's efforts to show off Margaret's musical skills, awkward though they were, only increased her daughter's disdain for
being forced to do what did not interest her. The success she had in oratory made
her an expert elocutionist, but the fine art of speaking *accompanied* a career or a
profession; it did not make one's career. Nevertheless, by the time she turned sixteen, her parents had come to understand three things: their daughter was excep-
tionally bright; she was determined to have her way; and, finally, whatever career
path she chose, it would have something to do with her writing.

Walker had begun her college studies just as NOU launched a successful campaign to bring in the best Negro students from throughout Louisiana. Despite
severe financial worries resulting from a Southern economy hit hard in the aftermath of World War I, a situation made worse by the Great Depression, the school
had attracted a large number of highly competitive students. Violence against
Blacks created a climate of fear as efforts to increase funding at Negro schools
grew. A renewed effort to make more money for higher education available to
Negroes might lessen the desire to attend white schools, or so it was believed.
The effort was consistent with the South's rigid social codes, which had approved
government sanctions for legal segregation in schools, housing, and public accommodations. Further, institutions like NOU benefited from individual local
philanthropy and from large private foundations such as the Rosenwald Fund
and the Phelps-Stokes Fund. A positive side effect was the concentration of talented Black faculty in the all-Negro schools, whether private or state-supported.
Those who may have received their graduate education in the nation's most prestigious Northern institutions—prevented from attending Southern white institutions by law—could never expect to secure employment at any Northern
university. Instead, Negro educators like Sigismund Walker could expect to
remain at Negro schools where they spent their professional lives and were invested in students eager to learn and advance the race.

Though much has been said about the plantation politics of the Negro schools,
which sometimes took on the character of little fiefdoms, faculty expansion and
curriculum development went hand in hand with an equally important concern
for artistic and cultural development. Sigismund Walker's position as a teacher
of philosophy and religion made him an important contributor to the academic
advancement of the students, but Marion had a broader impact in her position
as director of the university's twenty-piece orchestra and its Choral Club. The
latter specialized in performing music by Negro composers, continuing a rich

musical tradition that had enjoyed a long history in even the smallest of these schools. Thus, even if the schools were producing the "talented tenth," the impact colleges and their students had in the Black community's cultural enrichment was immeasurable. Public venues were closed to Negroes in New Orleans, like all Southern cities, but the chapels and auditoriums at Negro schools easily accommodated huge audiences for lectures, recitals, and performances where the nation's best-known artists and speakers routinely appeared.

Social segregation, as it was practiced in New Orleans, and in most of the South, rarely restricted the activities of whites because it was mainly and forcefully directed toward Negroes. In this regard, NOU was an important experiment

Marion with her NOU orchestra

in interracial cooperation, not unlike a number of other Methodist Episcopal schools founded in the late nineteenth century. While the Walkers worked there, President Kriege attracted a young and vibrant Negro faculty who worked alongside their white colleagues. NOU was, therefore, on par with Fisk, Talladega, and Morehouse Colleges, Howard and Lincoln Universities, all of which emphasized a classical liberal arts education for those who were deemed qualified to attend these schools. When Walker's parents insisted that she go to NOU, they were not settling for a lesser school, as Kriege had reminded them earlier. On the contrary, they were consciously selecting one of the strongest liberal arts colleges for Negroes in the nation at that time. After she left for Northwestern, Walker agreed that her NOU education was at least as good as anywhere else, if not better. She knew that no place would have provided as much support. Ultimately, she agreed that her parents had been right.

Walker took particular pleasure in the Bible classes she took from her father. Since he retreated to his study so often, the contact with her father was limited to the class she had enrolled in and it was where she could demonstrate her extraordinary skill at memorization and discussion of biblical characters. She also tended to avoid him more after she had been forced to remain at home. Now and again, he would discuss philosophy with his students, and although he thought that girls were naturally unsuited for such topics, he must have been immensely pleased when his daughter offered insights gained from her reading of the assigned texts. Because she was still struggling with the issue of a vocation, she put her feelings aside and used the time with her father to think about the relationship between his intellectual gifts and passions and her own. In her 1973 volume, *October Journey*, a collection dedicated to her father and Langston Hughes, she published "Epitaph for my Father," a poem in which she explores their relationship and the tensions derived from it.

She excelled, as expected, in the composition course and received first prize for her final class essay in her freshman year. Two of her teachers, both white women, were most impressed with her writing ability. While her parents may have been encouraging her to set her goal on a career that would bring economic security, they encouraged abstract thinking and rewarded her imaginative efforts. One of them, Miss Ella Fluke, would be instrumental in encouraging Walker's parents to send their daughter away to school. "Margaret is head and shoulders above all the rest of her class," Fluke told them. "You should get her out of the South," by which she meant sending her to Northwestern, the school from which she had graduated.[2]

As the fall semester of her first year in college drew to a close, Sigismund received a call asking if NOU would be willing to sponsor a young Negro poet who was currently on tour. Tulane had been unwilling to bring a Negro poet to their all-white campus, and there was no other place in the city where he could speak to an integrated audience. The poet was Langston Hughes, who had just published his novel *Not without Laughter*, and had recently returned from Cuba and Haiti. He was on his first tour of Southern colleges at the urging of Mary McLeod Bethune in Jacksonville, Florida. When Bethune met Hughes, she insisted that he should get to know the South and believed that even during the Great Depression, he could make a living reading his poetry to Negro audiences. Hughes might also have been looking for an escape. A disagreement over the disposition of the play *Mule Bone*, which he had written with Zora Neale Hurston, had ended their friendship and affected his relationship with their shared sponsor Mrs. R. Osgood Mason. Without Mason's support, he had become financially destitute. His poems had appeared in leftist periodicals, and his play about the "Scottsboro Boys" had also targeted him for some sharp public criticism. It was a good time for him to be out of New York; he accepted the invitation and planned his first visit to the South beginning in fall 1931.

Sigismund Walker was well aware that hosting the visit of such an important figure was more than a job for him. Looking for ways to heal the wounds in their relationship beyond the judicious praise he gave for his daughter's performance in his Bible class, he brought her a book home one day. She recalled that afternoon her father came home "with a little paperback book called *Four Lincoln Poets*. President Kriege had given it to him and daddy brought it home to me. For the first time I read the poems of Langston Hughes, Waring Cuney, Ernest Silvera and Frank Williams [William Allyn Hill]. Looking back now, I know I became saturated with those poems and came under the influence for the first time of Langston Hughes."[3]

Four Lincoln University Poets was volume 3 of the *Lincoln University Herald* and dated March 1930. The college that bore the name of the famous American president had been in existence since 1854, when it began as the Ashmun Institute, the first institution to provide higher education in the arts and sciences for male youth of African descent. The poets who appeared in the special issue had all gone on to illustrious careers, something the Lincoln administration was eager to promote and celebrate. *Four Lincoln University Poets* was the brainchild of the university's president, William Hallock Johnson, whose generous introduction called attention to "four young men who have been diligent in cultivating the Muse. . . . Their work . . . will make a contribution even more significant to the artistic and literary life of their country, and will win in larger measure both for themselves and the group they represent the respect and recognition of the world."[4] The periodical was sent to libraries, Lincoln alumni, and friends who would have quickly recognized the name of Langston Hughes, who was already identified with the cultural and intellectual ferment in New York. Far from the sounds of Harlem, Lincoln was an oasis for somewhat loosely supervised, free-spirited Black male students whose tutelage at the feet of white professors gave them a self-assured authority. The freedom they were allowed imposed a higher sense of honor and morality than any that would have been insisted on from without.

Hughes elected to complete his college education that had been short-circuited at Columbia University at the southeastern Pennsylvania college, arriving in 1926. By the time he graduated in 1929, he would have two books to his credit and a novel nearly completed. Hughes may have taken the energy he derived from Harlem to Lincoln, but Lincoln was as much the site of exciting cultural and intellectual activity as Harlem, which was known as the "Negro Capital of the world." Hughes was one year ahead of well-known US Supreme Court Justice Thurgood Marshall and Nnamdi Azikiwe, Nigeria's first president; Kwame Nkrumah, Ghana's first president, graduated a year after him. Their matriculation at the school helped to form the nucleus of distinguished graduates who gave Lincoln a reputation as the "Black Princeton." In 1954, one hundred years after its founding, it could boast of producing a larger share of Black physicians; attorneys; college presidents; leading ministers; ambassadors; and federal, state, and municipal judges, along with other public officials than any other school in the nation.

Everything about *Four Lincoln University Poets* intrigued her. She was already beginning to react to contemporary events and any news about writers. While Hughes was just beginning to make a name for himself outside New York, his appearance in a school magazine endeared him to aspiring writers throughout the Negro college network. Walker read the brief biography that appeared in "Notes on the Writers." Of the four poets, the description of Hughes's life was the most colorful and exciting. "Before coming to Lincoln," it read, "he worked as a seaman to the West Coast of Africa, Holland and the Mediterranean."[5] These places were part of a world about which she knew nothing, and here was a Negro poet who had already traveled to them. The book was a map and Hughes a guide to all that she knew she wanted to explore. What struck her about this poet in particular was his ability to engage a world of learning and letters without sacrificing his passion and zest for life. As someone upon whose life order had always been imposed, Margaret saw Hughes as a kindred spirit, someone who followed his imagination more than the expectations of others.

She stared at her father in disbelief when he told her that he and Marion would be hosting Hughes at NOU, the only engagement the poet would have in New Orleans. Walker had already decided Hughes was to be her model. For the first time, she could see that artists could exist in separate worlds that did not necessarily have to conflict. It was possible, she believed, to become a well-known poet and to do so without alienating those who were part of one's community. Hughes had remained steeped in the traditions of Negro life, traditions that he respected and sought to share through his work.

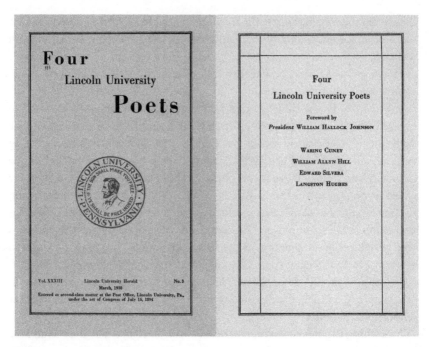

Front cover and title page, *Four Lincoln University Poets*

She read and memorized his poems in the book. "Cross," "Youth," "Mother to Son," and especially "The Negro Speaks of Rivers" had such a profound effect that she added them to her repertoire, so she could practice reading them whenever invitations came to recite poetry to audiences throughout the city. Reading Hughes's poetry gave her more reason to transform from that thin, sickly girl into a strong and forceful presence in her performances. When she came home from a reading, often after winning a local oratory contest, she was energized and ready to write her own poems in her daybook. She had never expected to meet Hughes but was already feeling his impact.

There are no distribution records for *Four Lincoln University Poets*, but the current holdings of many libraries suggest that the volume enjoyed a wide circulation. Hughes's warm reception by Black students, as well as the Black and white faculty on the campuses of many of the smaller Negro colleges, lent support to the growth of small literary journals that enjoyed a lively existence at many of these schools. They were part of the expanding cultural focus on the performing arts, a significant part of the curriculum in many of the Negro schools. As much as Harlem may have dominated the Black art scene in the 1920s, the explosion in Black culture was by no means limited to Harlem, or New York for that matter, as evidenced by the tremendous activity in places like Lincoln University and

NOU. Even towns like High Point, North Carolina, where Walker would spend the early years of her marriage, could boast of a "Cotton Club in the South." One didn't have to go to Harlem to see Cab Callaway and Duke Ellington, who performed to some of their largest audiences outside of New York.

The Lincoln anthology also gave her a sense of where and how poetry could be understood within the context of her own time. Most of what she had been reading was limited to earlier male poets in anthologies of British and American literature; now she became more interested in living poets. She could see her early college years as the promise of greater exposure to more living artists and writers. NOU could be for Walker what Lincoln had been for Hughes. To her repertoire of Hughes's poems she offered in the performances she began to add others, but it wasn't long before she would recite her own poems and write articles for publication. She was getting nearly as many invitations to read at church and community events as her sister got to perform music. By the time Hughes appeared in New Orleans, Walker had already claimed him as the model she wanted to follow.

Hughes's visit to New Orleans followed an exhausting schedule that included schools in Maryland, Virginia, North Carolina, South Carolina, Georgia, Alabama, Florida, Mississippi, and Tennessee, as well as other stops in Louisiana. This whirlwind tour by car in less than three months had also resulted in some important reunions. He had seen James Weldon Johnson at Fisk University in Nashville, and his old friend Arna Bontemps at Oakwood College in Alabama. The tour also gave Hughes renewed energy and the raw materials for some of his more satiric verse like the poem "Christ in Alabama." Only one incident had caused some controversy, exposing the nature of Southern relations. Allen Tate, who praised Hughes, saw to it that the reception for Hughes at Vanderbilt was canceled, so firmly did he hold to his belief in social segregation. Hughes's biographer Arnold Rampersad noted that Tate had made an insulting remark when he compared the possibility of seeing Hughes socially with socializing with his Black cook,[6] which he believed everyone would have seen as a true violation of southern etiquette.

NOU was the perfect venue, an institution that understood well its role in bringing events of cultural significance to the wider New Orleans Negro community. Sigismund and Marion were careful to schedule the New Orleans reading so as not to invite negative publicity. At the same time, the sponsors wanted to maximize the opportunity for Hughes to meet an audience of eager listeners. Hughes was set to appear on February 11 at Peck Hall.

Walker listened intently as the plans were being made for the visit, secretly making plans of her own. She was sixteen and still impressionable, but aware enough to recognize the opportunity that presented itself. She organized a sheaf of her poems, just in case there was a chance to share them with Hughes, writing in her journal nightly about her choices. But she was not the only person with a hidden agenda. Marion had two daughters who needed exposure, and she was intent on seeing both of her daughters get their just due.

Peck Hall was packed on the night of Hughes's appearance. The committee had been concerned that they could not meet Hughes's speaker's fee, which they certainly could not do in advance. The Walkers, as cochairs of the host committee, had asked Hughes to accept payment from the money raised from the tickets they sold, and were overjoyed when they realized the huge turnout would allow Hughes to be paid more than he had originally requested. Marion had organized the program in the college's typical lyceum format, which called for students from the college to showcase their talents before the featured speaker or performer. It was no surprise that Marion had Mercedes performing first with a piano solo. Walker joined the choral group that sang a few numbers under Marion's direction, but then receded into the background until the end of the program. She'd never forgotten that evening:

> I had carefully concealed my date-book with all my poems in it and three times I went through the receiving line trying to get enough courage to speak to him. The first time I could not lift my eyes. . . . Next my English teacher went to introduce me but I still lost my tongue. . . . Finally, I plunged forward again. . . . Mama who remembered why she had gone through all this work, told him I had my notebook and wouldn't he take a look and see if they were any good. He did read my poems one after another and said they were very good. And he punctuated these remarks by echoing Miss Fluke's words to my parents, "You really must get her out of the South."[7]

The words shot through Walker like a bullet. It was a moment she had been waiting for. Hughes had not only become her model, but also the voice of authority. She no longer had to challenge her parents. Hughes had done it for her. His words, spoken so resolutely and supported by what her English teacher had already said, seemed to be directed at her parents. She knew that Marion was listening, so she could not be accused of lying, or of having a "wild imagination"—something they told her often. Now she had the ammunition she needed to convince her parents that she had a reason to leave, that had everything to do with her future.

By "getting out of the South," Hughes was not casting aspersions on the land he was seeing and learning about for the first time, but rather sharing his sense of what a writer needs to do in order to grow and develop. He would have said the same thing about a writer from any other place. It was what he knew, his roots in Kansas, growing up in Cleveland, spending time in Mexico, and finally moving to New York, only to find new opportunities opening up for him as he traveled around the world. Had he never left his own home, Hughes was convinced that he would never have become the writer that he was. His advice to Walker was heartfelt and sincere. This turning point in her own life tells us much about the importance she placed on literary influence as she began to define her place in the world of art and imagination.

Walker remained under Hughes's spell for the rest of her time in New Orleans. Little did she realize they would remain friends for life. The most important public statement that she made about Hughes came much later in her 1986 preface to Hughes's autobiography, *I Wonder as I Wander,* published twenty years after his death. She must have been thinking about how much Hughes had given her a sense of connection to a world beyond the one she knew when she wrote: "I heard from him around the world wherever he went, notably from Carmel-by-the-Sea in California, from the war in Loyalist Spain, the revolutionary movement in West Africa, and his beloved New York City. There was a kaleidoscopic nature of his mind and experiences."[8] At the end of Hughes's life and throughout her own, she considered him the "Dean of Black Literature."

Shortly after completing her sophomore year, Walker was asked to write something for the Colored Juvenile Delinquent Rescue Association of New Orleans. The August 1932 issue of its publication *Our Young Magazine* included essays and poetry written by local young people. She decided not to submit a poem for the issue, but instead she wrote a statement that she thought would represent the ideas of her generation:

> A good and sure way to succeed in our various occupations is to apply our knowledge wisely in our environment with a view to bettering conditions there. Thus, we follow the principle and words of our great teacher, Booker T. Washington, "Let down your buckets where you are." A further inference from these words may be summed up in this manner: The Negro has a bucket, the tool is in his hand, he has used it and given it to others all over the world; his manual labor has brought enormous profits and stupendous results to nations who have used him as the tool to realize their dreams and ambitions, to materialize their ideas and plans. Now he must use what is his own for himself, he is putting his brain to school daily, it should and it must supply him with the idea, the scheme, and the plan. And now the two together—his brain and his brawn—must work out his own salvation.[9]

Entitled "What Is to Become of Us?," the essay was aimed at the students who were graduating, and who, according to Walker, "have been thrown into life by their Alma Maters."[10] Although she had only completed two years of college, the use of the collective "we" marks her willingness to accept a role as a mature adult and a leader of her generation, just as it tells us about the person she had become

"What Is to Become of Us?" *Our Youth Magazine*, vol I: 5 (August 1932), 9–10

by sixteen. The essay advances the thinking of Booker T. Washington at the outset. "We make a mistake when we think any one of us may be either a doctor, lawyer, preacher, teacher or social worker. All of us are not made to fit into some one of these. But if after careful observations and searchings we are able to definitely ascertain whether we have an intellectual or industrial trend of mind, a college education can then make a better cook or gardener or farmer or nurse."[11]

Walker *seems* to be saying that too much of the wrong kind of education is a bad thing for the race; she then makes the connection to Black business and economic growth, and secondarily to individual achievement. Although the first part of this article appears to be a fairly transparent promotion of ideas identified with Booker T. Washington and Tuskegee Institute, Walker gradually introduces a strikingly political subtext, expanding if not reversing the perspective. She refers to "our great teacher, Booker T. Washington."[12] Washington's frequently quoted phrase from the Atlanta Exposition Address, "Let down your buckets where you are," correctly identifies a position that can bring the Black community financial gain and independence. The agricultural climate and rural sensibility that made this phrase so forceful in the late nineteenth- and early twentieth-century South is not the emphasis that Walker has in mind, however.

"The Negro has a bucket, the tool is in his hand," she offers, "he has used it and given it to others all over the world; his manual labor has brought enormous profits and stupendous results to nations who have used him as the tool to realize their dreams and ambitions, to materialize their ideas and plans." The repetition of the words "bucket" and "tool" in this passage signifies Walker's own radical revision. The phrases "all over the world," "enormous profits," "stupendous results," and the word "materialize" imply systematic and worldwide economic exploitation. She refuses to limit the discussion of exploitation to a Southern context, and heightens our political awareness of the relationship between Black labor and economic development on a worldwide scale.

This was Walker's first instance of her recognition of the essay as a most effective rhetorical tool for engaging in the public debates of her time; it would be decades before she embraced it as one of her preferred forms of expressions. Until then, she had seen poetry as a private domain, deriving from the imagination. Hughes had given her a first sense of poetry as a public discourse. But because he wrote in a Black idiom, giving renewed respect to and celebrating an African American cultural and racial matrix, she might have seen his poetry as having a certain kind of interiority. "What Is to Become of Us?" is a different kind of attempt at self-definition; she wanted to put into permanent form something that symbolized a mature, thinking individual who is intensely concerned with the politics of race and class. Because she did not return to essay writing until many years later, after years of enforced silence in fact, this essay signals an important moment in her creative development. Inserting herself into such public debates, tactfully deferring to and then countering the vision of such a renowned figure as Booker T. Washington, Walker demonstrates that she was as attentive to other factors as she was to those governing her inner life.

Choosing to name and, in a sense, to write *against* Booker T. Washington without any mention of W. E. B. Du Bois became more significant in time. Walker would later describe Du Bois as the most profound intellectual influence in her life, noting "how seminal [his] mind was for us all," in her poem "Giants of My Century."[13] But in 1932, a lot more was at stake that prevented an immediate embrace of W. E. B. Du Bois, the noted proponent of liberal arts education. She was well aware that her father had begun his educational journey at Tuskegee, and that it was her father's disagreement with Washington's educational philosophy that led to his departure for Atlanta to continue his studies. Sigismund Walker's tenure at Gammon Theological Seminary corresponded with that of Du Bois, who joined the faculty of Atlanta University in 1897.

Her essay and its commitment to education and uplift confirmed Walker as a member of the talented tenth. The requirement for membership included the establishment of one's public voice, leadership potential, and the need to use one's "native talent and equipment . . . to greatest advantage."[14] To do so would ensure, she concluded in her essay, "a high plane of intellectual and spiritual growth."[15]

Her rhetorical style would intensify, but not change fundamentally, in years to come. Her examples of the Black experience look to the past at the same time she advocates change based on that history. The seed for her poem "For My People" is here in bold relief as she charges the youth of her own generation with the responsibility for bringing about necessary change. Although it does not have the calculated artistry and poetic intensity of "For My People," "What Is to Become of Us?" introduces the central tension that she explores in that classic work.

It is this tension—between one's knowledge of the past and one's sense of responsibility for the future—that initiated a new phase of her life, one that looked backward and forward. The past was an omnipresent influence, and the present a constant challenge. Here is where her sympathies lay. The experience of her childhood in Birmingham and New Orleans defined her subject matter for her, drawing her to a life of social commitment.

> Most of the solutions to our problems and much of the discoveries on the road to our goal will and does depend upon us. True, we have a hard road before us with many heavy odds against us but we are encouraged when we think of the splendid progress made so far and know that in proportion to the difficulties our fathers faced and the hindrances we face today, we are indeed fortunate. Let us bear in mind that we . . . shall be part of the cause for the coming generations asking and facing the same question as we do, "What is to become of us?"[16]

Challenging the orthodoxy of early twentieth-century Southern racial thought, her voice may speak the words of Booker T. Washington, but her heart belongs to W. E. B. Du Bois.

To see this crucial moment in her intellectual and emotional development is to understand that the sixteen-year-old who wrote "What Is to Become of Us?" is conscious of the need to speak as an adult, not as a child needing the protection of her parents. Surrounded by Black intellectuals who founded and taught at Black schools and who established and built influential Black churches, she listened to many adult conversations. A host of Black educators, many of them women, provided immediate models. These women had very public images and could match any male preacher in rhetorical power. Through public service, these women understood they could do what was not available to them in other professions. It was public service her parents believed in and practiced. She seemed, at least at this point, undaunted by any negative sense of patriarchal authority; she wrote and spoke because she could and had the means to do so. This is what she might have meant when she said she always felt confident in being her father's child. When we add to this her consciousness of the moral and ethical authority of educated Black women of her day, it is easy to see how she grew comfortably into the role of a cultural spokesperson.

As the quintessential race woman, Walker's fulfillment of her intellectual potential was commensurate with the progress of the race. She had begun college with this strong sense of her own intellectual resources, but she was preoccupied with the need for more training to become a writer. Two years later, she became filled with a desire to be a credit to her race. The social proscriptions might prevent her from achieving her goal, but individual talent did not. The function of education was to cultivate individual talent—her family had instilled this in her from the beginning. Her two years at NOU provided the opportunity to continue her development. With a few exceptions, she had white women teachers who took pride in challenging her intellect and instilling in her a strong identity as a professional woman. She realized later that these women paralleled those role models that extended from her family.

While her grandmother gave her the rudiments of a Black female education, teaching her fundamental domestic chores, her mother fulfilled the role of a professional woman. Marion's lack of domesticity offered an unanticipated advantage. Female teachers at Gilbert Academy encouraged intellectual pursuits and represented the mastery of subjects she so thoroughly enjoyed. This juxtaposition and blending of roles, played by the important women in her life, made Walker far less conscious of the boundaries that limited most Blacks and women of her era. When she chose to leave her budding career, marry, and raise her family, it was to teaching she turned with a great deal of fulfillment. When she could not write, she could claim an equally important identity as a teacher. In one of her autobiographical statements, she made this clear:

> I am the example of a family of three generations of teachers. My great-uncle, Jim Ware, and my maternal grandfather, the Reverend Edward Lane Dozier, taught school one hundred years ago in Greenville, Mississippi. My mother and father taught more than fifty years ago in Meridian, Mississippi. . . . My family has been involved in education in Mississippi for at least one hundred years. . . . I am a product of southern black teachers, mostly women, and as a result of those good teachers, my image of the teacher is reflected in what I am today.[17]

"What Is to Become of Us" as the first appearance of the budding writer might have been hypnotic had it not come as a surprise. Since the issue that contained the essay did not come out until August, the summer months were filled with anticipation. Between June and August, she experienced another emotional crisis—this one more severe than before and triggered by her anxiety over leaving home and going so far away for school. What made it worse was her desire to keep it contained. She had learned that it was better not to express these feelings openly. To do so would give reason for her mother to think that she might still not be sufficiently mature. And yet it was the idea of leaving home that frightened her, the place where the constant surveillance of her parents provided a buffer zone of protection. The idea of losing that buffer brought her talent, desire, and ethical responsibility into an irreconcilable conflict. She felt paralyzed by misgivings, self-recrimination, and guilt.

In the wake of her seventeenth birthday, she experienced an intense renewal of religious faith that helped mitigate the crisis. On June 5 she recorded, "Nearly every hour in the day my soul is crying out in desperate need for the love of Christ in my heart and the presence of His Holy Spirit in my soul. . . . Help me sweeten my temper and conquer my many faults and careless ways."[18]

The entry on June 6 exhibits a more prayerful tone: "I am so weak but I desire thy strength to charge through my body and soul like electricity and fire me with devout love, faith and truth. Make me humble and send someone to talk to me, to counsel and comfort me, bless those I love and widen my love and teach me the way."[19] This crisis of conscience seems unbearable until near the end of this period of intense introspection, when the darkness begins to subside. Relief comes as she feels the "light within my soul once more!"[20]

Although Walker continued to desire more freedom to be and do as she pleased, this did not include freedom from religion. In fact, one of her greatest fears was to feel the presence of God's spirit without being able to sustain it. "Dare I believe when in a few hours I may be on the rack again?" she asked herself.[21] These feelings were accompanied by intellectual affirmation. In addition to the Bible, she was attracted to several books on faith, including E. Stanley Jones's Christ at the Round Table (1928), which appealed to her need for divine love and forgiveness, at the same time promoting an activist faith. She needed to hear what others had to say when they experienced a loss of faith or found certain religious ideas wanting. Jones's book guided her search for certainty. Her natural instinct had always been to question, and in religion she found many things to question. One is required to have faith, she believed, but because faith can come without understanding, one may not always know what was right or wrong in any particular situation. Now, facing the uncertainty of a new stage of her life, she needed evidence that reconciliation of conflicts was indeed possible. More than anything else, Walker seemed drawn to religion out of her need for assurance that she could lead a moral life regardless of whatever choices she might make, and that she could do so outside the watchful care of her parents. She had grown up in a rather strict household, and whether or not her parents subscribed to the Calvinist belief that a person was born in sin—always the disobedient, resistant child—she was not easy to control. If there were no external penalty imposed upon her when she exceeded boundaries, she was not sure she would know how to respond. So thoroughly indoctrinated was she with the belief that if she did something wrong, which was often, she would logically associate it with the presence of evil. At these times, she would be expected to, and always did, seek forgiveness and repentance through constant soul searching and prayer.

At seventeen, all of her social contexts had derived from church and school, or tied to her parents' outreach activities in the New Orleans community and the surrounding area. These existed on a religious continuum that was fairly predictable. It was the thought of exchanging predictability for uncertainty that must have been so terrifying, that incited such dread, and that made her vulnerability more apparent. To add to this, she felt the mounting pressure of a career choice. She had talked of being a poet, but understood well the need for a career that could support her—a point her parents had made often. She was unsure if becoming a poet could do that, but believed that she had no choice but to take this venture into the unknown.

The dangerous ground on which she stood seemed ready to explode at any moment. A journal entry is telling: "I know that I must serve my people," she says, "yet I have been fighting against the task that I feel is calling me."[22] The "calling" to serve one's people is undoubtedly spiritual in nature. We can only speculate about the resistance here. Poetry is often identified with a world that encourages self-indulgence, if not decadence; and freethinking, if not liberation. The collision between expectation and desire, between family ties and spiritual needs, is not altogether clear here. What is clear is that moving outward and forward was not easy for her, no matter how much she longed to leave what she considered to be a stifling environment. Her center of gravity was shifting, and even if she found herself "so far away in thought and deed from the master," she felt "duty bound to follow [her] own conscience."[23]

A journal entry on June 28 brings the uncertainty to an end: "I believe that men are the tools for the working out of [God's] great plan. . . . I commend my soul to him now, henceforth, and forever."[24] With this, she welcomed her seventeenth birthday with the full recognition that she was about to close the final door of her childhood, "and that in a little while, a mere matter of months and days, I shall be a woman."[25]

5

Goodbye New Orleans

Of the 360 poems Walker recorded in the daybook she had received from her father in 1929, nearly half of them were written before she left New Orleans in August 1932. When she packed her bags, she put the daybook in last, expecting to have a lot to write about during the long drive. All she could think about now was going to the place that would make her a writer. In later talks and remembrances about her time in Chicago, she routinely referred to it as "the place where I found my voice."[1]

What Walker had been imagining for a long time was about to come to pass. In "Goodbye to NOU," she bade a final farewell to the place that had done so much to cultivate her dreams of becoming a writer. The occasional poem would always be a fallback form, given her need to memorialize particular moments and events and her public sensibility. Cloaked in sentiment, it showed her strong attachment to the romantic legacy that dominated her youthful reading:

> These are the last dear days!
> Soon shall the past envelop them
> And pleasant memories they'll be
> Like unto some unused gem
> Exotic cologne from life's tree
> Per chance we idle while they pass
> These golden hours elude our clutch
> How much we'll pay in tears, Alas!
> Who knows how little, half how much
> These are the last dear days![2]

She penned "Goodbye" sometime in June 1932. Along with a sizable collection of juvenilia, these short, nostalgic pieces about her life in New Orleans up to the time of her departure never appeared in print. They provide a permanent record of her thoughts and feelings associated with a particular period in her life that became fixed in her imagination, lending the raw materials for some of her most important work. The rhymed couplets modeled the nineteenth-century Romantic poetry in the textbooks for the literature curriculum of high schools and colleges. She had NOU to thank for offering her such a large sampling of models from English poetry, which continued to provide the structures she

The House Where My Soul Lives. Maryemma Graham, Oxford University Press. © Oxford University Press 2022.
DOI: 10.1093/oso/9780195341232.003.0005

relied on heavily in most of her unpublished poems. Margaret had yet to use the free-verse forms that would characterize her earliest published poetry, but she was highly conscious of the need for structure in a poem, even at the expense of awkwardness.

She had secretly wanted to take the train to Chicago, for she had never forgotten the experience of that first train ride from Birmingham to New Orleans. Having decided that their two daughters should go together, the Walkers considered the ritual of taking one's children away to college for the first time a most important one. Marion remembered the loneliness she felt with her departure from home and arrival in Washington, DC, without family, knowing that she would not see them for at least two years. She came home only once, never to return, even though the reason at the time was a valid one. But time had given her a new perspective, and she was not about to allow anything to stand in the way of a smooth transition for the two daughters whose hopes and dreams she had worked so hard to nurture. But four train tickets to Chicago would have been prohibitive. Moreover, her parents had no intention of riding Jim Crow cars through the Southern states. Instead, Sigismund Walker bought the family's first car for the trip. The action not only made for a unique bonding experience, giving the Walkers the ultimate satisfaction of seeing their daughters appropriately settled. Above all, for Marion, appearances were also important. Her husband had graduated from Northwestern, and now he was returning to enroll his daughters in the same university. By any standard of measure, he had achieved success, and the car became one of the most visible material possessions that Negroes in the 1930s could have. Walker well understood the sacrifice that her parents were making and was determined to show that "the talent he [God] has given me shall not be lost but more added to it."[3] As if it were needed, further justification came with her belief that this was her calling, one that was as religious as anything else. "My life is not my own alone . . . but for fallen and helpless humanity," she wrote.[4]

Despite the unevenness of educational opportunities for Negroes in the first three decades of the twentieth century, Walker considered her formal education to that point full and rich. She always held her teachers in high regard and believed none was better prepared to give her what she needed in her early training. When she chose to begin teaching years later, "knowing that I would not be able to eke out the barest existence as a writer," she felt no indifference or loss, but rather tremendous excitement at finally having earned the right to be part of such an esteemed and select community.

Her English teachers throughout high school had been women, just as women had been her teachers in her first years of college—women who fed her desire to write and always nurtured her talents. A contrast here is the life of Richard Wright or the unnamed protagonist in Ralph Ellison's *Invisible Man*. The lives of both men, as they reimagined them in their fiction and autobiographical works, represent critiques of Southern Black education, or in Wright's case, the lack thereof. Walker was leaving the South, not in anger but in deep and full appreciation for what it had given her, and for instilling in her the belief that she was and could be the best of what the South had to offer.

Nevertheless, this seventeen-year-old, tiny coffee-colored girl with hardly the look of a woman-to-be had mixed emotions as she left New Orleans. Stories, good and bad about the North, were legion, always larger than life. Her first impressions of Chicago appeared in a later essay:

> I had been told that Negroes in the North were better off than Negroes down South; they had more sense and more opportunities; they could go any place, enjoy recreational facilities such as parks and movies, eat in restaurants without discrimination; there were no Jim Crow transportation restrictions, and if Negroes were subjected to any indignity, they could sue the person or company involved; there was no such thing as lynching. Best of all, Negroes could vote.[5]

Such impressions were common among migrants traveling north for the first time. But Walker had more to reflect on than the rumors she had heard about life "up North." She had learned to assert herself and to have confidence in her abilities, but she had always lived in a Negro world. Going to a white school frightened her, accompanied by a growing sense of self-doubt.

She was in deep thought for most of the drive. She contemplated her future and the meaning of the past she was leaving behind. In the South she was full of questions, and at least she knew someone was there to ask. To whom would she go to ask her questions now? She also knew that going to all-Negro schools brought with it the assumption that no matter how good they were, they would never be as good as white schools. "I might prove backward as a result of my southern training," she feared. At the same time, she acknowledged, "I had become anti-white myself and I feared coming into close contact with white people."[6]

She had learned the irrationality of race prejudice; for despite her parents' careful monitoring, it reared its ugly head without warning. She remembered the owner of the white grocery store at the corner of their Perrier Street home, who was always friendly to her, and who believed in drafting Black men into the army to fight for their country. Yet he was adamant in his belief that whites and Blacks should not fight in the same ring together. Then there was the story of a family friend, a story people shared with whispered breaths. An accusation that she was keeping the acquaintance of a white man sent a mob tearing into her home intent on teaching her a lesson. When her family found her, she was covered with turpentine, tarred, and feathered. Neighbors had heard her cries as the mob tortured her and alerted her distraught family who found her barely alive.

In her young mind, too many in her community held the view that "This is a white man's country and the black man ain't got no place in it."[7] She had heard Black people put themselves down, making themselves easy targets for white racism. For every Roland Hayes, Marian Anderson, Paul Laurence Dunbar, James Weldon Johnson, and Langston Hughes, there were Blacks who saw themselves as "cursed by God, sons of Ham, scared to stick up for their rights, distrustful of all other blacks."[8] Similarly, racial prejudice had distorted her view of Southern whites: "In the South I had always thought that, naturally white people had more money than colored people. Poor white trash signified for me the lazy scum of the marginal fringe of society with no excuse for poverty."[9]

If leaving New Orleans and going to Chicago stirred up certain fears, it also heightened anticipation of a new kind of freedom. She would be leaving Jim Crow behind. Her skin would mark her identity but would no longer limit her opportunities. Determined and headstrong, with the values her family had bequeathed to her, she had every reason to feel confident. Their religious principles and stern morality would keep her focused and deeply spiritual just as the racist practices in the South had heightened her cultural awareness. They had taught her to be thrifty, which together with self-reliance would make her fearlessly independent. Growing up with parents who were educators, committed to a life of service, inspired in her a deep respect for Black leadership and a corresponding commitment to social change. In her own life, she would undergo struggles against poverty, illness, defeat, and disappointment more taxing than her parents had known. Yet the family's Christian optimism would always provide the strength she needed.

If the South had satisfied the hunger for knowledge and her passion for truth, it had given Walker an intellectual maturity well beyond her years. But now a fierce ambition was driving her to succeed. She was aware of the acute situation of her race. As the oldest child and role model for her younger siblings, she knew intuitively that she could not accept a marginal position in society. She, therefore, approached this journey as if it were her destiny. The die was cast. There was no turning back.

We do not know when the Walkers made the decision to send not one, but two daughters to Northwestern. Even though she kept copious notes on all the relevant conversations among her parents to which she was privy, there is no record of what may have transpired between them on this issue. As parents, the Walkers were full of ambition and expectations for their children but without the resources to see them materialize. Several weeks before their departure, she had filled out an application for admission. One week before their departure, however, her father confirmed that Northwestern had admitted the two sisters. Without asking any questions, Margaret and Mercedes knew that they had to begin packing right away. Sigismund still had contacts from the summers he had spent in Evanston completing graduate school, but it was probably Marion who decided to set up a boarding arrangement with Mrs. Lyda Landers on Emerson Street where the Walkers had stayed in the summer of 1928, when they both attended Northwestern's summer session. Marion trusted Landers to follow the instructions she left, "They don't dance, play cards, nor receive company."[10] The girls were thoroughly embarrassed when their mother insisted that the landlady enforce a ten o'clock lights-out policy and expected to be the laughingstock of their peers.[11]

That Victorian standards should prevail was not unusual for parents who were leaving their two adolescent girls alone for the first time in a major urban city a thousand miles away from their home. What a difficult separation this must have been for Marion who had always been extremely protective. Walker wondered if her mother had felt the same way when she left home in Pensacola twenty years earlier. Like Mercedes, Marion was also fifteen, but the welcoming environment that Nannie Burroughs had provided her girls in an all-Negro environment was no comparison to the uncertainty of what her daughters would be going through. She had come as close as she could to finding a parallel situation for her daughters with the Landers boarding house arrangement. Fears that she may have had subsided whenever she thought about what this new opportunity would mean for her two very bright and talented daughters. Her duty was to prepare them well to take their place in a world unlike the one that she had known. She could continue to enjoy their successes as if they were her own.

She was probably more certain of Mercedes, who at fifteen, seemed more mature than her seventeen-year-old sister. It is also doubtful that her parents would have allowed their oldest daughter, despite her ambitions and ability, to leave home alone. Regardless, Walker believed she had *earned* the right to leave home. In her mind, she was showing signs of greater maturity and religious convictions, pleasing her father immensely. She hoped that her parents would have noticed the calmness that she began to display and a fervent desire to embrace a more public faith. She no longer giggled during family prayers, one of her worst habits, and she had learned to contain the outbursts that found their way into those adult conversations in which she knew she was not included. Her fight against the old belief "that children should be seen and not heard" had been a personal crusade. Whether or not she had allayed their earlier fears about her maturity, the likelihood that Walker could leave home increased dramatically by the time her sister had graduated from Gilbert Academy. Mercedes had advanced beyond the musical training that Marion was able to give her and needed to go to a musical conservatory. The Walkers were not expecting their daughters to achieve simply conventional success. They had so carefully orchestrated the children's education that there could be little doubt that they approached this moment with as much excitement as their daughters did.

That they had done so reveals much about the state of Black education before World War II and the tumultuous events that culminated in the 1954 *Brown v. Board of Education* decision. While there were Northern universities where Blacks could attend much earlier, like Alain Locke, who had entered Harvard as an undergraduate in 1903, for two young Black women to enter a white university such as Northwestern was rare in 1932. Thirty years later, Southern white universities would still be fighting violently to prevent even token integration in all-white schools. Because of the terms of the relationship between the South and the North resulting from the Civil War, like most people, the Walkers accepted that at a certain point, one had to cross the Mason-Dixon line to further one's education. The question was always when. Sigismund Walker had crossed that line to pursue his graduate education, as was the case for Marion, who had taken a postgraduate course in Northwestern's music school after her graduation from Xavier.

Walker already knew about Northwestern from her father. But when she entered Miss Fluke's class that first year at NOU, Fluke had made it a point to share her own her experiences as a student at Northwestern. After winning the five-dollar prize for the best freshman essay, Walker found in Fluke more than tacit support in her effort to leave home. Fluke told her parents that their daughter needed to be more challenged, and that Northwestern would be a good place for her to go.[12] Fluke also made it clear that one could go to colleges such as Northwestern for reasons other than the ministry. The encouragement caused Walker to quickly forget about Fisk and Talladega as Northwestern began to take center stage in her mind. Her parents considered the possibility only because they knew Northwestern, whose Methodist affiliation was especially appealing, even if sending their daughters there seemed a remote possibility at the time.

* * *

In 1932, Northwestern had 11,000 students enrolled, forty of them Black. As was the custom of the day, admission of Negro students into the university came without housing privileges. The university provided a list of homes that accepted Negro students as boarders. In some cases, these students sat in a different section of the classroom, where they could expect to be ignored more often than not. To avoid the extreme prejudice and unprofessional conduct from other students, the small group of Negro students found it easy to keep to themselves.

Preoccupied with crafting a career for herself as a writer, Walker was at times uncomfortable but less concerned about the racially hostile environment. She noted, however, one incident that illustrated the mood of the times. When a group of young Negro students wrote to Northwestern president Walter Dill Scott, citing specific acts of discrimination and racist behavior, he wrote them back an earnest reply that she recorded verbatim in her journal: "You are such a small percent of this student body you have no voice whatsoever."[13] She would always remember the helplessness she felt when white students confronted her, insulting her with impunity.

Other aspects of her Northwestern experiences were atypical. She may have been extremely self-conscious of not being as pretty as some other girls, but she had never felt subordinate because of her gender. Though she had complained that her parents seemed to favor Brother, who could do anything and everything he wanted, she felt no imposed limitations on her desire to pursue her studies or a career. At Northwestern, her professors offered her full encouragement, and she seemed not to be aware of sexual barriers until much later in her life. Moreover, her parents were rather unusual in that they had no intention of educating girls only to see them married off. Likewise, throughout her time in Chicago, her parents warned her against men who "might turn her head" or otherwise distract her from complete devotion to her studies. That Marion had married after high school rather than continue her studies seemed to make her more determined that her daughters not repeat the error.

Walker remained starry-eyed and eager as she began her first classes at Northwestern in September. She passed the placement exams comfortably and didn't need to repeat any classes. Despite her achievements and ambitiousness, however, some self-doubt persisted. A strong belief in her own abilities wrestled with a characteristic sense of Black Southern inferiority in her mind. She needed constant affirmation that she was indeed as good as any white student there. She admitted that the classes were difficult, she earned fewer A's and when she did, she found it extraordinarily challenging. Yet she had few expectations that first year of getting anything other than the best training she could have for her professional development. She remained very focused, and though she was the older, more responsible sister, she knew that she was extraordinarily naïve. "I surely did not know how to powder my face nor comb my hair and I had never worn lipstick," she remembered. "I only knew that I wanted to learn as much as I could about writing. If I had remained in the South without having my chance at Chicago and Northwestern, my future as a published writer would have been an impossible dream."[14]

The sisters grew closer that year. They accepted their reality: Northwestern was the place where they attended classes and nothing else. When Northwestern's highly competitive School of Music failed to admit Mercedes, they vowed always to support one another. This made it easier to counter the isolation they felt. Grateful for their host family, they became part of a community that revered them, and relying on their father's connections in Black Evanston, they developed a heightened sense of loyalty that brought numerous commitments. Involvement in the Methodist Episcopal Church where their father had often served as a guest minister left them little time for rest. When Mercedes had some

degree of flexibility playing piano for various churches, Walker was too preoccupied to be a reliable accompanist, which her more moderate skills would not
have encouraged, in any case. Living with the Landers offered the assurance, at
least for their parents, that they were at home away from home.

The sisters were surprised that they found the religious atmosphere of the
Landers's home comforting. Thankful and happy for the most part, Walker
turned to Psalm 27 whenever she felt herself succumbing to feelings of self-
doubt. Drawn to lyrical quality she found in the Book of Psalms, the meditation
on the value of isolation and the need to stand firm when facing difficulties reminded her to remain steadfast, patient, and fearless, and to distinguish between
those times for rebellion and defiance and a need to surrender. The words would
have provided some comfort when, even after a year there, she and Mercedes
had made few acquaintances and almost no friends aside from those they met
at church. Walker still found herself in a narrow social world, one not designed
to bolster her self-confidence. She acknowledged no interest in men, those that
she saw in church or elsewhere, thinking that they had no reason to be interested
in her.

If at the beginning she felt out of touch among her fellow students, her observations about her difference from those who had more clothes and more money
than she ever thought was possible sharpened her sense of social class. She could
rarely find clothes to fit her girlish frame and had grown accustomed to a wardrobe her grandmother, mother, and her aunt had designed for her. The same
clothes that once drew admiring looks and compliments for the seamstresses,
when compared to her female classmates, now caused her to feel badly dressed.
What she saw in their attire and physical appearance was breeding, if not
upbringing.

Had she been living on the campus of one of the Negro colleges, she would
have been socialized into an entirely different culture, one where the sharing of
trade secrets about clothes and especially the taming of "kinky" hair were essential components. Her mother had often told her stories of her life at the Nannie
Burroughs School, stories that had no parallels in her life at Northwestern. At
best, some of the Negro women students who lived in private homes met to take
the elevated train into Chicago to access the services of a larger Negro community. With limited funds, this happened rarely for the Walker women.

Walker never quite learned to control her hair; it was too soft to hold the
smoothing effects of the hot-iron straightening comb, the familiar way to bring
most types of black hair into conformity. While other taming options would become available in the years to come, she elected to mature into Negro womanhood with the widely accepted practice of wearing a fashionable hat as a mark
of distinction. In her early days at Northwestern, however, to imagine herself
dressed in the same finery as those around her would mean that she was the same

as they were, and that, ironically, she had nothing extraordinary to contribute. This sense of social inadequacy, together with a decided uniqueness, brought renewed confidence in the rightness of her personal and professional goals. She was not destined to marry and fall in love, but she would feel proud of being a Southern Black girl, poor and unknown, who would excel in those areas that had yet to make a place for a Black woman.

Walker's first year passed with a great deal of excitement that had very little to do with Northwestern itself. She had begun school during the campaign for the presidential election of 1932. Franklin Delano Roosevelt had received the nomination in Chicago as the candidate from the Democratic Party. His tag line, "We have nothing to fear but fear itself," helped to usher a nation demoralized by unemployment and economic distress into a new era that showed how a government and its people might be more responsive to the needs of its poor and disfranchised. Growing up in the Republican South where Negroes had remained faithful to the party of Lincoln, Walker saw, for the first time, Negroes working for the Democratic Party. The New Deal politics that Roosevelt promoted was her introduction to American political culture, and while she could not yet vote, she joined the jubilant crowds who paraded in the city on the night of the November 1932 landslide election. The challenges that lay ahead of him were pushed to the background for the moment. She got a close-up view of the process, however, since one of the boarders at the Landers's home was intimately involved in the election campaign.

Witnessing this shift of power at the national level, and getting an introduction to the nature of political participation, was one of the advantages of living in one of America's major cities. Without knowing it, Walker was getting her orientation to the work she would later do in Jackson, Mississippi, at the local and state level. Randall Ware, the character she created in *Jubilee* from the bits and pieces of family history, was taking shape in her mind. She would imagine Ware as the first Negro elected to a post in the Reconstruction government, providing her with an opportunity to explore the meaning of political participation in the postwar South.

The political activity that accompanied her arrival to Chicago also made Walker aware of the larger world. Early in 1933, she began to read about Adolf Hitler in Germany. While she had full exposure to the English classics, and to some extent the study of philosophy through her father, she now found a new passion for history as she saw it taking shape before her eyes. But this new passion would have to take a respite when her parents ultimately realized they could not support two daughters at Northwestern for a second year. Neither of the sisters was willing to go without the other. They chose instead to sit out that second year together.

PART II
GROWING OUT OF SHADOW
1933–1938
(Chicago)

6

The House Where My Soul Lives

Leaving New Orleans had done what it was supposed to do for Walker, who was now about to enter her eighteenth year. Spending a year away from home had left her more prepared to accept life's contingencies. She was more aware of who she was and who she was not, and she was able to see something she had either not seen or had failed to understand before about her parents. Marion and Sigismund Walker were now openly contentious in their behavior toward each other. Her father, once proud of his multitalented wife, now expressed anger and resentment toward her. Marion Walker had not given her daughters a ringing endorsement of an autonomous domestic life, for she was a woman who refused to confine herself to home. She found her life beyond the domestic sphere as a musician and teacher perhaps richer and more fulfilling than the one she had at home. As the family faced this financial crisis, Grandma Dozier continued to manage routine domestic chores while Marion was committed to increasing the family's income. Although this made sense, the implication that Sigismund Walker was unable to take care of his family was the source of conflict.

She noted in her 1934 journal entry: "My mother is the innocent victim of my very jealous and hardened father. For years he has masqueraded in the name of my Lord, and in his old age, he slanders the mother of his children and seeks to break her will to his own."[1] While she may have felt some guilt about being partly responsible for the circumstances in which the family found itself, for the first time, Walker expressed outrage at her father. Years earlier, it had been her mother who was given to rages and unprovoked outbursts. Now, she sensed an ally in her mother whose drivenness and ambition she recognized in herself. Too close to the scene of conflict, she found little relief being back in New Orleans, a city that became more important to her once she left.

By 1933, New Orleans was best known for two things: violence and Carnival, the familiar term for Mardi Gras among the citizens. Its ritualistic past would overshadow the city's growth into a viable community. Walker would not have been aware of it, so cut off was she from the city's more secular culture during her early years, but New Orleans had mastered the art of exclusion, of masking, and of performance. It had not come by this easily or lightly. It was a city where chaos and disorder were constantly redefining themselves, played out in increasingly more public forms. She was a member of a Protestant community in a Catholic city where divisions by politics, race, culture, and class were all visible.

The House Where My Soul Lives. Maryemma Graham, Oxford University Press. © Oxford University Press 2022.
DOI: 10.1093/oso/9780195341232.003.0006

In 1934, the ethos of Jim Crow became more evident in the city than ever before through the instrument of Carnival. King NOR, an invention of the white community for its children, became a regular feature of Carnival. King NOR parades, however, excluded Black participation; they required white children to appear in blackface to "represent" the history of Blacks in New Orleans. The response on the part of Black New Orleans was to organize the Zulu balls, focusing the Carnival activity in the heart of the city's Black districts.

Walker had been looking forward to the annual event since it meant a loosening of the family's typical social restrictions. The Great Depression was still a reality in the nation, and no less in New Orleans, a city that had hardly recovered from the devastating effects of World War I, the federal government shutdown of the Storyville district, and the outlawing of alcoholic beverages. Without the physical and mental resources to return a highly successful Carnival to its former self, the New Orleans in which Walker spent her first official year of adulthood was a more refined version of the Jim Crow South—more brutal and unforgiving.

Yet she found her creative and moral center in the midst of these myriad conflicts, gravitating toward them, almost as a duty to herself. On the one hand, the situation with her parents wore heavily on her; on the other, the social realities of New Orleans stared her in the face. What made all of this unique was her attempt at self-definition through these conflicts, one not bound to her mother, her father, or a Jim Crow world. It was the first time she had felt compelled to mark her independence, which she did, not by speaking her mind, but once again by keeping her silence.

During the months she was home, she found herself in a state of virtual noncommunication. She felt, saw, knew, and thought too much about everything, none of which she seemed to be able to process fully or comfortably. It was impossible to come to terms with it all, whatever the label—confusion, guilt, egotism, disappointment, or was it loss of faith? Her body reacted physically as it always did, and she was alternately hyperactive and lethargic. She could see her life moving ahead without herself as its guide and felt trapped in a life-and-death struggle over her duty, her family's expectations, and as-yet-to-understand emotions that appear to be connected to equally unfamiliar desires. Her only outlet during this period was her journal, which recorded her movement toward greater clarity. She came gradually to a consciousness of her inner voice, with multiple competing components that could only find coherence in the spiritual realm:

> I do not know how many rooms there are but I like to think there are many, like a labyrinth. I like to think that in the last room of the house my soul lives. And where my soul lives there is a keeper. One who delights in restoring my soul with the life-giving bread and water of life. The rooms of my house where my conscious self first dwells with assistants and then where my subconscious

mind dwells with all her silent helpers . . . all these rooms must remain spotless, there must be no filth. For the lord of my soul stands guard over my castle.[2]

Effective and moving metaphors like those in this passage were becoming more common for Walker. "Soul" was a porous term that signaled her need to protect herself against unwanted impulses, and redirect and redefine them as a form of interiority. Initially she sought only to process and preserve everything in the "mental castle." Now she began to see a dynamic inner force, constantly renewing and transforming itself, subject to new and different experiences, even as it remained subject to a higher authority.

The distinction she made was a crucial one for our understanding of the kind of poet that Margaret Walker became. Hers was an intellectual and artistic awakening as much as it was a physical one that affirmed her identity as a young Black woman. Art was her sense of connection, a convergence of individual will and creative spirit bound together by the needs and expectations of her family, community, and her race.

It was in this moment that Walker disengaged with the concept of a writer as a free spirit. Words like "house" and "castle" suggest that she did not wish to— nor would she—reject the provincial morality or the dominant values of the era in which she was born. She may not have seen marriage as a goal, an idea her parents supported, yet marriage and family became a central part of affirming her sexual as much as her social identity. She was grappling with what it meant to be an artist and a Black woman in the first quarter of the twentieth century.

She had the example of her mother who, despite her father's late-developing paranoia, had carved out a place for herself within a marriage that allowed her considerable mobility. When she thought of the woman she might become, then the example had to be Marion Walker—an educated, highly accomplished pianist, and an energetic teacher and organizer. She would not have linked the pursuit of a career in any way that threatened her relationship with familial and other social networks. Wherever the life of an artist took her, it would not veer uncomfortably away from those things that had been part of her enclosed world. She knew, even at eighteen, that she wanted and needed to be nurtured physically and emotionally in those ways that mattered to women who believed that marriage was necessary for their protection and the completion of their identity.

Her words foreshadow her future life as a poet as much as they do her preference for the conventional life of a typical mid-twentieth-century woman. When the passage turns toward the biblical—"One who delights in restoring my soul"—Walker is making a strong statement of her beliefs. She will not abandon Christianity and seeks closer communion with God through her art, fearing perhaps that the world in which she might find herself has many "rooms . . . like a labyrinth," which created unnecessary distractions. To become an artist requires dedication and determination in the presence of distractions; it requires an awareness of a "conscious self" consisting of its own insights and perceptions. That the soul's place "must remain spotless" is no doubt a reference to the avoidance of sexual temptation.

In fact, Walker's heightened awareness of her sexuality frightened her, leading her to believe that it, like her soul's art, needed protection. At this moment, she seemed to be aware of every faculty that she possessed—a feeling that could not have been very pleasant. The prevailing image is one of control, suggesting an urgent need to create order out of chaos and those hormonal urges that she felt. Interestingly, she doesn't seem to imply that the "house" is a site of a struggle, though in 1934 it was. By the end, however, she has shifted from "house" to "castle," a difference in degree, if not necessarily in kind. A castle is indeed impenetrable, while a house might be entered into rather easily; a house is more inviting, while a castle is unapproachable. She indicates that she desires to be open and receptive within the context of specifically articulated boundaries.

The effort to name an abstract thought or feeling as "the soul," "the conscious self," or "the subconscious mind" is an early indication of Walker's attentiveness to her own mental state as she tried to reconcile the innocence of childhood with what would become a troubled state of young adulthood. At eighteen, she no longer considered herself a child, and a return home was a painful reminder of how uneven the transition from adolescence would continue to be.

In late January 1934, when the conflict became unbearable, and she began complaining of nervousness and chronic fatigue, her parents took her to the doctor. The condition was probably severe depression associated with a hormonal imbalance and sleep deprivation, both of which contributed to her anemia and low blood pressure. The prescribed cure, typical of the period, was not to address any internal symptoms, especially if they were associated with young women, but to concentrate on external activities that could redirect or deflect those feelings. The prescription was to do more social work, change her daily routine, and become engaged in some form of constructive activity to focus less on herself and more toward others. Following these orders, therefore, she began working in a community children's center, angry at having to do so, but surprised when she actually began to enjoy it. There were lively discussions about what to teach young children and when actual schooling should begin. Surprised by the level of dialogue, Walker began to spend more time in Dryades library to see if she could learn more about the subject. In addition, the library allowed her to read *The Crisis* and other Black newspapers without censorship.

Later that summer and shortly after her nineteenth birthday, Walker accompanied some friends on a weeklong leadership training program at Camp Knighton, a Methodist retreat in Alabama where she would return often in later life. Describing the week as "the jolliest and most carefree days I have ever spent . . . the spirit of friendship—good comradeship and refinement were splendid things that stand out as never to be forgotten bits of happiness,"[3] she found for the first time true friendship among other girls her own age, friendship her parents did not censure. The camp was a refuge from the outside world surrounded by a natural landscape that pleased her immensely. This was probably one of the few coeducational social experiences she had ever had outside the control of her parents, which at nineteen, was long overdue. She learned to relax, play cards, and even dance a little—activities that her parents had strictly prohibited. In the end, she believed that Camp Knighton had been the cure for her ailments; she had even learned "to keep my tongue better than before . . . to make myself look dressier . . . to mingle with boys and girls of my age and feel alright and not out of place . . . to make myself try to do things I have always been too sensitive and self-conscious to attempt . . . the feeling of slight inferiority gone."[4]

Walker recognized that while her parents had encouraged her intellectual pursuits, she had pushed herself even more. Camp Knighton became her much-needed transition into adulthood that gave her a new comfort zone away from studying and books. Her self-confidence and social skills improved, and she learned the importance of reciprocity in friendship. When she returned after the week, she composed a poem for her journal to indicate her new self-awareness:

> Now I want to bend, to mix, to know
> I am tired of fighting
> Now I want to take, to have, to hold
> I am tired of striving
> Let me work, let me live, let me laugh
> Let me love
> I am tired of hating.[5]

She had grown, what seemed like overnight, into a more carefree person. If the need to revolt existed because she did not feel comfortable in herself, that same need dissipated when she began to enjoy the new self that was emerging.

After Camp Knighton she found that what had once been a chore, like teaching Sunday School, suddenly brought pleasure. She was beginning to understand that the upheaval she was experiencing was part of her own creative development. She no longer saw her weaknesses as wrongs she needed to right, but as pieces of her life that provided the entryway to new and richer forms of expression. Everything that came at her she gave back to her journal, analyzing and explaining as fully as she could all the dimensions of the conflicts and their resolutions. While her tone revealed her sense of danger and betrayal, it only fueled her passion to capture every moment, to have at her disposal as authentic an account as possible.

What also lifted her spirits considerably was the news that a poem she had submitted to *The Crisis* magazine would appear in its late-spring issue, 1934. She had heard W. E. B. Du Bois give a talk her first year at Northwestern. He wrote provocative editorials in *The Crisis*, challenged the NAACP's conservative position on integration, and designed a course at Atlanta University on "Marx and the Negro," creating more alarm than pride for many. His radical views had cost him his teaching position, and Du Bois had left the university under duress but not before having initiated a series of major publications on the history of the Black race that he called the Atlanta University Studies.

His role as editor of *The Crisis* made him especially interesting to Walker. She had been reading the Black writers he published, and now at only nineteen, she saw herself joining their ranks. She sent him the poem she had written, and although she would revise it for its reappearance years later, "Daydream" showed a mature poet prepared to meet her first public audience:

> I want to write
> I want to write the songs of my people.
> I want to hear them singing melodies in the dark.
> I want to catch the last floating strains from their sob-torn throats.
> I want to frame their dreams into words; their souls into notes.
> I want to catch their sunshine laughter in a bowl;
> fling dark hands to a darker sky
> and fill them full of stars
> then crush and mix such light till they become
> a mirrored pool of brilliance in the dawn.[6]

"Daydream" was a wise choice for a first poem since it placed Walker squarely in the modernist camp. The poem has a quiet, meditative quality not unlike the earlier religious verse to which she had been so wedded. But it also has a strong sense of inner movement. The last line, "a mirrored pool of brilliance in the dawn," is not only about the creation of art, but about the artist as well. As Eleanor Traylor points out, the poem prefigures Walker's "signature: the concrete imagery, the fusion of meter, internal and near rhyme, alliteration and assonance; the prominence of verbs second only to nouns . . . the music of the poem sings a dawn song." It is the moment of conception that begins "the journey of a people and the voice of an age," Traylor concludes.[7]

If we consider "Daydream" as her earliest poem, we have to conclude that Walker started out as a far more polished poet than she really was, leaving much of the backstory in the shadows. Yet the backstory becomes important to the foreground since it helps us to locate those critical moments of growth that help distinguish between her lengthy writer career and the relatively short periods that constituted her publishing career.

Before and after the poem appeared, *The Crisis* became a staple in Walker's reading diet. She received notification of the poem's acceptance but was not certain about the date of its appearance in print. The only choice was to read all of the issues that came out. If *The Crisis* was not at her home, she would go to Dryades Library, pleased to discover other Black periodicals she did not know existed. Walker was gathering more and more evidence of her sheltered childhood and teenage years, which the experience at Camp Knighton had initially confirmed. Now two years into adulthood, she relished the fact that she could go to the library and stay as long as she wished without any questions asked. The opportunity to take advantage was hard to turn down. On one of the visits she read an obituary of Lucy Craft Laney, a name she knew from her family's discussion of Black women educators. Laney's death in the fall of 1933 had generated a sizeable amount of press about her work and impact, especially the somewhat unusual educational system she had created in the South.

The appearance of the poem and Walker's growing discovery of the kind of attention that other Black women were getting made the reason for returning to Northwestern in late August 1934 even more important. A senior and now a published poet, Walker was eager to make up for the lost year. For the second time, the sisters were going together to Evanston, but for the first time they would not be at the same school. Mercedes had gained admission to Chicago Musical College in preparation for a career as a concert pianist. Wanting to offset any appearance of parental favoritism that allowed her, rather than her sister, to return to Northwestern, Walker was determined to work doubly hard. She viewed it as a privilege because she, not her sister, would graduate from their father's alma mater. Whether there was any tension between them resulting from this decision is not clear. Her lingering discomfort from decisions over which she had no control seemed to have eased.

One of her fall courses was English poetry taught by Edward Buell Hungerford. She did not know yet that the experience would change the course of her life and the lasting impact that Hungerford would have on her. For the first time, she was among other young poets like herself to whom literature, especially poetry, seemed to matter more than anything else. They were all eager to learn and none of them could have been a more diligent student. Hungerford was a small man, gallant, always dressed in a suit and tie, who observed a formality of manner to which she had grown accustomed. He reminded her of her father and, like him, had a commanding presence; he rarely raised his voice except to emphasize a word in a sentence or poem he was reading aloud. His students listened intently to the carefully planned lectures that he composed, which he eventually published in 1966 as *Recovering the Rhythms of Poetry*.

After his first lecture, Walker believed she was not mistaken in her decision to become a poet. What she didn't know was the world of choices that were open for her, all having to do with the conventions of language and form. She had become a poet because she loved the sound of words, most of them associated with the idioms of music or the biblical cadence of the religious sermon. She loved reading rhythmical clusters of words and arranging them on a page, having come to poetry first as oral forms. Her father and teachers routinely read poetry aloud, and it was the audible quality that appealed to her. Even though she had been writing poetry since childhood, her predisposition was to imitate the sounds she had heard. Perhaps for this reason, her discovery of the ballad would have strong resonance. It was the ballad that brought her the closest to what she was most comfortable with, words that were either spoken or sung. The ballad could also accommodate the characters and stories that emerged from memories of her childhood in Birmingham and New Orleans, translations of the stories that her grandmother had passed on.

She was the only Negro in her class, and she could tell that Hungerford took an instant liking to her. When he discovered how easy reading aloud was for her, he called on her often. She had learned early to speak in two different voices: one for regular conversation, and one for reading publicly. Her experience in elocution classes—which had often focused on eliminating the dialect patterns in Southern Black speech while retaining a certain dramatic quality—now made her the envy of her classmates. Since Hungerford did not limit his instruction to the elements of poetry—how to count accents, determine rhythm, and memorization of metrical patterns—she began to grasp the technical language from what he called the "moderns." She quickly mastered the scansion system, never tiring of the recitations that accompanied them.

Sitting beside better-dressed girls, who were clearly from wealthy families, bothered her less than before since it did not seem to affect the relationship she had with Hungerford. Although she was not writing much poetry, she was quickly imagining herself as part of a larger community of writers. Langston Hughes was still her model, but no longer the only source for her understanding of poetry as a form. Hungerford had succeeded in getting her to think in terms of stanzas and traditional meters, and she was as drawn to the metaphor, symbolism, and allegory in the longer poems in the Romantic tradition as much as she was to the compression and containment in the shorter lyric.

Her attraction to Shakespeare's sonnets, the odes of Percy Bysshe Shelley and John Keats, and the long poems of William Wordsworth gave positive reinforcement to her transformation into a poet. It would be these forms specifically to which she would turn when preparing her first manuscript, especially the sonnet, the ode, and the long poem that would always show her best work. To some extent, she mirrored Hungerford's preferences for poetry steeped in the Greek tradition and those poets whose work demonstrated a similar kinship. Her class notes for the discussion of Shelley in November 1935 not only show Hungerford's meticulous praise for the English poetic tradition, but they also confirm Walker's enthusiasm for a long work such as *Prometheus Unbound*.[8] The lives of these poets fascinated her; at a very young age, they defied moral authority and social convention, developed a significant body of philosophical thought, and championed the creative imagination. Even if she did not see herself like them at all, she was drawn to their youthfulness, their impulsiveness, their extraordinary productivity, and their revolutionary ideas about poetry and about society.

In the winter term, she enrolled in her second course with Hungerford, creative writing. While he continued to present examples from the Romantic and Victorian tradition, he put more emphasis on those contemporary poets whose work had begun to appear in *Poetry*, making it clear that he was eager to nurture young talent. Still relatively young himself, Hungerford had been first exposed to the new poetry movement that was sweeping the nation while he completed his studies at Harvard. His arrival at Northwestern had given him and his students direct access to the legendary Harriet Monroe, who had branded the movement with her own stamp of prestige and power through the journal simply called *Poetry*.

Monroe was scheduled to give a reading at Northwestern that semester, and she was in the class that Hungerford took to the reading. The appearance of Harriet Monroe, the poet, meant less than Monroe as a powerful woman editor in Walker's mind. *Poetry* was a leading publication in Europe and the United States, and Walker could not help adding publication there to her wish list. If we count the initial publication in *Our Youth* in New Orleans; the somewhat imitative poems that had appeared in *Modern American Poetry*, poetry annuals edited by Gerta Aison; and "Daydream" in *Crisis*, Walker had now published in three places in three years. She had the impulse for poetry and, with the upcoming visit by Monroe, began to see a pathway toward her publishing career as a poet.

After Monroe's visit, she realized the meaning of Hungerford's mentorship for her growth as a poet. She had survived the first stage of her own evolution as a poet of sentimental, religious verse, and it was time to move on. As this last semester of college came to a close, she asked herself a question without having an answer, "Where do I go from here?" Hungerford had opened the door to a world that included a cluster of successful women poets and influential women editors. He confirmed for her that young female poets could have realistic expectations about an audience for their work. He did not signify any difference between her and other white poets, at least none that she could remember.

Walker's affinity for these women was absolute. While she found Shelley, Keats, and Wordsworth important in her discovery of poetic form and the

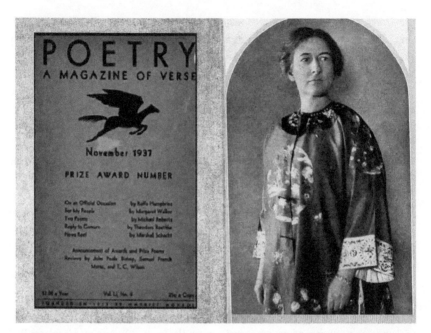

"For My People" first appeared in November, 1937. Harriett Monroe, founder/editor of *Poetry* magazine

shaping of her opinions about poetry, she was more attracted to Edna St. Vincent Millay, Sara Teasdale, Amy Lowell, Mina Loy, Gertrude Stein, Marianne Moore, Genevieve Taggard, Lola Ridge, Elinor Wylie, and Muriel Rukeyser, whose poetry she discovered in the pages of *Poetry*, *Broom*, *Vanity Fair*, and *Dial*. That women poets accounted for nearly 50 percent of the content in the poetry anthologies and journals published in the mid-1920s is a commentary on the fate of women's poetry in the decades that followed. Seeing women as professional artists, with established careers as poets, made Walker's goals seem more achievable and certainly within reach. Genevieve Taggard and Lola Ridge, as women poets on the Left, would also figure prominently in her life when she began working in Chicago after college in 1936.

Hungerford told her that publication in a respected journal was an essential step in confirming her transformation to a new stage in her developing career. There was much he did not know about her poetry background, however, and she decided that it was important to keep it that way. Her poems in the *Modern American Poetry* annuals were undistinguished, she believed; neither was the publication a very respected one in her opinion. Far better for her to appear as a novice to her professor, she concluded. Walker wanted him to see her as a serious poet and accepted the situation that imposed certain limits on her. There was a proper way to enter poetry, and she was intent on following that path, even if it meant leaving parts of her publishing history undisclosed. Her youthful enthusiasm now gave way to a more mature wisdom in order to position herself for the training that she desperately wanted. Hungerford himself was just beginning to publish, and Walker was careful to keep the boundaries between teacher and student absolute.

No correspondence survives concerning her earliest poems in *Modern American Poetry*, the annuals edited by Aison. Because the poems differed significantly from her later work, Walker could relegate them to her period of apprenticeship that had served its purpose, but not to be considered serious poetry. Yet they matter to her beginning professional career and to our understanding of the evolution and demographics of American poetry in the early twentieth century. "Aspiration," "Laughs from a Brown Throat," and "Lost" appeared in the 1932 inaugural edition of the annual alongside the work of 131 poets, with a larger percentage of women than men.[9] Three more poems appeared in the 1933 edition. Gerta Aison had distinguished herself as a popular editor during what she referred to as "a renaissance of the poetic fervor to create" intended "to bring the cult and culture of poetry into American homes." Aison proclaimed poetry "a necessary and vital force for people."[10] Her plan was to complement the annuals with a series of nationwide radio programs that not only introduced the poets, but also emphasized the aesthetics of poetry. There is no indication that Walker either knew or corresponded with Aison, and it is likely that Marion was behind the effort to get her daughter published *somewhere*, just as she had managed her husband's professional career. Aison's belief in poetry as a public form had a strong connection to Walker's vision of what poetry was and should do, offering a glimpse of her future.

With these first appearances in print, Walker found herself in the company of women who were responsible for the phenomenal surge of women's creativity that began after World War I, but would all but disappear before the beginning of World War II. That most of these women have been forgotten says less about the quality of their work than it does about the lack of an accompanying critical apparatus to explain the dynamics of the movement, and thus carve out a secure place for it in literary history. Most of what we know and teach about twentieth-century American poetry begins with the modernist movement, identified with and defined by leading male figures such as Ezra Pound, T. S. Eliot, Wallace Stevens, William Carlos Williams, and Robert Frost, but which contrasts sharply with the reality of the period.

The earlier published poems by Walker, therefore, matter greatly for we might call the rise and fall of women's poetry in the period. While we can tease out the transformation from Walker's religious meditations and the poetry of personal emotion to the style that became more characteristic of her work, she would suffer a similar kind of planned obsolescence like many of these earlier women. The poems she wrote before and after "Daydream" share a common desire to validate a public voice, a critical element in all of Walker's poetry, and another characteristic of this cohort of women.

From the time she arrived at Northwestern, she continued to write furiously, and during 1933 she recorded more than seventy poems, all with single-word titles. "Journey," "Music," "Teach," "Fear," "Entreaty," "Illusion," "Lust," "Futility," and "Soaring" are the kinds of poems that mark an adolescent world of ups and downs, one that was finally coming to a close.[11]

A discernible shift occurs in her style as early as January 1934 during her year in New Orleans. The three-page long poem "Decision" is both shapeless and precise, as Walker attempts to bring the poem under her control. The three poems recorded in the poetry notebook that follow immediately after "Decision" move her further away from the imitative forms of the past. In them, she pushes the boundaries of experience as well. "Caravanserai," "Saki," and "Mushtari" are titles that show the influence of her reading in Middle Eastern and Asian literature during her first year at Northwestern.[12]

Walker had little familiarity with the conventions of modernism, especially the use of free-verse forms, when she wrote the new poems "For Black Women" and "I Am Hungry for Love" within a few weeks of each other in March 1934. They tell us two things: first, she was adopting a radical posture in her use of the word "Black" at a time when "Negro" was common parlance. Second, she had begun to openly express her feelings about romantic love, a subject about which she would never have entertained a discussion at home. "For Black Women" is a marked departure from the "women's poetry" of the period as well. Although there were by 1935 multiple traditions in women's poetry, much of the writing still remained cautious about self-presentation. Respectable poetry by women, and in this case poetry by a Black woman, should not offer explicit affirmations of identity. And even though the 1920s had unleashed the poetry of women poets like Anne Spencer, Georgia Douglas Johnson, Helene Johnson, and Gwendolyn Bennett, they continued to exercise restraint. A display of excessive female emotion was to be avoided. If you did not, as was the case when Georgia Douglas Johnson who gave the bold title *The Heart of a Woman and Other Poems* to her 1918 volume, you were subject to the dismissive male critics who dominated the established literary networks. It was of course even worse for Black women poets. Johnson's work was not rediscovered until the 1970s during the Black Women's Literary Renaissance.[13]

This period of furious writing builds Walker's confidence so that new titles like "Nocturnes," "Difference 1 & 11," and "Song of My Soul" reflect an openness that her earlier poetry lacked. This immersion into a new phase of writing poetry is very visible from the entries in her 1934 journal, almost all of which are new or rewritten from an earlier period.[14] Hungerford saw this collection of rewritten poems, a solid body of work that could easily have been attributed to his influence. This reconstruction of her identity as a practicing poet might have given Hungerford more credit than he was due, but it was in keeping with the sort of authentication strategies that had long been part of the African American literary tradition.

African American writers, beginning with Phillis Wheatley in 1773, were dependent on white sponsorship for support and validation before gaining mainstream recognition. This legacy of slavery haunted virtually every writer, even after the period of enslavement ended. William Dean Howells had introduced Paul Laurence Dunbar, who was already writing poetry, when his patronizing introduction provided Dunbar the credibility he needed to appear before a disbelieving, mainly white American audience. Even Langston Hughes had given his poetry to Vachel Lindsay, from whom he hoped to gain sponsorship. Walker continued the practice as late as 1942 when she entered the Yale poetry competition and won. Her signature volume, *For My People*, published by Yale University Press, included a preface by the reigning dean of American poetry, Stephen Vincent Benét. That she chose to keep Benét's original preface when she collected and published all of her poems in 1989 suggests the importance that she attached to the tradition.

When we reflect on the emergence of women's poetry in the early decades of the twentieth century, giving consideration to her earlier work makes it easier to place Walker as an important member of that first wave of women poets in America, to which Alicia Ostriker brought much needed attention.[15] As Ostriker notes, male professors taught and revered male poets as models with a system of approvals and disapprovals—a veiled gender bias—that made it difficult to acknowledge certain kinds of originality or difference.[16] As Walker would also discover, like these women, connecting writing to political activism extended one's writing trajectory, but sometimes at the cost of critical acceptance.

Nevertheless, Walker's personal story illustrates the curious history of the surge in women's poetic creativity. While male teachers were her teachers and mentors, it was the works by women writers that fed her creativity. Women were playing crucial roles as poets, playwrights, artists, and editors. They operated as a network that claimed recognition for each other, and for other women who helped to shape the direction in which American modernism was going. Many of them chose a bohemian lifestyle, one that Walker firmly opposed. She distinguished herself from these women even as she admired the freedom and the points of view that their lifestyle permitted. Breaking free of the conventions and restrictions that bound women was something that Walker struggled with for most of her life. At nineteen, however, she bolstered her confidence as she saw women gain greater control of a world that had kept them invisible. She was in the midst of successful women, and she was determined to become one of them.

Within this context, Walker found her first encounter with Harriet Monroe both exciting and confirming. Monroe had given her life to the work she felt destined to do. But Walker could not take her recent success for granted. She could see only signs pointing to further success; matters of race seemed minor in relation to all that was possible. Meeting Monroe was, therefore, one of those critical moments that paralleled her experience at Camp Knighton, affirming her growth as a woman filled with purpose and promise. She would write that she was "indescribably happy, my face smiling. I want to cry out for sheer joy. I have to clench my hands and sometimes press my mouth to keep from doing so."[17] Walker continued to attribute her physiological reactions in these moments to the "peaceful assurance of the Holy Spirit in my heart," interpreting the experiences as "spiritual energy that God wants to put to some practical use,"[18] with a period of intense writing activity to follow. She would confine herself to her room where the spiritual merged with the creative, allowing poems to come quickly. At her best moments, when the writing was going well, she could describe physiological reactions in great detail. "My body feels light, and quick, electric-shock like vibration running through my upper body and limbs." Her musings led to equally insightful commentary. "If I were a Catholic," she confided to her journal, "I would be a nun but I thank God I am Protestant. If I were a man, I would probably try to feel myself called to the ministry, but I thank God I am a woman."[19] In any case, she made a promise to herself in a New Year's resolution for 1935: she would publish in Harriet Monroe's *Poetry*.

Hungerford's class was most important for her newest revelation: every idea she had for a poem could and must find its own form. With this understanding, she began to work more toward perfection of those poems that she wanted to publish. That she was headed in this direction was already clear from "Daydream," the trademark for the kind of lyric poetry she would continue to write. "Daydream" did what all her poetry was intended to do: announce itself in no uncertain terms and insist on familiarity with the reader with the use of the first person. In writing "Daydream," she probably drew as much from her memory of Dunbar's poem "Sympathy" as she did from anything she learned during her years at Northwestern. And while Countee Cullen questioned why God would "make a poet black, and bid him sing,"[20] Walker felt challenged, if not empowered, by her sense of responsibility for becoming the collective voice of a race. The challenge would not go unanswered.

Walker gives specific insights about the intellectual and creative origins for the development of her poetry in relation to her emerging consciousness in her provocative essay "Growing Out of Shadow." Most significant to her growing awareness was an understanding of class *and* race:

My background was so thoroughly petty-bourgeois that I had not understood the people who worked with their brains were also workers. . . . As soon
as I began working in close contact with whites, I discovered startling things
peculiar to both racial groups: that whites suffer psychologically from the
problem of race prejudice as much as Negroes. . . . The second step toward understanding what it means to be Black in America . . . the Negro vote assumed
significant proportions and in many instances proved effective in the balance of
[political] power. . . . A third came from a growing world perspective. As a child,
reading the history books in the South, I was humiliated by some unhappy picture of reference to a Negro. It was as if we were cut off from humanity, without
sensitivity. . . . Now that we are engaged in a global war, it is even more essential
that all peoples of the earth gain a world perspective and become conscious of
our common humanity and struggle to be free.[21]

This evolving awareness was critical in her second course with Hungerford,
where she alternated between poetry and prose for the writing assignments. She
felt confident in the poems she turned in to him, but less so in the 300 pages of a
novel based on her family's life during slavery that she had begun to write.

The story told of Hetta, a woman who, at twenty-nine, was dying as she gave
birth to her fifteenth child. She couldn't get the story out of her mind and was
worried that it was not on par with her poetry. Rather than waiting for his comments, she went to Hungerford's office. He was pleased with what she had written,
he told her, but she was still afraid that her work was not of "A" quality. She asked
him what she had to do to get an "A." He responded that she had already made
the grade. That night, she asked for God's forgiveness for her arrogance, "I am
not humble. I know how terribly unnecessary I am how insignificant a place I fill.
And yet since I must live," she adds, "why not as widely [and] as well as I know
how by God's grace and as he wills."[22]

Hungerford did more than wish his student well. He was also willing to break
the rules for her. Only after her graduation did she discover that he had lobbied
to get her into the Northwestern chapter of the Poetry Society of America. No
Negro poet had gained admission before her. With this act, he had ensured that
she would be linked with the contemporary movement in poetry and would have
access to the broadest possible context for bringing her imagination and creative
will together.

Walker completed her work for graduation by August 1935, confident that she
had gotten all that she had hoped for from Northwestern. She had not made all
A's, but she did in all the classes that mattered to her and had failed nothing.
The Negro arts community now knew her from her publications in one of its
most reputable journals. She had found the intellectual stimulation she needed
to push her work forward, and she had found a mentor whom she trusted and

who was willing to guide her career. Many of her Northwestern teachers had left her feeling cold and distant, but in Hungerford's literature and writing classes, she had come alive. The dialogue was rich, and she never tired of the close analysis that Hungerford forced his students to consider.

Five days before she was to finish, she had a panic attack. Consumed with the fear of failure, she wrote, "I have worked myself into nervous frenzies and dilemmas over my school work. If God sees me through this, it will truly be a miracle and I am expecting nothing else of him but that. I know that I am unworthy and that if I fail, I alone am to blame."[23] But there was a logical reason for the panic. Sigismund Walker was coming up, expecting to take his daughter back home, but she had yet to tell him or her mother that she had no intention of returning to New Orleans.

A visit to St. Matthews Methodist Church, surrounded by old friends, was a welcome relief from the endless round of questions her father had been asking. She simply did not know what she was planning to do and was afraid to suggest anything that would put more financial strain on her parents. She had identified some job prospects that she hoped would produce positive results. None of this mattered when she noted her excitement in her journal the day after she picked up her diploma. Jubilant, she imagined writing her first book that was going to make her famous, bring financial security, and allow her to purchase a fine home and a car . . . all, of course, after she married the right man and had given birth to twins. Her storehouse of daydreams was still full, and they knew exactly when to kick in.[24] In this case, the timing could not have been better. With no job in sight and no longer able to rely on support from her family, daydreams gave comfort.

She had just turned twenty, proudly claiming her new status as a college graduate and a poet who had a lot to say. She had learned that poets looked to form to give them the space to feel that which is most private, but poets had no limitations on where their meaning came from. Emotionally, she did not believe she had been fulfilled, and she continued to acknowledge certain fears. But she was determined not to retreat to the security of home, understanding that if ever she needed to remove herself entirely from her parents, it was now. She saw no future in a return to her mother's control and her father's silent complicity. Though she had nothing in a material sense, she had the strongest sense of a mission and her own place in history. Feeling the first real freedom she had ever known—freedom from school and family, as fearful as it was—she allowed it to drive her every ambition.

7

Brave New World

The enjoyment of writing fiction had grown on Walker during her last term at Northwestern. Without the required page limit, she felt a new sense of freedom and was less prone to have the negative feelings and her typical second-guessing herself about the decision to stay in Chicago. She continued her church activities, though not always with Mercedes whose ability to play any type of music landed her jobs not only in churches but in an assortment of recitals and concerts. Walker was free for the first time to explore the city and learn more about Chicago overall. She was eager for new experiences and with more time to get to know Chicago, her confidence in her creativity increased. The coherence between the African American experience of her childhood and the place she now saw as home confirmed that she had made the right choice. She was determined to follow up on every suggestion people made to see or visit in Chicago, and for as long as she lived, Chicago was the only other place that she never grew weary of visiting.

One experience would push her to think more in terms of race than ever before. She accepted an invitation to speak to a group of white Methodists in a small community north of Evanston. Sharing what she thought to be her experiences as a Southern Methodist growing up in the segregated South, she was horrified when a woman in the audience asked if she were bitter because she was a Negro. It was not so much the question that shocked her as the expectation that she should say "yes." After she came to know Richard Wright, she would begin to understand how deeply the experience of growing up in the South could damage one's psyche.

Perhaps because she had come to know the South through her symbolic imagination as a child and through the imaginary world her grandmother created for her, Walker came to understand the Black experience in dual ways: both tragic and romantic, a sacred spirituality and a secular humanism, filled with anguish and exultation. Or perhaps because she was seldom witness to the severe degradation that so often described life in the South, she could more easily transmute those feelings. In any case, coming to Northwestern in her late teens and leaving as a young poet opened up new possibilities. She began to think of herself as a "struggling artist."

What she added to this was her strong sense of personal obligation to her sister Mercedes, who had two years of college remaining. It was important for

The House Where My Soul Lives. Maryemma Graham, Oxford University Press. © Oxford University Press 2022.
DOI: 10.1093/oso/9780195341232.003.0007

Walker to ensure that Mercedes complete her studies, since she felt some continuing guilt that her own progress had come at her sister's expense. Although finding a job was her first concern, the more time she spent in Chicago, the more eager she was to experience the vitality and energy of the city's intellectual and political community. She began thinking even more about the kind of writing her work represented in relation to the work of other Black writers.

Margaret and Mercedes left Evanston and moved to 315 Wendell St. in Chicago. Aunt Hattie, as they affectionately called their landlady, was anything but a Bible-toting Christian. Unlike the Landers boarding arrangement, there were no rules. Aunt Hattie never checked on their comings or goings and even encouraged her new tenants to go to movies and parties with friends. During these early days in Chicago, Walker found the city seductive and familiar. In some ways, it was like being in the South but discovering a new street she'd never been on before. With no money, she discovered riches that she never knew existed in her visits to museums, concerts in the park, and art galleries. "I was like Alice in Wonderland," she wrote, "skipping down the primrose path in a dreamworld."[1] Understanding that Northwestern had been a new beginning for her, she pulled various elements of her history together to create a distinct narrative: "For a Southern black girl, poor and unknown, to dream of a future as a published writer was at that time like dreaming the utterly impossible, and I am sure if I had remained in the South without having my chance, it would have been an impossible dream.[2]

She was ready to turn another page in her life, since staying in Chicago "made the difference."[3] Hardly a day went by that she did not see someone she thought she recognized. The faces of the people in the city seemed little different from those she had seen at home, just as she heard her the same singsong rhythms in their voices she had grown accustomed to in Birmingham and New Orleans. The difference seemed only in degree, not kind.

Not for an instant did she regret her decision to stay in Chicago, even when she found it impossible to get work. Neither did she get homesick, since everyone she met seemed to form a portrait or topic she could see herself writing about. She found a dynamic Black culture, with Negro artists, writers, actors, painters, dancers, sculptors, and musicians who, like her, were young and filled with a sense of limitless possibilities, talking endlessly about a future of fame and fortune. She was self-indulgent in her journal, learning how to interpret this new world through the voice and vision of the artist. Every new experience was either "exciting," "magnetic," "contagious," or filled with "the glowing imaginative fire." Her consciousness absorbed everything, giving it poetic form. Her concern with crafting a strong poetic sensibility and her need to expand her circle of writer friends received affirmation in Chicago. It was in Chicago where she ended "a world of isolation, closed-in and separated from my fellow human beings."[4]

Keenly aware that this was precisely the kind of environment that would nurture her talent, Walker believed Chicago was the test she must pass before she could move on with her life. In her unpublished poem "I Shall Remember Chicago," she gave the impressions of a starry-eyed girl trying to confront idealism with optimism.

> I shall remember Chicago
> From the first as being
> A place of settling dust and grime
> Of alleys running through the town
> Of motorists who drive at madcap speed
> Of Yiddish women wearing black head shawls
> Of brightly lighted streets
> And great sky skewing shops
> At the back ways of tenement houses
> Of long ugly winding steps.[5]

Chicago was also different from Evanston; she began to see it as an historical, linguistic and cultural extension of the South, a place that easily felt like home. For the first few weeks after her graduation, she acted as if she *were* back home. She did nothing but sleep, her body recovering from the exhaustion that was second only to the acute anguish of her mind. She had learned to repress her feelings; if there were any disappointments, frustration, and disillusionment she'd wrap them into an invisible ball that was there and not there when necessary. Sleep washed away her anxieties and unpleasant memories, leaving her with renewed vigor. When she awakened, she felt comfortable in a way she had never been, even though there was no assurance of what the day would bring.

She was beginning to understand that what she repressed could itself become the poem. The poet's task was to move beyond self-indulgence, to shape it into a form that gave it aesthetic relevance in a more general sense. She was learning to trust her powers of description and the autobiographical voice, seeing them in a complementary relationship, something that was to be one of the most striking characteristics of her poetry. She not only saw, but she felt, heard, and read the landscapes as they appeared before her. The South had given her such a strong sense of the natural world that she was struck by the transformations from natural landscapes to the built ones, and the many people it took to make complete the process. What she was seeing was texture, and it was Chicago alone, she believed, that could give her that.

Walker went on government relief, an experience that gave her a connection that would prove useful in the days to come. More than once, she stood in the breadlines at the soup kitchens when their food ran out. She'd bring home some bags of yellow meal and yellow grits, dried figs, and unmarked cans of milk and beans for a meatless meal. Christmas came and went, and by early 1936, she could count the miles she had walked in search of a job. Six months from turning twenty-one, she bore the weight of a much older woman on her shoulders since she had responsibility not only for herself, but also for her sister. It was this thought that alerted her to another sense of Chicago, the place of "pain and hardship and fiery trial."[6]

When she began to assess the meaning of her individual experience beyond the context of a cultural and racial paradigm is not clear. What reinforced that urgency was Chicago's distinct social and political climate. She found it difficult to separate herself from other Black and white unemployed people she saw everywhere around her, people she knew had even less than she did. She quickly acknowledged the limitations of being petty bourgeois, which prevented her understanding of a very real socioeconomic divide, the ways in which race served as the dividing line between the Black and white poor. "To understand the issues out of which [prejudice] grew became my life's preoccupation," she later wrote.[7]

Chicago, like every other large city in 1935, was still in the declining years of the Great Depression. Masses of people remained unemployed, and the government could only provide a modicum of relief. Sometimes, she recorded in her journal, she would smell the aroma of food cooking as she walked by a restaurant and would go home to sleep it off. But the images of hungry, poor people reserved another place in mind. One of the poems that she wrote during this period of unemployment is "People of Unrest and Hunger," which appeared in *New Challenge* in 1937. It was one of her earliest attempts to respond to the perceived hopelessness of poverty.

> Stare from your pillow into the sun.
> See the disk of light in shadows.
> Through fingers of morning Day is growing tall.
> People of unrest and hunger
> Stare from your pillow into the sun
> Cry with a loud voice after the sun.
> Take his yellow arms and wrap them around your life.
> Be glad to be washed in the sun.
> Be glad to see.[8]

The original poem shows some awkwardness in these first experiments with new subject matter. She tries to reverse the pattern she had used in "Daydream," where she established a personal context before introducing a metaphor. Here the personal context is absent, and the poem charges ahead after she announces the title, speaking directly to the "people of unrest and hunger." It emphasizes action and assumes a certain authority over those to whom she speaks. Trying to shift emphasis away from the material reality of poverty, she offers compensation from nature. Although the individual metaphors such as "disk of light" and "fingers of morning" are effective, the poem overstates the possibility of relief from human desperation through blind faith. It forecasts a better future: "Day is growing tall." She holds on to her belief in the consistency of nature, the never-ending cycle of creation and transformation that shapes the human experience. In its insistence that faith in nature provides comfort, the poem appears to reflect an insensitivity or dismissal of that which is more immediately devastating. Abandoning the first person, it breaks the connection between the self and the other, the inner and the outer world. The return to nature seeks to bring order out of chaos, resisting the feeling of hopelessness and affirming the spiritual connection with nature and its presumed power over the material universe. "People of Unrest" found Walker still struggling for the right subjects to address and the method for doing so in her poems.

A lead for a job with the Chicago Institute for Juvenile Research, where she had worked as a volunteer during college, failed to come through. As a last resort, she signed for jobs doing day labor. On one occasion, she worked in a nut factory, sorting shelled pecans. Fearing that she would cut her hands and not be able to type diminished her productivity considerably, and after only one day, she was fired. Fortunately, by that time, she heard through some friends that there was to be a Chicago unit of the Federal Writers' Project, but a start date had not been announced. Mercedes, having heard about a similar program for college students, applied for and received support from the National Youth Administration, which provided funds for her to continue school.

Despite her dreadful experience of not knowing where the next meal was coming from, the space that unemployment afforded was useful. During the weeks and months between her graduation from Northwestern and her first real job, she became a member of Chicago's literary world, one that was as flamboyant as it was intense. Her journal records the parties, lectures attended, and people met, often noting her awareness of her change from a "very devout and passive Christian . . . to a conscious and alert or belligerent [human being] striving for action."[9]

Another advantage was the time unemployment provided for reading works by those who would become legends—T. S. Eliot, Ezra Pound, Wallace Stevens, and William Carlos Williams—but she remained more interested in the lives of women poets she had discovered earlier. Her desire to be part of a community of literary women in 1935 was not difficult to fulfill. The less secure she felt financially, the more she embraced the cosmopolitan and erudite qualities in those she met. The political engagement by women poets intrigued her, like Edna St. Vincent Millay and Lola Ridge, who had been arrested for picketing the Massachusetts State House on behalf of Sacco and Vanzetti in 1927.

Her circle was widening, and the list of social events seemed endless. When she accompanied a friend to a party one winter evening, she was surprised to discover herself at a celebration for Muriel Rukeyser, who had just received the Yale Series of Younger Poets Award for her 1935 volume of poetry *Theory of Flight*. The event was noteworthy for two reasons. Rukeyser, whom Walker saw as an exquisite speaker and committed poet, provided her with another exemplary artist model. She wrote in her journal that night a second literary goal: to win the Yale Award.

The job search went on for seven months. Not having yet turned twenty-one, she hadn't realized that age was a factor in her job search until one day she learned that a job she was certain she'd gotten suddenly went to another woman. The woman had made sure the supervisors were aware they were hiring a twenty-year-old Negro girl with a college degree and no work experience. Even the day work had dried up. Just when she was about to give up, the Works Progress Administration (WPA) announced the start date for the Chicago unit of the Federal Writers' Project.

She quickly submitted her application but expected that they would be slow in hiring Negroes until she found out about the Office of Negro Affairs. The FWP workforce had barely 100 Blacks out of nearly 5,000 workers and, as a result, there was much discussion in Chicago about segregation, especially for those units based in the South. The WPA director, Harold Ickes, had pleased many people when he hired Sterling Brown as head of what became known as the Negro Unit. Brown's job was to see to it that Black employment was increased and that they would develop projects of particular interest to the Negro community. Brown was well respected and made a point of identifying locations in the North and South with large populations from which the WPA could draw. He wanted to get maximum exposure for those who gained employment and for the WPA. Once they met, Walker and Brown would remain close friends, personally and professionally.

Increasing the ranks of the Negro Unit in Chicago was not difficult, for the city was filled with talented young artists and intellectuals. Whether they came for school or for work, they were, nonetheless, part of a steady stream of Black folk, most of whom had come from the intensely segregated and economically depressed communities in the South. The Great Depression had swelled the numbers in most Northern cities, but a particular group in Chicago in the 1930s—writers, artists, students, and intellectuals—soon discovered their common purpose and connectedness. This second generation of New Negroes quickly began to affiliate with organizations on the Left, secure employment through the Writers' Project, and publish in multiple literary magazines and journals. While it would take decades to generate the most appropriate term for the explosion of cultural activity that characterized the period, since it was over-shadowed by the Harlem cultural awakening of the 1920s, it is best described as the Black Chicago Renaissance. In later years, one could not speak of Arna Bontemps, Willard Motley, Katherine Dunham, Theodore Ward, William Attaway, Margaret Danner, Frank Marshall Davis, St. Clair Drake, and Allison Davis, and Richard Wright without remembering that they all knew each other and had lived and worked in Chicago. It was this larger community of writers Walker would meet when she joined the project. Few of them could have imag-ined the significance of their mutual discovery of one another.

She knew exactly where to go—downtown to Erie Street—when she re-ceived a notice on March 13 to report to the Chicago Unit of the Federal Writers' Project. For weeks, in eager anticipation, she had done nothing but gather in-formation about the writers employed on the project. Some Negro writers had already been hired, she learned, but there had been a delay in processing the paperwork for the additional people who were needed. The month before she had received her notice to report, however, some friends from the University of Chicago had invited her to attend a gathering of the first National Negro Congress (NNC). The February 1936 event was a foreshadowing of her new life just about to begin.

The meeting at the Old Armory Building on Chicago's South Side grabbed her attention immediately. She had no idea what to expect, but she had never heard people who were overtly political expressing themselves in such a forceful way, sometimes pounding on the table. Aside from the NAACP, she had heard of no public organization that announced its racial composition so openly. The NNC was one of the rapidly growing mass organizations in the 1930s with active Communist participation. An association with the Scottsboro Case brought at-tention to its work against racial violence. The mobilization effort in support of the nine Black teenagers accused of rape drew heavily from artists and writers who found the case to be a rich source of material for their work.

A few years earlier, she might have found this first encounter with communism far less appealing. The American Communist Party (ACP) had originated as a splinter group of the Socialist Party in 1919, as one of three parties all claiming al-legiance to the Communist International. After establishing a strong base of op-erations in labor during the 1920s, the Socialist Party became embroiled in bitter disputes with other older and newer groups. The factionalism did little to bring members on board or to enhance its reputation among the American masses. Any organization on the Left discovered quickly that its popularity increased in direct proportion to the effectiveness and speed with which it responded to the world economic crises of the 1930s. In the United States, experiencing the greatest depression it had ever known, radical ideas about the cause of and ways to solve the crises were easily embraced. Because the Left in general was prepared to act quickly on hardcore issues, their numbers swelled.

The ACP was in the forefront of the unemployment movement by the early 1930s, due to its ability to rally huge numbers of unemployed people for public demonstrations. While many such events ended with violence, they had the positive effect of creating local martyrs. Their unemployment councils, organized by neighborhood, city, and state, became a common ground where card-carrying Communists and non-Communists alike could meet and work. They had similar success with their work in the antifascist movement, where they led united-front efforts that were not bound by Communist Party membership. By 1935, its work with labor unions, the American Youth Congress, and the struggle for equal rights made the ACP the leader of the leftist movement in the United States. Most mass organizations in Chicago and other major cities could expect to have a solid representation from Communist ranks.

ACP members were present in full force at the opening session of the Congress, along with an assortment of other groups that she knew nothing about. Her single motivation for going was Langston Hughes, the keynote speaker for the occasion. Remembering his visit to New Orleans, she was eager to see him again, now that she had done exactly what he had said she should do—leave the South—and was now a published writer. After he wrote *Scottsboro, Limited: A One-Act Play*, a small volume that circulated widely, Hughes visited the nine young Black men, still in their adolescence, who were awaiting their death sentence in Kilby Prison in Birmingham, Alabama. Hughes had been prevented from speaking about this during his tour of southern Negro schools, but as president of the Communist-front organization, the League of Struggle for Negro Rights, he was the natural choice to speak at this first Congress.

Walker was little more than an observer of what went on at the initial sessions. She had extremely mixed feelings, feeling both attraction and revulsion as she witnessed what could only be called intellectual fire. Without knowing who he was, she watched Harry Haywood, a well-known Black Communist, manage the oddest-looking group of people she had ever seen; some looked disheveled, while others had suitcases and bags of flyers, newspapers, and magazines. They talked incessantly, interrupting one another, and their laughter seemed orchestrated. She had been to church conferences, where she'd seen a lot of bickering, but this was different. As they called the roll of delegates, a representative would answer, "I represent the Communist Party of the United States of America." Then there would be a burst of laughter. She was bewildered and yet intrigued by it all.

When she returned for the sessions on Sunday, she finally saw Hughes. After he spoke, she rushed over to talk to him, trying to get his opinion on her newest poems she'd brought along. When Hughes discovered that she had no copies, he would not take them. He was surrounded by a group who seemed to be his friends, including Richard Wright, whom Walker had yet to meet. She remembered that Hughes "turned to Wright . . . standing nearby, listening to the conversation and smiling at my desperation."[10] Langston urged Wright to include her, should they get a group started. She was ecstatic, not only because Hughes had given her such a recommendation, but also because this was her first opportunity to be part of a group of Black writers. Introductions came in quick succession, but Arna Bontemps and Augusta Savage were the only ones she later recalled. Her excitement wiped clean her mental slate of names as quickly as she heard them. What she did remember was Wright agreeing to Hughes's request, "don't forget to include this girl."[11]

By the time she showed up at the Writers' Project office in mid-March, she had been well schooled on the two people who worked with the Federal Negro Theatre, Theodore Ward and Richard Wright, the name that seemed to be cropping up everywhere now. Both had been working nearly a year. She also knew that the WPA had underwritten a large race-relations project on Chicago's South Side, headed by scholars from both the University of Chicago School of Sociology and Northwestern. The intention was to look at social welfare, economic, and cultural issues in Chicago, and those pertaining to the Negro race particularly. The project called for twenty research students and an additional 150 WPA staff workers. It meant that WPA workers were all over the city, doing a wide range of tasks.

On her first day at the job, Walker walked across the bridge at Wacker Drive and entered the main office at 1011 Wells Street, where she met Louis Wirth, the first director of the Chicago Writers' Project. Because the project drew heavily from its base at the University of Chicago's School of Sociology, there were regular exchanges between those employed on the project, those who were attending school at the University, and Chicago's radical Left. Friendships developed easily, observing few boundaries. Her receptivity to the Writers' Project, to people she did not know and to ideas she found foreign, says much about the importance of Chicago as a laboratory for the development of socially conscious art and explicitly political writing in the 1930s. She was open to doing whatever it took to further her development as a writer, and now that she was employed, she had no reason to doubt her ability to support herself as an independent woman and an artist.

In the office on Erie Street, she met other new employees, including Studs Terkel, Jack Conroy, and Nelson Algren, and renewed her acquaintance with Saul Bellow, a classmate from Hungerford's class. Conroy was the most political of the group and had the more authoritarian air, but Algren, at twenty-six and only a few years older than she was, had just published *Somebody in Boots* (1935), the first of his several novels about life in Chicago. She read the book right away so that she could join in the lively office discussion about the new realism and proletarian literature that they were all reading. It intrigued her to know some-body who already had the designation as a *novelist* and was working alongside her on the Writers' Project.

She began as a junior writer making $84 per month, just as Bellow did. She worked alongside Frank Yerby, who would go on to write almost exclusively about the South, and who seemed to have the least interest in the left-wing pol-itics that preoccupied most WPA writers. Although he appeared in some of the early journals alongside Walker, Wright, and others, Yerby was on the Writers' Project for less than a year before he left for a teaching job in the South. When he resurfaced in1946, he did so with his first and highly successful novel, *Foxes of Harrow*, marking the beginning of a lucrative career—recreating the romance and history of the antebellum South. What made him famous to some, with three dozen novels over the course of his life, isolated him from both his fellow writers and one of the most important literary movements of the twentieth century. Walker could not have predicted his success, but none of her colleagues under-stood the tastes of the American public as well as Yerby.[12] His ideas drew consid-erable criticism, which he simply passed off as too highbrow. Neither did Yerby find it necessary to advertise that he was a Negro, since he was writing the kind of fiction most associated with Southern white writers.

Chicago native Willard Motley, having gained something of a reputation for his column in the *Chicago Defender*, became interested in the new proletarian lit-erature and wrote several innovative novels. Beginning with *Knock on Any Door* in 1946, he looked at social conditions such as poverty through white characters but, like too many of the writers of their generation, was quickly forgotten. In fact, none of the other Black writers with passion and commitment to the cause of social justice reached the level of success that Yerby did, if we measure suc-cess by commercial standards. While they were all poor, they were also idealists, believing that one must never do anything just for money. Yerby belied their ide-alism; he took a risk and won.

The exception among them, of course, was Richard Wright. While poverty was as real for whites as for Blacks, Wright's success with dramatizing its conse-quences in strikingly racial—meaning Black—terms set the standard by which Black writing would soon be received and judged. Yerby's approach—to write "white" fiction and remain anonymous—suggested how complicated racial boundaries could be. Nevertheless, Walker, Yerby, and Motley were paid less than many of the people she met who had already become supervisors, making as much as $125 a month: Jimmy Phelan, Stuart Engstrand, Jack Scher, Sam Ross, Nelson Algren, Katherine Dunham, and Arna Bontemps. Although Richard Wright had less education than any of the others, he had been publishing since 1934 in little magazines and, therefore, qualified as a more experienced writer, a category that carried considerable weight. It had allowed him to start out as a writer in Public Relations with the Federal Theatre Project, then move to the Writers' Project, no doubt with the support of his friend and WPA director, Louis Wirth. Walker correctly assessed it was his "personal entry" that made the difference. That "was how the political machine worked at that time," she wrote.[13] Later, Walker realized that Wright was earning more because he was the sole support for his family, his mother and younger brother, while Walker could not claim Mercedes, who had received financial support from the National Youth Administration. Nevertheless, while he was more experienced, as she noted in her journal entry, as a federal program, pay scale in the Writers' Project was determined by both experience and need.

Considerable attention has been given to the role of the WPA in advancing the careers of many writers. For Walker, the political education that came alongside her participation in the Writers' Project resulted in an extraordinary level of productivity and a boost to her professional writing career. Jerry Mangione talked about its effects in *Dream and the Deal*, but the stories of individual writers remain to be fully explored. Living in Chicago and working for the Writers' Project provided a unique safety net, a place where her emotional fragility and lack of confidence could find constructive ways of working themselves out. She could lose herself in her work at home, at her office, or in the library; go to the museum, the park, or to the movies; or simply spend an entire afternoon at the *Poetry* offices. Everything she did seemed to move her in the direction that she wanted to go: meeting editors and other writers, finding rich materials for her poems and stories, and having an active social life with friends who understood and could match her intensity.

Walker met Margaret Taylor and Bernard Goss during this period. They were the perfect artist couple, as she saw them. The two Margarets were the same age, Goss a New Orleans native who had moved to Chicago with his parents as a child. The connection to New Orleans made the newlyweds' coach house Walker's second Chicago home. Goss became one of her closest women friends, her unofficial guide to both the day- and nightlife in the city. Although eager to talk about "girl stuff," she was laying the foundation for her future work as a formidable force in community and arts organizations in Chicago. Her interest in African arts, as well as in African American history and culture, led to the founding, with second husband Charles Burroughs of the famed DuSable Museum of African American History in 1961.

Every party at the Goss home was an event that people remembered and talked about long after. One entered what was at once a gallery, coffeehouse, and restaurant, with paintings and prints by the couple themselves. Hanging from the ceilings and walls were works by other black artists making their house the perfect setting for the lively discussions that took place over the pot of chicken gumbo with oysters and rice, or some other Creole dish, which was always on the stove when the guests arrived. They would sometimes spend the entire night eating and reading poetry, drinking, and laughing.

At one of these parties Walker first heard the sultry sounds of Billie Holiday, whose tragic life would be repeated by some of her own friends. In comparison to Walker, Goss was urbane, politically sophisticated, and not nearly as emotionally fragile. The friendship that developed between them grew even stronger after Walker had left Chicago, making her frequent returns to Chicago always a reminder of one of the most exciting periods of her life. Goss knew every Negro writer, artist, and musician in Chicago, and anyone who claimed to be such. When Walker accompanied her friend to meetings, she never knew whom she might meet.

Once they went to a literary club meeting at a private home, the hostess was Gwendolyn Brooks, barely eighteen, and already a published poet. Brooks, like Walker, had begun publishing early and was widely known as Chicago's child poet. Although both Walker and Brooks would earn the distinction of being the first African American women poets to appear in *Poetry*, they followed different paths toward literary recognition. In 1950, Brooks became the first African American writer to win a Pulitzer Prize. Since Brooks lived at home and was not employed by the Writers' Project, Walker saw less of her than she did some of the other writers. They were never openly competitive, but the space for Black women poets was so limited that being in the same generation gave the appearance that they were.

Although the Great Depression had destroyed much of the evidence of Chicago as the "literary capital of the United States," a phrase coined by the journalist H. L. Mencken, it was still the place to which many writers migrated and settled as they began to carve out a distinctive American voice. Works by Edgar Lee Masters, Margaret Anderson, and Vachel Lindsay were celebrated because they brought attention to small towns of the Midwest and the prairie in their local color writings. Carl Sandburg and James T. Farrell had focused exclusively on Chicago, as had Theodore Dreiser in earlier years. Hamlin Garland, Upton Sinclair, and Floyd Dell had all established a rich legacy that Chicago writers could claim. This rich tradition of literary and cultural expression in Chicago was not lost on the writers employed by the Chicago Writers' Project. Many of them represented the very people they began to write about, foreign-born or second-generation immigrants. The tools of literary realism and naturalism appealed to their humanistic sensibilities, allowing them to explore old and new modalities, and to speculate about the American dream and myth of success.

Likewise, Black writers had been identified with Chicago a generation earlier, such as poet Fenton Johnson. But because the first major period in twentieth-century Black writing is associated with the Harlem Renaissance,

Chicago writers were described as pre-Renaissance or extensions of the Harlem Renaissance well into the 1940s. Chicago writers like Marita Bonner and Frank Marshall Davis, for example, were quickly claimed by the Harlem Renaissance.

Arna Bontemps was among the first to recognize the importance of Chicago as a site of its own Black Renaissance. The writers and artists employed by the WPA, those who came to Chicago to advance their education, arriving from Black Belt states, especially Mississippi, all intersected in the city. The Black Chicago Renaissance would clearly distinguish itself from the earlier Renaissance because of its grounding in a new set of social and economic realities. It is true that Chicago did not have an Alain Locke or a James Weldon Johnson to popularize the "New Negro," which implied a division within the race. An extraordinary level of productivity sometimes overshadowed its built-in elitism and the privileging of the few without the benefit of a trickle-down effect. The political intensity of Chicago fed a broad-based cultural phenomenon from the bottom up. Its vibrant art scene and community-based cultural institutions produced a wide assortment of individuals for whom art and social change were joined at the hip. Walker knew and revered the writers and artists from the Harlem Renaissance, especially Hughes, but she took her worldview from Chicago where every gathering was an opportunity to learn and organize, write and participate, and where conversations led to concrete action associated with some form of transformation that would benefit working people. Living in Chicago presented Walker with a diverse and complex world, one that forced her to go beyond the fairly narrow Black and white interpretations that she had absorbed:

> Now I discovered there were poor white working people exploited by rich white people . . . that all Jews were not rich . . . all Negroes were not even in the same economic class. Negroes who made money by exploiting poor Negroes . . . had some of the same attitudes toward them that rich whites had toward poor whites and that prejudiced whites have toward all Negroes.[14]

Whether at her workplace, the parties, or meetings of literary clubs, the Chicago Federation of Arts and Professions, or the Writers' Congress, she was reading literature and meeting people who shared these sensibilities. Many of those on the project acknowledged an ethnic affiliation—Jewish, Negro, and Irish, in particular. Like her, they recognized the importance of preserving cultural traditions, especially those customs that designated a distinct ethnic heritage. She met no one who wasn't glad to be in America, yet they all proclaimed that their ethnic identity had made them who they were. The sheer preponderance of writers meant that Walker was meeting new people all the time, sharing her work and expectations, and gaining a broader perspective on areas of American life and culture that she saw as parallel to hers as a Negro in America.

She soon moved up to the position of senior writer, which increased her pay to $94 a month. She was now the breadwinner in the family; she could make regular contributions to her sister's expenses and sometimes send money home to her parents. Most important of all, she had established a routine at her job that gave her time to write. She would report in the morning to the Erie Street office to receive her assignment, initially entries for the *Illinois Guide Book* and *Cavalcade of the American Negro*.

She found the research useful since she was learning more about Illinois as a state and was surprised to discover new facts about Negro history. The writing was also easy, since it was basic reportage and the library was such a familiar place for her. She found that she could complete the assignment by noon and have the rest of the day to roam the library, read, and revise the poems that she was submitting for publication.

The offices of *Poetry* were also located on Erie Street. She had already submitted a poem to that magazine and received a polite rejection note signed by Morton Darwin Zabel, rather than Harriet Monroe. Her disappointment came not so much from the rejection itself as from the shock that Monroe had died suddenly. Well into her seventies in 1936, she had gone to Peru to attend an international writers' conference and died there. *Poetry* was now in the hands of a member of the editorial collective, who had sent out the rejection note.

By the time George Dillon was appointed the new full-time editor, Walker had paid for her subscription to the magazine and read every issue carefully. One day, rather than going to the library from the Writers' Project, feeling especially self-confident, she knocked on the door of the *Poetry* offices. She introduced herself to Geraldine Udell and met George Dillon for the first time. She talked about having met Monroe as a student and said that she was now working on the Writers' Project. Dillon showed her around the offices and told her that she would be added to their mailing list. In the meantime, he said, if she were serious about writing and publishing in the magazine, she should read some of the French Symbolist poets, because they were having an important influence on American poetry.

She left the office eager to return to the library to find a copy of Baudelaire's *Les fleurs du mal*, Rimbaud's *Une saison en enfer*, and Mallarmé's *L'après-midi d'un faune*. She was so confident in her proficiency in French that she paid little attention to whether she should look for them in French or English. She read with admiration poetry that was more intricate than anything she'd ever seen. She understood why Dillon had sent her to the French writers; they were not afraid

Gathering at the home of Margaret and Bernard Goss, Chicago. Standing
(L to R): Marion Perkins, Vernon Jarrett, Robert Lucas. Seated (L to R): Margaret
Brundage, Tom Conroy, Fern Gayden, Gwendolyn Brooks, Margaret Taylor Goss.
Courtesy of Chicago Public Library, Harsh Collection.

to play with language, yet their images were sharp, the voices magisterial. Even
when they were being colloquial, they were elegant. Then she read the poetry of
Marya Zaturenska and Dylan Thomas and reread Muriel Rukeyser. She saw poetry now in terms of both taste and tone, and she was beginning to understand its
significance in the contemporary world in a new way.

Walker had always found writing poetry an easy endeavor because she enjoyed it. What it took to be a professional poet or novelist was both fascinating
and frightening. Her desire for recognition was not only a powerful incentive,
but also a fiercely competitive one. While it had been her dream to be a poet, the
world in which she saw writers operating was different from the one inhabited
by ordinary people. She saw writers collapse in the face of rejection when they
needed only to rewrite a piece but could not, some of them never getting over a
minor disappointment, forever seeing themselves as hopeless failures. She witnessed personalities go from tender, passionate, and caring to violent, suspicious,
and bitter. There was one drawback. She was not ashamed of being traditional,

and thus found the constant exposure to Bohemian culture that was rampant at *Poetry* receptions distasteful. Was this rejection of traditional values just for the sake of rebellion? If she were going to benefit fully from the education she received through her association with *Poetry*, how could she find a way to be in this culture, but not of it? It occurred to her that most of the Negroes she knew could ill afford or sustain the life of a bohemian. It boiled down to who you were. Blacks would be distinguished from whites no matter what the situation might be. And on this matter, she was willing to part company.

Her longer poems began to show the influence of the experimental poetry she was reading. Working with newer forms and free verse in particular was more difficult than she had imagined. What drew her to poetry originally was the ease with which she could compose and turn a phrase. The words and phrases took more time when she was in free verse, and she'd begin numerous poems without being able to finish them. Feelings of self-doubt returned, and she began to question whether her work would ever be worth anything, whether she would ever have anything published in *Poetry*.

Thinking about her novel eased some of the doubt, since she was meeting more writers of fiction. She pulled out the 300 pages she had written for Hungerford's class, but *Jubilee* had not become consolidated in her mind. Part of the difficulty was her sense of urgency about contemporary social issues. A Civil War story seemed inappropriate for the times and no longer excited her as it once did.

What did seem to make sense was related to a project in which she had been involved during her final year at Northwestern. Volunteering with the Institute for Juvenile Research brought the same sense of satisfaction and renewal as her experiences with the children's center in New Orleans during the year out of school. The Institute was designed as an experiment in cross-class contact and utilized some of the theories developed by Robert Park, a noted sociologist at the University of Chicago. The program's focus was on Black youth who had been negatively affected by the Great Depression. For Walker, working with a group of young girls who either were prostitutes or who had a criminal history was eye-opening. When she later described it in an interview with Nikki Giovanni, it didn't occur to her that she was doing work since her job was to "pal around with in order to see what kind of influence a person with my background and training would have on them."[15]

A new assignment for the Writers' Project required a creative work based on Chicago's Negro community. Should she consider creating a fictional character based on one of the young women she had met? Was this the kind of artistic license that was acceptable, not ethically questionable? Like most of her peers, Walker was becoming heavily influenced by social realism, the belief that art must portray life as it was. Social realist writers were drawn to working class subjects, and while Walker's own situation placed her in that same class, she was not surrounded by negative influences. She still had her dreams. One of the young women talked about her desire to be a musician, but her need to survive led her to make choices that shattered that dream. The idea for the story would follow her life and the experiences leading to her downfall and her dream destroyed. The models she could rely on would have been popular reading from the period, proletarian literature, as it was called. Although not explicit from her notes, Walker may have been thinking about Theodore Dreiser's *Sister Carrie*, a popular Chicago novel published in 1900 that brought attention to the conditions of young women who dream of an escape from rural life, come to the city, only to succumb to forces beyond their control. Walker would also have had a steady diet of proletarian literature from Chicago during the 1930s, from colleagues like James T. Farrell, whose *Studs Lonigan* trilogy set in the Chicago's South Side Irish community was required reading for anyone on the Writers' Project. She was familiar with the leftist magazines *Anvil* and *New Masses*, and would later meet *Anvil's* editor, Jack Conroy, on the Writers' Project. Conroy had already published two novels, *The Disinherited* in 1933 and *A World to Win* in 1935.

Within the context of Chicago and exposure to its popular fiction, Walker also wanted to identify with her character. Equally curious was she about what her mother referred to as "bad girls" when forbidding her children from associating with those classmates Walker always found fascinating. Thus, the job assignment and a degree of voyeurism merged as Walker began working on "Goose Island," the place where the young woman lived—which Walker took as the title of her new project. "Goose Island" became the framework for the story and the major cause of the young girl's descent into a life of prostitution. Despite working on it throughout her time on the Writers' Project, she had at least one completed manuscript. It remained, however, unpublished. "Goose Island," she concluded, was too sentimental a piece. The story line was transparent and unsophisticated, so modeled was it on the mechanical sociological descriptions she typed up during her volunteer work. While it fit the period's proletarian literature because of its method of social realism, the characters were flat and the dialect, which she believed to be essential to its authenticity, was unreadable.

Yet something about "Goose Island" encouraged her to write consistently. The story became the subject of her conversations at parties and meetings. At one such meeting with a group of writers she'd first met at the National Negro Congress, she learned about a plan to start a magazine associated with the Chicago Federation of Arts and Professions. Eager to publish more, she submitted her poetry and began working on a short story. Two ballads "Big John Henry" and "Bad-Man Stagolee" would eventually appear in the new journal *Creative Writing* in 1938. [16]) Jack Conroy, *Anvil's* editor and her colleague at the Writers' Project, published the short story she finished, but "The Red Satin Dress," did not appear until 1939 after she'd left Chicago.

Working comfortably in fiction gave Walker permission to return to poetry. When a writers' group that met in the Chicago Loop asked her to read some of her poems, she found that reading poetry aloud again brought back the excitement she felt in front of an appreciative audience. Although she no longer lived in Evanston, she continued to get postcards about the meetings for those groups associated with her membership in the Northwestern chapter of the Poetry Society of America. She returned to Evanston to one of them and gave a stunning performance.

The Writers' Project sponsored a host of activities: Black productions of Shakespeare's *Macbeth*; a production written and directed by Gertrude Stein; and Theodore Ward's *Big White Fog*, about life in the Deep South. But it was Katherine Dunham's *Bal Negre*, a spectacular performance of Black dance utilizing the folkdance forms from the Caribbean, that captured Walker's attention more than the rest. Dunham introduced dance forms that became central not only to Negro cultural expression but also to modern American dance. Since she could actually include it as part of her Writers' Project assignment, which had her covering shows at the Chicago Art Institute for the *Illinois Guide Book*, Walker became an instant Dunham fan, making it her project. The opportunity gave her exposure to WPA painters and sculptors. Learning more about art became a new adventure, especially when she discovered the Italian Renaissance paintings and the Art Institute's copies of paintings by Raphael, Tintoretto, Tiepolo, and the Flemish painters Rembrandt, Van Dyck, and the German painter Dürer.

There was another kind of education that came when the two sisters moved from the Near North Side to 6336 South Evans. Their relocation to the heart of the Black community expanded opportunities on a number of levels. After a first exposure to the game of bridge, Walker was hooked for the remainder of her life. With a kitchen and a sitting room, Walker began to practice what became her long-standing tradition: preparing sumptuous meals for friends who would marvel at her culinary skills. When does a young poet have that much time to spend in the kitchen? For Walker, it was a distinction she could bring that linked her to her Louisiana roots and Southern hospitality, another practice that brought her great pleasure throughout her life.

The family from whom they rented had come from the South early in their marriage. Mr. Hyames had secured a job at the post office and bought a home, a common pattern for many migrants. Hyames did not want his wife to work, since her duties were to care for their home. They had no children, but the sizable residence could accommodate several families, another common practice that assured newly arriving family members of a place for short visits or long-term stays, at least until "they got on their feet." But as Hyames began to realize, even with extra shifts at the post office, they were struggling to make ends meet. And, as the Walkers would soon discover, both husband and wife had a few bad habits. The only solution was to rent rooms, and their preferred boarders were young women coming up from the South for school or jobs. They had done well by the standards operating in the Negro community: he had never been laid off, and since he had a civil service job, he was guaranteed a retirement pension, which meant long-term security. Thus, even though Hyames didn't have much education, his job made him equal to those who did.

Walker had not seen this side of the world before, nor had she thought about the relationship between lack of education and job security. Education was important, she had achieved it, and those who hadn't had no one to blame but themselves. It did not occur to her until she met Richard Wright that structural limitations existed that made many things impossible for Negroes in the 1930s and 1940s.

The Hyameses lived comfortably, and the Walker sisters closely observed the dynamics between the couple. Mrs. Hyames knew that she was well cared for, and she had a fondness for bridge and gambling. By insisting that his wife stay at home, Mr. Hyames had fed her gambling habit, since most of her friends worked during the day. Unlike them, she had little to do once she had completed her household chores. No longer critical of card playing, the sisters began to perfect their bridge game. Mrs. Hyames knew all the tricks, and with her strong encouragement, they began to understand some of the pleasures it afforded. Bridge parties were all the rage in Chicago at the time. Walker later remembered having gone to one party when she was still in college and leaving almost immediately when everybody rushed to the table to locate their bridge partner. Even the person who had brought her to the party disappeared and didn't notice when she left. Now, she understood what she had missed.

Under the tutelage of the Hyameses, the Walker girls became unbeatable bridge players. The word spread quickly throughout the South Side social network. Walker's self-image as a social misfit was no longer compatible with her mastery of the game. She was in demand as a partner, especially when her sister had to go to school or practice for a concert. On some of the days when she did not have to go into the office, she had time to practice her skills with her landlady, hoping to dissuade her gambling habit. At this time in her life as a single young Black woman with a job, playing bridge and playing it well satisfied her adventurous spirit; it did not require breaking free in the traditional sense. Had she viewed herself as more attractive, the social importance of the game might have been far less significant. In any case, it had become the one thing that tested her mental abilities at the same time that it gave her a decided social advantage.

She often included lighthearted descriptions of the Hyameses in her notes for her stories. One she recorded began, "When he opened the door every afternoon he would say, 'I'm home honey!' If she had won [the lottery] she would be beaming and have porterhouse steak but if she had lost, he could tell by the look on her face. The next day he would come home drunk. I don't think she ever recognized the connection between the two because she rationalized that she was always breaking even; win or lose, she broke even."[17]

Nonetheless, the couple provided an important access to a life from which the two sisters had been so carefully guarded. Viewing Mrs. Hyames as an "inveterate, congenital gambler"[18] made it easier for Walker to spend her weekends going to a round of parties, and only rarely to church. It was not unusual for her to leave home on Saturday afternoon headed for a book reception at the *Poetry* offices, then to a second party on the South Side, and end up on Sunday with old friends and schoolmates, spend the night, and then leave in time to get to the Writers' Project for her Monday morning sign-in. On one occasion, after returning home from one of these marathon weekends, she noted that even her sister and her landlady were "shocked into stony silence."[19]

This time of complete freedom was rare; Walker knew that it had come at a particular moment for her and that it would never happen again once this moment had passed. She felt no guilt, because she was doing nothing really wrong. It was also easier and cheaper not to visit her parents in New Orleans during this period, although she did send money to bring Brother to Chicago for a visit, an act that signaled, more than anything else, how well she was doing.

Certain memories stood out from this period. She remembered the first time she had heard the name Adolf Hitler. Mercedes provided the details of the man who had risen to power in Germany, giving a whole new meaning to her understanding of race. Since she was now reading about the history of Stalin, Mussolini, and Churchill, following the headlines and the comic mockery aimed at the exiled Haile Selassie became more important. As civil war broke out in Spain, she met people rallying for the relief of Ethiopia and Loyalist Spain. She even met one Negro nurse from Harlem who left school to go to Spain to serve. Her days at Northwestern had been so isolated that now every moment and every experience brought a new and welcome awareness.

Because of her doctrinaire religious beliefs, Walker now concluded that the deeply religious phase of her life was a natural part of childhood, which logically should transition to a new stage for an adult, which she now was. She did not denounce religion; it simply began to recede from her immediate consciousness. Maturing as a writer and as a woman, she believed that her growth required an expansion of her thinking. What was becoming available to her she may have taken initially at face value, because it gave her a language that connected her with a literary community, a connection she had been seeking all her life. But she soon began to absorb and include in her conversations more analysis of the political climate and expand her thinking about race, the Black Belt, and social systems. She surmised that whatever this new knowledge might have cost her, the good far outweighed the bad. She would not quote mindless jargon; rather, she read the literature and then used her journal extensively to tease out interpretations and pose questions that she intended to seek answers for. Her library card was her most treasured possession, because it supported her intellectual liberation. She was acutely aware of her own transformation and the voice it allowed her to have. Whatever unspoken readiness she might have felt, her own desires seemed to find confirmation in those public declarations that she adopted as her own. Perhaps the clearest one appeared in her journal after almost a year after joining the Writers' Project:

> I found myself rather wholeheartedly adapting the Extreme left socialist or communistic way of thinking—of thrusting off the shackles of a passive and blinding religion; of recognizing the necessity for economic re-construction under the leadership of the proletariat coming to ascendancy in the face of decadent capitalism which received its death blow in America in 1929; of accepting the right of self-determination as the way out for the American Negro nationality; of working toward the enlargement of a group actively among artists, musicians, and writers, and all such cultural builders as a means toward producing a cultural renaissance in this country, of bringing the masses through reeducation to a new consciousness of the significance of current affairs to an awareness of a sense of their duty and a stand for the respect of their human dignity.[20]

The capability of self-determination brought her private world and the public one together in ways she was only beginning to imagine. For now, she was eager to accept what she saw simply saw as her fate.

8

Colleagues and Comrades

South Side Writers

Almost two months after she had begun working at the Writers' Project, Walker received a postcard inviting her to the organizing meeting for a group of Negro writers. The card was signed "Richard Wright." Although they were now coworkers, most of what she knew about Wright came from conversations with others rather than with him. She doubted if he'd remembered her from the American Writers Congress meeting where Hughes had introduced them, but she was nonetheless pleased to be identified as part of a group who would soon have its own moniker, "South Side Writers."

The meeting was less than a month away. The time and place, like those who were invited, had been carefully selected. She had yet to meet Robert Davis, another writer on the project, who had agreed to host the event at his home on South Parkway. Despite being the undisputed leader of the newly formed group, Wright continued to live in a small apartment, which he shared with his brother, mother, grandmother, and aunt, one unsuitable for visitors. In contrast, the Davis home was in the more upwardly mobile Bronzeville, the name that had come to signify Black achievement and opportunity as Black migrants settled in Chicago's Third Ward, an area that extended from 14th and State Street southward to 60th Street and westward to Paulina. South Parkway, the major thoroughfare passing through Chicago's South Side, was an identifiable part of the "Black Belt," the phrase social scientists had coined when they began to map the social geography of this overpopulated urban ghetto. Chicago's Black residents preferred the classier designation, Bronzeville, comprising many individually owned homes; Bronzeville formed a city within a city, where businesses flourished and on the basis of which the new arrivals began to amass some political power. The importance of South Parkway was signaled half a decade later by its name change to Martin Luther King Jr. Drive.

There were younger children playing in the yard as she approached the Davis residence in late May, and she realized that Davis was still living with his family. Suddenly her own sense of importance increased, since, at twenty, she was working and living on her own, and unlike Davis, was not dependent on her parents. Nevertheless, Walker took an instant liking to Davis, one of the members whose career she would continue to follow.

The House Where My Soul Lives. Maryemma Graham, Oxford University Press. © Oxford University Press 2022.
DOI: 10.1093/oso/9780195341232.003.0008

Counterclockwise from top: Frank Yerby, Walker, Fern Gayden, Richard Wright, Alden Bland, Arna Bontemps, St. Clair Drake, Russell Marshall, Frank Marshall Davis, William Attaway, Marian Minus and Dorothy West, Robert Davis [Davis Roberts], Theodore Ward. South Side Writers Group and Friends. Collage by Earl Richardson

She walked into the room to the sound of a man's forceful voice and stood still as the stream of swear words trailed off his tongue. Recoiling "in Sunday-school horror,"[1] she saw that she was one of three women in a room full of men. The initial shock passed quickly, and she felt connected immediately. For Walker, that first meeting and the events surrounding it along with the emotions it evoked remained etched in her memory.

> Twice I left the house and turned back, the first time out of great self-consciousness because I felt I looked abominable. I had nothing to wear to make a nice appearance, and I was going to the far South Side, where I felt people would make fun of me. But my great desire to meet writers and end my long isolation conquered this superficial fear. I made myself go.[2]

The South Side Writers Group (SSWG) was the brainchild of Richard Wright, who had been in Chicago for a decade. He was the same age as Walker was in 1936—nineteen—when he came from Memphis to live with his aunt. By the time the group met, Wright was moving up the ranks as a post office employee, the only one in the group who was not college-educated. He had a lot riding on him as the sole support for his extended family. Desperate for a context in which he could develop as a writer, he had listened to his white post office friends and joined the Chicago chapter of the John Reed Club, one of a chain of similar organizations around the country and the breeding ground for writers on the Left. The clubs had not been especially successful in recruiting Blacks, and Wright was a prime target; he was from the rural South, naturally bright, talented, and most of all, he fit the profile of the urban working class, the "proletariat."

Wright's experience upon arrival to Chicago, however, was not entirely unlike Walker's. As a member of several leftist groups, he found new relationships and an accompanying political education. Walker found that to be the case as well. What was different was Wright's *training* as a writer. Having grown accustomed to writing for a variety of small leftist magazines and receiving strong encouragement from the officials within the John Reed Club, Wright became one of the John Reed Club's elected officials, which marked him for Communist Party leadership. His style, therefore, had derived both from his experience growing up in poverty in Mississippi and from learning how to use words in a compelling manner. The style, new to Walker, singled Wright out for her immediately. Because he had begun his career as a poet, he and Walker had something else in common.

What mattered most to him, just as it did for Walker, was the opportunity to publish, to receive the affirmation and the kind of social immersion necessary for writers. Being surrounded by other writers fed both of their ambitions. Wright became a card-carrying member of the Communist Party, persuaded by its members' genuine interest in him and the ideal of revolutionary social change, which put them, at least in his mind, in the forefront of the battle against Negro segregation. Pouring all of his anger and hostility into stories of capitalists and oppressed workers, Wright wrote some of his most powerful poetry for left-wing journals in the early 1930s.

After several years in the leadership, Wright also discovered that the perception of him as an intellectual with bourgeois aspirations was in sharp conflict with the party's expectations. American communism, at least the version practiced in Chicago in the 1930s, fashioned ideologies of proletarianism that locked people like Wright into a prison of definitions and preconceived notions of class and class behavior. There were working-class intellectuals, but these positions were generally reserved for the white leadership; in contrast, Black leaders were to look and were assumed to be less educated, making them appear more like those workers, both Black and white, whom the Party hoped to recruit.

In fact, Wright was far less interested in the tasks of a mass organizer; he saw himself as a writer, first and foremost. His growing discontent, however, did not affect the enthusiasm with which the communists promoted his writing as exemplary proletarian literature. Once Wright gained the friendship of white artists and intellectuals, learning how they operated, he began to seek out other like-minded Black intellectuals, believing that Negro artists in particular had an important role to play, one that was not understood by the leadership of the Communist Party. He found them first at the University of Chicago, where he became an unofficial student of Louis Wirth, one of the professors working with Robert Park, whose research had helped to transform the field of American sociology. Close friendships formed, like those with Horace Cayton, a Black graduate student from Seattle, Washington, who was working as Wirth's assistant and was the first to write a major study on Negro workers. Cayton introduced Wright to St. Clair Drake, another graduate student in the program. For Walker they all became part of her close network of activist intellectuals who would continue to support each other's work.

Walker connected immediately to Wright's ideas, after having discovered the power in his prose. In his view, the network of Black intellectuals at the Writers Project had an opportunity to envision a different context in which Negro writing could develop. The John Reed Club was the model for the SSWG, and, in Wright's view, the ideal of communism did not necessarily have to be unifying factor among them. What communism did for him in part was to demonstrate the importance of collective work. Wright especially wanted to be among other Black artists and intellectuals, who stood for the academic achievement and social mobility from which he was excluded as a youth but which he now sought. His job at the Federal Theatre Project, as the only Negro hired without a college degree, made him acutely aware of his position among other Negro intellectuals. Wright would not have seen the opportunity as being unfair—as some undoubtedly did—but rather confirmation that there were at least some sectors of US society where racial and social privilege did not apply. Moreover, it was appropriate that he assume a critical role among other Negro artists and intellectuals, both as a member of the proletariat and as someone who had a history of self-advancement.

She recognized Wright as the leader from the moment she entered the drawing room of Robert Davis's home. They were all ready for connection and community. The SSWG followed Wright's independent spirit, which the communists had discouraged, but which could now proceed unhampered in carving out its own path. If the members of the group thought they were trying to keep alive, if not resurrect the spirit of the New Negro Renaissance of the decade before, they knew that in 1936 they were confronting conditions different from those of their predecessors.

The New Negro era had spawned organizations like the NAACP and the National Urban League, which focused on improving the conditions of Blacks in the United States, but the dominant belief among many was that the steady rise of Black excellence and the Negro's ongoing contribution to American culture would not only enrich the United States and world but would also have a positive trickle-down effect that saw greater racial harmony. The Post–World War I era nurtured the optimism and energy of a newly minted talented tenth who found their opportunities expanding at a time when the national economy was eager to exploit and expand new cultural markets. There was academic and cultural capital to be had within Black America as the migration routes led from farm to factory and from small towns in the South to large cities in the Northeast and Midwest. There were tons of danger signs many people would ignore, focusing instead on the steady rise of individual Black talent with hungry publishers, eager sponsors and leading ideologies shaping a narrative of racial exceptionalism.

The danger signs were harder to see going into the Great Depression, but when the dust settled, a world economic crisis revealed itself in no uncertain ways. Few traces of that movement that had allowed Black artistic and cultural contributions to reach a high-water mark were visible. Publishers had stopped pursuing the writers, many artists had left to seek their fortunes in Paris and elsewhere, and financial support from wealthy New Yorkers quickly dried up. What became known as the Harlem Renaissance had not so much ended as it had been overshadowed by more practical concerns, concerns that were paramount for most working Americans.

Among those working Americans was a large Negro population composed mainly of migrants. In cities like Chicago, they were barely a generation removed from their roots in the Deep South, especially Louisiana and the Mississippi Delta. Those who met at the Davis home that day could count themselves in that number: they were simply more educated than most Blacks and had different experiences and aspirations. Moreover, while the unemployment rate rose among the masses of people, these writers had been fortunate to get support from the various programs associated with the New Deal. Many of them also received support from philanthropic organizations like the Rosenwald Foundation. They had, in effect, greater access and opportunity than other Negroes they knew.

From the beginning of their meetings, Walker kept notes on all the people who came, making a distinction between the "regulars" and those who came occasionally. There was the tall, strapping Midwesterner Frank Marshall Davis, whose lanky frame belied his sophistication. Frank was one of the most socially conscious among them and followed the Langston Hughes tradition of seeing poetry as a kind of jazz improvisation. He had published his first collection, *Black Man's Verse* (1935), and was working on his second, but he made his living as a journalist for the Negro press.

Arna Bontemps had already earned a reputation as one of the poets of the Negro Renaissance and had added considerably to his reputation with short stories and his 1931 novel, *God Sends Sunday*. After leaving a teaching position at Oakwood College, a Seventh-Day Adventist school, he landed in Chicago in 1934, hoping to secure a position at another Adventist school, Shiloh Academy. He continued to work on his historically based second novel, *Black Thunder: Gabriel's Revolt: Virginia, 1800*, which appeared in 1936. With two published novels, Bontemps was considered one of the most successful members of the group. He had been among those who received a Rosenwald Fellowship that helped to sustain his family when the Chicago job fell through. He made good use of it, finishing a third book only a year later. By 1938, he had a job as editorial supervisor with the Illinois Writers' Project. Walker, therefore, had an opportunity to develop a relationship with Bontemps, whom she saw often at work. They would grow closer later when both took positions in historically Black colleges in the South.

The two attractive brothers Edward and Alden Bland, born in New Orleans, had come to Chicago with their parents as children. They were closer to being native-born Chicagoans than anyone in the group and were friends with other natives like Gwendolyn Brooks, who may have made one or two visits to the group, though Walker does not seem to have recorded any. Alden had gone to college at the University of Chicago but worked at odd jobs before landing gainful employment at the post office. Walker remembered Edward, the poet and critic, more than Alden, an aspiring novelist, no doubt because of the kinship they shared as fellow poets. Edward's death in World War II brought an abrupt close to a promising career. At the time, Alden was working on *Behold a Cry*. The novel appeared in 1947, regarded as an important if overlooked migration novel that suffered from the timing of its appearance. Wright's *Native Son* overshadowed it, and while *Behold a Cry* was wedded to a proletarian sensibility, it was less explicit, if not forcefully anti-communist, in its message. Even the watchful eye of his editor, Maxwell Perkins, who had helped to shape the careers of major American writers such as Ernest Hemingway, was not sufficient to provide Bland with the necessary literary capital the book needed.

Another member Ted Ward, a small man whose voice bore the unmistakable sound of his hometown, Thibodaux, Louisiana, would figure prominently in Walker's life over the next few years. She had first met him as a fellow worker with the WPA. Ward's sole ambition was to be a playwright, and having spent four years in the Creative Writing program at the University of Wisconsin, he had come to Chicago in 1935 to seek his fortune. Like Richard Wright, he was attracted to the John Reed Club and followed its ideological lead in producing socially relevant work. Among the members of the group, he and Wright were the most alike politically and traveled in similar social circles, especially as the first two Negroes hired on the Federal Theatre Project. When Wright asked for a transfer to the Writers' Project, which he believed was ignoring Negroes, Ward remained and saw his controversial play *Big White Fog* in a stage production in 1938.

Wright encouraged his fellow postal worker Russell Marshall, whose strong interest in writing drew him to the group. He, like Wright, displayed a popular proletarian style that the group found fascinating. They often shared vivid stories from working their postal shifts, which they referred to as "the Black man's university."

There were few women, but among them was a young Fisk graduate, Marian Minus, who was then a graduate student in the anthropology program at the University of Chicago. Walker surmised that Minus seemed to have more than a passing acquaintance with Richard Wright. While her time with the group was short, she played a key role for the group after she returned to her home in New York. Once there, she began working with Dorothy West, beginning their lifelong friendship. West wanted to include the SSWG's work in her new magazine, *Challenge*, which began publishing in 1934. Minus was probably directly responsible for West's official sanction and recognition of the SSWG. In the April 1937 issue, in addition to featuring Minus's essay "Present Trends in Negro Literature," *Challenge* editor West identified "a young Chicago group. . . [who] hold meetings regularly, where their work is read for open discussion." She concluded, "The meetings, we are told, are lively and well attended."[3]

The only other woman who was a regular, and with whom Walker would become close, was Fern Gayden, a Chicago social worker. They had both graduated from Northwestern, Gayden preceding Walker by a few years. Gayden, like Frank Marshall Davis, was a native Kansan, had come to Chicago to pursue a career in law, but found too many doors closed to Black women. After graduating, she found it much easier to take a position in social work, a highly respected job in a period when so many families were on relief. Gayden was not a writer, but she felt a strong connection to the activist spirit she found among the group. She came to know Wright through his family, which was on her caseload. The group reflected Wright's interest in reaching out broadly to those with a shared interest and need to come together, and that included people like Fern Gayden.

After their first meeting, the SSWG group agreed to convene twice a month and confirmed the Abraham Lincoln Center on Oakwood Boulevard as their regular meeting place. Each member would bring some work for others to critique. Wright showed himself to be a committed, forceful leader. His ideas about the value of an independent organization—which is how he defined the SSWG group—and not a "communist front" were all new to Walker. He talked disparagingly of the political activities of the communist groups with which he had been involved, yet he was clearly as political as any of the communists she had met. For Walker, with limited associations with men outside of her father and brother, being in the company of this group of select individuals was an unforgettable experience.

The SSWG attracted a great deal of attention. Famous visitors like Langston Hughes would show up to read or there would be lively discussions with the group of social scientists from the University of Chicago, usually led by St. Clair Drake. With his Rosenwald Fellowship, he was beginning field research for a book that would eventually be published as part of *Deep South* (1941).[4] Drake would make his more visible contribution in *Black Metropolis: A Study of Negro Life in a Northern City* (1945), which he coauthored with Horace Cayton, whose visits always generated talk about Negro workers. The presence of these younger writers interested in researching and writing about broader social concerns, about how society was structured into classes, and the employment of Negroes, and especially the racism in the North, ensured a great deal of cross-fertilization.

What Walker found most interesting were the explanations from sociology, psychology, and psychiatry that related directly to her earlier experiences at the Institute for Juvenile Research. Sometimes Drake and Cayton tested their own theories with the group, which meant that everyone was reading broadly, venturing into disciplines that were new to them. These experiences would be helpful when she began to write more social criticism. They provided a great deal of insight into a range of topics, most of which she'd never thought about. She took pride in her ability to think independently and embraced the circumstances in which she found herself. She'd often write in her journal a well-developed analysis of a subject as if she were in conversation with someone about it. She had relied on her journals for composing poems and recording events, but she found herself chronicling her own times as her need to confess merged with her need to test the knowledge she was acquiring in both the political and social realms. Her ability to listen to and debate different points of view became useful practice for her later years as a much-sought-after speaker with a capacity to draw in a large and diverse audience.

The SSWG's commitment to social realism, at Wright's encouragement, was an appropriate framework for presenting their poetic, fictional, and theatrical work. Like her colleagues, Walker read the literature of the Left, embraced its principle of collective responsibility, and felt a renewed commitment to do something important with her talents and vision. That this was taking place in Chicago presents a contradiction worth noting, since the city saw its Black population increase in reverse proportion to the opportunities available to Negroes who continued migrating there to improve their lives. The SSWG's youth and energy, combined with their growing political consciousness, put them in the spotlight as agents of change, a new generation charged with the responsibility of creating a future. Their idealism was contagious, for it made them more acutely aware of their own agency, fearless in the face of circumstances that, in another time and place, would have stopped anyone short in their tracks.

To the outside observer, were it not for the enormous productivity of these South Side writers, it might simply have been another club that was organized and disbanded as time moved on. Although it would take fifty years before they would be assigned an identity or recognition, it was for Margaret Walker, as for others, the beginning of a full season for African American cultural production. Even without the towering figure of Wright, the SSWG's role was singularly important. Arna Bontemps, one of the first to remember this period in print, saw it as the second phase of Negro literary awakening,[5] no doubt because of his own connections to Harlem in the 1920s.

What distinguished this group of writers seems to be several commonalities. First, there was the presence and influence of the WPA, for which most of them worked. There was also the radical political climate of Chicago to which they all responded; the distance from their own youth, but not necessarily from the struggle of their recent past; the success of an earlier generation of Black writers from which they were not far removed; and their affinities for each other and their concern for their collective achievement. What seemed to bind them together was their utter disdain, at least on the surface, for any art that was not connected to its source.

Walker understood the years 1936 and 1937 as the context and the means for her greatest productivity, a time when her lyrical abilities were in high gear. At no point in her life would she find a situation where the nurturing of her art was as mutually satisfying, not even at the University of Iowa, where she would go in 1939 to refine her craft. In Chicago, she felt such deep emotional and social connection that even moments of despair offered creative inspiration. With few responsibilities other than those connected with the life of an artist, her confidence meant that she did not hesitate to share new work. Getting the feedback that she needed as quickly as possible meant that she learned to take the criticism and the praise in equal measure. The SSWG provided both.

Wright presented the greatest challenge to the SSWG, for although Bontemps had published more, Wright was getting all the attention. When the group began meeting, Wright had been publishing in left-wing journals, and he was beginning research for the short stories in *Uncle Tom's Children*; he had not even conceived of *Native Son*, his major novel. But it was clear that interest in his work fueled interest in theirs. William Attaway's novel *Blood on the Forge* (1941) and Willard Motley's *Knock on Any Door* (1947) were all wedded to the concepts of Black proletarian fiction that Wright's work was beginning to make popular.

Literature was not the only area of art that embraced a proletarian ideal. Katherine Dunham, for example, had founded a dance company on Chicago's South Side, suggesting how far-reaching was the belief in the superiority of art derived from the deepest sources of Black culture. Dance was not merely for entertainment but could also serve a socially constructive purpose. Based on her field research in Haiti, Black dance first gained attention as an art form.

* * *

Working on and sharing the poem "Southern Song" was one of Walker's most positive experiences during her time with the SSWG. At their second meeting she had announced she would read from her work, so eager was she to publish the poem. The fear of what might happen following her reading had not set in. "Southern Song" was one of her newer free-verse poems, which she had feverishly reworked for the occasion. Being in Chicago, she discovered, had made her even more conscious of her Southern roots. She composed the poem in first person:

> I want my body bathed again by southern suns; my soul
>   reclaimed again from southern land: I want to rest
>   again in southern fields; in grass and hay and clover
>   bloom; to lay my hand again upon the clay baked by a
>   southern sun, to touch the rain-soaked earth and smell
>   the smell of soil.[6]

The poem moves closer to the form that would find its full evolution in "For My People": long incremental free-verse stanzas followed by a series of indented lines that elaborate the meaning. The alliteration of "s" sounds and repetition of "southern" give the poem needed emphasis, and the catalog of images undercuts what at first appears to be a tranquil, pastoral scene. Though the group members were not especially fond of nature poetry, they would have recognized the poem's social intent, as the final lines make clear:

> I want no mobs to wrench me from my southern rest; no
>   forms to take me in the night and burn my shack and
>   make for me a nightmare full of oil and flame.
> I want my careless song to strike no minor key; no fiend to
>   stand between my body's southern song—the fusion of
>   the South, my body's song and me.[7]

"Southern Song" is a statement about voice, one that synthesizes the natural and social worlds. Since Walker is speaking from a specific cultural matrix, her vision is inclusive and holistic. The poem establishes a connection to that which is primal, as the mythic voice struggles to make experience intelligible and give order, meaning, and unity to the images, chaos, fragments, and phenomena from a dismembered culture. Her memory of the South permits Walker to enter history and make it sacred.

Guided by their youthful revolutionary spirit, the SSWG would have seen this poem as a far cry from many of the sentiments that appeared in the pages of the leftist journals. Walker demonstrates a remarkable ability to remain historically grounded and technically skillful at the same time. She was not shying away from racial concerns. In fact, the poem locates itself in a reality whose overtones are clearly racial: "forms to . . . burn my shack," and "nightmare full of oil and flame." What this piece achieves, it does through the compactness of the sensory details and the precision of its imagery. While the subjective aspect of the poet's desire is achieved with a repetition of the opening phrase, "I want . . .," the action centers around the author as agent reclaiming the South through a sensory experience, the sounds and smells of Southern earth.

By juxtaposing a pastoral image with the South's "other" reality, Walker shifts the mood from desire to resistance. The contradiction is established linguistically: the object of desire expressed longingly in the first stanza, "I want my body bathed . . .," then shifts to strident denunciation in the second, "I want no mobs. . . ." What is at first an open embrace becomes rejection and resistance in the third and fourth stanzas. To evoke memory and imagination is also to risk the painful thought of violence and destruction, the "mobs that wrench . . . from southern rest." The resistance expressed is doubled-edged. The nightmare of the past must not be repeated; neither must the past be allowed to cause psychic divisions. The poem, therefore, ends with reconciliation: "the fusion of the South," the integration of the self and memory—"my body's song"—and history—"my body's southern song." Thus, while the threat of the violent past is evoked in a "careless song," the resistant imagination asserts the humanistic self.

After she had read her poem, she steeled herself for the criticism that was to follow, having seen the dynamics in the meetings. When she finished, she looked out at the faces. There was nothing but silence. Ted Ward and Wright both offered comments that were surprisingly kind. Wright then asked her if she thought the poem was ready to be seen in print. Though she considered it one of her best poems, she hesitated for a moment, not wanting to appear overly confident. Before she could answer, the others chimed in with generous praise.

The next reader was not as lucky. The criticism was sharp, and Walker wondered how she would bear up if this had been aimed at her. It was then Wright's turn. She had expected to hear another one of his hard-hitting poems like those she'd seen in *New Masses*. He had not read aloud from his work in some time, and she was eager to hear something new. "Big Boy Leaves Home" was nearly finished, and he read the opening sections to the group. Wright's prose exhibited a power that she did not know how to describe at the time. "I kept thinking, my God, how that man can write,"[8] she wrote in recalling that experience. She was very discerning in her sensibilities as she listened to various readers. Some of the writers seemed to enjoy the shock effect on the audience. She had grown comfortable enough by the third meeting not to let her initial shyness prevent her from speaking. After that, her strong personality and forceful opinions never failed to evoke surprise.

During the following year, Walker attended every meeting. Without knowing it, she had become part of a radical movement, as well as one of Wright's closest friends. But it would be a mistake to assume that her political development was exclusively a function of their relationship. Even before they met, she was actively attending communist-supported events and meeting many people on the Left. After attending the National Negro Congress, where she'd heard Hughes, she had attended the Conference of Midwest Writers that met in downtown Chicago in June 1936. She was yet to make a direct connection between "communist" and "writer" and probably wouldn't have had it not been for Frank Marshall Davis's questions at the next meeting of the SSWG. Davis asked about the "communists" who spoke at the conference, knowing that Wright had been one of the speakers. It was only then that she realized that Wright must have been a communist! "The whole thing sank in gradually. I honestly didn't know what Communism or Marxism meant. . . . My sister knew more about Hitler and Stalin than I did."[9] Confusion about who was a communist and who wasn't led her to read more. But it also led to fellow staff Jack Scher's warning one afternoon as she was leaving the project office. "Margaret, I hope you will get to know all these people on the Project without getting to be a part of them and all they represent. Observe them; don't join them," he said.[10]

Although Walker's poetry was not political in the same way as Wright's was, most notably his poem "I Have Seen Black Hands," she summarized their joint practice: "Suspended in time somewhere between the Writers' Project and the South Side Writers' Group . . . three forms of writing took place in our consciousness, conversations, and action. We sat together and worked on the forms of poetry, the free verse things, and I came up with my long line or strophic form, punctuated by a short line."[11]

The "consciousness, conversations, and action" to which Walker refers do not imply a division between artistic validity and political message. The group members never questioned their roles as representatives of the masses, nor the source and value of their art. The Great Depression was for them a cultural marker and a signifying moment, the context drawing them into the orbit of radical ideas. The process of their radicalization was genuine, not faddish; Blacks and communists sought common solutions to their problems, common answers to their questions.

Reading back from today, we see a legacy shaped by the narratives of modernism as it in turn was given shape and meaning by New Criticism as a literary trend. In order to fully recognize and appreciate the poetic innovations of T. S. Eliot, Ezra Pound, and William Butler Yeats, who came to personify the modernist impulse, much of that which fed and fueled its development had to be ignored, if not rejected. By offering an alternative vision of "radical," shifting away from the sphere of the social to the sphere of the imagination, that is, literary experimentation, modernism created a privileged space for its most visible practices, which many considered the domain of "pure art."

Both Black artists and women had thrived on a kind of free-spirited radicalism with the advent of World War II, and their work had exploded. Modernism became consolidated and gained its authority by establishing rigid definitions and categories that defined as "political" one set of ideas. Political for them came to mean denying the validity of any associated artistic production. As multiple forces in the 1930s gave shape to ideas about greater inclusiveness, justice, and equality, the distinctions between "political" and "apolitical" art grew sharper; it was "political art"—meaning any art that espoused social ideas—that had less aesthetic value. Likewise, all legitimate criticism of the Left became undifferentiated as anti-communist propaganda.

For the SSWG members, distinctions between the "political" and the "aesthetic" were ultimately less important than their own existence as writers at a particular moment in time. Theirs was a generation without any real precedent; to realize their ambitions as writers and artists meant that they existed on a continuum between their individual experiences and their collectively bound histories. But it is also possible to attribute political meaning to everything they did, in the sense that they knew their writing was a negotiation for power and a place in the world; it was an explicit statement about their human, civil, and equal rights. Their process was more eclectic than strictly ideological, as Walker's work demonstrates. They were in search of tools that would best shape their literary art and give them access to a broader public. It is significant that Walker, who was the least sophisticated member of the group in traditional political terms, never found herself isolated or alienated from those who knew far more than she did.

Wright's conflicts with the leaders of the Communist Party, who wanted him to organize, recruit, and distribute the party's literature, maintained a shadowy presence over the SSWG. He did not want anyone to tell him how to write, although he had clearly learned a great deal about the craft from his party affiliation. He was especially concerned that there be no restrictions in the development of something quite new, "Negro literature."[12] His refusal to accept and willingly execute without question his assignments caused him to eventually withdraw membership from the Communist Party, whose leaders routinely criticized his individualism. He believed that socialist realism, though important, was too limiting for depicting the African American experience. Thus, he had come to the SSWG with a deep need to assert an independent voice, hoping to find common ground.

That search became part of their collective practice in another way as well. They spent weeks working on a document that Wright believed they should publish as the group's manifesto. They wanted to craft a language that would explain the relationship between art and the social movement, between the literature of the past and the present. It was to be their "blueprint" for Negro writing offered as the statement of their generation. Unity around the document was impossible, however, because they were engaging in a debate over issues that had been gaining increased attention in the twentieth century. While they understood that their writing needed to be different, they lacked a critical apparatus for discussing this outside of what Wright, steeped in communist ideology, provided. They were never able to reach a consensus, but Wright was determined to see the piece in print.

"Blueprint for Negro Writing" made its first appearance in what was to be the final issue of *New Challenge*, fall 1937, with Wright as the sole author. The issue included work by four other members of what was referred to as "the Chicago group": Frank Marshall Davis, Robert Davis, Allyn Keith, and Margaret Walker. Minus had done her job well, for her name appeared on the masthead as one of the editors for the journal, and she supported Wright in getting West to shift from its original name, *Challenge*. By the time the issue appeared, Wright had moved to New York, and his name is listed as the journal's associate editor.[13] West maintained that Wright's interest in taking over the journal made her extremely cautious. They had differences that could not be resolved, which eventually led to the journal's demise.[14]

If his decision to list his name alone disturbed any of SSWG, there must have been some consolation for the names of the most frequent attendees alongside Langston Hughes, Alain Locke, Sterling A. Brown, Owen Dodson, Ralph Ellison, Henry Moon, and Eugene Holmes. More important, "Blueprint" appeared as the first essay in a forum that included "A Note on Negro Nationalism," by Allyn Keith, a pseudonym for an unidentified SSWG member, and Holmes's "Problems Facing the Negro Writer Today."[15] Both are little-known essays from 1930s that parallel Hughes's far-better-known 1926 essay "The Negro Artist and the Racial Mountain," indicating a certain self-reflexivity that looked ahead to the future of African American literary discourse. Because of its association with Wright, "Blueprint" is the only essay from the volume that has seen multiple reprintings, with little understanding of its origins. It remains, nevertheless, the most important literary record of the SSWG's existence, as much as it prefigured the major lines of argument taking shape in the Black Arts Movement of the 1970s.

New Challenge was a singular opportunity to bring attention to the SSWG as individuals and as a community of writers. They had vetted each other's work within the group and seen its evolution into print. Walker had four poems in that issue, including her favorite and most important poem to date, "Southern Song." While the SSWG would be short-lived, their sense of community was not, since most members continued to maintain close ties to one another.

The amount and extent of the SSWG's collective work cannot be overestimated. Drake, Cayton, and Wright worked together closely in encouraging Wright to complete *Twelve Million Black Voices* (1941), the folk history he wrote to accompany Ross Suskind's photographs. Wright later repaid the favor by writing the introduction for Drake and Cayton's *Black Metropolis: A Study of Negro Life in a Northern City* (1945). Other members collaborated outside the collective. In the same year, Bontemps teamed up with Jack Conroy to publish *They Seek a City*, another study of the formation of Chicago's Black community. Because many shared both a WPA and SSWG history, these crossovers between and among them occurred easily and often. Those who did not meet at Lincoln Center, or whose visits were so infrequent as to be negligible, like Willard Motley, William Attaway, and Frank Yerby, were nevertheless part of the extended family of Chicago writers and artists who were invested in a process that prospered into an impressive legacy.

In its meetings, the writers of the SSWG created an independent space to comment on issues and concerns that were part of a larger public dialogue. It allowed Walker to recognize her sheltered world. Now, only nine months after moving to the South Side of Chicago, she better understood a city stripped of all pretensions. The writers saw themselves as members of a race that had survived slavery and its aftermath, and they felt challenged to find ways to articulate both the consciousness and the experiences of Black people in an accessible language. They did not call for a rejection of social realism—as evidenced by the sizable number of writers who were influenced by the tradition of the "protest novel," a tradition attributed to Wright. They recognized the need to tell their own stories, and they searched for ways to capture the meaning and nature of the Black experience through them. Richard Wright, Ted Ward, and Frank Marshall Davis all spoke in the familiar rhetoric of the Left, a language that Walker grasped quickly. None of the SSWG members disavowed Wright's orientation toward writing as the weapon of the masses. While many differences were apparent in the group, especially over the role and relationship of the Communist Party to the Black community, they never argued about the antiracist nature of artistic expression.

An inventory of their publications from this period suggests that the SSWG writers did not limit themselves to periodicals on the Left. Their work appeared in Negro newspapers like the *Chicago Defender*; familiar Black journals, *The Crisis*, *Messenger*, and *Opportunity*; and they also made frequent appearances in a host of Black journals long since forgotten such as *Abbott's Monthly* (1930–1933), *Brown Magazine* (1936–1945), and *Mirror* (1936). The writers of the

Harlem Renaissance had been announced in a special issue of the *Survey Graphic* devoted to the "New Negro" in 1925. But the SSWG's association with the Left prevented it from having such mainstream support in the 1930s.

Most of the group members were little concerned about the wide-ranging and often negative response to literary radicalism. For one reason, the Left had control of certain media and a well-established publishing apparatus that enabled its voice to be heard above most detractors. It was difficult to find in Chicago in the mid-1930s a force strong enough to refute the claims of those who supported fundamental social change and revolution. Considering the networks established through the WPA, together with the communist movement, there were more publishing opportunities in the 1930s than in the previous decade, although the opposite has been the common perception.

Perhaps the most-sustained speculation about this period has to do with the relationship that developed between Margaret Walker and Richard Wright. Walker recalled that after the second meeting of the group, Wright asked her if he could walk her home and gave her John Reed's *Ten Days That Shook the World*. Although he was at odds with the Communist Party, he talked about it incessantly, something that continued to baffle her. Talking to Walker, a neophyte on political ideas, Wright could assume the role of teacher. He explained to her the relationship between racism and class struggle. The popularity of the labor movement in Chicago made their discussions lively. She respected Wright's keen intelligence, and because he had only a grade school education, she was constantly in awe. She trusted his suggestions for books to read. They discovered they could and did talk about everything. She found his social theories strange, his radicalism at times frightening. He accused her of confusing the search for a spiritual truth with the truth about violence and racist oppression that confronted Black people daily. She saw some good and evil in everyone and insisted on maintaining her belief in rational humanity. She thought that Wright saw things too narrowly and was too quick to form opinions about Southern whites. He confessed to hating the South, but he did his best writing out of that feeling. Their disagreements kept them in constant dialogue. They met at work, walked home routinely after the SSWG meetings, and discussed common readings. To Walker, Wright was a brilliant and dynamic artist who was already in the limelight. He critiqued her writing; she did a considerable amount of editing of his work. Wright was careful not to violate her sensibilities, for he learned quickly how much she hated obscene language and sexist jokes.

Independent-minded and yet naïve, Walker found intriguing the depth and range of Wright's questions. The result was an expansion of her thinking, as illustrated by one of her journal entries exploring the relationship between aesthetics and propaganda:

Art is a wholistic [*sic*] enterprise, it is aesthetic, personal, social, and technical; the artist can no more divorce himself from his art than he can his personality from the medium of his art. Art reflects the social trends and conditions or ideology of the artist's time. Technique is the tool. Art is never only one of the four. All art forms have proportion, movement, variety, tone, and color, only the medium is different. The greater the art, the greater the propaganda.[16]

The two spent hours debating these topics with each other and with other members of the group as well. She engaged in these dialogues not only because she was genuinely interested, but also because she wanted to be more than that *girl* that got included in the group only because she appeared to conform to the ideas they proposed.

The word she most often used when referring to Richard Wright is "amazing." His hunger for knowledge seemed to be insatiable, driven by what he did not have or had been prevented from having. Just as Wright would count on good friends Allison Davis, Horace Cayton, and St. Clair Drake, he had aligned himself with young Jewish intellectuals he encountered in the communist movement. Both groups found it difficult to explain Wright, someone who lacked formal education and seemed superior to them all. She would always believe she understood him more than anyone: Wright would throw himself into whatever was presented to him so convinced was he that nothing was too difficult for him to master. He could talk and seemed to know about every subject and was as comfortable around the writers as he was the intellectuals, a distinction commonly referred to during the period. At twenty-seven, Wright had probably done enough reading to have earned him several degrees. He was an intellectual giant, as much as he was the "daemonic genius"[17] that she would later write about.

Out of this intense desire to learn and educate himself, Wright had become a model of organization. Once when she had stopped by his office desk so that they could go to a SSWG meeting together, he was on a writing binge and didn't see her standing there. She watched as he wrote a line on a half sheet of paper, his cigarette dropping a chain of ashes to the floor as he inhaled more smoke. A moment later, he would ball the paper up frantically and toss it into the wastepaper basket. Sensing that he was unaware of the time, she cleared her throat to get his attention. He clinched his fists, squared his shoulders, and looked up at her wearily. She thought to herself, how is he ever going to have the energy to run tonight's meeting? He looks as if he's been fighting a bull. He stacked the papers on his desk, emptied the ashtray one more time, and grabbed his coat, signaling that they should go. He was silent for most of the walk to Lincoln Center but became very animated when the meeting began. As they concluded, he told the group that he thought Walker should serve as the convener for the next session. Everyone looked around at each other but said nothing. On the way home, she

learned that he had passed the exam for the post office, which meant he had received notification to return as a permanent employee. He was troubled and she
remembered asking him if he wanted to be a postman all of his life as well as his
response. "Bad as I need money, it was the hardest decision I ever made in my
life. . . . I want my life to count for something. I don't want to waste it or throw it
away. It's got to be worthwhile," he told her.[18]

When she reported for her WPA assignment the following week, she learned
that she had been given a promotion. It meant that she could now turn in chapters from the new novel she had begun, "Goose Island." Eager to let Wright know
the good news, she went to his floor, only to learn that he was home ill. She had
never been to his house, since they always met at hers, but she knew the address
since she had been doing some mailings for the SSWG. On Indiana Avenue, she
climbed the stairs to the third floor that opened up to a series of doors very close
together. She knocked at the door bearing the number she had been told and discovered Wright in a tiny space he called his room. There was no place to put the
soup and the oranges she had brought and no place to sit. No, he did not have a
kitchen, he told her embarrassingly; he had moved there to give his mother, aunt,
and brother more space in their apartment that had only one bedroom for the
four of them.

Walker had about 300 handwritten pages of the novel, all of which had been
inspired by her experiences in Chicago. The group had been discussing the use
of folk materials in writing, and those working on novels agreed to try this. She
wanted a direct connection to the spirituals and the folk literature she had grown
up with and decided to use lines from these songs to title her chapters. Wright
had already begun "Big Boy Leaves Home," where he could apply the Southern
folk dialect in an effective manner in a scene with the boys engaged in playful
banter among themselves.

She decided to try something different. Following the idyllic opening scene
of her novel manuscript comes a sharp contrast. There is an accidental death, a
chase, and a lynching, all violent acts that follow the young boys' brutal awakening to Southern racism. She did not realize how closely her story sounded like
Wright's, and when she asked him what he thought, he was not very forthcoming.
We wonder, however, what might have happened if Wright had been more encouraging about these early attempts at fiction. They had perhaps become com-
petitors in his mind, although Walker saw herself far from being the developed
artist that she had planned to become. It was clear that his fiction, at least in their
conversations, was to take precedence over hers. By telling her that she should
stick with poetry, now that he had left it behind, he eliminated any real competition between them. Wright would have realized, too, that poetry occupied a different and, some believed, smaller place in the literary hierarchy. She concurred
with him that her forte was poetry and was happy to see herself as a beginner,

a less-developed talent. This is not to say that Wright minimized her brilliance and her ambition. He was generous with praise at the same time that he was a stern taskmaster. When her poems began to appear later, he had taken her out to dinner, quoting T. S. Eliot to her and announcing her as his logical successor. The irony is that bending to the pressure of a subordinate role, she could accept the full benefit of Wright's rigorous instruction and advice. In warning her of those who would try to defeat her, he made her stronger. When he told her that a Negro need not expect to publish in *Poetry*, it made her more determined to do so.

Margaret Walker understood that Chicago had been her Renaissance. It paralleled her Southern home environment—affirming, intellectually stimulating, and filled with opportunities for training. Yet, it did not replace the South. "Southern Song" had enabled her to work through the contrasting feelings she harbored for that native South: her deep emotional connection to the land and its people, her hatred for the social landscape that she had now learned to express in unequivocal terms. The poem had given her the tone and framework of "For My People." She sensed that she now had the tools for expressing this dilemma. Unlike the nineteenth-century writer Ralph Waldo Emerson, Walker never gravitated toward a life of solitude, though she would later understand the importance of a quiet place to work. Her poetry, under the nurturing of Richard Wright, the SSWG, and the cultural and political environment of Chicago, came to allegorize the relationship between the personal space of the lyric and the often painful facts of history. She felt the forces of conflict, but she was learning to balance them in her poetic voice.

Immersion in a political ideology has been severely criticized by those suspicious of the Left and its subsequent impact on American life and culture. Many believe that the Communist Party and its multifaceted programs represented powerful opportunists who took advantage of unsuspecting innocents. In Walker's case, transformation or immersion identified a deeper need that she was unable to comprehend. Her vulnerability, if it can be called that, was in fact a functional release. She seemed to be perfectly willing to repudiate her traditional academic background and revel in a newfound freedom associated with studio parties and radical intellectuals, the professional world of struggling young writers, painters, musicians, dancers, actors, journalists, and even the occasional paid functionaries of the Communist Party USA. These were not ends in themselves, as they would be for far too many during this era, and Walker demonstrates that the means can indeed produce positive results.

One indication of this transformation and immersion occurred less than a year after she'd become a SSWG member. In February 1937, she joined the Young Communist League, confirming her political engagement on the other hand and at the same time believing this to be a step toward increased productivity and publishing success. Even if she later regarded this decision as naïve, she made it with conviction and a sense of her empowerment as a woman. Her decision followed the self-acknowledgment of all she had learned about Marxism, communism, the revolutionary movement, and the labor movement. She was anti-fascist and believed that this heightened awareness required greater responsibility on her part, especially as a woman. Confidently she wrote in her journal:

> I'm on my way to communism, into class consciousness. I feel impelled to do and speak for all womanhood, especially working womanhood through my voice as a Negro woman. I had begun to see what a grave responsibility has been gradually settling down upon me. I must speak for the maid, the cook, the washer-woman, domestic servants. I must speak for the midwife and muse, for the farmer's wife and for the young girls struggling for an education. The human being who is exploited sexually and economically first because she is a woman and second because she is black. I must show what an awful psychological effect this has had on us and how we must find our way out. I SEE MY JOB.[19] [emphasis original]

At twenty-one, she could not take this revelation lightly. What she did not know was that Wright was preparing her to take over leadership of the SSWG. He had given his energy and his voice to the group, serving as its pivotal center, but as an organization, it would have to form its own legs and grow and to defend itself against the charges of being a "nationalist deviation," the phrase communists attributed to ethnic and racial groups who wanted an exclusive organization. The SSWG saw its work as crucial for creating an independent voice for Negro writers. In a few months, Wright would go to New York, testing the group's ability to survive the departure of his powerful influence. But the door was already open to her liberation, and Walker came to believe that what she needed could be fulfilled from within. That the instrument had been her relationship with a card-carrying communist motivated by his own ambitions does not matter. What does matter is that she resolved the dilemma that had been troubling her for some time. The birth of her new political awareness was simultaneously the birth of a more committed poet and artist.

During her four years in Chicago, it seemed to Walker that the city was full of young Negroes, working for the WPA, studying at the University of Chicago and other nearby institutions, and participating in radical movement activities. In many ways, Walker was correct. That the emergence of so many Black writers, enough to constitute a second Renaissance, was coterminous with a migration that had increased the Black population by 400 percent meant that Walker was simultaeously typical and atypical. She was younger than most of her peer group, but like most of them, she was from the South. Despite the devastating effects of the Depression, interest in race and ethnic relations and in Negro life and culture had increased since the Harlem Renaissance. That interest in the 1930s was of a different order. The artistic creativity that had been so visible in New York and elsewhere now added an intensification of active will, a directed sense of purpose and ambition that was contagious for a generation that would extend well into the 1940s. If the young Negro social scientists offered serious challenges to the prevailing racist interpretations of Negro ability, they also helped to fuel the literary imagination of people like Margaret Walker. It was also true that as Negro intellectuals they had had less time—and could ill afford—to create the kind of hierarchies and exclusions mirroring the broader society; they, therefore, welcomed each other's presence, relishing in the growth of their numbers. Concentrated in Chicago, there were enough of them to create a defiant, visionary, radical ferment. The most optimistic interpretation was that Negroes were reaching their full potential at long last.

Even though the majority of the SSWG did not join the Communist Party, their curiosity drew them into the party's orbit. As aspiring Negro writers and graduate students alike, they traveled in the same circles, showing little cautiousness in an era before McCarthyism became a hardened anti-communism. Wright's radical allegiances were never masked, and Walker believed that Wright invited individuals to join the SSWG precisely because of the likelihood of their shared perspectives. Neither was the group limited to writers of poetry, prose, and plays. They were united around their belief in the need for a collective response to the deep social and economic crisis that threatened Black achievement. Communism might have been the "working man's religion," but it was not entirely free from the racism that permeated the larger society. Bound together by a sense of empowerment as much as by their search for a distinctive expression and a set of ideas to guide them, the more they talked, the more passionately they became. Not as communists, but there was something attractively subversive about what they were doing.

If Chicago during the 1930s was the shaping-place that caused Arna Bontemps and Robert Bone to refer to a "Chicago Renaissance," then the SSWG, which would last nearly two years, must be considered its incubator. There was no need for pretense among the newly arrived to Chicago, whether they had the benefit of a college education or not. They had each experienced the leveling effect of the Great Depression. Their differences gave them inspiration, and they formed friendships and partnerships that would last beyond any specific ideology that had brought them together. Gayden and Russell Marshall, in fact, would reunite with Walker at the University of Mississippi on the twenty-fifth anniversary of Wright's death in 1985. Both spoke warmly of their time as members of the group—looking directly at Walker—and of being aware that they were doing something very special indeed.[20]

There is some speculation as to why Gwendolyn Brooks, a native Chicagoan, did not figure prominently in the South Side Writers group. Further speculation surrounds whether there was any competition between Brooks and Walker, the first two major Black women poets in the twentieth century. Except for meeting at a house party, Walker made no other references to Brooks during the four years she remained in Chicago. Born two years apart, there were some significant similarities in their lives. Both grew up in Methodist families, met and were encouraged by Langston Hughes as teenagers, were local celebrities as teenage poets, had mothers actively promote their careers, were in writers' groups that met at the South Side Arts Center, and had major poems published in *Poetry*. Walker's mentor at Iowa, Paul Engle, would become a reviewer for Brooks's books. Their awards distinguished them, although not in equal measure: Walker was the first Black writer to win the Yale Award and Brooks, the Pulitzer Prize. Those who knew them saw two different personalities: Walker was talkative and engaging; Brooks, quiet and shy. The Brooks and Walker families fit the profile for many upwardly mobile Black families of the period, who measured their success in terms of aspirations, not their financial status. These class perceptions carried over into their friendships and acquaintances and parents who were fearful of "bad influences." Brooks and Walker benefited from a strong elementary and secondary education, which ensured their successful careers. The conclusion that most people came to is that for all their similarities, the two women were acquaintances rather than friends.

The differences between the two women provide useful insights into the social networks South and North, and publishing choices for Blacks during the period. A thriving arts community in Chicago not only had a leading journal, *Poetry*, but also an active community of influential patrons, like Inez Cunningham Stark who knew Brooks before she enrolled in her South Side Community Art Center's (SSCAC) poetry group in 1941. As a cultural institution centered in the Black community, the SSCAC was a stimulus for art, culture, and politics generally. In addition to Brooks, the group included burgeoning artists who at that time already had name recognition. Margaret Taylor Goss was an artist who also wrote poetry, while Edward Bland and Margaret Danner were both poets. When Brooks joined the group, she had completed only two years at Wilson Junior College, married a fellow poet, given birth to her first child, and was well placed to take advantage of all that Stark had to offer. Bland's early death left Brooks and Danner, also a young published poet, and who would eventually become an editor at *Poetry*. It was Brooks with whom Starks developed a close working relationship and whose career she enabled. Through Starks, Brooks met the right people, made contacts in the publishing world, and soon signed with Harper's, whose impressive list of writers included Wright. Elizabeth Lawrence, Brooks's editor at Harper's, was dedicated to getting Brooks the best advice in shepherding her work through to publication. After her first book, *A Street in Bronzeville*, Brooks sent Lawrence two manuscripts, *Maud Martha*, under another name, and the future Pulitzer Prize–winning *Annie Allen*. We would have to conclude that Lawrence's knowledge as an editor was an appropriate match for Brooks's talent as a poet, when she rejected *Maud Martha*, but sent the *Annie Allen* manuscript to poet Genevieve Haggard whose eight-page review carefully outlined revisions. Brooks was an attentive listener and appreciative student for whom the process worked well. From Taggard and Lawrence, Brooks's collection had the careful vetting from those most familiar with the literary climate and hierarchical nature of commercial publishing world. Brooks's network included three major women writers and editors, just as *Annie Allen* drew the attention of major reviewers. *Maud Martha* came on the heels of the prize-winning volume, only adding to Brooks's acclaim. These personal and professional networks served as gateways to greater success and sustained public recognition. According to biographer George Kent, Brooks's "adventure with the white liberal critical consensus would continue its present course for seventeen years and become the most extraordinary one experienced by a black poet."[21] Brooks's singular success would foreshadow what could and did happen with a generation some decades later.

In contrast, Walker, who had already left Chicago by the time Stark inaugurated the poetry workshop, experienced few if any professional benefits of a social network before she left the South. That network for Walker was a direct result of Chicago's radicalized political culture during the 1930s, one that Brooks carefully avoided. As the only woman writer at the initial meeting of the SSWG, Walker played an organizational role, especially after the departure of founding member Richard Wright, when she served as convener. Because of the number of people who dropped in for a session now and then, and the kinds of political debates among the members, sessions were not always dedicated writing workshops. Had this not been the case, they would have produced far more work with greater visibility.

Walker's interest in poetry as a child was more or less contained just as racial segregation precluded a young Black girl a wealthy white patron or a sponsor during her years in New Orleans. Her only choice was formal education as an entry into the writing world, the one she actively pursued. Any sponsorship she had came through academic mentors, Hungerford at Northwestern, and Engle, and to a certain extent years later, Norman Foerster at Iowa. She won the Yale Award through her own persistence: she would submit her work three times before getting it. While Walker benefited enormously from the Iowa Writers Workshop, and received tremendous support from her professors, for both of her advanced degrees, she was practical: she needed security, and a teaching career was the best choice for a young educated Black woman who was not married and lived in the South. During the era of segregation, most of Walker's generation who received advanced degrees found their calling in Negro colleges. It meant joining a community of unusually talented individuals with grand visions and limited opportunities. Walker was considered one of those poets between two worlds, as R. Baxter Miller called them, who entered their careers between 1940 and 1960, often carrying the remnants of both with them. For Miller, Walker and Brooks joined a host of important but ultimately lesser-known poets, including Melvin Tolson, Owen Dodson, Dudley Randall, Margaret Danner, Robert Hayden, and we might add to this list expatriate poet James Emmanuel, along with a number of college teacher-poets who wrote and published independently without the expectation of much recognition. Brooks had departed from the tradition of formal, advanced education. With the support of well-connected social networks, Brooks could move more easily from early identification of her extraordinary talent into a professional career.

When we take out of the equation a judgment about the quality of their work, none of these writers reached the status or acclaim that Brooks did. One wonders, for example, why Robert Hayden, who came closest to writing in the tradition of American modernism that American critics privileged, did not receive more critical attention earlier. Alain Locke seems to have been correct in his assessment in a 1934 essay that Black artists were the "victim[s] of two vicious extremes—uncritical praise or calculated disparagement."[22] There was little in between, and few Black poets could expect to have their work garner serious critical attention, especially in the middle of the twentieth century. The Brooks exception teaches an important lesson. Sustained social networks and an accompanying critical apparatus—which was not available until years later for most Black writers—are essential ingredients for the kind of career goals that only a few of these writers achieved, and which many more desired.

Walker's world found what she believed to be an adequate parallel in her formal education. If we consider the alternative, the measure of success would have to be different. Walker would eventually have a woman editor who showed real interest in her work, Dorothy Santillana at Houghton Mifflin, but neither the will nor the way for developing a sustained professional relationship was possible at that late stage in her career. Her academic identity was already formed, and her fierce independence would not allow submission to the authority of others. By the time *Jubilee* was published, her personal and professional goals had shifted. Though Santillana prodded, offering advances on future books that Walker considered and even started to write, she was unable to deliver much more for the commercial publishing market after 1966. She could not easily shift gears. Her dual identity as an educator and a professional writer she could not separate, and the former was in charge. In addition to her academic training by all white men, Walker's goal had been to publish a single book at each juncture of her life, which is what she did. She may have wanted to build an empire of sorts, at least a legacy one could detect through others. "To teach is to lead, to learn is to change the world," something she wrote years later, could have been her motto.

Lerone Bennett, Walker, Gwendolyn Brooks, Margaret Burroughs, and Val
Gray Ward often saw each other at Chicago gatherings

Brooks and Walker did, however, become friends and were part of a more informal yet highly visible intellectual community in later years that included the
historian Lerone Bennett, artist Margaret Burroughs, and actress-producer Val
Gray Ward. Except for Brooks, they were all associated with Mississippi, and their
gatherings were legendary. Just as the surviving SSWG members would meet one
more time, Walker and Brooks met for the last time in March 1994. Margaret
Burroughs, who had founded with her husband the DuSable Museum of African
American Culture, asked them to do a joint appearance in a symposium appropriately called "Women of Arts and Letters in the Chicago Renaissance." When
asked to talk about the SSWG, Brooks made clear her preference for tracing
her identity to sources other than the leftist movement and the WPA. Walker
gave full credit to the SSWG, and her WPA and leftist associations during her
Chicago years. Both women understood who they were and the pathways they
had elected to follow had begun by the time they had met each other in Chicago
during the 1930s.

9

Marriage Is a Green Apple

Even though most of her time was spent going to meetings, working, reading, writing, and studying with Wright, Walker had begun to respond to the advances of a young minister James Russell Brown sometime during 1936. A journal reference to a young man her friend Ernestine Smith had introduced to her suggested that she had met him at St. Matthew as early as 1935 and they had a brief conversation, during which she admitted that she "could not do without church . . . a habit . . . a necessity . . . every moral, physical and intellectual act is motivated by something spiritual.[1] This was probably one of the last mixers she attended before she stopped going to church altogether. Brown, who soon became the "JRB" of her journals, had completed his undergraduate education in Wichita, Kansas, and, like so many other young Negroes, came to Chicago to further his education. He had written a thesis on Christianity and the Negro at Howard University's School of Religion and now wanted to complete his training in order to assume a leadership role in the African Methodist Episcopal Ministry at the Chicago Theological Seminary. Many of the smaller seminaries with high enrollments of Negro students had an agreement with the University of Chicago's Divinity School that allowed them to take classes at both institutions. Students mingled freely with one another on the combined campuses, adding to their sense of themselves as a critical mass of talented individuals.

Typical of those in his generation who believed that ministers must be educated, Brown would become part of an available pool of administrators for Negro schools and colleges. After active duty in the US Navy, he held appointments in Kansas, Colorado and California and became Dean at the Bishop Williams School of Religion in Kansas City. Because of the strong connection between religion and education, Negro seminaries were in abundance, making the history of Black education, then as now, inseparable from the history of the institutional Black church. Because Walker was a symbol of this connection, having grown up on the campus of New Orleans University, she would see in Brown aspirations similar to those her father had. In one sense, Brown was the right "fit": an ordained minister with an advanced degree in theology, which ensured his ability to shuttle between a career in higher education and one as the pastor of one of the larger churches.

The first meeting with JRB left her very impressed. But he seemed captivated the moment he saw her, a smart young Negro woman, whose father also

The House Where My Soul Lives. Maryemma Graham, Oxford University Press. © Oxford University Press 2022.
DOI: 10.1093/oso/9780195341232.003.0009

happened to be a minister. That there was a physical attraction between them was clear at the outset. But she was a novice at negotiating relationships with men, which produced a great deal of anxiety whenever they saw each other. Her work with the WPA and the circle of associated friends she had met made demands on her that included regular attendance at political meetings and rallies. When Brown first learned this, he was more fascinated since he had yet to meet any Negro women who were as openly assertive as she was.

On the morning she saw him after an absence of many months, she felt immediately drawn to him, and they talked for nearly an hour. "It reminds me of our first league days in Birmingham," she wrote in her journal. "Only there is something more thrilling now, more intensely interesting. It almost frightens me." Moving into unknown territory intellectually and socially, she was very cautious, especially since it reminded her of those times when she was "hungry for someone interesting to talk to or write."[2]

On the morning in question, she sensed that he seemed more interested in her work than before, asking about her poetry in particular, even though the conversation eventually got around "to the Christian endeavor again." Soon they were seeing each other regularly. She admitted feeling a little frightened, "but I do not want this budding friendship to get away from me. This fellow JRB is most charming affable and promising."[3]

Walker made detailed entries in her journals on their activities between their meeting in 1936 and summer 1937. She struggled with her feelings from the beginning: a strong sexual attraction demanding fulfillment and the need for restraint required by custom. She had to weigh these impulses against everything else that was occupying her time. The WPA job was going well, and she was writing constantly, experiencing success and support. But she saw herself falling hopelessly in love with JRB. Seeing her sexual attraction to Brown as a danger sign, Walker began to question if they were moving too fast. A first adult relationship that could in any way be described as sexual caused her to feel morally compromised.

Because they were both drawn to each other, they knew that as a couple they had to resist their desire for intimacy; each was, therefore, committed to protecting the other. "The ache in my heart was so intense for him a whimper crept to my lips and he urged me not to excite myself. . . . We were so happy together . . . over and over we tried to say goodnight. Finally he said he could not bear anymore. He cared for me too much. He is sure that I have excellent control for both of us."[4] The courtship quickly became official; dinners, movies, and her return to church, and through it all, a sexual tug of war. "Maybe we are just growing up, maybe sexual repression is better, maybe this is not love, but it will have to do until the real thing comes along,"[5] she concluded. On Valentine's Day in 1937, Brown proposed. Her response was typically analytical. Why me, she asked herself? The answer that came made sense: he was impressed by her intelligence and she had the right pedigree. There was the inevitable conflict. "I've known him for nearly a year . . . and I know it is unwise to think of marriage very soon and equally as unwise to continue our friendship without marriage in view."[6]

Nevertheless, she took full responsibility for the emotional part of the relationship. "I must not fail him, but I must not ruin him," she wrote. "I am striving hard to have him pay for all he gets and earnestly striving to keep before me the standards I must observe and live up to for both of us."[7] Heated declarations and high-style adorations fill the pages of her journals: "I shall never love anyone more than I love JRB," "There will never be a finer character, a nobler integrity, a cleaner personality, a more splendid soul." Realizing that the freedom she had longed for could not be fully realized in a sexual sense, Walker grew increasingly more frustrated in the relationship. "I am only human"; "This is trying to get the best of me"; "We are bursting with desire . . . how long can a man and woman go on like this. . . . I can sublimate sex into art or religion no longer," she confessed.[8]

Five months before turning twenty-two, Walker was on the threshold of romantic adventure. But moving into unknown territory intellectually and politically as she was increased her fear of parallel movement on a personal level. Her response was immediately to try to control what was at once thrilling and frightening. She reported in her journal that Marion agreed to give her consent to her daughter's marriage in three years and *only* if Brown had demonstrated the ability to "properly take care of me."[9] When they went together for prayer at Hilton Chapel at Chicago Theological Seminary where he was studying, he expressed concern about her retreat from faith. She had missed a few church meetings that they had promised to attend together and made him upset. Two days after her twenty-second birthday, Walker came down from an emotional high and considered the changes her life had undergone in the last year. Brown had no connection to her radical activities. She claimed that space for herself—and for Wright—and she needed to devote more time to her writing.

The fear that emerges before taking such a big step was normal. The first stage of romantic attraction confronts reality. The truth is that they were alike but also very different. Brown was following the dictates of the Black clergy in the 1930s, preparing himself for the leadership of the Black church. Walker was pushing against an inherited tradition as much as she was bound to it. Conflict between them was inevitable. Their relationship had emerged at a period when Walker was concentrating her intellectual energies on her development as a writer and as a political being. Moreover, she was beginning to ask new questions about her identity as a woman. Her independence was crucial to her development, and anything that disrupted the process was distasteful to her. Her continued involvement in political and literary events, which were of no interest to Brown, consumed more and more of her time. To get her work done, she needed rigid discipline. But her time with Brown required discipline of a different sort. In early summer 1937, when she broke a date with him to go to a poetry reading, he became livid. When his proposed solution to what he saw as their conflict was to go to chapel, listen to organ music, and pray together, she suddenly realized that their worlds, even with all that they shared, were growing further and further apart. The most important thing they needed to share—goals and expectations—they did not.

James Russell Brown was a first love, that necessary interlude in one's life where, for a time, nothing matters but the thing itself. Her resistance got his attention, making him relentless in pursuit of her affection. The timing was also appropriate; she had finished college and was no different from countless other women who thought of marriage as a necessary next step to a fulfilling life. But Walker did not see herself as "countless other women." The courtship between them represented a logical sequence of events in the lives of two young people who met under similar conditions and were in the same place at the same time. Walker entered it willingly, for she immediately recognized that Brown would meet her parents' approval. But Brown was a minister in training for a career in the AME Church; he was looking for a life partner, someone to help him reach his own career goals. They were both products of a Southern Black religious culture, both understood clearly the expectations for that others had for them. Walker, a well-trained daughter of a well-trained theologian, represented the ideal he was looking for. From all outward appearances, Walker's profile was that of a progressive minister's wife: she was well-read in the Bible and religious literature, she had cultivated an observable religious practice, she played the piano and had substantial exposure to high culture. Her extraordinary intelligence added to her appeal for a man with his ambitions.

Their relationship, as Walker understood it at the time, was about the struggle between love and passion or lust, as she sometimes called it. Love must be triumphant, she believed, and it was altogether different from passion. She confided the private, inner story of the relationship with JRB in a thirty-two-page journal entry, in which she speaks honestly about her own sexual urges and the corresponding impact of sexual repression. "What an age of confusing standards in which to be born,"[10] she began. This entry is as much a statement of their breakup as it is a clarifying moment in her understanding of the antagonism between men and women. It anticipated a deeply emotional crisis of female power in relationship to men. She had idealized what a relationship should be: finding one's intellectual equal, the perfect union of the emotional, the physical, and spiritual. When they alternated between expressions of undying love for one another and bitter insults, she found herself easily persuaded by the roses that always appeared immediately after one of these battles. Moments later, she admitted feeling disdain at the idea of being conquered by a man, believing this to be God's test of her ability to find her moral strength.

They had prayed and made a pact between them, to gain strength from each other as they continually renewed their faith in God. What Brown had not counted on, or had completely misunderstood, was the extent of her ambitions. As they began discussing plans for the future, one evening she responded to his question about her future without flinching, "I have no plans except to finish these two books,"[11] and she offered the manuscripts for him to read. Unprepared for her forthrightness, Brown was crushed. Humiliated to be so ignored, he became defensive and bitter. He accused her of having no religion, of thinking herself his intellectual superior. Once again, Walker's mouth had got her into trouble. Marriage and a professional career were simply out of the question for a minister's wife. "You don't want to be married, do you? You look as if you might be intelligent but not the other part. . . . You are still a little girl and you won't be a woman until you have done two things: had a man and had a baby,"[12] she remembered him saying. Despite the explosion, they unleashed their passions, feeling entirely uninhibited as they never had before. She did so, knowing that they were breaking up, feeling no shame in expressing what she truly felt.

Afterwards, she invited him to her reading at the George Cleveland Hall Library the next evening. He agreed to come but appeared only in time to take her home. He had never heard her read publicly and didn't seem to want to, a clear sign that the relationship was over. The coldness that she felt toward him was undeniable, but she did not want to give in to these feelings. It was a time for silence and prayer, a reminder that one should never put man above God.

She had believed Brown to be her physical mate, "that with him love would be ecstasy,"[13] but once she determined "I must go on with my writing, my poetry, my novels," she knew that the space, now afforded her by her separation from Brown, could be used for engaging the very ideas that he believed made her so "unworthy."[14] She would always add "of being a minister's wife." There was no better person to help her give shape and form to these ideas than Richard Wright, who believed that Brown and Walker "had nothing to run from except shadows."[15]

In late April, Walker summed up the experience and considered the whole thing foolish, refusing to allow any emotional fragility. Instead, she participated in an unconscious dualism. What she was incapable of accepting in her personal life she more than made up for in her path toward intellectual growth and social commitment. Accordingly, her thoughts turned immediately to Wright. "He has been my first and best teacher in Marxist principles and aesthetics. DW is teaching me many valuable and important lessons about writing. I prize his criticism. He is the best teacher I know."[16] Less than two months later, under the heading "The Dream Is Restored," her journal entry noted that Richard Wright helped to provide "proper perspective and an approach to technical facility"[17] that she did not have.

The other factor in her decision to refuse Brown's marriage proposal was equally important—her growing awareness of the limitations and expectations for women of her generation. While Walker would never use the word "feminist" to describe herself, she realized that she had been too optimistic about the equality that was possible in marriage. But her bitterness was evident in her comment that men "smelled and straddled a bitch and moved on."[18] Only after the optimism wore away did she begin to ask questions about her own awareness of gender as a social category. When their relationship had ended, Brown had told her, perhaps out of anger, that she was far too ambitious for a woman and that her career would have to be abandoned if she got married, not just to him, but to any man.

In a moment of startling recognition about that part of herself that had become attached to Brown, she quickly let go. The knowledge that marriage would go hand in hand with suppression of her creativity trumped all other knowledge and all feeling. Like a sign she had been looking for, it made her determination to end the relationship even more fierce. "Marriage is an obstacle and an unfortunate thing for the artist,"[19] she told herself. The challenge was learning how to go from the personal to the political, and she needed a bridge to help her cross.

For the last weeks of March and early April, Walker carefully copied in her journal the several letters she sent to Brown; any anger or bitterness on her part had disappeared. She knew she could not accept his proposal and that she had to end the relationship, that it was her "sincere hope that we never meet again, never see each other, never correspond."[20] Yet she ultimately believed it had been uplifting, giving her something she had never had before. Confessing her undying love, she spoke of being

> still in a fiery daze of happiness . . . regardless of what the future may be. . . . I feel as though my heart will burst from my bosom with such fullness, such immeasurable happiness. . . . Oh, I cannot tell you how much I long for your complete happiness always, that someday you may know the fullness of joy, exquisite delight and incomparable ecstasy. Over and over I tell you how much I desire your life to be radiant with the best. No matter what woman may open the gates of sweetest paradise to you and bring you all . . . I shall be happy if she makes you happy.[21]

In a sophisticated "Dear John" letter, Walker poured out her heart: "I wish I could promise you beauty and strength and peace. It is what I wish for you. But these have not yet manifested themselves in me and I know I must feel them here first just as you must before we can know happiness. I remain ever yours alone,"[22] she ended her final note to him. Later she would remember the bitter words and even more bitter scenes, when he called her "Margaret Walker the untouchable . . . coldly analytical, selfish character . . . callous . . . unworthy of [him] and [his] profession," to which she had responded coyly, "I accept your verdict. I bow before your will."[23]

She would see him once more. Brown came to visit her in Iowa City in 1939, when she was nearly finished with *For My People*. He asked if she had reconsidered his proposal. It had been three years, the amount of time that Marion had asked her daughter to wait before accepting his early marriage proposal. As if he were following her mother's wishes, he believed that she would feel differently than before. They were now free to marry. There had been no communication between them, and he had hoped that after completing graduate school, she had accomplished all that she wanted. "What do you want next?" he asked. In her unpublished autobiography she repeated their conversation and her editorial commentary:

> I said, "I want to publish a book." Obviously that was the wrong answer. He literally flew into a rage.
>
> "Publish a book, a book! Here I came clear across the country to ask you to marry me and all you want is to publish a book. No man can speak peace to your soul. All you want is to satisfy your ambitions."
>
> I was upset to see him so distressed. I thought I loved him but I knew he wasn't right for me. He had told me once we were married, my career had to go. No writing, speaking, teaching, I must be satisfied being a wife to him and a mother to his children. And how many children did he want? Maybe a dozen. I remember laughing at that. True his kisses were my first emotional awakening—the first hint of sexual arousal, and I was twenty-one. And now the minister said as if to rebuff and hurt me, he was going to find another woman to marry.
>
> "You're too brown for me anyway. I'm going to marry a little yellow gal with red hair." Which he did.[24]

At the conclusion of the visit, the words of a fortune teller came back to her, "Marriage for you is like a green apple on a tree—it's not ripe yet."[25]

It was no accident that her breakup with Brown came during the period when Wright was preparing to leave Chicago for New York. She had not been dishonest, but had misjudged her capacity to balance emotionally and psychically relationships with two very different men. In rejecting the man who wanted her, she asserted her independence as a woman. The two men had met each other on at least one occasion. When she had broken a date with Brown, who insisted on coming to her house to change her mind, he arrived just as Wright was leaving. It was natural for him to be jealous. She used Brown's behavior as the reason to see him in terms of what he was not. Doing so pushed her interests toward Wright even more. She convinced herself of how important her relationship with Wright was to her development. "I have discovered a world at my fingertips through DW. My rationalistic yearnings and artistic inclinations have assumed shape and meaning and crystallized into consciousness through his careful guidance to Marxism. More than anything else I still need to live and live dangerously. . . . I think now of how much he has said to me in these months, how much he has shaped my attitudes and purpose, how much he has helped me to understand myself, how much he has shown me about the necessity of utilizing my only weapon in these days of impending disaster."[26] That weapon was her writing, and she was determined not to let anything stand in the way of its development. It was the one thing she knew that she could not live without.

Walker's bravado with Brown provided her with a useful mask. The day Wright left for New York, she wrote, "He has fed me the very bread of existence at a time of great disillusionment and confusion."[27] Repudiating herself for moral weakness in succumbing to pleasures of the flesh with Brown, Walker felt as if she had barely escaped from a fearful monster in a dark forest that had nearly trapped her in its clutches.

What made her relationship with Wright so desirable was the degree to which he supported her work and understood what it took to be an artist. In contrast, what made Walker's relationship with Brown so problematic was the satisfaction she derived from spiritual, emotional, and sexual fulfillment with someone who neither believed in nor supported any of her ambitions. She felt bound to make a distinction between the physical desires she struggled to contain and the crystallization of a heightened political consciousness of her "rationalistic yearnings and artistic inclinations."[28] The latter was superior in her romantically derived imagination and demanded at this stage of her life her undivided attention in order to accomplish the proper transformation.

Although Walker still did not fully comprehend how to respond to her sexual urges that she found frequently distracting, she believed her responsibility was to redirect her energy toward the creative. The practice of restraint has a long history, and she was one of its most observant pupils. She could interpret those feelings of passion as stemming from several different places, and she could choose where she wanted to apply them. Her commitment to being a writer produced a newfound faith, "in life and people, mostly in myself."[29]

Fearing the emotional and sexual dependency she saw developing with Brown, Walker became susceptible to an ideology that claimed the full attention of her intellect at the same time it harvested her creative powers. The positive result was a sense of liberation from the expectations of conventional womanhood. She entered in her journal her new motto:

Justifying my existence as a woman, as a human being, capable of thought and feeling capable of action and unified consciousness, capable of mental and emotional discipline, involved, recognizing understanding and using all of my human heritage, body, and soul. Justifying my existence as a Negro involves the same recognition and an understanding and use of social heritage. Justifying my existence as a writer means an awareness of centuries of artistic heritage and cultural heritage and implies working with technique until I find a suitable expression for this personal, social, and cultural heritage.[30]

This was work that she knew she still needed to do.

10

The Author of "For My People"

In July 1937, Walker turned twenty-two, and what she could not confront earlier, she began to comprehend, though still unable to confess. The absence of two men in her life left a void that she could not easily fill. She spent her birthday reading, writing, and playing the piano, to escape from some of the busywork that came as she grew more conscious of acting as Wright's substitute at the SSWG meetings. Despite the confusion of what kind of relationship she had with him and where it was going, its by-products were most beneficial. Her growing radicalism motivated an intense work ethic that allowed her to divide her time efficiently between the Writers' Project and her own writing. She was learning to focus her creative energies and work on the "northside novel." Knowing poetry to be her strongest artistic form, the most likely to bring recognition, she was committed to improving her skills in fiction writing as much as she could.

Anyone at the project office would have noticed that she had more time on the days she was there to turn in assignments. Nelson Algren and James T. Farrell were becoming closer friends and trusted advisors. But it was probably her friendship with Vivian Harsh, librarian at the George Cleveland Hall Branch of the Chicago Public Library, that brought the most opportunities for readings at other Chicago branch libraries. These events prompted her desire to publish more frequently and in journals that carried more prestige. Harsh also introduced her to Zora Neale Hurston's *Their Eyes Were Watching God*, a book that Wright disliked as much as he did its author, whom he believed catered too much to the white establishment.[1] Because she already knew of Hurston, Walker apparently had read the book before Wright wrote his review and "enjoyed Hurston so much I was surprised."[2]

Walker was receiving invitations to read her poetry more often as Hurston's book began circulating in 1937. *Their Eyes* created quite a stir among those on the Left. She was fascinated by Hurston's depiction of a Black woman's life in the South and her struggle for independence, especially regarding marriage, something that resonated with Walker's recent experiences. Reading Hurston undoubtedly precipitated an interest in the works of Black women writers, and now that she saw a work by a Negro woman novelist she considered well written, she thought that her own fiction seemed shallow and infantile. Hurston's political beliefs did not bother her, for they shared a kinship that went deeper. They both had a psychic connection to African American people in the South. The

The House Where My Soul Lives. Maryemma Graham, Oxford University Press. © Oxford University Press 2022.
DOI: 10.1093/oso/9780195341232.003.0010

manifestation of that connection was to be found in their deep appreciation for Black folk expression and the Southern story-telling tradition that could not be reduced to ideology.

What she had first felt, she could now name as *feeling tone*, the special quality that African American culture transmitted through expressive culture. The real task of the Negro writer, she believed, was to capture this idiom and feeling; it began with becoming well versed in Negro folklore. "I want to express the life and language of my people as they have not been expressed, to unify the various parts of this folklore, the song and dance and tale," she wrote in her journal.[3] The more she learned about Hurston, the more she saw an important model. What Hurston would later do, Walker was already imagining herself doing, "to write an authoritative book on Negro folklore from research done in the Carolinas, Virginia, Louisiana, Mississippi, Georgia, Alabama and Texas, in addition to the West Indies, perhaps the Virgin Islands." She intended "to write folk tales in deep southern vernacular in the present tense with limited time and point of view."[4]

Yet she understood how much a threat Hurston, now on her third book, was for Wright, who was getting repeated rejection slips. It was not until December 1937 that Wright learned *Uncle Tom's Children* had won the nationwide *Story* contest, which assured its publication with Harper & Brothers. He watched as Hurston's novel received highly favorable reviews, one of them written by his friend, Marian Minus.[5] Feeling betrayed, Wright resented Minus's lavish praise of Hurston, especially since be believed that Hurston represented the kind of writer that "Blueprint for Negro Writing" had criticized. What Walker said in her Wright biography is worth noting—that his distrust of Minus was due to questions being raised about her sexual orientation. But Wright must have been infuriated that Hurston's third book preceded his first by six months; anyone showing a preference for her work might give a bad review to his. The gender politics could have been operating on several levels: Wright's competition with a Black woman writer, and his rejection by Minus who may have been bisexual. The intensity of the review is hard to explain beyond thinly veiled jealousy as well as frustration over the progress of his career. Hurston did not take his comments sitting down, however; she repaid the favor when she criticized *Uncle Tom's Children* in her review of the book, calling it bleak, negative, ideological. Where was his pride in the race, she asked.[6]

Reading Hurston's novel confirmed for Walker that shifting her attention to fiction projects and the use of Black vernacular expression was the right thing to do. The discovery of work by others who explored the vernacular offered new models. She knew, for example, that Katherine Dunham was introducing students in her studio to what later became the "Dunham technique," a series of distinct dance movements based on Dunham's keen observations and research on African and Haitian religious and secular dance forms.

A benefit of Wright's absence, even as she existed in his shadow, was the strength of her convictions she began to feel alongside expectations that her career would parallel his. When he wrote that he was submitting the stories (novellas) that became *Uncle Tom's Children* to the *Story* contest, she prepared to submit some of her newer folk pieces to *New Challenge*, work that she saw "as a direct influence of your influence,"[7] she told Wright. She was trying to reproduce Black folk speech as she remembered it, an activity that turned out to be excellent practice for *Jubilee*, where the dialogue was important for authenticating a story about slavery and Reconstruction. Dorothy West, however, "was none too enthusiastic."[8] She found that while she worked on the folk stories zealously, she had exactly the opposite experience with her novel "Goose Island," which continued to proceed "more cautiously and with more anxiety. Sometimes I have been so anxious that I have felt like chucking the whole thing. I get the feeling that it is getting worse and worse. I know that now I should be sure of what I am doing and not blindly fumbling in the dark but sometimes I get panicky and think maybe I haven't taken in any of the new working theories I have discovered or had discovered for me in the past year."[9]

What she didn't know was that Wright's influence was affecting her ability to make inroads into fiction publishing, just as his negative relationships would transfer to her. She had grown somewhat accustomed to the backbiting in the SSWG and attributed it to envy. She was less prepared for Dorothy West's reaction to her fiction submissions. Wright had envisioned a partnership between the New York group, a carryover from the New Negro Renaissance and the SSWG. The name change from *Challenge* to *New Challenge* signified this development. While she was never privy to what transpired between Wright and West, there were rumors about a love triangle: West and Minus, both lesbians,[10] and Wright who had also dated Minus. We do know that West fiercely resisted what she saw as a communist takeover. This, coupled with mounting criticism of Wright, gossip about his affairs with women, including Walker, and his overwhelming ambition to be in control of anything he was a part, made it difficult for Walker to continue her defense of him. Her naïveté was a major handicap. She could only hear Wright's point of view since she was only in dialogue with him, failing to understand what West was up against. That West had managed to put out six issues of *Challenge* by herself between 1934 and 1936 naturally led her to resent his intrusions. When, in her late seventies, she was interviewed by Hazel Rowley, West still blamed the demise of *Challenge* on "a raid by Chicago gangsters,"[11] while Wright saw the financial problems as the real reason for the failure of the journal to fulfill its promise.

Several months after the September 1937 issue of *New Challenge* appeared, Walker still did not understand the extent of the difficulties. Looking at the masthead listing Wright as associate editor, Walker showed her unquestioned

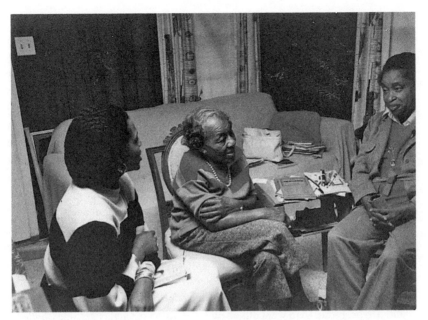

Author arranges for Walker and Dorothy West to meet for the first time at West's home in Oak Bluffs, Martha's Vineyard,1990

allegiance to Wright with her comment, "who is D. West and who is M.M.? Anybody with any literary awareness at all in America knows that those two names are utterly unknown just as much as you are known."[12]

When Walker and West met for the first time in 1990 at West's home in Oak Bluffs on Martha's Vineyard, however, Walker admitted her ignorance and offered an apology for the part she unknowingly played in "the raid by Chicago gangsters."[13] West immediately pulled a copy of the issue and turned to four poems by Margaret Walker, drawing a huge smile from the author. Walker had forgotten that she'd published these poems. Although she had the largest number of poems in the issue, she was the only poet whose poems were not listed by individual title. The table of contents simply listed "Four Poems" by Margaret Walker, suggesting that the group of poems shared a common theme. By contrast, Frank Marshall Davis, Sterling Brown, and Owen Dodson were identified with "Snapshots of the Cotton South," "Ole Lem," and "From Those Shores We Have Come," respectively. What she had said about Wright seemed to apply to her: Margaret Walker's name was as utterly unknown as Davis, Brown, and Dodson were known, thus justifying the slight. Ironically, two of the poems were among the best written during the period, notably "Southern Song" and "People of Unrest and Hunger," both presented before the SSWG.

West and Walker, however, did agree on several things during their conversation more than half a century later. With the exception of a few pieces, they
believed the fall 1937 issue of *New Challenge* was a very bad one. The writing
was very uneven and, as West was soon to discover, Wright's editorial skills were
far from developed. West wondered, therefore, how he could write so well, but
Walker refused to betray him even then, keeping her silence. Both also realized how remarkable that project had been. Theirs had been perhaps the only
magazine in the 1930s where Negro writers might continue "to make a place for
themselves . . . to make themselves heard . . . and to bear a tremendous force
for breaking down stereotyped ideas about the Negro, and for creating a higher
and more enlightened opinion about the race,"[14] *Challenge*'s proudly stated
mission. West was fighting to preserve the journal's independence and resisted
the surrender to more dominant voices throughout the Depression. To take
an ideological position, she believed, would compromise their work and cause
greater dissension rather than serve as a common ground for ideas and a unifying force among the community of Negro writers. She fought for this independence, hoping to preserve a unique space for Negro writers to be what they
wanted to be, rather than what others dictated. Instead, *Challenge/New Challenge*
became yet another battleground, with Negroes fighting each other rather than
addressing the larger social problems. Remembering her own battles within the
SSWG, Walker couldn't agree more.

Giving her time to the activities of the SSWG may have made Walker feel that
her contribution was similar to West's, who was one of the many little-known
women playing critical roles, especially in giving shape to a literary landscape
as visionary editors and leaders. The experiences Walker took from her work
in Chicago during the late 1930s had lasting effects, though unnoticeable at the
time. Most of the SSWG members were discouraged and offered little help when
she proposed ideas, if they did not outright reject hers. They spent their time
complaining about what they could not do, as splits within the group increased
with each meeting.

Finding little satisfaction with the SSWG, Walker spent her time attending
meetings of the League of American Writers, the Youth Communist League,
and the seminars at the Workers School, where she could take a full course of
study. These added to her responsibilities at the Writers' Project. She found herself "caught up on the maelstrom of meetings. Writers Unit meetings and Union
meetings . . . and class meetings and every kind of meeting." She complained to
Wright in one of her letters, "I think [one] of these days some of us are going to be
sitting in meetings and they'll be fighting in the streets and have to throw a brick
in a meeting to let the rest of us know that things will have started. I cannot keep
this up."[15]

It was not unusual for Walker to walk into a meeting when a lull in the conversation quickly turned into a deafened silence. She tried to dismiss the innuendoes as the musings of the ill-informed and was compelled to respond to those who wanted to know as much about Wright as they could whenever she attended any meetings, they had previously gone to together.

Given the pressure she was under, one might expect slow progress on her own projects, but she remained highly productive. Because she was much further behind in learning the craft of fiction than she was in writing poetry, and far behind Wright in gaining recognition, she may not have wanted to appear uncertain of her mission as a writer and, therefore, limited her updates to him on what she was finishing or had already completed. "I intend writing twenty of these, maybe twenty-four [folk sketches]," she wrote in an update letter to him on August 28, 1937, already beginning to see a thematic sequence for some of her folk sketches. Six were ready, "at least I think they are." "Two Gun Buster and Trigger Slim," "Yalluh Hammuh," "Example," "California Special," "Be a Bum," and "Skipper Gib[b]s" are then listed.[16] She had yet to fully conceive what she intended this work to become. The transformation that the sketches needed did not occur until she went to Iowa in 1939: they became folk ballads that form the second part of *For My People*.

Hughes and Wright were among the Black male writers who were regulars in the local proletarian journals, *Anvil*, *New Masses*, and the like, but seldom did one see the work of a Black woman. Walker was very pleased to be one of the few Black women getting her work published in the same journals.

Accustomed to filtering everything through Wright's thought and activity, she probably did not connect the respectful attention she was receiving, or the lack thereof, to her relationship with Wright. She continued to be present at all the major leftist events. Her journals describe in detail everything that happened. She encountered people who had differences with Wright about one thing or another. While some were wary of expressing them in his absence, others expressed their differences as outright hostility toward her, especially at SSWG. Her response was to question their loyalty to the organization, explaining the problem as those "people who have talent for writing but who do not want to take it seriously enough to create a craft group where we can work out individual and national problems of contemporary literature and writers."[17] She was even contemptuous at times, "I know niggers is deceitful and evil too and I'm counting on that knowledge," but also regretted working in a context with "malicious personal feeling . . . a striving for dominance and control on the part of opportunistic and pseudo-intellectual people warped and distorted out of all natural and decent proportions."[18] She was disdainful when meetings, like those of the SSWG, served only as social outlets, or a "bourgeois fad," rather than opportunities to reinforce "writing as a social and individual necessity."[19]

Hoping that having people hear her own voice would discourage them from seeing her as Wright's ear and mouthpiece, Walker tried to be more vocal at meetings she attended. She criticized the actions of people who seemed, in her mind, to lack a proper ideology, without always being aware that she was mimicking Wright. Airing her criticisms openly won her little support, and she was constantly confronting SSWG members Bob Davis and Russell Marshall, who were inseparable. In the absence of group unity and eager to get her work out, she began sending off materials, including that of others without their permission, and was unconcerned when anyone reprimanded her. In much of the SSWG work, she could count on few people, other than Fern Gayden. Walker found herself doing more and more work alone, pushing against anyone who refused, only to find herself isolated and embattled.

The struggles within the SSWG wore her down. Urged by both her doctor and her mother to get more rest because "my neurosis is threatening to become a psychosis," she recognized that "I will have to cut down on going . . . I need more energy to write."[20] Resolving to slow down, she told herself and Wright, "I'm turning individualistic for a while."[21]

In her detailed letters to Wright, she calculated the Writers' Project layoffs, described the plans for a Negro movie company and a Negro Cultural Collective on the South Side that she'd heard about, and detailed vicious union struggles. Although she was never afraid of confrontation, she often asked for Wright's intervention. "I fancy you can have a little more influence," she had written, hoping to gather momentum for a project she was involved in. Even if her ongoing work in communist-front organizations, work that Wright had introduced to her, was difficult and a distraction from her own writing, Walker was loyal and thoroughgoing in those duties she gave herself or believed were given to her.

Because she believed "Goose Island" marked the height of her involvement in the communist movement, its completion near the end of 1937 was a significant achievement. She showed it to John Frederick, the Chicago branch WPA director, and was pleased that he thought it was good enough to search for a publisher immediately, which she did. The entire process, however, was frustrating, and again, she found her confidence diminishing.

> I get thoroughly disgusted and the importance of the thing reaches such distorted proportions in my own mind that I feel I'm just messing around with everything that spells my life and work. Writing that I can laugh it off as ridiculous, . . . I want to do what I do as well. . . . I work almost like a dilettante which I am not. . . . The only thing that encourages me is the sure knowledge I have within myself that nothing is going to make me quit until I do what I've got to do if it takes me till I'm thirty-five to have my first real achievement.[22]

Fortunately, she did not abandon her poetry while diligently working on the novel and folk sketches. A brief reference to "one [poem] in particular they liked,"[23] referring to her colleagues at the Writers' Project, is the first indication that she believed she needed different advice beyond her usual networks. She shared it with Nelson Algren, Jack Scher, and Abe Aaron. Scher and Aaron deferred to Wright, suggesting that he should be the one to help to her "to give it that final charging . . . to put the power in those last lines where the poem needs it so badly, and to effect a thorough crystallization of the emotional elements in the poem." She was unusually tentative. "Perhaps I shall send it to you,"[24] she said in a letter to Wright. But she did not.

Composing poetry typically made Walker analytical, leading to moments of extreme self-examination and confession. She could be brutally frank with herself, as this journal entry indicates: "I believe my feverish intensity and desire for life overrides my discretion and I am unwilling to wait for an opportunity to normally relax and quietly satisfy my sexual desire. . . . I am determined to plunge ahead into unnatural and abnormal ways of living out my childish masturbating habits."[25] After her relationship with Brown, however, she believed she needed to find a satisfactory explanation for her sexual urges, which, as normal as they might have been, she had been trained to see as abnormal. Walker craved sexual intimacy, whether it had been fulfilled or not, she could confirm. She no longer feared it, as she had been taught to do as a child, but she had yet to feel comfortable when the feelings presented themselves. She felt safe attributing sexual desire to the artist's psychological makeup; she could own her feelings rather than be ashamed of them.

Experiencing this openness about herself provided the context for one of her most crucial realizations. The birth of the poem "For My People" signaled the completion of her apprenticeship as a writer. She had assimilated an entire philosophical system that invited her to give voice to her commitment. When Walker sat down to write "For My People," in July 1937, she was feeling the weight of her life in a way she had never felt before. Wright's departure and her refusal of marriage to James Russell Brown had sent her into a tailspin but had also been emotionally liberating. Once she began to sense this new freedom, her experiences for the past twenty-two years seemed to come together at once. Her education was complete; she was a woman who did not have to subordinate herself to anyone. The ethical and moral sensibilities that had guided her inner life were now conjoined with a compelling social vision. For a moment she was on edge, her body commanding her to act quickly. Sitting down at her typewriter, words seemed to be gushing out of her. Each phrase that she released kindled another thought in her imagination. She was typing frantically, trying to maintain the rhythm as it gave shape to each new line. It seemed like only fifteen minutes had passed. Before she could stop, she had written fifty lines. It was her longest poem

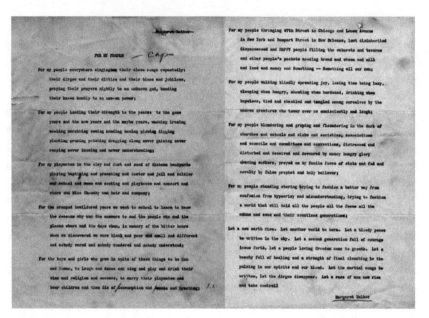

Typescript of "For My People"

yet. The young woman, who at five years old had announced to the world that she would become a writer, now saw her talent come to full maturity in "For My People."

Oddly, Walker never divulged the full experience of writing the poem. She shared almost everything with Wright for two years, but not a word about the composition of "For My People." She glibly mentioned a poem the SSWG had liked. Perhaps she was so driven to write that she was unaware of her own actions. Years later, she could speak only of the moment she stopped writing, unable to find a suitable conclusion for the poem. Her telling of the story, like the poem itself, became classic.

Into "For My People" Walker poured an entire history as she had come to understand it. Her memory held the images of the people she wanted to write about; her voice carried their words and stories. Her rigorous training in the modernist forms permitted the freedom of expression that she needed to create such a poem when the nineteenth-century poetry that had nurtured her childhood could not. She knew she was in the right place at the right time. The poem's time had come.

Critics have called "For My People" Walker's best poem. They were not alone, since its author offered her own prophetic lines when she finally told Wright, "I believe it is the best poem I have ever written."[26] It is the one that she herself claimed as her "signature piece," and it appears in more anthologies than any other poem by a Black writer. It resonates in every movement since the time it was written. Walker's ties to the Left did little to endear her to those who wanted to present poems that offered a neutral position on history and social change.

One question that emerges here is how the poem, written in 1937, could continually renew its relevance for multiple generations. For the most part, this derives from the poem's powerful opening lines and its final stanza, "Let a new earth rise, let another world be born." The association of "For My People" with social protest came naturally from its origin in the 1930s. Walker responded to a question about the poem's origin, however, in a 1982 interview with John Griffin Jones, presenting a very different view of the poem. "I don't think my writing has grown out of anger or hostility. I think it has grown a great deal out of a kind of brooding, intuitive, internal questioning and seeking answers. When I look at Wright's work and see what you produce out of anger, I know that we were thinking differently."[27] "Thinking differently" for Walker was her way of commenting on literary history as it is written and presented. With more than forty years to think about the poem, she had come to understand that everything written by Black people in the 1930s and 1940s had been viewed in terms of "anger" and "protest." While Wright was protesting a condition of Black existence, he became the subject of narrow interpretations that called for an exclusive model for African American writing.

She had come of age in the period when she absorbed Marxist ideas that taught her principals of fundamental social change. Yet her poetry was often contemplative. In "For My People," however, Walker disrupts the contemplative voice with an imperative statement at the conclusion. When she wrote it, she had been thinking and writing "too much, too easily, too soon, too fast."[28] Rather than working within more familiar forms—the sonnet, the short lyric, and the folk ballad were to become her favorites—she began to think of herself, rather than the poem, "as the instrument for the sounding and testing of raw sensory experience . . . a juggler of words, a dreamer with spoken dreams, a fire-maker who blows the sparks into flame with magic bellows," as she put it in a 1974 essay."[29]

"For My People" is written in the narrative mode, with the sweep of an epic revealing itself more as a meditation. Ten identifiable stanzas alternate between five and six lines up to the eighth stanza. Stanzas eight and ten have seven and eight lines respectively, framing a ninth stanza that returns to the five-line pattern. The characteristically long lines are punctuated by a series of short lines that sets up a certain tension as the poem moves through a catalogue of images in rapid sequence. Because the poem is a reconnection to the past while bringing into focus life in the present, Walker had to find a way to bring the two landscapes together, without viewing them in opposition to one another. To write in third person would have created a speaker other than herself, establishing a distance between the sensory experience and its expression. The simple opening line "For my people" resolves this dilemma, since it is not a statement to be processed but rather a gathering together for the presentation of what is to come. The preposition "for" suggests it is a gift, something that is being shared willingly.

Walker was exercising the freedom afforded her through free verse, and the poem in some ways signaled the arrival of a second phase of the Modernist movement, one in which Black writers would struggle to become more visible. An earlier phase of Modernism exhibited a decidedly exclusionary tendency and sought to set itself apart from the leftist politics of the period. By their very silence, however, a particular group of Modernists, especially Ezra Pound and T. S. Eliot, became suspect, and suspicions were often confirmed through the actions that many of them took. An important part of the movement became consolidated and retreated to the South, to Vanderbilt University, focused around a magazine, *The Fugitives*. Situated within a racialized culture, Modernism developed its own manifesto, a core following, and a set of structures through which it easily sustained and transmitted itself. There was little chance of expanding once it became part of the South's agrarian past, so dependent on a slave economy, for it was a world that was also fighting to regain ascendancy. To its credit, however, it also produced a writer like William Faulkner, who would help us see the psychological dangers inherent in a culture and a people living in and with the terror of its own past.

As a young writer, Walker read T. S. Eliot, first in college, where she found him dull, and then again with Wright, who prompted her to reconsider this poet that he admired. She preferred to read the fiction of André Gide, Emile Zola, Guy de Maupassant, Honoré de Balzac, and André Malraux, French writers who wrote about human suffering, demonstrated a very controlled narrative style, and were fascinated with the psychological aspects of experience. "I wanted to do the same thing Zola did in *L'Assomoir*,"[30] she had written to Wright, seeing herself as an American Zola, an astute observer of human nature, creating fictional landscapes that mirrored the world around her. Chicago offered the kind of laboratory that she needed and provided the energy that went into her work on "Goose Island."

She had come to poetry, on the other hand, through the individuals she had encountered, like Langston Hughes, E. B. Hungerford at Northwestern, and Harriet Monroe at *Poetry*. They exuded the same passion for language that she had always felt, but because poetry had come easily to her, she often questioned whether it was the thing that would be the ultimate test of her creative abilities. She was not consciously writing out of the Modernist tradition so much as she was consumed by it. This is best illustrated by "For My People," where Walker embarked on familiar territory in an unfamiliar way, driven by the desire to bring her own life, everything she had learned, and all that she felt to a kind of fulfillment. The poem presents a thesis and an antithesis that do not come quickly or easily.

"For My People" opens with the sound of music, "slave songs, dirges and ditties, blues and jubilees," bringing two important elements of Black culture together: music and religion. The poem embraces the reader, serving as an historical odyssey of slavery, migration, and life in the urban North. We are caught off guard from the very first words, "For my people," since structurally we might expect the prepositional phrase to come at the end of a statement, rather than at the beginning. It becomes, therefore, the poem's chorus, opening each of the nine stanzas that follow.

What is so successful in the poem is its ability to reflect the ebb and flow of a collective Black history through its inner structure. The poem literally moves through space and time as it goes from the general to the particular:

> For my people lending their strength to the years, to the
>   gone years and the now years and the maybe years,
>   washing ironing cooking scrubbing sewing mending
>   hoeing plowing digging planting pruning patching
>   dragging along never gaining never reaping never
>   knowing and never understanding;[31]

In this second stanza, the structure of the lines highlights the continuous, non-stop work over which Black people had no control. Walker is not willing to let the negative images overwhelm the reader; it becomes necessary, therefore, to assert the affirmative. The stanzas alternate between these negative descriptions and the affirmative ones. In the third stanza, the poem begins to invoke the memories of childhood, as the author refuses to distance herself from those about whom she speaks:

> For my playmates in the clay and dust and sand of Alabama
>   backyards playing, baptizing and preaching and doctor
>   and jail and soldier and school and mama and cooking
>   and playhouse and concert and store and hair and
>   Miss Choomby and company;[32]

Speaking in the collective voice allows the poem to build in a crescendo-like fashion, since this is not an individual experience but rather one drawn from people everywhere. Walker's task was to merge the individual self with a collective experience. At the same time, general experiences must be particularized, so that there is immediate connection to a sense of place and time. She does this by shifting from the more general "my people," to "my playmates," in the third stanza and then in the sixth, to "the boys and girls who grew in spite of these things to be man and woman."[33]

The movement in the poem is precise and methodical, with a visible tension between the individual lines and the substance of the poem. It is as if the insights that have occurred are obliged to follow a structure, one that cannot contain all the necessary meaning. Thus, it must look like a poem on the page, without sacrificing the dramatic effect of the message. This is most apparent in the third stanza, as the lines move effortlessly with few breaks, thus heightening the effect of the whole, leading us to the conclusion that "nobody cared" or "wondered" or "understood":

> For the cramped bewildered years we went to school to learn
> to know the reasons why and the answers to and the
> people who and the places where and the days when, in
> memory of the bitter hours when we discovered we
> were black and poor and small and different and nobody
> cared and nobody wondered and nobody understood;[34]

The tension here is between expectation and reality, the monotony of the changing sameness.

In the fifth stanza, the poem moves up to the North. The shift invites the roll call of urban cities filled with Southern Black migrants—"47th Street in Chicago and Lenox Avenue in New York and Rampart Street in New Orleans"—heightening the contradiction with what has been established in the poem's exposition. Faith moves people, sustains them, justifies their blindness, and even compensates by defining a somewhat happy existence as people go about their lives:

> . . . walking blindly spreading joy, losing time
> being lazy, sleeping when hungry, shouting when
> burdened, drinking when hopeless, tied, and shackled
> and tangled among ourselves by the unseen creatures
> who tower over us omnisciently and laugh;[35]

The predatory nature of this process is revealed is the eighth stanza, where the exposition builds to a climax:

> For my people blundering and groping and floundering in
> the dark of churches and schools and clubs and
> societies, associations and councils and committees and
> conventions, distressed and disturbed and deceived and
> devoured by money-hungry glory-craving leeches,
> preyed on by facile force of state and fad and novelty,
> by false prophet and holy believer;[36]

The church and the state help to perpetuate this helplessness, poverty, and powerlessness. This revelation is set against the more benign descriptions that begin the poem. This is the greatest moment of despair. While she must go forward with the poem's argument, Walker is unable to leave the reader in such a cynical state. She creates a space here for a kind of interlude, as she imagines a more hopeful existence for her people:

> standing staring trying to fashion a better way
> from confusion, from hypocrisy and misunderstanding,
> trying to fashion a world that will hold all the people,
> all the faces, all the adams and eves and their countless
> generations;[37]

Several accounts document that Walker was unable to complete this poem in one sitting. Because she had been so swept up in the language of the past, in describing what she knew intuitively about Black life, she had not looked outside of that experience to gain a different perspective. She remained part of it, feeling no need to counter the narrative she had created. As a result, the poem begins to indulge its own bleakness; "enough," it seemed to be saying to her. She knew only to stop, not knowing how to move beyond the descriptive catalogues in order to take the poem further. She had spent the better part of the day thinking about the ending. When she told the story of "For My People," she always called it her "fifteen-minute poem."

The "fifteen minutes" are more symbolic than real, for she needed to have a way of explaining the rush of spontaneous emotion that she associated with the poem. It was one of the few times that a subject she had been thinking about had begun to unfold in series of images that translated into words almost instantly. The process would have been going on unconsciously; the poem took shape in her mind in a way that other poems had not, moving from idea to development, through the sounds and images before it revealed itself in the actual words. But spontaneity alone does not a poem make.

Since Walker made no entry in her journal on the day she wrote "For My People," we have only her version of the story she told to interviewers and audiences many years later. It was written "a few days after my 22nd birthday [July 7]," she said repeatedly. It is clear that Walker understood the need not only to tell the story, but also to give it agency, "that final charging," to those to whom the story belonged: the poem had almost thrust itself upon her, but in order to make it her own, she had to exert control over it. She had stopped writing when this occurred to her, knowing that she had so identified with the speaker of the poem that she could not find her own voice. To move out of this writer's block, she turned to her fellow writers at the Writers' Project. As Walker later told the story,

Nelson Algren asked her the critical question, "Margaret, what do you want for your people?" Having decided not to send the poem to Wright, she took Algren's query to heart, but the conclusion to the poem was about what she had learned from Wright and what she had not. The poem could not *end* until she could answer that question, which meant finding a response appropriate for the historian, poet, and the ideologue to blend their disparate voices into one.

Yet a second voice was also necessary in this instance, one not content to meditate and describe, making its way through recollections of lived experience. The second voice has to present other words in another tone; it would have to talk back to the first. Without knowing it, Walker was replicating the familiar call-and-response pattern that was a major structural component of Black oratory, especially music and sermons. The poem felt incomplete because it lacked the rhetorical design that gave it cultural approval. Going deep into the expressive modality of Black folk, she remembered the music in the churches and hearing Protestant ministers extol an old-fashioned religion that demanded public affirmation from eager listening audiences. The sensibility she wanted to capture needed the distinctiveness reflected in the biblical cadence and parallelisms that Black sermons relied on so heavily, just as those same patterns would be found in the sermons and addresses of Martin Luther King Jr. in years to come. To ignore this tradition would leave the poem open to misinterpretation. The entire experience of composing this poem had jarred her moral sensibilities as much as it had challenged her creative ones.

The final stanza would have to be the poem's centerpiece. While it is necessary to tell a story about the past, to praise the ability to endure the countless horrors and indignation, the poet's job is to do more than feed complacency and hopelessness. The poet must seek to break with the pattern, to be an agent of a new kind of process, creative and transformative. The tone of the final stanza is aggressive, each sentence establishing a new action. The call-and-response pattern gives the poet a new role. Moving from its thesis to the antithesis, Walker demonstrated a dual function. Unlike the previous stanzas, there is no stated subject here; a series of forceful assertions create an orderly, rhythmic succession, each coming after a simple "Let" at the beginning. The journey through memory and history has been a cleansing, cathartic process; the speaking about pain and suffering is not an end in itself. It must be transmuted into something else. This is what that she meant by "a thorough crystallization of the elements of the poem." The "elements of the poem" are also part of an interactive cultural process. The poet or speaker is part of these two domains, the world of art and imagination, and the world of historical meaning, which cannot be separated. The revelation comes to us in the last stanza's dramatic break with the tone of the first nine stanzas. After the truth-telling, "the dirges" can and must indeed "disappear." Passive acceptance must give way to active resistance. The role of art is to imagine this possibility, to move beyond reality in the reader's mind. After composing this poem, Walker knew that she did not need to learn anymore from Wright; she needed only to listen to her inner voice, since she knew as well as anybody that art could be the bridge between the truth of past and the vision of the future.

> Let a new earth rise. Let another world be born. Let a
> bloody peace be written in the sky. Let a second
> generation full of courage issue forth; let a people
> loving freedom come to growth. Let a beauty full of
> healing and a strength of final clenching be the pulsing
> in our spirits and our blood. Let the martial songs be
> written, let the dirges disappear. Let a race of men now
> rise and take control.[38]

She had good reason to be pleased with the results of the poem. Simple elegance makes it readable, and yet it does not compromise those literary qualities that Walker, both as a diligent student and later as a teacher, considered important. The poem's definite structure and its rhythms have effective power derived from "an ethical idea realized aesthetically," as poet and critic Mary Kinzie explains. Kinzie also warns us about looking at the poem through the writer's eyes, "always the perfectly visible unfolding of a success story in which certainty and completion overcame doubt."[39] In this case, however, it turns out to be true. In "For My People," Walker did overcome the doubts she had about herself, doubts borne out of her recurring depressions, the conflict between her religious faith and physical desires, and the uneasy relationship between her emergence as a woman and a writer.

If we track the beginning of her career from "Daydream" in 1934 to the birth of "For My People" in 1937, we gain a better appreciation of what had changed. The two poems are connected in the sense that "Daydream" is the announcement of the event, while "For My People" is the event itself. The difference between the two is temporal and intellectual. One speaks in terms of desire, the other fulfillment. One begins where the other ends. "Daydream" is personal, while Walker cast the net far beyond herself in "For My People," going deeper into the essence of the human experience. She would state it clearly in a later journal entry, "I want to express the soul of my people. . . . I want to speak for them as one of them, among them, and with them. I want to become whole within, whole of mind and body and spirit."[40]

The reading of "For My People" as protest literature, which it is, must carry with it an understanding that the claims of history and the claims of aesthetics are often at odds. Jerry Ward admonishes us that the world in which writers like Margaret Walker and Richard Wright emerged saw no distinction between creating a "weapon against culturally sponsored ignorance as well as a medium for expressing . . . intellectual and artistic vision."[41] The difference is not within either claim, one for history or for aesthetics, but only in the way we have come to view them. For Richard Wright, who dominated the period, anger and protest went hand in hand. In creating her signature poem, Walker had found her mission: she had achieved the awareness of her heritage that could invite effective expression.

After she appended the final lines to "For My People," she took two poems to George Dillon, *Poetry*'s editor. He immediately accepted "For My People," without even taking a look at the second poem, "Summer." "For My People" appeared in November 1937. She received that issue when her mother was visiting her in Chicago. She had distanced herself from her family, especially her mother, whose resentment had grown stronger as her daughter exercised more and more independence. The tension between them had been thick, and Walker's only solution had been to make fewer and shorter visits home.

After an absence of four years, Marion recognized that her dutiful, but strong-willed and even contemptuous daughter had now become a successful poet with national visibility, one whose creation she could take some responsibility for. It was a triumph of a special sort, one that provided the reconnection both mother and daughter needed.

"For My People" confirmed what Wright had said about the two of them making it big together. He had warned her against having high expectations of publishing in *Poetry*, a journal that he believed was reserved for more elite, white writers, who cared little about Negro literature or its writers. Ideologically, it might compromise a writer who published there, if she considered herself on the Left, he thought. She did not want Wright to spoil the moment. If Walker had any hesitation, it may have been due to the embarrassment at having succeeded too well and avoiding any accusation of any opportunism on her part, something Wright would quickly charge. She was also sensitive to his feelings of rejection. But when the news leaked that he had won the *Story* contest, which promised its winner a publishing contract, Walker felt comfortable telling him her good news as well.

She had learned from "For My People" that she wrote her best poetry when she was able to find a balance between her submerged self and its reemergence in an appropriately public form: a collective identity coalescing with an individual one. Because Walker could write in a voice that was undeniably Black without explicit racial or gender markers, the poem qualified as universal, while announcing its particularity. It also ensured its long-held reputation for being aesthetically precocious and boldly executed. Rooted in the materialism of history, the imagery is not only compelling, it is also both regionalized and periodic. It is an African American story that moves rhythmically through a range of human emotions from "despair to joy to triumph."[42]

Walker also paid her debt to the popular American poet Walt Whitman, perhaps without knowing it, with her active use of the literary catalogue, a popular technique for modern verse poetry. In the last stanza, the poet is the prophet, endearing herself to all people by invoking their innermost thoughts and fears. Like a modern-day Moses, she was leading her people to a new vision of what the world could be. The myth of reinvention and recreation, which her biblical and moral instruction had instilled in her from childhood, had also served as the guardian of her poetic sensibility. The author of "For My People" had learned how to negotiate between the private world of the spirit and the public world of action.

PART III
NO ENEMIES SAVE MYSELF
1938–1943

(Iowa; New Orleans; New York)

11

Dear Dick

Margaret Walker and Richard Wright had been many things to each other, but she observed the necessary restraint by referring to herself as a "sincere comrade and friend" in the letters that she wrote to him after he left Chicago in May 1937. The correspondence had started immediately after his departure for New York. Since he wrote first, she felt obliged to respond immediately, confident that a first letter coming so soon was an invitation to her to write back and often.

An immediate effect of his departure was her heightened desire for books to read, since that had been the source of lively conversations that would continue uninterrupted, as they left together at the end of the workday. She continued what she had been doing each payday: taking part of her check to pay for the books she had placed on layaway, books that Wright had recommended. She managed to get copies of Gorky's novels quickly but was still paying for the basic list that Wright had compiled: Marx's *Kapital*, John Strachey's *The Coming Struggle for Power* and *Philosophy of Nietzsche*, and Adam Smith's *The Wealth of Nations*. J. W. Beach's *Twentieth Century Novel* and Babette Deutsch's *This Modern Poetry* were two books that became "must-reads" on a list that included James Joyce, Joseph Conrad, Marcel Proust, Gertrude Stein, and John Dos Passos, books that she had learned about during college.

She bought books that she thought needed to be a permanent part of her library, but she spent just as much time in the Chicago Public Library. The George Cleveland Hall Branch, walking distance from the WPA offices, became one of her routine stops on her way to and from work. Her borrowings included Dostoevsky and Tolstoy, along with Erskine Caldwell, Thomas Mann, D. H. Lawrence, André Gide, Henri Barbusse, and Henry James. She knew about and had already read the works of Herman Melville, Stephen Crane, Emile Zola, Guy de Maupassant, Honoré de Balzac, Anatole France, and André Malraux, but since much of her college reading had been modern poetry, she began to adopt Wright's taste in fiction, reading works by Maxwell Anderson, Floyd Dell, James T. Farrell, Clifford Odets, Paul Green, William Faulkner, and Ernest Hemingway.

The theories of Freud, Jung, and Alfred Adler, which had had an enormous influence on Wright's fiction, would find their way into *Daemonic Genius*, the Wright biography she would write years later. Although their views on religion were quite different, she and Wright both read and discussed the Bible. Wright, for all of his resentment of the Seventh-Day Adventist faith in which he was

The House Where My Soul Lives. Maryemma Graham, Oxford University Press. © Oxford University Press 2022.
DOI: 10.1093/oso/9780195341232.003.0011

reared, had an appreciation for the Bible as literature, but Walker remembered him quoting extensively from Job.[1] For Walker, rereading the Bible connected to her studies of folklore and Marxist dialectics. She was drawn to José de Ortega y Gasset's *Revolt of the Masses* and, for purposes of craft, Henry James's *The Art of the Novel*.

Walker never felt that she needed Wright to tell her anything about poetry that she didn't already know, but she discovered a new appreciation for Carl Sandburg when she learned that he had left school at thirteen, become a laborer, then a successful journalist and a socialist. These facts that made him exemplary as a writer on the Left. Her own choices included Aristotle's *Poetics*, all of T. S. Eliot, and Harriet Monroe's *The New Poetry*. She maintained a keen interest in structure, which Hungerford had always emphasized in her classes at Northwestern. Louis Untermeyer's "The Forms of Poetry," a 1926 essay on the shifting status of American poetry in the 1930s, was one of her go-to's for models of free-verse forms that she favored. French and American classics, Voltaire, Rousseau, and Emerson were as important to Walker as Negro history, especially W. E. B. Du Bois's *Souls of Black Folks*, Booker T. Washington's *Up from Slavery*, and Carter G. Woodson's controversial *The Mis-Education of the Negro*, the book she had discovered the year she sat out of college.

Dialogues about folk forms drew Walker's firsthand testimony—acquired from her grandmother—just as growing up in Alabama and New Orleans provided the basis for her intimate knowledge. She might not have argued that folk forms were the true expression of the masses, as did the Marxist intellectuals she met, but she was convinced that "If I succeed as a writer, it must be with this Black idiom that is me. Black writers . . . must be themselves, a natural-born woman or man writing about a world we sometimes understand, interpreting ourselves as Africans in a hostile white land, trying to make the society in which we live less inhospitable."[2] What she had said in her 1932 essay "What Is to Become of Us," she never fundamentally altered: "A good and sure way to succeed in our various occupations is to apply our knowledge wisely in our own environment with a view to bettering conditions there."[3] Given her work schedule, there was time to fill in the gaps in her knowledge and to locate a broader context for her development than her family or her church provided. Her strong interest in leftist ideas did not surprise her, for she saw it as part of a process of maturity.

One could say that Walker embraced Marxism fully, in part because she enjoyed the intellectual respect it afforded her among peers. Understandably, the role she played gave the appearance that her convictions and positions were based on Wright's, who was himself indebted to the Communist Party for giving him a life that he could not have had otherwise. What this perception overlooks, however, was Walker's childhood reality. She had grown up reading literature and history; they were the subjects in which she had always done well. She had, in comparison to most Negroes of her generation, a privileged life. When she was fourteen and wanted to read philosophy, her father had discouraged it, insisting that she had neither the maturity nor the logical reasoning it required. Reading Marxist philosophy now appealed to her not so much because it was a radical philosophy, but more because she was intellectually curious and motivated to challenge her father's early assessment. If four years of college and living on her own in Chicago did not make her mature, then what did? "My father had a tendency to choose courses for all of us, and we never went wrong if we followed his advice."4 She wondered if her father questioned certain abilities because she was a woman, although he had never discouraged her intellectual development or her interests. By the age of twenty-one, Walker believed what her father had once called a "puberty urge" may well have been "the mark of a genius,"5 so confident was she of knowing more about herself than her father did.

She did read Marxism, knowingly in part because of Wright, and no doubt began to share his critique of unthinking, party-line followers, especially among Negroes, and his growing dissatisfaction with the Communist Party itself. Being Wright's confidante during the height of his involvement with the Communist Party in Chicago gave her unique access to certain fears they both shared: an ideology and accompanying practice so dominant that it could stifle creativity and sensitivity. Racism may have driven Wright out of the South, but the Communist Party, which he discovered to be equally repressive, drove him out of the country. Moreover, Wright's involvement in American communism encouraged her participation in a radical experiment vicariously, while simultaneously allowing her to maintain a guarded distance.

Despite the time they had spent together, Wright must have given Walker reason to think there was more to his relationship with her than there actually was. He never overstepped, they never spoke of intimacy or love, but she believed they had a language of inner perception that was expressed through their work and art. To Walker, Wright was naturally brilliant, a full, undivided human being who wanted to become somebody and was very clear about his goal. He was the artist's artist, which she found irresistible.

After reflecting on her own sexual psychology when her relationship with Brown had ended, Walker may have been cautious about how she should exercise the freedom she had chosen to give herself. But since Wright was everything that James Russell Brown was not, she could not see any of the weaknesses that Wright might have had. Instead, he was above that level of comprehension. In her journal entries, she contrasted her memories of Brown with the excitement she felt when she spent time with Wright as if to further justify her decision. One required her to surrender; the other, she believed, taught her to trust herself and develop her abilities through a new code and philosophy of life. She saw her relationship with Wright as intellectual and spiritual, noting that it begged for a physical component that Wright simply repressed, or so she believed. She gave reasons for this repression in her biography of him, believing that Wright's relationship with women forced him to confront the psychic wounds of his childhood and his hostility toward the women in his life. Because they happened to be Black, his only escape was to marry white, she had finally concluded.

She believed that she had come to know Wright in a way that no one else did. Only later did she begin to analyze her idealized portrait. His passion for his work, his irrepressible desire to succeed at all costs made him highly attractive to women. She included herself in that group. He set himself apart from most people and, which made him more desirable *because* he was seemingly unattainable. Understanding the history of their relationship shifted her focus on his turbulent personality, her belief that he was a man tortured by anxieties, if not decidedly schizophrenic. The Wright she knew for those three years loomed larger and larger in her own mind until his "daemonic genius" was as real to her as her own existence.

Her friends at the SSWG and the Writers' Project remained curious about her relationship with Wright. Margaret Taylor Goss [Burroughs] was more direct. "How can anybody spend six hours talking to someone and still call it platonic?"[6] she asked her one day. It startled Walker as much as it made her angry at times, since she was determined to keep her intellectual and creative activity apart from anything that would disable the identity they had established as writers. The feelings were there, but she worked hard not to put them on display. Because her relationship with Wright gave her everything she could have asked for in a companion, and her traditional views about sex translated into sexual anxiety and unnecessary torment, the healthy choice was to assume that her creative life could and would grow undisturbed.

For these reasons, the components in what Walker defined as a platonic and intellectual friendship are difficult to sort out. She was very aware of learning valuable and important lessons from Wright. But because his education had ended at ninth grade, he also became dependent on her. He had grown up poor and alone with a dysfunctional family life. His relationships with women included an emotionally unstable mother and an inordinately strict grandmother wedded to religious fundamentalism. Thus, Walker offered him all the respect and affection that he craved from a female figure, none of which he received from the women in his family.

She remembered Wright asking her to join him when he announced he was moving to New York in May 1937. According to her journal entries, she agreed to make periodic visits, just as he had planned to return to Chicago when he could. When friends suggested jokingly that she go to New York to marry Wright, she was embarrassed, not because of their teasing, but because she was unable to control the emotion she felt at the very mention of his name. Their separation had more of an effect than she had anticipated. By July 1937, Walker's entries had become increasingly confessional. Initially, she had attributed some of the passion and yearning to the sexual explicitness of *Sons and Lovers*, the D. H. Lawrence novel she was reading at the time. Her response was to consider the place of sexuality in the life of an artist:

> This thing called artistic temperament or the artist's Personality beyond a doubt involves both his perspective and his sexual life. Perspective covers the mental attitudes and degrees of consciousness and these are determined by the sexual reactions upon his physical self. This means that again according to Freud, sex is the strongest motivation in human life. As DW says, the typical feminine temperament is diffuse and vague and general. The business woman is forced to organize and direct her energies toward one focal point, success in her occupation. This hardening process necessarily unifies her personality and tends to make her less feminine in her manner as she becomes more efficient in her business. Exactly the opposite may happen with the masculine personality. An artistic interest may tend to soften the emotional impulse as art appeals to their softer rather than sterner natures. The artist has a tendency to be quite intense in his likes and dislikes—the extreme psychological case is a killer, a schizophrenic, a sexual maniac or fiend. On the other hand, the artist prides himself in forming the cultural minority of society, the gods of the earthy, measuring that through emotional perception. They alone excel and understand. They create the only aristocracy, the aristocracy of the mind. The artist has a tendency toward inversion in temperament which must be overcome and must triumph over sex. We use our minds more than our bodies, suddenly we are warped, introverted and frustrated people because we do not engage in natural things. Regarding sex, we can only expect to harness it to our needs.[7]

What is remarkable about this period is the way she revealed—mainly in the letters to Wright—her taste and judgment on virtually everything. Her attention to detail in reporting to Wright suggests an intense relationship where language was supremely important. The passionate banter and mutual criticism made them allies in creating each other's work, and their participation in a movement focusing on the relationship between race and society made them comrades who wanted and needed to find a common space in which to share and learn together. Their social and emotional experiences, on the other hand, caused them to react quite differently to the political and ideological landscape they encountered. The instant attraction to each other's intellectual and creative gifts could easily have concealed an elaborate masquerade to avoid getting drawn into a sexual relationship. Wright's conflicted sexual attitudes toward Black women, which presented themselves very early, and Walker's dormant and repressed sexual impulses were easily transmuted during the year they spent together and the two additional years in which they corresponded.

Wright had begun to outline his ideas for *Native Son*, based on the Robert Nixon case, a Negro who was accused of murdering a white woman in Chicago in 1937. It was his first novel, and he shared his excitement with her. She chose her words carefully in her response, wanting to approach him about some gossip she had heard indirectly:

> If you think I should offer congratulations I shall be glad to do so but if you have been able to write 175 pages on a new novel and appear as thoroughly absorbed in it as I am led to believe on top of getting married, you must be a superman![8]

At the same time, she assured him that she was not affected by "any such poppy cock as this."[9] She spoke the truth about his working hard. She had already seen and congratulated him on his novella *Bright and Morning Star* that had appeared in the May 10 issue of *New Masses*. "Yes, this is revolutionary. This is the fastest moving, most powerful and violent of all the prose pieces," she told him.[10] His essay "High Tide in Harlem" in the July 5, 1938, issue of *New Masses* was a discussion of Joe Louis that "made my very toe nails glad," she wrote him the same day she read it. "It's exactly what all of us feel but have never had a chance or the ability to express."[11] Winning the *Story* magazine award for his novella *Fire and Cloud* had assured him publication of his first collection of short stories, *Uncle Tom's Children*, in 1938. He had shown high regard for her with his "offer to push my stuff"[12] in *New Masses*, Walker said as she thanked him. He would also introduce her to an editor at Doubleday and Doran, where she had planned to send her "Goose Island" manuscript. Her output was small compared to Wright's but was growing and important. She had also demonstrated that she could stand on her own, writing and submitting poems without his support or input.

Just as he planned, Wright made several trips back to Chicago, and his dependency on Walker increased. He needed her help, and she was happy to comply. His letters to her followed in rapid succession, several of them by airmail, with requests to send him copies of the published documents about the Nixon case and individual contacts he should follow up on. Wright dedicated most of 1938 to *Native Son*. Each return visit to Chicago involved research on the novel, with her assistance, which required them to spend time together. She set up appointments with informants and forwarded trial transcripts and news clippings, responding to his ideas as he composed the novel. From an outsider's point of view, those visits drew them closer than ever.

After each visit, Walker was unable to resist the fantasies which thoughts of a relationship with Wright provoked. Now and again her journal's controlled analytical prose is transformed into long, rather gushy entries describing the intensity of her emotions. She only knew to call them one thing: "If I am not in love, then at least I am in hell and passion is a terrible thing,"[13] she says, referring to Wright in May 1938. When Wright's collection of short stories, *Uncle Tom's Children*, appeared in 1938, she was swept up in the wave of excitement:

> His name is on the lips of half the people I know. . . . He has become the byword on literary lips all over the country. I'd give anything to have the happy privilege of being his wife, and until I know definitely, I cannot hope to be, I'm afraid no other man is going to interest me seriously. I don't want to be caressed by anyone else. There is no one else's opinion I value more highly than his and no one else I wish to please more than I wish to please him.[14]

The excitement over the appearance of *Uncle Tom's Children*, and Wright's forthcoming visit to Chicago in late fall 1938, caused her to shift from one set of troubling thoughts to another. She needed to think much more about the role that she would continue to play in Wright's life. "I want his friendship as much as I want his love," she wrote in her journal. "I must discipline myself before he comes so that I may be able to meet any unexpected situation emotionally and otherwise. . . . I dare not impose myself or will upon him."[15]

Weeks before, she had poured out her romantic feelings about Wright for what was probably the final time in her journal. It took the form of a poem and must have been written sometime between September 4, 1938, Wright's actual birthday, and September 9, judging by its placement among her journal entries. There is no evidence that she ever sent the poem, "To Dick on His Birthday." It is far more explicit in its declarations of her love than she would ever say to him directly. The poem borders on the sexual and, as an ode, uses the conventions of direct address. The beginning catalogue defines the addressee in six couplets, "You whom I love better than I love my life . . . / You who bring me peace and hope and strength and courage and light." She then responds as the speaking self: "I will catch my breath and think . . . You will be here. / I go on ever desiring only to . . . be sure that our kiss is real." In the poem's final stanza, Walker moves from acknowledgment to uncertainty and finally loss:

> Things that were precious
> Grown dim and clouded
> With the fear of war
> And the torment of love
> And the misunderstanding that is
> Father to hate.[16]

The poem plays with the concepts of platonic and romantic love, using nature as the common point of reference. It was Walker's praise poem for Wright, and it offered a metaphor for the world in which they found themselves in 1938, one surrounded by "the fear of war." War makes things "that were precious . . . dim and clouded." Shifting the discourse to the more personal, identifying "torment" with "love" and *not* war, the poem suggests that the responsibility for change in the state of things is social, as well as political and personal. "Misunderstanding" results when we fail to create a proper relationship between the two, and it can bring extreme consequences; it is indeed the "Father to hate." Because the highest form in which she sought to express meaning was poetry, and because poetry creates its own space between the real and the abstract worlds, she considered the poem her way of communicating the feelings she had, while maintaining a level of secrecy.

Walker believed she had already confronted her fantasies by the time Wright made his final trip to Chicago in May 1939. His *Native Son* manuscript was finished. Because she had provided assistance with this novel, she felt jubilant over its completion. As a show of his gratitude, Wright invited her to attend the American Writers Congress (AWC), which was to meet in New York in early June. The League of American Writers had initiated its biennial congresses in 1935 to provide a common ground for artists, scholars, and activists to showcase their work and to have a focused discussion of the relationship between art and revolution. The leadership for the AWC brought together those employed on the Federal Writers' Project and members of the Communist Party, with people frequently associated with both. It operated more as a united-front organization where non-communist groups had time for their dedicated presentations, just as it was one of the most important gatherings for the members of the various Writers' Projects throughout the country.

She had seen the announcement of the Congress in *New Masses* but had thought New York was beyond her reach. This opportunity for a first visit delighted her. Eager to meet with publishers, she would take two manuscripts, the poetry, "For My People," and "Goose Island." She had planned to submit the poetry manuscript again to Yale for the annual Younger Poets competition but was also interested to hear what any publisher might have to say about it.

It is hard to disentangle what might have been Walker's vicarious enjoyment of Wright's successes from those she imagined having. Because they were both part of a select community of young Negro intellectuals identified with the Left, various kinds of relationships existed within the group and with each other. She had accepted her role as his protégée and placed him on a pedestal. He had gone far with very little and was extraordinarily sensitive about this fact. The communists did not have a place for him in their organizational hierarchy that met his expectations. Although only seven years her senior, Wright's lived experience made him much older; he would have seen himself as the wiser, nurturing older brother that she never had. Collapsing the boundaries between their personal, political, and professional seemed natural.

Was Margaret Walker in love with Richard Wright? Undoubtedly, she was. She was certainly aware of her feelings but also the need to guard them closely, fearing that any anxiety might jinx the possibility of a relationship that was other than platonic. It was only after Wright's departure for New York that she realized the depth of those feelings, however, and read his numerous letters as a sign that the relationship was moving to a new stage. She believed she had encouraged him, assured him that he was not making a mistake by leaving, especially after he had received notification about a permanent position at the Chicago post office. She knew that he *had* to go to New York. They might have made it big together, something he may well have told her. But it was his time, not hers. "He grabbed both my hands and said goodbye," she had remembered.[17] Such displays of his vulnerability only affirmed the special closeness that she felt they had.

"Will it develop into a romance and if so what chances are there for marriage and when?"[18] she wrote in her journal after one of Wright's return visits to Chicago. Even if Wright had been uncertain about what he did feel for Walker, when he left Chicago, he saw himself as moving forward with a new life, the life of a famous writer. She admitted noticing the shift in the tone of his letters, especially as he neared the end of the *Native Son* project. His letters were shorter, more distant, and less frequent, all of which she attributed to his increasingly busy schedule. There were also the regular rumors about the women in his life, but he dodged questions whenever she confronted him. A review of their two-year correspondence neither confirms nor denies the charge leveled by some that Wright led Walker on. It does indicate the extent to which Wright had come to rely on Walker's efficiency and how much he benefited from her loyalty to him.

One thing is certain. Walker was always guarded about her successes when communicating with Wright, especially those in magazines that were not part of leftist circles. She was in the most creative period of her life but allowed herself to indulge her inner thoughts and feelings only on occasion. She waited until "For My People" was published in November 1937 to mention it to him:

> Last Sunday was the first time I have done any real creative writing since August and then I wrote three sonnets. I am rather glad although I know they probably need a great deal of reworking. I was becoming afraid of "running out" and as this was the first time, I have missed more than a month writing some sort of poetry since I began scribbling a good seven years ago, you can imagine how worried I was.[19]

The understated tone contrasts with her roll call of names, those who had won prizes from *Poetry*—Louise Bogan, Franklin Folsom, and William Pillin—raising little doubt that she expected to be included in that number at some point. On the other hand, she continued to make her ongoing political education a point of reference and self-criticism: I have not "done well with the Dialectical Materialism at all. . . . I don't think, nor act, nor reason dialectically." She needed to work harder, committing herself to taking "three months and just read this stuff over again for myself until I can begin to comprehend just what it's all about."[20] Although she had been able to contain her excitement over the publication of "For My People," in a letter to Wright on December 21, 1937, she admitted, "Well, you did get around to reading my poem. I knew you hadn't read it before because I felt if you had read it, you would comment, and here I was almost sick inside just hunger for a good word from you about it."[21] By this time, Wright was busily preparing for the publication of *Uncle Tom's Children*, getting a different job, moving to a new place, and writing much less frequently.

The closer she got to the departure date for New York, the more forced the trip felt. She had no money, borrowing from several people to get enough to buy her train ticket, and then had to depend on Wright once she arrived. Wright had secured housing for her with the Cooks, the family who had welcomed him to their Edgecombe Avenue home in upper Harlem. He had met Marvel and her husband Cecil first, when they had invited him over for a home-cooked Southern meal. Well-known in leftist circles, Marvel invited Black and white friends to gatherings at their home. Marvel's sister, Zelma, who lived with them, would be sharing her room with Walker. She arrived later than she had hoped on Friday morning, the conference was already in session, and she was so exhausted that she caught herself dozing in the sessions on folklore and literature, those she had especially wanted to hear.

She made contacts during the social gatherings between the sessions, and had lunch with Ralph Ellison, who reached out to her after recognizing her name from her poems in *New Challenge*. She also met Eugene Gordon and Eugene Holmes, who were active communist organizers in the New York area; Wright; and "a young Jewish woman who rather attached herself to the party."[22] Later Ellison took her on a tour of Harlem before dropping her off at the Cook residence. Exhausted, she was unable to sleep for the endless visitors who came by over the course of the evening. She enjoyed this New York scene; the pace was much faster than Chicago's, and she met writers she did not know existed. She saw Langston Hughes on her second day at the Writers Congress; now considered an old friend, Hughes introduced her to Alain Locke, whose name she knew from his association with *The New Negro*, the special issue of *Survey Graphic* magazine that served as the model for their special issue of *New Challenge*. She also met, for the first time, Sterling and Daisy Brown, with whom she felt a strong connection. They all shared a common interest in the use of folk idiom in poetry and gravitated to the folklore sessions, where she met Angelo Herndon, who had achieved an important position in the Communist Party. The session that drew all of them together was a presentation by Alan Lomax, who offered some of his recent taped recordings. Lomax worked on the New York Writers Project and would become a leading expert and collector of Negro folklore.

She spent more time during the AWC with Hughes, who accompanied her home after the evening sessions. Wright, at least it seemed to her, was avoiding contact. This was a point of discussion at the Cook home, but Walker believed that it was because he was avoiding Zelma, with whom he had had a run-in and who was dating Ted Ward. Zelma was also a notorious gossip, and since Wright was attracting a lot of attention, much of what Zelma had to say was aimed at him. Noticing that he had invited Walker to New York and was rarely escorting her anywhere, Zelma saw this as further evidence of his arrogance; he had let success go to his head. She had even seen an invitation to Wright's wedding that didn't happen, but she reported that the bride was some "prominent bourgeois girl."[23] Not certain as to why she was being told this information, Walker was equally curious about Zelma's investment in all of this.

Zelma went further to say that Wright's behavior toward Walker was unacceptable, and she proposed to tell him as much. Not wanting Wright to think she had put Zelma up to doing this, Walker became immediately defensive. "I begged her not to say anything to him, particular about me because I was sure he was doing everything he knew to make things pleasant for me,"[24] she had told her. Her response was understandable, but she could hardly disagree that Dick Wright was certainly no down-to-earth guy like Langston or even Ted Ward. Nevertheless, Zelma provided updates on the progress of Ted Ward's plays, which were to be produced in Philadelphia by the Suitcase Theatre, a company Hughes had started. Then she dropped the lug: Ward and Hughes, in an effort to be economical, had planned to move in together. She took the news coolly, especially when Zelma boosted her ego with "you [are] going farther than Dick Wright anyway."[25]

The next day when she saw Wright, Walker could not figure out a way to broach the subject of his impending marriage. Knowing that she was sharing a room with a gossip, Wright, in turn, wanted to know what was being said about him, after sharing a run-in he had had with Zelma. Without thinking, Walker blurted out what she had heard, that Ward was going to move in with Langston Hughes. Although they went to eat afterwards, Wright quickly dropped her off at the Cooks and rushed off to handle other business.

What happened after this is reported in an extensive journal entry of June 11, 1939. Before going to a play, Walker accepted an invitation to accompany Zelma to the hotel where Wright and Ted both had rooms. As Walker tells it, she went with Zelma to Ted Ward's room and without knocking, Zelma opened the door to find both Ted and Wright sprawled comfortably on the bed. Ted jumped up, startled by the unannounced entry. Wright seemed nonplussed by her fumbling apology for the intrusion. Feeling the need to justify her presence, she asked if he would accompany her to the play. Wright's refusal was followed by another awkward moment when Ted Ward rushed her out the door and escorted her to the subway. After the play, however, back at the Cooks', Wright came by and asked Walker to have a chat. Sitting outside on a park bench in a deadening silence, Wright was the first to speak, "I think the best thing for you to do is pack your things and get out of here in the morning." Startled, she asked him to clarify what he meant and then, trying to shift to something more reasonable, asked what she was supposed to do with her novel if she left. "Well," Wright responded, "that doesn't concern me any longer."[26] The words stung, but more than that, Wright continued, "This thing has gone on for three years. The relationship between us is at an end. . . . And I don't want any hysterics." Her pleas for more information about what she had exactly done only made Wright more agitated. "Search your conscience and you'll know the answer," she remembered him saying. Her reluctance to accept this finality provoked him, "Do I have to call the cops to keep you from following me?"[27] and he walked away, as she stood there in disbelief.

Her next actions were driven by pride. She went to the hotel, waited, and was beginning to write when she saw him approaching. They exchanged more words and Wright literally ran away, ducking to get rid of her. That night and the next day were a blur, but Walker finally got up enough nerve to talk with Marvel Cook, who encouraged her to return to the purpose for the visit: getting the book to a publisher. Marvel's obvious distraction nearly worked until that afternoon, when she received a telegram from her sister: "Come home at once. Will explain later."[28] When she followed up, she learned that Mercedes had sent the telegram after receiving two from Wright, asking her to insist that her sister return to Chicago. Walker saw the telegrams as "undue presumption, an overstepping of prerogative,"[29] all part of Wright's false bravado he could assume when he wanted to hurt someone.

After some rest, she was awakened by Marvel, Zelma, and Jane Newton, a white woman who was a friend of Wright's. Together, they would get to the bottom of this and map out a plan of action. It was then that Walker realized what had set Wright off: seeing Ted and Wright together in an uncompromising position with gossip already circulating about Ward and Hughes being gay. Wright thus became a target of suspicion. Because she had been eager to tell Wright what she'd heard from Zelma, Wright immediately had no idea what else she might say about any of them. Marvel's suggestion was to write a letter of apology—no, she was not admitting guilt, only that she understood how easily things had been misconstrued. Walker agreed, finished the letter, and mailed it before leaving for Chicago.

The letter was as much an earnest desire to clarify a difficult situation as it was her personal therapy. She was sure she would never see or speak to Wright again. But she did have a sense that she was at a critical juncture in her life, that she needed to assert her own authority by putting some order to this irrational state of affairs. Writing did that, and though it was not the rhythm and progression of poetry, it was driven from the same impulse—emotion and release. Their relationship had a history, and she was never more conscious of its importance and meaning than at the moment when it ended. She intended to take the high road, to be very explicit about what remained after such a loss as this. "As a matter of fact," she had written, "my whole personality has been influenced and conditioned by yours in its most noble and finest realities. What you have done for me has been merely to help the latent and somewhat confused elements of all these personal equations emerge—my life, my work, my faith, and my integrity—and by association I daresay you have enriched and ennobled all these even if it now seems just the opposite."[30]

She wanted their friendship to last longer, but such was not to be. The brutal world that had been his childhood taught him how to disengage instantly when he sensed conflict or danger. He had a survivor's instincts that were neither polished nor cordial. The experience of betrayal for someone who has difficulty trusting others is impossible to forgive. And she would betray that friendship. Nothing else after that was possible. In the end, to Walker, Wright became cold, heartless, and a wanton opportunist.

The letter, dated June 7, 1939, was seven single-spaced typed pages, and it would be her last letter to Wright. Ultimately, she had written a full apology, detailing everything as she understood it, and signed it "your comrade and friend." Because he would never tell her what had happened, only that she *had to know* what it was, she affirmed what it was that she did know. This required her to recount what had happened between them in the course of their three years together.

All of the precipitating events she identified were connected to gossip: either she reported to him something she'd heard to him or had been guilty of repeating something someone else said without questioning it. Wright must have attributed her actions generally to mean-spiritedness and jealousy. She remembered that within a few months of Wright's departure, the sexual politics operating inside the SSWG quickly caused the group to disintegrate. Members projected their stress and anxieties onto the more vulnerable members of the group. She was an easy target, because she had been the least aware of all the dynamics that were operating in the first place.

The latest round of gossip about Hughes and Ward, and implicating Wright and Ward, took her back to the SSWG tensions. Walker would have to share some blame for exacerbating these tensions. Was she to blame also for Ted Ward's exclusion from the special issue of *New Challenge* they had all worked on? The reason given for why she had done so was her resentment of Ward's dramatic adaptation of Wright's short story "Bright and Morning Star."

If Walker had little understanding of the sexual dynamics that were operating in the SSWG, Wright himself might have been naïve or unconcerned about the pressure his own success put on all of them. It didn't help that Ward and Wright both dated several women in the group, Fern Gayden, Marion Minus, and Alberta Sims among them,[31] which only heightened the tension. All she could see was that Wright was trying to get her to believe the worst about herself, "a wretched woman capable of utter dissimulation, most horrible deception, and thoroughly callous and reprehensible. Well, I do not propose either in the deepest reaches of my own personality or in the consciousness of the comrades whom I have deemed my friends . . . to allow myself to be bullied and intimidated into such an awful picture of myself. I beg the privilege of pleading my case if not trial by jury," she wrote.[32]

Belief in her innocence in relationship to all of the dissension in the SSWG seems surprising. Her sense of responsibility for being Wright's ear may have blinded her to the impact it may have had on her decisions and the way in which others saw her, especially after she assumed the leadership role in the SSWG in his absence. Her initial letters to him in New York had typically summarized the SSWG's goings-on and what was happening in Chicago, and Wright hadn't seemed to mind her reports at all. Within the context of the New York incident, however, her earlier actions took on a different meaning. Certainly, a man with a troubled history with women would have reacted negatively to any suggestion of a sexual relationship between two of his male friends in an era that relegated homosexuality to the closet. Would not implicating two of his closest male friends implicate him as well? This incident may have given him the excuse he needed to end a relationship that was becoming more complicated than he wanted or needed it to be.

Her final letter to Wright was the fiftieth she had written over a two-year period, completing the cycle of an intensely political relationship and affirming the trust and affection they had for one another that was as deep as it was complex. We know only one side of this relationship or what happened, since Wright's letters to Walker have not survived, or at least they were not included in the archival materials that were transferred to the repository at Jackson State. However, the employment of certain rhetorical devices indicate that Walker and Wright responded to each other in kind; he apparently wrote to her nearly as often as she did to him. Most of her entries begin with "So glad to get your letter today," the specific date of receipt of a letter from him, or the answers to certain questions and requests he had made. The suddenness of their breakup suggests that only a romantic affair could have such an effect on a person.

What casts a shadow over this discussion or at least has become the source of considerable controversy is related to what happened after the failed friendship. Wright's subsequent marriages to white women, a first secret marriage to Dhimah Meidman, and following his divorce from her, a more public marriage to Ellen Poplar with whom he had two children, have led to interpretations of Wright's negative attitudes toward Black women. As one of those Black women, Walker took it upon herself to explain Wright in her later biography, a decision that would bring her neither favor nor praise. For those who take the biographical details of his life and attitudes expressed in his autobiographical and fictional work to mean a rejection of Black women, Walker seemed to be at least one concrete realization of that rejection. Neither would *Daemonic Genius* change the general opinion about her relationship and feeling for Wright, or Wright's attitudes toward women, since it was based partly on research but also on her journals that she kept from their time together. It is easy to assume that the years never eased the pain she experienced from the loss of their friendship, and that it was unrequited love in one form or another. Equally as easy has it become to believe that Wright would not, could not, marry a Black woman because his own feelings about Black people were so conflicted, feelings that he transferred to Black women. He never wrote to her again. She wrote to him only once more, a brief note congratulating him on the publication of *Native Son*, the book that she had helped make possible.

When her relationship with James Russell Brown ended, Walker did not allow herself to linger in the bitterness it had caused. She had determined that she would have felt far too restrained in a marriage with Brown, especially after she had begun to think of herself as a rebel; she could thus justify her choice to reject him. However, she began her social and political transformation in a combination of idealism for the work itself and idealization of Wright; the failure of their relationship was far more difficult to comprehend, because it caused her to question her allegiance both to an ideology and to the individual who personified it.

Those who knew Dick Wright, including Ted Ward, noted that Wright let friendships go easily, no doubt owing to his own insecurities that developed into a full-blown paranoia in his later years. Casual friendships never came easily for Wright, but easily ended. Walker opened up about their relationship at a meeting at the University of Iowa in 1970, and her talk became the basis for her essay "Richard Wright" in *New Letters* in 1971, which she expanded into her biography published seventeen years later. By the time Walker began talking about Wright, she had opted for a psychological reading, one that allowed her to maintain a distant and objective tone. "I think we were "rather good friends . . . a rare and once-in-a-lifetime association . . . rather uncommon in its completely literary nature,"[33] she wrote as she opened her essay.

She may have taken the high road in her June 7 letter, but her journals reveal the emotions she was reluctant or unable to express throughout their two-year correspondence. Her ability to maintain these separate spheres, marking her political life and her private thoughts, was an important part of the discipline she had developed. Although her letters to Wright were personal, they are also filled with dutiful reminders about taking care of his health and dressing properly for the weather, just as they contain chatty gossip about Communist Party politics and the machinations of the SSWG. Though her letters are private, Walker considered them her principal connection to the person who had been her best teacher, and who saw her as his most trusted reader. The tell-all nature of her letters and the journals are, however, different. The latter remained a true record of her life without concealment.

12

As Low Down as the Blues Will
Let You Be

Despite what Walker thought about herself in 1939 after she returned to Chicago, the literary world had opened its doors to her. "For My People" continued to attract major attention. She was no longer a struggling young poet, but one with a growing reputation, which no one could question after *Poetry* published two more of her poems, "The Struggle Staggers Us," and "We Have Been Believers." Their successful placement affirmed her poetic talent, making the fiction she thought she needed to write much less important.

For reasons not connected to Wright, she was giving more attention to what she read in *New Masses*, the "mouthpiece in the struggle for a better world."[1] There she found feature articles by women that were not limited to women's issues and was excited to discover women on its editorial board. *New Masses* welcomed Black writers, especially since there was considerable discussion about the Negro struggle for freedom and the Democratic Front. One could count on the magazine to cover all the major political issues with in-depth commentaries, and it featured articles by the leading members of the Left worldwide. Despite being under communist control, she could expect to see multiple perspectives on social and economic developments and reports on a wide range of cultural events. One of its largest sections was devoted to reviewing relevant literature. It never apologized for being in the forefront of the "battle for the common people."[2] Work by Langston Hughes was a regular feature, as she enjoyed essays and reviews by Ralph Ellison, Eugene Clay Holmes, and William G. Pickens, with guest appearances by E. Franklin Frazier and Harlem Renaissance poet Gwendolyn Bennett.

Despite her interest in women's writing, Walker was not prepared at this point to identify more closely with women artists and writers, preferring to admire them from afar. She had all but lost touch with the men in the SSWG, but also with most of the women. Thus, she found it easier to restrict her friendships to women outside the SSWG group but continued to strongly identify with women in areas other than the arts, like spiritual leader Mary Baker Eddy, one of her favorites. Efforts to relate to white women, no matter how hard she tried, were difficult because she saw them as being too different from her. She was genuinely uncomfortable with the fraternizing between Black men and white women. She

The House Where My Soul Lives. Maryemma Graham, Oxford University Press. © Oxford University Press 2022.
DOI: 10.1093/oso/9780195341232.003.0012

did not believe that most of them were able to give "one's life to a human cause even to death [as] the greatest bravery."[3]

With three poems now having appeared in *Poetry*, Walker began to feel a stronger connection, if not comparison to some of the more popular women poets, Louise Bogan, Elinor Wylie, Edna St Vincent Millay, Dorothy Parker, "and all the tribe of women" she read, "sometimes with relish." On the other hand, she told herself, "I don't want to be influenced too much by any of them. I'd rather be influenced by men if I have to be influenced by anybody."[4] That she could define herself as a "rebel, against convention, against formal religion and religious institutions, against planned morality, and false superficial standards,"[5] yet remain so wedded to the idea of male dominance, suggests the unevenness of her development and the difficulty she would have shifting gears when there was a more active women's movement. Even with her practice of continual self-interrogation, Walker remained grounded in a male-centered world, which in many ways made her more vulnerable because of the trust she put in them.

The world of communist ideas and activism had educated her, strengthening her desire to see "the good life begin and the mythical kingdom of heaven be realized on earth . . . with peace and plenty for all."[6] Her reference to the "sure faith we can keep"[7] makes it difficult to distinguish between a deep spiritualism, grounded in her own religious history and the visionary goals of a radical social movement, since she comfortably operated between the two. Thus, when she faced the bitter infighting in the Writers' Project, brought on by the growing resistance to WPA reformism and Democratic control in Congress, she could speak about "the gradual deterioration in morale . . . on the Project" and conclude, "The project is my bread and butter and I must not endanger myself there," but added quickly, "I look on it as a means to an end."[8] The decision was a wise one, because as soon as she decided not to worry about the battles at work, she could focus more on her own writing.

Walker spent the weeks before her twenty-third birthday conducting an inventory of her activities, reassessing her goals, and identifying her strengths and weaknesses. Despite recurring health concerns and exorbitant medical bills, she had learned to take better care of herself and had been able to turn her nervous energy into productive work. The psychotic episodes that plagued her childhood were happily down to a minimum. Sounding less like the new and fanatical political convert that she had been at first, she defined her progress in three important areas: political, personal, and professional. She had increased her understanding of a Marxist approach to literature; she was more self-assured and aware of her limitations; her relationship to her parents had shifted from blind loyalty to a healthy love and respect; and her publication list was steadily growing. To add to her excitement, audiences were demanding her public appearances, always wanting her to perform "For My People." Because reading aloud was her standard practice, "For My People" was a poem written to be read. She found herself gaining as much pleasure in the reading as her audiences did in hearing it. When George Dillon, the editor of *Poetry*, included her as one of the readers in a live radio broadcast, "For My People" began its first venture into the public poetry world. Walker and "For My People" thus became inseparable as a couple, for better or worse.

She concluded her musings in her birthday journal entry: she wanted to "express the soul of my people . . . speak[ing] for them as one of them, among them and with them." What was left was to become "whole within," she wrote, "whole of mind and body and spirit." The entry is a mandate as much as anything:

> I want to become adjusted to society and I want to live in perspective with clarity of vision to see my world and others as well as the whole. I want to bring happiness to those who trust me most and whom I love devotedly; I want to relieve my family of strain in every way, I want to become their helper, their champion and their pride.[9]

Ten months before the New York incident with Dick Wright, the Walker sisters had left Chicago for their first return to New Orleans after a four year absence, a reward they both believed they deserved. It was August 1938, and Mercedes was nearing completion of her studies, having given several successful recitals. But the oldest daughter in the Walker family, whom most would remember as a rather nervous girl, was now a recognized and published poet. And she knew that Marion was eager to vet the invitations her daughter would get to read while she was at home. She felt a strong desire to test her new identity as a writer within the context of her home community. On August 12, she and Mercedes boarded a bus in Chicago bound for Memphis, not having enough money to take the train. There they would change buses to go to Jackson, Mississippi, and finally take another bus to New Orleans.

She knew Mississippi to be the worst part of the journey, the state where almost any action by a Black person could cause trouble, and one never knew what or how severe the punishment would be. The stops in Memphis and Jackson were sharp reminders of what they'd left behind and to which they were now returning, since Jim Crow officially began or ended there, depending on which direction one was headed. In Memphis, they went straight to the back row, joining other Negroes who were already seated.

Having traveled mostly by train, which their parents believed to be safe, neither of the sisters was prepared for what they soon encountered. As if to keep Blacks and whites from breathing the same air, a celluloid screen separated Black from white. Segregation advocates wanted to be sure to get their message across. The screen did its job so well that it allowed very little fresh air to enter their part of the bus, making Walker feel faint, since the temperature was over 100 degrees. Before modern air-conditioned bus travel, bus companies could only alleviate this situation with frequent rest or comfort stops. In this case, the bus stations after Memphis had seen fit only to maintain the restrooms for whites; the Negro passengers saw no "colored only" signs anywhere. Remembering the pride instilled in her by her parents, Walker refused to suffer the indignity of going outside to a grassy meadow to relieve herself. She was determined to wait until they found a suitable restroom. She asked only to stop for ammonia to fight off the fainting spells and continued to suffer through the journey, getting sicker by the minute from the combination of heat and the need to relieve herself. She depended on Mercedes to contribute for both of them to a group exchange that took place among several old school friends, who also boarded in Memphis. By the time they got to Brookhaven, Mississippi, they knew most of the people in the colored section, but she ate none of the food they had packed to bring along.

Their stories reminded her that returning home was a ritual of singular importance. One's hope was always to have a job, so that returning home marked the transition from childhood to adulthood and independence. Families could brag about those who now worked "up North," and though they may have had jobs with little distinction, they had escaped field labor, exchanging it for a factory or service job earning a decent wage. Whether one took the train or bus, one could also expect to meet a wide assortment of people, and this trip was no exception. Walker found herself surrounded by people whose stories won her interest: a beautician, who fancied herself as the next Madame C. J. Walker; a teacher, whose school was the only one in a sharecropping community; and, the less-hopeful fourteen-year-old boy, who had already witnessed two lynchings. Nevertheless, she admired the glamour of their attire—freshly pressed hair, bright gingham dresses, wide lapels on newly purchased suits, and brand-new pointed-toe shoes. These people kept her from completely giving in to her misery as the trip continued.

The conditions she had to endure incensed her, causing her to respond in a lengthy journal entry once they arrived in New Orleans. "It would be better if they refused to sell us seats and did not take our money at all rather than put us on those back seats that were not fit for dogs much less human beings."[10] She was, nonetheless, very conscious of making such a statement in Louisiana and not Mississippi, where the racial consequences of appearing to express those feelings in any form of action would have been far too dangerous.

By the time they got to New Orleans, they were exhausted, dehydrated, and in dire need of a bath. Walker fell into her grandmother's bed and slept for fourteen hours straight. Her father had taken on ministerial duties at a local church in Alexandria, where Marion had joined him, leaving uninterrupted time with

Grandma Dozier, the thing Walker enjoyed the most. Her energy was quickly restored, and she reemerged in excellent spirits.

Then began a whirlwind of activity, as Walker accepted as many reading engagements as she could. Marion was in stage mom heaven, marveling at how comfortable her daughter felt in front of people, without the least bit self-consciousness as others showered compliments on how well she looked. Once shy and embarrassed by what she perceived as physical unattractiveness, she now saw her looks as appropriate for the poet she had become, invigorated by each reading. Each hearty round of applause was an affirmation. She was also proud of fulfilling her mother's desire: Marion was able to promote her two daughters who could now perform together, one as a musician, the other as a poet. Dividing her time between social events and parties in her honor sponsored by friends, as expected of her, Walker acquiesced to separate readings to Black and white audiences, pleased that the numbers in each audience were comparable. She read her poetry for a live broadcast on KALB radio in New Orleans, which also featured her mother's musical group. For four days, she turned down no request to speak at a school or for a local group.

These Southern audiences gave Walker the opportunity to perfect her public readings of "For My People." For as much as her Chicago audiences enjoyed the poem, the real test of her ability was on the home front. She knew that at each home reading she was not representing herself. Rather she was the personification of others, everything anyone could ever imagine themselves to be. Her heightened awareness of the place and the people therefore drove her to connect as deeply as she could in readings to the New Orleans Black community in particular. The lyrical quality of the poem meant that she easily varied the pitch and tone of her voice as she moved from stanza to stanza. She replaced her audience's expectation of rhymed lines, to which most of her audiences were accustomed, by focusing on the rhythms embedded in the phrases. She had an old-fashioned sense about these things, taking her chances while reading by inviting her listeners with her eyes, hand gestures, and body movements. She began the last stanza quietly, building up gradually until she was almost singing the final lines. Each performance achieved the effect that she desired, since the final crescendo was climactic, drawing an immediate reaction from the audience. Those to whom she read needed no deeper understanding of political theory or knowledge of aesthetics to appreciate the work. The poem may have evolved out of her political activism, but her message needed no translation. "For My People" had become its own thing, capable of generating new meaning with each reading.

With the success of her visit home and committed to returning for a longer visit at Christmas, Walker returned to Chicago renewed. She felt more prepared for the turmoil in the Writers' Unit of the Communist Party. The battle to save the New Deal programs, and especially the WPA, had everyone on edge. Moreover, every organization to which she belonged had several members who were on one or more of the relief programs supported by the government. Most people were still too close to the Great Depression to hold out much hope that they could survive the storms that were forming on the horizon.

The excitement and sense of renewal she brought back to Chicago was quickly offset by widespread criticism of the Writers' Project. Its employees were being charged with having too much political clout, and the WPA was in imminent danger of losing its funding. Controversy came from inside and outside the Democratic Party, which had generated broad public support for its large-scale federal works programs, conceived during President Franklin Delano Roosevelt's administration. Republicans were outraged at the way the popularity of the relief programs so easily translated into votes. They argued—with substantial supporting evidence—that individuals employed by the WPA programs used their influence to coerce, intimidate, and press for votes. Communists did not control the WPA programs, but they were on the payrolls, and their political activities invited increasing suspicion. Even the Democrats were somewhat in agreement about the degree of federal corruption.

In 1939, Congress passed the Hatch Act, sponsored by New Mexico senator Carl Hatch. Intended to halt the presumed misuse and abuse of public funds designated for relief or public works, the Hatch Act gained a reputation as a response to the threat of communism, since it stated specifically that membership in "any political organization which advocates the overthrow of our constitutional form of government" was forbidden.[11]

Walker followed the lines of argument as much as she could, mostly from the viewpoint of the Communist Party that came from *New Masses*, but she found it all very disconcerting. Still confused on ideological matters, she had not gained clarity by attending the Workers School, since most of its sessions had focused on the trade-union movement. While she did understand that the attacks were not aimed at any individuals, she did not know to which side of the issue she belonged when she heard distinctions between supporters of the trade-union movement and cultural projects. While both had coexisted in the WPA Writers' Project and in many of the mass organizations that had informal ties to the Communist Party, varying degrees of practice without absolute unity around ideological positions existed. Some wanted to read, some to write, and there were those who were working as organizers. Those who joined the party, however, were expected to work in the mass organizations. If they did not, they were chastised.

She went to meetings but found that heated debates and infighting caused further confusion for her, or she would be singled out among those criticized for being too undisciplined. Her attendance at Communist Party meetings became spotty for another reason. Money was scarce, making it impossible to keep her membership dues current. She nevertheless had considered herself a card-carrying member of the party since late 1937. Because the communists were considered the root of government corruption, while the affiliation provided her with support and opportunities earlier, she found little protection for herself now. She carried all the wrong labels: a communist and a WPA worker. Like all WPA workers, she was under careful scrutiny and faced a mountain of suspicion.

She began to reflect on her venture into the Communist Party. Five reasons emerged from her list: to attain greater knowledge about the craft of writing; to advance her understanding of political, economic, and social questions; to gain a certain discipline; to work more closely with those interested in "the Negro problem"; to serve as a guide to her living. Now she could only see that she had energy to continue her writing. "I intend to stick [with it] as long as I feel there is a reason I should," she wrote, "but I realize that no movement could exist and continue if all were like me."[12]

Her fears were well-founded. While *New Masses* could celebrate the "mushroom growth of the army of socialist partisans" and "Radicals in Rompers" in July 1937, a year later, Earl Browder, head of the CP-USA summarized the November 1938 election results by pointing out that "Nothing is ever gained by underestimating the effective forces of the enemy. And we must say frankly that the people suffered many defeats."[13] Roosevelt's upper-class supporters began to desert him, adding to the Republicans' "flank attack" against the New Deal. In the end, Republicans gained control in eighteen states, representing more than a 100 percent increase. The crumbling forces among leftist organizations, as well as conflicts and splits within the local American Federation of Labor chapters, the trade-union leagues, the Congress of Industrial Organizations, the Non-Partisan League, the Socialist Party, the American Labor Party, and other progressive organizations all contributed to the shift. Exacerbating the tensions was the spread of Trotskyism, which challenged the CP-USA line. Demoralization within the leftist movement and widespread confusion among the masses of voters gave the upper hand to the opposition forces.

Martin Dies, one of the New Deal's most vocal and influential opponents in Congress, helped to plant the seeds of anti-communist hysteria. In 1937, he had formed the Dies Committee, later the House Committee on Un-American Activities (HUAC), installing himself as chair from 1937 to 1944. Dies worked with the Senate Committee to Investigate Election Practices, producing enough evidence to permanently designate communism as a well-designed plot financed by "Moscow gold" and hell-bent on destroying America. Red-baiting became standard fare, and communism was stripped of all that had been good and decent about it.

She found herself pulling back from it all, unable to find a comfortable place. Her familiarity with the communist programs and methods for attaining social and economic equality for Blacks had come through its organizations. The American Negro Labor Congress, the League of Struggle for Negro Rights, the International Committee of Negro Workers, the National Negro Congress, the Southern Conference of Human Welfare, and the Southern Negro Youth Movement, among others, had been the context in which many Black leaders had emerged. Some had sought membership in the Communist Party, while others were certainly "fellow-travelers." Given the framing of the work for most Negro leaders as race radicals, and perhaps less so as confirmed communists, Blacks felt increasingly alienated as the Communist Party closed ranks to save itself. The issues became more complex as communists themselves began thinking in terms not so much of socialism against capitalism, but rather of democracy against fascism. Communists also saw the practicality of a broad-based united-front effort to defeat the spread of fascism as a worldwide threat, but it did little to reduce the latent fears about themselves as enemies of America. The Communist Party also failed to maintain the confidence of many of its Black constituents when it redirected much of its effort toward the fight against fascism, pushing the struggle for equal rights further into the background.

She remembered having lashed out at Wright before their correspondence had ended, "You had convinced me that as a Negro and a writer the program of the Party would be best for me," she wrote.[14] Now her observations as she faced possible unemployment were real. First, she had found it difficult to separate her emotional state—the normal crisis of a twenty-three-year-old—from everything that was happening around her. Second, writing—the very thing that had brought her into the party—was the source of the greatest dissension in virtually every group of which she was part. She was simply not prepared for the hostility toward creative writing and art from those who saw themselves as educating the masses.

As always in her journals, she began to analyze and comment in greater detail on the "trouble and turmoil" she was experiencing. What became clearer in her own mind was that she had been foolish, and that any real security she could expect to feel lay in the freedom to make choices in her own life.[15] Now, she had no security and felt embarrassed by her actions. She needed to find a way for these revelations to guide her actions from that day forward.

How those who considered themselves progressive thinkers realigned organizationally and ideologically in the face of the attacks and misrepresentation of New Deal programs and policies and the fear of a world takeover by Adolf Hitler and Benito Mussolini is difficult to judge. Walker's sense of abandonment was total, having lost the one person who had made sense of it all and the group of writers who shared the same sensibility. That larger context, therefore, began to interest her less and less, as she refocused her energies on writing. Her disillusionment symbolized the failure of communism to take root and remain a dominant force in America and the extent to which reactionary forces will go to prevent any lasting social change.

Keenly aware of the tentativeness of her own position, Walker began to see the value of leaving Chicago. The WPA was a job, a very good job, she told herself. It paid the rent and put food on the table, and it brought the first truly satisfying relationships she had ever had. But she seemed to have lost sight of what now seemed larger. She was still unable to contribute very much to her family. Realizing how much her family had sacrificed for her and her sister's education, she felt selfish and insensitive that she was only occasionally in a position to support them. Paying off her own college loans little by little, along with huge doctors' bills for her chronic psychosis, made her financial situation more precarious.

When she and Mercedes returned home to New Orleans for Christmas in December 1938, Walker felt that her mother was finally treating her as a young adult, with fewer complaints about her behavior and attitude. During most of their two-week stay, her father was in Scotlandville, a small town near Baton Rouge. Their parents' positions at New Orleans University had ended when NOU became Dillard University in 1935. Marion had been eager to start her second music studio, this time in New Orleans, where she had a large clientele and a solid reputation as a music teacher. Sigismund Walker renewed his Methodist affiliation and accepted a church in Scotlandville as his official church appointment. The church was within walking distance from Southern University, another Negro college in the region, but Sigismund was no longer able to manage a teaching job and tend to the needs of a congregation, no matter how small it might be.

Walker and her sister were still in Scotlandville when the students, many of whom attended Sunday services and the Sunday evening youth fellowship at their father's church, returned from Christmas vacation. Walker was amazed at how eye-opening her conversations were with these young people, most of whom were her age. Having spent much of her time among highly sensitive writers who were often unable to manage their own emotions, she saw level-headed young people whose friendly banter provided welcome relief. She saw young women and men chiding either other, who expressed few fears about where the next dollar was coming from. Suddenly she saw a distinction between what she regarded as weak, insecure artists, afraid to take responsibility for their own lives, nagging and complaining most of the time, and those hardworking students from rural towns in the South whom she met. Eager to learn all they could in the basic subjects, some had ambitions of becoming doctors and lawyers, and many felt they had been called to the ministry but knew that a formal education would give them better options in life.

At home with her parents, she sensed her mother's discomfort with the unexpected costs associated with their change of status. As former college teachers, the Walkers struggled to reestablish themselves in a lower-income bracket at the same time her father began to show signs of ill health. Walker's instincts told her that she needed to take over the mortgage on the home her parents had purchased in Scotlandville. She wanted to demonstrate her ability to be a responsible, if not financially successful, daughter. She knew her mother would not object. But how could she do this?

They returned to Chicago in the bitter cold of mid-January and learned that the Writers' Unit of the Communist Party was scheduled for dissolution in April. WPA employees, including those in the SSWG, were being reassigned to the street units and ward branches that had little use for writers.

There was some good news: Benjamin Botkin had read her folk sketches. A leading folklorist who served as the national Federal Writers' Project folklore editor, he was already writing landmark essays about folklore. He had begun work on *Lay My Burden Down*, which would later serve as an introduction to the WPA slave narratives, some 2,000 of which were collected in 1937 and 1938 under his watch. She would likely have read his essays, such as "The Folkness of the Folk" (1937) and perhaps "The Folk and the Individual Creative Reciprocity" (1938), and she knew about the huge oral history project on ex-slaves. Botkin was impressed with the work she had done on "Goose Island," and though encouraging, he had little time to give her advice.

She knew hers was the heart of a poet. But the spark for fiction had reignited itself. She continued to be drawn to the idea that her development as an artist was dependent on her mastery of the art of fiction. Given her attitude regarding Emile Zola and her reverence for Wright's fiction, she may have felt that she lacked the passion and control required to produce on the level she felt necessary to claim competence, at least at this stage in her life. "Goose Island" was solid experimental practice, though her mastery of fiction would not be fully realized until she completed *Jubilee* in the 1960s. Furthermore, she had thought a lot and had much to say about writing poetry, an important source for the prose essays she produced in her later years.

She continued to read from a booklist she had developed several years earlier and to get suggestions from her friend Vivian Harsh, who accepted her role as a midwife to the literary movement by actively cultivating various literary networks. Given the highly racially segregated environment in America before the Civil Rights Movement of the 1960s, the branch libraries in African American communities often became a common space where Black readers and Black writers could meet. Walker understood that maintaining relationships with Harsh and other librarians was valuable to her career. Looking ahead to the publication of her books, she knew that even if bookstores did not stock her books, branch libraries had the freedom to acquire books by those authors in whom their constituencies would be interested. These branch libraries often did more to introduce authors to their reading public, since Negro churches or schools might deny a Negro author's visit if they feared repercussions from white funders on whom they frequently relied.

Walker knew that she needed to prepare herself to accept greater responsibility for her family's security as well as her own. With so many ideas milling around in her head, while the novel form seemed an excellent medium, one more likely to provide a lucrative income as a writer, she recognized that she had been unable to develop and stick with a set plot or dialogue. Even with models she used, Hemingway, Stein, Dos Passos, Hurston, and Wright, "Goose Island" remained heavily indebted to the sociological studies she had done while interning at the Institute for Juvenile Research. It was imitative and mechanical, typical WPA-inspired fiction, she said to herself. She was writing a folk novel, but she was trying to follow the criteria for proletarian fiction. Reading the reviews of fiction that regularly appeared in *New Masses*, she understood that she had to create a socially relevant context inspired by the economic situation of the country.

Arnold Shukotoff's [Shaw] summary of the characteristics of proletarian fiction in the January 1939 issue of *New Masses* asked the writer to consider three problems: how to suggest group experience through the presentation of individual experience; how to convince skeptical readers that the unbelievable experiences of the underprivileged are real and not fictitious; and how to communicate to the reader, in addition to the sense of participating in the life of fiction, a desire to understand and participate in the life of social action. Shukotoff asserted that a distinction needed to be made between the psychologism of the 1920s and the preferred social realism of the 1930s. "The neurological dissection of inner disturbances has yielded in attractiveness to the dramatic analysis of social forces that create disturbances. Moments at which life stands still have become less interesting than moments of change,"[16] he wrote. Walker would have taken careful note of Shukotoff's assessment, since at the conclusion of his essay, he cites models, starting with Richard Wright.

"Goose Island" is the story of Roberta, a talented young Negro woman who is unable to escape the influence of the social conditions that surround her. She has dreams of using her musical talents to advance a career but living in the Division Street area of Chicago brings her into contact with a criminal element, including pimps, drug dealers, smugglers, and other undesirables. Walker wanted to make clear that these people had limited choices that forced them to eke out an existence the best way they could. With no positive reinforcement or opportunities coming her way, Roberta marries and abandons her dreams. She steadily drifts into the life of prostitution, as her life goes downhill. The plot is simplistic, but Walker believed that she could present case studies of each of the characters in Roberta's world and weave their stories together into a single narrative. The idea was ahead of its time and one that Black women writers would later embrace.

A generation earlier, another Chicago writer had produced a set of sketches based on the city's Negro population. Marita Bonner wrote what eventually became *Fry Street and Its Environs*, which was never published during her lifetime. Bonner was practically unknown until her rediscovery and the book's publication in 1987,[17] when she benefited from the renewed interest in women's writing. Significant parallels exist between \ Ntsake Shange's *For Colored Girls who have Considered Suicide with the Rainbow is Enuf* (1976) and Gloria Naylor's *Women of Brewster Place* (1982) to suggest that an experimental narrative form had much appeal to Black women writers much earlier. James Nagel indicates its growing popularity among writers of color, especially women.[18] For Walker and Bonner, the women's lives and their stories are best captured through interconnecting narratives, often without a central plot, and set in an urban environment.

Roberta's story was important, but not one that found a receptive audience before the 1970s. That neither Walker nor Bonner saw their narratives in print during their lifetime—Walker's "Goose Island" is still a manuscript—invites questions about the critical environment in which Black women writers were operating in the early decades of the twentieth century. Zora Neale Hurston, who became famous as a recovered author long after her death, remains the best known Black woman writer who published in a period dominated by Black men before the 1940s. Although she chose a rural South folk setting, Hurston's experiences and the negative critical reception of her work forecast what Bonner and Walker may have anticipated had their work emerged sooner.

When Walker talked about "Goose Island" with Jacqueline Miller Carmichael in 1992, she admitted that "it wasn't a well written novel and it wasn't organized."[19] She was looking for a way to bring two sets of experiences together: her work at the Institute for Juvenile Research and her studies of Marxism and dialectical materialism, which she had struggled to grasp. "Goose Island" was the result of her political activism, but it would take much more experience than she had at that point as a writer to turn her ideas into art.

Walker judged her fiction by the expectations she had been able to achieve with her poetry, which had taught her how to maintain lyrical control in the language of a structured poem. Her failure to gain this kind of control in "Goose Island" led to her increasing dissatisfaction: her narrative voice simply did not have the power of her lyrical voice, she concluded. "Goose Island" was an apprentice work that afforded her good practice, and it allowed her to fulfill her WPA writing assignments.

She ultimately put the "Goose Island" project aside, believing it was for the last time. Walker knew that the only chance she had was with her poetry. Now it was time for her to return to it. Her fiction had grown out of the collective process; she and Wright had worked together, but somehow it seemed to have benefited him far more than her. She would soon be unemployed, having saved no money.

She could not help herself or her parents. She was now alone, feeling emotions that had been reluctant to present themselves earlier. To keep the fears and sense of loss out of her mind, she submitted to the words that spilled out in rhythms, relying on symbols to call forth a state of mind. Here her spirit could refresh itself and channel the emotions into an organized form. She could not cast off the uncertainty that she confronted, and she sensed her soul needed healing. She had reached one of those moments where she was feeling a "as low down as the blues will let you be."[20]

13
Time Is a Mighty Healer

Walker's existence within a group of New Negroes whose early achievements defied the norm for Black America brought with it a heightened sense of duty that often wrestled with feelings of desire. Her father's educational achievements, especially his advanced degree from Northwestern, had become the model: it was her duty and a clear expectation that she would return for a second degree. Her parents had brought their gifts and talents to Negro institutions, where they could play an active role in uplifting the race, as it was understood at the time. This coalescing of the practical, the social, and intellectual had not been a choice for most of those who might have been considered members of the Negro intelligentsia a generation earlier. Walker had pushed open a space for an education of a new type, and her expanding political awareness brought a distinct set of abilities. None of this changed fundamentally who she was. The public Margaret Walker could live in a world of political action and exhibit a radical identity; she was a professional poet and a credit to her race. The private Margaret Walker never diverted from her introspective moods, the tendency toward self-analysis and reflection. She had mastered the art of interiority, relying upon herself alone to know what to do and who to become. Looking deeply inside herself with the assurances of the last two years laid bare, she could always resolve any tension between duty and desire. Searching her soul gave her the key to enter a new house that she would need to find how to build.

The voice that she had found while living in Chicago affirmed her existence as a poet, and she could not let that go. That writerly identity expressed itself in an enormous output between 1932 and 1939, most of which remains unpublished journal poems from the Chicago years. They reflect her characteristic soul-searching, for which they were intended, not for public dissemination. One in particular stands out:

> For then you seem
> A perfect looking glass [in] which I see
> The image of my soul
> My moodiness
> That others do not fathom
> And edges where the roughness is not gone
> And most of all

The House Where My Soul Lives. Maryemma Graham, Oxford University Press. © Oxford University Press 2022.
DOI: 10.1093/oso/9780195341232.003.0013

My troubled search
For that illusive something
These groping hands of mine
Reach out in vain to grasp[1]

The poem stands among the twenty that she wrote focused on Chicago as a place of significance for Walker's literary imagination. The first relationships she had formed outside of those dictated by her parents were in Chicago, and it was the first city with which she and her sister would become familiar as young, independent women. But it was also Chicago that gave her the emotional distance to publicly acknowledge the power of the "fire burning within," the necessity of finding a form giving it full expression, and the rightness that it should be shared with others as one's life work.

Chicago, therefore, continued to loom large in her imagination as the place where her career expectations could be fulfilled. An early thought, therefore, had been studying sociology at the University of Chicago because of the friendships she shared with St. Clair Drake and Horace Cayton, who talked excitedly about their work with Robert Park. She accepted the view that Chicago could serve as a laboratory for studying the lives of Negroes. Ideas from her discussions with Wright, Drake, and Cayton had found their way into many of her WPA writing assignments. "Goose Island" she might have seen as the most important beneficiary if she were to pursue a degree at the University of Chicago.

As part of Walker's routine practice of using poetry as personal reflection, we can see the same group of unpublished Chicago poems as looking both forward and back at her life. "On the Road" honors the journey from Louisiana to Chicago, while another poem is an elegy to the stillborn sibling that the family never discussed. The poems show a variety of emotion and themes, love, the consequences of sin, and nature. Still searching for a form, the use of end rhyme is fairly consistent.

The WPA was being eliminated, and Chicago had served its purpose for her. The thought of leaving invited deeper reflections about the years she had spent there, what she had learned, and what more she might need to realize her full potential as a poet. Furthering her education as a way of increasing her job security was a practical consideration. A 1974 autobiographical essay, "My Creative Adventure," explains the stages of her life in the context of her growing understanding of creativity. The essay begins with her informal and formal education and professional training and experiences, out of which Walker extrapolates a process that includes psychological and personality-driven factors, one that is both conscious and unconscious, and that requires God-given talent accompanied by learning and developing a craft. Her own process might have begun with her "desire and determination" as a child, but it had to evolve into "perceptual and conceptual thinking," in order to effect "new knowledge and invention," the success of which is measured by the "aesthetic reaction."[2] Although this is one of several places where Walker reminds us that finding her voice came only after graduating college and while working on the Federal Writers' Project in Chicago, that cerebral process nurtured by a rich cultural and intellectual environment was incomplete. She had yet to discover "for myself the kind of thinking that makes a poem or the way to organize any imaginative writing."[3]

Walker believed in the romantic idea that poets bore the responsibility for translation. This idea began to figure into her understanding of creativity and the subsequent role of poets: "to make, create, fabricate . . . cooperating with the creation energies of the universe and using the total personalities to accomplish this fact."[4] She acknowledged the source of her views, especially William Wordsworth, whose work her father had introduced to her as a child, and whom she had also studied in college.

When we put the reflections and uncertainties in the unpublished Chicago journal poems together with later essays that reference the critical period leading up to her departure from Chicago, we see that Walker had not taken for granted her status as a successful new writer. She knew, more than anyone, that "For My People" had become a singular work for its time. She knew, too, viewing the poem in relationship to her developing political consciousness during 1930s was not in itself a bad thing. But she also recognized that leaving Chicago needed to provide new grounding for her, to confirm that "For My People" as a single poem was not a one-time thing, and to guarantee a way for her to create and produce work that would always be timely in any period or any place. Walker turned to Wordsworth because he explained best how the poet can bring the subjectivity of feeling to a series of recurring objective experiences. Wordsworth, in Walker's words, had seen the spontaneous "emotion, image, meaning, movement, beauty reoccur" which are all "recollected in tranquility."[5] She transferred and used that process in different ways time again and again, starting with the 1937 appearance of "For My People," in Poetry, with subsequent poems there a few months later, and still others in Opportunity, the leading Negro arts and culture magazine for more than twenty-five years. She needed to prepare herself to produce work that would last.

What she does not say in the 1974 essay was that these appearances of her poetry, in the leading white magazine and a leading Negro one, had broken the color barrier for her. The sense of this new status fueled her desire to focus exclusively on developing her craft, quickly replacing the need to continue revisions for "Goose Island." The active dialogues with Wright about those revisions were now a thing of the past, although Walker later believed that Wright's interest in the project had more to do with implications for his own work, rather than hers. Ultimately, finding her voice in poems like "For My People," "We Have

Been Believers," and "Southern Song" was as much an achievement as it was a revelation, the thing that was necessary but not sufficient. In time that "troubled search" to which she referred in the Chicago poem would continue as she sought to sustain herself as a person and an artist. If she lacked the confidence to do anything, she could not make it public; rather she had to demonstrate that she could do it better than anyone.

At such critical junctures in her life, when there was no clear option, Walker's parents had insisted that she come home. She had been able to stay in Chicago because her sister was in school. This would be the first time she refused to surrender to their demand, or to the possibility of failure or fear. Her only choice was to try to make it on her own, even if it meant stepping outside of the comfort zone that characterized the lives of most college-educated Negro women in the 1930s. Walker described her situation as a fusion of "rationalist yearnings and artistic inclinations,"[6] propelling her to take a leap of faith. Soon to be unemployed and with no job prospects in sight, having rejected the offer of marriage to one man, and being rejected in turn by another, she knew only to follow the path that presented itself at that moment.

Walker probably learned about the University of Iowa from one of her former Northwestern professors. Although it was past the application deadline, she told her parents that she had planned to begin graduate school, sounding confident enough that they asked few questions. She was not expecting any financial support, which relieved some of the pressure they would have felt. Simultaneously she wrote to Norman Foerster at Iowa's School of Letters, who was a key figure in the new humanist movement and a prolific spokesman for the consolidation of American literature. Though nearly four decades into a new century, American literature had been slow in gaining the respectability as a field of study in US universities, which remained dominated by European history and British literature.

She needed to dream big. Getting into Iowa would provide some of the access to publishers she believed was lost when her friendship with Wright ended. She would certainly have been motivated by a desire to prove to Wright that she could advance her career without him. At the same time, as the child of educators, she knew that her parents would approve any effort to ensure her security and gainful employment. Her determination overshadowed the reality since she had no idea how she might finance this education.

Walker actually knew very little about the Iowa Writers' Workshop and asked only about the possibility of entering the graduate program in English. Although she sent manuscripts to Foerster, it was the second person to whom she wrote, Paul Engle, recently appointed dean of the School of Letters, who had been most encouraging after reviewing samples of her poetry and prose. Neither Walker nor Engle knew what was in store for them. For Walker, Engle became her professional advisor for the remainder of her career, someone she could turn to at critical moments. For Engle, Walker became one of his most successful "experiments."

She heard from Engle and Foerster around the same time she got the notice about the layoffs at the Federal Writers' Project. Although she had no confirmation of admission into the program, she proceeded to make plans for her departure. When her final check came, she was able to clear $50, but $20 of that was already committed to Northwestern for the transcript that would not be released to Iowa without it. With another $20, she put down enough money for two more weeks of rent and bought several weeks of groceries, which she hoped could spread out even longer. Mercedes was still living at the Hyames', but a full-year scholarship and work aid—more than she'd ever received before—could allow her to complete a second degree to better prepare her for her musical career. Mercedes would continue to supplement her income by playing for churches and serving as an accompanist at recitals.

Even though Walker had Mercedes's full support in her decision to leave Chicago, Walker's old guilt about abandoning her sister surfaced once again. It is likely that the senior Walkers had pressed this point, since they had only agreed to let their older daughter remain in Chicago to help out with her younger sister's education. While this was not the *ostensible* reason, she could never forget that it was her return to Northwestern, and not her sister's, that her parents supported. Her feelings alternated between guilt and distress. They had shared a room all their lives, had gone through high school together, left the South together, and had grown even closer together as a result of their experiences at Northwestern and living in Chicago. Facing separation for the first time would not be easy. Walker's need to put some very negative experiences in Chicago behind her, a need to avert what appeared to be visible signs of a nervous breakdown, propelled her forward. She drew strength from what she later perceived as a weakness, a fear of being alone, of never having the benefit of "purposeful living and planning."[7] She became more obsessed than ever with a sense of accomplishment, of survival beyond "the possible collapse and the probable ailments."[8] With her remaining cash, she purchased her $4.50 train ticket to Iowa City and looked at it daily until she packed the last of her bags. When the day for her departure came, she launched into her usual litany of self-doubt. "What am I going to do? What is to become of me? Where do I go from here? . . . I wish I knew, yet no one can tell me because no one knows. Perhaps there is dawn just over the hills or the awakening I desire, perhaps the services I must give or the happiness I must have."[9]

She had spent the week saying her goodbyes. The SSWG that had so occupied her time had disbanded; no vestiges of it remained. Nobody asked her anything about Richard Wright. The eerie silence she encountered when she met old friends told her everything she needed to know. She wanted desperately to put all that was negative behind her. One unpublished journal poem from this period is telling. While the subtext may indeed center on loss, the most sustained image is one of self-rejection:

> I have no gifts to offer you
> Nothing save the single catch of fear at night
> Til I feel you breathe
> I have no words to bring you
> Nothing save the empty muteness on my lips
> Where you are near
> I have no beauty dear to dedicate
> Like some high priestess on an altar fire
> No strange and regal power of force commanding you to pledge
> fidelity in me
> I have no gold nor incense nor wiles to cast a spell
> I am a dreamer, all my wealth is wrapped in love for you.[10]

When Russell Marshall came to pick her up to take her to LaSalle Street Station in Chicago, she was relatively calm. It was just after Labor Day when she boarded the Rock Island train, promising herself that the first thing she would do when she arrived in Iowa would be to purchase a new journal. She would have to mark this next and all-important phase of her long and difficult journey in the way that mattered to her the most.

The thought of such a critical transition, living without her sister for the first time, made Walker tense, her mind "full of many things—my body . . . nervous and restless . . . the night . . . a veil of perplexity covering everything."[11] She considered the ending of the Writers' Project as commonplace, tied directly to the end to her seven years in Chicago, signaling that her "days of schooling and probation as a dependent are over." Far more important in this journal entry is the connection she draws between a renewed sense of independence—"I go forward on my own to make my own way" and the world being "once more at war and the high seas are not safe."[12] She was referring to September 3, the day before Labor Day, when France and England had declared themselves at war with Germany in response to Germany invasion of Poland. Two weeks earlier, Germany and the Soviet Union had signed a nonaggression pact, to the consternation of the entire world.

She had to save the "dreamer" that she knew herself to be somehow, and it meant extracting herself from the abyss into which she saw herself falling. She had repeated the words "I want to write a good book, publish a good novel, a good book of verse, an authoritative treatise on Negro folklore" many times before, but beginning a new life in Iowa made them both familiar and new. She was turning inward even more, allowing her thoughts and feelings to gestate.

Walker, who had just turned twenty-four, stood on the train platform in Iowa City and followed the instructions she had received in Chicago. She was to go to the home of Helen Lemme and inquire about a room. But Lemme had filled her rooms with Negro men for the year and directed her to Frances Culbertson's home. Similar to Northwestern, Iowa welcomed Black students by ensuring that they were well placed with Negro families or local teachers. Despite this capitulation to overt segregation, Walker knew that she would have a homelike atmosphere, an introduction to a community where students had genuine support, and the social life they needed to balance an otherwise sterile existence. Frances Culbertson lived in a two-story frame house, most of whose occupants were her immediate and extended family. Culbertson rented one room to Elizabeth Catlett, who would become Walker's roommate. The Culbertsons' residence would be Walker's home for the next ten months at Iowa.

Catlett was in her second and final year of her graduate program. Having studied at Howard University with Lois Mailou Jones and James Porter, Catlett was determined to become an artist and enrolled as one of two Negro students in the Art Department studying under Grant Wood. Brief introductions were followed by Catlett's general advice about registration and the first weeks of classes. What Catlett remembered most, however, was having to stay up all night, as Walker disclosed her painful tale. Finally, able to grieve without anyone judging her, Walker claimed Catlett as her ideal listener. For Catlett, it was an introduction to the woman with whom she would share a close friendship for the remainder of both their lives.

> It was almost like listening to a priest sitting there listening to all that. I was trying to sleep and she was up on her elbow on her bed. I knew some of the people who were involved . . . it was terrible. I did not know who Richard Wright was. Her main point was that he had stolen an idea she had for a novel. I don't remember the name of the novel, but it was about one scene, with the frying pan. She said he took it right out of her book, right out of her manuscript and it appeared in <u>Native Son</u>. She had a crush on him, but I don't think they were any kind of lovers.[13]

Catlett regarded Walker as "old school" and confirmed Walker's expectation that a certain kind of relationship with Wright would materialize. When it did not and ended badly, she continued to reflect on the lessons she believed she had learned. The details that Catlett remembered Walker repeating were like those in Walker's journal. Walker was prepared, however, to gain a new understanding of what had happened in New York. According to Catlett, Walker believed she had committed the ultimate crime by insulting a still-unsure Wright with her allegations about his manhood. It was not simply malicious gossip to announce that

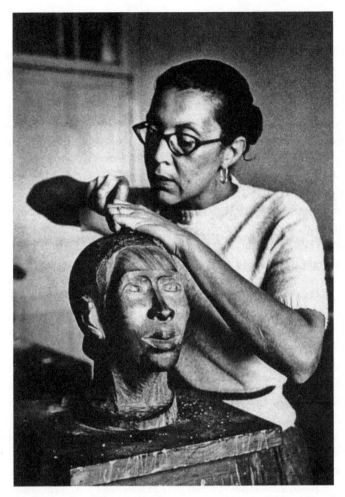

Elizabeth Catlett and Walker met at Iowa and became lifelong friends.

he was living with another man; it was also emasculation made worse because it had not come from white America, and treachery because it came from a woman of his own race whom he considered a close friend and colleague. If Wright had entertained any thoughts of acting upon feelings other than platonic that he had for her, this act obliterated them entirely. His fierce antagonism toward Walker in that instant, was made comprehensible to Catlett, at least in the retelling of the whole sordid affair.

Her move to Iowa City was the right thing to do on many levels. It allowed her to resist and finally escape the prison of self-rejection that she had begun to fall into, even though it was only visible to a few. By moving, she exhibited her growing capacity for transformation, proceeding with direct clarity of mind, as if there were no shifting sands beneath her feet. Going to the University of Iowa was also timely, since Walker joined a cohort of African American artists and intellectuals who would become central to Black culture and institutions. In addition to Elizabeth Catlett in the Art Department there, Negroes were enrolled in the programs in theater, education, and social work, in particular. She formed new and lasting friendships with Carolyn Hills Stewart, Clifford Lamb, Catherine Shaddock, and Luella Margaret Wright,who had become the first Negro faculty member in Iowa's English Department. If the Negro women who came to the university did not stay in private homes, they would more than likely stay in what Catlett referred to as the "girl's house,"[14] which supported the development of a close-knit community, defined as much by exclusion from the more mainstream activities as by certain social and practical needs. Many of the women came to the university only in the summer to complete their graduate degrees between sessions in the schools where they worked during the year.

The friendship between Walker and Catlett began in a way that we might see as typical: one woman listening to another woman's pain. On the one hand, Walker's sleeplessness and periodic health crises made it difficult to share a room with anyone; on the other hand, it made them closer friends. Walker had endured the silence, speaking only to her journal for so long she did not recognize the relief that talking to a stranger provided. While Elizabeth did not replace Mercedes, who knew but rarely spoke openly with her sister about her feelings, she had become the confidante that Walker needed. That a new stage of her life was beginning was clear, as she announced in the first entry of her new journal, "This book was bought with the intention of continuing excursions into the subconscious."[15]

What was not new were the financial worries. Graduate School dean George Dinsmore Stoddard was not the only person shocked by Walker's boldness: first, that the woman who had written a letter introducing herself was a Negro; second, that she came without any money. Walker had come, as she told Stoddard, because she fit the profile of those students that Iowa was trying to attract: creative individuals who would submit a creative project for the master's degree. By the time she had applied, however, she had missed the deadlines for all of the financial awards but was hopeful when she read Paul Engle's encouraging words. What was left was a research position, but the challenge was finding someone willing to hire a Negro. Paul Engle served as her most aggressive advocate, matching Walker with Luella Margaret Wright, who had already begun her tenure on the faculty and who was preparing articles for Iowa's state historical society journal. Engle also pointed out to Walker that she was eligible for support from the Methodist Church. When one of the local churches heard about her, the minister took up an offering that allowed her to register for the semester.

Her initial success was not without some difficulty. Walker was constantly quarreling with the one person without whose support she could never have remained at Iowa, Paul Engle. Their weekly conferences were a war zone, with each taking sides. "I thought he was insulting and condescending to me. He thought I was rude and sharp and bitter, and above all, ungrateful."[16] Not wanting to repeat her experience at Northwestern, forced to leave when her finances ran out, she elected to take more courses in her first semester in order to complete all of her requirements faster. Her plan backfired. She spent too much of the little money she had, without planning ahead for the start of the next semester.

Her greatest distraction at the beginning of 1940, however, came in a different form. Someone had given her a copy of *Native Son*. When she began reading the novel, she welled up with anger, to a state of near collapse:

> I sat in my room reading the novel and I slowly went out of my mind. All of the past three and a half years burgeoned back up and over flowed. For two weeks, I didn't do anything. I ceased to function, I scarcely ate, slept, or bathed. At the end of a week or ten days, I called the Health Center and told [them] my mental condition or state of mind. I was out of school and didn't know it.[17]

In a session with the college psychiatrist, Dr. Gottlieb, to whom she was referred, she began to calm down. Gottlieb drew out of her the emotional torment that embarrassed and consumed her. His analysis helped her finally to understand her real feelings for Richard Wright. She had indeed fallen in love with a man who did not love her. Despite the lack of emotional or physical feelings, theirs was a psychic involvement, Gottlieb explained. In one version of her unpublished autobiography, she summarized the most important lesson from her sessions with him:

> I had unconsciously willed for [Wright] the same kind of success I had potentially from birth willed for myself, and that I felt robbed and cheated not only of my ideas and material and my success, but of myself which in fact I was perfectly willing to sacrifice if that had been what he wanted. Once I was washed and purged and drained of this emotional torment, I faced my school situation.[18]

The "school situation" to which she referred caused further embarrassment. In her frenzied state, she had not only missed classes, but she had also missed the deadline for paying her tuition. When she returned to her classes, she never thought about paying her tuition. In a tearful encounter with Dean Stoddard, who chastised her for not taking care of business, she found someone much less sympathetic than Engle, especially because she acted "proud and independent, quite self-assertive and uppity . . . [not] a bit like [they] thought a Negro woman should be." Once she got over the "wave of pain and shame," she recognized that "time is a mighty healer . . . also a mighty revealer."[19] She did not graduate in June, but the mishap would give her more time to polish "For My People," to send it for a third time to the Yale Younger Poets Competition in the spring of 1940, having been rejected in 1937 and 1938. Not only did she finish her courses that summer, but she also joined a study group that became essential for passing her graduate exams.

The discoveries she made that year had most to do with maturity, self-knowledge, and a kind of cleansing that opened up new possibilities. At the encouragement of some friends, she took a small role in Paul Green's *In Abraham's Bosom* when the Experimental Theatre Iowa produced the play. She enjoyed taking on the character of someone else, giving her the freedom to express feelings that she dared not claim for herself. At twenty-five, Walker's "wild days of youth [were] over. Must clear debts and settle down,"[20] she wrote. She had lived in Chicago for six years and Iowa for one. Emancipation for her meant finding a job and earning a living. Despite her emotional distraction and financial troubles, she completed her course work at Iowa, passed her orals with flying colors, giving, according to Paul Engle, a "brilliant oral, absolutely brilliant."[21] In the meantime, she sensed that something wonderful was about to happen, but not without one more disappointment.

Desperate for some personal attention, tired, and sick, Walker felt let down when no one in her family could afford to come to her August graduation. She had gone to Iowa with ten dollars in her pocket and had earned scholarships from the Methodist Church and National Youth Association to pay tuition. She had asked for money only once, and her father had written to say he did not have the five dollars she needed. To make ends meet, she had typed other students' theses and dissertations, even while she was typing her own manuscript for both the master's thesis and the 1940 Yale Competition. She didn't win, but Stephen Vincent Benét wrote her a personal note on the returned manuscript: she was sure to win the next year, he told her.

Now, her mother had written to say they could not find enough money to send someone to attend her graduation. She cried the entire afternoon that she got the letter. The next morning, she got up feeling hurt and alone. Fortunately, the commencement was over in an hour. Too weak and tired to resist the urge to return home to New Orleans, she quickly packed and took the train to Chicago, changing for the southbound train to New Orleans. It was night in the Jim Crow coach, and she could sleep until morning. She'd be in Jackson, Mississippi, by 3 P.M. and New Orleans by 6 that next day. When she saw her mother standing at the platform, she could hardly hold back the tears. By the time they had taken another train to Scotlandville, she was ready to collapse in her father's arms.

July 2, 1940, was the last regular journal entry recording Walker's activities between the completion of her degree at Iowa and the beginning of her home retreat. Except for a few entries between March, six months after her arrival in New Orleans, and December 1941, we have only Walker's memory from a distance of nearly fifty years, in the form of her unpublished autobiography. Although the period between July 2, 1940, and January 24, 1942, is impossible to verify, the change in Walker's demeanor is significant. As she made her regular entry near her birthday in the July entry, a twenty-five-year-old Margaret Walker "closes the chapter on her formal education" and looks forward to getting a job and a husband.[22] So specific is she on the date of a proposed marriage—June 22, 1942—it is difficult to reconcile the Walker who left Chicago with the one who spent nearly two years with her parents. With no existing journals, did Walker, who grew increasingly conscious of documenting her life as she aged, elect to keep this record of her life permanently closed?

Walker could not have prepared her parents for would happen over the next two years. The expected glorious return for their oldest daughter turned out to be disastrous. It had been seven years since she had lived with her family for any length of time other than brief vacations. She was overworked from a demanding year at Iowa, made even worse because she succeeded in completing the year-and-a-half requirements in ten months, had earned extra money typing for other students, and rarely had time to sleep. The emotional and physical fatigue left an anguish gnawing at her heart that she could not understand, let alone express. She felt none of the fire that had brought her to Iowa, or the firm resolve about her future as a poet. Her parents expected her to find a job, but nothing materialized. She remembered her sister's earlier warning not to return home: "There is nothing there,"[23] Mercedes told her, when she had urged her to go to Iowa. How right Mercedes had been, she soon realized.

Returning home was the ultimate acknowledgment of failure. She was rewarded in her bold decision to go to Iowa, and she had completed a full manuscript of poems. She had learned discipline and focus, and she had produced the first book that would make hers a household name. Yes, she resigned herself to accepting her parents' help in securing a teaching job. She had to support herself, and teaching was the only path left open for her now.

She lost one job to a Black male PhD at Talladega College, and before she could pack up to leave for San Antonio for a junior college position there, she was notified that the position was filled. A position at Southern University in Baton Rouge looked promising, but it too fell through. Secretly, she was glad not to have a job to commit to, for she was not only physically drained of her energy, but also manifested signs of the psychic damage in the form of depression. Her grandmother still saw her as a little girl and expected to monitor her activities more closely than Walker preferred.

Living in Scotlandville with her parents was dull, making it easy for Walker to disengage. She didn't know anyone and didn't care to. Her journal had always been her safe house, balancing out her frequent tirades, and keeping her secrets; now her mother, who had encouraged the practice, considered days spent reading and writing as laziness. When she appeared at the dinner table with book in hand, or set her notebook by her plate, recording notes that kept her face downward, her family protested angrily. They were appalled at such a wanton display of arrogance. She had little regard for others, it appeared to them; they saw idleness, a temptation to be resisted at all costs.

Always in need of money, her family could not understand why a daughter with degrees from two of the most reputable white institutions and poetry published in major journals was unable to find work. Walker understood that Marion was blaming her for the condition she was in and jumped on her without provocation. Her mother's anger pushed Walker further inward, as she found herself sinking deeper and deeper into depression. Both mother and grandmother watched and commented on every move she made or did not make. Even when she tried to assist with meals or clean up, she remembered, nothing she could do was right. They simply pushed her aside.

As confirmed by Mercedes, one spring day in 1941, Walker took a hatchet and began chopping at parts of her body. Her father stopped her, patiently holding this child who had his intensity and resolve. The family listened to her sister Gwen's proposal, although they did not act upon it: "Why don't you have her committed to an institution. Can't you see she is crazy,"[24] her youngest sister was convinced.

This dramatic display of self-hatred caused everyone to regard her as a threat to herself and the family. Things began to change slightly when Mercedes came home from Chicago for a short summer visit following her graduation. The sisters had been together long enough to balance out each other's anxieties. But this situation had an added dimension. Walker had been hiding her pain for years, and although she had some success in containing it, each disappointment pushed against a wall that now refused to absorb it. The place that had been the refuge for her soul's most intimate yearnings had nothing to offer her. Her stillness and silence were as unbearable for Walker as it was for her family. It was as if she had a wound that not only did not heal, it also grew deeper with each day.

In September, Walker, Gwen, and their grandmother returned from Scotlandville to the New Orleans home. The family home, rented during the time the Walkers worked in Scotlandville, had lost its last tenants after a fire. Despite the polio that had left her disabled, Gwen was socially active, happy to be back in New Orleans with her college degree in hand. She got a job at one of the local elementary schools and made enough money to take care of herself and repair the damage to the house. Walker, by contrast, seemed a social illiterate, with no job prospects. With Gwen spending time out of the house for parties and carnival events, Walker was alone with her grandmother.

When Elizabeth Catlett, who had moved to New Orleans after Iowa, learned that Walker had returned home, she called her. On one rare occasion, Walker visited Elizabeth Catlett in the French Quarter and spent the night—without telling anyone. When Walker returned, her infuriated grandmother became physically abusive. Attentive neighbors alerted Gwen, who had been out at the time. When the Walkers arrived a few days later, the "crime" was reported by her grandmother: "She was 'no good' . . . and did nothing but read and write all night and waste electricity."[25]

Her father came to her rescue, explaining that she was not well and was nervous about not being able to find work. He did not regard his daughter as no good. In a surprising display of support for her, he ordered the grandmother not to embarrass the family in front of the neighbors, as she had. He threatened to send her to a nursing home if she continued to act in an abusive manner. Watching her grandmother cry, Walker appreciated her father's intervention. She needed his support now more than ever.

Years later, Walker would realize that her grandmother, like her mother, feared losing control. Her grandmother had lived with her most of her life, had taught her how to cook and sew, and had told her all the stories she had begun to write about. Her grandmother's words were woven into her life. But now, she watched her grandmother's fear of growing old turn into abuse. What would happen to her now when nobody seemed to need her? She was unable to understand this child she had raised from birth. The rift was impossible to heal. Although Walker made peace with her grandmother when she finished *Jubilee*, she died before its publication.

Walker could do little to satisfy her mother. Marion Walker had always been the dominant one in the family; she told her husband what to do. If he disagreed, which he sometimes did, he did not let her know it. When Marion realized she was no longer in a position to dictate to her daughter what to read or what to say, she found her behavior unacceptable; she criticized her daughter's slovenly existence that she believed could only result in her downfall. Whenever they were together, they quarreled repeatedly; Walker, pushed to her limits, would not take her siblings' advice and just "be quiet." Her stubbornness made it worse. The only solution was to keep their distance, and Walker allowed herself to bask in the quietness of her room in New Orleans.

Another experience shook her remaining self-confidence. One day she read in the *Chicago Defender* the announcement of James Russell Brown's marriage. She remembered he had questioned her ambitions as a woman. She had rejected his marriage proposal, but his words, spoken out of anger and bitterness, remained with her. The two men, Richard Wright and James Russell Brown, who might have been eligible for her to marry, she now realized were beyond her reach. Wright had insulted her no less in marrying not one but two white women. She never regretted having refused Brown's hand in marriage. Now, broke and unemployed, she felt worthless and helpless. The thought of having no prospects for marriage in sight intensified these feelings.

While Walker rejected the belief that children should be seen and not heard, which she acted out in an embattled and hostile relationship with her mother for most of her life, she learned during her time in New Orleans that she did not reject the basic values that her parents shared: their deeply religious faith; the stern, moralistic code of duty and responsibility; and their Protestant work ethic. Returning home reinforced these ideas, including those about marriage. She saw her family doing moderately well; all four children had either completed or were completing college and all, except her, were gainfully employed; and her parents were highly revered members of the New Orleans and Scotlandville communities. These prompts could only force her to begin to think about a family for herself. But her mother was controlling, her temperament never mellowed, and she was resentful and angry at her daughter's willful disregard of authority. Marion had been successful in controlling the lives of Gwen and Brother, who lived at home and never married, and Mercedes, who eventually moved to Brooklyn to become a music educator but who also never married. What had made it so difficult to gain control over her oldest and most difficult child?

The Protestant ethic that the family observed was part of what drove her mother's anger and Walker's emotional response. Knowing that she should be working, Walker came to appreciate the break that the eighteen months at home provided. The tension between her desire to work and her inability to find a job, coupled with the constant criticism from her family, triggered conflicting emotions. During a time when she might have been meeting new friends, Walker found herself continually depressed and self-absorbed. Her writing career also lagged. She felt everyone had let her down.

When Walker returned to her regular journal writing, she offered reflections of her time at home. The anger and bitterness are gone. Without more details, we can assume by her tone that the depression had run its course, that she found appropriate help, or more likely, she was bolstered by the appearance of "For My People" in *The Negro Caravan*, edited by Sterling Brown, Ulysses Lee, and Arthur P. Davis and published in 1941. The anthology was the most important and most comprehensive Negro-authored anthology ever to have been published and replaced *The New Negro*, which had been published in 1926 by Alain Locke. Just as Locke had consolidated the era with his stewardship of writers of that period, Brown, Lee, and Davis published newer writers who were immediate forerunners for the Civil Rights Movement. That she was the youngest writer to be included was not lost on Walker, who was elated to appear in a list of greats—and many close friends—like James Weldon Johnson, Charles Johnson, Langston Hughes, Zora Neale Hurston, Arna Bontemps, and Richard Wright.

The final journal entry from New Orleans in January 1942 noted that none of the things she had planned during the two years at home had occurred, but she appeared hopeful. That she felt stronger after this forced retreat and had the opportunity to focus on her health and healing left her grateful. The girl she had been was now gone. Her transition into full adulthood had been an especially painful one, which paralleled, with greater intensity, what she had experienced first during her adolescence and again during the year she sat out of Northwestern. The first she had interpreted as a religious awakening, the second, a social and psychological one. Without any models, Walker had spent seven years devoted to becoming the person she had imagined herself to be, often trying unsuccessfully to find the image she sought in others. She had studied hard, worked too much, and written herself into existence as a nationally recognized poet. But she could also see a new stage of her life as a woman emerging. Having been blessed with friendship and affection, she had failed at finding love, which, many women in her generation believed was required to make a woman complete. Mapping this new stage now seemed more important than any other stage. No one knew her better than she did, and she need only transfer the determination that had made her a poet to becoming fulfilled as a woman. She recapped her life in the journal entry with a chronology of the events that had occurred since her arrival in New Orleans as a nine-year-old in 1925. Nearly every year she could enter a major achievement, the last of which had been her master's degree from Iowa in 1940. In her twenty-seventh year, Walker had far more than most women, and was exemplary among Negro women. But she believed she could not yet call herself a real woman.

14

A Year of New Beginnings

On the day following the Japanese attack on Pearl Harbor, in December 1941, Sigismund Walker handed his daughter a telegram from President W. J. Trent of Livingstone College in Salisbury, North Carolina. Trent had learned about Walker through a fellow clergyman and invited her to join the faculty of the small Negro liberal arts college. The semester would start in January, and Walker was to report to school soon after the start of the new year. Still dependent upon her family, she was not able to buy a ticket to begin her new life and swallowed her pride as she turned to her mother for help. With borrowed money and a small suitcase of clothes, most of which she had brought with her from Chicago and Iowa, Walker again boarded the Jim Crow coach of the Illinois Central, going north. She was in good spirits, but having had teaching jobs disappear no sooner than she learned about them on multiple occasions, she understood there were no guarantees. The train ride made up for any of her trepidation since it always provided the solitude that allowed her to write. This trip, however, brought an additional pleasure that she took as a sign that her fortune was about to change. When she entered her assigned car, she immediately recognized Jacob Lawrence from pictures she'd seen and the news articles about his paintings that featured scenes from African American history.

Walker was surprised how young he looked. At twenty-five, Lawrence was already married; he and his wife Gwen were in route back to New York after spending the year in New Orleans. He had been awarded a fellowship from the Rosenwald Fellowship, known for its support of African American education in the rural South. The name Rosenwald was attached to Sears, Roebuck and Company, the leading distributor of merchandise and services in the South, with its home base in Chicago. Serving on the board of Tuskegee Institute and his immigrant background prompted his philanthropic interests. In addition to his support for Black education in Southern states, Rosenwald was a major source of funding for artists, writers, and scholars who were engaged in research on the African American experience. Lawrence's project was a series of paintings on Black migration. During the year in New Orleans, he produced sixty panels that formed the *Migration Series*. Nothing like this had ever been done, and Lawrence had been invited to open the exhibit at New York's Museum of Modern Art, making him the first Black artist to do so. Two years younger than Walker, he would soon become the most celebrated African American artist in

The House Where My Soul Lives. Maryemma Graham, Oxford University Press. © Oxford University Press 2022.
DOI: 10.1093/oso/9780195341232.003.0014

the United States. The Lawrences did not know her, but quickly asked what she did and where she was going. Her journal entry shows that she had fully accepted the person she was preparing to become. Visions of grandeur about her literary career had not receded from her mind, but she was more pleased to announce that she was headed to her first college teaching job.

Walker was coming to the rather startling revelation that who she was and what she wanted to be might have had little meaning in the 1940s within the larger context of an average Black person's life. She had been nurtured in one of the most politically intense periods in American history at that point, and she was very aware that her writing self would never disappear, but that more immediate was the necessity of earning enough money to support herself. The encounter with the couple served as a vivid reminder that she was living in the Jim Crow era in the days before the passing of the Civil Rights Act in 1964, the official date when public accommodations were deemed illegal by law, although not necessarily by practice. That Jacob Lawrence's reputation had already begun to supersede many artists of the period did not change the realities of segregation. Gwen and Jacob Lawrence, Walker, and other Negroes found themselves traveling together, since distinctions were based on race not class. She met other passengers on the trip to Salisbury in January 1941, but she talked mostly to Lawrence and his wife because of what they represented. The extended conversation with them took the edge off her fears about the new job. She had left home thinking she was about to give up her dreams but meeting a model couple made her hopeful that she was not.

Her arrival in Salisbury in the middle of the night, however, rekindled those fears. When no one met her at the train station, she took a taxi to the girls' dormitory and banged on the door for a half hour before she got a response. After settling in and with only three hours of sleep, the dormitory matron welcomed her with an announcement that she was to report to her 8 A.M. class—information about which she knew nothing.

Coming from a family of college teachers and having been taught by single women throughout high school, Walker was well aware of certain traditions and prevailing expectations. Unmarried women faculty could not live off-campus but only in those accommodations the university provided for them. Serving as models for the young women whom they taught, single women teachers had to comply with the social codes and demonstrate knowledge of proper etiquette. Although the world she was now entering was a familiar one, there was a sense in which she was settling for what was always to be. Her parents had tolerated her wild years in Chicago, but following tradition seemed to come natural to her. To be honest, she felt a renewed sense of purpose in the work that this expected career path required. The teaching schedule was intense, with classes virtually every hour, and whatever time was left the administration tightly controlled by assigning a variety of committee and college-wide responsibilities. Her situation was made more difficult because she was replacing a favorite faculty member. Whatever the reason for that faculty member's departure, faculty and students alike blamed Walker. Her only solution to avoid the side glances and less-than-friendly comments was to remain in her room and write when she was not in classes.[1]

African American teachers in the 1940s constituted a growing Black middle class whose jobs and education gave them a sense of security never before imagined. Because Walker did not consider this achievement unusual, she did not rate it as highly as many of her colleagues. In her mind, having a job was important but what excited her more were the students who wanted to learn and to hear her read and teach them about literature. But those with whom she worked seemed to view the status that the position offered as most important. As a result, they worked hard to maintain their very volatile positions. One served at the discretion of the president, who was in the unenviable position of having to maintain peace, order, and decorum among a mostly disgruntled faculty who were severely underpaid simply because they were Black. The dual system of education had a compliant group of state politicians who helped to preserve it. Private Negro colleges were generally supported by Negro church denominations, like the African Methodist Episcopal Church with which Livingstone was affiliated, but they generally followed the same practices as the state schools.

The precarious position that Negro College presidents found themselves in required that they operate with a characteristic duality: one for the politicians and business leaders whose support they needed to keep the schools open; the other for the faculty and students whose interests they intended to serve. To their faculty, many presidents at Negro schools in the 1940s seemed concerned only about keeping the status quo, fearful of drawing undue attention from watchful outsiders on whom their survival depended. Given the unevenness of the education for Negroes especially before the desegregation of schools, students came from a wide variety of backgrounds, had equally varying abilities, and often battled with their own sense of inferiority. To counter this, the Negro system of higher education, separate though it may have been, operated with the assumption that the education of Negro youth, especially in the South, was essential for maintaining a Southern power base, possible only with an educated citizenry. Thus, one could find sympathetic whites who supported progressive policies and made significant contributions to schools, many of which took the name of the benefactor by custom.

One drawback that also had its benefits was the absence of higher education for Negroes in the Southern states. In such cases, state funding was available to cover the cost of advanced degrees for teachers elsewhere, in any state outside the segregated South. Within this very complicated environment, all-Negro schools became sanctuaries for training in the cultural arts, political leadership, scientific discoveries, and religious instruction, rarely imposing any limits on the potential of the students in their care. That the students were there, no matter from what circumstances they came, was sufficient reason to give them all that was possible to give.

Walker quickly discovered her young students to be remarkable inside the classroom, which in turn became her private domain, allowing her to ignore much of the pettiness that she felt surrounded her. She followed the rules for the most part. According to the custom of the day, she did not go to public places other than church or lectures. Salisbury was neither Chicago nor New Orleans, and it did not offer the kind of intellectual community she had found in either of the three cities in which she had lived. She taught, ate in the dining hall, and returned to her room to write. Since she was teaching only until May, like the rest of the unmarried women faculty, she had to locate a summer residence for the three months that school was not in session and return to the dorm when school reopened in the fall. She doubled the amount of writing in her journals during this period, for as she would later explain, "Sometimes I write to unburden myself, to find a ready and willing listener who would remain silent, to express emotions and ideas I could not speak abroad to other people."[2]

William Trent was somewhat atypical of Negro college presidents. He knew who Margaret Walker was, and he was determined to keep the young poet at Livingstone. He had hired her because he needed someone to teach English, a subject the colleges held in high esteem. The field not only focused on reading and discussing the classics, but on elocution, diction, and interpretation. In other words, it gave one access to a larger stage, where there were too few Negroes represented. He certainly would have been thinking of those figures of note who had combined academic and public careers like W. E. B. Du Bois, as well as those who were seen as representing the best of Negro culture, like Langston Hughes and Marian Anderson. Negro institutions at that time competed for the best talent, but Walker had yet to earn the reputation of someone like George Washington Carver, Alain Locke or James A. Porter. She had appeared, however, in *The Negro Caravan*, by Sterling Brown, Arthur P Davis and Ulysses Lee, the anthology which so many of the schools were using. Thus, Trent saw decided advantages for the students, the school, and himself in hiring a published author.

A few months into the position, Trent called her into his office, Walker expecting the worse. Since she had been intentionally dismissive of the gossip and the women who issued it, she had begun to think that she was sowing seeds of dissension that could have negative results. To her surprise, at their meeting in March, he asked about her professional career, and proposed that she attend her first meeting of the College Language Association (CLA). CLA was only five years old but had quickly grown as the only organization serving the needs of

African American teachers of language and literature. The Association for the Study of Negro Life and History was at that time the largest and most familiar, but it focused primarily on history, with its constituent population high school educators. Its founder, Carter G. Woodson, had founded Negro History Week, which was the major goal of the organization at its founding. Singular in its purpose, Woodson had brought "Negro History" to the schools as an academic subject. The campaign for Negro History had been a bottom-up process, one that was very communal and allowed for a great deal of diversity. Woodson's orientation was not elitist or academic, but centered on giving the Black community something they could control entirely through multiple forms of expression.

By contrast, the College Language Association was founded by college professors and was academic and professional in its goal. Inspired in part by the exclusionary practices of organizations like the Modern Language Association that was founded in 1883, and the National Council for Teachers of English founded in 1911, CLA made clear the need to create an independent group. Its birth was a deliberate attempt to counter these negative experiences with racial exclusion with positive opportunities and networking that would benefit members of the organization and develop a body of intellectual work. Neither was CLA at the outset interested exclusively in Negro Literature, but rather concerned to demonstrate that Negroes were just as good as their white colleagues in studying and writing about the same materials. CLA did not make a conscious effort to exclude whites but found its niche to be the sizeable body of Black academics who were employed in Negro schools at the time. The organizations used MLA as their model in meeting annually and soon added a publication, the *College Language Association Journal*, which roughly approximated the *Publications of the Modern Language Association*. Their goal indeed was to ensure that their members could appear more regularly in print.

In her fifty-year retrospective, then CLA president Marie Buncombe maps other notable developments in the 1930s, which makes Walker's appearance at the 1942 annual CLA meeting and what happened there significant. According to Buncombe, the founding of CLA was also part of a larger effort to redefine literature within the context of a race-conscious American society. She points to the 1935 meeting of a select group of Southern writers at Louisiana State University for the "Conference on Literature and Reading in the South and Southwest." Perhaps the most important outcome of that meeting was the launching of *The Southern Review*, reaffirming a "new school of poetry, New Criticism (most notably championed by T. S. Eliot), agrarian sympathies, and such contributors as Eudora Welty, W. H. Auden, Allen Tate, William Faulkner, and Ernest Hemingway." *The Southern Review* . . . subsequently became "the most prestigious and influential magazine in modern British and American letters."[3]

Even as the group of Southern white writers were meeting, the literary land-scape of America had been altered by the enormous growth and expansion of Black writing, much of it by writers from the South. Yet their discussions of American regionalism and the South proceeded with the conspicuous absence of Black writers themselves or any reference to their work. We would have to assume that it was not ignorance among such an impressive group, given the enormous attention that Black writing and culture had received during the 1920s. Not only had Alain Locke's 1925 *New Negro: An Anthology* originally undergone a series of reprintings, but the 1930s would extend the list of publi-cations with a special emphasis on the South. Sterling Brown's *Southern Road* (1932) was followed quickly with two critical studies of modern Black poetry and fiction; James Weldon Johnson's autobiography *Along This Way* and Carter G. Woodson's *Miseducation of the Negro*, both appeared in 1933; and Zora Neale Hurston's novel *Jonah's Gourd Vine* was published the next year. Three of the men involved in the LSU meeting had all published in *Poetry*, just as Walker herself had. As Buncombe further noted, Alain Locke, who was Harvard- and Oxford-trained and a well-established critic, specifically placed Sterling Brown "in the advance guard of younger poets . . . and the new school of American regionalist literature."[4] *The Southern Review* was yet another example of the many marriages between benign neglect and segregation.

Those who had come together in 1937 to form what would later become CLA were fully claiming themselves as participants in the larger literary culture of America, whether recognized or not. They were prepared to call themselves "Negro writers," but not yet consolidated around the term "Negro literature." The discussion predated Margaret Walker's appearance at the annual meeting and was likely influenced by the editors of *The Negro Caravan*, who believed that the term "Negro Literature" was not entirely accurate because they considered "the bonds of a literature tradition to be stronger than race."[5] It was not yet the time to determine how to best present the burgeoning field in its own right. Such an action would make its dismissal in its entirety far too easy. The willingness to fight the battle of meaning and interpretation had to be done on the same turf, although there was no question about the value and importance of those writers among them like Margaret Walker who were actively publishing.

Oddly enough, the founding of both the *Southern Review* in 1935 and the Association of Teachers of English in Negro Colleges in 1937[6] had similar goals: both wanted to cultivate and give shape to the growing body of writing by those who shared a clear sense of identity. And where explicit or not, both were movements that sought to redirect a conversation about race that was al-ready happening. Their difference was that they operated at different ends of the spectrum. The founders of the *Southern Review* in their recapitulation as "New Critics" associated with "New Criticism" made it easier to shift the terms of discourse, place it under the control of a regionalized whiteness, and gain a stronghold in the American academy with lasting implications. The founders of CLA took their directive from America's broader social landscape as it underwent a radical shift. Issues surrounding race were becoming increasingly more central to the future. The 1930s, mired in controversy over the Scottsboro Trial, also saw the rise of the National Council of Negro Women by Mary McCleod Bethune and the Southern Tenant Farmer's Labor Union. These two constituencies would help lay the foundation for a new America. Margaret Walker identified with both.

William Trent's insistence that Walker become part of an organization just five years old reminded her that, like her years in Chicago, choosing the right stage for her work was a crucial consideration. She knew the world she had now entered better than most, and she was no newcomer to political organizing. As a young woman teaching in a Negro college, she joined a new generation of educators who would witness the transformation of American education. Two parallel systems for knowing and understanding the world and one's place within it had developed. Historically Black Colleges and Universities, as they came to be called[7], often accepted the duality in practice if not in theory, since they were preparing students for the real world. To their credit, those who organized and would sustain CLA preferred not to focus on their exclusion, but rather what a tightly knit group could accomplish. Becoming part of this new formation gave Walker a sense of community, replacing the one she thought she had lost, as she met people who believed in what she was doing as a teacher and a writer. It was important for her to know that President Trent supported her, even if the colleagues in her department allowed their jealousy to spoil any meaningful relationships. Three months into the job, she was feeling that she had made the right decision, and she eagerly looked forward to joining the organization and attending the conference.

Meetings of the organization were held on the campuses of HBCUs, which allowed its members to avoid some of the more overt encounters with racial discrimination. Walker was aware that she was a newcomer and would be under close scrutiny. Though she could see that it was a predominantly male-run organization, she felt welcomed and appreciated when she arrived at Hampton Institute, Virginia, for the 6th annual meeting in early March 1942. As would become her custom, she brought a few new matching outfits to wear. She first saw Arthur P. Davis, who taught at nearby Virginia Union College in Richmond, and with whom she had communicated about permission to use "For My People" in *The Negro Caravan*. He extended an invitation to give a poetry reading— something she had not been able to do in two years. Davis saw himself as a mentor for the newer generation of writer-educators and, unlike some of the older faculty with whom she worked, he was very encouraging.

She also met a fellow poet, Owen Dodson, and since they had similar backgrounds, she was eager to get caught up. He had completed his degree in poetry at Yale while she was at Iowa. Dodson had taken a job immediately after graduation and had been at Howard University for two years. In a short period, he had earned the respect of younger and older poets as a leading member of a newer generation whose work was more stylized, showing the influence of modernist aesthetics. But the catching-up she had expected was a lot more. He greeted her, not by name, but as the next Yale Series of Younger Poets awardee. Walker was in disbelief. Since no one outside of her family and her professors at Iowa knew she had applied to the Yale Competition multiple times, how was it possible that he would presume that she'd won?

A short while into the conversation, she remembered that Dodson had known Stephen Vincent Benét, and it was Benét who headed the Yale competition and acknowledged all of her submissions. Benét had apparently taken Dodson into his confidence and was eager to share that he would be selecting Margaret Walker for the next award. While there is no indication that Benét's eagerness to share might have been prompted by Walker being the first Black writer to receive the national award, he was clearly very pleased with his choice. Walker had received Benét's gracious note following her third and last submission of the "For My People" manuscript, but ultimately decided that losing out for a third time was sending a clear message that her work was not sufficiently competitive. At this point, if what Dodson said was true, she was also suspicious of the change of heart. Her conclusion was that Benét, like many white scholars, was simply patronizing her. Dodson, however, who offered insight into his former mentor, assured her that she had won. To play it safe, Walker felt that a cavalier attitude would protect her from yet another disappointment.

Two months later, in July, Walker received a rare letter from her father rather than her mother, who was the usual family correspondent. She opened it, hardly able to contain her excitement. She was indeed the selection for the 1942 Yale Series of Younger Poets Award by Stephen Vincent Benét. She knew that Dodson had been correct, although it is unlikely that he knew the full story. Archival evidence, however, points us to several key factors. In a telegram dated June 18, 1942, that Benét had sent to the Press, we get a sense of what had transpired. Some of the language from the original telegram was repeated in the version relayed to Walker but not all of it. Benét provided an important factor in his decision, "For Yale [Younger Series Award] this year I am picking FOR MY PEOPLE [caps original] by Margaret Walker of Scotlandville, Louisiana. Miss Walker submitted a manuscript last year and I have just recalled it as this year's lot was not promising. Walker is a negro and most of her verse is concerned with the problems of her people. I am in Stonington if you want *more dope right away* [emphasis mine]."[8] Without knowing the specifics of the intriguing "more dope right away," we might assume that it included a discussion of Walker's repeated submissions and even an unwillingness on the part of the committee to select a deserving candidate who was Black any earlier, and the reasons they believed they could now. Benét's choice, then, was a calculated one. With the major obstacles removed, and with Robert Frost having won four times already, Benét saw a window of opportunity with minimal conflict. Benét's choice was acceptable because Walker was not taking away a spot from a preferred, new white candidate. In addition, the decision may have reflected the heightened sensitivity to the changing nature of race relations in the crucial years between the Depression and World War II and leading into the Cold War, when legal challenges to and active organizing against discriminatory practices were well underway. Benét does deserve credit for knowing excellence when he saw it.

The Yale Award was the validation that Walker needed. As always, she reminded herself that she had worked hard and that "anything I want I am willing to fight tooth and nail for it. . . . I'm not a sore loser because I always play high stakes to win."[9] These were indeed high stakes, and the win was big. She secretly thanked Dodson for bringing her the news in advance and entered a prayer of thanks to God before she read the telegram again closely to make sure she was not dreaming it all up. Benét asked her to forward the manuscript immediately so that the award could be official. Production would have to begin right away in order to stay on the publication schedule of a mid-October release date.

The flood of memories came back as she processed what was happening to her. She had submitted "For My People" for the Yale competition in 1937 and 1938, and skipping a year, decided on a third submission in 1940. But the fear of another failure and embarrassment at disappointing Paul Engle drove her to forego the usual request to him for a letter of endorsement. The Yale Series of Younger Writers was not only the oldest poetry competition in the United States, but Engle himself had also won in 1931—both facts adding more pressure. Would it be too forward of her to apply yet again? "Forward" had often been Engle's choice word for Walker in their frequent disagreements, and he would draw such tiffs to a close with the more deadly term "arrogance." The only solution in her mind was to craft a letter to Benét on her own, explaining that the manuscript was to be her thesis under Engle, and she wanted Benét's critical opinion as she prepared the final version of the thesis to complete the requirements for her degree. The not-so-subtle approach was a characteristic Walker ploy whenever she wanted something. She did not say explicitly that she was submitting for the competition in 1940, only that she thought after two earlier submissions, he could provide some useful advice. Her strategy apparently worked since it reminded Benét that she had submitted previously, that she was from Iowa, and that she was Engle's student, all of which might not have mattered in the same way earlier. She always believed that her risky behavior worked to her advantage in this case since

Benét might not have taken a second look to see the manuscript with fresh eyes. It would not have been lost on him that he would get an enormous amount of credit at having selected the first Black poet to win this prestigious award. The Yale Award was as much about predictability as it was about visibility.

She rehashed all those experiences leading up to and associated with the award, which centered primarily on the Chicago years: failed expectations, the lost friendships, the rejection she had suffered. Suddenly, the pain and unhappiness were worth it. She ran to her room, pulled the manuscript from the dresser drawer, and then headed to the post office to send the insured package to Benét at his New York address. She had promised President Trent that she would teach summer school, and she had only a few days to take care of the details surrounding the release of the book. A photograph of her had to be taken and her biographical sketch prepared. In a week, she had mailed to Benét everything he had requested.

Walker considered this success the result of her hard work and sacrifice; her faith in God, in whom all things were indeed possible; and the excellent teachers who guided her. Although she had left Iowa vowing never to return because the experience had been so difficult, she now thanked the three men who had tested her patience throughout that year. Austin Warren, who had been collaborating with René Wellek to publish *Theory of Literature*, she considered one of the most brilliant men under whom she ever studied. Paul Engle, with whom she had battled most over the ballad form, but realizing that he had pushed her to do something she would otherwise not have done. In turn, the ballads became part of her signature. And Norman Foerster, who had introduced her to literary criticism, something that was entirely new to her. Because it matched her tendency to be analytical and dissect everything, she discovered criticism to be one of her major strengths.

The official release date of *For My People* was October 20, 1942, but news had spread much earlier and very quickly, especially on campus. Until then she had been a nobody on campus or confronting petty jealousies. Suddenly all people heard was talk of Margaret Walker. Job offers began coming in immediately. Just a year ago, she couldn't find a job. Now, she couldn't decide which one to accept. But a job decision was not hers to make. When summer school ended in late July, and she went home to New Orleans, she learned that her parents had accepted a position for her at West Virginia State in Institute, West Virginia. Her salary was $200 a month, and her mother "felt it was her duty to grab it before somebody else did."[10] She felt a sense of obligation to William Trent and wanted to return to Livingstone, but West Virginia State offered far more money. This was one of those occasions that she would agree with her mother and wondered if this was a good or bad sign. But Marion Walker understood the meaning of her daughter's success, and for once she offered no complaints. Rather she was delighted to be in charge of any decisions that would shine light on her daughter's success, and, therefore, her own as an attentive parent. It would take some years before Walker would understand how to negotiate her value, but Marion, who had absorbed all the characteristics of a stage mom with her children from the beginning, was well prepared. If her daughter did not recognize her own worth, it was up to her to make sure she did.

An advance copy of *For My People* arrived in the mail after Walker had begun her teaching duties at West Virginia State. Holding the hard cloth binding in her hand, she fondled it over and over again. She sat quietly reading the poems and remembering the stories of each. The volume was an amalgamation of her own journey as it blended with the larger history of Black life. Walker was translating experiences through the people and the places over time. The title poem had become larger than life because it had been so successful bringing all that she felt into a single structure. Reading it, she remembered that day in the office of the Federal Writers' Project, in desperation to bring the poem to a close. Nelson Algren's prompts had pushed her toward the ending, and ironically, it was he who became one of the reviewers for the volume.

The Benét affiliation brought Walker a good deal of immediate attention. His foreword was generous but cautious, with the prediction, "I should be very much

First edition of *For My People* and official press photo

surprised if this book were all she had to give." She liked his focus on the title poem in his foreword, which was additional affirmation that it was an example of her best work. Benét recognized in "For My People" the "controlled intensity of emotion and language that at times has something of the surge of biblical poetry." This was a most accurate description of what Walker was trying to achieve, and his assessment that "language . . . comes naturally to her and is part of her inheritance" suggested that he knew a bit more about Black poetry than most. Although Benét did not have an academic affiliation before he became editor of the Yale Series of Younger Poetry in 1933, he had already won a Pulitzer Prize for the epic poem "John Brown's Body" in 1928, was enormously prolific, and was, thereafter, regarded as one of the most influential poets of his generation. He was certainly the most widely read in a period that had begun to embrace the idea that poetry's accessibility was not necessarily a sign of its lower quality. Indeed, Benét better than anyone helped connect poetry to the reading public in a way it had not been since the days of Henry Wadsworth Longfellow.

What might not have been quite so obvious at the time was the similarity between Walker's poetic style, choice of themes, and especially her use of the ballad form and Benét's work. They both focused on themes from American history and were not opposed to using rhymed verse alongside more experimental forms. Benét represented a line of thinking that Walker demonstrated throughout her life—a belief that poetry should have a certain emotional and imaginative power, that it had the capacity to move people, especially if the forms of communication were familiar or accessible like the fable, legend, and ballad. The skilled writer had the advantage of the lyric form, which had similarities to music and allowed a reader to follow a feeling or idea that grows in intensity from beginning to end.

Walker followed a distinctly African American tradition in her preferences for forms and Southern imagery, even as her understanding of poetry became more advanced. Leading with the visual and the internal rhythm through sounds rather than end rhyme, she saw her poetry as a form of movement: from the perceptual to the conceptual, from the working up an idea to a more complete thought. She had become more technically proficient without alienating readers, contrasting longer lines to express deep feelings with shorter lines that reflect more musicality. Critics who knew little about that tradition or the rhetorical power attached to a Black sound, whether secular or sacred, would have missed the significance of a Langston Hughes, a James Weldon Johnson, or a Sterling Brown, who paid close attention to these matters.

Despite the recognition that the Yale Award gave her, the volume drew lukewarm reviews, especially from traditional critics, almost as if to discredit the award and Benét for his selection. Several reviewers capitalized on the idea of her "public poems," with reference to "urban poetry" that was still "biblical in language." Some found her sonnets superior but found the ballads weak, noting that while "crude," they were "effective," or "not above average." Others saw the sonnets as the "weakest feature of the book," and the folk ballads "far and away the best." Arna Bontemps, the only Black reviewer writing for the white media, refused to divide the volume, highlighting the organic relationship between the different sections of the volume and putting the onus back on the reader by validating the selection, commending Walker's "understanding" of the importance of folkways. He ended his review by quoting Benét directly: "*For My People* is part of our nation speaking." The worst review was by Louis Untermeyer in the *Yale Review*, and the one that Walker elected to quote in her preface to *This Is My Century*, the volume of her collected and new poems published in 1989. In an opening gesture that showed some generosity, his carefully chosen words describe the poems as revealing "vigor and undeviating integrity." Untermeyer quickly shifts to the judgment realm, finding the sonnets "commonplace." His last few lines were intended to sting: "The dialect verses which compose the second section are faltering imitations of gutter blues, swaggering ballads, and hearty folk-stuff; they are like nothing so much as *Langston Hughes turned soft or Paul Laurence Dunbar turned sour* [emphasis mine]."[11] The truth is that Walker understood and respected her audience more than the reviewers.

Margaret Walker had become a celebrity overnight, inviting praise and criticism. That she was Black and a woman gave most of the Black media an opportunity to praise the volume and acknowledge the importance of her achievement in terms of a literary tradition and race. What mattered to white Americans and what mattered to Black Americans differed in kind and degree. And no one knew this better than the Black media. The leading Black journals including *The Crisis*, *Opportunity*, and Black newspapers of the day like the *Chicago Defender* saw Walker as the new talent on the horizon. All were in agreement that their primary obligation was to highlight the achievements of the race, which would otherwise go unnoticed. It's difficult, therefore, to make a general assessment of these first reviews as a whole. What we can say is that the reviews were important in different ways for different audiences. While Isaac Anderson included Walker in his list of "Forthcoming Poetry" in the *New York Times Book Review* in August 1942, Elizabeth Drew's review in *The Atlantic* paid more attention to technique. What Walker could not say was that she was ignored. What did not change was her commitment to those communities she knew and respected throughout her career: the religious community and the educational community, both she knew to be largely identified as Black. In turn, she earned the respect of Black media, who remained largely responsible for her growing popularity. The racial divide that defined this reality was not one that Walker or other Blacks had created. Rather, it was a meaningful response to the conditions that existed, and an opportunity to build a network that nurtured and valued its own.

Perhaps the most revealing thing that Walker took away from the publication of her first book was a strong sense of belonging to a distinct community of Black poets—all of them men. Owen Dodson and Robert Hayden had both published their first volumes of poetry in 1940, but it was she who had won the Yale Award, suggesting that she was highly competitive. This trio played an important role in gaining African American poetry new audiences in the 1940s, paving the way for both Walker and Brooks. Dodson, Hayden, and Walker were also alike in that they were the first professionally trained Black poets— academic poets, if you will—who had brought significant attention to the field itself, which had lost some ground since the New Negro Movement. Of the three, Walker was considered the most readable and a bridge between two traditions: a vernacular one and a Modernist one, the latter of which was being actively promoted by the New Critics. In 1942, she could not be excluded from any literary discourse because since she revitalized an older tradition and demonstrated that it was possible to focus on the interior of Black life through a new lens that afforded more contemporary uses of imagery and sound.

Her most supportive audience aside from her family were those individuals at West Virginia State and the surrounding community, where she had barely lived for two months. The library at West Virginia State held a book reception; her church in the town of Institute invited her to read to its members. The local Black press created a curiosity about the puny little girl who had published an award-winning book. Although many people congratulated her personally, her success did inspire jealousy in some. The chair of the English Department, who believed she was in immediate danger of losing her job to someone with more reputational capital, treated her with disdain. She was a small woman who had waited a long time for her own success but had seen few signs of it. Having become chair of the department, watching others receive greater recognition more quickly only intensified her insecurities. The situation did not improve when she realized that she had no control over Walker's schedule, which required her being away from school for the book launch.

Meanwhile, Walker had fears of her own. Returning to New York would rekindle those negative feelings. Leading up to the trip and even during it, Walker "felt in the grip of very compelling urges—the whole unhappy business of 1939 and Wright crowded in on me."[12] Whenever the feelings surfaced, Walker would turn to her Bible for reassurance, if not comfort, hoping that the gratitude for her good fortune would help drown out any backdraft. Ultimately, excitement about the official release of *For My People* in late October overwhelmed her. She was facing a full schedule of promotions and related activities in New York starting in late October. The preparation time quickly turned to considerations of what would be considered appropriate attire. Traveling by Pullman, she bought and wore her first Stetson, one of many hats that would become her trademark. The alligator shoes and bag filled with enough money for her trip expenses made her ecstatic. She was aware that people were expecting an award-winning poet, but also they were looking at a Black woman: she had to make the best with "what she had," and that meant paying close attention to her hair and her outfits so as to make the right impression. She also knew that she would be meeting the Black intelligentsia and encounter many whites associated with the Yale Award and its Ivy League sponsor.

The first reading allayed her fears and confirmed all of these expectations. J. Saunders Redding and Merze Tate joined her. Redding was the leading Black literary critic who had written a major book in 1939 on Black poetry, *To Make a Poet Black*, and was regarded as the expert in the field at the time. Walker had met Redding at CLA, but he would have been on hand at occasions like this for another reason. He was already identified with a tradition of Black intellectualism: a scholar and educator, but also a public figure whose ideas and opinions on relevant topics were promoted and shared in the independent Black press. Redding used his regular column in widely circulating *Baltimore Afro-American* to cover civil rights and World War II, and never feared calling Jim Crow instances in the government's actions. He may have gotten ideas from *For My People* and the exchanges at their dinner for a forthcoming essay "A Negro Speaks for His People," which appeared in *The Atlantic Monthly* a few months later in March 1943. Walker met Merze Tate for the first time and was immediately impressed by a woman she immediately saw as a model for her future. Tate, nearly ten years older than Walker, had already established a reputation for firsts: the first African American woman to attend the University of Oxford, first African American woman to earn a PhD in government and international relations from Harvard, as well as one of the first of two female members to join Howard University's History Department.

While in New York, Walker paid her first visit to the special collections department of the New York Public Library, which had been named after Arthur A. Schomburg two years earlier. She knew Lawrence Reddick, head curator, from her Chicago days. They had both worked for the WPA and he was among the graduate students she'd met at the University of Chicago. Reddick's interest in New Orleans had eventually become a dissertation on the history of Negroes in the city, which led to an appointment on the faculty of Dillard University for a few years before accepting the job in the New York Public Library's Special Collections Division. The reunion served them both well. Reddick was in a position to introduce her to other important Black New Yorkers, and reconnect her with old friends, making the book launch a true coming-out-moment after her period of hibernation. They had many friends in common as well, like Elizabeth Catlett. Learning that she and her husband Charles White were residing in Harlem, Walker quickly tracked them down. New York confirmed itself for

Walker as the major center for Black life and culture, and exactly the place where her first book needed to be launched, keeping at bay any of the residue from the 1939 debacle. Those feelings would have likely surfaced when she agreed to do a book signing at the Schomburg at Reddick's request. Yet, she was delighted to give him an opportunity to raise the profile of the Special Collections Division, which he expanded during his nine years there.

Another event provided Walker with an opportunity to express her appreciation to Stephen Vincent Benét directly. He was among those who attended the *New York Herald Tribune*'s Book and Author Luncheon a few days later. Walker read "For My People" before 1,500 people, the largest audience she'd had to that point. When she saw him, she wasted no time going over to thank him graciously. He was surprised that such a small woman in stature could have such a "big talent."[13] She often thought that she was equally as surprised at his small stature and manner, although she would never say it aloud. Even though she had not given a reading in some time, her energetic performance captured the audience who gave multiple rounds of applause. She then took her seat at the head table with Benét and journalists Lewis Gannett and Quentin Reynolds. After the reading, she met Phyllis Moir from the National Concert and Artists Corporation, who telegrammed her the day after the luncheon, offering her a contract to go on tour for five years. She told her that the pay would be three times what she was making at West Virginia State. The offer sounded appealing, but she would make no commitment without careful consideration.

Walker noted a range of social outings with Black literati on her New York itinerary, including a dinner with Henry Lee and Mollie Lewis Moon. Henry Moon had begun his career at New York's major Black newspaper, *The Amsterdam News*, but Walker had met him when he worked for the WPA. The Moons were important New York socialites as well, and their reputation only increased after Moon went to work for Robert C. Weaver, a young Harvard-trained economist who served as race relations advisor for Franklin Delano Roosevelt. Moon then secured the position for which he became best known, the long-serving editor of the NAACP's *Crisis* magazine. While Walker counted the Moons as old friends, she enjoyed a fashionable tea date with new friends Mrs. James Weldon (Grace Nail) Johnson, widow of the famous musician, author, civil rights activist; and Mrs. Aaron (Alta Sawyer) Douglas, who would soon go with her husband to Fisk University, where his career as an artist and teacher would open up a new era for Black art in the United States. One of Walker's most enjoyable experiences during the New York trip was meeting the dancer and choreographer Pearl Primus. Having developed an interest in Black dance during her Chicago years after meeting fellow WPA worker Katherine Dunham, Walker saw dance as performance-driven like poetry. It required the use of sound and images, which were combined in an organized rhythmic structure. She had followed Dunham's ongoing career, but a younger dancer had emerged with a focus on African dance. Primus was actively preparing for the debut of "African Ceremonial," scheduled for February 1943. It is likely that Walker saw the production of *Strange Fruit* in which Primus performed, and it provided the two of them an opportunity to meet after the concert at a downtown café.

After the New York engagements, Walker continued to attend welcoming events in New Haven. The Yale Press dinner and reception were as noteworthy as those in New York. Yale's president Charles Seymour congratulated her personally. She also took some time to visit her cousin Samuel during the weekend in Boston after a bookstore signing in the city but returned to New York for an early Thanksgiving dinner with Elizabeth Catlett and Charles White. She arrived back in Institute after nearly three weeks away exhausted, but exhilarated. The exhilaration came from sharing her stories with her students who sat in awe as she repeated the famous names she rattled off, her reunions with old friends, but mostly being treated as a celebrity. They did not see a woman whose sense of accomplishment created distance between their teacher and themselves. Instead, they felt more attached than ever to someone who pushed boundaries they never knew possible.

Between Thanksgiving and Christmas 1943, in between her teaching duties, Walker attended to mail and sent out acknowledgments and thank-you letters, following her mother's advice: no matter how well known she should become, there were always the little ways in which she should stay the same. She had planned a big homecoming for Christmas, the first visit since the book's publication. She was confident that she could offset any potential conflicts with her mother. To save money, she decided not to take the Pullman to New Orleans. She got on the Jim Crow coach, changing trains in Memphis as usual, then on to Jackson and New Orleans. Everyone was there to greet her this time. She could see that they were excited, and she could even see through her mother's semi-hostile expression. They managed to get through the holiday with little quarreling. When Walker told Marion she would be sending her part of her royalty checks to help with the mortgage, they both felt a sense of satisfaction. That her daughter had maintained her sense of obligation to her family without being prompted confirmed for Marion that her oldest daughter had finally grown up. Even though Walker felt this to be more symbolic, her mother's expectations became real. She would continue to provide substantial support for her parents from her royalty earnings, though meager, until both parents died—her father in 1953 and her mother thirty years later, in 1983.

Walker had agreed to do a few readings at HBCU's in the spring of 1943, as the invitations continued to come from her new CLA colleagues. Increasing her visibility was not the only reason why the readings mattered. Her first model and mentor had been Langston Hughes, and she could not help remembering that evening at Peck Hall a decade earlier where she met him for the first time. Still angry that her parents would not allow her to leave home for college, Hughes's visit made staying home to attend NOU that first year well worth it. He had been the perfect example of what a poet must do to keep himself grounded. She would have been thinking of Hughes as she weighed the pros and cons of accepting Phyllis Moir's offer from NCAC. And it was probably Hughes who encouraged her to accept the offer. She was a writer now, he reminded her, and she could expect more opportunities to come her way.

Hughes was making a prediction. The following spring, some of her most serious writing was done during the week at the Yaddo artists' community in Saratoga Springs, New York. She had kept in touch with Hughes, who was now seeing her as his protégé. That he was at Yaddo that same week suggests that he may have had something to do with the invitation she had received. Most of theYaddo group spent time in their rooms writing, coming together only for meals and brief readings. But Langston Hughes's presence made for an especially lively experience. They took long walks, and she spent more time with him than anyone else. When she recapped her experiences in her end-of-the-year summary in the journal, she remembered promising herself after she had left New York that she would not stop writing. She had intended for her next year to be better than ever. Yaddo had allowed those words to ring true.

When the school year ended at West Virginia State, having accepted the NCAC offer, Walker took a leave of absence from teaching. The fall would include a six-week tour. Starting from New York, she would travel by train first to Fort Valley, then continue to Alabama with lectures and readings at Alabama Agricultural & Mechanical College, Talladega, and Alabama State Teachers College before her first break. A second round of talks she'd give at Atlanta University, Knoxville College, where her sister was now teaching, and then head to Pine Bluff for a talk at Arkansas Agricultural and Mechanical College. She'd circle back to the schools in North Carolina, speaking at North Carolina Agricultural and Technical College and Barber Scotia, then have a second break before heading out to New England. She knew the trip would be grueling. Connections between cities were not well developed, and since most of the trains in the Southern railway system only offered the day coach service for Blacks, she would have to get off the train, stay with friends or at a local YWCA, and wait to board the next leg of her journey. Trains were also notoriously late, which one had no way of knowing in advance. To say that travel by train was an adventure was an understatement. As she quickly discovered, every college hosted her well. The accommodations, meals, and receptions existed alongside extremely large and grateful audiences. Many old friends and new friends were teaching at the schools and she looked forward to these reunions.

Walker at Yaddo, with Hughes and other resident artists in 1943. Courtesy of the Yaddo Corporation

The NCAC tour was Walker's first big tour, her rite of passage. While the salary was significantly higher than her college teacher's salary, she had a clear schedule and payment worked out in advance. For the first time, she had no reason to be worried about money. Many of the lectures paid upwards of $250, and even those that were added late would bring in an extra $125. With all of her expenses paid, Walker saw her standard of living rise considerably. She looked forward to it with a certain amount of nostalgia, but mostly with a feeling of a necessary reimmersion in the region that was so central to who she was. Being validated in her native South, not New York and even Chicago, mattered more to her than she realized. Little did she know that she was opening a new chapter in her personal life as well as her professional one.

15

October Journey

On October 15, Walker left New York for Fort Valley State College by Pullman car. She did not want to forget what it felt like, and she recorded her perceptions. It was the beginning exercises of a volume of poetry that would not appear until 1973 as *October Journey*, but the descriptions would also ready her for *Jubilee*, whose principal settings are Georgia and Alabama. For now, it was part of her mind's eye. "From New York through New Jersey, the trees were a riot of color. Nature's aura is a masterwork in the East at this time of the year. After New Jersey, the land seems more subdued," she wrote, then quickly shifting to a different reality, "After a couple of years of pullman travel, I'm accustomed now to the stares I get from white passengers."[1] She would enjoy the Pullman until they crossed the Mason-Dixon line, where, according to custom, one got off the train and awaited a morning train that would take you deeper South. The stop was in Baltimore, and Walker was lucky because she had a network of friends with whom she could stay.

The early morning train offered a lot of writing time, and by the time she reached Georgia, her descriptions had also changed:

This Georgia country is ugly, barren soil. Old cornstalks and ole cotton stalks remain in the fields. The land is faded. Even the cattle of necessity looks poor. In perpetuating a jim crow system the South has been so busy it has become the poorest section of the country whereas it could have been the richest.[2]

The contrast between what was and what could have been, were it not for systems of oppression, makes clear that Walker's sense of historical timing was always on point. Her first stop at Fort Valley State College was a reminder of how intentional those oppressive practices were as Southern states put in place a rigid two-tier educational system. Blacks nonetheless could take full advantage of them, especially in the 1940s as they became concentrated and exclusive sites for the social and intellectual development of that new generation who would envision a new world through some of the most sweeping social changes in twentieth-century America. For Walker, this first visit to one of Georgia's Negro state schools was also a reunion for her. She and Horace Mann Bond, the first president of Fort Valley State College, had connections that dated back to New Orleans and Chicago. Bond was a part of the cohort of young Black men at the

The House Where My Soul Lives. Maryemma Graham, Oxford University Press. © Oxford University Press 2022.
DOI: 10.1093/oso/9780195341232.003.0015

October Journey was published in 1973

University of Chicago, which included Lawrence Reddick and St. Clair Drake, both of whom alternated between graduate school and teaching at Negro colleges until they completed their degrees. Bond had completed his work by 1936, and it is likely that Walker had only heard about him. But Drake, Reddick, and Bond had been among the first hires at the newly named Dillard University, as NOU was phasing out. Bond's father was also minister, and she and Bond had both graduated from college at nineteen. While they both would have been considered part of the talented tenth as educators, Bond's family and background placed him squarely in the Black middle class. She remembered how quickly he had become dean at Dillard in 1934 and was rising rapidly in the leadership of Negro schools thereafter. Bond had brought to Fort Valley an ambitious plan for expanding the school's budget and providing new experiences for its student population. One of them was a Lyceum series that invited W. E. B. Du Bois as its inaugural speaker. Walker was delighted to follow his footsteps as the second in the series.

She was appearing at a time when many of the Southern-based institutions had transitioned from the "industrial and normal" school model to comprehensive colleges serving the state's Black students. Typically, Southern states won a double victory by acquiring preexisting independent institutions, founded by Blacks for Blacks. Since most Southern states made no provision for public education for its Negro population, the consolidation of a segregated system for lower and higher education ensured at least a modicum of funding, which would meet the demand created by the postwar boom. Southern Blacks were not waiting on the states to provide any education at all, which often meant that formerly independent institutions were prepared to take bigger steps with state support. Fort Valley was one such college.

That she had been educated in a two-tier system, with the added benefit of an advanced degree outside of the South, Walker did not take for granted. Rather, it meant that on her NCAC tour, she took special care to engage as many students as possible. The first reading at Fort Valley set the tone for the others that followed throughout schools in Georgia, Alabama, and Tennessee. She packed in as many events as she could, rarely allowing herself enough time to arrive in town, prepare for and give a lecture and reading, have dinner with her hosts, and leave on the train early the next morning. Remembering the days when she had no readings, and little motivation to do anything, she felt no hesitation in embracing the intensity that such a tour required. She was also accustomed to riding the train and knew how to make good use of her time. Rest was possible, but she wanted to have a series of different talks that she could give. Her goal was to spend at least two days at most of the schools, speaking to classes as well as to the large public audiences. She did a radio program at Fort Valley, which would happen at several of the other schools. Radio was one of the most important forms of communication media, and white-owned radio stations, like newspapers, reserved time for their "Negro news." Walker didn't expect to see Therman and Lillian O'Daniel, who had come to Fort Valley before moving to Morgan State College in Baltimore. They had been among those she'd met at her first CLA meeting, which provided a network to which she would find herself indebted time and time again, the place where her personal and professional networks continued to expand.

Being on the stage in front of an audience energized her no matter how tired she might be. Her performative style had a special appeal to Black audiences. The ballads were the all-time favorite, and the practice in New Orleans in front of all-Black audiences now paid off. Her code switching between characters and voices came more easily and it had begun to feel natural. She could sometimes hear the cadences she'd learned when reciting the popular poetry of Paul Laurence Dunbar creep in. Although her own ballads were not replicas of Dunbar's poems that were written in traditional dialect, they still required more effort in order to give her audiences the feel and sound of the people whose stories she reimagined. Any Negro college at this time attracted as many students as it did community residents for such public events, and Walker's designated status as poet generated the same attention that a tent revival would. People came for the communal re-affirmation and uplift that events provided, whether spiritual or secular. What Walker understood and had mastered was an ability to capture their attention with skilled performance. Though only a year following publication, the title poem "For My People" had made the rounds, and everyone recognized her as its author. After priming the audience, she would read it, drawing rousing applause.

Walker's journal notes from this period indicate that she was also expanding her own professional options. The poets Countee Cullen and Langston Hughes, like Saunders Redding, all had columns in the Black newspapers. Black women had yet to claim that type of authority unless they were career journalists. Walker realized that NCAC was giving her a comparable platform. Many of these ideas—about audience markets, promotion venues, lecture tours before the days of tele-vision and social media—she had gained exposure to during her time in Chicago, without fully understanding the impact of launching a career with leftist affili-ations as she did. A book review in one of major media outlets, a literary award, and the patronage system were the major components for a successful career, and Walker had two of the three. She was confident enough to believe that she could make up for the third. Thus, the NCAC tour emerged as an opportunity to establish her own social network that she might draw on as her career evolved. Using herself as an example, she also believed that there was a greater need for "political education" in the South, especially among youth. She would usually do a poetry reading as a single event, and while she felt equally prepared to give talks on different subjects, she often chose topics of particular relevance for the Black students. She was comfortable talking about the crisis of the Negro, a common subject at the time: the contributions of Negroes in American literature and cul-ture; the role of Negro youth; or critiquing the idea of the talented tenth, all of which showed the marked influence of her Marxist readings and study groups from the 1930s. Walker understood this to be an important part of the students' education, remembering her own experience in those early college years, espe-cially her encounter with Langston Hughes. She wrote and was prepared to share more than was always possible. Conditions were different at each school, and one had to gauge the type of leadership she encountered on an individual basis. For example, in 1943, emphasizing the importance of the Black vote at a Negro College in Georgia would have been considered heresy. But her need to write her ideas out, regardless of the opportunity to present them, explains why she left such a massive body of unpublished material. Many of the essays that appeared in the two volumes published in her last decade derive from these thoughtful encounters during the October journey. The writing, like the tour itself, was an opportunity to remind herself of who she was, sometimes sounding like her comrades at the South Side Writers Group.

Her notes for one lecture read: "The writer's responsibility is to his people; he must have social conscience and perspective, personality and integrity; the writers must have more than talent." The words almost exactly parallel those in the collective document the SSWG had worked on. She upheld the importance of Black and white cooperation, referring to Du Bois's idea of the talented tenth as "an old idea . . . intellectuals did not save Europe from fascism. . . . Nothing will happen without definite and concerted steps [being] taken toward organized and mass action."[3] It was clear that Walker was talking to young people, and while she made a connection to poetry, her appeal was strong:

> Negro youth must become intelligent about the race problem, understand it, economically, politically and socially, develop self-respect and dignity, pride in the human race, personal heritage and destiny; must be alert to danger and militant for complete Negro rights all over America—protest, agitate and fight. Must be prepared educationally and have world perspective.[4]

No record survives of the talk or the radio interview at Fort Valley, but it would become a common practice for Walker to write down extensive thoughts, which she polished over time, and eventually produce a typescript. As a poet and writer, she saw no limitations on her intellectual curiosity. In contrast, she believed it was precisely the writers' responsibility to engage more deeply with ideas and broader spheres of knowledge. Conceiving of and expressing them in writing was at times sufficient. With a generative mind, Walker captured thoughts that became ideas that found expression in a way that was acceptable for her time. If she wrote them out, there would be an opportunity to express them when the time came.

As she continued her tour from Fort Valley to Huntsville, Alabama for a fifth appearance in a week, Walker found she was more exhausted than she realized and slowed down her pace. The respite evoked a rush of prose, which was the only way she could process the conflicting images that the physical landscape offered:

> We are passing through Georgia country, the Tennessee Hills, mountains, valleys, and hillside flaunting autumn colors and we came through a tunnel of solid rock. . . . In the distance the hills are blue and blazing in the golden fire of the trees. There is a baby laying in a yard and a child running to wave at the train—a miserably bleak and poverty-stricken house—almost a shack. Each body of water, great or small, and we have just crossed the Tennessee river—is like a mirror reflecting tender idyllic and pastoral sight in a land torn with social conflict and with undertones of violence underlying all life and threatening

reprisal in case of race friction. The sun is setting and the earth is glowing as though lit from coals of some secret Mediterranean fire.[5]

The recording of these initial impressions became a constant reminder of how well Walker read and visualized the South, how intimate and personal it was for her. She was coming to a new revelation. Her calling became more specific—she had an obligation to become the voice of the South.

She was eager to return to Alabama, remembering her childhood there. The train ride brought recollections of her nine-year-old self, riding from Birmingham to New Orleans where the family was reunited following her father's decision to take a college teaching job. The first stop was at the State Normal School in Huntsville for a short visit before heading to Talladega. The reading and a reception following did not have the benefit of the books, which was an experience she would have fairly often during the tour. But she considered the event a success, noting the terms "refined and cultured" when referring to President Joseph Fanning Drake and his family, the school administrators, and the students in the dormitory where the reception was held. Rather than an indication of her judgmental predilections, the phrase would have had a fairly specialized meaning in the 1940s as a way of affirming the aspirations and standards of Black educational leadership in the Black Belt South. To be "refined and cultured" had a double meaning.

Walker was well aware at the time that she was entering the eye of a political storm. Southern states hoped to keep the lid on legal segregation and maintain white minority rule, which required suppressing any desire for Black voting rights. Supporting Black education was often part of an intended compromise. Yet the tension and growing activism on the campuses of Black schools could easily be disguised under "refined and cultured" behavior. It was up to Black college presidents to decide which side of the political aisle would serve their positions best, and most would play conciliatory roles in public. Similarly, it was up to Walker to decide how open she would be in sharing her views on race matters. Black college presidents would have been aware that the guests they brought to campus could express positions that were not the views of the administration. Yet many were eager to have others express such views and for their students to hear them. The time at Huntsville, however, was too short for one of her topical lectures.

She had learned to take in stride the peculiar nature of the railway system in the South. The train did not stop in Huntsville, which was only four hours from Talladega, which meant driving to Athens an hour before to take the train at 5 A.M. The inconvenience was rarely worth a comment, except when she missed the train, as she did in this case. President Joseph Fanning Drake had been her escort for the entire trip, and when she missed the train in Athens, he agreed to drive her by car to Talladega. She learned during the four-hour drive that he was one of the longest-serving presidents of a Southern Negro college. Arriving in 1927, he came to the State Normal School, a land grant college, and oversaw its transformation to Alabama Agricultural and Mechanical College; he continued as president until 1964. But it was at Miles College in Birmingham where he met the Walkers. Drake and her father had crossed paths when Sigismund taught summer school at the small Christian Methodist Episcopal School. She realized that the president had approached her visit as if she were his family.

The four-hour car ride was an introduction to the Alabama Walker did not know. Driving into the sunrise made the trip more important as a point of return. From the conversation during the drive, she concluded that Drake represented a tradition different from Horace Mann Bond and the generation of whom she was part who had received their education in the Midwest. She also learned why he was eager to drive her to Talladega, his alma mater, where he continued to have strong ties. Once he left Talladega, he had gone North and was befriended by a white benefactor who enabled him to further his education, returning the favor by taking the benefactor's middle name as his own. Drake then returned South, was appointed president of the State Normal School at the age of thirty, and commuted to Columbia University from Alabama to complete his doctorate. His final connection to the Walkers and New Orleans was an invitation to interview for the presidency of Dillard University, a position that was given to Albert Warner Dent. Drake, eager for Walker to know his side of the story, provided extensive details.

Journal entries on her readings at Talladega and Alabama State Teachers College in Montgomery suggest that she again encountered former acquaintances among the faculty from CLA or during her time in Chicago and Iowa. She got better at managing the energy each stop required as well. In addition to reading and giving selected lectures, she responded to requests from students asking, "Who do you know?" She'd tell her Langston story, being awestruck by Du Bois as a college student, and what it felt like to meet Stephen Vincent Benét himself. Preparing too much heightened her expectations, while being flexible brought pleasant surprises, especially when she could easily comply to a request. The Talladega visit was also exceptional because she gave her lecture in the library surrounded by Hale Woodruff's six murals, which President Buell Gallagher had commissioned. Gallagher was another of those presidents who was committed to producing excellence; his tenure began with the implementation of a rigorous academic program. The only unpleasantries occurred in those cases where the administrators did not present her with a check but sent it to the NCAC's New York office instead. She saw this as distrust and disrespect, which led to a practice from which she never departed for the remainder of her life: requiring payment at the time of any speaking engagement to which she had agreed. When this expectation was not agreed upon in advance, she discovered, sponsors easily took advantage, sometimes explaining after the fact that the money would not be available at all. Receiving payments at the time of the appearance offset any unfortunate situations and discouraged dependency upon people who made her uncomfortable.

Walker would have expected to go to Birmingham, where a talk had been arranged for Miles College. As she rode South from Talladega, the more she remembered the smoke-filled city she knew as her birthplace. While she could find some beauty in all that she saw, the closer to Birmingham they got, the more ugliness she saw. They passed one place that served as a cement worker's town, but so completely covered with dust, it was barely visible. "Even the trees were grey. One knew there was nothing healthy in that dust."[6] Again, she found that her stature as a noted poet gave her special treatment. The president of Talladega, Buell Gallagher, drove her to what he thought was Miles College, passing through Avondale on the way. That the drive took longer didn't bother Walker as much as it did Gallagher, who was embarrassed at not being able to find the school. For Walker, visual memories returned quickly, passing the viaduct, the Masonic Temple, and the unexpected pleasure of stopping at the city's small library. Gallagher took advantage of his need for directions by stopping there, only to discover that the librarian, who had issued Walker's first library card two decade earlier, was still there. These memories replaced any nervousness she felt at being 15 minutes late.

The Miles engagement prepared her for a series of experiences that constituted the homecoming that she was so nervous about. The patient and eager audience gave her the welcome that she needed, putting her in her comfort zone that neither the delay nor the somberness of the ride could challenge. The reading at Miles, in her estimation, rated as the best; her flow of words were smoother, and the audience response was the most enthusiastic. She interpreted this as their appreciation, devotion, and pride in welcoming a native daughter. It was exactly the preparation she needed to make the pilgrimage to her birth home. It was very much as she remembered it. It was late October and still hot in Alabama. She visited West End, the place where she had been born and the Southern Youth Center where she had spent a summer restoring her psychological and emotional health and accepted that the forced retreat had accomplished its purpose. With a certain amount of melancholy for the past, she quickly returned to the present, knowing that she had come full circle.

Birmingham had far more to offer, however, than a most welcoming return for its native daughter. Walker had learned previously that Marian Anderson was scheduled for a Birmingham concert and quickly added it to her itinerary. After the Daughters of the American Revolution had refused to allow her to sing to an integrated audience at Constitution Hall in Washington, DC, the 1939 concert became a cause célèbre. The National Association for the Advancement of Colored People and the Black media attracted the attention of First Lady Eleanor Roosevelt and her husband Franklin D. Roosevelt—but not until Zora Neale Hurston published a public statement against the First Lady's delayed reaction. The intervention resulted in Anderson giving an open-air concert on the steps of the Lincoln Memorial on Easter Sunday, April 9, with 75,000 people in attendance and a radio audience in the millions. Aside from the publicity, little changed for Anderson. Like Walker, her hosts were a Black family in Birmingham since the law prevented her from obtaining hotel accommodations. Walker's enthusiasm resulted in a twelve-page summary of the concert, so completely moved was she.

She did not expect to have a friendship with someone like Anderson, but they would meet at a gathering at the home of Anderson's hosts after the concert. What her report of the concert shows is a remarkable knowledge of classical music, no doubt owing to what she had absorbed, in part by force, from Marion Walker. She wrote that she who had "never been so completely moved" recognized that "something extraordinary was taking place." She cited each song individually, each in the appropriate foreign title, and inserted her knowledge of major and minor keys and forms like the aria and vocalese, which her mother had first introduced her to. Anderson followed the tradition of Black classical musical performers by reserving the final portion of a concert to a selection of Negro spirituals. The practice was intended to make a statement—that traditional Black music was an equal and important part of the classical tradition. But it also showcased a wide assortment of arrangements of familiar Negro spirituals by different composers. In this way, established Black artists could introduce the work of newer and/or lesser-known composers, which would quickly begin to circulate. Having heard Anderson on two other occasions, Walker was eager to hear her favorite spirituals, and Anderson did not disappoint.

Why this third attendance at an Anderson concert claimed so much attention had as much to do with Walker's own sense of having achieved a certain status as it was the need to claim some models in a period where there were so few, especially among Black women. A transference effect would have been natural for her, as she thought about Anderson's full stage presence, including her choice of clothing. We hear Walker, Black woman artist, talking in most favorable terms about another Black woman artist:

> There is so much more to a Marian Anderson recital than just the singing as if that were not enough. What she wore, how she walked on that stage, the little way she kicked her train in place. Only a woman of absolutely erect carriage could wear a dress like that and never step in it—never stumble. No queen ever walked more regally—most queens are too short and too fat—not statuesque

like Marian Anderson. . . . I shall never forget the way my heart jumped each time she appeared. It was like something electric, something unforgettable. I found myself making comparisons with other recitals and noting the amazing fact that, although each time I thought her voice was divinely perfect—there is still something added—something indescribable. . . . It was as if a chalice of liquid yet golden fire had been offered by a high priestess before a sacrificial altar to the great God Art—worshipful and prayerfully.[7]

While the white media had given extensive coverage to Anderson, known to break barriers as the first Black person to perform in all-white venues, Black audiences like these they ignored. Only in the Black media would there have been notices and elaborate praise citing the achievements of its own people. At times, trained musicians who existed at almost all of the Black colleges would contribute articles. Walker's unpublished commentary becomes all the more important within this context. Her witnessing confirmed an important fact in Anderson's career. While Walker remembered and named the two previous accompanists for Anderson's concerts, she was very aware of making comparisons. Listening to her first Anderson concert accompanied by Franz Rupp was notably different:

But with Rupp this art is being created—not worshipped. There is something more intellectual involved—something equally as objective as the former was subjective. This is not merely an emotional experience, not merely an intellectual experience, not merely an aesthetic experience separate and above either of the two; it is a mingling of the three. It evokes from the audience each of the three—something so emotional so as to be physical, something so spiritual as to be almost ecstatic and something so intellectual as to be reached almost by a completely rational process. You know that back of this native talent there is great training and intensive study, yet it has not taken out of existence the depth of feeling—the rich pools of passion and more than these there is revealed obviously the great personality, a sensitive and supremely intelligent woman, a woman of great dignity and integrity.[8]

Rupp would remain Anderson's accompanist for the remainder of her career. Reading through these lines gives some sense of how Walker wanted others to view her.

It is hard not to read the high degree of self-consciousness in these lines, especially in the comments about what happened at a gathering after the concert. Though hesitant, Walker joined a group of women, and was reluctant to mention that she had met Anderson previously, believing it would be "vulgar boasting" to do so. Yet she was in the midst of a successful book tour, which at least one of the women knew and somehow felt snubbed. In Walker's view, the women were making fools of themselves in an effort to impress Anderson. Finding the behavior reprehensible, she referred to one woman whom she knew as a "cheap hussy and gorgeous whore, whose art when compared to Miss Anderson's degenerates to cheap showmanship."[9] To her credit, there is an equal attempt to balance her own outburst on the page with some objectivity as she wrote up an account of the entire event:

> Of course, I have, too, my own self-consciousness and smallness and riddled with inferiority complexes. I have to learn how to protect myself a little and not blurt out something I may regret. Such a repression becomes an inhibition or protective covering which I cannot lose even in the face of a great woman like Miss Anderson. Consequently, I said nothing about having met her. There were at least a dozen people in the room, and I was sitting almost in the door when she opened it and entered the room. Before I could get on my feet those big eyes of hers dilated in surprise and she recognized me, took my hand and saying, "My dear Margaret Walker," and stooping she KISSED ME ON THE CHEEK [emphasis original]. Well, Lord, have mercy, my heart jumped in my throat and my cheek tingled. She still held my hand and was saying she knew I was in the South but had no idea I was in the house.

Anderson's attention to Walker had changed the tenor of the room entirely. "The room was frozen and of course I had not yet regained my composure to stand up as I should have." Walker remembered their brief exchange, as Anderson asked that she be remembered to one person or another that they knew in common.

What happened afterwards was expected. Some of the women quickly introduced themselves, having realized that they had been too busy trying to compete for Anderson's attention to notice the poet Margaret Walker. A series of "I don't believe I know you's" then led into a brief conversation. Others simply spoke to her out of courtesy or embarrassment, which required nothing more than a smile and acknowledgment. Walker countered what would have been publicly embarrassing behavior on these occasions, illustrating one of the purposes for her ongoing journal writing, the place "to express emotions and ideas I could not speak [aloud] to other people."[10] Although it was a bit early in her career, she knew that her strong views and her inability to hold her tongue would be tested time and time again. Adding a layer of fame meant paying attention to how she was perceived and how she perceived others. The lessons from the Marian Anderson encounter she would continue to think about. She knew that the practice of self-censureship would be a routine.

The last Alabama engagement was at Tuskegee Institute, a school associated with Booker T. Washington. Although Walker spent only a short time there, the agricultural model that was the basis for its founding had already changed. It was perhaps because of that image that she did not expect the reading to attract much attention. She was wrong. The students, faculty, and local community turned out in large numbers, making her wish she had arranged to stay longer. But the tour was so tight, and connections so poor, such adjustments were impossible.

To get to Atlanta, for example, for her next talk, she had to go to Cheraw, South Carolina where she took the train in order to make it in time for a talk at Spelman College. Admittedly tired, she was eager to continue on to Knoxville for a planned visit and reunion with her sister Mercedes. The Spelman audience, in contrast to others, she considered more conservative, and Walker was "not sure people liked everything I had to say."[11] But two guests at the lecture would have offset any repercussions resulting from anything she did say. The first was William Stanley Braithwaite, who had assumed a professorship in creative literature at Atlanta University, and was himself a leading poet, anthologist, editor, and critic. The other was Marian Anderson, who came to the reading and greeted Walker personally. It confirmed for Walker what she already knew, that Anderson was the most gracious and refined woman she had ever known.

She had been to eight schools in two weeks, with too many one-night engagements, and too much time in a car or on a train. The housing accommodations were terribly uneven, at times limited to the student dormitories or makeshift guest houses, which included eating in the dining halls. The good thing was that these were rare opportunities to talk with students, given how limited her stays were. The best arrangements were those at faculty residences where meals were often arranged with the president and his family. Having to get up at the crack of dawn to take trains and then continue on a lengthy car ride to arrive at the schools, most of which were located in rural areas far away from the cities, made her eager for a break that was not tied to a speaking engagement.

The break came in Knoxville, where the sisters would have three days before Mercedes was scheduled to leave for New York. Knowing that her sister's career was beginning to take off provided a balance to what each of them may have been feeling; there could be neither jealousy on Mercedes's part nor guilt on hers. She was intent on being there to support and help her sister pack and prepare for the New York debut, just as Mercedes had been there to encourage and support her decision to leave Chicago for Iowa. The two sisters had both learned to live with the reality that while they could consider themselves artists, their lives were bound to teaching jobs, which they were fortunate to have. After three days together, spending time on the campus of Knoxville, watching her sister carry out her responsibilities as the school musician, Walker concluded that Mercedes's situation was far more dire than hers. She saw teaching school "killing and destroying her bit by bit," and decided she must find a way to keep Mercedes in New York, the only way she was going to get any recognition as a pianist. Success could not be Walker's alone; it had to enable her sister's, whose career had been delayed because of the family's choice. The experience years before was never far from Walker's mind. Both had sat out a year and returned to Chicago, but it was only Walker who was able to complete her degree at Northwestern. Mercedes was forced to find a less expensive schooling option for the education that she desired. Now Walker had the opportunity to take two years off out of the classroom for a lecture tour. She wanted the same for her sister.

The train to Knoxville allowed an extensive set of definitive reflections to emerge about the Deep South tour. Having lived so long with the perception of others that living in the North was inherently better for Blacks than living in the

Mercedes Walker's press packet

South, she now had evidence for seeing the South differently. That difference mattered for someone who had always rejected that perception. In Southern cities, there was a density of the Black population that united them in many ways. In places where half or more of the population was Black, like Mobile and Birmingham, she was not as impressed by the rising and seemingly influential Black middle class, which was important enough to mention only briefly. What stood out much more was industrialization, a change that gave Black workers, once forced to seek employment in the mines for little more than slave wages, the opportunity for advocacy through organized union activity. She'd been gone less than two decades, and now concluded that Birmingham, a city leading the country in coal, iron, and steel production, needed Black people. As a result, it was forced to support integrated trade unions, which was not the case in any other city in the South. Mobile's shipping and welding industries added to her image of the South as a progressive region on the move. Finally, she understood the emergence of the Southern Negro Youth Congress (SNYC) as a logical successor to the National Negro Congress, which she had attended, so it brought back the excitement she had felt. Any associated racial tensions were only a necessary "disturbance." It was reported that SNYC was now claiming 700 members with an ability to hold rallies that attracted some 7,000 persons in "race riot proportions," which she took as a positive sign for change. SNYC was in fact a rural-based movement, which fit the South where the majority of the US Blacks still lived in conditions akin to slavery. Not unlike the National Negro Congress, members of the Communist Party were present, which in her mind made their work more viable because it represented a united-front organization allowing Blacks and White to work together.

Although there were students from the Negro schools in the South who were involved with SNYC, Walker was careful about where she expressed her more political views. There were times when she recognized a politicized advance guard, which bore many resemblances to and considered a definite predecessor to the later civil rights activism. The South was already involved in various levels of organizing; there were boycotts against discriminatory practices for Black workers, anti-lynching campaigns, resistance to voter suppression, and efforts to secure legal representation for those unfairly treated. This Southern-based movement would become clear evidence to her that the more popular era of civil rights—the 1960s—was an extension if not a watered-down version of what was already going on a full two decades before the historical term "Civil Rights Movement" was coined. While she was not on most of the college campuses long enough to be aware of any activism, whenever she made references to student activism, her comments were well received by the students.

She would continue these reflections as she left Knoxville for a Pine Bluff, Arkansas engagement and a final reading at Jackson State College, which was close enough to New Orleans to visit family before heading back to North Carolina. The train line she took to get to Pine Bluff was the longest, retracing the Alabama route and adding Mississippi. She left Knoxville for Athens, then up to Chattanooga, Huntsville, and back up to Memphis, changing for a final train to Pine Bluff. While Walker saw it as an "odd line," the major motivation was to get to Jackson and then go to New Orleans, where she would stay for two days. The unwieldly ride was so long, however, that it allowed her fatigue to emerge in full form, bringing along with it a spiritual surrender. She had been moving fast and saw the trip as the reminder to be grateful for all the blessings that she had received. Seeing Mercedes and feeling such joy was only additional cause to show gratitude. That sense of gratitude was accompanied by a tendency to exaggerate. Each reading was the "best that I've given yet," but there was something about that phrase that must have been true at her Jackson State talk. Walker met enough people there and made such an impression that the invitation she received to join their faculty six years later might not have been as much of a surprise as she would come to think.

But she was near home, and the sense of bringing this phase of the tour to an end renewed her energy. As always, she was initially pleased to see her family, especially since Brother was to be inducted into the army the next day, an indication that he was finally grown up and was now a man. It did not take long, however, before she found herself saying too much, getting overly emotional. The visit was both too short and too long, and she sought comfort on the ride from New Orleans, since one of her neighbors was the Pullman porter. He brought her breakfast to her, and Walker settled in for the long ride to North Carolina.

During this leg of the journey are glimpses that Walker's creative energy had returned. She was rested enough to feel the inspiration, her mind free from other distractions so that the lyrics came through with some degree of fluency. Mostly she found herself recording flashes of thoughts as they came across her mind, merging with feelings prompted by certain memories. But she had enough visual images to start "October Journey":

We rode through rain swiftly and secretly as silent wells
The trees
Scenery
Ravines
Mountain ranges
Gulleys
Bare
Barren sticks and holes
Soldier take my heart away to distinct shores of Tripoli to battle scenes.[12]

The last line was likely directed toward Brother, who was leaving for the army at the same time she was heading back to North Carolina.

The remainder of the tour of North Carolina schools: Winston-Salem Teachers College, Greensboro A & T, Fayetteville State, and Barber-Scotia College in Concord were not burdensome. Livingstone, where she had taught previously, had not confirmed a reading as she had hoped. But it allowed for a day's rest in preparation for the journey back to New York.

What the Southern book tour had done was to present Walker with new possibilities for a place she could call home. It was not New Orleans, which always reminded her of the forced retreat. But as she summed up each visit in the Southern cites, the region began to present itself as a whole, filled with changing politics and promising new possibilities at a pace that seemed to be about right. The tour became its own form of reclamation. She was both home and not home; it could not be both.

PART IV
THE POET AS WOMAN
1944–1962
(North Carolina; Jackson, MS)

16

Find Somebody to Love

In an early unpublished autobiographical fragment, Walker reflected back on the meaning of her sudden rise from a nobody to a somebody after the publication of *For My People*:

> I found myself one day on fifth avenue in New York City with nearly a thousand cash dollars in my purse; more money than I had ever had before in my life and I could not think of a thing I wanted to buy. I was so lonely I could have cried. I did not know a soul to whom I could turn and I had no friend with whom I could even share a movie. I said to myself then I may be on my way to fame and fortune, but if I write more books and travel far and remain so lonely I will die unhappy. I am going to find somebody with whom I can share my life, otherwise I will die miserable.[1]

The excitement over her success was insufficient to mask the loneliness she saw on the horizon. Fame was not unwanted; she was fully prepared to embrace it and would have been disappointed had she not received such public attention. At twenty-seven, ordinarily she would have expected to be married. Seeing and meeting Elizabeth Catlett, who had married, gave no indication to her that marriage and a career were not compatible. The provisions for single women to which she was subjected—like living in a dormitory reserved for unmarried women, most of whom gossiped too much for her—she saw as an infringement on the freedom she believed her education and achievement warranted. Walker, therefore, found herself implicated in a complex posture toward the protocols of race and womanhood unique not only to Black women in mid-twentieth century but especially to someone who believed that marriage was the fulfillment of womanhood. Her violent opposition to the same view when JRB had presented it could hardly disguise her firm belief in it.

The contradictions that had begun to surface probably became more visible while she was traveling. Although writing was her major preoccupation during those long hours on the train, she was very observant, and most of the people she saw were men, families, and couples. The women she saw always had children in tow. Whatever she did and wanted to do for the rest of her career, Walker remained a modern "race woman," breaking barriers, a leader and a model, someone who placed a priority on what contributions she expected to make for

The House Where My Soul Lives. Maryemma Graham, Oxford University Press. © Oxford University Press 2022. DOI: 10.1093/oso/9780195341232.003.0016

Early photograph of Firnist James Alexander and Margaret Walker

the benefit of her race. All personal feelings aside, Walker would have been well aware of her own history as a member of that critical mass of Black women who would be identified by that term,[2] like Mary McLeod Bethune, a familiar name in the Walker family because of their Florida roots. In the way that Darlene Clark Hine, Evelyn Brooks Higginbotham, and Paula Giddings have explained, the important work that Black women did in the late nineteenth and early twentieth centuries was possible in part because of their unquestionable moral and social character. Now that she was becoming a more public figure, that tension between the need to protect that public image and the desire to be a full and completely sexualized woman pushed up against the legacy of nineteenth-century Victorian ideals. She had learned to manage that tension for most of her life with regular prayer, asking guidance from God, and writing as a form of release. And when that didn't work, masturbation. What she did was acceptable because she was under the protection of a higher authority, her faith was the assurance of that protection, and she remained pure. If she often found herself acting out of passion and then later regretting it, she adjudicated the situation by entering into a full-blown confessional mode. The journal was always the place where she could lay bare her soul, without fear of consequences. It remained the house where her soul lived, an appropriate metaphor that she had offered up early in life to explain the way she would learn to manage competing priorities, needs, and desires without losing her grounding. The house protected her, no matter what path she took or decision she made; her soul would remain the pure essence of who she was and would always need to be.

The last leg of Walker's journey took her to North Carolina, where she took a brief break. It hardly felt like home since she had only spent so little time in either of the two places where she had worked, Salisbury or Insitute, before the tour started. Yet, being away and returning impressed upon her the remarkable nature of what she had done. Fear of what might have happened, interestingly enough, only emerged as the tour was drawing to a close. She doubted that had it not been carefully arranged, and the conditions of travel were such as they were—by train and not bus—it would have worked as well as it did. Could she see doing this kind of thing again, alone? Somehow, the fear was like an alarm that she could not shut off.

Walker had been fortunate. There is no known record of any Black writer other than Langston Hughes taking a tour of Southern Negro colleges as Walker had done before the start of the Civil Rights Movement. She had had the experience of traveling by bus, which she and Mercedes had done often, and she could remember those being some of her worst experiences: first because the space did not allow for two sets of bathrooms that were then required—one for Whites and one for Colored. At some point, she would have found herself without a seat, since Blacks would have to give up a seat to any white passenger who boarded without one. Bus travel along Southern roads covered with tar rather than cement or a smoother gravel would have wearied her even more. The railway system, segregated as it was, represented a major improvement, as it was a newer form of travel before the desegregation of public accommodations brought assorted benefits for Blacks. Walker experienced those benefits on her tour. First was the presence of Pullman Car Porters, an exclusive Black male enterprise. And while they were hired to lend assistance to the mainly white passengers that used them, it was widely known that the porters took care of their own.

Immaculately dressed and thoroughly accommodating, Pullman porters emerged almost simultaneously with the railway transportation system, taking their name after one George Pullman, who quickly saw the benefits of recruiting Black men to put those skills learned during slavery to good use. Guaranteed employment and a service orientation combined to create a communication network of considerable importance, both politically and socially. Whites traveling expected exquisite service, but Blacks traveling got the benefit of joining a human link between Black communities in the South and North. Managing the affairs of the "Jim Crow Car" could mean just about anything: handlers for the growing number of Black artists and musicians, protectors of African American families, connoisseurs and promoters of jazz and other forms of Black urban culture, and transmitters of ideas of a nascent Civil Rights Movement that had yet to name itself. Black women traveling alone, as Walker was, would be sure to get the attention of a Pullman porter, who understood implicitly their job as protector. It was not unusual to know one or more of the Pullman porters when traveling regular routes, as she did on her visits to and from New Orleans. Pullman porters were "teachers" bringing books and magazines, if not radical ideas otherwise banned in the South. A wage-earning job and built-in travel could translate into upward mobility. Moreover, their exclusion from the American Railway Union membership prompted a spirit of activism. Their sheer numbers, camaraderie, and sense of physical independence made it easier to organize a major movement that radically transformed America's unions.

Unlike Hughes, who traveled by car on his tour in the early 1930s, Walker had the benefit and comfort provided by Pullman porters—even if one were riding in the segregated car that began at the Mason-Dixon line going South and stopped at the line going North. The porters paid careful attention to the unaccompanied passengers and families, and they understood what it meant to exude the pride in a highly respectable job. They were skilled raconteurs for any children traveling, could assist in matchmaking when appropriate, and could be trusted with sources of critical information that often had no other form of transmission.

Walker was among those who trusted her safety to Pullman porters when traveling alone. In a period when sexual and other forms of vulnerability were still very real for Black women, Walker could be assured that she was under a certain surveillance of the Pullman crew. Every porter was a good conversationalist, part of their stock in trade, and did as much flirting as they did matchmaking. The NCAC tour by train brought her in contact with many people, and Walker took advantage of occasions to meet fellow passengers, dining with some of them, which the racial segregation facilitated. Likewise, Pullman porters made it their business to know who of note was on board. If the Walkers discouraged their daughter from communicating with any random male she met on a train, Pullman porters mediated those conditions by providing the safe space for that to happen after tipping off young men about a single woman aboard the train. Not surprisingly, Walker's journal notes alternated between comments on the landscape and those people she encountered. She had become a trusted daughter to a train system. And it was not unusual for her parents to give her some money during her college travel days with a reminder to "tip the Pullman Porter so he'll be sure to take care of you."[3]

This first extended tour by train was a major reason Walker always preferred train travel. Even when air transportation became available to the general public, she opted for train travel. Only after the train system entered its declining years did she express a preference for the car, accompanied by her willing husband as her driver, and after his death, her youngest son. Train travel allowed the pace for thinking and writing to which she would become accustomed. On the "October Journey," as she began to refer to the book tour years later, Walker saw herself as coming into her own. The long stretches of travel time gave her the opportunity to look back at her life and look ahead.

But those long stretches of time spent traveling allowed for another important observation: men noticing her. This boost to her self-confidence was unmistakable. Not knowing any of the people around her meant that she could be who and what she wanted to be, peeling off layers of the respectability veneer as needed. Part of that confidence was associated with resolving the tension between her public and private selves, the woman writer and the woman who needed and wanted to be loved. Her first inclination was to take her cues from others: "It is becoming very obvious to all my acquaintances that I need emotional release—actually sexual or physical love—some of them tell me—others merely look and see it in my eyes," she wrote in her journal after meeting Catlett in New York. She was accustomed to being the center of attention, having people notice her as if she were the voice of authority. Poetry had been the first medium to do that. But she also learned how to code switch, giving advice on writing poetry as easily as she analyzed the social world, which gave student audiences in particular advice on how to become agents of change. The metaphor of the "growing out of shadow" no longer seemed appropriate. People listened to her and men looked at her, the latter, she presumed, because they saw something they liked.

The consequence of the attention that was now coming her way as she traveled, however, was something for which she was not prepared. She had been steeped in notions of romantic love, but because her two experiences with men had been so different, and because of a carefully overprotected childhood, she was less than experienced in the art of male-female relations. What mattered, at least based on what she had been taught, was intelligence, which is what she had in abundance, not physical beauty, which she had always been told she did not. In fact, she believed she was "homely," which meant unattractive to men, having few choices, and sometimes feeling forced to marry anyone to avoid being an "old maid." For Walker, being homely was not necessarily bad, since marriage had never been a high priority. The demand for excellence in school and subsequently in one's chosen career was all that mattered. If you aren't pretty, as her mother had reminded her, you'd better be smart if you want people to pay attention to you. She took from this logic the view that an intellectual compatibility would be her basis of any successful relationship with a man were she to ever have one. It did seem to explain or justify what had drawn her to Wright, and him to her. In JRB's case, it was precisely her intelligence and her ambition that he wanted her to suppress. Perhaps in both cases, the issue was competition. Who was to say? What was clear to Walker as a twenty-seven-year-old young woman who had yet to become sexually active, was the arousal she felt when well-dressed, educated men with polished speaking voices reached out in a graceful gesture to shake her hand. The excitement she felt was more erotic, which she knew spelled caution. "Love, I want but may not get—Respect is something I must have and will get,"[4] she concluded. The most important lesson she had learned was to let her fears go. She summarized the lesson from those previous failed relationships and the book tour:

> One thing I believe I have truly lost is gross fear. I am no longer afraid. If I get caught up short, I know I can still go on facing life with courage. If death over-takes me with unfinished business, nothing else will matter anyway—and up to then I want to be able to say—I did my best considering.[5]

Walker was determined to come to a clear understanding of the relationship between her public and her private selves, and work-life balance. She began to see more clearly what control she did have. As she made her lists, she concluded that the problem with work was discipline, something over which she believed she needed to gain more control. And while she may have gotten over her fear, she was as yet uncertain about having gotten over the hurt. But it too was impor-tant on the personal side of her checklist.

> Will a man's love help me? Will it be enough to blot
> out the hurt that has eaten my heart out these four years?
> Should I ever bring myself to have an affair? Tonight I
> heard of two new marriages. They set up the same deep
> yearning inside me.[6]

Believing in love and believing that one can be loved for Walker were very different. She began with what she thought was an objective analysis. She offered this self-description: "Nobody can deny that even if I do walk like a farmer, wear crooked, wrinkled stockings, keep dirty fingernails, have an occasionally B.O. and halitosis, have bad dandruff and hair that kinks too often, and know an-ything about makeup . . . I am a charming person."[7] "Charm," "intelligence," and "beauty" occupied very different places in her understanding of social relation-ships. Her perceptions about what it means to be a very successful woman who wasn't pretty, but who attracted men nonetheless, began to change. She no longer greeted men in passing. Instead, she took stock of all those she met.

The next stage in Walker's growing awareness of her relational identity with regard to men led to an assessment of the men she had met on the Southern book tour.

> I have met four men on this trip who have claimed an interest in me and who have interested me in varying degrees. First the soldier Harry, lowest in intel-ligence and training, probably an unskilled laborer before the army got him, yet magnetic. The soldier Alex, who scarcely struck a responsive chord in me, sat beside me and slowly went berserk in typical soldier fashion . . . bought me

two chicken dinners and then tried to take me in his arms and failed. Then the teacher of science at Atlanta, Warren Henry who handed me a lie about his having taken a tumble for me. . . . He was way up in the academic scale yet did not interest me one whit.[8]

While her usual practice of making lists seemed just a matter of course, Walker was clearly impressed by the fourth man, one of the college faculty she met at the lecture she had given at North Carolina Agricultural and Technical College in Greensboro:

[Bernard] Mason is crazy. But I like his craziness and I am almost positive I am going to see him again. A concert pianist, he has the most gentle and sensitive hands I have ever seen on a man. . . . He saw in me what I want myself to be, not merely appear.[9]

Walker was duly impressed by Mason and his musical training at Oberlin. He told her he was in line to become the next chair of the Music Department at A & T. The next five journal pages describe their time together, and she vowed to "bend heaven and earth to hear him play in Washington at Howard [University] on December 16." It was Mason whose words were "touching and tenderly beautiful," words that "paid such tribute to me, I only wish I were half as worthy of it as he thinks I am."[10] Always anxious and guilt-ridden about any sexual feelings, Walker expressed none of her usual trepidation. Mason mesmerized her; he made her hopeful and joyful about her future. Amused by her own behavior, she commented that she enjoyed hearing him talk so much that she remained unusually quiet.

Bernard Mason was the most suitable of the four men Walker had met, not only because he was well educated and ambitious, but also because he understood and executed the rules of amorous courtship that anticipated Walker's desires. After her program, they went to dinner and returned to her guest home where he began "quietly and too seriously making love to me," she wrote in her journal. The lavish descriptions sound more like an affair of someone who had fallen hopelessly and helplessly in love.

What seems odd about this passage is Walker's casual use of "making love," a phrase that seems to refer to anyone demonstrating a romantic interest in her. Since she used the phrase in several other reports of her encounters with men, it is likely that she enjoyed being wooed and found some qualities of the men she was meeting attractive, while others, not so much. She rarely depicts a lovemaking scene in which she participates, only one in which a suitor is making love to her. She might imagine herself, after all, a member of an elite group of Black women who could expect to have their choice of male admirers. She had inherited romantic notions of all kinds beginning in childhood and the only marriage she might have was still one that needed to meet her parents' approval. The new experience as a successful and mature woman was intoxicating and liberating. Walker makes clear in the entry her desire for physical affection, knowing that her body was ready for a sexual experience. Her journal was indeed her confidante.

> He talked until all hours. . . . I can't repeat half of what he said—some of it I simply want to remember as he said it. It would have no significance for anyone else but me. . . . I know I shall remember what he said all my life. . . . The more I saw of him the higher my estimation of him grew. . . . He talked as if there would always be tomorrow, next year and the next. I know nothing of the future is promised. Today is all we have. Yet he makes me hope for the goodness and the happiness of the future. . . . I liked to hear him talk. I remained quiet to hear him talk. I actually hated to say goodbye. He said he couldn't ask me to stay another day because he knew it would be selfish. He knows I have my work and that my work is important—that I must go on doing for other Negro youth and saying to other Negro youth what I said and did at A & T.[11]

Whether or not the lengthy discourse was real or imagined, she was carried away by what she would describe as an affair. By the end of the entry, the experience elicits comparisons, "secret and hopeless—greater than the memory of Wright or Brown and against which all other men are dwarfed while he remains immeasurable."[12] To experience something that was very real, but which may have violated her moral arsenal, could only be written in the journal. She cannot resist the urge to give words to the experience, but only in the most private inaccessible way. The report of this short but rather intense experience let Walker know that her heart was ready for love.

An important entry during the Salisbury break seems to confirm that Walker encountered several soldiers on the train, not uncommon given that Fort Bragg, the only US military base in North Carolina, was the largest at that time. It was the middle of World War II, and the number of Blacks serving in the armed forces was at an all-time high, even though they were still subject to the Jim Crow laws, especially in the South. Clusters of them were routine on the train, and they stood out dressed in freshly pressed uniforms and spit-shined shoes, enjoying the camaraderie with each other and the other passengers they met. It would have been difficult for them not to pass through Fort Bragg on their way to or from basic training or deployment, or, as was the case for one Firnist James Alexander, on their way home for a furlough before shipping out to an overseas location.

Greensboro was the last stop on her North Carolina lecture tour before Walker's planned break at Salisbury. She could not help noticing the soldiers as they passed by her. At least they were conscious of her, quietly observing her intensity while she was either reading a book or writing in her journal. Some dared to "disturb" her by speaking. She still wasn't certain if she had just been oblivious earlier, but winding down the first month of the tour, she was more exhausted than usual, and with no more talks for a week, she was more willing to entertain a conversation to make the time pass faster. More important, she was beginning to enjoy the attention she was receiving, now believing herself to be more than reasonably attractive.

A photograph of her taken by Carl Van Vechten shortly after the release of the book pleased her enormously, and it would have been that image of Margaret Walker she hoped that men saw. The upsweep hairstyle actually gave her height and framed a face that displayed a pensive look. While she did not have the patience for care that such a look required, she was content knowing that she could be attractive and that some men thought so. As she matured and had even less time, Walker settled for hats that gave her more height and control over her unruly hair. Walking suits completed that attire that gave shape and form to her body that became rounder with age. The Van Vechten photograph was often used to promote her readings, and while it might have misrepresented her appearance slightly, her memorable readings forgave any attempt to misrepresent what she looked like. The attention she was getting made her feel different about herself, and as she gained more confidence with each reading, she concluded that she needed to dress for the talk itself *and* for the men who might find her attractive. For many of those in the audience, Walker was the only real Black poet they had ever seen, and not knowing what a poet was supposed to look like, made her appear both familiar and strange. She was aware that people viewed her closely, each group for different reasons. Barely seeming to be out of her teens with her education and literary acclaim, for the men she encountered, Walker would certainly have been considered "a prize catch."

She had now been traveling long enough to gain more practice with being under observation, learning how, for example, to pause from her writing and turn slightly to the side to see who might be looking her way. What might have appeared calculating was for her to have more curiosity about who those observing her were. Her encounters with men had been limited to the graduate students who were usually in the University of Chicago divinity school, and the artist-activists. But her sense of herself as a woman being admired by men in general fascinated her. She had some understanding of the rituals of courtship and marriage, but after such negative encounters, whatever she had associated with the protocols between men and women and how to read them were no longer available to her. She thus approached this new experience more openly and with a willingness to trust her instincts. After having become the poet she wanted to be, she felt some sense of liberation in the possibility that there was still a chance that she might now become the woman that she needed to be.

A noticeable gap in Walker's journal entries leads us to wonder whether Walker saw Bernard Mason again since he was in nearby Greensboro. What is clear, however, is that she did have an encounter that made a major impression on her. The journal reports a prayer of gratitude that appears after the arrival in Salisbury: "All day I have been blessed with such a sweetness in my heart. I felt a need for spiritual refreshment, for the Presence of God in my soul and truly he has blessed me."[13] What follows is a lesson, one in which she finds examples from religious history to confirm her faith. The prayerful conclusion is for God to watch over her, "I know thou art my God—that thy spirit walks with me—I know my heart belongs to thee. I am dedicated to thee and consecrated to the doing of thy will."[14]

Something happened that marked the end of Walker's Southern journey just as she was beginning the Northern phase. For the few days she was in Salisbury she continued to express idealized language in her journal entries, but with a remarkable shift from the human to the spiritual.

* * *

By the time Walker arrived at her next reading in Springfield, Massachusetts, fourteen days later, her mood had changed:

> I have a million and one things to say. Time goes so fast and things happen to me now so quickly I can hardly realize it is only a week today since I left North Carolina. It seems at least a month—more like something in a distant past vaguely remembered and faintly realized.[15]

She chastises herself for "behaving in an unbecoming manner in a way alien to my true nature and character." There is a rather unusual sign: the absence of painful monthly abdominal cramps, which by her calculation should have occurred two weeks earlier. After a visit to the doctor, she agreed that the lateness was attributed to the stress of travel. But the fact alone brought on her usual attack of self-loathing and a rejection of all that she had seen earlier as positive. She directed her comments at Mason, with whom, in her words, "nothing actually happened," yet fearing that she had left him with the impression of her as a "free and easy woman," letting him see "too much of how I felt. Another bitter lesson learned. Dear God, when will I learn?" she asked.[16]

Although the entry is connected to some comments about Bernard Mason, with whom "nothing actually happened," she refers to "something . . . vaguely remembered and faintly realized," that she could only talk about in these allusive terms. The yearning for the man she loves to be a child of God would have been someone with whom she felt she was in contradiction, someone like the soldier Firnist James Alexander, who was different from anyone she'd ever known. He was the object of the words "I am in love. . . . I feel my heart yearning for him to be a child of God and one to whom I can go for spiritual companionship as well as physical sustenance."[17]

Walker carried these feelings with her to Troy, New York, and Mt. Holyoke, where she gave talks during the Thanksgiving week. Despite her physical exhaustion, she gave brilliant performances and spent time with students. Mt. Holyoke students were especially attentive to her. She rested a bit and had a visit from her friend Elizabeth Catlett. But her thoughts, recorded in her journal, continue to reveal more than she says. Before describing her Christmas plans, she noted thoughtfully: "If I marry, I will be lucky and must just let nature take its course." [18]

When she returned South, Walker had something else on her mind. The soldier Firnist James Alexander, "Alex," had made an impression. While she was delayed in recording these early impressions, their chance meeting eventually became one of her favorite stories. In the most commonly recited version, she admitted not having ignored the light-complexioned soldier who beckoned to her when she got on the train in North Carolina. Startled, she quickly found another empty seat. Confident that she had heard him, the soldier ran to the seat to join her just as she placed her bag in the overhead compartment. She felt like a dwarf next to him. Handsomely attired in his military uniform, his curly hair was slicked back, brushed away from his face until it was nearly straight. She couldn't help looking at him, wondering who this man was, a man who couldn't stop talking to her. They talked as though they had known each other all their lives until he got off in High Point. He asked her if she would contact him when she returned from her tour. Trying to be coy, she brushed him off at first. High Point was near Salisbury, he said, and he thought they could get together. "Get together for what?"[19] she asked. She was uppity and she knew it, but he liked her aggressiveness and was determined to get to know her better. Walker was somewhat unnerved by his proposal and kept his face in her mind. If he's really interested, he will just have to find me, she thought.

Alexander was a tall, handsome man with reddish brown hair. He was technically biracial, born in Union City, North Carolina, in 1910 to a Black mother who worked for the white farm owner who fathered her children. Alex, the name that she would always use, was a self-assured man who had gone to work at the age of eleven. When his mother left the farm and moved to High Point with her five children, two girls and three boys, Alex had already manifested his independence. He knew how to earn money from odd jobs to supplement his mother's income. When World War II broke out, he enlisted as a twenty-seven-year-old infantryman. The army was his education, as he traveled to Scotland, Wales, and London. He was on furlough when he met his future wife.[20]

A missing journal makes it difficult to confirm when Walker and Firnist actually met. Those journals in which he does appear suggests they might have first met in late 1943 during the North Carolina leg of her lecture tour. She makes clear that she had met and fallen in love with a man who expressed deep affection for her and was not intimidated by her intelligence but was in fact proud of it. He wanted intelligent and cultivated children, he had told her, so he expected his wife to be both of those things. She knew that she saw possibilities in this relationship, and she was ready for marriage.

Given her experiences with the traditional African American middle class in Chicago and at the schools where she taught, Walker believed she had what the traditional middle class wanted and more: the satisfaction of knowing she could command attention as a poet. Marrying a man who matched her class status was less important to her than marrying a man who worshipped her. Members of the Alexander family in High Point saw the couple as an ideal match. "Because he was good looking and she was in academia, they accented each other." Both facts could neutralize those conditions that would make for jealousy in a relationship. Josephine Rogers and Dorothy Williams, Firnist's cousins, remembered Walker as very sweet and down-to-earth; she was not "stuck up. Firnist was willing to work around her schedule; he would quit his job so he could take her wherever she wanted to go."[21]

Women's poetry critic Alicia Ostriker explains the experience of the woman poet in the 1940s and 1950s as one of conflict: "To be a creative woman in a gender polarized culture is to be a divided self."[22] Some women chose to name the division in their art; others, like Walker, found a way to reconcile that division by reinventing themselves within a socially acceptable context. Though Walker revered Black women artists of the Harlem Renaissance, she recognized their anonymity. The major American poet whose image prevailed in literary America was the secluded Emily Dickinson. Walker could accept neither anonymity nor seclusion. She would not be a "madwoman in the attic."

With one book published and widespread recognition, Walker believed her identity as a poet to be secure. She was far less secure about her identity as a woman. In her mind, romantic love and fulfilling her destiny as woman, wife, and mother were not in opposition to her life as a poet. It did not seem difficult or unusual that she should pursue the first ideal out of her need for professional satisfaction and then set her goal on accomplishing the other when she was both mature enough and emotionally ready to do so.

She had found it easy to respond to Alex's advances. He would make a good husband, in her opinion; he was unpretentious and kind, and she sensed that she could lead her professional life without fearing undue intervention or control.

In a later essay, "On Being Female, Black, and Free," she identified some specific problems of African American women. The problems, however, never caused her to wish to be anything other than a woman. "I like being a woman. . . . I have learned from the difficult exigencies of life that freedom is a philosophical state of mind and existence. The mind is the only place where I can exist and feel free."[23]

There was no question that Firnist James Alexander made her feel like a woman, not the girl who had left the South to find her voice and become a poet. She had always feared her sexual feelings, following the dictates of the Victorian sensibility that had shaped her upbringing. But Alex made her feel warm and safe, and nothing seemed to be beyond the bounds of propriety in their relationship. Unlike other men, he did not appear to want to conquer her. He was generous and extravagant with his time and—having been given a disability pension on his release from the army—with his money. She could see him in public situations when he was angry and defiant, but with her his gentleness was foremost.

Anger and defiance were learned characteristics. Black men like Alex who served in World War II were part of a cultural shift in the nation. They had gone to war to defend democracy abroad, and after experiencing the freedom in Europe that they did not have at home, few were unwilling to accept the dehumanization. Alex had a temper, Walker discovered, but he learned to keep himself out of harm's way. When he would refuse to go somewhere or do something, she knew it was because he believed the situation might result in a confrontation of some kind or another. He liked to choose his battles. When he did, he always won.

When Walker looked back at the years 1942 and 1943, she remembered that she returned from the Christmas holidays in 1943 to find a letter from Alex waiting. He told her that as a result of an injury, the army was going to release him. When he came home, he said he intended to make her his wife and the mother of his children. She wrote back that she had enjoyed meeting him, but that she could make no such commitment without getting to know him better.

Her students quickly realized that something was happening to their teacher. Walker was brilliant as always in her lectures, but now she smiled easily and seemed more at ease.

What happened next is also unclear. In an early draft of her autobiography, Walker wrote that immediately after his release in late February 1943, Alex drove to see her, invited her to High Point to meet his sister Daisy, and gave her a firm kiss. She remembered thinking it must be the French kiss they are talking about. She hadn't experienced anything like this before. She found she could talk to him easily, and although they did not discuss intellectual topics, he was full of stories of his sojourns during the war. He was lighthearted and fun to be with, and he knew how to entertain her.

The meeting with Daisy was pleasant enough, and she could tell that they were very close. But when she asked Alex to take her to his own house, he refused. He was embarrassed to tell her that he had no furniture, no place for her to sit. Later she found out that he had been married and that when he had asked his wife for a divorce, she left, taking all the furniture with her. Walker and Alex never spoke of the matter again.

The courtship lasted a little less than two months. Walker would visit Alex in High Point for the weekend; they would go to church and Sunday dinner at Daisy's and take strolls around the countryside. One Sunday she did not get back until late and missed a call from her parents. When they finally reached her, they asked if she had been away giving a reading. She told them she was simply out; it was none of their business. She dared not tell them about Alex, for she knew immediately that he would not meet with their approval. He didn't have money, education, or family status—the basic requirements for a good husband in their eyes.

But she did not need their approval, so complete was her rebellion against them by then. They had told her where to go to school, picked the clothes she was to wear, selected all her classes, and signed two job contracts for her. No, they were not telling her whom she should marry. Alex was completely committed. When they were together and she was talking, he listened intently, glowing as if something of rare beauty was on display. For Walker, being with Alex was so different from anything she had ever imagined that she found herself discovering new things about him daily. He understood people and could judge situations instantly. He was focused and good with money. Above all, Alex gave her a sense of permanent security; given the uncertainties of her life over the last nine years, she was thrilled at the thought of putting that life behind her for good.

The decision not to tell her parents more about Alex grew more difficult each day. She dreaded hearing what they would say. It all boiled down to "He wasn't good enough." They had brought her up to be an educated woman, and now she was thinking of marrying an illiterate man, the bastard son of a white man. She had hoped that, in time, her parents might be reconciled to the idea of her marriage to him. In the meantime, she learned that her application for a Rosenwald Fellowship had been approved; she could finally begin some research she wanted to do rather than return to teaching. While she continued her NCAC tour, Alex returned to the army for the final tour before his release.

We *can accept* the following facts Walker revealed about her experiences that December 1943. She took a break from her NCAC tour, and together with Mercedes, spent the Christmas holidays in New Orleans. She had dreaded going home, and for the two weeks she was there, she felt "sick, worried and badly unorganized."[24] She was hardly able to think about any writing at all. The NCAC tour would end in April, and then she'd go to New York, since she needed to spend time at the Schomburg Center of the New York Public Library. Her next stop would be the Congressional Library, and finally Georgia to complete the tracking of Randall Ware, the major male character in the novel she was calling *Jubilee*. Completing a draft of the novel in the last six months of the fellowship was the ambitious goal she set. The home visit had brought her good fortune. Her grandmother, who was declining in health, had withheld some pertinent information. For the first time, Grandma Dozier revealed where she was born, and Walker felt she had a place for *Jubilee* to begin. This was the last piece she needed, and her grandmother seemed to know that it was the last fragment of the story she had remaining to give to her granddaughter. The rest would have to take care of itself.

Everything was on schedule except her body. Walker was in the middle of a deep emotional crisis, constantly telling herself otherwise. She was too upset to write and "weighted down with sin."[25] She pushed herself to finishing the tour, expecting to find the necessary relief in New York where she had planned to slow things down for a while.

Comparing several versions of her personal history and government documents, what seems most likely is that Walker had learned that she was pregnant sometime in November 1943; she kept it well hidden but refused to let it disrupt her plans. Firnist Alexander's army enlistment records confirm that he was still on active duty. His status was listed as "separated" (apparently from his first wife) and with "dependents" since he was the oldest son in the family. He had expressed his desire to make Walker his wife early on, but would have to complete the divorce from his first wife.

At barely a hundred pounds and given her emotional history, trying to maintain her composure through such a turbulent time would have been difficult for Walker. In New York, she had supportive friends, Elizabeth Catlett and Langston Hughes among them, since going home to New Orleans was not an option. Her journal entries make clear her distressed state of mind. "I need God now more than I have ever before . . . for strength and for moral victory, for courage and faith and cleanliness . . . joy and peace and constant love." Her self-identity as a "repentant sinner" precedes the list of problems and failings that resulted in her having "no right to be called God's child."[26]

Margaret Walker and Firnist Alexander had their own truth, one that never changed. As their children remembered it, their mother and their father had both said they had fallen in love at first sight. He was the man she wanted to marry and father her children; she was the woman that he wanted as his wife and the mother of his children. Everything else they expected to negotiate.

Elizabeth Catlett was the first person who realized Walker was pregnant. She had arrived in New York in early January to continue her NCAC lecture with engagements in Pennsylvania, Ohio, Illinois, Massachusetts, Maine, Rhode Island, and New York. She wrapped up final engagements in Missouri and Minnesota believing that by April, she was too large and was showing, which eliminated further travel until after the baby was born. Her plan was to stay in New York, accept the Rosenwald Fellowship, and pick up the tour again in midsummer. No matter how small she was, the pregnancy barely visible on her tiny frame, according to Catlett, they did go to the hospital to confirm that she was indeed pregnant. Since Catlett's husband Charles White was in an army hospital nearby after contracting tuberculosis on active duty himself, she invited Walker to move from Harlem to her Bedford Street house in Greenwich Village between Carmine Street and 7th Avenue. They never discussed any details once the pregnancy was confirmed. Walker explained that Alex was overseas on active duty, and she divided her time between writing and her favorite pastime—cooking. "When I was at school," Catlett recalled, "I would look forward to coming home to all these delicious meals."[27] During those months, Walker saw Hughes often. "One night I got home and Langston was on the top bunk with her. She had become rather close friends with him and Arne [Arna Bontemps]. By then she was way out there and Arne was shocked that she was pregnant. I don't know why,"[28] Catlett offered.

Bontemps's shock was quite understandable, however, since he would have been familiar with Walker's relationship with Richard Wright from the time he spent in Chicago. Since she had not told anyone about her pregnancy, including her parents, she could not risk the news getting back to them. Her parents' opposition to Alex, the man she intended to marry, would have required sharing as little as possible about their relationship. She loved Alex no less, and since he had asked for her hand in marriage, their engagement had already begun. That the marriage was delayed was due to reasons beyond their control.

She remained with Catlett, who saw her through the pregnancy and birth of her first child on July 19, 1944, at 12:45 P.M., weighing six pounds and twelve and one fourth ounces, recorded in her journal. Her water had broken early, and Catlett had taken her to Harlem Women's Hospital, expecting the baby to be born the next day. By the time Catlett came home from work, however, Walker had given birth to Marion, given Elizabeth as her middle name, and Catlett the status of godmother. The addition of a crying baby, however, put too much pressure on the small apartment, and Walker, who had finally told her parents about the birth, wanted to be in her own apartment by the time her mother arrived. Fear of the confrontation with her mother, who was already preparing to give the baby up for adoption, encouraged Walker to put off her mother's visit as long as possible. The stalling tactics she used with her mother included a proposal to move to Chicago and stay with Mercedes, whose career was in full bloom. Because she had to continue her NCAC tour, however, Walker needed to remain in New York as her base and therefore moved into her own apartment, hiring someone to care for the baby. It did not take long before she realized that she could not afford the joint costs of an apartment and full-time child care in order to continue her tour.

Returning to New Orleans was not an option, but a decision to move to Boston to live with her Aunt Abby and cousin Samuel seemed to satisfy her mother. She was also able to let her mother know that Abby needed someone to care for her while she was in the hospital, and Samuel could babysit while she was with her aunt. Marion Walker, therefore, did not make a visit to see her first grandchild.

Walker experienced some post-partum depression, but mostly she was consumed with the fear of being left alone, an unmarried woman with a child. She was, on one hand, self-critical—how could she have become such a sucker? She needed to be through with men, who would try to control her. "I do not want to be obligated, to have to knuckle down to somebody else," she wrote. "Men are perversely made to be treated harshly, the worse you are to them, the more they think of you and the nicer they are to you. . . . Their lies are liquored and honey—beware of a man's lies." In her worst moments, she resolved "From now on my method with men will be this, get all I can get out of them and give them nothing. Use their money and them for convenience, push them around, don't let them push you around. This is the age-old wisdom of the experienced woman born wise and what the fool has to suffer to learn."[29] Coupled with these thoughts is a desire to be independent from family and friends, having her own home, and a room of her own. As always, Walker's desires are followed by a prayer for strength and support.

Staying with Aunt Abby, and Marion's severe colds during the Boston winters, pushed some of those feelings about men aside. But Walker had a more important reason for restoring her confidence and the rightness of what had happened to her. Supported by her growing belief in signs and reading astrological charts, she could remember that Grandma Dozier had died after the sisters' last visit to New Orleans. Now a child had entered the world in her grandmother's place. What the connection between the parallel events were, she did not know. But it could not simply have been an accident that the death of her great-grandmother, Margaret Duggans Ware Brown, preceded Walker's entry into the world as the family's firstborn just as Marion Elizabeth's birth had come following the death of her great-grandmother, Elvira Ware Dozier. Recognizing these parallels provided just cause for Marion's birth. What was a mistake was now part of the plan for the universe, the necessary line of succession of women in her family. With this discovery, Walker let go of much of the self-loathing into which she could so easily fall. It also would gave her reason to construct a new narrative for this new part of her life that at first seemed so unplanned. The only people who knew she was unmarried were her parents. The version that she began to tell so often was the only story that she was willing to accept as her own. In this version she and Alex were married in 1943 before his return to active duty. She was in New York when she discovered she was pregnant and had remained with Elizabeth Catlett while Alex was away but moved to Boston to live with her aunt following the baby's birth. The story continued, in Walker's version as Catlett and Marion Walker both went to Boston for the christening for Marion Elizabeth Alexander in the spring of 1945. The ritual for becoming a godmother had been completed.

In truth, the next time that Catlett saw Walker and her godchild, they were passing through New York on the way to High Point. According to Catlett, Alex did indeed come for Walker and Marion Elizabeth in June 1945. The journal entry confirms that Walker was in High Point by September where she had returned to teaching at Livingstone College. What we know is that a marriage ceremony took place. The Walkers were not invited; Mercedes was not there. Three

Walker and baby Marion before reuniting with Firnist

people were present: the bride, the groom, and Daisy, Alex's older sister, who offered her home for the marriage ceremony. They took no pictures.

Walker's outline for her autobiography places her marriage in June 14, 1943, the date she continued to celebrate. The Guilford County Registry records the marriage between Firnist James Alexander and Margaret Abigail Walker on June 14, 1945, following his honorable discharge from the army as a disabled veteran. The factual inaccuracy became an insignificant detail that never mattered to either of them. What did matter was her belief in herself as the woman who accepted all that she had been given, the good and the bad. "I have no enemies save myself,"[30] she had once said.

In her relentless mental recounting of the events that had transpired, when she wanted to express deep emotion, or explain herself to herself, Walker typically complemented her words with passages from the Bible. Her choice of Psalm 27 helped to answer questions and allay her fears at the moment she felt alone. Thirteen years after leaving home to complete college, she believed she had cleared major hurdles and achieved most of her important goals. But she was now venturing into an unknown future complicated by unexpected pregnancy and a husband. Was this "the time of trouble . . . When my father and mother forsake me?"[31] She had asked for mercy and forgiveness, believing that the Lord had answered her. What had happened had its purpose. She could lift her head once she was married and recommit herself to a faith that had always guided her. Although a mixed blessing, what was required now was that she "offer . . . sacrifices of joy . . . [and] sing praises unto the Lord."[32]

17

Every Child Is a Book I Didn't Write

By midsummer 1945, Walker's life was moving forward rapidly. She had become widely known as a poet, completed a whirlwind tour of ten states, embarked upon a lifelong career as a teacher, fallen in love, given birth to her first child, and weathered several personal storms. The Margaret Walker who emerged from this period was radically different from the one who had lived in the world of possibilities. Now that those possibilities had produced a new reality, how was she going to adapt?

"Growing Out of Shadow," an essay invited by the editor of *Common Ground*, was the first publication that indicated a major shift in Walker's thinking and publishing activity. Its appearance in 1943, written in an autobiographical voice, offers a useful summary of life as she had known it. The journals now provided the text she would use, and the discovery that people were as interested in the woman behind the poetry as much as the poetry itself came as a pleasant surprise. "Growing Out of Shadow" introduces us to a precocious child: "When I was five, I was busy discovering my world, and it was a place of happiness and delight." Suddenly a shattering of innocence occurs, a violent act that signifies racial otherness: "a white child shouted in my ears 'nigger' . . . and I was startled. I had never heard the word before."[1] The vivid contrasts depicted in the paragraphs that follow the description of this encounter build up to the end of the essay, which is the best portrait of Walker as the young artist-in-the-making. Her narrative unfolds in long paragraphs that repeat a refrain and build to a climax at the end of the essay. In the conclusion to "For My People," she called for a "new earth to rise." Similarly, "Growing Out of Shadow" calls for a "new type of spiritual understanding."[2] The need for change in the material environment is coupled with change of a higher order. A familiar pattern of rhythm and repetition is visible in the last paragraph:

> Once the human spirit is washed clean of prejudices, once the basic needs of people are considered, and not the pocketbooks of the few nor the power of a handful; once institutionalized religion is liberated into religious meaning, of necessity there must begin to bloom upon the earth something spiritually more durable than any of the mystic conceptions of religion that humankind thus far has brought forth.[3]

The House Where My Soul Lives. Maryemma Graham, Oxford University Press. © Oxford University Press 2022.
DOI: 10.1093/oso/9780195341232.003.0017

The Alexander children: Margaret Elvira, Sigismund, Firnist James Jr., and Marion Elizabeth

While the growing public admiration for Walker's work had prompted the essay, it would also mark the beginning of an extended literary silence. The essay's importance lies in what it offered to readers whose only reference to a Southern Black writer at that point came from Wright's "The Ethics of Living Jim Crow." Walker accomplished two goals with her publication: she confirmed herself as a young Black woman confident in a career that had begun to fulfill its promise, and she set herself apart from Wright, a friendship with which she knew she would be linked. She identifies the importance of Chicago, the WPA, her growing understanding of class, her political activism, all as part of her growth as a writer. "Growing Out of Shadow" gave her ownership of the self she had learned to articulate, and an alternative view of the life of an artist coming of age in the Black South and urban North. Although Zora Neale Hurston had also provided an alternative view in her essay "How It Feels to Be Colored Me," which was published in 1928, interest in her had waned significantly following negative reviews of *Their Eyes Were Watching God*.

But something else happened that Walker did not know, at least she gave no indication that she did. What we now know is that Walker had been nominated for the Pulitzer Prize in 1943, seven years before Gwendolyn Brooks became the first Black person to be so honored. Instead, the decision was made to award Robert Frost his fourth Pulitzer that year, ruling Walker out altogether. The story behind the story is that Wilbur Cross, professor of English at Yale who served on the committee, submitted his assessment: "*For My People*, by Margaret Walker, a well-educated colored woman, now a college professor of English: Stephen Vincent Benet has given her a conspicuous place among the younger American poets. Miss Walker writes of her people with deep emotion, lightened here and there with humor. No one of her race, I think, has done better for them in verse."[4] Forgiving Cross for his political incorrectness—he was born during the middle of the Civil War—one cannot help wondering what might have been. That Frost knew all the major members of the selection committee raises some interesting questions. But this recent revelation points to the realities then as now regarding social networks and how they function. Winning would certainly have complicated her life at the time, but one would think in a good way. Yet Walker had accepted what fame had given her. Although she had worked hard for it, she could not let it be the driving force in her life. The making of a poet and the making of a woman were now in sharp competition.

In "How I Wrote *Jubilee*," another autobiographical essay that appeared in 1972, she gave an updated account of her literary journey, one that also invites parallels to Wright's "How Bigger Was Born" as a literary practice typical for the times. Focusing on *Jubilee*, Walker described as "living with and imagining its reality . . . most of my life."[5] Her motivation, however, had been different from Wright's. She had an urgent need to provide a counterweight to prevailing assumptions about a stalled career. She was reemerging at a critical moment in the history of Black letters, stepping back onto a stage that she had left. The stage, however, had changed. She had done it once and believed she could do it again.

"How I Wrote *Jubilee*" gives the deliberate impression of her relative stability during the long gestation period of the novel, but also a life and career that she consciously plotted and managed. She carefully describes her activities in 1934, 1942, 1944, 1947, 1948, and finally in 1953, when a Ford Fellowship gave her time to complete her research. "How I Wrote *Jubilee*" traces the path from *Jubilee* to "Goose Island" and back again before quickly bringing that period of her life to a close in the next paragraph. There is no reference to what happened in Chicago beyond the WPA. "Sooner than I realized, three years had passed, and in 1939 . . . I discovered I was a boondoggler and must get off the government's payroll. . . . I decided I must go back to graduate school and work toward a master's degree in English so that I could go south and teach in a college."[6] Finally, the absence of journals from October 1942 to October 1943, the only major gap in the entire record, makes it difficult to understand how Walker really managed this critical turning point in her life.

Looking back on her life in 1972, Walker does make clear that a shift had occurred in her mindset, if not her vision. She admitted that she still "wanted more than anything else to write," but her father's wisdom had prevailed: "I would have to eat if I wanted to live, and writing poetry would not feed me."[7] The motivation for this sobering thought, aside from her father's persistent reminder, seems obvious enough: the loss of a job and a close relationship that had nurtured her earlier idealism. Without either, she could not escape her legacy— "three generations of forebears who had taught school."[8] In the end, she saw limited choices.

The highly ordered "Growing Out of Shadow" and "How I Wrote *Jubilee*" belie the reality. Walker's need to reconstruct a particular kind of narrative, to impart a compelling personal style, and her decision to abandon the perceived objectivity of the third person for the first-person singular promises authority and authenticity. She turns a perceived liability—absence from the literary scene—into an asset, and in this case, a quest narrative. "How I Wrote *Jubilee*" fills the gaps for the public, as her thoroughgoing research into the details of her family history reveal. The search is her story as well, blurring the lines between historical method, autobiographical urgency, and personal desire.

What critic Mary Kelley has termed "literary domesticity" might well apply here. Walker was very conscious about the need to keep her life private, while presenting a well-honed view of herself to the public. Kelley proposes that nineteenth-century female writers were "literary domestics . . . unwitting witnesses to both the public event and their own private experience," engaging in a range of discursive practices that included their published writing and their unpublished letters, journals, and diaries, where they "reported on their own phenomenon."[9] The resulting neglect of these women writers had much to do with literary scholars not knowing what to do when they could not acceptably label women's writing "sentimental"—if they were even recognized. The larger problem was questioning whether women as emotional creatures could actually write books at all. The recovery of women's texts, women writers, and reclaiming the domestic experience has certainly helped to put women back into history, but old habits die hard.

Walker's choice to embrace a domestic life in full bears some consideration in relationship to her critical reception. As she began to retreat from a more public life, she was careful to self-censure her public prose to present an ordered existence that would raise few doubts about her literary worth. She knew that she was emotional, but she found that writing provided an emotional release. But she had misjudged her ability to balance her creative mind, her emotions, and her ability to translate both onto the page. Her pathway was always academic, her networks were always white males, and she would remain self-driven. She would have to either catch up or be left behind.

What Walker had hoped would happen was an additive effect. In a hand-written draft of recollections for 1940–1942, she comments on a "hiatus" that was as "special as it was "significant" in transforming her life following her return to New Orleans in 1940:

> Eighteen months passed and I felt depressed, feelings dormant in hibernation, futile and hopeless. All my dreams were still unfulfilled. I wanted a job, to publish a book, to get married, and have a family—children, a husband, most of all, a happy home. Instead I was sick, broke, without friends, and so depressed I felt suicidal.[10]

The successful publication of *For My People* and its critical reviews gave her all the affirmation she needed. The explanation given is entirely personal. The losses after 1945 were great. She produced little poetry, turning ultimately to *Jubilee*, her novel. Although the prose pieces are guarded about her personal life during these years, they do confirm who she knew herself to be: an ambitious, driven woman who refused to let the oppressive conditions of her life diminish her potential. She became her own contradiction: the strong Black woman who must discover the limitations of her strength.

Walker had grown up with the language of poetry; the most intense period of her development had been in Chicago, where her access to language, the ability to create, discover, and express found a nurturing political and social environment and an accompanying audience. She would only return to poetry when she found a similar context, one that guaranteed an audience of listeners, in the 1970s. This makes even more critical the function of *Jubilee* as a work-in-progress.

The evolution of *Jubilee* was both strategic and symbolic. Strategically, it existed between the author's more restricted daily life and her desire to assert a professional identity, one that stood in danger of being lost. For a Black poet before 1950, winning the Yale Award was the highest achievement. With no guide to tell her otherwise, in many cases, Walker was making it up as she went along. What she saw was the growing popularity of Black fiction. Wright had proved that. Shifting to fiction for an achievement comparable to poetry seemed logical. *Jubilee* was the symbol of her maturity as a writer who was breaking her silence.

Yet the public attention to fiction made Walker wonder if her decision to drop "Goose Island" had been wise. If she complained to Elizabeth Catlett that Wright had stolen her work, what greater revenge could she have than achieving success with her own novel, giving her the distinction of making a name for herself in two major genres? *Jubilee* had always been harder to write than her poetry and had received more criticism from her teachers, who saw poetry as her strength. Knowing that it would take her some time, even if the story had always been there, Walker believed that she needed something more expansive than "Goose

Island" and should be set in the South. *Jubilee* thus became a book of historical necessity and personal desire. She also hoped that her reputation as an established poet would carry over into *Jubilee*, that the critics would welcome it, and that the publishers would option for it.

Thoughts of *Jubilee* provided balance between the reality of Walker's new life in High Point and the one she had dreamed. While she joined the population of migrants who lived in High Point's colored district, it was far from the small version of Harlem that residents liked to call it. On the other hand, a visible middle class found it relatively easy to enter into commercial ventures to meet the needs of an expanding Black community. The train station on High Street was near the Washington Street area where the famous Kilby Hotel stood. Black-owned and operated, the Kilby booked local groups, as well as major entertainers for sold-out events virtually every weekend. The music was a special feature of the Kilby, so much so that when young John Coltrane was growing up in High Point, his one ambition was to play at the Kilby. Playing regularly on weekends while still in high school jumpstarted his career.

By contrast, High Point's middle class residents, who lived near East Washington Street and owned the shops and businesses there, kept themselves separate from their customers. Many of these customers were first-generation Blacks whose land came from their color and mulatto status or their ability to take advantage of business opportunities that a strict system of legal and social segregation facilitated. A number of towns fed into High Point, which had its share of funeral homes, insurance companies, newspaper publishers, beauty parlors, barber shops, and other Black-owned businesses.

Black workers, Black businessmen and -women, and a color-conscious Black middle class were all part of her new world, but not one in which she could actively participate. She was by all standards poor, but she would not betray her education and religious background. Any previous transgressions she attributed to her reckless youth, something that her marriage fortunately helped to dissolve. Her logical place in the community would have been among its educated elite. In addition to public education, several area colleges provided post-secondary opportunities, creating a reserve of trained teachers and ministers.

High Point's Black community, however, had given her a lukewarm reception at best. They heard that a well-known writer was living among them, but she was an outsider, not always genteel or appropriately deferential in her encounters with the residents. With a residual supply of leftist political leanings remaining from her relationships and experiences in the 1930s, she was understandably suspicious and critical of the pretentiousness and preoccupation with light skin and "good" hair, neither of which she had. Despite representing what many of them wanted—education and professional success—High Point coloreds left her alone. To them, she was an uppity brown skin-colored woman with two degrees who had married a white-looking man. Between 1945 and 1949, she apparently did not receive an invitation to join any social or colored women's clubs. Or if she did, she declined them all. Despite all the culture and entertainment, High Point was neither Chicago nor New Orleans. It was a home to Black workers with more money than they were used to, and it provided a gathering place for people to hear popular singers and bands on weekends.

But living in High Point had a singular advantage: she was less than two hours from her future. Going on a research trip was foreign to anybody she talked to. She certainly did not discuss it with Daisy so soon after her marriage. Alex would not have openly complained, for continuing her work had been a condition of their marriage. Besides, Alex would be kept busy building their new house on Graves Street, on the land he had purchased in a Black residential section of town. Working full-time left him little time to devote to the house, which required the full use of his carpentry skills.

Living with her sister-in-law was drudgery. Daisy's devotion to her brother precluded her acceptance of anyone he would have married. That he had married someone who probably thought herself better than any of them simply made it worse for Walker. Daisy knew her brother's reputation for getting any woman he wanted and didn't really believe his vow that no woman would ever faze him again. For Firnist Alexander, Margaret Walker was the pinnacle of his achievement. "She had been very protected and he knew he had a gold mine because she was untouched," according to his cousin Josephine Rogers. "He called her his soulmate. She called him her 'sweet patootie' because Grandma [Daisy] had petunias growing all around this house."[11] Walker knew that she had found a man who was not jealous of her doing what she loved. Josephine remembered Alex saying about his wife, "That's what makes her go . . . when I see her up on that stage, it's electrifying."[12]

Whether this educated girl who wasn't anything to look at would change his ways remained to be seen. Daisy, Alex, and Walker did agree that a newly married couple needed their own space, their own house. Although Walker saw little that she could do to improve her in-law relationships, Alex, for his part, was determined to offset any criticism from his in-laws. Her family might remain angry once they learned that she had married an uneducated man, but they would never forgive Alex if he did not give her what she wanted. As Alex's cousins understood the relationship between the couple, they had many things in common, not the least of which was a "common goal to make it work. [Uncle Firnist] was also determined to prove that he could provide for his wife. He was stubborn about that. He wouldn't touch a penny of what the Walkers gave them. He knew he could provide for his wife and his children and he did."[13]

Walker spent the early months of her married life as excited about her new motherhood status as she was about the opportunity to begin *Jubilee*. After a few unsuccessful attempts to locate pertinent information in several North Carolina libraries, she turned her attention to mending the situation with her family. She decided to go to New Orleans with the baby but without Alex, who had vowed never to set foot in the Walker household. If all went well, she expected to resume her research in the fall.

She arrived in New Orleans for the first time as a married woman. Her father's characteristic silence left too much space, which her mother's cynicism and renewed outrage at her choice in marriage quickly filled. Yet it was an important moment that she could not have wished for. The entire family was aware this grandchild had come on the heels of the great-grandmother's death. Elvira Ware Dozier's absence inserted a much needed calm into an otherwise tense atmosphere. The strangely familiar experiences gave Walker impetus to stay on the *Jubilee* trail, no matter how long, and no matter the costs.

Marion Elizabeth Alexander's early experience was also like her mother's. She had the nurturing and support of a world of women who honored the firstborn as a gift from God. Both births had been fortuitous, in a way that Walker did not understand at the time. But it offered her the death/birth symbolism that became the opening framework for *Jubilee*. The death of her great-grandmother in real life—whose story *Jubilee* told—and the death of her grandmother, the narrator, would be the most logical context for the written narrative. In this way, the birth of her own daughter Marion was the beginning of a new generation of Randall Ware's descendants and symbolically also the beginning of *Jubilee*. Infusing this symbolism unique to women into the novel, complemented by Walker's own experience with childbirth, gave *Jubilee* the one ingredient that would distinguish it from any other novel written before or after. Hetta's death in the opening chapter of *Jubilee* symbolized the deaths of all those enslaved women who had been similarly exploited by their masters; it was Walker's organic connection to her own text. Two generations of Ware women had given birth, just as the generation immediately preceding them had died. *Jubilee* became an act of creative birthing in the same way.

The visit to New Orleans served its purpose well. Naming her firstborn after her mother pleased Marion. To the delight of many, the baby was so light-skinned that the nurses thought she was white. The birth softened Marion a bit; surely the child was a positive sign from God. She could not hide her joy that her first grandchild had Alex's color and, hopefully, she quickly added, her mother's intelligence. No matter what disagreements Marion had with Alex, they shared equal excitement about their firstborn. Short of having a male child, a girl child who looked like her father was "born for good luck."

She soon returned to High Point, where she accepted Daisy's help in caring for young Marion. This strategy, she hoped, would allow her to spend more time in the libraries, but this new life offered little balance. The less time she had to continue her research and writing, the more she felt overwhelmed by her new parental responsibilities. She did her share of the housekeeping; Alex's constant praise of her good cooking fed his expectations and her desire to fulfill them; she prepared large meals daily, baking buttermilk biscuits in the morning and fresh rolls in the evening to accompany his favorite dishes. When she found herself frustrated at the cooking, she delighted in his praise. She had grown accustomed to hearing her friends marvel at her skills, but now she had her favorite customer, just as Alex had his favorite chef. Compliments about her culinary skills added to Walker's enthusiasm about housekeeping, but the days were long since Alex was working overtime at the local mill.[14] When her heart was not in it, she was ineffi-cient, and she daydreamed. Daisy was a careful observer, and on more than one occasion Walker found it impossible to accept the secondary role that her sister-in-law deemed appropriate.

Over the next year, her energies seemed to dwindle even more. Keeping up with Marion, who was cranky from her allergies, and attending to the household tasks took all the energy she was able to muster. Before long, she discovered she was pregnant again. It was clear that she was not going back to work, something she had hoped to do when Marion was a little older. She could not expect support from Daisy, who would see her as weak and eager to offer an anticipated "I told you so." After all, when Daisy was twenty, she had moved away from Monroe, North Carolina, to High Point, bringing her brothers Rufus and Alex, and her sister Minnie, along with their mother. At no point had she complained about taking care of any of them.

Although Daisy was only fifteen years older than Walker, by mid-1940 stand-ards, she was already an old woman and could not remember being young. Daisy took Alex's side in everything, making it impossible for the women to ever be on good terms. Walker felt she had intruded on a somewhat complex relationship that made her an unwelcome outsider in her own family. The Alexander family had light-skinned members, and Walker, even as light brown, was unacceptably dark. On the other hand, the Alexanders were defensive about their lack of edu-cation. These unexpressed tensions cast a shadow on all of their encounters.

Walker could comfort herself in other ways, however. She worked on *Jubilee* at home whenever she could steal a moment. It did not take her long to confirm that her grandmother had been born in Dawson, Georgia, and that the best place to do research on the nineteenth-century South was right there in the state of North Carolina. Why a mother with two young children and an overworked hus-band would want free time to read and write made no sense to Daisy. But Walker knew how essential the emotional space was to keeping her sanity. Torn between her parents' fear, as well as her own, that her career was falling into ruins, she found her self-confidence waning. Just a few years before, she was the talk of the nation's literary scene, an award-winning author of a stunning first collection of poetry. She was the first major poet to emerge since Langston Hughes and the Harlem Renaissance nearly twenty years earlier, the movement that was all but destroyed by the Great Depression.

Alex completed the Graves Street house in early 1946 allowing them to move in before the new baby arrived. With a second child, and now with a home of her own, when she compared her situation to other Black women, Walker had little to complain about. The house was small, only three rooms, but it had an inside toilet, which was still somewhat rare in Negro homes in 1940s High Point. She and Alex were excited about being in their own home, the one he had built for her. No doubt Alex was ecstatic about the birth of their first son in May 1946. Although Alex knew his wife's devotion to her father—and the need to repair a torn relationship—they agreed to the customary naming pattern. They had planned to have other children, and the first son, Firnist James, became known as James Jr.

The birth of a second child did little to offset Walker's impatience, because she could not spend time at the University of North Carolina's Southern Historical Collection. She got up at dawn to prepare Alex a full breakfast, make his lunch, and then turn her attention to Marion and James Jr. General housekeeping she let go, a practice that she would continue. There were few neighbors nearby, and the backyard was a favorite spot for the children and her. This was marriage, what she had prayed for and got, she said to herself when she began to indulge in self-pity.

In their excitement over the newborn son and the new house, she found herself pregnant a third time within a year after James's birth. Her small body—she was still barely over a hundred pounds—needed more time to recover from childbirth. She was too weak to carry a pregnancy to full term. A miscarriage left her frightened and despondent. She knew Alex had wanted a large family, and he had accepted her as a woman who insisted on a career. That never caused any disagreement between them. But now she wondered if she could manage it all. She was beginning to feel that Alex was not happy unless she was pregnant—"barefoot and pregnant," she would say. In desperation, she confided in the doctor who had delivered James and handled her miscarriage. He, in turn, agreed to talk to Alex. She needed to take a break from the babies, he warned a confident father. Privately, he told Walker that her depression could cause serious consequences if she did not do something to counteract it. When he asked her if she was happy in High Point, her reluctant answer brought another suggestion: that she should consider moving to a place where she could find a job that she enjoyed. She left with the thought ringing in her ears.

With Alex's encouragement, Walker accepted a speaking engagement in Albany, Georgia, which put her back in touch with the NCAC. Her first year with them had been successful, and they were still getting requests for her readings. Alex had already agreed to drive her anywhere she needed to go. The idea of traveling satisfied both their needs. She would not have to make a choice between leaving her husband and following her career. It also gave Alex access to a different world, one that he accepted eagerly. He had served as a caddy in Florida earlier where he had learned to play golf. Trying golf courses in the places where she spoke, especially when he could easily pass for white, provided a pastime he fully enjoyed. Their trip to Albany was eventful and helped to shift his thinking about how well she could manage her career and her family.

That fall, she made a visit to Durham, hoping to convince Alex to move there as soon as the children could both go to nursery school. Then she could continue her research. While there, she met John Hope Franklin, a professor on the history faculty at North Carolina College (NCC), who had made national headlines with the publication of *From Slavery to Freedom* a year earlier, a book that told a different kind of history of the American Negro. Walker saw herself as doing the same thing, except through a work of fiction. She was not writing factual history, but she needed the facts of history to tell her story. The contact was a good one; NCC had the Martin Collection, containing interviews and narratives with ex-slaves, a product of the WPA.

Slave narratives were just emerging as the authentic voices of Blacks, and archives were developing as WPA interviewers sought out individuals who were still alive and could share their memories. It meant that her grandmother's unwritten narrative held even greater significance. "I knew then that I had a precious, almost priceless, living document of my own. There are hundreds of these stories, most of them not written, but many of them recorded for posterity. These written accounts tell of the brutalizing and dehumanizing practices of human slavery. They recount such atrocities as branding, whipping, killing, and mutilating slaves. All of them contain crucial information on slavery from the mouth of the slave."[15] She devoured the narratives she found in NCC's Collection. After returning to High Point, she could not let go. Lines for the novel's story began to emerge in unsuspecting places. The last line in the book came after this first trip. One day, they were visiting Daisy's new home in Rest Haven, a few miles from High Point. Daisy had envisioned land for her children and for posterity. The backyard was filled with chickens and rows of corn, tomatoes, sweet potatoes, string beans, onions, and collards. From the bedroom where she and Alex stayed, she would wake to the sound of Daisy's voice in the early mornings:

> Come biddy, biddy, biddy, biddy,
> Come chick, chick, chick, chick!

Walker knew that she had come to the end of the story conceptually. Here in Rest Haven was the calm that they all wanted. She wanted Vyry, the name of the story's protagonist, to have what Daisy had now: her own place, her own land where she could grow things as she wanted. Rest Haven even seemed to make the tensions in her relationship with Daisy dissolve. She wondered if she could get to this point in her story—where Vyry would have all the tensions in her life resolved, be in her own place, a place of peace. She kept the words for the story, committed more than ever to bringing Vyry's story to the same resolution, with the same words.

Walker was given access to the Martin Collection, but she feared that the Southern Historical Collection at the University of North Carolina was still segregated. John Hope Franklin had used it, and he encouraged her to do so, offering to write a letter of introduction for her. The collection, just like the university, had a unique history with African Americans. Although the university was not integrated, the presence of Paul Green and his interest in Black folklore attracted many visitors. Sterling Brown and Zora Neale Hurston were among its early ones.[16] If she were to gain access, she would, therefore, not be the first.

On her next visit, Walker entered the Southern Historical Collection, knowing that she was looking for the other side of her story. She had what she considered the "Negro viewpoint," since the overall narrative and the folk voice that she needed were in place. At Northwestern she'd learned about the standard histories of slavery, those by Ulrich B. Phillips, Frederick Law Olmsted, and Francis Kemble. At Iowa she had begun to immerse herself in Civil War history. During her Rosenwald Fellowship, she had talked at length with Lawrence Reddick, and he, like John Hope Franklin, had encouraged her to pursue the Georgia laws enacted for Negroes during and after the Civil War. But none of these opened up the white world in a way that she could embrace for her story.

The discoveries she had made during her Albany trip provided more clues to support her grandmother's birth story. By her calculation, Randall Ware, who would have been her great-great-grandfather, had lived well into the twentieth century. The visit to nearby Dawson had led to positive results: A free Black man by the name of Randall Ware, who was a blacksmith, had lived and died there. This discovery prompted her immediate desire to learn as much as she could about Ware, Vyry's first husband in *Jubilee*. Walker reported that she saw Ware's smithy, his grist mill, and his homeplace.

But the impetus to tell the story needed more than the discovery of Randall Ware. Ware was only one character, and she felt comfortable with what she had learned about him. It was his counterpart, white characters and a white world, that she needed to enter. On another speaking engagement that took her to Greenville, Alabama, which was close to Dawson, Georgia, she retraced the steps of her family's postwar migration from Dawson to Greenville. She was looking for anything: a name, a family, a house, a store that could bring the story to life. She had seen an antebellum home in Bainbridge, another town near Dawson and concluded that it was located on the likely site of her great-grandmother's slavery home; it could serve as the model for the Dutton plantation in the story. The trip to Dawson was still in the back of her mind when Walker made a return trip to the Southern Historical Collection, realizing that she needed to find out more information about Southern white families living in antebellum times.

She discovered Nelson Tift's diary by accident. Tift combined philosophy with personal dreams, objectives, and political opinions. He was someone who, like Walker, needed a place to express his deepest feelings, those he dare not say out loud. Tift's diary, therefore, not only provided the content for *Jubilee*, but Tift also became a companion and a refuge for a young woman struggling to resolve the question of her identity in relationship to a project that was beginning to define her life.

The "Nelson Tift papers . . . letters, bills of sale, and other personal papers of [the] wealthy white Georgia planter" gave concreteness to her thinking because Tift had been a resident of the area where the story was set. Even though she "spent months on the material and took numerous items for the book,"[17] it is questionable that her process was exactly as she described. One thing is certain—Walker experienced a relationship with Tift through his diary. This relationship allowed her to construct a white male planter, using Tift as a model. She had found a realistic portrait to make the novel convincing.

Who was this silent partner, this kindred spirit, who aided Walker through a troubled time? Nelson Tift had decided to write as a way to save himself from financial ruin. Although there is no indication of the extent of his formal education, it appears to have been minimal. At twenty-five, he was extraordinarily perceptive about the world of men and business, having already lived in Key West and Charleston where his inexperienced youth undoubtedly accounted for several failed business ventures. It is likely that Tift reminded Walker of Alex, who was thirty-three when they married. Both lacked any formal education and considered themselves self-made men.

The sensibility of a self-made man intrigued her. Tift's move from Dawson to Augusta, Georgia, brought success. He rented a building and opened a dry goods store, and later he accepted a clerk position in a store in nearby Hawkinsville, where he became a property owner and a business partner. By his twenty-sixth year, his diary records that Tift was successful enough to acquire land in Baker County (Albany, GA), soon extending his holdings to Macon and Bainbridge.

After becoming a partner in Rawls, Tift, and Co., Tift married and, as was the custom, built his first plantation. He bought and sold slaves, although his diary focuses on those whose use appeared to be limited to the household—personal servants and cooks. In time, he became active in local politics and, when asked to represent the citizens of Albany at a state convention, he authored a progressive bill bringing equality to state banking and lending procedures. Because his earlier life had been negatively affected by bad debt and crooked moneylenders, Tift was concerned that others not suffer as he had in establishing financial credit, essential to a successful career. After apprenticing as a lawyer, he was elected justice of interior court, which positioned him for his later election to the Georgia legislature.

Although Tift shares his brief encounters with young women—he is, after all, a most eligible bachelor—he does not describe a courtship that led to his marriage with Nancy Maria Mercer, daughter of one of Albany's well-to-do merchant/planters. Reading Voltaire, and displaying strong antislavery tendencies, he started a debating society for which he served as chair. Tift's forays into poetry must have caught Walker's eye. She had recorded her efforts in her journals just as he did. His nineteenth-century stanzas, employing conventional rhyme, resembled her early efforts. His progressive ideas won him both enemies and friends: he authored a bill to educate the poor and indigent and was responsible for incorporating the city of Albany, winning even among great opposition. In short, he was the father of Albany and a champion of public education for the masses. Tift had transformed into a hardcore plantation owner, displaying the necessary emotional distance that would allow him to be a good slave master. By the end of his diary, he resembled John Morris Dutton, the plantation owner in *Jubilee*.

Nelson Tift was a white man—Northern-born, Southern-made—a poet, an intellectual, a compassionate landowner. He knew when to be the evil master. This dialogic fascinated Walker; she would come to express it clearly in *Jubilee*'s structure. In it, the Southern "way of life" quickly inverts itself during the war. The fight against slavery is the fight to destroy a system and those who support it; it liberates those who have been oppressed by that system. The humanity of the individuals remains firm, however. Nelson Tift affirmed that complexity.

Walker never met anyone in the Tift family, but Nelson Tift's diary gave her what she needed: a man she could come to know through sensibilities she could accept. Soon she was making regular visits to the collection, which Alex's support made possible. Each new page of Tift's diary inspired passion for a story she could now envision. Tift was not only telling her a story, but his life was amazingly close to her own. Tift began his diary at twenty-five, having been inspired in much the same way as she had been as a young child. He loved language just as she did.

She had been determined to follow a lead. Her hunch was correct; what she found was more thorough and compelling than anything she'd seen.

It may have been her discomfort with her own near-poverty situation that made her escape to Tift's diary necessary. If she found herself snubbing people when she was out in public in High Point, she was simply keeping a protective distance. She got what she gave: they snubbed her back. Whenever she mentioned returning to work, Alex assured her that he could take care of them. The children needed her more than the students she was eager to get back to, he would often remind her during those days. Nevertheless, when their finances reached an all-time low, she did return to Livingstone College for a semester, until her pregnancy demanded that she quit. It was unusual for women to be married and teach then, and even more unusual that they should work while pregnant.

Walker used her work to protect her emotional space. As soon as James was old enough to walk, she made the decision of putting both children in nursery school to make more time for her research. Whether Alex agreed or not, he saw his wife's determination, and he was eager to find a solution to her depression. He even encouraged her to accept other speaking engagements. More than an act of chivalry, it satisfied both their needs, and Alex would not feel left out of the life that she had as a professional writer. They grew more comfortable leaving the children with Daisy. Having time alone strengthened the bond between them. Gaining a measure of freedom for herself helped to put *Jubilee* on course. She was confident that she would prove Arna Bontemps wrong when he saw her pregnant for the first time in New York. "Every child is a book you didn't write," he'd said to her. Every time she grew weary, she'd remember his prediction.

18

The Walls of My Prison House

Even though she made her public and private declarations of renewal each January, Walker's growing dependency on Alex, the creative lull, and endless domestic responsibilities combined into emotions that not only overburdened her but also aggravated whatever ailment she had, even a simple cold. Post-partum depression accounted for some of her mood swings, for which she received ineffective treatment. What made matters worse was her refusal to ask her parents for help; to do so would have required her to admit failure. The physical compatibility and love that she and Alex felt drew them closer, but too often she concluded that "this dulls my creative and religious impulses otherwise but my love will not let me leave."[1]

The result was that they fought often and in different ways. Walker's sharp tongue could insult, belittle, and provoke Alex. When she was angry, sometimes covering what might have been envy she felt for others, she lashed out as if he were responsible. She and Alex began to repeat scenes of rage and reciprocal abuse—hers always verbal, his physical. Their fights always ended in reconciliation, but she admitted, "I bear the marks of it on my face."[2] She recognized that she was an incurable romantic, idealistic about a marriage that contradicted the reality of her life. At the end of each episode, she would remind herself, "If anything is sacrificed, I do not want it to be my marriage."[3] Of this she was absolutely certain. On one occasion, his abuse was so severe that she considered taking out a warrant for his arrest, but she could not face the options: leave right away or lose face. She also surmised that she had nothing to gain by leaving since going to New Orleans would add to her misery and allow Alex to claim desertion. "I feel as though I were living through days of inner darkness. I grope for the four walls of my prison house without hope."[4]

Walker's routine of self-therapy steeled her during these years. She told herself that bitterness, envy, and jealousy were the most self-destructive feelings. The thought of turning thirty-two that July gave her some hope that "The venom of hate that [had] never before corroded my soul would pass."[5] More typical was her fatalism. "I don't believe I will live much longer," she told herself. She was at war in her own marriage. "It means I must submit or be destroyed. Marriage slowly tells me that one of the other of us has got to give in."[6]

Even if she exaggerated in those moments of acute distress, equating her marriage with slavery, for example, she took marriage and motherhood as a given

The House Where My Soul Lives. Maryemma Graham, Oxford University Press. © Oxford University Press 2022.
DOI: 10.1093/oso/9780195341232.003.0018

rather than an option. She complained but resigned herself to the new life and all that accompanied it, giving herself practical advice. "There's no need thinking [Alex] is going to be the nice quiet kind to submit, and all of my intellectual superiority and academic advantage won't get the better of him." There was also the positive side: Alex had a good head for money, sound judgment, and "excellent wisdom with children. He can give emotional and financial security,"[7] what she felt she needed the most. She was probably more likely to see her sufferings as God's test. Moreover, she always came back to her belief that "Alex tried to do the decent thing by me even though we were strangers. He provided a home for me and our children." She saw many of the conflicts between them as a result of her being "not his type of woman,"[8] with the caveat that she could not be compared to his first wife. Such revelations followed lengthy deliberations in her journal.

For Walker, marriage was the "result of something apart from my life . . . altogether aside from my rearing—training, education and former way of thinking."[9] Seeing her isolation from the kind and class of people she was accustomed to knowing stalemated her career. "My knowing Alex has put a question mark after my name,"[10] she could say only to herself. It would have been difficult for Alex not to know that she thought this way, and while there was no justification for his physical abuse, she made her objections known. "I have never had to do drudgery work . . . constantly with no thanks from anyone but constant criticism, nagging, griping and complaint, abuse, cursing and beating."[11] She was especially displeased that he drank and did not feel the same way she did about religion or the institutional church. She was therefore obligated, or so she thought, to pray for his salvation. Yet, she also admitted that being dependent "galls me . . . almost makes me ill, depresses me and makes me despondent. I have almost lost my grip."[12] On the other hand, marriage "is a compromise and an adjustment." One married for love, in her view, but one stayed married for one's children. This married love was what she saw herself striving for and believed she would achieve.

The situation must have become unbearable when Walker decided to go to New Orleans with both children in June 1947. She stayed six months, hearing from Alex only once until he sent a train ticket for them to return. In December she ended what she called a separation, although she had told her parents that Alex wanted to work around the clock to finish their new house, making it a good time to visit. Marion, who had made her first mother-in-law trip to High Point for Firnist's birth, suspected otherwise. In her uncertainty, Walker read her astrological chart religiously, observing that the full moons brought flare-ups.

Her constant question was whether her marriage was worth sacrificing her career. She analyzed the question closely, weighing both sides in the dialogue with herself. Interestingly, Walker came to the conclusion that (1) she should not pursue divorce, but (2) she simply needed to make some money, and (3) that she was in a better position to do that than Alex. If she were the major breadwinner, then she could regain some of the independence in their relationship that she believed she'd lost. With the ultimate goal of reestablishing her writing routine, her short-term solution was to secure a more stable teaching job. That meant looking beyond High Point. To contain her frequent blowups, she turned to the *Daily Word*, the staple of her religious literature.

Walker got an unexpected surprise when Langston Hughes included High Point in his tour of area schools. His visit gave her a boost, and she'd remembered his inclusion of her as one of four poets in a column he had begun writing for the *Chicago Defender* in 1942, adopting the name of the fictitious character Jesse B. Semple. Hughes called the column "From Here to Yonder" and by the advent of World War II, "Simple," as he was better known, became the vehicle through which Hughes educated America. In his columns, he mused about the war and Black people's involvement in it, Black culture generally, and his favorite topic— white people. Her visits with Hughes always fortified her, and this national plug restored her confidence that her career could move forward.

Walker's New Year's resolution for 1948 focused on what she had achieved in the seven years since she had completed *For My People* at Iowa, rather than a laundry list of complaints. She continued to spend more time in New Orleans than High Point, successfully avoided another pregnancy, and enjoyed the space it gave her to write and think without having to feel completely obligated to Alex and her children. Because the children were the center of their two doting grand-parents' attention, buffered by their young aunt and uncle, Walker's differences with Marion seemed far less distracting and blew over quickly. She even felt her-self working hard to change an age-old habit, which she hoped would carry over when she returned to High Point: "bridle and control my temper and tongue," which meant "a complete overhauling of myself."[13] The recognition that Alex might be correct about both of them acting instinctively before thinking star-tled her. She could finally admit that if Alex had a "fighting nature because his circumstances have put him on the defensive," then her own inability to "exercise intelligence and have enough sense to control myself"[14] was certainly not more worrisome. Later, she referred to this period of her life as a temporary separation from Alex, a time to think about what mattered to her and to what extent she was willing to compromise. She finally set a major condition of her return: he would have to include her and the children's names on the deed to their house. Because the lot had been purchased before they had married, the names of his mother Ella and sister Daisy remained on it. She considered the need for security for her-self and their children of utmost importance.

Spending more time in New Orleans afforded her other literary advantages as well. She became close to Marcus Christian,[15] the New Orleans poet whom she had learned about when she worked for the WPA. Christian was among those who encouraged her to return to her writing. She had chosen to be a wife and mother, but she would not be happy until she satisfied her passion to write, he told her.[16] She had always thought that her desire to be married and have a family would be a driving passion once she became a published poet. She began to understand that her family—her husband and children—provided emotional security that neither competed nor conflicted with her art. What she considered her emotional picture was incomplete without her art. The frequent New Orleans trips helped her restore this sense of balance. No longer seeing herself as suffering from a profound sense of failure, she stopped looking for explanations for what she could or could not do. That sense of failure fed into her fears that Alex was unfaithful, fears founded upon a reality that her long and frequent absences over a two-year period made possible. That the solution to all of her problems lay with her and her alone was her most important revelation.

She continued to carry with her the rough outline of *Jubilee* that she had written at the Southern Historical Collection. With four sections outlined and most of the scenes in place, she decided to make a trip to New York to meet with Bernard Perry, an acquisition editor for poetry at W. W. Norton, soon to become the founding director of Indiana University Press. Even though she had not touched the outline in two years, she had a clear plan in her head and hoped to secure a contract to finish the book. Her parents had agreed to keep the children, and she spent a week visiting friends in Atlanta and then made a brief stop in High Point to visit Alex, before leaving for New York. For the first time in a long while, her exuberant mood spilled over in lines of verse she posted in her journal on June 4, 1948: "Such happiness is like a pear / A golden pear that hung upon a tree / Of unripe fruit among and / Hanging there."[17] The poem anticipates her arrival in High Point, where she would explain to Alex why she must go to New York, and that the decision to do so did not lessen her commitment to her marriage and their family, but rather made it stronger than ever.

She could not have made a better decision under the circumstances; Alex showed a renewal of his commitment by buying her train fare. Walker was beginning a journey she would make many times in the years to come. Taking the Southern Railway line out of High Point, she had stopovers along the way when she visited with friends in Washington and Baltimore, before arriving in New York on September 29. Staying at the YWCA, she embarked on her mission as if there had been no interruption in her writing life. She met with friends and learned that Elizabeth Catlett had remarried, moved to Mexico City, and was now the mother of a young son.

Her meeting with Perry went well. He had shown interest in her, and she left their discussion believing that he would do his best to convince his board to take *Jubilee* and give her an advance. Walker got in touch with Thelma Warlick, her new contact at NCAC, to return to the lecture circuit that had been so successful for her. She quickly learned that NCAC could give her access to additional publishers such as Holt, Rinehart Winston; Farrar Straus; and Macmillan, so that if Perry was not successful, she would have other options. What surprised her was her total fearlessness about the entire visit. She had very little money and turned to Langston Hughes, who lent her enough to cover another night's stay at the YWCA. She felt comfortable using what was left to see *Finian's Rainbow* and *Hamlet*. She wrote in her journal that night, "The spirit of prosperity and success has entered into my affairs and my whole visible supply is increased."[18]

In between her visits to friends, spending a day with Langston, and meeting the editor of *Common Ground*, who requested that she send them something more to publish, Walker had to get Marion's birth certificate to begin school the following year when she turned six. Her itinerary had her going non-stop, including visits to the Schomburg Center and dinner at Gwen and Jacob Lawrence's home, all while making follow-up phone calls. In the few days she was in New York, she managed to see all of her friends for the first time in several years, recalling fond memories with each one. She had no hesitation in wiring her parents for money for the train fare home. Her mood only changed when she began preparing to leave, knowing that what lay ahead of her was hard work, work that would have to be finished in High Point.

The world was opening up in ways she could never have imagined, and the thought that it could shut down just as easily discouraged and depressed her. She had poetry, a new novel based on her family history, a new idea for a novel she called "Mother Beulah," and a series of long short stories all waiting for her to finish them. She comforted herself by recounting her memorable week, as-suring herself that she could "turn a new leaf."[19] What she needed to do at home in High Point, she simply listed alongside her expanding catalogue: "getting Alex's clothes for Xmas; fixing up the house; mailing poems and manuscripts; perfecting one hundred pages of the novel; [going]to the doctor and dentist for exams."[20] She knew exactly what she wanted to do with her career and was confi-dent that she could do it. Likewise, on the train going home, she began to plan a dream house, laying out "precisely what I want."[21]

The list continued once she returned to High Point. The dream house and the writer blended into a single image. She added her plans for setting a writing schedule to be implemented immediately. It called for her to write six hours every day, with a morning and afternoon or evening stint. She wanted to become a "writer for life," the true vocation she now saw for herself. She needed only dis-cipline, believing there was "nothing to hinder me and necessity driving me."[22] Similarly she began her treasure map for the dream house. One could not happen without the other. She had a rude awakening when after a few days she had done no writing. What she had done instead was "scrub my kitchen floor, cook and wash dishes . . . fighting discontent, disappointment, discouragement and resent-ment."[23] The old feelings quickly returned, and in the absence of her children, they intensified. But dreams cost nothing, she concluded. "I can dream myself away from this and I can work to make my dreams come true."[24]

Before the week ended, however, a profound spiritual experience left her transformed. Out of curiosity, she had gone with Alex to a revival meeting in nearby Jamestown where a faith healer was conducting a service. Her book about a faith healer, "Mother Beulah," might have been in the back of her mind, although she did not indicate this in her recall of the event. She did express doubts about the power that such a person could have, since it was too easily confused with the power of God himself. As an observer, however, she decided to reserve her opinions until she could see for herself. At the revival meeting, however, she found herself so moved that she jumped to her feet and began to speak. Not since her childhood had she experienced anything like this moment when she felt so filled with spiritual joy. Walker's journal entry was part personal testimony and part reportage as she described what she saw and heard, as Black and white participants were healed. A twenty-three-year-old woman and mother of three children who "had never heard nor spoken from birth . . . I saw that girl open her mouth and speak plainly. The girl continued to answer questions and to turn her head and answer when her name was called. I left witnessing it as a miracle."[25]

The events that night removed the one obstacle that Walker believed stood in the way of her marriage and her future. Alex had been equally moved. His experience made hers complete as she wrote in her journal:

> Last night it was a joy to hear my husband speak and witness to the power of the Holy Spirit in his own heart. At last my prayers are being answered. My married joy is complete for with a Christian husband who not only loves me but also loves God I have all I can desire. Nothing is more precious to my soul tonight and nothing else seems as important.[26]

Walker responded more formally by writing a letter of gratitude to *Silent Unity*,[27] to whom she had written asking for prayers to bring peace in her home. In the eight-page letter, she summarizes the "face-to-face talk" she had with herself, especially about Alex's abuse:

> I saw how I kept drawing abuse to myself and how at bottom I was at fault for much of the trouble between us, also my fear of him brought on worse things. I realized how I created a point of irritation and antagonism with many people—certainly members of my family as well as my husband.[28]

Her creative imagination took its cues from the experience as well. Margaret Walker had been bred in the middle-class culture of the Black South. She grew to womanhood with the understanding and possibility of an ordered life within a distinct social network. Through marriage, however, she had become a new person, facing new contradictions and self-discoveries. All the while she clung to the religion of her childhood, the one thing that kept her centered. Her commitment to write about the poor and about poverty required that she not write "in a spirit of degradation or hopeless depravity." She would name it her humanism: Walker saw her characters "even in their lowliness [to] have something of the sublime, of the nobly divine."[29] These qualities applied to Vyry, *Jubilee*'s protagonist, in particular:

> Vyry must be such a woman. She must emerge a victorious woman, her life meaningful because of her deep and abiding religious faith. Even though she is first a slave and grows up ignorant and oppressed, she must emerge into heroic statue. Likewise, Randall Ware who is conscious and aware must also be a hero. Mother Beulah must be such a woman. Through a mystic spiritual power she emerges triumphant over life—against all odds.[30]

She continued to name characters in her future work, paying special attention to the women. She knew what her characters should be but was uncomfortable working in prose as opposed to verse. This issue preoccupied her as she continued to develop the story of *Jubilee*. For several months, she read books with religious themes, some of them, like *St. Elmo* by Augusta Evans Wilson, she had known since childhood. Wilson's popular 1896 novel followed the precepts of nineteenth-century womanhood: the woman bore responsibility for her family and for her faithfulness and influence over an ungodly husband. Although Walker admitted that *St. Elmo* when judged by literary standards was overly sentimental, she liked the compelling narrative and the romantic element as she looked for models to emulate. She had already ruled out many prose writers of the period whose novels about Southern Negroes were too wedded to naturalistic techniques, Erskine Caldwell and Richard Wright among them. She found the work of Marcel Proust, William Faulkner, and Thomas Wolfe more suited to the style she was hoping for, especially their long sentences that she could punctuate with her own short staccato ones. But she also realized that *St. Elmo*'s story confirmed her own experience and the lessons learned: a woman's emotional hunger could not be satisfied until she found a husband. The subtext for all of this was that her own sexual frustration—from the failure of two previous relationships—drove her to Alex, a relationship that came at the right time and for the right reasons. She, therefore, needed to preserve it at all costs. In any case, the issue for her now was time. Since the children were still in New Orleans, and Alex left for work early in the mornings, she had most of the day to write. Although she chastised herself constantly, "My house is dirty and untidy, dinner yet to cook," she did "have the nerve to sit down and write."[31]

She sent poems to magazine editors and filled in more scenes in the first section of *Jubilee*. Even when the number of rejection letters began to mount, she was not especially upset since her list of possibilities was steadily growing now that she was back in regular touch with editors in New York. She had yet to send anything to *Common Ground* and she had planned to send at least three poems to *Harper's Bazaar*. A surprise letter from Langston Hughes suggested that she send the photograph Carl Van Vechten had taken of her to *Ebony*, for the magazine's special issue on Negro writers.

Walker was pleased that she and Alex were beginning to meet and entertain some friends. Her skill at reading astrological charts made their home a popular nightspot. Along with it came a lifestyle different from the one she'd known and deemed appropriate. She had not grown up with alcohol, something that was forbidden in her parents' home, but changing her attitude was a small price to pay for a happier existence with Alex. Since they did not have a phone, she began to welcome the breaks from the overwhelming projects she had set for herself. Among their new friends, she never talked about *Jubilee*, and although they sometimes knew she had published a book of poetry, compartmentalizing became easier than she had realized.

By day Walker dreamed of painting the Dawson, Georgia, landscape with words or reading Du Bois's *Black Reconstruction*, Charles Beard's *Rise of American Civilization*, and Arthur Lee Cole's *Irrepressible Conflict*. Lawrence Reddick had promised her to send whatever she needed when she visited him at the Atlanta University Center, where he had recently become head of the library. She had already contacted someone at High Point College about using their library, although it was a white institution. She was eager to work and had most of each day to be Margaret Walker, which would not conflict with the joy she felt in being Mrs. Firnist James Alexander, the identity she wanted and needed to keep her whole. Alex never let her forget that it was Margaret Walker he had fallen in love with and married, and that she would remain that person always. Invitations to read at nearby institutions came as well, making it more comfortable to honor both women that she knew herself to be.

Except for their financial problems, Walker might have felt they were truly just beginning their lives together. Alex saw himself as the breadwinner, however, and as their funds became scarce, he grew more irritable and angered easily. When he did, she knew to stay out of the house until he calmed down. By November, what had seemed like their second honeymoon was clearly over. He suggested that they store all of their personal items and rent their house out furnished to bring in additional income. Walker could not bear the thought of returning to Daisy's. She resolved to find a job and to take it, no matter where it was. She knew that when Alex was making money, he was seldom annoyed. With her education, she could supplement the income and put an end to their quarrels.

Fate was not something Walker could control, and as hard as she relied on the predictive ability of her daily astrological readings, what others might have expected always caught her by surprise. She became pregnant again, the first time after the earlier miscarriage. The timing could not have been worse since it would prevent her from getting a job. With another mouth to feed, she felt an eruption of pressures that had been accumulating. She had hoped that James was her last child, after having been told after her miscarriage that she should not have another. She was confident that they could educate and rear two children, providing them with social and cultural advantages and a minimum degree of comfort. Alex found her option—to have an abortion—totally unacceptable.

The holiday season came and went. She did not have an abortion, and in a state of severe emotional distress, she sought respite in New Orleans. Symptoms of the neurosis that had incapacitated her earlier reoccurred. She was alternately depressed, given to sudden emotional outbursts, drowning in self-pity and melancholia. Although her parents had taken her to the doctor for this problem when she was eighteen, as far as they were concerned, she had recovered and was now a responsible adult. They saw her breakdown as a response to her marriage that never should have been. They seemed, at least to her, to have little sympathy, making it clear that she had become a financial burden on the family who would soon become responsible for taking care of three children and her. Marion's response was immediate: sue Alex for divorce, child support, and alimony. Before she realized it, Walker had struck her mother, so completely unhinged had she become. Descriptions of the various emotions she experienced with her response are quite detailed in her journals. Ultimately, she turned inward and began to plan a method for self-healing.

Had she been more connected to the established literary world or had the money, she might have gone to one of several sanitariums that specialized in treating emotional disorders associated with writers, especially women. Some of her models, like Sarah Teasdale and Louise Bogan, both of whom had what was referred to as "nervous conditions," frequented treatment centers on expansive country estates where they convalesced and returned to the selves they needed to be. Instead Walker had to utilize a different approach, seeking comfort in prayer, her subscription to the services offered by Unity Church, and writing in her journal.

She saw herself at another critical juncture when she could either "become integrated and give my life its greatest meaning or disintegrate physically and emotionally."[32] She designated two activities—writing and rearing children—as integrative functions. If she were to lose either one, she would become more ill emotionally and lose her mind totally. Since she was more distant from her writing, she took that to be the necessary focus of her healing ritual. From this thinking came plans for her "new cycle." For complete recovery, she determined that she would not only need psychological treatment, but also "a chiropodist's

Marcus Christian, a New Orleans poet, became an
early mentor

adjustments to balance her body and mind, nerves and muscles, blood and glands; astrological advice from Grant Lewis; and Unity."[33] From its writers she would request more prayers and reading literature.

The creative side of her took control, and by the middle of May, she had planned a children's magazine, *Bronze Kiddie*, which would initiate Bronze Kiddie Clubs. She saw the birth of a national project that could provide a source of income and travel and identified a potential editorial board along with a staff for the journal. Ultimately, she put the journal on the back burner, and she never returned to it. At some point her overburdened emotions finally became lighter. Her creative musings were cut short when she got a job offer from Jacob Reddix at Jackson State College in Mississippi, one that she and her family decided she should take. Reddix had heard that she was an unemployed writer and might be available. The offer came on the heels of the birth of her third child, a second son. She named him Sigismund after her father, as she and Alex had agreed.

President Reddix promised an untenured position, a room, and tenure in three years if her work was satisfactory. He was not fully confident that Walker would fit what the college needed, especially since very little of her higher education had been at an historically Black institution. But he was short on faculty in the English Department, and school was to begin in less than four months. By the time the job offer came, she was desperate. Moving to Jackson was her only hope to break out of the prison she found herself in.

19

All My Roots Are Gathered in One Place

The promise of employment shook Walker out of her disheveled state, keeping her busy with this major transition for herself and her children in a short period of time. Her parents seemed to be satisfied that she would be gainfully employed. She made a promise to send money from her paycheck regularly if her parents would keep all three children with the help of a housekeeper. Their agreement allowed her to see her life moving forward.

She was fortunate to have all of her classes on Tuesday and Thursday, which meant she could dedicate Wednesdays and Fridays to her writing. Alex intended to remain in High Point, suggesting more than a temporary separation. Walker's only family commitment, other than sending her parents money, was to go to New Orleans from Saturday to Monday. Having a job, the ability to control her own money, the privacy and peace that a room brought, and seeing her children as often as she could gave her a new sense of independence, which pleased her parents. Wary of including Alex in her plans, she saw an impending divorce and began preparing herself for single motherhood. In September 1949, she weaned Sigis—the name everyone would call him—and prepared for her departure for New Orleans en route to Jackson, Mississippi.

On September 28, one day after she began her classes, she made a vow to herself in her first Mississippi entry into her journal: "I can write my novel this year in this room and I am going to do it."[1] Almost as soon as she made this commitment to herself, Alex called to issue an ultimatum: either she quit her job and come home to High Point or else. She was prepared to resist without the emotional entanglements. High Point had become a dead end for her. She was determined to find a new way, her own way, but it would have to be without him.

While she was generally pleased with Jackson State, she was less confident about her relationship with its president Jacob Reddix. After one month and several encounters with him, she was convinced that he expected to fire her after the first year. It is more likely that Reddix thought an award-winning poet with a national reputation would leave for a better job. Thus, he took little interest in getting to know her or going out of his way to appease her. Some of this she brought on herself. She was not around very much since the temporary situation she had created for her children lasted for the full year. Neither did she find any

The House Where My Soul Lives. Maryemma Graham, Oxford University Press. © Oxford University Press 2022. DOI: 10.1093/oso/9780195341232.003.0019

time to return to her writing. She made twenty-six visits to New Orleans in the first thirty weeks, but did not work on a single project. Her publishing was at a standstill, the career she wanted, in limbo.

Yet if 1949 was the year that Margaret Walker chose an unlikely place to rebuild her life, no one could have predicted what she could and would do with that choice, as she transformed herself from a writer to the voice of an age.[2] Her comment "Nothing exciting or evoking excitement,"[3] in response to those who did what she had wanted to do—publish more books—can be taken at face value. WPA colleague Nelson Algren's *The Man with a Golden Arm* became a best-seller and Gwendolyn Brooks published her second collection of poems, *Annie Allen*, winning the Pulitzer Prize. Her coolness toward both was less a sign of jealousy than it was an early indication of how deeply attentive she was to other matters, with her remarkable capacity for clarity in *predicting* cataclysmic changes in the social order at the half century. Entirely uncertain of her own future, she offered her perspective on America:

> Now with a world in flux, the old ideas are dying and the new are still in the birth throes we need a writer to clamor from the housetops, someone to give us hope and our lives new meaning. America is already solidly fascist from New York to Florida. So many are not aware of the outbreaks of violence around us nor of the rapidly developing police state enforced by brutality and rigid laws enforcing prejudice and segregation. . . I do not believe that Russian Communism will work in America. I do believe, however, that we are going to war with Russia within the next three years. I think our way of life in America is going to change. Prejudice, segregation and Jim Crow are in for a death struggle and I hope they will die. Our schools will no longer be separated; neither our churches. Acts of prejudice in commercial places like stores and hotels, places of amusement etcetera will be punished as crimes against the people. I think it will only take a mere ten years for change to take place. Atomic energy is going to change our lives from drudgery to wide-spread leisure. The electrification of farm homes will be increased . . . our cultural lives broadened. Our youth will have great opportunity. And all our lives will have greater Freedom.[4]

On the personal side, her mantra to "publish books steadily, to have another degree and to have a high degree of economic independence"[5] steadied her. She understood the uniqueness of her chosen place and the role she believed she had been given. The 1920s and 1930s had been good to her, but now she needed the balance of hard times and the necessary suffering that the subsequent decade offered.

She tried not to worry about her marriage, and meeting new friends who lived in the row of faculty apartments helped. As far as they were concerned, Walker was extremely fortunate: her parents were caring for her three young children, and she could socialize with others as a single woman for the most part. She met Luana Jean Clayton and Ernestine Libscomb, two women whom Jackson State had also recently hired and who would become close friends. She shared with Clayton a love of gossip and bridge: both were deeply committed to transforming higher education. In Clayton she confided her innermost feelings about her marriage. It was Clayton who encouraged her to reunite with her husband and helped Walker identify property on Guynes Street in an upwardly mobile West Jackson. The idea of building a new home—a permanent home—renewed her desire for marriage and the family as necessary elements of her life. Ernestine Libscomb was Jackson State's librarian and someone on whom Walker relied as she returned to her writing and research. Her social life improved when she reactivated her membership in the Alpha Kappa Alpha sorority. Its members were excited to have an established writer as a sorority sister. She felt her life was falling into place once she joined Central United Methodist Church, where she would later teach Sunday School for many years.

Slowly, Walker created a base that would keep her stable. When she reviewed her astrology charts, she identified her earlier years as an obscure domestic period that would be followed by another fifteen years when she would maximize

Walker with early friends at Jackson State, Cleopatra Thompson, Head of the School of Education, and Ernestine Lipscomb, Head of JSU Library

her career, with more writing, academic achievements, and public visibility. Alex continued to protest her move but she never returned to High Point, nor did she back down on her word. Someone had to give in, and she was determined that it would not be her.

What we know is that in the summer of 1950, Alex left High Point and moved all of their possessions to Jackson. She brought the children from New Orleans, and they began to see themselves as a family for the first time in three years. As they saved up enough money to build their permanent home on Guynes Street, they got an apartment in the college's faculty housing, a series of converted army barracks originally built during World War II. Alex's return meant that he had accepted her terms. For Walker, it was confirmation that she was now in control of their lives and was free to map their destiny with greater certainty. In Jackson, she had pulled herself back from the edge and could stand with her feet firmly on the ground.

Although they were still financially insecure, she had become adept at finding meaningful ways to reinvent herself as she exited a traumatic period. She was a married woman with three children, and she needed to reclaim herself as a successful writer. First, she made sure that Alex completed his training at the GI trade school and that he received the small compensation from the army to supplement their income. She then returned to her dreams, intent on making them a reality by finishing the books she had begun earlier and someday leaving teaching behind to become a full-time writer. Religion was typically her operational base, but she could also find comfort in those parallels from the natural

2205 Guynes Street became the family's permanent home in West Jackson. Courtesy of Charlotte Mormom

world, winter giving way to spring and finally summer, or in recapitulations of the lives of those great figures she so admired. When she taught Paul Laurence Dunbar, the brilliant poet whose suffering cost him his marriage and an early death, and W. E. B. Du Bois, wrote so beautifully about the painful loss of a first-born child, she could see her own suffering in a new light. These were not so much comparisons as they were reminders of her terrible dependence on pride, that moral indiscretion that prevents us from seeing something greater and more powerful than ourselves. She believed in the mystery of the universe but thought it was important for each of us to know the difference between "what is authentic and what is not."[6] What became real after her move to Jackson was a renewed vision of the importance of family, with children who would grow up and transition into adulthood, in a house that was also a home, which they would eventually leave to begin their own lives. Grounded with this new understanding, she committed herself to no further moves.

In an interview years later, recalling her arrival in Mississippi, she told Jerry Ward, "Mississippi spells for me all my roots gathered in one place. This is where I put in from the sea. I put down roots here; I came to stay here; I looked at Jackson, MS, like a harbor. After going from place to place and literally tossing on the sea of life, I put in at this harbor. And it has sometimes seemed like a dead-end street, that I'm going no farther. This is my place."[7] The South's restorative function made itself known in her poetry. Many of her verses echoed a surrender that brought strength. "Jackson, Mississippi" was one of the first from this period in which her physical and emotional landscapes coalesce into a single image:

> I give you my heart, Southern City
> For you are my blood and dust of my flesh,
> You are the harbor of my ship of hope,
> The dead-end street of my life.
> I give you my brimming heart, Southern City
> For my eyes are full and no tears cry.[8]

Bringing order to what had been a very chaotic existence invited feelings of permanence, security, and assurance—and would end her seven years of obscurity.

That obscurity, however, would not officially end until she completed *Jubilee*, the dream that haunted her constantly. While she saw Jackson as the launching pad for a "new and greater life," she also worried about her discipline, about having "missed the boat, [being] too lazy to fulfill talents."[9] While planning *Jubilee*, she found the courage to do everything else she wanted and needed to do to bring her real and ideal worlds together. The first of a list of projects she hoped to complete appears in her journal, one that she would return to again and again over the next four decades. She meditated and observed her own thought processes, commenting on them regularly. Should she see the return to a writing career as a childish fantasy, something that she needed to give up now that she was both full-time mother and teacher? She fought with herself, insisting that she should be better at all she did: a more loving wife, a more attentive parent, a more caring teacher, a more respectful colleague.

As part of renewing her identity as a writer, Walker accepted responsibility for organizing the seventy-fifth anniversary of the founding of Jackson State College, which was held in 1952. She was buying goodwill, so that any future requests that she had begun to enumerate would receive a favorable review. A literary festival would also highlight the most well-known writers in Mississippi and the South, at least in her initial thinking about its organization. She was asked to compose a poem for the occasion and decided on "Litany for a Dark People," one of the first long poems from this new period. In keeping with her tradition, "Litany" consists of a series of four long stanzas alternating with repeated refrains. Echoing the familiar catalogues in "For My People," the poem moves through the space of Black historical memory, but the tone is more religious and the unevenly rhymed lines are predictable. "Litany" seems to be a less successful poem within her larger body of work. The pattern is classic Walker, however, with the apocalyptic message as the poem draws to a close:

> From grasping of the helping hand the writer brother cast;
> From building empires of our own with brain and brawn and prayers;
> From working to enlarge the gift of him who gladly shares;
> From lifting fallen brothers and rising as we climb
> To build a race of leaders and a nation more sublime;
> From giving our talents in measure full and free
> To speed the coming of that day when all mankind shall be
> United under God in love and charity
> And Thy Kingdom shall abide on earth through all eternity;

And then the final refrain:

> O God of earth and sky and sea,
> Great God of love and majesty,
> Thine humble servants everyone
> In mercy have we come.[10]

The first appearance of the refrain turns the poem into a prayer of thanksgiving, serving several purposes. A celebratory occasion and commemoration for Jackson State, the poem was also an opportunity for Walker to publicly acknowledge her own gratitude for the new beginning Jackson State had offered her. The refrain begs for participation, befitting the occasion for which it was written and ensuring the enactment of an important cultural ritual—call-and-response. "Litany" was the first of several occasional poems that would become her forte. Walker enjoyed writing them even as they had less aesthetic value than her larger body of work because they did strengthen the sense of purpose for her life and her work at a time when she needed it the most.

Her original plan for the festival was to invite William Faulkner, Eudora Welty, Jessie Hill Stuart, Dorothy Thompson, Ruth Draper, Lewis Gannet, Vincent Canby, and E. B. Hungerford. Except for Hungerford, she had chosen Southern writers with whom she wanted to be identified. She had already begun to accept speaking engagements throughout the state and came to see herself as similar to these white authors, if not in terms of what she had produced but what she could. It is unlikely that Walker issued invitations to any of them except for her former teacher, Hungerford. Those who came were writers she knew, some of them quite well, including Langston Hughes, Arna Bontemps, Sterling Brown, Robert Hayden, Melvin Tolson, and Owen Dodson. She had included William Gardner Smith, Willard Motley, M. Carl Holman, Frank Yerby, Gwendolyn Brooks, Era Bell Thompson, J. Saunders Redding, and Ann Petry in her planning notes for the event, but it is likely that funding limitations affected who eventually came. The poets were mentors, like Hughes, or members of her cohort. The photograph became legendary: it was the last time these leading Black poets would be seen together. Her vision of a literary festival was not only radical, but also the first of its kind, and all but impossible in the 1950s. Only she could have pulled it off, just as she would do two decades later in setting another precedent.

From the time Walker arrived in Jackson, she was creating a treasure map for each year, identifying the benchmarks of her success and achievement. Her plan was to take classes in a range of institutions, progressing toward the doctorate of philosophy by 1956. Her projected itinerary would begin with a visit to Chicago where her sister Gwen was finishing her MA in 1952. In successive years, she planned to take Old English at UCLA, French and German at the University of Michigan, and return to the University of Chicago for a qualifying exam for the PhD as an experiment, just to see if she might pass. She had hoped to end up at Yale, where she'd actually get the PhD. Like her plan for the literary festival, she felt free to dream the impossible, knowing that with adjustments, those dreams would eventually come true.

When it came to her observations and self-analysis about the future of her life with Alex, her dreams were far more pragmatic. She did expect them to have a life together, but she knew that they could not sustain their marriage unless she maintained control. She did not expect happiness in the marriage but accepted the choice she gave herself: she had to become the breadwinner and Alex would have to sell their house in High Point to put money down on the Jackson home.

Back row, left to right: Arna Bontemps, Melvin Tolson, Jackson State president Jacob Reddix, Owen Dodson, Robert Hayden; front row: Sterling Brown, Ruth Dease, Margaret Walker, and Langston Hughes at JSU in 1952. Courtesy of Jackson State University

A final condition she made during their reunion year was not having another child. These were the reasons her decision to remain at Jackson State made sense. She knew that she and the children could succeed, even if Alex did not agree to her terms.

A Ford Foundation Fellowship offered her a year off in 1953 and 1954. She convinced Alex that they could all move to North Carolina once again to finish the research she had begun at the Southern Historical Collection. She could use Durham as her base for the additional research trips, but in the back of her mind was the idea that being near High Point would make it easier to sell the house. On her thirty-eighth birthday, the family moved to Durham. She purchased a camera and a tape recorder and wrote letters to all of her contacts. Her concern about being so far away from New Orleans was that another year would go by without seeing her parents. They had not seen the children since she had brought everyone to Jackson. The Walkers had opposed her reconciliation with Alex and were helping her get back on her feet—without him, they believed—and they saw no good coming from her decision to allow him back into her life. Sigismund had taken the stronger position, encouraging her to leave the children in New Orleans, where she could come as she had been doing. It would free her up to continue her writing career and make life much more comfortable for the children. Her mother suggested that the children could spend summers with her, and they could travel; Marion was getting old enough to help with her research, both parents argued. Her decision to stay with Alex had caused another major rift with her parents.

It was her father she thought about as they prepared to move to Durham. She had never made any professional decisions without his advice and, although she felt the need to call him as they left for North Carolina, she had resisted. The decision would be one she would always regret. That August, one month after they arrived in Durham, Sigismund Constantine Walker died. Father and daughter had gone for the longest period of their lives without speaking, a fact that she couldn't reconcile. She remembered her last conversation with her father. Walker and Alex had agreed on one thing when they reunited: the children were never to be separated from them, so she dismissed her father's suggestion. Now she thought that her father had worried himself to death. Although he had been ill for some time, he was overjoyed that he had grandchildren, something he never expected. Having the children around, he seemed to get younger. She knew that his final years were among his happiest, but he remained the quiet contemplative man he always had been. She should have given more credence to what he said, for no one knew her better than her father. Mixed together with her grief were feelings of selfishness in needing to have her own way, and sinfulness in giving in to her own sexual desires. She had disobeyed the one person who had been right about everything he'd told her. The heaviness eventually lifted, but not without much prayer and self-recrimination.

As they returned from his funeral in New Orleans, she was more somber than she'd been when they'd left for Durham earlier that summer. She worked steadily, but by Christmas realized how difficult the task of completing the draft of *Jubilee* was going to be. Two children were in school until early afternoon, Alex was working, and her childcare for Sigis was inadequate. Now that she was eager to finish the book and had support to do so, everything seemed to be getting in the way. Her mood swings were more extreme than usual, and her bouts of depression lasted much longer. When the depression made her downright sick, she went to the doctor, only to discover that she was pregnant. Her parents were right, and she was angry with herself for not having had more self-control.

Seeing no choice now, and against Alex's wishes, she took the children to New Orleans, since the effect of the pregnancy was to diminish her emotional control when she was with them. She was embarrassed and now had to face her mother alone for the first time without her father. Feeling as if she needed to make amends for earlier decisions that went against her parents' wishes, decisions that brought consequences they were correct in anticipating, she found it easy to make a difficult decision for herself—one which they both had fully encouraged. She would leave Alex for what might be the last time and make her way alone. It was early in her pregnancy, and she could still make a trip to New Haven to meet with Yale University Press about her new poetry manuscript, *October Journey*.

Alex objected to her traveling. His expressed concerns about her health increased her resentment and drove a further wedge between them. They parted in angry silence. He went to High Point to work, and she repeated the cycle of her first pregnancy almost exactly. Then, she had a Rosenwald Fellowship, became pregnant, went north alone, and relied on friends for help and comfort. Now, she had a Ford Fellowship and was going north again alone, was pregnant, and would have to rely on friends for help and comfort. On June 17 she was in Harlem Hospital for a second time, giving birth to a daughter who came a little earlier than expected and weighed less than six pounds. She consulted neither Alex nor her family. This was her child, and she named her Margaret, with the middle name Elvira, after her grandmother. Because she was premature, "little Margaret," as she was quickly dubbed, gave her mother a longer stay in the hospital, which brought no complaint.

In fact, she was not alone. By this time, Mercedes had moved to Queens, New York, where she had begun teaching. Walker remembered how concerned she had always been about her sister, whom she left alone in Chicago after deciding to go to Iowa for graduate school. She had always seen herself as watching out for her younger sister. Yet Mercedes had achieved the independence that Walker had not, having chosen what appeared to be a far less complicated life. Mercedes knew that it was time for her to return the favor by taking care of her older sister. She moved the two from the hospital to her home in Queens. She packed up the belongings from the New York apartment where Walker had been staying and assured her sister that she could stay as long as she needed.

Her recovery from childbirth, however, was as emotional as her pregnancy had been. She would flare up unexpectedly, refusing all calls from Alex, who had found her forwarding address when he paid the hospital bill. Her frustration over this pregnancy and not being able to send her mother money for the children made it easy to transfer all blame to Alex and to tell herself that she wanted nothing else to do with him. "This is the end of the road, I cannot bear any more and have done all I can do."[11] When a new contract came from Jackson State, she was relieved. "Despite the emotional problem of severing myself from Alex, I see much ahead—peace, prosperity and real success.[12]

She would have to turn her weaknesses into strengths, and in the throes of a premature midlife crisis with such visceral overtones, no amount of cultivated indifference on anyone's part could contain them. She needed all the discipline she could muster and could not afford to lose control over anything, whether it was her financial or personal affairs. The time with Mercedes proved to be good for her on several levels. She was away from demanding responsibilities, with uninterrupted time for reflection and reassessment, enough to conclude that she needed a change in attitude and a set of new strategies if she expected to achieve any positive results. She began to see a coalescing of the intellectual and professional brought on by her "mystical contemplation and spiritual strength."[13]

The confirmation of a positive outcome came as she read her charts: Saturn was in the Seventh house. The return to a deeply meditative state brought her relief, and she willingly accepted the second part of the reading: only one more year of trial by fire. Her suffering now assuaged, Walker recognized the recurring physiological and psychological stress that came in these moments of emotional intensity. She remembered she had fallen into a deep neurosis coupled with depression, although her mental health diagnosis was not precise in the 1930s. But her parents had known to take her to a physician who recommended a work-based therapy. Now, with remarkable objectivity and detachment, she carefully analyzed her feelings, summarizing her own history of what she referred to as "backsliding"—including her radical "aberrations" during the 1930s—noting that they were always followed by an upward journey, a necessary return to faith. The loss of faith, she concluded, makes us vulnerable to anguish and clouds our judgment.

During the two months she spent with Mercedes, she began to feel renewed, fully present in herself, to herself. Suddenly everything fell in place. "I want a tranquil home where I can live and write in peace. I want peace in my job and freedom to be an adult, not a child. . . . The past is gone, but the future looks wonderful. I am neither resentful nor complaining,"[14] she told herself. The calmness brought more poems that she preserved in her journal before she departed for Jackson to begin classes in September. She also revised her timetable. She would concentrate on getting *Jubilee* published before returning to *October Journey*. Concerned that her new poetry might not be as good as *For My People*, with which everyone would compare it, she determined that it was far better to let the world know that Margaret Walker was still alive with a different project altogether.

Thinking ahead, after establishing herself as a writer of fiction, she would be ready to finish the stories for "Goose Island" that she had started in Chicago. Her mental notes turned into an outline with new ideas for some of the book's characters. She wanted to foreground individual types she had encountered in Chicago. There was Smugs, the Smuggler; Steeplehead, the pimp; Wheels, a gambler; Fingers, the pickpocket; Rosalee, the prostitute; and Sadie, the shoplifter. In addition, she extended her descriptions to include a story about a male harlot, a narcotics peddler, a numbers runner, and a bookie. Writing was good therapy since it brought her full circle. She had spent a year away and felt she had something to show for it after all.

That she would return to Mississippi in the fall of 1954 had not always been certain. One month before her daughter was born, the Supreme Court ruled that racial segregation in public schools was unconstitutional. "Ever since, Mississippi has been in a worse state than the world has been over the atom bomb," she wrote.

> I could have gone against honor and changed my mind about coming back. The tension and fear, incidents of violence, intimidation, reprisal, indignity and gross injustices would fill a huge volume. Teachers have lost their jobs. People have been killed. Others have been harassed, and this harassment has included real bullets to back up threats. We on our job at Jackson College have been told that if we make a front attack on segregation, we will not get our checks. Very few of the faculty members belong to the NAACP. A veritable reign of terror has truly begun in Mississippi. And it includes every sphere of white life—churches, schools, politics, press, radio, televisions, and the hated Security Councils, later called the White Citizens Councils, which are new Ku Klux Klan formed to put the economic squeeze on Negroes.[15]

Her analysis of the causes and consequences of social change is extensive and well informed. She wrote as if she were a commentator on a broadcast whose audiences trusted her judgment. She closed the discussion with the role of communism and religion and supporting her claims with an astrological reading. The *Brown* decision signaled a monumental moment in civil rights history. For Walker, it was accompanied by "turmoil and strife, civil and social disturbance. Everywhere there is this disquiet, this lack of ease, whether locally, nationally or internationally. . . . When, where, and how it will all end nobody knows and few dare to predict," she wrote.[16] Yet, it was not like Walker to refrain from predicting, especially given her astrological predilections:

> In these next six months all major planets are moving and that means universal shakeups. Africa and Asia are in for more wars and there will surely be many revolutions because they are in the path of all major eclipses for the past several years. America's problems are manifold and they include in the order of their importance . . . financial . . . labor . . . unemployment . . . Meanwhile Neptune [is] going into 5th or Scorpio emphasizes children and education so that integration is a foregone conclusion, which 15 years of adjustment will make permanent in America. But sex crimes and perversions increase and children especially need protection from these. There are also terrible problems with natural bodies of water such as storms, hurricanes, typhoons, floods, and other unnatural cloudbursts. . . . As for the Negro we will fare worse where Neptune

is most afflicted. . . . Freedom for Negroes will become a reality in these next 15 years in most parts of America, but nobody is betting on Mississippi, the last stronghold of barbarism.[17]

She could not be content with the world she described. "This is the raw stuff out of which I have written poetry. Not to be allowed to speak or write as I think means creative death to me."[18] Her return to Mississippi had the potential for the greatest period of creativity for Walker.

The *Brown* decision also encouraged her to review her personal connections to events in Black education as someone growing up in the era of segregation. Her family had been involved in education in the South for three generations, and she saw that story as one she would eventually need to write. Schools like Jackson State were a concession to Southern segregation, but they had thrived because they filled a need at a time when the desire for education among Negroes was at its height. If there was going to be a change in the education system, and she believed that there would be, a *new kind* of education would be in demand. She was not sure what this meant exactly, but she asked herself what she could be and do were she to remain in the South, especially at Jackson State.

She was not sentimental when she wrote, "We who are black and have suffered—we know what it is to have been belittled—to have been chastened and above all to have been spiritually nourished—for surely only those who have suffered can also know healing of the spirit and by the spirit."[19] She never hesitated to explain the world that she saw, expose the contradictions within the democratic ideal, and criticize with severity those who stand against human justice, those who act violently because they "fear that [their] civilization is crumbling and 'way of life' fast disappearing as non-whites are becoming increasingly aware of the terrible problem of color and moreover growing more alert politically and economically."[20] She came to her conclusions instinctively, and they were frighteningly accurate, but without a platform, they remained in her head and in the pages of her journal. She knew that her return to Mississippi offered her a ground zero view of painful, violent, yet exciting change. Events like the murder of Emmett Till triggered both her political and creative sensibilities with an intense desire to champion a new social order, to live in and make a world with positive human energy. There was no other place that Margaret Walker could see herself.

The impact of these events caused her to shift her thinking about what she needed to do in order to play a more crucial role in them. Because she was not writing, what was once a possibility—earning the PhD—became an obsession. She faced a big decision: resuming her life with Alex or returning to school as a single woman. "One mind says no, never again, while another said, think about the children,"[21] she wrote. Could she, as a middle-aged woman, on whose income her family depended, realistically expect to return to school? She reviewed her history again, weighing her odds. Could she repeat the success she had had when she was twenty-four? Would the faculty at Iowa allow *Jubilee* to be her PhD dissertation, as they had allowed her poetry manuscript to serve as her master's degree? She had never heard of anyone doing that before, and she feared the faculty she had studied under were no longer there. If they were not, she would have to get to know an entirely new team. The logistics of a leave to complete her PhD were even more problematic. In a few more years, she would be eligible for sabbatical, but she needed to begin her planning well in advance. Even if the sabbatical came through, the money would have to be the source of her family's support. How could she sustain herself for a year, even two, away from home? She drew another treasure map, calculating the time when she might leave home with minimal disruption to her family.

Walker took baby Margaret to Jackson with her while the other children remained in New Orleans. She had given up her apartment and needed to find a place large enough for the five of them. By the beginning of the next year, however, Alex returned to Jackson. He was eager to see his new daughter, and the time away from him had softened Walker considerably. He was also much more compliant. They were bound to each other and to their four children; she needed him as much as he needed her, he maintained. She made clear what her expectations were for the marriage and her own future plans, including leaving home to pursue another degree. They signed a contract to begin building their house in Jackson, and she went to get the children.

Although she may have felt some tension, the certainty that the dark years were behind her quickly dissolved it. She sincerely believed that she was entering another important period of personal and professional growth. She would recite her own history like a catechism: her early life until the family moved to New Orleans when she was ten, joining the church at twelve, her baptism at fifteen, and her first major spiritual awakening at seventeen, the slow years from seventeen to twenty-one, the years of heresy and apostasy in Chicago after college, and finally the years of her married life, which, though rocky, she saw as moving steadily toward new opportunities, contemplation, and illumination. She remained convinced that there was at least one more stage of her life that she needed to complete.

In hindsight, going to Mississippi in the late 1940s provided Walker with new possibilities that were more than personal. She was moving to a state that would soon erupt in forms of violence that would rock the nation. Even the excitement about the move could not blind her to certain realities. Yet those realities would begin to coalese with a new sense of purpose as she returned South. Certain freedoms came with a steady income, one of which was reestablish connection with her Chicago friends, starting with Margaret Burroughs, who filled her in on their social group. After she sent Marion the first monthly stipend for childcare, she quickly returned to what would become a lifelong habit, ordering the books she wanted to read. On the the top of her list was *Deep South, A Social and Anthropological Study of Caste and Class*, the book she knew about from its early planning stages. St. Clair Drake had been in the research group led by Allison Davis, the main author of the landmark study. Reading the book was one way Walker prepared herself for life in Mississippi. She knew who she was; now she knew more clearly where she was. As an eternal optimist, reading the factual information about Mississippi sharpened the outline of her dreams. She believed that her past struggles had been necessary for the journey that lead her to the place she was meant to be.

20

Turn Loose and Sink or Swim

After they resurrected their marriage, Walker observed her husband as a changed man. The new conditions of their relationship made her comfortable enough to engage her work at Jackson State differently. Between 1955 and 1960, she worked diligently, looking for opportunities to exercise her vision for Black education in the South. She accepted assignments that demonstrated her ability to make things happen that she sincerely believed no one else had the ability or desire to do. She praised the new programs that President Reddix had allowed her to implement. He was eager for her to take on challenging tasks, knowing that she had a unique set of skills, thought creatively, and had a penchant for perfection. Nonetheless, her public criticisms of her Black male colleagues, who were very close to him, gave Reddix reason to distrust her loyalty. She believed and did not hesitate to say that these men were inferior and threatened by her intelligence—an intelligence that she proudly demonstrated.

She needed to undo the reputation she had earned: that of an outspoken woman who complained about everything and who was determined to undermine the administration. She argued with her colleagues on many topics: what should constitute passing grades, what kind of student should be recognized for achievement, the difference between training and education, and what kind of jobs they should prepare students for. Her ideas contrasted sharply with those expressed by the majority of people with whom she worked, and thus she had to be wrong. While they were all concerned about whether they would survive in a climate dominated by resistance to desegregation, she refused to allow that fear to dominate her thinking.

Walker was beginning to formulate views that would result in important essays published in later years. "Religion, Poetry and History: Foundations for a New Educational System," "Revolution and the University," and "Humanities with a Black Focus" showed a preoccupation with making education more relevant to the civil rights era, even in a climate of fear, although the first of these essays did not appear until 1968. She asked questions about the values of a society and questioned the assumptions that most of her colleagues made. Many of her ideas were intrinsic to her own education in Black and white religious institutions, and they were initially developed in the practice and teachings of her parents, who valued highly their own advancement and that of other Negroes. The Walkers did not recognize social limitations; they expected their children to

The House Where My Soul Lives. Maryemma Graham, Oxford University Press. © Oxford University Press 2022.
DOI: 10.1093/oso/9780195341232.003.0020

serve as examples of what one could and should do. Added to this was the larger education she'd received living and working within a network of artist activists influenced by a social movement. She had learned to ask questions and to read broadly for answers in all the humanities-based disciplines.

She saw herself in a rare position, listening to outdated ideas about what education should be, repeated by people who were looking backward, not forward. Most of what she heard seemed to have no connection either to a society undergoing radical shifts or to people who needed to think differently about themselves as a result of those shifts. She tried to convince others that something had to change, just as she saw herself as an agent of that change. She was convinced that if she did not know how to implement those changes, she could learn how, and she would then teach others.

Many of her colleagues saw her as disruptive, difficult to get along with, and arrogant—a word she had heard for much of her life. Given the dynamics of her personal life, most of her colleagues believed that she could ill afford to tell anyone else what to do since she could not keep her own household straight. Her arrogance derived from her profound disappointment with people who accepted their own inferiority, an inferiority they passed on to their students. It was this internalized racism she meant to disrupt, to disagree with. Every time she encountered dissembling behavior and self-negation, she was infuriated. She argued that they were preparing a new generation of leaders who only knew how to use old tools. What should have earned her respect brought backlash instead, something she never understood. She asked herself who was she to tell anybody what to do?: first as a woman, and second without a PhD? The third factor, what people said about the ups and downs of her marital relationship, she simply ignored.

Walker felt neither noble nor powerful in these moments. On the contrary, she had the ability to be open and honest with herself, occasionally loathsome, aware that she could never will herself into a state of normalcy defined by others. She put her marriage in this last category, something she never expected anyone to understand. But she did display many of the characteristics that had come to define women who were approaching what was considered middle age in the 1950s. Given to periods of brooding, Walker experienced neurotic urges that consumed her as her hormonal shifts set their own course, sometimes alternating between emotional paralysis and delusion. She took sick days often to contend with these conditions, fighting them in isolation, while the children were at school and Alex was out of the house. She was intent on finding strength inside the weaknesses, pushing through the things that seemed to hurt her most.

She knew she had to address the money question. The family needed every penny she earned, and she didn't see that changing soon. When she thought of returning to graduate school, she immediately asked herself how she could justify doing anything that put her family in jeopardy. The answer came through prayer: "A perfect life in God must also be sacrificial," she reminded herself.[1] The poverty she felt was more spiritual than material—although it was true they had very little money. Walker surmised that a change of attitude would address both issues directly. In practical terms, with her track record for receiving fellowships, she thought she might apply to at least two places: the Southern Education Fund and the Guggenheim Foundation to support the completion of *Jubilee*. She would ask President Reddix, in a carefully constructed letter, to supplement her salary while on a two-year leave. She would have to tread lightly on the explanation she offered: she had been promised a promotion based on her creative work but realized that the university would find greater use for her talents and abilities if she pursued her PhD.

After preparing several drafts over a two-year period, Walker wrote Reddix her first letter requesting an official leave with pay in 1959, and another in 1960. As she anticipated, he denied both of her requests. Regardless, she was determined to go to Iowa, taking more than 300 typed pages of *Jubilee*, most of which she had written in Hungerford's class in the fall of 1934. A decade later, in 1943–1944, she'd written more as a result of the research she'd conducted in North Carolina, Georgia, and Alabama while under contract with the NCAC. Ten years later, in 1954, she added the last pages while on a Ford Foundation research fellowship. A promising, unfinished manuscript would have to be her calling card. She had drafted about half of the book manuscript even though she believed it wasn't any good. But she knew that Iowa was the right place to make it as good as it was going to get. Time was not on her side, but she was on a mission: she had to get the PhD to earn a promotion and secure her teaching career.

Her inner satisfaction became her most important consideration as she looked ahead. *For My People* had emerged two decades earlier, when the accumulated experiences in her life needed to find a way for release. By 1960 she had begun to feel that intensity again. She was still that writer, but more mature. She was living in the heart of a nation that needed a guardian. In the mirror she saw herself as a woman who had honored her drive and her God-given talent. She had accomplished her goals: professionally, she had fulfilled her dream of becoming an award-winning poet; personally, she had found satisfaction in marrying the man she loved and having a family. Still, the professional and the personal could be in conflict in the court of public opinion. As a poet, she could be famous. As a wife and mother, that individual identity had to be submerged as her children and family became her priorities.

Although many women continued their careers uninterrupted by motherhood, it was rare and virtually impossible if they were Negro. She seemed to have appropriated a nineteenth-century model of womanhood. Typically, these women, some of them writers who became public figures early in life, found it necessary to transform or put aside that public identity after marriage. Walker made the adjustment by becoming an educator, the one career that was open especially to Negro women. Her parents had been teachers too, and she was aware of many Negro women educators who could serve as models. In Florida, where she spent a lot of time with her mother's family, she would frequently hear about the work of Mary McLeod Bethune, who had opened in 1904 the Daytona Literary and Industrial Training School for Negro Girls, which later became Bethune-Cookman College. Although Walker did not meet Mrs. Bethune until the 1940s, she knew her reputation well as an educator and early civil rights advocate. Bethune, like many other Negro women educators, had studied under Lucy Craft Laney, who had founded her own school—Haines Normal Institute in Augusta, Georgia—in 1883. She remembered learning about Laney's life the year she was back home in New Orleans and was intrigued by her story as a pioneer in early childhood education. Bethune went on to found a professional nursing school for Negro women as well.

As a child, Walker remembered that Marion took great care to explain that Booker T. Washington was not the only influential Black educator, especially since his industrial school model was highly contested within the Negro community and a point of discussion within their own family. She knew her father's experience with and opposition to Washington's "Tuskegee Machine," as it was later called. At the same time, Negro women educators expanded Washington's model by adding studies in the classics, history, literature, and the arts to the standard home economics curriculum required of their female students. While W. E. B. Du Bois had the most widely publicized disagreement with Washington over the strategy for Black progress and the nature of Black education in the beginning of the twentieth century, Negro women seemed to care less about the debate than about establishing their own schools. Lucy Laney, Mary McCleod Bethune, and Nannie Helen Burroughs inspired those they taught and generations of later women educators by offering models of engagement that resonated with the Woman's Era. As a result, Negro women demonstrated an increased intellectual and cultural influence after the 1890s, a period that saw the rise of the Black women's club movement and publications like *The Woman's Era*. Many of the ideas espoused by these groups had found their expression in Anna Julia Cooper's *A Voice from the South* (1892), a book that Walker read and greatly admired.

Walker thought about her mother for reasons other than the different lines of argument about Negro education. She began to fear that she might be repeating her mother's mistakes, as much as she had tried to resist them. Marion's Washington, DC, years were a constant reference in the Walker household, and Walker knew that her mother's ideas about what girls should do to become proper women had come from her early school experience. Like Nannie Burroughs,

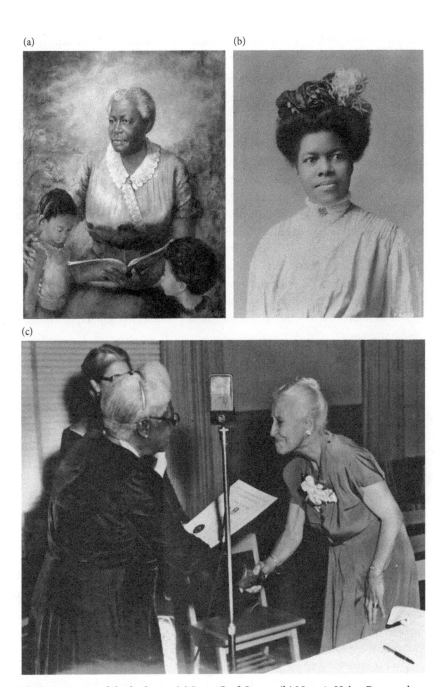

Black women models clockwise (a) Lucy Craft Laney, (b) Nannie Helen Burroughs, and (c) Mary McCleod Bethune with Mary Church Terrell. Courtesy of the Lucy Laney Museum and Bethune-Cookman University Archives

Marion Dozier Walker was a self-starter and had the first independent Negro music studio in New Orleans. Walker also recognized and criticized the energy and optimism required by her mother's career that often left little time for her own children.

Women like Laney, Bethune, and Burroughs lived and worked at a time when education for Negroes was largely unavailable, especially in the South. But none of these women had husbands and families to contend with. Bethune, who did marry, was separated from her husband by the time she began her school. Lucy Laney never married, and neither did Nannie Burroughs. When Walker elected to teach, she was following this long-established tradition of Negro women educators who embraced their work with a missionary zeal. At one time, a missionary career had appealed to her, giving her life in service to others. But missionaries were forbidden to marry, and marriage, she believed, made one a complete woman. It was not something she was willing to forgo. Yet she was like these women in the sense that teaching was a path to freedom for those she taught, directly tied to upward mobility. She knew that her mother believed that as well: upward mobility and respectability were extremely important for a Negro woman.

So why was she not content with the career choice she had made? Why was there such a persistent need for something more? Had she not done everything she wanted? If *Jubilee* were never finished, her life was still fulfilled. She was a woman who had produced a major work; *For My People* proved that and more with its awards and accolades. She had done what other Negro women writers of her generation had not, with the exception of Gwendolyn Brooks, with whom Walker was often compared.

However, thoughts of her mother brought back feelings of unresolved conflict. She believed her mother saw a boldness in her daughter that she needed to contain. Although she hated to admit it, she was like her mother in her drive and hunger for something more, something she did not yet have, which outward appearances could belie. Walker knew that her mother had not reached her highest goals in a professional musical career, but that she had found immense satisfaction in her life as a musical educator. What Marion did do as she sublimated her impulses was to transfer those higher ambitions, divided between her two daughters. Sister Gwen's polio as a child, and Brother being the only son and born to an older Marion spared them from their mother's intensity, which became muted over time.

Walker remembered the absence of both parents, especially when they were away at work or pursuing their degrees. She did not want this for her children, yet she had benefited from having her parents care for her children, just as Grandma Dozier had been the consistent single presence in her childhood. However, she did not equate being relegated to the care of her grandmother with what her children had experienced. Rather, she saw this as the protection that a caring grandmother provided against Marion's frequent outbursts that could easily overwhelm them all, especially when they were aimed at Walker, which was most often the case. She concluded that her mother simply had few motherly instincts, the same ones that *she* had taken great care to cultivate. At times, all of the Walker children may have seen Marion as a mother who operated more out of duty and obligation than love.

Other matters concerned Walker. The death of Emmett Till had shaken the nation up, alarming anybody living in Mississippi. Negroes with teenage sons were terrified. Her final fear was real. Recounting an incident involving her son in a journal entry, she described an attack by white boys, who slapped and knocked James off his bicycle. He did not fight. "It takes so little on a Sunday afternoon in Mississippi to make or provoke a tragedy,"[2] she wrote. Her objectivity could easily fail her when something was this close to home, enough to make her question whether she had done the right thing in choosing to raise her family in Mississippi. It was hard for Walker not to identify with Mamie Till Mobley, the mother of fourteen-year-old Emmett, who must have been the bravest woman in the world to take on the state of Mississippi. She read Martin Luther King Jr.'s *Stride toward Freedom* as soon as it appeared and was in full agreement with his ideas but wondered, "How long can this wide sweeping social revolution remain bloodless. Thus far it has been fought in the courts. We pray it will not begin to be fought in the streets."[3] Her predictions were only a few years from reality.

Worries about her children, especially her oldest son, and assorted physical ailments affected her emotional state. In 1960, her condition was so severe that she required hospitalization. She had an infected kidney that needed to be removed. The possibility of losing her job seemed more real than ever, and without enough money for the household bills, she let the telephone go. In the summer, feeling cut off from all communication with the outside world, Walker dealt with unresolved tensions in her marriage, leading to her renewed accusations of Alex's infidelity that, whether true or not, became a subject of considerable discussion within the Jackson Black community.

Her children were all at an age where they could openly react to her explosive moods with moods of their own. In June, the children went to New Orleans with her mother, and Walker and Alex both entered the hospital, he for repair of a hernia and she for kidney surgery. The two weeks in the hospital resulted in her self-proclaimed mandate: "Be calm, do not fight and fuss or complain; refrain from agitation. No more wasting of myself without rest and sleep and proper food. Now I am 45."[4]

In 1961, she was beginning to understand more about her parents, and why her mother was the most vehement in her objection to the marriage. She had defied them earlier, only to discover now how correct they were, even if it had been for the wrong reasons. In her deliberations, she experienced a gradual letting go of the resentment she felt because her mother could not accept Alex. What had prevented Walker's understanding earlier was a failure to see their similarities—she only saw how different she was from her mother. Her mother was eighteen years old when she made a decision about the life she wanted to live. In contrast, she was twenty-seven and very much an adult woman capable of making choices for herself. Marion would have seen her daughter, in whom she had placed her own hopes, making the mistake she herself had made as a young woman in love. But Walker had reached the point where she did not fault her choice of marriage to Alex; rather it was her failure in learning how to be married. Had she not done things differently from her mother? She remained home with her children and had resisted returning to school until now. Her sense of urgency had as much to do with making the family more economically stable with a secure job as it did with the realization of personal goals. In contrast, her mother's drive got in the way of their family a great deal. Marion had spent most of their childhood trying to recover what she had lost.

How strange it was now for Walker to recognize that she would become that same ambitious woman and mother, with possible consequences for her children that she dare not predict. If she returned to school, she would likely have to separate the children. At most, she could take the two younger ones. She could not see leaving any of them if she returned to Iowa, but realized that Marion and James had enough independence and maturity to help their grandmother with their younger siblings if she were to leave all four children with her mother. Marion was entering her senior year and was sure to get a scholarship for college. Walker began to explore colleges in Iowa that she thought might be a good fit for her oldest daughter. If she succeeded in gaining admission to the University of Iowa PhD program, having her daughter nearby would create less tension within the family and make it easier on her mother, who would have responsibility for three, rather than four children.

In her mind, she had very few choices. She knew that she would have to work for a living, and her father had always insisted that she understand this fact. His goal was for his daughters not to be dependent on a man, even if they chose to marry. Marriage was also something they need not rush into, he cautioned. Yet he had also questioned whether she could actually earn a living as a writer. He nevertheless provided her with the skills and education that ensured her independence. When she realized that her father was correct, that writing would not provide a stable or consistent income, she had allowed her emotions to stand in the way of maintaining her independence. Becoming dependent on a man was the mistake she had made; about that she was clear.

That clarity had caused Walker to successfully change her strategy. Reclaiming her independence, she had been able to maintain her marriage simultaneously. Teaching had accomplished that purpose and another as well: it provided a way for her to satisfy her intellectual needs and a respectable profession that secured one's independence. Although the literary world had all but forgotten Margaret Walker by 1960, and she was disliked by some of her peers, she was a hit among the students. They respected her sense of authority and commitment to her teaching at a Southern Black college. Her presence made them feel special. They flocked to her classes, which were always oversubscribed, and they waited patiently for her, even though she was repeatedly late. If her colleagues were jealous of her popularity, her reputation among her students more than made up for it. Ten years at Jackson State had only whetted her appetite. She was reading and teaching the literature that she loved; she needed to write it as well.

Despite the joy she felt in the classroom, the 1960–1961 year had been her worst yet. Run-ins with Reddix and the feeling of being underappreciated rose to the top of her list. She was not certain she could return to Jackson State in the fall. Had she been able to redirect her energies to writing, she might not have felt that her "creative destruction"[5] was equal to her economic one. By the end of May, she felt the "pressures . . . crushing like iron hammers mashing human skulls. There is no hope, no mercy, no love and no redress."[6] When she regained her composure, she had clear reasons for leaving: she had to get her PhD to continue teaching and to maintain her credibility and demand a competitive salary. Even though the Black colleges did not award tenure and promotion on the basis of publication for the most part, not having a terminal degree could be a stumbling block in anyone's career. In the end, the question became not could she do it, but when? These were her thoughts as she made up her mind to exercise the only choice she had: go to Iowa in summer 1961.

After her classes had ended and the children were out of school, Walker made arrangements to borrow money to cover the cost of the Iowa summer session. She took Marion and James to New Orleans and headed to Iowa City with Sigis and Margaret. She needed to prove to herself that she could still hold her own in a rigorous academic environment. She reasoned that if she could get through the intensity of summer school classes and do well, she might be able to convince the admissions committee to admit her into the PhD program in the future. Taking her mind off Jackson State gave her courage to face one remaining challenge.

The transformation that would mark her independence at this stage of her life was driving to Iowa alone. They had bought a station wagon a few years earlier, and she had finally succeeded in getting a driver's license. Even though she was not an experienced driver, she was amazingly calm for the entire trip to Iowa City, while Sigis (twelve) and Margaret (seven) entertained themselves. It was the first trip of many trips to come, and it was the first long trip without their father, who had always been the designated driver. They asked questions repeatedly. Young Margaret was concerned that she would miss her friends, and Sigis was eager to see if any of the boys were taller than he was. Given a chance to be the big brother for the first time, he was excited that his tall stature might be a positive factor.

They moved into graduate student housing on the University of Iowa campus that was only slightly better than the barracks that she remembered during her early days at Jackson State. Her children, living in an interracial community for the first time, easily adjusted to the housing since it was teeming with young children, mostly free of prejudiced thinking. Sigis and Margaret enjoyed roaming freely in and out of their small apartment. The intimacy of apartment living and their new acquaintances brought the strange and unfamiliar that the rituals of childhood could easily accommodate. Walker enrolled them in summer programs to allow herself time for her classes and homework. The long, hot days of the Iowa summers meant that the children were never at a loss for outside companions, and she could count on the evenings and afternoons being relatively free from interruptions. With only the three of them, she could adjust her schedule to her own needs, no longer cooking daily. The three of them ate less and had plenty of leftovers since she found it hard to break the habit of cooking for twice as many people. It had been years since she had so much time to devote to her reading and writing.

She enrolled in two courses that summer: "Cultural Ideals of the East and West" and a fiction workshop. The introduction to Vedic philosophy in the cultural ideals course was especially intriguing. Not only did it represent the kind of intrinsic philosophy that she found compatible with her own, but it also deepened her curiosity about world philosophies and religions. She saw herself discrediting her father's view that women were naturally attracted to the arts, men to philosophy.

Verlin Cassill taught the fiction workshop. Because she had focused on poetry when she was there earlier, it was like working with him for the first time. She needed to know if *Jubilee* was worth the wait and if she really could find a voice for the story. When she turned in her draft of the first chapter of this novel to Cassill, he was discouraging. He advised her to read the Russian novelists to better understand how historical novelists create a relationship between the events of history and individual lives of their characters.

She wrote and rewrote the first chapter. Because their apartment was small, she did most of her writing in the library, claiming a table the first week of classes. She found it waiting for her each day she returned to write longhand in lined notebooks, crossing out sections and then writing them anew. She would not stop until she could see the difference between what she had turned into him and what she now wrote. Then she would return her new version to Cassill.

The long road she had traveled with *Jubilee* now had a clear direction. Each meeting with Cassill confirmed forward movement. She had been away from the book too long but was still relying on childhood memories. Separating the memories of the real from the wholly imaginative was a difficult undertaking. The characters would have to interact with each other, so she had to apply the skills of a psychologist, as well as an artist. She needed more detachment, Cassill told her. This was not poetry, where emotion is a good thing, he would remind her. Emotion has to be contained to avoid melodrama in fiction. He was pleased with the revisions she brought him and agreed to be her advocate when she met with Paul Engle. Although she was certain she wanted the PhD, she needed Engle's approval to create a combined approach to courses and workshops that would fulfill the requirements of a degree. The faculty in the literature program needed to be convinced that the content of the workshop program was sufficient to warrant the terminal degree in English studies.

Cassill had provided Engle with an overview of what Walker had done in the workshop, the basis for which she believed *Jubilee* could serve as her dissertation. She had little convincing to do. She was already developing a reading list that would become the literary component. She would focus on coursework for a two-year period, but her major objective would be to learn how to write historical fiction. She also had studied with Paul Engle before, but now as director of the Iowa Writers' Workshop, his time for teaching was severely limited.

She was still feisty and determined, without a "pot to pee in," she imagined him saying when they would meet. She remembered how green she was during her first stint at Iowa immediately following the Federal Writers' Project. She had grown, and Engle would have to believe that she was even more prepared to beat the odds than she was as a much younger woman. She hoped that he would not hold her lack of productivity against her.

Could she do it in two years? Walker was elated with his affirmative response and willingness to set up admission arrangements for the following fall. She was a veteran teacher. Without her children or husband to care for, she could teach two classes and go to school easily. She had begun this process without the certainty that she could leave home. At the end of the summer, she felt completely capable of making a firm decision to return to Iowa. Her debt to Engle was now doubled. He had known her as one of his favorite students, and the forty-five-year-old mother of four he saw that summer had lost none of her fire.

Walker was in an exuberant state after the summer session ended, and it continued following her return to Jackson. She had exchanged her normal life for a return to a writer's life, and she knew it could give her a future. Though it had been twenty-two years since she'd been a student, some of what she now felt was the same as before. That giddy girl who had ventured to Iowa when she was twenty-four had not disappeared. She also knew she was entering another period of self-discovery. *For My People* had been about her birth as a professional writer. *Jubilee* would be about her rebirth.

Once she returned home, the thought of being alone for two years chastened her. Self-doubt and fear resurfaced. What had she done? A married woman in her middle forties leaving her family to follow a dream?

> Was this just an ambition motivated by intellectual pride—a psychological need for achievement—to compensate—to preen myself rather than humble myself. . . . Will it really lead to good for the children, for my people or merely for myself? I ask only that God's will be done—and that if this thing be not a good thing, take away this gnawing proud desire.[7]

She convinced herself that it was the right thing to do at the right time. After all, she was the perfect wife and mother. Hadn't she cooked every meal that Alex and her family had eaten? For twenty years, she had written virtually nothing. She was loath to return to Jackson State where she felt despised and unappreciated by an insensitive administration who resented her abilities and her vision. Didn't she deserve more?

The one person's advice that was no longer available to her was her father's. He would have known exactly what to say to calm her recurring fears. He read,

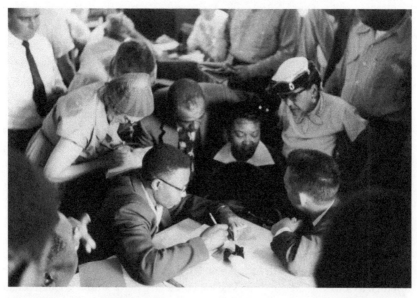

Mamie Till Mobley with lawyers and the press in Mississippi, 1955. Courtesy of the Ernest Withers Collection

thought, and wrote, led by his characteristic pensiveness, reserving his words of advice for special occasions. She could easily recall the wisdom he shared on her career matters. He had told his daughter early that people respect two things in Negroes: an education and a handle. The more you get, the more people respected you. That philosophy drove him to return to Northwestern for those four long summers—for more education and a handle. From her father's point of view, getting the PhD would bring her the approval and respect she wanted and needed. He was no longer physically in her life, but she could take his ethics of improvement from his beloved Ralph Waldo Emerson and apply it to her own life. She was Sigismund Walker's daughter, and that would never change.

PART V
A NOT SO QUIET RADICAL

1962–1974

(Iowa; Jackson, MS)

21

Jubilee

A Community of Memory

Never had there been such fierce competition between the two sides of Walker's self than after her return from Iowa: the writer committed to a public art, and the wife and mother on whom her family was almost entirely dependent. The tension between duty and desire was the constant driving force in her life, feeding her creative energies. As she grew older with increased responsibilities, any reconciliation of her separate spheres through her art was harder to achieve. The impossibility of that achievement Walker saw as failure. And if she failed herself, she failed others—an option that did not exist. When she was in her twenties, Walker had embraced a vision of the world that taught her how to see and understand it differently; through that vision, she found her voice. That kind of integration was what she always sought. The country faced a depression that drew people into its orbit regardless of who they were. Her conversion experience in the political environment of Chicago allowed her to produce a socially conscious art that spoke to the period and for the people for whom it was written. In contrast, returning to the South had given her an emotional comfort zone that suited her sensibilities, even as its fixed and predictable social world camouflaged the violence and terror that sustained it. All of that had become unhinged by the early 1960s, putting Mississippi at the center of the national stage, as the representative of all that was bad with America. Black, white, and Native all drank from the same water, but each had their own identities, nationalisms, and border. Each struggled to find common ground with the other and with the rest of the world.

Being in the middle of a South that was becoming unhinged offered another form of productive tension in Walker's life, one that fed a belief that she might take up where she had left off decades earlier. It may have felt like her Chicago period, where writers and artists heard a call and answered it, resulting in an unprecedented level of cultural production. In her mind, a return to Iowa was intended to replicate what she had done before, except with a different outcome. Just as she had left Chicago feeling at the end of her rope, she was at the end of her rope in Jackson. She had learned as much as she could in Chicago, but she needed a new structure to bring it all together. Likewise, she had exhausted the possibilities for any reconciliation of her duty and her desire at this new stage of her life. She trusted Iowa to provide the structure she needed. Still, she was as yet

The House Where My Soul Lives. Maryemma Graham, Oxford University Press. © Oxford University Press 2022.
DOI: 10.1093/oso/9780195341232.003.0021

Walker receives the first copy of *Jubilee*

unsure if she had fulfilled the promise she made to herself as a "woman, writer, and person."[1]

Walker's doubts about herself and her literary output—her belief that her career was in serious decline—was in some ways inconsistent with the reality. The constraints she was under, namely her inability to maintain her contact with editors and to complete any of the promised essays and book manuscripts, did not mean that she was invisible. While she was not as active as she wanted to be, she did make regular appearances in print during what she referred to as her silent years. Poems from *For My People* were routinely reprinted in the 1940s and 1950s, and the title poem would begin its journey as the most widely quoted and recited poem in Black America. She had also published some new poems that she'd written during her NCAC lecture tour. "Harriet Tubman," "For Mary McCleod Bethune," "A Litany for Dark People," "Dear Are the Names That Charmed Me in My Youth," and what became the title poem for a future volume, "October Journey," made their first appearances in both small magazines and leading Black journals during the period. In other words, readers enjoyed a steady diet of Walker's poetry before and following the publication of her 1942 volume. She had also begun to diversify her output further. A personal essay, "How I Told My Child about Race," appeared in 1951 in *Negro Digest*, the most widely circulating Black periodical of the era. It became the second of her most popular essays before the appearance of "On Being, Female, Black, and Free" years later. The essay worked because it represented the kind of reconciliation between her private and public worlds that would become central to *Jubilee*. The infusion of autobiographical elements that had been so successful in "Growing Out of Shadow" was a method that she would continue to use, drawing heavily on her material from her journals. Since *Negro Digest* featured articles by the most famous Blacks at the time, Walker not only affirmed her connection to the Black intellectual tradition, but she also allowed her readers an opportunity to keep up with a new stage of her life during one of the most crucial periods in American history. The public/private integration was the underlying element, the coalescing of the spiritual and physical in single house.

If *Negro Digest* would ensure that Walker would become everywoman, the placement of two other essays offered a chance to elevate her status as a literature critic. "New Poets" appeared in *Phylon*, a journal whose subtitle, *The Atlanta University Review of Race and Culture*, made clear its intent. Du Bois had founded the journal in 1940, giving scholars who shared a unique intellectual history an entry point into the debates of the period. Up to that point, race scholarship had been primarily a phenomenon of the social sciences, in large part dominated by Robert Park at the University of Chicago. *Phylon*, as one of Du Bois's initiatives, would become a site for burgeoning new voices and scholarship on race. That the editors turned to Walker for a critical assessment of Black poetry between 1930 and 1950 suggests at least two things. First, they were aware that readers would trust what an award-winning poet like Walker, whose work had already appeared in *Phylon*, had to say. More than the familiarity, however, was the belief that a critical review of the period following the Harlem Renaissance was in order. Her essay would appear the same year that Gwendolyn Brooks would win the Pulitzer Prize, which demanded more attention be paid to poetry by Black writers themselves. Important, too, was the 1941 publication of *Negro Caravan*, the most comprehensive Negro anthology to date, and its editors Sterling Brown, Ulysses Lee, and Arthur P. Davis had given a major boost to the academic study of Black poetry. An accompanying critical apparatus necessary for the institutionalization of Black literature was slowly emerging.

The *Phylon* essay did exactly what it was intended to do for Walker and the field: it introduced a protocol for examining Black poetry on its own terms, specifying the trends within a movement and distinguishing it from others. The formalized study of Black poetry was still in the making. Thus, many were starting from ground zero—that a tradition of Black writing existed at all was new. The idea that literary periods existed—beyond what most referred to as the New

Negro Movement—was highly suspect. Showing her intimate knowledge of the poets and the poetry of her cohorts—she included her own poetry—Walker offered a critical interpretation that took into account craft, style, and ideas, seen against the changing landscape of the post-Depression years through the Cold War era. Since she had already made an appearance in *Phylon* with a poem, "Harriet Tubman" in 1944, Walker took great care to carve out a space for the poets of her generation, who neither claimed an affinity with the social protest poetry of the 1930s, nor would abandon their strong preference for Black subject matter. The maturity, as Walker notes, is visible in both the form and the content of a new body of work. About the writers from the 1940s, she said, "Negroes not only have grown up as poets technically, with volumes of poetry showing a growing concern with craftsmanship, social perspective and intellectual maturity, but they have also begun to reap the reward in the form of laurels due to them for their labors."[2] Her focus on showing the differences between poetry of the 1930s included Sterling Brown and Frank Marshall Davis, for example, and her peers whose volumes appeared in the 1940s, Robert Hayden, Melvin Tolson, Owen Dodson, and Gwendolyn Brooks. Three poets who have remained shadowy figures from the period, David Wadsworth Cannon, Bruce McWright, and Myron O'Higgins, Walker also discussed. Her inclusiveness is important, despite the glaring absence of other women poets outside of herself and Brooks. Her inventory of poets included the male poets, with none of the poets from the Chicago period, like Margaret Danner. What she followed was a protocol that considered only poets with published collections, no matter how active their career seemed to be. But she was also aware that inclusion of too many of the still publishing poets from South Side Writers Group would have challenged her views about the movement away from the social realism of the 1930s period and the legacy of Richard Wright. The designation "New Poets" ultimately meant that Walker accepted the role for which she seemed naturally suited. Trained in close reading as she was, she was most knowledgeable about poetry of the modernist movement. Thus, her inclusion of T. S. Eliot, W. H Auden, and Robert Lowell does not seem surprising, since she also wanted to make a point about the religious revival that those poets reflect, as distinguished from the Black poets she had mentioned. In contrast to what would become common in literary criticism, Walker did not start with a comparative approach to those known modernist poets, but on the features of the poets under consideration. Only after the analysis does she note a tendency within a group of Modernist poets that she had yet to observe among the Black poets already mentioned.

Establishing herself as a literature critic early gave Walker a decided advantage, but not one from which she would fully benefit. As one of the few, if not the only, Black woman writer in that period, she joined the field of widely known and influential male critics, including Alain Locke, J. Saunders Redding, Arna

Bontemps, Lorenzo Dow Turner, and Richard Wright. To complement her new critical position, she also published a review of *The Nausea of Sartre* in the *Yale Review* in 1953. While it was common for white writers to comment on Black literature, the reverse was a rare privilege. Recognizing the invitation as an opportunity, Walker took advantage of her connection to Yale. She needed to show through her own writing that "Race . . . is used as a point of departure toward a global point of view. . . . The tendency is toward internationalism rather than nationalism and racism . . . our world has shrunk to a small community of nations and mankind is forced to recognize the kinship of all peoples."[3] It did appear that Walker was trying to gain some leverage with crossover literary appeal.

The critical intervention she was making may have simply come too soon for Walker to take fuller advantage. She was equally as concerned about the slippage in her literary reputation and more practical things like job security. She was a well-known poet, and it does seem surprising that she did not return to the familiar form for which she was best known, when she found herself again at the crossroads of duty and desire. She was willing to give up on "Goose Island" but not *Jubilee*, the project that challenged her sensibilities as much as it had been practically writing itself. She had been living with it all of her life, "long before [it] had a name,"[4] she was fond of saying. The novel became an allegory for her experience as a woman, and many of her earliest preoccupations resonate in the story. Like Walker, the protagonist Vyry had a difficult childhood, an older female figure taught her how to be a woman, and the mistress of the household despised her. Vyry also settles into a more traditional life as a wife and mother after a failed relationship with a man who represented the revolutionary ideal. Yet, the turn to *Jubilee* was more than allegorical.

Walker could not have ignored the cultural shift during the postwar era. The 1950s had seen important novels emerge: Ralph Ellison's widely acclaimed *Invisible Man* in 1952, followed immediately by James Baldwin's *Go Tell It on the Mountain*, the first of four novels he would publish in the next fifteen years. It is also likely that her preference for the folk forms, the sonnet, and free verse had been surpassed by the technical artistry she saw in poets like Hayden and Brooks. But she did see possibilities for innovation in the fiction that was emerging. And although Walker would have noticed the rumblings in Chicago among a younger generation, she remained an academic poet,—that is, a professionally trained one at predominately white institutions; however, she was not always certain that her work would cross over well.

She had already spent a good deal of time researching the novel. The biggest push had come from her grandmother just before her passing in 1944, but her father's death in 1953 had set off another one of those fires that was burning within. The many pieces—a 300-page fragment from college, multiple stories from her grandmother, and scenes she had written in North Carolina—represented the accumulation of three decades of work. Even as new networks were beginning to open up for her, she needed to seek comfort in the familiar. Her life was too complicated to take too many unnecessary risks. Thus, she turned down additional invitations to write articles and settled on her plans for the next stage of her life.

She also had the benefit of those revelations that came after years of self-critical brooding and her journal exhortations. At *Jubilee*'s center is an internal monologue that guides the protagonist without always revealing itself. Vyry is the ideal listener to Walker's longings as they reveal themselves in the desire for self-making and through Walker's own practice of remaking. Although the novel began as the coming-of-age story of a young girl enslaved from birth, she gave more focus to her Vyry's interior life as a mature woman, mother, and wife against the backdrop of slavery's demise, the birth of a free Black community in the South, and the choices that people made—choices that were neither easy nor always clear. *Jubilee*, as an analogue for historically situated slavery-to-freedom-and-after encounters, verified through painstaking research, defies sentimentality, even with its love triangle. Her preference for irreverent portrayals of people on both sides of a terrible system lends credence to her belief in the "integrity or wholeness of the creating personality . . . brought to bear on the raw materials of human experience and chaotic physical phenomena."[5]

Before the novel could become a reality, however, Walker had her own reality to contend with. The payoff for a return to Iowa would be the completion of *Jubilee* and another academic degree. The changes could not be too radical. Nor could it suggest instability. She was equally clear that before presenting the plan to Alex, she would need to know where the money was going to come from. He was an ultimate strategist in these matters, brutal in his questioning. What if this were just another one of her flights of fantasy that, left to her own devices, could leave all of them completely groundless?

Thinking more strategically, after she had returned to New Orleans to pick up Marion and James in August 1961, she talked with her mother, Gwen, and Brother. Marion would be leaving for Western College for Women, the Ohio institution Walker had carefully selected for her daughter. James had one year of high school left and was already independent. Only Sigis and Margaret would need attention, and since Sigis had grown accustomed to looking after his sister, she told her family that having the two children there would not be an onerous task. With their support for three years, she knew that she could finish the coursework for the degree, write her dissertation, and publish it as the novel *Jubilee*. What was unsaid was that it was her own fault that she had taken this long to finish the education she had talked about doing long ago. She expected to have to withstand their verbal abuse to get what she wanted. Yes, she had married a man who made it harder for her to achieve her goals, she had expected Marion to say in much stronger language. But her mother no longer felt the need to badger her daughter, for they had reached a rapprochement long ago. Marion could not resist one final comment, though: she was glad to see her come to her senses. Her family would help in any way they could. The matter was settled.

At home, Alex felt her restlessness before she began to talk with him about her plans. Their marriage had become predictably stable, and he had lived with her long enough to know that when she decided to do something, nobody would have any peace until she'd done it. She was relieved that he agreed so easily with her plan of returning to Iowa and that he would stay in Jackson. She told him her thinking, assured him that she would not go unless Jackson State agreed to pay her full salary for the two years she was away, and that a teaching assistantship would cover her tuition at Iowa. Because they had been so saddled with financial problems, she did not want to add to his concerns with her pipe dreams. She felt at that moment she was fortunate to have a husband who understood her passion and was willing to let her go.

Firnist Alexander did not have the mind of a writer, but he knew his wife's heart, and he paid attention. He knew, too, that the famous poet he had married had been absent from the literary scene. Even though "For My People" continued to be popular, he recognized that his wife was receiving fewer and fewer speaking engagements and seldom got invitations to actually read her poetry anymore. Since most of what was being published were reprints, Alex recognized that he hadn't seen anything new published in a long while. For whenever she did, they would always celebrate together. Her family's continued hostility to him got the best of him sometimes, but Walker mediated it well. Maybe they were right: Margaret Walker had become a has-been, and he was partly responsible. The truth of the matter was that over the years of their marriage, he had become more and more amazed at his wife, a woman who had given up a career in full motion with much promise ahead to marry a man who was neither socially nor intellectually her equal. She never complained, at least not to him directly, about what she had lost. Walker, in turn, had learned that she had to make Alex feel that she needed him, which was never hard because she did. Their differences were something her parents had pointed out repeatedly, but Walker never felt that he embarrassed her. Their love offered them a common perspective that each of them alone did not have. At the same time, that love gave each of them an intimate understanding of the other. But Alex knew she needed something else, something he could not provide. It was his time to let go. He felt neither threatened nor abandoned. She needed to go to Iowa; she should not worry about the money. They would find a way, he assured her.

These were times when Walker knew that the worst part of their lives had ended, that the dissension between them had bound them together. She also understood something else: that his anger was not directed so much at her, but rather from his fear that he could not make her happy. He was experienced with women and knew how to make them happy. He was, therefore, unaccustomed to feeling that his wife was the one exception. Whenever this feeling arose, it translated into his need to exert more control and drove his fits of jealousy. Walker was not a woman who could be controlled. She had fought him with her quick tongue and sharp wit, which was all she had to counter his physical strength. He was a giant in comparison to her small size.

Neighbors recalled hearing them fighting constantly through the thin walls of the faculty barracks where they stayed in their first years in Jackson. What drove their passions was always the fear that they could not be what the other wanted or needed. She respected his strengths, his wisdom, his ease with the children that she did not have, his astuteness in matters of art and design, his gracefulness, and, of course, his attractiveness. She believed, and we have no evidence to suggest otherwise, that he loved her unconditionally despite an occasional indiscretion. He had even finished high school because he thought it would make her happy.

Walker knew that he was sexually appealing to other women, but she was confident that she was always first. At a time when women did not speak of intimacy, she admitted that Alex was all "man," someone who gave her complete sexual satisfaction. She was fully compliant and comfortable with him and knew when they met that she could never be with anybody else. Their relationship made her a richer, more substantial person. For these reasons, Firnist James Alexander could feel comfortable with his wife leaving for two years without his objections. Theirs might have been a flawed love, but it had replenished itself and reached near-perfection with time and, therefore, sustained each of them individually and together.

These thoughts about Alex would not be her last excursions into the past, but they released her from feeling that he was the most critical factor in her slow rate of accomplishments. This illumination that accompanied the subtle growth of experience was not unlike her recognition that the problem in writing *Jubilee* reflected a problem in her life, one of methodical organization and discipline. "It is not just a question of self-control in health, finances, emotions, tongue and energies, but now a real need to channel all these with real economy and conservative effort and restraint into the true and complete meaning and realization of all my life's purposes. . . . Now I not only have my finger on the problem, I know at long last what to do about it,"[6] she counseled herself.

Such breakthroughs typically came on or near her birthday on July 7, as this one did, marking a shift in her thinking and action. Because she was preparing to leave for several years, she knew she needed to recite for herself the lessons to take with her, knowing that the intensity of the years 1962–1965 would test her time and again.

She ended the 1962 school year at Jackson State on a high note. Once again she applied to President Reddix for a leave with pay, and this time he agreed to her terms: a two-year paid leave, after which she would return to JSU permanently. She wasted no time in preparing for the multiple departures. Marion had returned from Western College exuberant but tired. In between conversations with her daughter about the woes of being a college freshman, Walker packed for everybody. She calculated what James would need for one more year before heading off to college, and she packed almost everything that Sigis and Margaret needed for their long-term stay. She carefully organized her own clothes, paying the most attention to the books she wanted to take with her. She was not taking a car this time, so most of her things would have to be shipped. She and Alex had a final discussion about finances, with one remaining item: she needed a place to stay. She quickly wrote Alma Hovey, whose acquaintance she had renewed during her initial return, to tell her of the good news, and wondering if she wished to have a boarder. She would study on campus, remain quiet, and entertain no visitors, she told her. Hovey, now retired from the English Department and living alone, wrote back quickly. She looked forward to welcoming her into her home.

In fall 1962, she left for Iowa, moved in with Hovey, and began classes. "Miss Hovey," whom she had met when she first arrived at Iowa in 1939, was one of few women in a department filled with men. She had befriended Walker, the young girl from the South, right away. Their friendship was mutually beneficial and it would last until Hovey's death in 1986. In her response to Walker's request, Hovey had only one requirement: that she buy her own food. She was not planning to charge any rent. She assured her new tenant that she was thrilled to be seeing her again at a different stage in both their lives. Walker did not realize what kind of gift had come her way. When she shared her plan of completing the work in two years, Hovey was determined to help make it happen. Alma Hovey became Walker's accountability coach in modern-day terms, keeping close tabs on her schedule. *Jubilee*'s success would become Alma Hovey's as well as hers.

If *Jubilee* gave Walker a way to express what it meant to be a woman and a Negro in America, the search for a form for the novel was a far more difficult process. Telling the story was easy enough, as each of her teachers had tried to explain to her, beginning with E. B. Hungerford at Northwestern. Norman Holmes Pearson, with whom she had worked during her Ford Fellowship semester at Yale, had repeated that message in 1953, and now the voices of Verlin Cassill and Paul Engle at Iowa were a chorus in her ear. A first-time novelist rarely needed to discover what she needed to write. In fact, as Cassill and Engle reminded her, often the writer knows the story too well. What one needed to learn, and a primary reason she went to Iowa, was to understand how to show that story.

She knew her great-grandmother's life by heart, and after completing her first fiction workshops, concluded that her form would be that of the historical novel. Then she began her search for a narrative voice. She had considered first person, in the tradition of the slave narrative, but thought she could do more using the third person to capture Vyry's evolution as a young woman in the epoch-making periods she had planned the novel to cover. As an ancestral novel, it would become a composite of her many selves as extracted through her maternal kin. On the one hand, she was eager to celebrate the story of a survivor who could look back and look forward. On the other hand, conflicting feelings about constructions of Vyry's identity plagued her. In her earliest attempts at the novel, she always created Vyry through a series of the facts she gathered from her research. Engle was repeatedly critical because she did not allow the reader to see and feel the story, he told her. She tried to follow Cassill's advice not to overwhelm the story with emotion, but it created so much distance that she failed to make the character believable. How was she, an educated Negro woman, going to make an illiterate slave convincing to a reader? Nowhere in literature, at least up to 1961, were there stories of these women's lives under the system of slavery. The most popular novel, Margaret Mitchell's *Gone with the Wind*, was exactly what she was NOT trying to replicate.

The year went well, but the turbulence in Mississippi kept her attentive to matters at home. Just as her first year ended, she learned that her neighbor, Medgar Evers, whose family they had befriended and who had drawn significant public attention as field secretary for the Mississippi chapter of the NAACP, had been murdered in front of his home, with his wife and children inside. She had grown closer to his wife Myrlie, who had become a member of the Neighborhood Garden Club. The nation mourned as his young widow and their three children dealt with this terrible tragedy. Walker's youngest children and the Evers's children had been playmates. She knew she had to write to still her anger as much as to grieve for someone she had come to know well. "I have written an article that is both a tribute to Medgar Evers and an expose of the whole Mississippi story, but I dare not print it now. My family would be in danger, and there might be all kinds of reprisals."[7] The article never appeared in print, but in an unmarked journal entry in the same month that Evers was killed, Walker wrote:

Now, if ever there was a time to write and speak out for Negro freedom, it is now. Negroes in this country are in an uproar—the whole country, not just the South. And, yes, at last we are able to articulate and express our militancy in the South. Negroes everywhere are not only ready but demanding justice. Freedom—Liberty—Equality—Fraternity—the watchwords of the French Revolution are the words of Negroes today. We are all part of a world revolution—but we are also in the midst of a tide of revolt that is only one of the historical imperatives of the moment. This is the hour and this is the time—time and tide wait for no man—this is the tide and now is the time. The full tide of the Southern Revolution for Negro Freedom is now sweeping over America.... What Medgar Evers hoped to do, now seems to be started: The conscience of America—better thinking America—and men of good will be truly aroused. The general belief in gradualism and everything in due time is being thrown out of the window. Negroes want full rights and right now not tomorrow. As one newspaper article says: This is tomorrow![8]

When the formal part of this unpublished essay ended, she commented in her journal, "more essays and articles on the race issue propping out of my mind and on paper." More informally, she remarked that she had seen tension building since the Emmett Till case in 1955. "Nobody feels like waiting any longer."[9] But the tragedies began to compound themselves. The following November, President John F. Kennedy was brutally assassinated in Dallas. She noted in her journal for November 24 that Kennedy was "shot with a rifle much like the one

Funeral of Medgar Evers. Courtesy of the Ernest Withers Collection

that killed Medgar Evers. We all share the moral responsibility for such evil and violence in our midst."[10]

By her second year at Iowa, four little girls had been killed in the bombing of the 16th Street Baptist Church in Birmingham, the city of her birth. Freedom Summer had created a groundswell of activism in Mississippi. Enough momentum had been established to pass the Civil Rights Act and the Voting Rights Act, both in 1965. Knowing that the violence would not cease immediately, she began to think ahead to a new ending for *Jubilee*. Writing this book in the middle of such civil violence offered unique inspiration. As a Negro, a native Southerner, and adopted Mississippian, she shared the deep and profound sense of rage that was growing in the nation as a whole. Mississippi had become America's metaphor for all things evil.

Could she write a historical novel in which her readers could see the past truthfully exposed by imagining a different future? She began to feel that the novel had been called into service for a cause greater than she had imagined. She had answered the call once before; she knew now that she could not rest until the story was done. But *Jubilee* would be about the past, and she was filled with a sense of urgency about the present. She would resolve the tension between the two by returning to what felt familiar to her. An invitation to read at the annual meeting of the United Negro College Fund a few days after President Kennedy's assassination became her prayer "to God who will judge us for our actions . . . accounting for our stewardship."[11]

To give herself a break from classes and her novel writing, in 1964 Walker wrote two new poems. In the first, her preference for free verse combines with the formal elegy in a communal poem. "Epitaph for My Father" narrates the life of a man through the images of a world he left behind, a world he remembers for his daughter. That sense of loss becomes his permanent refuge and his source of strength. The more she wrote, the more memories of her childhood began to flow. "Epitaph" is one of the longest poems Walker ever wrote, filling five pages of the slim volume she published in 1973, *October Journey*, her most personal and, many believe, most unsuccessful volume. The mixed assortment harks back to her earlier work, which "Epitaph" attempts to do, and combined with the tribute and occasional poems does not make for a coherent volume. "Epitaph" does not achieve the dramatic power of "For My People," as it fuses her deepest memories with scenes of the familiar and familial. It is at once her father's story, her mother's story, the commencement of their love and life together, and their shared autobiographical journey. First comes the sense of place:

> Jamaica is an Island full of Bays
> Like jeweled tourmaline set in the sea.

> The Caribbean coasts are washed with dazzling sand
> So blinding white the sunlight flashes fire,
> And trade winds lash against the palm-strewn shore.

Then it establishes the connection:

> When I was very young and still quite small
> My father used to take me on his knee
> And say to me, "My little one; I wish that you could see
> The land where I was born—so beautiful!
> With fruit so sweet and land so rich
> Where black men, too, are free."

The poem plays freely with a range of feelings and emotions—gaiety, hopefulness, humor, her father's whimsical nature and spontaneity, his sadness and grief. Refreshing moments of satire emerge:

> And when he said, "I wish your verse were more religious,"
> I pertly said, "It can't be what I'm not!"

but return quickly to the reverential:

> And I belong to all the people I have met,
> Am part of them, am molded by the throng
> Caught in the tie of compromise, and grown
> Chameleon for camouflage. Yet I have known
> A noble prince like man for all my life.

When Walker remembers her father's final days, she reclaims the poem's central metaphor, a pilot of a ship setting out to sea. Death alone can reverse the profound sense of loss, as he symbolically makes that return to Jamaica from America, his final reunion with home as the poem draws to a conclusion:

> When suddenly the shades of night began to fall
> The ship at sea was tossed and buffeted
> He stood and watched the light
> That beckons every pilot to his harbor's home
> In resignation to the will and fate
> Of providence, the destiny of Men.[12]

"Epitaph" is not anchored in heightened allegorical meaning or abstraction. It is more emblematic and suggestive, making an emotional parallel between Kennedy's death and the loss of her father ten years earlier. The poem is the most biographical Walker would be in describing her father, in her poetry or prose. His influence and the nurturing of her early creative impulses made this a seminal poem for the new volume. Ultimately, however, it seems misplaced, perhaps an indication of what happens when the urgency of the moment takes over before the form of a poem has fully evolved. In terms of length and subject matter, it comes from another time. It does, on the other hand, fit perfectly her contemplative mood at the time it was written. Her response to the loss of two men, one a personal hero, the other a national one, came from her need to let go. She knew that both men were not ready to die. Walker notes her father's joy at having grandchildren, a joy mitigated only by their arrival so late in his life. The suddenness and circumstances of the loss of a national leader made her personal one more real. In order to accept the reality of her father, the first one, vivid memories of whom remained, she must accept both. "What we must understand is that [their] work was done . . . [they] had fought well, it was destiny and we must bow to the will of God."[13]

She mentions a second poem in which she wanted to do more truth telling about the evil and violence that led to the Kennedy assassination, questioning why people get illegal firearms to do so much harm to others. No title appears in her journal entry. Nor does the content match any later poem published— although it does point toward some later essays. What it tells us more directly is that she was actively writing poetry again. The events of the 1960s would have been reason to do so. But other reasons contributed to this revitalization. The days during her holiday school break provided much reflection time, confirmed by her daily journal entries. A course on Romantic poetry had reminded her how much she loved John Keats and the English Romantics in general. They were her father's favorite period in poetry and the first poetry they read together when she was a child.

The idea of "poetic genius" appealed to Walker immensely, prompting the words "I have never reached my peak of creative expression and fulfillment and now I feel myself on the verge of it."[14] Keats had died at twenty-five, only a few years after establishing himself as a major poet, and his young life provided a parallel to her own. Both were from poor families, had gone away to school, and excelled in the classics and history. Although he was emotionally unstable, he bore much of the responsibility for providing for his family's financial security, something that troubled him throughout his short life. Keats's brilliance came early and fast, accompanied by declining health, making further parallels to her situation. He had mastered the sonnet, the form that came to bear his name, a form she routinely used. Walker had read closely his biography and commented in her journal on his "sad life," no doubt feeling a strong kinship with his bouts of depression, anxiety, and recurring financial worries. She concludes one entry with "If only I may be allowed to finish my work before the time comes for me to die."[15]

The death of Evers and Kennedy as young men became an occasion for this kind of transference between and among the poet, national leaders, and greatness. Nor did she hesitate to see a likeness between herself and Kennedy, drawing inspiration from a remarkable man whom she believed belonged completely to the twentieth century, as she did.

Praising Kennedy's New Frontier initiative, Walker remembered her own youth and her first essay, "What Is to Become of Us?" Writing on the train as she headed home to spend Christmas 1963 with her family, Walker was confident that she had new poems for another volume. That book would have to follow *Jubilee* because she was close to the end, now that all of her coursework was done. As always, she knew that approaching the end of a project was often the sign of a new beginning. With the return to poetry, the self was reborn, and Margaret Walker began to approach the half-century mark of her life with a calm that she had never known before.

She returned to Iowa in January 1964 intent on enjoying her last six months of classes. Everything had gone smoothly up to this point. She had done well in her studies, and the *Jubilee* manuscript was progressing. The second of her children had entered college; James was at Grinnell, whose long tradition of social activism she was familiar with. She could spend time with her two oldest children as adults in a way that was not possible when she was in Jackson. Preparing a favorite meal on their occasional visits without feeling any sense of obligation was restorative. She had begun to enjoy this freedom from attachments with time to focus on her writing. Miss Hovey continued to hold her accountable. At their weekly dinner together, Hovey wanted to know if her schedule for writing had changed in any way. If not, the completion of *Jubilee* was going to be their shared joy.

What was to be her happiest time at Iowa, eager to see it come to an exciting close and signaling the success of her plan, changed when she learned she had failed her Latin exam. Her aptitude with languages had not helped. The French and German exams came easily, but she ended up taking the Latin exam twice before passing it. She concluded that racism in the Classics Department bore more responsibility for her failure than she did. But so much had gone right at Iowa that she did not complain. Instead, she and other students—all Black— commiserated their fate together. They studied together and determined that it was not likely that they could all fail if they took it at the same time. The strategy worked, and she believed that the climate of the times had probably influenced their decision about whether to fail a group of Negro students who had all done superior work. She did not waste her time, however. While waiting to take the Latin exam, she continued to visit classes on the novel and took notes on her approaches to *Jubilee*. By the spring, Walker decided to set her notes for *Jubilee* aside so that she could prepare for the comprehensive exams that the Latin exam had held up. Before she did, she spelled out the place that she saw *Jubilee* occupying in the pantheon of Southern writing in particular and historical fiction in general:

> Mark Twain uses a folk motif in *Huck Finn*; Faulkner grasps the sociological and historical; Margaret Mitchell has authentic Georgia dialect for whites but not philosophy or point of view; Tolstoy has the greatest canvas of war in *War and Peace*; the Russian character studies of dramatic scene and situation, and there is endless variety in Turgenev, Gorky, and Chekhov. I need to turn to the Greeks, the Bible for individual characters. The parallels between the Old Testament Hebrews and *Jubilee*'s Christian myth of redemption, with John's temptation in the wilderness, his deliverance, and baptism, blood and fire. Vyry must learn from her suffering and grow in tragic awareness because of all the senseless violence and cruelty. Ole Missy is also a suffering human being but a mean mistress; we have to see a reason for what happens to her. Marster Dutton must be seen as weak, ineffectual, conscience and sin-ridden, never overtly cruel but often evasive of his duty. Vyry is his conscience and symbolizes shame and embarrassment.[16]

Walker was excited, writing quickly and had switched a biblical reference and failed to clarify her meaning—not the book of Hebrews, but the Hebrew people of the Old Testament and Jesus, rather than John, was tempted in the wilderness, or rather the desert—nevertheless making her point. She left *Jubilee* right where she needed it to be. When she returned to writing, she would be ready to assemble the book without stopping.

As the summer approached, although she was preparing for the last hurdle, the comprehensive exam, she remained close to the growing Civil Rights Movement in Jackson. By the time she arrived home in June, three civil rights workers had been brutally slain by members of the Ku Klux Klan. James Cheney, Andrew Goodman, and Michael Schwerner would be the subject of her tribute to them that later appeared in *Prophets for a New Day*, her book that forced her into a mood she could not resist.

During the summer break she met Fannie Lou Hamer, Aaron Henry, Unita Blackwell, Mrs. Victoria Gray, and Mrs. Annie Devine, all of whom would go to the Democratic National Convention in Atlantic City, New Jersey. Walker was most impressed with Hamer, who was a towering presence over the movement, and one of the few members of the older generation that the younger activists seemed to respect. Following Hamer's speech at the convention, the state of

Fannie Lou Hamer singing "This Little
Light of Mine" before speaking in
1968. Courtesy of the Ernest Withers
Collection

Mississippi and its climate of violence was on everyone's mind, not only as the last
bastion of racism, but also as a place where martyrs were made. In her first poem
in what became *Prophets for a New Day*, Walker's imaginative powers displayed
this revelation. The voice for "Street Demonstration" is that of an eight-year-old:

> We're going to be arrested
> And hoping to go to jail
> We'll sing and shout and pray
> For Freedom and for Justice
> And for Human Dignity
> The Fighting may be long
> But Liberty is costly
> And Rome they say to me
> Was not built in one day
>
> *Hurry up. Lucille. Hurry up*
> *We're Going to Miss Our Chance to go to Jail.*[17]

Pleased with this new turn of events, Walker renewed her strength as she completed her exams in the fall of 1964. Though physically exhausted, her creative energies were at their fullest power. Finishing *Jubilee* would be a testament to the process of change and growth for her and for Mississippi at a time that seemed very dark. Fate that had too often dealt harshly with her was now offering her its gift. As the insurgent movement gathered speed in Mississippi and the nation, so did Walker's pen. Except for the Christmas holiday break, she worked continuously, writing furiously. Working out all of the details of the novel did not allow any distractions. She wrote with the zeal of a religious convert. Her motivation was so high that she failed to recognize her body's signs of weakness. She had begun to experience more frequent infections, and she had learned to expect all that came with a hypersensitive digestive system, including complications in her stomach and intestines, as well as kidney and liver problems, compounded, if not caused by, stress. But through it all, she stuck firmly to her goals.

From mid-January to April in 1965, her words came easily. In her last classes, in which she had studied Melville and Southern literature, she took notes and composed her own reading list, adding essays and books about Negro literature that had not been included in her assigned readings. Most were by her friends, including *Negro Voices in American Fiction* by Hugh Gloster, and "Negro Characters in Fiction as Seen by White Authors," by Sterling Brown. To find the balance she was looking for in terms of tone, character, and style, she identified the individual elements she would take from Southern writers she had been reading closely: memory and vision from Thomas Wolfe, violence and distortion from Faulkner, fantasy and realism from Eudora Welty, and she added Tennessee Williams.

"One hundred years since Appomattox," Walker wrote on April 9, 1965, "I have at last finished the civil war novel at 10:20 AM this spring day and all I could do was fall on my knees and say thank you, Jesus, Thank God!"[18] She celebrated with friends and splurged, buying new clothes that she told herself she needed for Marion's upcoming graduation from Western College. The dissertation was finally done, and it was so large, it had to be printed and bound in two separate volumes, the first including Parts 1 and 2 and the second Part 3.

Walker was clear that the end was only a bridge to her next and most important step, finding a publisher. She had her mind set on *Jubilee's* becoming a Book of the Month Club selection, and even considered that it might be Pulitzer Prize material, so the book would need to circulate to possible publishers immediately. She was confident that her committee would give her the most important criticism for revising it, leaving little for an editor to do. She had a team of the toughest readers, including Vance Bourjaily, who accepted the invitation to serve without much prompting from Verlin Cassill. Under the watchful eye of these men, who, with the exception of Engle, were younger than she was, she

Walker's 1965 dissertation that became *Jubilee*

discovered instincts she did not know she had. Miss Hovey, however, as the older, wiser teacher, played a more central role than anyone else. Walker might still question Engle and Cassill, but never questioned Hovey, who spent as much time reading the drafts as Walker did. Cassill had already put her in touch with Dorothy de Santillana at Houghton Mifflin in Boston. Bypassing an agent, which would become her custom, Walker had written to her even before finishing the manuscript.

She was ready to let the novel go, even though the separation felt like she was losing a part of herself. She was so immersed in the period about which she was writing that she had become part of the characters she had created.

"The people became so real I could hear them think, see them walk, become involved with them and their problems."[19] She had promised to send the manuscript as soon as the revisions were done, and by May, she had completed all the requirements at Iowa, sent her books and clothes home to Jackson, and prepared to ship her *Jubilee* manuscript to Houghton Mifflin with a personal letter to de Santillana.

There was one more person she needed to call: E. B. Hungerford was excited but confessed his fear that she had waited too long. But she had not. *Jubilee* was finished when it mattered the most. Walker signed her note to de Santillana, "I shall eagerly await your reaction and I promise not to be thin skinned."[20]

The most important person that *Jubilee* needed to please was Margaret Walker. She offered her frank assessment:

> I am satisfied with the rounded out lives of my main characters—the creatures of their time and their place. I have realized situations and completely realized people. My language and dialect are my greatest strength. I have striven for a consistent tone, a consistent voice, and atmosphere . . . more than a folk novel, more than an historical or Civil War novel, more than a novel of social protest or outrage and yet it is all of these—it is a human document.[21]

Her "human document" was most certainly "important as a background and pre-history of the present-day Negro struggle, for civil and human rights. This is a story never before fully told, never before really known. . . . It is wrong to say this is another Negro answer to *Gone with the Wind*,"[22] she wrote.

Walker was breaking with the tradition of a recent trend in Black literature. Arna Bontemps had been the last Black author to treat the subject of slavery, three decades earlier with *Black Thunder*. James Baldwin and Ralph Ellison were her most obvious competition. But Walker believed she had provided what America needed in the 1960s, "an epic of a stirring, changing time."[23]

Jubilee is a history of slavery and reconstruction, as seen through the eyes of a female slave who was born on a Georgia plantation owned by John Dutton. Following the death of her mother in the opening pages, Vyry becomes the child of the plantation, cared for by various slave women in the quarters as well as in the Big House. Up to this point, *Jubilee* sounds like a typical Civil War novel: Dutton, the plantation owner, is her father, and the story moves through the events of the Civil War and the devastation of the Dutton household, and introduces us to a struggling group of Black and white characters who are trying to make sense of their lives in a system that has radically changed.

Walker sets up a love story to frame the development of the novel. Vyry's search is for Randall Ware, the free man with whom she falls in love, marries, and conceives two children. When Ware leaves, he convinces Vyry that she, too, must escape slavery by running away. Unable to part with her children, she escapes with them but is caught and remanded to slavery. After she is returned to the Dutton plantation, she never tries to escape again, raises their two children, and on learning that Ware is dead, marries another slave, Innis Brown. Together, Brown and Vyry share a life together, navigating post-slavery life and Reconstruction to become important forces in the several communities in which they become part. The novel ends with the return of Ware and a triumphant moment for Vyry, who must decide how she will help to give birth to a new Black nation.

Although it describes the general development of the plot, this brief summary of *Jubilee* disguises its most important features. Readings of the novel focus on a critique of Vyry, whose loyalty most critics found disturbing. By 1987, with the publication of *Beloved* by Toni Morrison, reconsiderations of the work of Black women writers were essential, and *Jubilee* became the predecessor to a new kind of literary fiction.

Regardless of her status during her hiatus, Walker wrote herself back into acclaim as a writer with *Jubilee*. From the beginning she envisioned Vyry's narrative as a success story. The novel not only helped her to revoice the past from a new perspective, but it also told the story of Black women enduring the most difficult period of history our nation has ever known. Walker knew that slavery was a repressive period for African Americans, but it was especially oppressive for Black women. One of the features of the novel is the array of female characters intended to represent the viewpoints of women and levels of slave culture. We watch as Vyry's subjectivity changes from an inferior status to a respected member of a community in which she plays a leadership role. At the time *Jubilee* was written, there were no narratives with women protagonists set during slavery written by Negro writers. Harriett Jacobs's *Incidents in the Life of a Slave Girl* had yet to be authenticated and therefore was not reissued until some years later. Hence Walker's decision to give Vyry a voice broke an inveterate silence in Black fiction on life before Emancipation. Similarly, *Jubilee* broke Walker's silence; she had invested Vyry with the kind of moral authority she believed women held in the domestic sphere, an authority that extended into the broader society.

In *Jubilee*, Walker was consciously writing herself into a text as a woman engaging the ideological debates of the Civil Rights Movement, which had some of its most intense moments in the South and specifically in Jackson, Mississippi. What Walker brought to the surface, long before its articulation among Black feminists, was the relationship of gender to all of these issues. *Jubilee* is evidence of the evolution and development of a woman's narrative voice, both inside and outside of home and community.

Walker's strong religious training grounded in the Methodist Church, accompanied by her ongoing practice, Bible reading, prayer, and assorted religious literature, support Vyry's characterization as a woman whose values transcend the temporal. The display of Christian humanism makes her both a target for radical attack and a martyr among women during Reconstruction. Vyry is a sacred voice in a secular world as Walker expands the domestic plot to accommodate her historical and ideological concerns.

Just as the conception of *Jubilee* was a series of oral exchanges between a grandmother and her granddaughter, so too does Vyry's growth reflect the knowledge gained through the exchanges between and among the slave women on Dutton's plantation. While Walker herself had often played the role of listener to her grandmother's original story, and the character Vyry plays the role of listener to stories from slave women in the Big House, we as readers become listeners to what these women tell us in the narrative.

The concept of storytelling is, therefore, central in the novel. Yet, *Jubilee*'s most distinctive contribution is the use of a folk voice as an authenticating strategy for a fictional narrative that explores race and gender in new ways. It allowed Walker to appropriate narrative authority generally assigned to white authors of Civil War novels like *Gone with the Wind*, and male authors of slave narratives like *Narrative of Frederick Douglass, an American Slave*. Unlike the genre of the conventional slave narrative, Walker presents the entire novel through the lens of folklore. In the nineteenth-century slave narratives, the acquisition of formal literacy symbolized achievement of freedom, thus making a distinctive break with the vernacular tradition. The slave narrator had to show the visible signs of a new self as a way of signifying a successful escape from the repressive system that made it illegal to teach a slave to read and write.

In *Jubilee*, the journey toward freedom is exchanged for Vyry's search for and journey toward a home that she can call her own. Each of her attempts to make a home meets with disaster, just as the slave faced defeat in attempting to escape from slavery before meeting with success. By reversing the male narrative of a runaway slave whose successful escape authorized his narrative, Walker suggested that the real narrative authority rests in one's ability to create and sustain community and to make a contribution in supporting the lives of others. After her own twenty years of marriage, Walker felt compelled to insist on a female voice emphasizing womanly concerns, believing that this kind of domestic feminism had as much of a right to a hearing as the more overtly political debates.

Later reviews of the novel missed Vyry's allegorical significance, a woman who serves as an exemplar carrying out a leadership role, as she exercises her domestic responsibilities. Although the political discourse in the novel appears to rest with Randall Ware, who runs for office during Reconstruction, Vyry doubles for Ware in the private world of the family. Her work in the community involves education and health care: she is a midwife whose concerns for human life go beyond the bounds of race. Moreover, by letting her son go away with his newly discovered father, she is giving her son to the cause of Reconstruction; undoubtedly he will continue the work begun by his father.

By extending the political discourse about the Civil War and Reconstruction into the domestic realm of gender relations, Walker made *Jubilee* more than a conventional historical novel. And yet it was with the historical novel that she began the composition history of *Jubilee*. As she read more and more works and researched the history of her own family in Greenville, Alabama, and Dawson, Georgia, the story developed its own narrative voice with characters drawn from her family history. Hence, *Jubilee* is both a moral and theological text, just as it is a social and historical one.

The autobiographical significance of *Jubilee* goes beyond Randall Ware and his descendants. Combining a family narrative with elements of the slave narrative gave Walker the flexibility to alternate between versions of lived history and its fictional recreations. But she made Vyry's ideas and belief system analogous to her own. Studies of the novel have failed to recognize this relationship, pointing out that Walker does not permit Vyry to move outside the boundaries of the stereotype of the loyal slave.

Walker's views of domestic feminism had evolved naturally. She had two distinct family models: her grandmother, who had performed all the responsibilities within the household, and her mother, who had been influenced by Nannie Helen Burroughs and a generation of like-minded Black women. For these women, racial uplift was the responsibility of working women as it was men. Marion Walker's talents and abilities were creative, and they allowed her to develop an identity as a public, working woman outside the home. Two of Marion's daughters followed her example in creativity: a skilled poet was comparable to a skilled musician. For Walker, both abilities affirmed the operation of a feminine principle, a balance in nature that the world required: "feminism and femininity: the sea, the earth, the air, fire, and all life whether plant or animal,"[24] as she would write in a later essay.

Women were also at the center of world religions, she believed, offering a more holistic view of history and the humanities in her essay "Chief Worshippers at All World Altars." In "Reflections on Black Women Writers," she placed women squarely within the humanistic tradition of African American literature where they embraced both the gothic and sentimental. Perhaps the most critical is her essay "Black Women in Academe," a scathing indictment of sexism in the various institutions where she had worked. She was finally able to bring herself to publicize her early experiences and name them clearly.

Some of these later ideas linked her to the growing feminist movement, but at the time she published *Jubilee*, second-wave feminism had already begun to take on more radical overtones that made her ideas unpopular. "No young writers had time for a black woman who remained loyal to a slave heritage that blacks were still struggling to overcome in the 1960s," Trudier Harris reminds us, explaining why many considered *Jubilee* "outdated from the date of its publication."[25]

The novel did have its share of enthusiastic critics. Hortense Spillers found "characters ... moving ... under the aegis of a Higher and Hidden Authority ... a theonomous frame of moral reference," and referred to the novel as a "long and protracted praise piece, a transformed and elaborated prayer . . . invocation to the guiding spirit and genius of her people . . . [with] no immediate precedent in Afro American literary tradition."[26] Other critics regarded the novel as overloaded with unnecessary details, which Walker did not fully integrate into the narrative. That such critics would assert a formalistic appraisal for a novel that "had no precedent" seems unusual indeed. Regardless of the novel's uneven critical response, Walker established a readership that was unparalleled, with book signings and appearances that provided continuous validation.

In a 1989 interview for WGBH in Boston, Walker talked about her creative process of writing a novel, as distinct from writing poetry. Because she had always been attracted to words and structures, putting poems together had come relatively easy to her. A poem's language was abbreviated and concise, and structure was important. Although the narrative form permitted more freedom with words, at the same time, it required greater responsibility for directing the lives of individual characters that made up the story. In addition, seeing herself as opinionated and outspoken, Walker did not attribute those qualities to the enslaved woman she wrote about. At the same time, she wanted to present a woman whose pervasive self-denial did not disguise her strength of character or will. Vyry would need to be sufficiently modest, so that her readers would see her as a woman of her era. But as a heroine, her voice would have to be central. Walker's intent was to depict Vyry's fuller life as a woman and mother in the context of a community at a critical period of change, as she saw in *War and Peace*, a novel she regarded highly.

She resisted the temptation to make *Jubilee* a tragic story, because she wanted it to be a celebration. Within the context of the downfall of one society and the birth of another, *Jubilee* delivers Walker's most important message about a woman who will not allow her philosophy of life to be undermined. Her inner strength ensures its permanence.

22

A Woman of Ideas

Walker saw the professional and personal success that she had achieved by 1968 as the fulfillment of a 1959 prayer:

> Dear Friends at *Silent Unity*, thanks for answering prayers.
> I ask for your continued blessing in this my 15th year of silence.
> I must publish, I must buy a car, I must get another degree.
> I must educate my children.[1]

Whenever her dreams came true, Walker took it as a sign that God had not abandoned her, and that all of her sacrifices had been worth it. Seeking affirmation through prayer requests to *Silent Unity* freed her from the judgments of others who might consider her too bourgeois or arrogant or who were simply jealous. She knew not to ask for much, but was bold and unabashed in her requests. Over the years, she had learned to find the balance between her need for personal success and goals that she set for her children and family. *Jubilee* was doing well, two children had completed college, and Sigis was about to begin his first year at Tougaloo College in Jackson.

Had it not been for the telltale signs of an aging body, at fifty-three, she would have seen herself as enjoying her new life rather than counting down the days before she would be "over the hill" as a Southern woman. She was comfortable, and with book royalties steadily coming in, her family had more financial stability than they'd ever known. Translation requests for *Jubilee* were mounting, and Yale had agreed to reissue *For My People*, which had gone out of print. Poets might be distant and abstract, some believed, but writers of fiction imagined a world that was, is, or should be. She was fortunate to be both a poet and a novelist at a time when the interest in Black history and culture was never higher. She became one of the most popular speakers because she could alternate between the writers and traditional historical figures, and speak cogently about contemporary affairs. It mattered that she *knew* most of the writers she usually talked about.

Walker's ability to move away from the usual literary topics demonstrated the sharpness of her intellect; she had unique perspectives on social issues and could offer them at will. Nevertheless, her age, gender, and personality did not fit comfortably the dominant model of the late 1960s. Those who earned the title of "Black militant" or "Black radical" were usually young charismatic males with

The House Where My Soul Lives. Maryemma Graham, Oxford University Press. © Oxford University Press 2022.
DOI: 10.1093/oso/9780195341232.003.0022

quick wit and fast delivery. Married to a revolutionary rhetoric, they exuded a distinct urban style, teeming with confidence and authority. They could be hot-headed, resistant, and inflammatory when the urgency of their cause demanded. In contrast, Walker was grounded in the history of ideas and interested in bringing information that helped people understand the nature of a world in crisis. She gave studied attention to whatever topic emerged, whether it had to do with war, politics, domestic concerns, or international affairs, always staying within the canons of good taste, refusing to betray her Southern etiquette, no matter how radical her ideas might be.

Walker was committed to remaining at Jackson State, but with a new role for herself. The face of higher education in the United States was about to change but was doing so in ways that most citizens were struggling to comprehend. Evidence of this at Jackson State, like many Negro schools, meant that a new breed of students were no longer content with the way things were. The Jackson State to which Walker returned displayed an activist sensibility, unlike the one she had left. By this time, white Southern leadership was accustomed to confrontations with resistant youth who had to be taught a lesson. It took very little on the students' part to prompt extreme reactions from the military and the police. The presumptions of the newly coined phrase "Black Power" wrestled with the law-and-order policies of the Nixon administration, resulting in deaths of unarmed Black youth throughout historically Black colleges and universities in the South. These actions far outstripped those in white institutions during the same period,[2] Martha Biondi's study determined. Those called on to quell the unrest on Negro campuses, for whatever cause, were "allowed to carry weapons of their choice to campus . . . [and] permitted wide discretion in lethal weaponry,"[3] leading to the ensuing blood baths and rampant killings of Black youth.

The excessive force and violence typical at Negro schools, directed exclusively toward African American students, seemed neither called for nor justified. Fear drove these actions: the same fears that made it illegal to teach Blacks to read under enslavement and the same fears that inspired miscegenation laws and brutal lynchings which found their parallel in the violence voting rights activists faced in Mississippi. According to Biondi, while national reports condemned the wanton display of disrespect for property and personhood, violent responses "far exceeded the danger"[4] the students presented. The extreme responses were examples that Southern states believed to be necessary to warn a younger generation in particular, against raising their expectations about a different South in which they wanted to live, and especially about expressing their newfound civil rights.

Over and over again, the Southern response and forceful actions equated with a license to kill. The cause did not matter. Students might have been conducting a sympathy protest in conjunction with the February 1968 killing at all-Black

South Carolina State College—the Orangeburg Massacre—that became the first instance of police brutality against demonstrators. Or, as was the case at Southern University in Baton Rouge, Black students could be protesting their severely underfunded education or inferior facilities drawing increased attention to the reality that separate continued to mean unequal. Even if Black presidents and administrators agreed with the students, they could not do so publicly. Southern governors and politicians believed it was necessary to validate white authority, and they did so by any means necessary. White Southern leaders appeared little concerned with how others viewed their violently repressive tactics.

With the exception of the Kent State massacre of June 1970, white students who boycotted, occupied buildings, seized properties, and presented demands to administrators received reprimands and were occasionally expelled, but they did not encounter the same viciousness by police and the military as Black students at Negro schools. These markedly different experiences at white institutions in the North, West, and Midwest caught Walker's attention, especially when they hit so close to home.

Her interest shifted from occasional journal entries about the racial turmoil in the nation to full engagement, as if she were preparing to complete a long-overdue assignment. Walker could bring a much-needed historical context to what she saw or heard in the news and on television because of her background. Feeling a deep kinship with the new generation, and thinking back to "What Is to Become of Us," she began to express her thoughts more openly and saw value again in the essay format. Many of the ideas would inform later published essays. "Religion, Poetry, History: Foundations for a New Educational System," for example, was one of her first attempts to explain what she believed was happening:

> Our young people today seem to be seething in a boiling caldron of discontent. Like the youth of every generation, they want to know, and they demand to be heard. Like youth in every age, they are the vanguard of our revolutionary age. They are the natural leaders of revolution, whether that revolution be of race, class, or caste; whether it is sexual or academic; whether it is political or intellectual. Today the revolution we are witnessing encompasses all of these, for the violence of revolution not only threatens but definitely promises to sweep out every corner of our outmoded existence. Violence today is more than a tool of tyranny, as it has always been; it is also the tool of revolution.[5]

"Revolution" was not a new concept for Walker. Although it had been thirty years since she'd read any communist literature, especially Karl Marx's theory of revolution, she was surprised how quickly the ideas came back to her. In most of the meetings at the Workers School she attended in Chicago in 1936, she had learned to apply a basic materialist analysis to US conditions. In her original thinking, the focus was on workers' revolution. She easily shifted her thinking to paint the kind of portraits she believed people needed to see. Young and impressionable, she had been drawn to the revolutionary rhetoric of her comrades during the 1930s, claiming their passion as her own. This gave deeper meaning to her experience writing poetry, although the landscapes remained in the South. Looking back at her earlier work, she saw images, while expertly drawn, ringing with nostalgia.

By the time she reactivated her revolutionary consciousness, her vision had broadened, but so had her creative interests. What she was thinking and needed to say was more expansive and more explicit than poetry. She asked herself if she could afford to be more aggressive, take more risks. The amount of social criticism that Walker produced between 1968 and 1992 suggests that she answered this question in the affirmative.

The questions Walker found herself asking were not new. As a child and a young woman, a fierce desire to find answers to those questions led her to make bold pronouncements in her poetry. "Let another world be born, / Let a race of men now rise and take control," she said at the end of "For My People."[6] Nearly three decades later, she believed that it was about to happen, even if no one knew what the world was to become. With the benefit of her enriched economic, political, and social understanding, she could pry issues apart and see far and wide. With the long period of obscurity finally behind her and sharpened sensibilities, she could reclaim her voice and deliver a more powerful message. She would see revolution in a new context. Keeping focused on the fundamental principle of dialectical materialism, Walker explained what she saw in ways that made the most sense to her:

> We are not only shedding the old ways of the past. We are overwhelmed by the problems of a new universe. We stand under the watershed of the twentieth century totally unprepared for the innovations of the twenty-first century already rushing headlong upon us. The historical process, of which we are a part, does not necessarily mark off the cycles of our progress with the man-made dates or hours we have set for change. The life of the twenty-first century has already begun while the debris of the structures in a dying twentieth century crashes all around us.[7]

These sharp analyses of politics, local and national, and ecological and environmental concerns about America and the world came easily to her, and they dominate her journals throughout the 1960s. Because she was invited to give lectures based on her reputation as a poet and novelist, these comments, though on point, did little to gain the attention of the mainstream media. The larger national conversation that was taking place in the late 1960s appeared to proceed without her. The leading voices in the media, who would become embedded in America's consciousness, were again generally male or based in the North, and far younger than she.

One of those voices was Stokely Carmichael, who had emerged as a leader of the demonstrations and student protests at Howard University. By the time Walker met him, he had graduated and joined other young activists in Mississippi. Stokely gave the phrase "Black Power" its biggest push in a speech in Greenwood, Mississippi. The strategy of nonviolence as a means of accomplishing social change was in its last days for these younger activists, and Stokely would help bury it. Walker was not a champion of violence in any form, but she did embrace the idea of "A Black University," a term gaining momentum within the Negro college community. The concept centered on the kinds of transformations necessary in those institutions whose beginnings dated back to the era of American segregation. The movement was not necessarily anti-integration, but it operated with the understanding that the majority of Negro students would continue to receive their education at Negro institutions and that these institutions had an obligation to prepare a different kind of student for a transformed America.

Contemplating how education might serve social change, Walker kept writing and sharing her ideas whenever she could. She wanted to create new institutional models that she could begin to implement. Her legacy would not be only that of a literary artist, but also that of a visionary concerned about the future of the nation and the world in which she believed Black people would be central. Her ideas, drawn from the copious notes scattered throughout her journals, focused on developing new intellectual practices that required studying, researching, and debating the Black experience from a range of disciplinary perspectives. By 1969, she was conceiving of what would become Black Studies, with the locus of her work in a Southern Black institution.

Although Walker began her project earlier and laid out a plan for execution that was more forward-thinking than many of those that followed in the name of Black Studies, public attention was directed elsewhere. The presence of a critical mass of African American students for the first time at Cornell, Columbia, Harvard, the City College of New York, San Francisco State, Berkeley, and Northwestern gave rise to dramatic events and labored intensity that would become the yardstick by which the movement would be measured.

Since she had returned to writing for a good part of each day, she had a speech that was always ready before she secured an engagement. "The Challenge of the 1970s to the Black Scholar," one of the topics that claimed a great deal of attention, showed the evolution of her thinking away from criticism of her colleagues at Jackson State and toward proactive solutions. In its published form, the essay puts the spotlight on the relationships between students and the scholars who teach them, especially at Negro colleges, which were now being regularly referred to as HBCUs. If Negro students were changing, she argued, then so must the Black scholar:

> I believe it is an absolute necessity that we develop a whole new generation of scholars and that they understand their obligation to black people as we seek to change our world and our society from what it is to what it ought to be. Let me begin by quoting from a scholarly journal a definition of the black scholar. The black scholar "is a man of both thought and action who thinks for his people and acts with them, a man who sees the PhD, the janitor, the businessman, the maid, the clerk, the militant, as all sharing the same experience of blackness, with all its complexities and its rewards."[8]

Walker presented a broad appeal to the intellectual community, securing her position as an agent of social change. Her battleground was education; the foundation of her authority, Black institutions. Her goal was to ensure their legitimacy and relevance in a period when far too many considered them products of a past era with no relevance in a post–civil rights America. Walker became an unassailable force in a new movement in American higher education, one she was uniquely qualified to see from the inside and out. She saw a "Black revolution" through several lenses. The apocalyptic perspective meant it was inevitable and unavoidable for a nation refusing to change its course. To ignore it would take the nation to hell and damnation. She also saw Black revolution as a clarion call for a new kind of aggressive action on the part of African Americans.

Many associated Walker, a writer who had reestablished her career in the 1960s, with the highly visible Black Arts Movement (BAM). BAM had set itself apart from the earlier and main current of American and African American literature, to which Walker had belonged. She respected those younger artists who had absorbed the ideals and the urgency of a Black nationalist sensibility, producing a new rhetoric and poetic idiom for the period. As a college teacher, she embraced the new art and its aspirations, although she preferred to remain largely outside the ideological debates identified with BAM's various configurations. Sharp lines were often drawn among the artists themselves and often depended on one's group affiliation and location. Chicago, New York, and San Francisco seemed to have the upper hand, although the movement was far larger in scope and cultural and artistic output. Howard Rambsy's reading of the period suggests a multifaceted movement, its impact hard to fully grasp because of divergent locales, the symbiotic relationship between various public dialogues, personalities, and inventive practices, and the range and type of its influence. "As a series of smaller movements," says Rambsy, "its legacies are continually unfolding."[9] Looking back at Walker's work during this period makes it difficult to comprehend its complexity because her specific accomplishments led to transformations that became a routine part of the social and educational environment, which were difficult to trace to a single person.

A most recognizable change was her deliberate shift from "Negro" to "Black" in her journals. She retained her opposition to violence but questioned the viability of the nonviolent platform of the Civil Rights Movement. Ultimately, Walker saw the 1960s as a new time to reclaim her earlier radicalism. Unlike the presidents of HBCUs, Walker did not need to become a skillful manipulator afraid to display any brilliance she had, or to balance the demands of a controlling white establishment, the needs of their local Black communities, and their students. She was, rather, part of a unique infrastructure within the institution. Black exclusion from white institutions before 1960 created the "indignant generation,"[10] according to Lawrence Jackson, a cohort of scholars at HBCUs who had prestige, but none of the privilege and access of their white peers. They saw limitations as something to be exceeded and were as demanding of their students as they were of themselves, believing, as Walker did, that their gifts and talents were representative.

Like other members of her generation, Walker exceeded the limitations imposed on her not only as a Black person, but also as a Black *woman* when she became one of the most accessible published writers and sought after speakers who remained at HBCUs. What made her distinctive was her unwillingness to reject anything she learned, even when it seemed diametrically opposed to what mattered most to her. She did not need to reject Marx's belief that religion was the opiate of the people, focusing instead on the theory of world revolution that a world in chaos will inspire the poor and disfranchised to rebel. This belief she took as both radical philosophy and divine prophecy.

Her ideas, therefore, reflect a characteristic dualism. While she might not reconcile Marxism with her return to a Christian religious faith, she consistently reaffirmed her belief that the nation was in a revolutionary period and expressed gratitude for the activists of the 1960s. She saw no contradiction between the artist and the revolutionary struggle, believing that artists and the arts had a unique role to play in transforming the world, and that her own work had been evidence of this possibility. "I do not stop writing to join the activists in the struggle, I *am* in struggle when I *am* writing,"[11] she vehemently announced.

In her journals, she continued to share her observations, pose questions, and search for answers, interspersed with readings from the Bible and the *Daily Word*. Quoting passages and excerpts heavily, her journal entries often extended for pages, her intensity increasing as her analysis deepened. Part of her intensity was due to a need to replace some of the fundamentalist Puritan influences of her childhood without denying their positive effects. She maintained her scriptural practice, daily prayer, and her preoccupation with perfection, which implicitly supported change and transformation. Fundamentalism she let go, seeing it as antimodern; wedded to a form of orthodoxy, it had no place for new interpretation or change. Walker was looking for validation and support from people with whom she could share her own anxieties, which she kept from plain view, because she associated them with weakness. The only choice was to follow different spiritual threads simultaneously, each one accounting for different aspects of her life.

She believed in penitence as well. Teaching a course on the Bible at her church was part of her religious practice by sharing her thoughts with others. Keeping a steadfast faith was directly connected to the blessings that God might bestow. Her ongoing search for a more self-directed faith, especially one that had both components of a scientific philosophy and prophecy, she satisfied through the ordered universe that her lifelong passion for astrology confirmed.

Rather than unsettling her radicalism, such activities nourished it. She pushed against the boundaries of knowledge, forcing herself to contend with ideas that she found challenging. She grew more comfortable with the analytical method that she adopted as ideas took shape in her mind. Often, she moved seamlessly across the lines of history, theology, political economy, and class analysis, creating her own philosophy. What she wrote was always a revelation, an interpretation at a critical moment, when no single field of study or knowledge was sufficient. Walker came to the idea of interdisciplinarity naturally, just as her formal training in the classics underscored her interpretation of the humanities, both of which became central to her organizational and institutional practice. All knowledge reflected a sense of the unity in physical and human nature, and she assembled the segments that supported her belief.

As an artist who wrote, studied, and taught literature, she had a composite view of knowledge, rather than a view of knowledge in separate spheres. Thus, when she superimposed her political and economic theories from the 1930s on the empirical evidence of late 1960s, she found support for her belief that the United States would become a fascist, military state. Such a state of affairs required further examination of those fields of study that gave people more insights into this phenomenon. When she tried to put these convictions into words, her poetry seemed stiff and forced, like the poem "On Police Brutality":

> I remember Memorial Day Massacre
> Nineteen thirty-seven in Chicago
> And I was in the Capital of D.C.
> May of nineteen seventy-one
> When they beat all those white heads
> And put two thousand souls in jail
> I wasn't in South Commons Boston
> Neither when Crispus Attucks died

Nor South Boston when the rednecks rioted
But I remember Boston
Where I couldn't buy a hot pastrami sandwich
In a greasy joint.
I remember living there in fear
Much as some would feel in Mississippi
I was neither in Watts, Los Angeles, California
In nineteen sixty-five
Nor Detroit in nineteen sixty-seven
And I remember all the fuss over LeRoi Jones
In Newark, New Jersey, too.
Now Santa Barbara, California, is remembered
As a separate incident, a separate thing
From Kent State in Ohio
And Jackson State in Mississippi
And Orangeburg, South Carolina
And Texas Southern.
But to me they were all of one piece
Of the same old racist rag.
And all of these things are part
Of what I call Police Brutality.[12]

This transition period in Walker's life, documented in her longer journal entries, served several purposes. She could employ the best practices she learned in her academic training for clarifying ideas, planning and outlining their implementation. Journal writing provided a silent partner with whom she needed to communicate when opportunities for open dialogue and discussion were limited. With an heavy teaching load at Jackson State, she appreciated a social and mental escape. The journal writing also gave her the voice that she thought had been lost, drawing her back to unfinished writing projects and new ones. Finally, her longer, free-style entries observed no limits or boundaries: she could write until she gave out, which she often did. She could explore ideas without committing to them, believing that her writing was best for bringing valuable new insights into what was happening in the country.

Becoming a woman of ideas gave Walker much pleasure, since it expanded her audiences beyond the readings at literary and civic events, and academic institutions. *Jubilee*'s lecture circuit included smaller towns more often than big cities. In smaller towns she met people who had not read her work, people whom others would have quickly dismissed. Walker treated them as if they were special, worthy of knowing more about and contributing to contemporary social and political topics. She knew how to vary her style, her rhythm, and emphasis without talking down to people. If Hughes was the people's poet, Walker had the people's ear, and she could be their voice. The smaller venues were lucrative as well since she turned no engagement down and traveled by car. When all the expenses were paid, she saw a profit. The small towns and those less educated kept her career in full bloom.

The public shift in Walker's journal writing reached the high point after 1968. Reciting personal history, reviewing current events, and making larger connections eliminated the need to focus on what others said about her. Helping others understand what the news media did or could not say gave Walker a new mission. The thinking aloud that she did with others eased her anger and bitterness at those colleagues whose respect she sought. She could let go of the need to prove them wrong, as other matters were more important.

Recurring thoughts about Martin Luther King Jr., recorded in a journal entry shortly after learning about his assassination, gave her material for one of her most popular unpublished speeches. She gave it often and in different versions, all of which she knew by heart. Her favorite was the one that made an important connection to Mississippi:

> The gun [that killed King] was similar to the rifle that killed Medgar Evers and John F. Kennedy. These three assassinations have all happened in less than five years. What can the world expect from America? Are we really a sick society so sick that this thing can appear again and again with no murderer caught or punished? What is the prognosis? For this non-violent movement and the Southern Christian Leadership Conference? For the Negro people, for the nation at large?

She saw King's death as a changing of the guard, and she rightly saw the struggle for new leadership as a major question in an organization dedicated to nonviolence in the midst of widespread national violence. Her musings continued:

> We American people must set this house in order but doing so is a herculean task. Our political future is insecure. Will Rockefeller run and name Reagan as his running mate? What about labor in its great support of Hubert Humphrey? Can the Kennedy family buy the Presidency again, this time for Bobby? What effects if any will George Wallace have? How soon before Senator Eugene McCarthy admits he's finished, kaput, and gets out of the race? What are the chances for Richard Nixon, and above all can President Johnson truly be drafted to serve the country for another four years?[13]

Her conclusion that "these questions lead to answers for the Negro People . . . and likewise whatever happens to us determines the destiny of America" had become by the late 1960s one of the most publicly acknowledged facts as the course of the Civil Rights Movement shifted from a race-based effort to a full-out struggle for human rights.

The political made personal was another way in which she made connections. Sigis had an Afro and wore one of the uniforms of the student movement, the Nehru jacket, which like the Mao jacket showed sympathy for the independence struggles of people of color—the Third World, as many referred to it at the time. But Sigis's outward changes were just a sign of things to come.

She was glad he had chosen Tougaloo, a private institution that stood at the center of the Civil Rights Movement activism in Mississippi, in keeping with the mission of the college's founders. Tougaloo had openly supported the Freedom Riders from their beginning in 1961 and provided support to those involved in the 1964 Mississippi Summer Project. A Tougaloo student, Ann Moody, had published her memoir, *Coming of Age in Mississippi*, in 1968 describing the causes and consequences of coming to consciousness as a Black student— especially as a Black woman - during the 1960s. It became the bible of the Black Student Movement in the South.

The assassination of Robert Kennedy in June 1968, two months after Martin Luther King's death, made Walker more keenly aware of her forecast: a troubled nation with no peaceful solution in sight. She asked questions that needed an- swers, and while she found political and economic explanations helpful, she was drawn to Black intellectual history. The Black Power Movement had con- verged with Walker's growing popularity and visibility, providing a platform she had longed for. Her keynote address at a centennial for the birth of W. E. B. Du Bois (1868–1963) was one of them. She spoke about Du Bois's dedication "to his people, the Negro race, those dark-skinned descendants of Africa and citizens of the African Diaspora and their struggle for freedom, justice, peace, and human dignity."[14]

She could link Du Bois not only with the founding of sociology as a dedicated field of study but also with the "great protest movement in the struggle for civil and human rights, for peace and racial justice."[15] Walker went further in naming revolutionary Black nationalism and Pan-Africanism as products of Du Boisian thought and philosophy. Her public acknowledgment of these highly controver- sial ideas earned her the respect of the younger generation. Her desire always was to provide a broader context for those ideas that became urgent in the late 1960s. Many of her colleagues at peer institutions were in conflict with the younger art- ists and activists, debating them openly and in print. One of the most famous discussions was between J. Saunders Redding and LeRoi Jones,[16] which was sim- ilar to the debate in the early twentieth century between Du Bois and Booker

T. Washington. But Walker had an added advantage: "For My People" was widely recognized as the movement's anthem. It had ringing words that spoke both brilliantly to the birth of a new generation and also to the ultimate goal of the movement with which they were associated. She had foretold what was to happen. For her, the younger generation was ushering in the world she had predicted, a generation that began "to rise and take control." She saw it as her duty to help design part of that world, for which she had so eloquently argued.

Walker had a strong sense of personal connection with the revolutionary fervor of the students at her alma mater, Northwestern. She had been the same age as many of the younger activists when she became politically active in Chicago, and she had also seriously studied revolutionary theories and movements. And even though an invitation to go to Northwestern as a visiting professor came at one of her busiest times, she could not turn it down. She had been a student there in the 1930s. What would it mean to return in this extraordinary period?

She had followed closely events that began taking place at Northwestern beginning in 1967. Active recruitment had resulted in a sizeable number of Black students from Chicago's south and west sides. But Northwestern was hardly prepared for the response it got when those same students responded in a less than appreciative manner. She began summarizing the events that later became part of the talk she would eventually give there:

> In the spring of 1968, Northwestern felt its first revolutionary thrust from the demands made by the black students on the Evanston campus. At that time black students on predominantly white campuses all over this country began to demand an education more relevant and sensitive to the needs of black people, more knowledge of African American history, and more understanding of black culture on the part of White America. They demanded more concern with the issues confronting America because of race and racism. In agreeing or assenting to these demands, the university promised to hire more black teachers and to try to recruit more black students.[17]

Her attention to the "painful state of revolution" in which Northwestern found itself coincided with what was happening in the nation as a whole. What she saw stimulated her: "Young black students, brilliant and militant, joined by equally militant and brilliant white students,"[18] which inspired her to do even more with whatever authority she had at Jackson State, where student activism had much less opportunity for success. Having more contact with Northwestern, where she could see change, elicited her support:

> Faculty members were concerned, administrators were harassed, alumni horrified, but the fact remains that the university faced change in every aspect of

curriculum administrative policy, and racial complexion of faculty and student body, because revolution promises ultimately to change all of our world society.[19]

She knew that the invitation she had received in spring 1968 was part of the negotiations between Northwestern's administration and protesting students who had issued a May 4th Declaration of Demands. When she contrasted two Northwesterns, the one she experienced in the 1930s and the one she encountered in 1969, her observations brought discomfort:

> My memories of my adolescent days at Northwestern have always been too painful to bear recollection. Young, poor, and black, my life at Northwestern was restricted to a very narrow sphere. I could not live on campus in any dormitory nor eat in any place in Evanston except the dime store. It was nothing unusual to hear a ranking professor tell "darky" jokes in the classroom. Very seldom did any fellow student who was not black speak to me. I made very few friends among teachers or students, but those rare friends I made have lasted a lifetime. I was not prepared for race prejudice in a great university above the Mason-Dixon line, in an institution founded by the very denomination of the Christian church to which I belonged. Then, too, I had never before seen such opulence, grandeur and obvious display of wealth. Naturally I was bewildered, and it was only after I was working in Chicago with black and white people that I began to understand.[20]

What had she begun to understand? And why was she so confident that "none of this grumbling is likely to stop permanently a worldwide societal revolution from grinding out necessary, even imperative change"?[21]

Walker agreed to go to Northwestern in the midst of preparations for a newly proposed project, a research institute for Jackson State. She was extremely tired from a grueling schedule of talks and appearances in the three years since *Jubilee*'s publication. Alex wanted her to slow down, and she had promised him she would. Northwestern offered a generous salary with housing provided, and an entire English Department and administration supported her coming. They did not expect that she would be willing to leave her permanent post at Jackson State, but it certainly have been in the back of their minds. It was best to simply take things a step at a time.

She was in her prime, her "peak years" she called them. Further confirmation of this came when Yale sent her an advance copy of the reprint of *For My People*. Her ostensible reason for taking three months away from Jackson was the possibility of having time to work on "Mother Beulah," the novel she hadn't touched in a year, despite repeated requests from Dorothy de Santillana. She also saw the possibility of gaining a different perspective of what she might do with her new project at Jackson State. If she were undecided, she would set all hesitation aside when she read the publisher's note in the reprint of *For My People*. The note gave new meaning to her poetry and work and confirmed her thinking about its continued relevance:

> "She has spoken of her people so that all may listen. Because in 1968, another generation, both black and white, is eager to listen, we take pleasure in making this volume available once more. Margaret Walker's voice deserves a new hearing in these new times.[22]

Walker's thoughts turned to the students she would encounter at Northwestern. The Black Student Movement there was making progress, and lending support to their struggle would certainly impact the continuing ones she faced at Jackson State. She had never seen a more courageous or mature group of young people, and she wanted to be part of the transformation. She already had in mind what she might say if anyone asked her whether the university had changed since she was a student in 1935:

> If Northwestern were not changing, nothing else would matter but my black skin. Do not misunderstand me to say that change at the university has been complete or even sufficient. Nor is it a fact that blackness could reaffirm such an untruth. Yes, the university was changing. You ask me how it has changed, and I answer I know that if it had not changed, I would not have been there. But there is a revolution taking place in the university, and hopefully a better society will be the result.[23]

The students were eager to learn and talk with her outside of class, regularly following her to her apartment across from the Orrington Hotel. Her fatigue was apparent on her arrival. Earlier that fall she had been on a whirlwind of lectures: the National Urban League meeting in New Orleans; the University of Buffalo; Tufts University in Medford, Massachusetts; and the Association for the Study of Negro Life and History meeting in New York, and she had spent a week at Howard University in Washington, DC, all before Thanksgiving. She continued to teach between her fall and early winter trips, finding that she had less physical and mental energy. A missed regular physical check-up and weight gain made matters worse. Whenever she got tired, she rehearsed the parade of previous and current problems and projects left undone, the second novel most of all. Surprisingly, the thoughts of so much to do lifted her spirit and gave her energy to keep going.

These personal concerns did not lessen her interest in and observations about the revolutionary movement. Left and right factions had begun to form even as the US military and FBI continued to sharpen their management of political repression. Most organizations that emerged on the political Left or Right expected informants in their midst. None of these impeded the growth of these groups or their activism. But the fear of communism and the anti-communist hysteria of a little more than a decade earlier had left a well-organized surveillance infrastructure that would serve the country well during the Black Power Movement. If Black people were enemies of the state in general, they were enemies of white supremacy in particular, a fact that loomed large in Mississippi.

Walker was especially mindful of this sharp contrast between Black and white institutions when she extracted herself from the climate of fear in Mississippi. If her arrival at Northwestern increased her fatigue, it also increased her investment in a desire to see firsthand what was happening. She fully appreciated the way Northwestern had honored its obligation to become a more diverse institution, given its status as an elite suburban university only a few miles from the inner city of Chicago. While she was there for those three months, she wrote that Northwestern was learning to deal with a Black city and "all its teeming millions."[24] She had been eager to go, indeed, contemplating the meaning and importance of the "great honor to be asked to return . . . even though at a difficult time."[25] She was making a triumphant return to an institution that was a family tradition.

She took with her the final edits for an essay requested for a new book, *Many Shades of Black*, by Stanton Wormley. With no time to produce something new, she elected to revise a previously written essay, "Willing to Pay the Price," even though the essay showed its age with her use of the term "Negro." While she may not have been aware of competing in a new market for Black writing, she did understand the need to be in the right place at the right time.

"Willing to Pay the Price" is one of the essays that responded to the highly racialized climate of the 1960s. Walker was concerned about how to define her role: "Am I a gradualist, an activist, a segregationist member of the Black Establishment or where do I stand?"[26] she asks. On the question of the role of the writer, she is, however, adamant:

> As a writer, my commitment has to be to the one thing I can do best, and that is to the business of writing. Civil rights are part of my frame of reference since I must of necessity write always about Negro life, segregated or integrated.[27]

She completed "Willing to Pay the Price" and "Revolution and the University" at Northwestern. These two essays reflect the structure and tone of essays to come. Leading with major questions, she describes social conditions, grounding her critique in a materialist analysis. Connecting to the audience through her personal history first, she transitions to a more public voice.

She did not work on "Mother Beulah," as she had hoped, but she signed a contract with Scott Foresman to complete an anthology of Black literature in a year, with a first installment due in six months. The project was dead from the start, even if it made sense. Foresman had acquired William Morrow, the major publisher of Black poetry; LeRoi Jones and Nikki Giovanni were among their authors. Walker imagined herself building an important relationship for her future poetry. Foresman promised an advance of $2,000 and a full $20,000 on delivery, with royalties down the road. She gathered notes but realized she would never take it any further.

In addition to getting to know some of the important leaders of the campus student movement, in particular James Turner, Kathryn Ogletree, and John Higginson, Walker renewed her friendship with E. B. Hungerford, whom she considered her major professor at Northwestern. Now retired, Hungerford still worked in his office. He had finally published *Rhythms of Poetry* in 1966, the same year she published *Jubilee*, giving them reason for a special celebration. They saw their careers as having taken parallel paths, with delayed publication projects and a commitment to educating students. Walker was pleased to give him credit for the birth of *Jubilee*. It was in the workshop she had taken with him in 1934 where she had written the first section.

The time at Northwestern was another of those periods for Walker when a beginning signals an ending. *For My People* and *Jubilee* were in print, but her dream of being a full-time writer moved further in the distance. Giving up remnants of her early self that she associated with this dream seemed less painful than it might have been, however; the loss did not mean failure. Perhaps the dreams deriving from childhood are like that. They seize you, turning into weapons that clear a path through the thickets of the world until such time when they can serve you better. You learn to put them away until they can become the tools for polishing the person you have become. In addition to being a writer, Margaret Walker had become a consummate intellectual.

The time at Northwestern confirmed that the context of her life had changed. Pondering her past and her possible future made the new phase of her identity clearer. Building a permanent legacy at Jackson State became more vital than ever. She had no way of knowing whether she would do badly or well and cared less about what challenges the task would bring. Nothing could replace the opportunity she realized she was given, one for which her mental and psychological preparation could not be more certain. Walker's life spirit was in full-renewal mode. At no other time would she draw on all of her resources and skills she knew she would need as she began to look toward a new future at Jackson State.

Northwestern was her past, and it helped usher in her future. Through mature, aging eyes and her skilled voice, she could help shape the dialogue for and map a new history of conscious change. Living in Mississippi with the ghosts of those who had sacrificed their lives, leading a new era of change was a birthright she could not deny. There was no lessening, then, of the creative impulse, only the form that it needed to take to meet new demands.

23

To Teach, to Lead, to Change the World

An unpublished poem written shortly after Walker returned home to Jackson in June 1969 reveals ripened insights and a renewal of her creative energies. "The Aquarium," a rare appearance among pages of critical commentary, social analysis, and planning notes, considers the impact of spatial confinement:

> We went to see fish in the aquarium
> under water, under glass
> strange mass of life
> water green and blue, marble-colored and yellow
> more golden than nuggets of sunlight caught in undertow
> glittering scales shimmering
> like jewelled light
> on strange phosphorescences
> no race conflicts of color here
> no wars and pestilence
> but deep serenity
> breathing day into eternity before birds and reptiles
> before morning of men rising on this planet earth
> I do not think I could live
> under sea
>
> breaking tank air and
> flapping frog fins on my feet
> even with many good things to eat
> better than algae or nourishment or many minerals
> my curiosity would fly
> not seeing birds nor hearing midnight trains
> but always watching and shifting
> rather I wish sunrise
> and skies dark with bright
> peering stars
> I have been locked in southern landscapes too long
> I cannot pull free
> But my land has lost

The House Where My Soul Lives. Maryemma Graham, Oxford University Press. © Oxford University Press 2022.
DOI: 10.1093/oso/9780195341232.003.0023

By the late 1960s, Walker had exchanged the years of literary silence for her status as a much sought-after speaker.

> cotton pickers, tobacco strippers, cane cutters
> now cotton picking machines devour delta land
> and rain washes ruts
> in red erosions
> now rotting shacks are deserted
> people pulling up stakes
> quit plows
> and catch trains to Chicago
> I wander here in an old land hearing old songs, old voices
> old melodies full of old tragedies.[1]

Because the poem remains unpublished, reading it as a thought-emotion piece within the context of a period of poetic barrenness opens up new considerations of what is lost and what might be gained from such a silence. Here, as she contemplates the image of a fish under water, Walker affirms her own creative writing process, one in which "she made up her own rules, ones drawn from the formal qualities of her signature poem 'For My People'—repetition, specific image or imagery, incorporation of the mundane into an individual and collective historical moment," according to Jerry Ward:

> Margaret does not follow the restraints demanded by the French forms rondeau or roundel; she moves in the writing into the territory of the Italian and English madrigal, but ignores even in that effort the rules about the accentual-syllabic. What we have is a 39-line poem that refuses to be a sestina. The poem is useful for gathering insights about Walker's transformations as a modernist writer, resisting the easy dismissal by too many critics who see her as too accessible and dated.[2]

Walker was as attuned to her psychic inner journey as she was to the compelling social, political, historical conditions of her time. One might consider her a resistant modernist, using this poem as evidence. Ward's analysis of "The Aquarium" connects Walker's sensibility, the formal structure of her work and its highly referential nature:

> Stanza one uses the collective "we" and stanzas two and three plunge into the lyric and individual "I." The aquarium may have been in Chicago, but Margaret's poetic mind was in the South. Walker's high regard for 14-line sonnet variation, seen in each stanza here, greatly influenced the writing, but she answers the call/pull of what Nathan A. Scott, Jr. described as "vision of presence" . . . in the final two lines of stanza three, she responds to the call of yearning in Jean Toomer's *Cane*. For does she not wish to capture for the present that which is passing and will be lost? I think she does. She is at once *der Dichter und der Denker*.[3]

If, as Ward argues, the poem's organic rhythm links different modal experiences in three successive stanzas of urban, cosmic, and rural,[4] several other rhythmic patterns are visible as well. Different elements of nature are connected, just as these overlap with the natural and built environment: the fish, water, Walker, the aquarium. The reversal of her own life pattern—starting from the South rather than the North—reflects the psychological moment of the poem's composition as much as it privileges her return to her native South. She is very methodical in her approach to knowledge as she explores the poem's theme of spatial confinement: from the descriptive and visual, to the perceptual, the experiential, and finally her confidence in her own poetic sensibilities. Ward asserts that "the agency is in the will of the human being not necessarily in the dictates of Nature—to be distinguished from typical heirs of Romantic poetry, putting Walker instead in the company of certain 20th century ecologists."[5] Walker's trademark in this poem, as in her best work, is her ability to create a rhythm and flow of the poem that evokes a corresponding rhythm and flow of history. The process is not linear, according to Ward:

> The image of the confined fish observed through glass in the first stanza carries over to the second. . . . "I don't' think I could live under sea /. . . I wish sunrise/ and skies dark with bright/peering stars." (stanza two) . . . The lyric "I" acknow-ledges the trope of migration and historical change but longs for the past made of Southern labor "pickers, strippers, cutters" (stanza three)) despite the promise of the urban North, the mecca, with "no race conflicts of color here / no wars and pestilence / but deep serenity" (stanza one). Yet, the Northern serenity is a lie, because the genuine serenity for Margaret is in the South where despite major disadvantages, the human being can engage in "breathing day into eternity be-fore birds and reptiles / before morning of men rising on this planet earth."[6]

The sharp images in the last stanza return us to a time past. Walker is remem-bering the life of her childhood in Alabama, the Deep South, more than the time in New Orleans, the North Carolina of her early years, or Jackson. She may have needed these memories to offset the physical and emotional stress of returning home to a demanding administrative job at the end of June, planning classes for a new academic year, but most important, the disappointment of not having worked on her novel "Mother Beulah." Instead, she responded to the call—a re-turn to domestic responsibilities. Memories of an earlier, freer time in her life helped her cope with her present condition. "The novel especially, this is my only hope to escape real bondage."[7] The term "bondage" here is telling. Given her complicated and demanding personal life, it would be easy for her to see herself as a woman in bondage. Because she took such pride in those aspects of her life that defined her Southernness, especially her family and her home, the reference is specific to her persistent financial worries, which she believed a second best-selling novel could resolve. Her return to Jackson had kept her safe from feelings of gloom, if not depression, for a short while only.

In reality, her return to Jackson State was anything but gloomy. The new ad-ministration was but a few months old. Reddix's long career had ended and with it most of Walker's major battles. John Arthur Peoples, the incoming president, knew that he needed to have her on his side, or she could be his worst enemy. He was a Jackson State alumnus, and although he had taken none of her classes, he knew her. A year earlier, before his arrival in Jackson, he had invited her to speak at the State University of New York at Binghamton, where he was then working. The opportunity to champion her work publicly had served him well. She saw in him a man who showed her the respect that she found difficult to get from her male colleagues in Jackson.

She had directed Peoples's inaugural symposium, at his request, before leaving for Northwestern. Planning the symposium gave both of them an opportunity to get to know each other better. She invited two good friends from her Chicago years, St. Clair Drake and Arna Bontemps, to speak. For the third speaker, she asked Matthew Walker, a charismatic young leader who had made his first trip to Mississippi as a Freedom Rider. These three men offered very different but critically important views about the history, culture, and future of social change. She and Peoples had bonded partly because of her choices: the combined message from the three men was exactly what Walker and the new president wanted the students and the faculty to hear.

The Symposium was an important moment in the history of the college. Among the guests present was Mississippi governor John Del Williams, a law-and-order man, and no friend to the state's Black population. He expected to speak, to publicly affirm his support of "the Negro people," which many saw as mere lip service. Walker watched closely as the young president managed the governor's appearance. What she saw proved to her that Peoples was the right man for the times. Peoples recalled that his plan came off without a hitch:

> I told the governor that with all the respect I had for him, I didn't want him to be embarrassed and that he would be booed if he said anything or was in the procession, which he wanted to do. I wanted him to be there, I said, but that he should come in the side door of the auditorium, remain seated, and let me acknowledge him. Any other way would be bad for us both, I said. He wanted to come so badly that he agreed to do it. He did exactly as planned.[8]

Peoples was thirty-eight and had waited patiently for the retirement of Jacob Reddix. While she had her criticisms of Reddix, Walker acknowledged the wisdom in his choice of a most capable successor. Peoples had been a popular student leader who, after serving in the military, completed his doctorate and began his career at the State University of New York at Binghamton. New York's governor Nelson Rockefeller had tapped him to be part of the new leadership of higher education in the state, which was experiencing burgeoning enrollments in its colleges and universities. Peoples, however, had other plans.

Peoples might have been an unlikely candidate for the presidency of an HBCU at his young age, but he was ushering in a new era of Black leadership. He had fresh ideas, and having spent considerable time away from the Jim Crow South, easily recognized and refused to accept, just as Walker did, the trickle-down effect of educational reform. Since eight out of every ten Black college students were enrolled in HBCU's in 1968, Peoples realized that the slow rate of change could lead to more violent confrontations. He had an affinity with Black students at Jackson State in 1968 and with Walker: he was dissatisfied with the quality of the education students were receiving, openly condemning the gross inequities that persisted, and was committed to the radical and speedy changes which many of her peers resisted. Peoples also knew, as she did, that the focus of public interest and hence the media in the late 1960s was not on students at HBCU's or the South generally. Ultimately, for John Peoples, Binghamton was too far away from the kind of cause that a rebel like him needed. He eagerly accepted when the call from Jackson State came.

If Peoples needed Margaret Walker, she needed him more. She could give him access to a network different from the one he had developed as an administrator, a network equally as valuable and no less national in its visibility. Peoples could give her the platform and the support that she needed to advance and implement ideas about education and social change, ideas that they shared. But she needed to consolidate her connections to a creative world, to realize greater benefits as the author of *Jubilee*, knowing too that any benefits that came to her would also come to Jackson State. As long as she was there, Peoples made it his goal to make sure she remained. She vowed that he would be the last president under whom she would work, making it clear that she liked what he stood for and the way he operated. Theirs was a mutually beneficial partnership.

She had volunteered to write an inaugural poem early for his January 1969 inauguration, seeing it as part of her duties as director of the inaugural symposium. Peoples felt honored. The celebratory "Ode on the Occasion of the Inauguration of the Sixth President of Jackson State College," was the first of many occasional poems she would write over the years. Her interpretation is both historical and apocalyptic. Like much of her poetry, "Ode" moves with a biblical cadence as the narrative is mediated through the second person. The poem affirms a power beyond the material word but remains grounded in historical reality. The mood is imperative as Walker emphasizes the rightness of the time, the need for change, as well as the man associated with it. Peoples's military background allows Walker to connect Black, US, and world history through images of darkness and light, blood and violence. That violence, whether manifested as war among people or among nations, is dialectical because it always anticipates peace. Freedom is dialectical as well. Both are lost when there are "black men born to die on foreign shores, on battlefields and on familiar trees . . . kindled to death by lynching mobs."[9] Freedom emerges through the toil and trouble of slavery, just as literacy is made possible for Mississippians with the founding of Jackson State. The well-known line from "For My People," "Let a race of men now rise and take control,"[10] shifts in this poem to an affirmative present. Hope lies with John Peoples, who belongs to "A race of men who can yet make the dream come true now in this time of truth."[11] She proceeds with cautious optimism that yields all power to a higher power in a prayerful conclusion with the appropriate humility and adoration for the new president:

Sing now a paean for this man
A prayer breathed on the wings
of shifting winds
that search the world
and bring the storm of change into our land.[12]

What united Walker and Peoples was their shared faith in possibilities through a "storm of change." Her ability to capture this sensibility in the language of poetry that he could appreciate bound them to the Jackson State of a new era. They would both have to accept the responsibilities for turning those possibilities into realities. Living in a state historically resistant to change, they realized the magnitude and tenuousness of their undertaking on the "wings of shifting winds." He could dismiss her reputation: her inability to get along with department chairs, her rightful displeasure with Black male leadership, her frequent wild rampages.

To Peoples, Walker was a perfectionist in an imperfect system. Her temperament did not matter to him. No one else at Jackson State would comply so willingly with the demands of change at the level that Jackson State needed. She had the broad intellectual knowledge for thinking outside of disciplinary boundaries. His task was to find a way to organize change, to centralize it while maximizing the involvement of as many units of the campus as possible. At the same time, he needed to have confidence that the work would get done without a lot of input from him, and that it would represent the quality that he demanded for his presidency. He trusted Walker to do that, and he could look to her as a model in hiring others. He knew, finally, that Walker was the kind of person who did not need people to like her when she knew she was right about something.

Peoples had inherited a board that was fearful and conservative, but its members fortunately respected him. "I was more angry than the students," Peoples said in an interview. "We had five consecutive years of riots in Jackson. The press called them that, but we called them 'police riots' because the police were the ones who would shoot. I didn't fight black power. I told the governor that I encouraged students to protest the conditions because they had a right to."[13] No president could make such a bold statement and expect to keep his job in Mississippi, but Peoples could because he was at Jackson State by choice. His credentials would easily secure him another job if he were to be fired. He stood up to the Mississippi State Board of Higher Education and his own board at the college. One of his first acts was to address the salary inequities of faculty at the Black and white schools in the state, a bold move. By the end of Peoples's first year, faculty got raises, and Walker finally got the major increase that should have come when she returned from Iowa in 1965. Jackson State received more state appropriations, much-needed construction of new buildings began, and the college actively pursued and received federal funding. Perhaps it was the confidence he acquired in the military that made him fearless in the presence of white authority, or he simply embodied the spirit of the people. "The government wanted law and order and they were used to black people being afraid. These blacks weren't scared,"[14] in Peoples's opinion. Walker believed John Peoples was a catalyst for change, and her opinion of him never changed.

Peoples saw Walker as a partner, someone with whom he could share his plans and whose opinions mattered. Well aware of what it meant to proclaim a "Black university" in the era of Black Power, he embraced her ideas and offered complementary ones: an interdisciplinary Black Studies program—and institute—that would involve history, English, music, and literature. Peoples took the proposed Institute for the Study of the History, Life, and Culture of Black People to the college's board for approval, making clear that he wanted Margaret Walker to be its director. Approval was granted, and she had only one question—who would be her boss? When Peoples replied that she reported directly to him, she was ecstatic.

He knew that she fumed at ideas she considered backward, drawing intense dislike from people for her presumed arrogance. He also knew that she brought to Jackson State more than the college at that time could pay for. The student complaints about her unreasonable demands—that no other faculty received—he saw as a positive rather than a negative. The Institute, he believed, would signal the kind of excellence that she wanted, just as he did, and he rightly assessed that she needed a larger, more focused space to realize her ambition. He envisioned an academic institution that could lead the nation in transforming itself from the top down as much as from the bottom up. "With Margaret Walker a person has to recognize genius when they see it," he said.[15]

Peoples had given Walker another important reason for not leaving Jackson State. Thus, she immediately resumed her planning once returning for the fall. The schedule was full of events to plan, grants to write, local talks to give, and, as typical of her practice, thank-you letters to friends in Evanston and Chicago. She found her match in Alleane Currie, whom she hired as the Institute's executive assistant. Mrs. Currie believed in achieving the perfection that Walker demanded. She was quietly forceful, wasting little time in small talk when there was work to be done. Walker could give as much time to the Institute as she needed since her personal life was shifting. James was away in law school, Marion was working in Chicago, and Sigis had gone to the Marines.

Just after classes began in the fall of 1969, threatened with kidney failure and complications caused by a malfunctioning parathyroid gland, Walker entered the hospital. Spending time in hospitals had become such a regular part of her life that she approached each stay as if it were the last. Resolute woman that she was, she diligently sought to understand as much as possible about how the world and the universe operated, but that resoluteness had been forged out of an abiding fear that her life would end before she had accomplished all that she desired. In those moments when this fear was greatest, she surrendered completely to a higher power, following her dictum to "prepare for surgery by preparing to die and hope God will let you live to come through it and wake up again."[16] Her ideas and beliefs existed on a continuum. The alignment of her Marxism and her Christian heritage was instrumental; knowledge and action were not dichotomous. She could go from the ideal to the real, from the theoretical to the practical with a margin of abundant and empowering ideas. Yet, as much as she understood the purpose and uses of religion, there were spiritual matters that lay beyond human control and best be left to God:

> God is for me the ineffable. His is pure spirit and His Kingdom is pure spirit— spiritual beyond the imagination or reason. His presence is with His own always, no matter where, but He chooses most to dwell within the Soul and mind and spirit of His beloved children, those whom He loves and who desire most of all to love and serve him.[17]

Her desire to *know* was not in conflict with the desire to *believe*. The lessons of the past served as her guide, but they were complemented by new forms of knowledge from science, technology, and her desire to make improvements in the world. Walker also recognized an in-between space that allows us to see the intersection of human world events and the positions and movements of celestial objects. She continued to find astrology valuable for explaining that intersection. The knowledge of God could only come through revelation, making prayer and meditation essential. In sum, she was an intellectual, and she devoured knowledge. But she also knew when it was time to let go and graciously submit to mystery in the universe and the divine power of God.

Fortunately, the hospital stay was exploratory, did not include surgery, and yielded an important new diagnosis. The overall imbalance in her body came from diabetes. To restore her blood sugar to stable levels required a radical adjustment in her diet and major shift in her lifestyle. To adjust her own fears, Walker immersed herself in reading Alex Haley's *Autobiography of Malcolm X*, a book she quickly put "in the class of great autobiographies," one that displayed a type of "tough honesty and tragic world."[18] Her assessment of the book both as literature and polemic provided a prism through which she could see the evolution of the Institute and its distinctiveness. She concluded that were she to make it out of the hospital alive, one of the Institute's courses would include *Malcolm X* and a selection of other books, each one created in a key historical moment to help students connect to history.

Though convinced that she could manage the diabetes, Walker returned to work burdened with a conscience that forced her to face her own mortality. "I thought I wanted to see the world, write a half dozen more books, before I die, but now I don't know,"[19] she wrote a few days after she returned home. With all the dietary changes and frequent loss of energy, she saw her ambition fading again. Without ambition, she found it easy to also lose the will to live. While she usually found ways of reinventing herself through reading her astrological charts and looking for patterns of beginnings and endings, she recognized that this bout of depression was not likely to end so quickly. When Sigis's twenty-one-day furlough ended around the time she was released from the hospital, the quality time she had so wanted them to have was severely reduced.

As 1969 drew to a close, her depression lifted. She began to receive job offers one after another. Atlanta University and Central State in Ohio, because they were so similar to Jackson State, she did not find attractive. It is doubtful that she gave serious consideration to accepting a position at Washington University in St. Louis or at the University of California at Irvine, although they were strong offers. It was enough to feel wanted. As a senior academic in the late 1960s, she faced an open market at predominately white institutions (PWIs) in desperate need of seasoned Black scholars. The production of new Black PhDs could not fill the demand, but PWIs were also wary of putting younger untested scholars— closer in age to the students themselves—in these highly charged environments. Most university administrations adopted a dual solution. Cornell, for example, successfully recruited J. Saunders Redding, already near the end of his career, as an endowed professor of English. They had also hired James Turner, fresh out of graduate school at Northwestern, to create and build their Africana Studies Program in direct response to the demands of student protesters.

But Walker was content to have a taste of this new experience for the three months she spent at Northwestern, as she watched many of her peers starting over in strange and unfamiliar places. She understood why they would leave, for they shared the same struggles at HBCU's: insensitive or jealous administrators who severely underpaid them, failed to see the importance of their work, and provided limited research resources. Redding had left Hampton Institute, Richard Barksdale left Morehouse College, Blyden Jackson left Southern University, and Darwin Turner left North Carolina A & T—all headed to PWIs. As Walker was quick to point out whenever she was asked about this: they were all men. They all had domestic arrangements different from hers, without responsibility for any children they may have had beyond the financial. Women like her, on the other hand, who were her peers, spent their careers in a single HBCU.[20]

In reaching the decision not to accept any of the offers—promising to do short-term residencies instead—she went through the routine process, taking stock of her general situation, parsing ethical and personal factors. Uprooting and having to build a new life in late middle age was not appealing. She surmised that since she was finally feeling productive and necessary at Jackson State, respected and working under a supportive president, there was really no need to move. Reimagining a way to translate her creative and intellectual interests with the least amount of personal disruption, which any move would require, gave her enormous comfort.

"The Brain Drain at Negro Colleges" by Alex Poinsett, which appeared in the October 1970 issue of *Ebony*, assessed this downside of desegregation in higher education. The exodus of talented Negro faculty from HBCUs to meet the demand at PWIs was rapid and extreme, the article argued, without an equivalent number of incoming or remaining faculty to fill the critical void. The prevailing view was that this process of commodification could only be detrimental, since it was a continuation of what had already been happening, as white institutions began by taking the best athletes, then the best students, and finally the best faculty.[21]

As it turned out, women who stayed at HBCUs had a major influence on subsequent generations. Poinsett was only partially correct. Rather than entering a critical void, a host of Black scholars and artists—including Nikki Finney, Joanne Gabbin, Paula Giddings, Nikki Giovanni, Trudier Harris, Deborah Mc Dowell, Bettye Parker Smith, Beverly Guy Sheftall, Jessye Norman, and others—encountered demanding teachers, model scholars and professionals, and caring mentors at HBCUs after the "brain drain." The "taking of the best" revealed a gender bias among other unsubstantiated facts that have their roots in long-held assumptions about racial differences. But Walker's experience was made richer and more substantial as a result of those relationships that she formed in Jackson that gave her an undisputed base of power. In addition to the working relationship with Ernestine Libscomb, she had neighbors and colleagues like Bernice Bell and Luana Jean Clayton. The arrival of Doris Saunders, who had left Johnson Publishing Company to create the Journalism program at Jackson State helped to complete a circle that included Mabel Pittman and Inez Morris Chambers. Walker also developed lasting relationships with a host of her former students like Ruth Campbell, Tommie Stewart and Doris O. Ginn. Her network extended to women like Charlotte Momom, an executive director with the Hinds County Library System; Jessie Mosley, civil rights activist and community leader; and Cora Norman, Mississippi Humanities Council's long serving Executive Director. Such a network that supported many of her successes would have been hard to replicate anywhere else . Because Walker operated as a "perfectionist in an imperfect system," John Peoples observed, she inspired more than she intimidated. Similarly, her ability to recognize potential gave those she mentored a decided edge.

Returning to a sense of security, her Mississippi "harbor," brought Walker back to her dream of extracting herself from working and following her passion to write full-time. Her children were old enough to fend for themselves, and Margaret would be leaving for college soon. Between 1968 and 1979, Walker had been repeating this promise to herself yearly: she was now ready to live her dream.

A December 1969 police raid of the Black Panther headquarters in Chicago, and the resulting death of the group's Illinois leader Fred Hampton, incited some of her strongest revolutionary rhetoric. Horrified by this overt display of police brutality under government sanction, and having no other outlet to express her rage, she turned again to her journal. In one of her legendary critiques of the US response to race relations, she argued the importance of revolutionary organizations for social change. She quoted relevant statistics: twenty-eight members of the Black Panther Party had been killed in the past year alone. Bobby Seale was on trial as one of nine defendants charged with disrupting the Democratic National Convention, Huey Newton was in jail, and Eldridge Cleaver was in exile. The siphoning off of the Panther leadership signaled a more repressive shift in the response by national security. In her New Year's entry for 1970, she wrote, "What we don't want to think is that change may be violent and that too many people will die—far more than the multitudes who died in the sixties. The sixties began a revolution, which may very well explode in the seventies. Welcome to the seventies!"[22]

In contrast to her earlier apprehensions, she now became understandably furious. "White racists dyed-in-wool conservatives, reactionaries and black middle-class snobs and toms have pushed poor black people to the wall."[23] She did not forego her usual piety, asking "God to save us all," but gave full force to a Marxist analysis condemning American capitalism. The January 1 entry is a renunciation of her more temperate thinking. With Black people so desperate and with no place to go, it was not hard to know what is wrong with America, she explained, adding that "people were busy learning what to do about it." The policies that the Nixon administration implemented made matters worse, she believed. "The Vietnam War together with the space program keep taxes and prices ever escalating so that inflation is past the point of return—too much money wasted while people are starving, homeless and with neither education nor jobs."[24]

Her rage evolved into the outline of a book over the next few days, describing the new stage of the revolution. She wanted to examine the decade of 1960s and the rise of a revolutionary consciousness, building a socialism for the twenty-first century. She had planned to incorporate information about organizations and contemporary politics, looking especially at the way crisis in society occurs when social institutions cease to function. Because political parties are social institutions, with a purpose of maintaining certain systems, she argued, when those systems malfunction, the failure and instability create a crisis in the economy. The book would be a systemic inquiry into individual, social, and institutional behavior. Thinking through the ideas was always easy for her. What was much harder was transferring the conviction of her ideas to the pages of a book.

Walker's mind travel expanded her assessment of the value of expository writing and the personal essay over and above fiction and poetry. She remembered shorter essays that had mapped the critical changes in her life, including her 1943 essay "Growing Out of Shadow" for *Common Ground*. Likewise, her 1951 essay "How I Told My Child about Race" provided the perspective of a young mother confronted with a decision of whether to protect her daughter from or provide an explication for race matters. Her solution, "I had to tell her that she is a Negro who can be proud that she is one of millions of colored people in the world and that she is a member of the human race,"[25] was typical of this period.

Using the essay as a way to accommodate the shift in her process of thinking was similar to her poetic practice. As a young poet, she was fond of figurative language and symbolic terms, having told herself that poets must think a certain way. The key question was what came first? She tackled the question in "My Creative Adventure":

> Concepts are first. . . . we conceive in pictures and feel the rhythms intuitively . . . learning different kinds of rhythms, whether patterns of the line or emotional meaning of words. I mastered many things unconsciously and automatically before I became conscious and self-conscious.[26]

Then, the more conscious she became, the more she felt a need to take into account the steady penetration of place, her life in the South, and her unfaltering belief in the impact of experience on the human mind. Walker had spent much of her early life training to be a certain kind of writer, and she had benefited from living and working among writers, most of whom believed as she did. Once she gained the confidence that she needed and removed herself from the active literary community, the new phase of her life required a new kind of training. Her sense of the *other* work that she needed to do became clearer over time, but the preparation for it was something that she must discover, in part, on her own. That she was on a journey different from other women she knew meant that she, alone, was in charge of her destiny, and that she would make the most of it always.

The process of thinking through her obligations, expectations, and the adjustments that one must make became a compelling reason for writing. She retained her love of ideas and a need to understand the ways in which they operated in the world. As her journal entries began to resemble personal essays more than spontaneous outbursts to calm her nerves, she found a balance between the Margaret Walker seeking clarity about that larger world outside of herself and the Margaret Walker needing to keep the complex dynamic of her inner world and demanding responsibilities in order. Her confidence could be as contained as it was intuitively visceral.

Once this balance was in place, her journal became a playbook for moving her new work ahead systematically and methodically. Writing with intent also helped her to break through the block she had experienced in completing overdue articles and essays. She could finally work on the literary history of *Jubilee*, which Dorothy de Santillana had been urging her to send to *Harpers* since 1966. Although she did not send it to *Harpers*, it was perfect for a talk at the Institute of the Black World in Atlanta, at the urging of its director, Vincent Harding. That essay "How I Wrote *Jubilee*" was later published by Third World Press in 1972 because she had decided to support the small independent Black press that had been founded by Haki Madhubuti (Don L. Lee).

The visit to the newly created Institute of the Black World in Atlanta brought more ideas about how to make the Institute she wanted at Jackson State distinctive. She outlined her goals, what the Institute should and should not do and be, and the local and national impact she expected it to have. For funding, she planned to match whatever Peoples gave her with contributions from organizations that had supported her previous work, especially the Ford Foundation. Her journal entries show a planning process that replicated her father's sensibility and practice, with more emphasis on the outline and enumeration as her organizing tools. Taking the experiences from her mother's planning of musical programs and events, she wrote about the importance of making connections among groups of people and building audiences. Everything she wrote started with an idea, posed as a question, then its historical roots explored, its practice in different periods, and the distinctions she saw in its current form. Once the background was in place, using propositional logic, she created various scenarios for programs that could produce the intended effect.

Her previous questions about the misalignment she saw in society came into focus as she planned the Institute, which was the most inspired of all of her projects. "What kind of education should we be providing?" was her overarching concern, and it was directly tied to her analysis of the university as a social institution. To solve the current problems in education, she believed, we must see where we went off track:

> There is a tendency of the school to become an isolated institution. Through inertia the school perpetuates the habits of an earlier form of society that were once relevant. But the school, having become segregated, maintained more or less independently from what is going on in the world fails to fulfill its social function.[27]

She drew from the ideas of John Henry Cardinal Newman and Alfred North Whitehead, whose work her father had introduced her to. Through her acquaintances at the University of Chicago, she had deepened her understanding of Whitehead's book *The Aims of Education*, which became the basis of Walker's philosophy of educational reform. Her attraction to Whitehead came from his emphasis on the importance of imagination and free play of ideas. According to Whitehead:

> Imagination is not to be divorced from facts: it is a way of illuminating the facts. It works by eliciting the general principles which apply to the facts, as they exist, and then by an intellectual survey of alternative possibilities, which are consistent with those principles. It enables men to construct an intellectual vision of a new world.[28]

In Whitehead she found a connection between struggle and activism, spirituality and educational reform—concepts important to personal life and professional work. While she drew liberally on numerous theorists, Whitehead's ideas helped bring the Institute's work in line with her own temperament. Not only did Whitehead have high regard for John Dewey, who was an important figure in her readings on education, but he also believed in an organized metaphysical system, linking God to the actions of human beings. Rather than a God who ordered the world to do his own bidding, God, according to Whitehead, is bound to the very idea of change, which is essential to human existence. While everyone has some measure of freedom and creativity, both are subject to the constraints imposed by the social structure. Hence, freedom always exists within limits. In order to realize civil and human rights, the condition of the world had to change. Although she did not adopt Whitehead's term "transdisciplinary," her use of the term "interdisciplinarity" embodied his meaning: education should help students make connections between real life and culture, which requires us to bring different areas of knowledge together into a learning system.

Making sense of the world in the seventh decade of the twentieth century helped her construct the philosophy for the Institute and also to grasp the underlying causes for the student rebellions as a worldwide phenomenon. Paris, for example, had experienced student uprisings at the same time as Northwestern. The Sorbonne's Disciplinary Council was far more severe, and students were subjected to brutality like that of white police and federal troops in response to Black student activism in the South. Seeing the larger picture worldwide made it clear to her that the goal of the movement for social change was not limited to civil rights or educational reform. She saw a movement that united students, the working class, and the underserved communities of people around the world.

Reading and seeing the news daily made far more relevant what she had learned in the early 1930s.

She wondered what might have happened had there been manifestos signed between students, the working class, and intellectuals as Jacques Lacan, Simone de Beauvoir, and Jean Paul Sartre had done in France. Would these alliances have made it more difficult to isolate and therefore delegitimize the movement? She was thinking especially of organizations like the Black Panther Party, with its origins among working-class Black students at Merritt College in Oakland, California. Had there been ties with more Black intellectuals, like the young Angela Davis, could there have been more unity between students at HBCUs and PWIs? Although the Panthers had strong support on some college campuses, like Yale, they were a separatist group far to the left of most student activists as well. Walker was probably one of the few Black intellectuals in her generation who recognized the relationship of various forms of activism.

Though she continued to insist that she was a writer first and foremost, and wanted to be remembered as a writer, Walker came to see that her new work would be "to teach, to lead, to learn, to change the world from an evil way."[29] Because she had been given license to do it, with student activism so woefully misunderstood, and yet so necessary to pull the nation out of its abyss, she allied herself with its cause. In this new literature of commitment, she felt her strong sense of obligation and responsibility as an intellectual who had lived long enough to see the past and the present from a unique perspective. That sense of responsibility would grow deeper with time.

In the midst of it all, the violence that she was trying to understand, the violence she believed most Mississippians wanted to get past, erupted uninvited, yet provoked. Nixon's announcement that he was sending troops to Cambodia outraged the antiwar community, as protest escalated throughout the country. The antiwar sentiment exacerbated the activism among Jackson State students. She was asked to appear on a local television show, no doubt as a voice of reason, the older woman for whom students had a great deal of respect, and to whom they would listen. John Peoples had deliberately avoided the media. His belief that students had a right to nonviolent protest was better kept out of the news.

Walker was cautious, knowing the media's expectations. When asked whether the protests were good or bad, she refused to condemn the students or predict anything, preferring to talk about the "disturbing and disruptive trend"[30] that frightened the American people. On the evening after her interview, however, a horde of fully armed Jackson police and highway patrolmen entered Jackson State's campus without warning and fired shots at the west wing of the women's dormitory that left Jackson State student Phillip Gibbs and high school student James Earl Green dead, wounding twelve others.

In her journal she referred to the days between May 10 and May 15 as a "five-day reign of terror" when "all hell broke loose."[31] Students had not initiated the pernicious violence, and they were unarmed; the violence came from the police. The telephone wires were cut, making communication impossible, leading everyone to believe that the police attack was deliberately planned. Her summary puts the tragedy in a global perspective:

> This whole thing has been used as a pawn in a political game—local, state, and national politics are all involved. School integration, civil rights and the war in Vietnam, Cambodia and Laos are all related to this particular incident. . . . The whole affair has shocked and stunned the people of Jackson—black and white people further apart than ever. The attack was totally unwarranted and directly connected with all the issues facing the nation. If the government does not resolve the war, we will have no country left.[32]

In terms of the impact on young people, she noted:

> Young black people are concerned that even as they received their degrees, they are drafted and sent to Vietnam. They feel that the white police are all their enemies and that the highway patrol is infiltrated with the Ku Klux Klan.[33]

That tragedy began to dominate Jackson State's historical narrative. Fifty years later when JSU commemorated the event in 2020, an exhibit was held at the Institute under its new name, the Margaret Walker Center. Those remembering that tragedy confirmed Walker's earlier observations. Nettie Stowers, who had been a student during that period, recalled, "It was a supercharged atmosphere because black men were being recruited and drafted to go fight the war in Vietnam. There were a disproportionate number of black men who died and who served in Vietnam, and a lot of them came out of the college ranks. That's where the pedal hit the metal for me at Jackson State and many others. The black men were being drafted right out of college and being sent straight to Vietnam."

Walker predicted, "Our very survival is at stake"[34] when she thought about what became known as the Jackson State Massacre. Her focus on documenting the events then proved the truth of that prediction. The national news media gave little attention to the event in 1970, but the full story would not only survive through the Institute but also become a constructive outlet for change.

* * *

Curtis King remembers going to the Institute on his first day as a freshman at Jackson State. Newly arrived from Coldwater, Mississippi, and a talented high school actor, he had mapped his future in New York. Like many students in

Mississippi, he had read *Jubilee* in high school, but he had never seen a Black author before. On his first day on campus, he stumbled into her office to follow up on a rumor he'd heard. "Someone told me that Margaret Walker, *the author*, is alive," he said innocently. "Does anyone know anything about this?" Apparently Walker, who had overheard the conversation—and King remembers her sudden appearance from the office and looking directly at him—responded, "Well, I can assure you, young man, I am very much alive."[35] That fortuitous meeting led to a lifelong friendship.

Those days for Walker were a whirlwind of activity; she was racing to and from meetings and kept a rigid schedule of appointments. But she found time for every student like King she encountered. As with many of the students she had grown close to, he took every course he could from her during his college years and supplemented his education by attending all the Institute's events. In 1972, the year before he graduated, he was one of the three students whom Walker took to Chicago for a major conference: the Black Academy of Letters, a summit for Black actors and scholars hosted by John H. Johnson, publisher of *Jet* and *Ebony* magazines. King confessed it was at that point that he realized who Margaret Walker really was. Her speech set the tone for the entire conference:

> This is not a time of joyous freedom, but a crucial time of unmitigated tyranny. An age of technological tyranny. Not a time of tranquility, but a stormy time of senseless war and killing. Militarism is the weapon of politicians and the lives of men have become a political football. There is no lull of mercy in the oppressor's brutality, as we move closer each decade toward a police state. Starvation and suffering exist in the midst of affluence and waste. Spiraling inflation ticks off the hours of economic instability. Death and destruction control all the nation while we fight against evils of injustice. Most people recognize the assassin's bullet and the racist's rhetoric as belchings of a sick society. We are threatened with annihilation of an entire planet because of the greed and short sightedness of one race in the family of man. A cancerous sore of white racism eats at the heart of all American life.[36]

It was almost like listening to a prophet, King remembered. She had included many of these ideas in previous speeches, but here her imagery and principle beliefs were clearly aligned in an exhortation, a call to action. The opening paragraph of this speech presents the facts:

> Five major issues daily headline the news: First, racial enmity and hatred generating violence; second, a perpetual foreign war dating from the beginning of the century; third, industrial contamination of all nature, earth, water, and air; fourth, the extreme dilemma of urban life with the new controlling economy of

Curtis King followed Walker's vision. In 1977 he
founded the Black Academy of Arts and Letters,
combining arts training with public engagement

crime and drugs; and fifth, political chaos and economic collapse, for the two
go hand in hand. Witness the three-ring circus of political primaries in White
America, while the faltering fluctuating stock market is sick enough to die and
prove it.[37]

That speech, "Agenda for Action," is important in understanding her vision for
the work at the Institute, the place where her growing outrage gave her form of
radicalism a permanent home. She knew that she had something to say, but her
exhortations were not semantic. She could not withdraw from the world or from
her duty to humanity. Nothing gave her more hope than the belief that a community of scholars, educators, and artists were at the forefront of change because of
the urgency of their cause. King carried that speech with him for a long time, and
it ultimately changed his life. He believed that "Everything she said in 1972 has
come true."[38]

She issued a call in this 1972 speech, understanding the Institute as the symbol
of all that education could and must do in a period of intense national crisis.
Hundreds of students like King would benefit from her tutelage, as they were

exposed to complex social problems that the Institute tackled in its range of activities.

King's assessment of Walker is astute: "I still remember her directives: ground your ideas with facts, don't trust all your information, and be clear. If clarity isn't there, the structure isn't going to be clear. She would look at a different person each time she repeated it, as if she were talking to you and you alone. . . . She was someone who would do her best work when she had a fight on her hands."[39]

If "the twilight of the Western world had come in 1972," as she told those attending the Black Academy's Conference on the State of Black Arts and Letters, "what does it mean for those of us who have yet to claim those freedoms long ago promised but never fulfilled?" Based on the strength of her vision, her optimism, and her multiple faith traditions, Walker saw a paradox, "a strange anachronism, and the handicapped horse that wins the race."[40] While her vision of art as a liberatory enterprise resonates with the cultural nationalism of the period, she was not popularizing other people's ideas, but rather echoing her own. Her greatest asset, to give language ordinary meaning in extraordinary times, enabled her to connect the human community through the Institute. "How can we talk about life tomorrow . . . unless we dare do something today to shape that life?"[41] she wrote. The Institute was what she dared to do.

Jackson State's faculty expanded with the arrival of John A. Peoples, president from 1967 to 1984. Peoples supported the founding of the Institute

Historian John Henrik Clarke at Institute workshop for teachers. Courtesy the Margaret Walker Center

24

The Institute

Race, Region, and a Mission Possible

While Walker continued to be bombarded with offers to leave Jackson State for a PWI, she had come to the conclusion that the Institute was the critical component of her intellectual legacy. She had the support she needed and a community it served. And it was also true that her popularity was greater than ever. If "For My People" had reestablished itself as the "rallying cry of the civil rights movement,"[1] as William R. Ferris noted, the fact is that she had too many ideas that could ensure her legacy off the page. To have those ideas become reality was now as important to her as the will to see her words on the page had been in those earlier years. A need to conquer the fear of becoming invisible and ultimately forgotten drove her. In Walker's thinking, one way to do that was to prove that remarkable things could happen in Mississippi that might not be possible anywhere else. This became her mission in the last quarter of her life.

The state's reputation for being the deepest of the Deep South states she embraced as an opportunity. Although she lived in the South, her sense of community, both in intellectual and cultural terms, was much broader. As a New Deal Democrat who viewed the world through the prisms of racism and fascism, she had a broad-based understanding of global and US politics. But it was her mastery of the double-conscious identities required of the modern race woman that made her who she was, an outwardly conservative appearance that easily disguised her grounding in a much longer, Black radical tradition.

She was bold enough to believe that it was up to her to make sense of an era that found it hard to step out of the shadows of its former self, to see those changes that civil rights activism had made possible. As a systems person, Walker was ideologically driven, which explained her faith in traditional Judeo-Christian religion and astrology, just as it fed her curiosity about everything else, especially the nature of social and political change. America was always in a state of change, but the intensity and impact of those changes could differ. That intensity and impact were most visible in Mississippi during the early 1970s, a reality that added a layer to her sense of purpose.

Opposition to desegregation, which escalated after the landmark 1954 *Brown v. Board of Education* decision, reached an all-time and well-orchestrated high during the 1960s and the election of Ross Barnett as governor of Mississippi.

The House Where My Soul Lives. Maryemma Graham, Oxford University Press. © Oxford University Press 2022. DOI: 10.1093/oso/9780195341232.003.0024

Early Institute staff: back row, left to right, Alvin Benson, Alleane Currie, Burns Machobane, Doris Derby, two unidentified persons, Marcus Douyon; front row, E. C. Foster and Walker. Courtesy of the Margaret Walker Center

Two successive governors, Paul B. Johnson and John Bell Williams, both vowed to protect Mississippi from racial desegregation, with an equal resistance to the Great Society programs associated with the Johnson administration. Williams, less visible on the national radar than Barnett, may well have been even more dangerous as an active partner in maintaining systems of oppression. Election to Congress in 1946 gave him a national platform for championing state's rights and racial segregation, linking him directly to vehement segregationists like Strom Thurmond. David Sansing, the Mississippi historian whom Walker most repected, remembered Williams for his public criticism on the floor of the House of Representatives following the *Brown* decision, where he viewed desegregated schools "as sites of anarchy." After twenty years in Congress, during which time his ideas became more racially polarizing, he returned to Mississippi to win the governor's seat in 1968. In 1970, two years before he left office, Williams was forced to follow the federal mandate to disband Mississippi's dual system of education and to create a unified one.

But all of this was not without struggle by the people of Mississippi themselves. For Walker, the founding of the Mississippi Freedom Democratic Party was essential in resisting the reign of terror in the state. Other local and national organizing efforts like Student Nonviolent Coordinating Committee (SNCC) unleashed the creative sensibilities of a younger generation, highlighting

Mississippi's resilience and potential as a model of activism and agency. What had been done was only a glimpse of what was possible through a systematic, well-organized effort building on that legacy at Jackson State. It was the only school in Mississippi's segregated system available to Blacks for post-graduate education, which meant that Jackson State was by definition a Black intellectual center. Bringing students and the community together to deepen their understanding of what a new America might look like not only for its Black citizens but for the nation as a whole, and what needed to be done to get there, was the real task of education in society. At least that was what Walker believed. And it was that vision that she imparted. The question was whether or not her Institute could become the center for this kind of transformation.

She may not have been conscious of creating a movement, but the evolution of the Institute converged with a long history of creating "safe" spaces for dialogue and debate about matters of importance to Black people. Rigid spatial boundaries and exclusionary practices had both benefited as much as repressed Black social and economic development and efficacy within the Black community. Despite political and religious differences among Black people, there had always been common ground.

The Institute was that common ground in the Deep South. It did not make explicit its ideological connection to any dominant position at the time. Rather, it was a concrete demonstration of resistance to repression through Black engagement by providing a constructive and creative think tank for the community. Walker continued to borrow ideas from the Institute of the Black World in Atlanta, which had been prompted by the assassination of Martin Luther King Jr. But she was more interested in attracting the larger community. The purpose? To educate and inform. What she had begun to realize, especially after the Jackson State Massacre in May 1970, was that being in the South put her in the middle of a critical transition from the Old to a New South. She felt a sense of urgency as she continued to craft this new public space. She was in the South, but not bound by the South's traditional ideas. Although she had always struggled against standard dismissals of and pervasive negative attitudes toward the South, Walker was not an apologist. She insisted that the South was simply more transparent in its irreverent practices, pointing out that other parts of the country were worse because of their pretense otherwise.

The new political and social landscape of a desegregating South presented an opportunity to think and dream boldly. The Institute would allow for a consolidation of her ideas that had been accumulating over time. She proceeded along three lines of thought. The first was educational transformation. From the published speech "Religion, Poetry, and History: Foundations for a New Educational System," she took a rhetorical approach. What is the role of religion, what is the meaning of poetry, and what is the worth of a people's heritage in developing their social consciousness? Her organization of ideas was not unlike a church sermon: one set out to make three points, to teach, or, depending upon the situation, to preach:

> One, the philosophy and aesthetic values of a society are fundamental to the development of certain basic institutions and the social phenomena of that society; two, when these social phenomena and institutions erupt in chaos, the basic philosophy must be reexamined and ultimately changed; and three, when the society thereby undergoes such violent change, the people are morally responsible to create a new set of values on which they can build better institutions for a better society.[2]

Walker's voice seemed tame when compared to the militancy of the period, since she relied on philosophers she admired. But her messaging was characteristically coded. In the "Revolution and the University," the speech she had given at Northwestern and later published in her 1997 collection of essays, she began with references to John Henry Cardinal Newman, John Dewey, and Alfred North Whitehead, but quickly pivoted to W. E. B. Du Bois's *Souls of Black Folk*. Without any mention of the *word* "race," she took Du Bois's quote on the function of education, "the organ of the fine adjustment between real life and the growing knowledge of life, an adjustment which forms the secret of civilization,"[3] he had said. Similarly, her emphasis upon the university as the "generator of ideas for all mankind" led directly into what she needed to "preach" regarding the formation of values and judgments. It was in this essay that she offered criticisms to her alma mater, Northwestern, believing that the contemporary university was "called upon to lead by example in learning what is just, what is true, what is real, and what leads to freedom and peace." If they could not accept this responsibility, she concluded, "then the university does not deserve to exist."[4]

The second foundational idea for the Institute derived from her understanding of the historical and political context of the period. What the nation had been, and what it was becoming, were always on her mind; any hope for the future had to begin with understanding the past. With the election of Richard Nixon, for example, Walker saw a return to the past. Her analysis of Nixon's presidency—never seen outside of the journal entry—would have currency for years to come:

> The Nixon Administration seems to be a repetition of the Rutherford Hayes period in American history. That is not a favorable time in government for black people. The Republican party is not only courting and winning the white South as Hayes did in his infamous compromise, but Nixon is trying to establish the Republican Party across the Nation as ultra-conservative, which is not only anti-labor, but also anti-Negro or anti-black people. The obvious first step is to change the Supreme Court from the liberal court which it became in the

1930's under Franklin Delano Roosevelt back to the nine old men who were on the bench before Roosevelt threatened to pack the court if he could not change it. But he changed it. As far back as Reconstruction when civil rights acts were passed for a decade after the Civil War, the Supreme Court has had cycles of liberal and conservative decisions—1875 civil rights laws were probably the last from those begun in 1865 and then in 1883 these were reversed until 1896 when Segregation was firmly established. In the early years of the 20th century, segregation took a firmer hold and the record of lynchings from 1900 through 1929 should tell the story. Nixon and his party expect to be re-elected in 1972 and they may be but if they are the country could be in open rebellion by 1976—the 200th anniversary of the American Revolution and the Declaration of Independence. White America believes now that it could put down a black revolution should it become violent and get "out of hand" and this is perhaps true, but white and black people know that coalitions would not be so easily beaten, put down, or destroyed. Just now black militants are against these coalitions because they do not trust any white people and, feel that black people must first be united as a people—close together because of all we have in common—our blackness, our economic and political dependency, and our cultural or educational lack and ignorance. A cultural revolution is necessary first—economic and political [realized] must be demonstrated—not merely measured as potential—and tight organization must follow awareness. **We no longer need a Messiah like King or Evers, or Malcolm X**—who have served a very heroic and tragic purpose. What are needed now is mass unity, mass understanding, mass strength, and mass power.[5]

Her experience as a journalist during her WPA days accounted for her news-style commentary that worked well for posting quick thoughts as journal entries, ones she had expected to flesh out later. While she had expressed no political ambitions at the time, she was an engaged and respected intellectual who remained an uncompromising voice on behalf of a socially just America. In her head and the pages of her journal at least, she held America's leaders accountable for creating oppressive conditions and condoning racist neglect. These were the conditions that required mass action as the only appropriate response, she argued. Her thinking remained consistent with the shape that America had taken under the presidency of Franklin Delano Roosevelt, whose progress on racial questions was mainly due to the interventions and influence of first lady Eleanor.[6] That era of radical social change with mass organizing at an all-time high became the standard by which she saw America and continued to judge its potential for change. It was, therefore, easy for her to advocate and support the student organizing that occurred under John A. Peoples, who remained Jackson State's president until 1984, and James Hefner, who succeeded him from 1984 to 1991.

The Institute's third anchor was a focus on what would come to be called the New Black South. She was ever guilty of South-watching,[7] a phrase coined by John Shelton Reed to explain the late twentieth-century preoccupations with ideas that reimagined the South. The New South, from a white Southern perspective, was always conflicted since it was often unclear as to whether it meant pouring "the old cultural wine of planter rule and white supremacy into those new economic and demographic bottles,"[8] according to Reed. For Walker, however, as a witness to all that was going on in the United States, she could focus on the transformative potential of the South, not the conflicts. For her it meant showcasing Black talent, some of the best-known and most-influential scholars, artists, and diplomats in the United States and the world who could tackle major issues in a changing America. For her, the South was no longer a no man's land. She belonged to a generation—if not partially responsible for it—who sought to demystify the South, a practice that would continue. For Walker, the South, along with its history, brought psychological complexity, inspiration, real and mythic landscapes, and vernacular culture, all of which fed an artist's imagination. Producing innovative forms of visual, musical, and literary culture may have been caused by a need to explain itself to the world, as some believed. But for the Black South, the externally imposed restrictions forced people to turn inward, tapping into a reservoir of cultural richness and spiritual strength. Living and working in the South for Walker provided renewable creative energy that could be put to good use. The Institute was, in fact, Walker's way of giving order to her imagination and form to that energy.

While on the surface the Institute's timing coalesced with those Black Studies initiatives emerging during the late 1960s at PWIs, it was significantly different from those for several important reasons. First, the Institute was not prompted by mass student protests. It was a seasoned approach to institutional and social transformation that evolved from her ideological grounding in the 1930s, and yet it was intentionally non-ideological. It could be seen as the physical manifestation of "For My People," since it was a way of recreating a world where the past and present could be understood and the future imagined. She complemented that with the idea of its being the repository for her papers and journals. Second, it was not exclusive: not only did it provide enormous opportunities for the students at Jackson State, it also gave others outside of the South a reason to come to Jackson for meaningful and productive intellectual and cultural exchange. In doing so, Walker had the ears of the Black media who followed the appearances of national and international speakers she brought to Jackson State. It was exactly what was needed to recenter and recover the Black South. As her Institute was the only remaining center of its type in the South at an HBCU well past the half-century mark, Walker had given the South back to itself in a way that everyone could embrace.

The term "Black Studies" encapsulated what she was doing at first because Walker, like many others, was looking for ways to advance a new field, she believed, by advocating for new systems of thought, new ways of teaching, and promoting Black knowledge production. She had long ago accepted her blended professional identity, the teacher-artist-scholar, shaped by her parents, whose lives epitomized an aspirational middle class with careers in Black higher education. That world brought not so much social status, as responsibility to provide Black youth with a solid training. In addition to earning one acceptance and, hopefully, respect among whites, a Black education brought enormous added value. Whether or not you took white culture, modified and adapted, as your own, such an education could succeed in meeting the needs of Black people in a rapidly changing world in the last quarter of the twentieth century.

Such thinking was at once practical and philosophical. How might she respond to the "call" for Black Studies? What could she bring to the table? She had the benefit of a classical education in a white university that came after her fifteen-year gestation period at Black institutions where education was both a right and a privilege. Could she be that bridge that was needed at a time when the ideal of America was in constant conflict with its reality? She described the Institute's broad and inclusive vision as "interdisciplinary, inter-departmental, and intercultural in nature and scope, . . . a humanistic approach to knowledge."[9]

An early indication of the "humanistic approach" appeared in an essay she contributed to a 1973 report on "Curriculum Changes in Black Colleges III," published by the US Department of Education:

Teaching European art, music, literature and western civilization exclusively is a crime against all humanity and particularly against black humanity. It is altogether misleading. It demands in the first place a truncated world and a truncated civilization which, of course cannot exist. It is like a worm with neither head nor tail, beginning in the middle of things. It divides the natural world into unnatural parts of East and West, then ignores and eliminates the oriental world and all its ancient significance . . . Humanities then obviously begins in Africa with black humanity. World literature begins with the ancient Egyptian *Book of the Dead* which predates all the epics of Homer and Virgil and obviously influences the Rhadamanthus legend from the beginning of recorded literature to Ralph Ellison's *Invisible Man*.[10]

The kind of intervention Walker was calling for had parallels in more public debates within higher education, but hers was unique in its focus on HBCUs. The essay's double-voiced nature was rhetorically provocative. On the one hand, she criticized the younger militant generation, "the impractical dreamers full of unchanneled emotion and imaginative fantasies," and proposed "that creativity . . . be channeled in various constructive ways." On the other hand, she argued forcefully:

> We need to strip ourselves of the unnecessary baggage clinging to our liberal arts education. We need to know how to do things well and with skill, first in order to survive, for pure survival; second, in order to liberate our people or actually accomplish complete social and intellectual freedom; and third, in order to entertain and occupy ourselves in times of leisure.[11]

Her revisionist model combined liberal arts education espoused by Du Bois, without refuting the value of the Washingtonian example of Tuskegee, which highlighted the more practical uses of Black education. She was in effect presenting a racial paradigm that presumed a socially segregated world. The use of pronouns "we," "our," and "ourselves" suggest her collective advocacy for the HBCU as a site of transformation and racial survival.

> The black student has a right to know how the black diaspora has affected the entire planet earth . . . the three moments in historical time when black people were cut off from their mother country—Africa—by the Roman Empire, by the religious wards of the Middle Ages, and by the colonialism and slavery inflicted upon us through European domination at the beginning of their modern civilization.[12]

A more important point in the essay is her critique against the use of technology to aid in the programming of what she called "mass ignorance . . . even for genocide. Jensenism, Shockleyism, Moynihanism to name but a few control mechanisms, are designed for our racial destruction,"[13] she wrote. Humanism was a positive and constructive weapon essential for the purpose of racial survival.

The slow-burn effect of her militant rhetoric was understandable and yet remarkable. Perhaps because she lived in a state with a sustained climate of fear, she expressed no fear in leveling these criticisms in a public document. Walker was impressed by the view put forth by the former *Newsweek* correspondent Sam Yette in a controversial book, *The Choice: The Issue of Black Survival in America*, popular at the time she was expanding her vision. Like Walker, Yette was a Southerner, educated at an HBCU, and once terminated from his position at *Newsweek*, spent the remainder of his career at Howard University. At the time, the book was viewed with suspicion by many Blacks who believed that conspiracy theories represented a radical fringe that detracted from racial progress. But Mississippi provided Walker with more than enough evidence to support Yette's view. While racial progress was evident in the state, Mississippi continued to have the highest numbers for Black infant mortality, illiteracy, and poverty, with staggering death and incarceration statistics that would only increase. Her intent was to show that any discussions about Black people had to start in Mississippi.

Centering a particular kind of discourse about race in Mississippi gave the Institute the legitimacy that it needed, elevating the importance of Jackson State, along with Walker's leadership. For planning the Institute's events, she drew on a familiar scaffolding: communal settings with people of different ages and sectors, individuals and families; a range of activities meant to nurture, educate, and entertain. The goal was to gather and share the accumulated knowledge within the Black community in a context that pushed the work forward.

The level of thought and attention that went into the planning of events, assorted venues, and choice of speakers was intentional. Jackson State was still in a very vulnerable position, and she knew that the university could use some positive press to counter the lingering effects of the Jackson State Massacre. She was mobilizing a community by bringing renewed attention to the critical role for the Deep South in forging a new era of cultural and intellectual activism that could parallel its earlier one as a center for the Civil Rights Movement. Since HBCUs were physically located in historic Black communities, she saw advantages and disadvantages. Tougaloo College was on the outskirts of Jackson and had established its reputation as a hub for the Civil Rights Movement and home for SNCC activists. Jackson State, therefore, had to establish a new identity for itself, one she could amplify with her sizeable number of contacts from around the country. It could become a galvanizing force for the entire Black community, a platform for transformative thinking, making Walker's role as its Institute's director central.

Doris Derby, a native New Yorker and early member of SNCC who remained in Jackson for nine years, remembers that Walker not only had a large and supportive local community network, but she also maintained active relationships with national organizations of artists and writers, and local and national politicians. Walker was very close, for example, with John Oliver Killens, whom Derby knew from New York. He had founded, along with Rosa Guy, John Henrik Clarke, Willard Moore, and Walter Christmas, the Harlem Writers Guild in 1950, a place where almost every working writer for several generations would pass through. Walker and Killens were not only the same age but also Southerners. Alex and Killens had also been in the army at the same time, which meant that John and his wife Grace were friends with the Alexanders on a number of levels.

As Derby explained, the Writers Guild would remain the largest network of Black writers, and many of the members made visits to the Institute at Walker's invitation. "I was almost always in attendance since I knew a good many of them," Derby said, "and I would attend the after events that were always held at Walker's house."[14] These events turned out to be Walker's signature, a lavish dinner at her family residence, no matter what the size of the gathering. Even if the event was too large for Walker to do all the cooking herself, which she often did, she would oversee every aspect of the evening dinner parties. She confirmed everyone's faith in Southern hospitality on the one hand, but she also circumvented any confrontation that could arise if those attending her events wanted to eat in the city's white restaurants. With her superb cooking hard to resist, Walker could play the gracious host while uniting people around a new idea or action she was already formulating in her mind.

Derby ultimately joined the Institute's staff to help expand its art-related programs, especially the summer art camps. A partnership with a fellow faculty member, Lawrence Jones, linked the Institute to JSU's art department, which Jones had founded. The addition of art to the Institute's activities was important since a long history of segregation allowed few opportunities for Black artists. Walker had known Jones from his days at the Chicago Art Institute, and he had worked briefly with the Federal Arts Project on the WPA. Their partnership had a mutually beneficial advantage: Jones could expand his program as more students became interested in art, and the Institute could exhibit more artists from the Africa diaspora.

Before the Institute emerged, Jackson had been primarily known to most white outsiders as the home of Pulitzer Prize–winning writer Eudora Welty, even as it began to make bolder efforts to step outside of its provincialism more than

Walker with Stephen Henderson, Howard University professor, and JSU students. Courtesy of the Margaret Walker Center

most of the South. Jackson would begin to "open up," as people often referred to the gradual desegregation of public facilities in the late 1970s. For example, a public auditorium built in 1968 was technically open to all, but it was not effectively so until Thalia Mara, an internationally renowned ballet performer, agreed to come to Jackson in 1975 to develop a professional ballet company and school, one of several initiatives to change Mississippi's image and a sign of more changes to come. The wise decision helped to turn Jackson into one of the most international cities in the South. Before that, however, no Black churches or performance venue was large enough to offer the kind of professional programming possible at Jackson State.

Jackson was the capital of a state bordering Alabama, Louisiana, Arkansas, and Tennessee, and equally close to East Texas and North Florida. In essence, the Institute was striking a blow in the heart of the Black Belt. Appropriately, Walker elected not to focus on a single type of event, but combined timeliness with variety. Even with a theme-driven program, the speakers list ensured a broad range of perspectives. The Institute's 1971 National Evaluative Conference, for example, the third and most important national conference on the topic of Black Studies, announced four basic goals: "to discover the nature of the various programs (philosophy and purpose); to establish lines of communication and organization; to evaluate educational outcomes and significance; and to use this knowledge to develop criteria for new programs that were rapidly emerging.[15] The degree of success in advancing social change on the campus and in the community was linked to each goal. Along with the keynote addresses by Chuck Stone, Congressman John Conyers, C. Eric Lincoln, and Alex Haley, Walker invited position papers from Vincent Harding and Stephen Henderson, Andrew Billingsley, John Henrik Clarke, and Wilfred Cartey. She asked William Strickland, Leonard Jeffries, and Nick Aaron Ford to give reaction papers, along with individual students from Jackson State.

Faculty at the college served as group discussion leaders. Special sessions took place with Black Studies directors, Black student organizations, and cultural centers. But what no one missed was Walker's emphasis upon place. She had her own version of what Thadious Davis calls "race, region and reclamation,"[16] which was evident in the proposal for funding she submitted to the National Endowment for the Humanities:

> This area between Memphis and New Orleans contains the heart of the Cotton Kingdom of slavery, the decisive battle fields of the western front of the Civil War, and is noted historically for the most egregious forms of repression of Black culture emanating from the systems of slavery and segregation. Black culture has its deepest if not richest Roots in the soil of this deep southern section.[17]

Typical post conference event at the Alexander home

Her argument emphasized the value she placed on the South in all of her work. For follow-up, she planned visits to participating schools, as well as a published report of the conference outlining the three-part structure of these programs: its philosophy, educational purpose and methods, and strategies for social change.

The event got a great deal of local attention. The discussions were rich and meaningful. For many who attended, the conference marked a turning point. But the Black Studies movement had become a turf battle that the South was unable to win, as programs in white Northern universities seemed to preclude the contributions that HBCUs made. With the exception of Howard University, few HBCUs followed the model established by Walker. The level of inter-institutional dialogue that she hoped to initiate did become a reality in the 1975 organizing meeting of the National Council for Black Studies (NCBS). Although some of those who attended the Institute's National Evaluative Conference were at the NCBS's inaugural meeting, the organization reflected a decided shift in two ways: toward younger scholars and a demographic base outside the South.

Nevertheless, Walker was staking her own claim in the Black Studies debate. Her overview for the conference pointed out "our mutual search for remedies, panaceas, and reasonable alternatives to violence, chaos, and anarchy."[18] Although she believed that Black Studies programs were a creative response to violence and racism, she felt strongly that we should not allow the reactive component of these programs to overshadow the need to examine them closely. She wanted to ensure their intellectual rigor, delineate their scope, and define ways for measuring what they do. Her philosophy of inclusion, rather than exclusion, continued to be at the core of her thinking.

While there were individual courses developed by scholars and writers who accepted positions in newly formed programs around the country, like Sonia Sanchez who taught the first Black Studies course at San Francisco State University, there were other concerted efforts to grapple with a radical critique of education on the national level. A Symposium on Black Studies held at Yale in 1968 and the resulting publication was one of the most celebrated. Armstead Robinson, one of the key leaders, edited and published the proceedings as *Black Studies in the University: A Symposium* in 1969. The Yale conference led in intellectual capital, but it was a Black Marxist collective, known as Peoples College, whose slogan "study and struggle" created a different model, at another HBCU, Fisk University in Nashville. Emphasizing the connection between social change and the acquisition and production of knowledge, the collective brought competing ideological views into a coherent "paradigm of unity." An early stage of their work brought together students and faculty from Fisk with members of the Nashville community, students and shop workers in shared dialogues about social change. The emphasis on grassroots organizing and their high visibility in anti-imperialist campaigns brought increased attention to global injustices. Exposing investments in countries supporting oppressive conditions by US corporations, including universities, often put them at odds with other groups. The Peoples College collective was the most consistent in sharpening the debate over the nature of Black Studies through their frequent appearance at conferences, ongoing community organizing efforts, a strong political education component, and the self-published widely circulating *Introduction to Afro-American Studies: A Peoples College Primer*. From a mimeographed course syllabus to a bound text and finally to an e-book, *Intro*, as it was called, gave a major push to defining an inclusive, precise discipline. The volume defined Black Studies as a "radical movement for fundamental educational reform," by asking the most critical questions that kept it grounded: "Afro-American Studies: Who, What, Why, and For Whom."[19]

Walker asked those questions in a different way. She understood that defining the field and giving it an imprint was a priority. Otherwise, those programs that were emerging in the late 1960s stood in danger of succumbing to the needs of each particular institution, preventing the field from having integrity. Bringing a greater sense of self-consciousness about the methods and scope of the work was what she sought. She addressed the key juxtaposition: the knowledge/action dichotomy with an imperative of social change; questions about teaching; and models for research. She believed that if she created a space for the dialogue, the answers to these questions could emerge.

For as much as she grasped the importance of shaping a new movement, what Walker did not realize at the time was her accommodation to and reification of a decidedly masculine world. In the early days of the Institute, her conference presenters were generally men, although her planning notes frequently listed the women she was considering. The legacy of the Civil Rights and Black Power movements had made difficult the kind of intervention she thought possible. Even if she held up Fannie Lou Hamer when she thought of the Civil Rights Movement, the field of Black Studies represented the hierarchical nature of the society. Walker was an established figure, but without the cultural capital or geographical advantage that a new era required. The Institute had provided her with a base of power, but it would have to wait to gain the respect it deserved. Her Black think-tank model was an early laboratory experiment, one that seemed out of reach to a new generation of scholars. When a shift did occur, the bases of operation were generally within white institutions.

The significant turn in the field that Walker had helped to accomplish had other important markers, however. The Ford Foundation had been an important source of funding Black Studies programs at HBCUs, including Fisk, Howard, Morgan State, Lincoln, and Atlanta. By 1982, however, Ford's funding priorities shifted away from the HBCUs toward PWIs, primarily research institutions, where they helped to grow programs through 2004. In a published report of its work in the field as a whole, Ford cited the Yale conference in 1968 as a key historical moment, making no mention of the 1971 Jackson State conference, the only one hosted by an HBCU.

The Institute for the Study of the History, Life, and Culture of Black People, on the other hand, had provided the professional rejuvenation that resulted in a personal achievement for Walker. Even as she gave up opportunities in order to keep her family and the Institute on track, notably a Fulbright Fellowship to Trondheim, Norway, what she received in return was arguably far better. For one, Sigis returned home from the Marines in June 1971, finally free to return to a normal life. For Walker, it meant, for the moment at least, relief from those daily fears that kept her up at night, worrying that she'd receive a call that her son had been killed in action.

Her visionary work at the Institute signaled something else personal for Walker, a return to poetry. Only a few poems appeared in her journals, but after the Jackson State upheaval in May 1970, she sensed the renewal of her creative unconscious, which took precedence over her rational sensibilities. Indeed, it would have been difficult to be rational about what was happening in the country, and especially at Jackson State then. The poetry emerging was her assessment of the 1960s, thoughts and images of the violence and tragedy throughout Mississippi during that decade of turmoil. The idea of modern-day prophets provided her theme. It is likely that she had begun to think about publishing something after Dudley Randall wrote to her when he founded Broadside

Press in Detroit in 1965. The first book was a tribute to the life and work of Malcolm X, who had spent his early years in Detroit. Randall's second reason for starting the press was a desire to publish Detroit-area and other poets of his generation whom he believed needed to have a voice alongside the younger writers. He hoped she would have something to send him. Randall helped her reconnect with Margaret Danner and Naomi Long Madgett, who were part of her cohort of poets.

The return of a familiar context, an opportunity to reunite with a community of poets, offered her the strongest motivation for writing new poetry. She finally replied to Randall when the spring semester ended in 1970. If she could send him something by late spring, he told her, he could have a chapbook out by summer. Randall reminded her that the annual meeting of the American Library Association was to be in Detroit that June, and he wanted to release the book in time for the event.

At the end of June, one week before her fifty-fifth birthday, Walker left for Detroit, expecting to see her first book of poetry in twenty-eight years. She enjoyed the conversations she had with young poets. She and Margaret Burroughs had been in lively dialogue about what the younger writers were doing. By the 1970s, the Chicago wing of the Black Arts Movement had become fully consolidated as a result of the activities of Chicago-based poets: Carolyn Rodgers, Johari Amini, Angela Jackson, and Sterling Plumpp, as well as Haki Madhubuti. Although Sonia Sanchez and Nikki Giovanni were not Chicago-based, they had a close association with the Chicago group.

It was probably Burroughs who had encouraged Walker to end her dry spell, pointing to the success of the Broadside's 1967 volume *For Malcolm: Poets on the Life and Death of Malcolm X*, a collection that helped to establish a new trend in American poetry. Finding herself among these younger poets, with a new book published by a Black press, gave Walker a more secure place in the Black Arts Movement. She believed it was important that the South be well represented in the poetry and other writing for a new age. Because of this, the poet with whom she developed the closest relationship in Detroit was Sonia Sanchez. Born in Birmingham, Sanchez was for Walker a new way of connecting to the South through one of its most respected writers. Her fascination for this daughter of the South who had followed such a different path never ceased: Sanchez became her literary godchild with whom Walker would always feel the strongest allegiance.

Walker's book *Prophets for a New Day* emerged from her experience of living in a violent era where loss was the norm rather than the exception. As its title suggests, the twenty-two poems that make up the volume connect history, struggle, and freedom, the spiritual map that Walker draws for the civil rights years. Stylistically, the poems aren't new, but seeing individuals as "prophets" gave them meaning far beyond their particular lives. Familiar events are all identified by the locations: James Meredith's attempt to integrate the University of

Mississippi in "Oxford Is a Legend," and the March on Washington in "At the Lincoln Monument in Washington." The practice of the movement also calls up spatial markers, as in the poems "Girl Held without Bail" and "Sit-Ins." The poem "Birmingham" is an homage to her birthplace, blending image and thought into an unpredictable logic:

> Call me home again to my coffin bed of soft warm clay.
> I cannot bear to rest in frozen wastes
> Of a bitter cold and sleeting northern womb
> My life dies best on a southern cross
> Carved out of rock with shooting stars to fire
> The forge of bitter hate.[20]

Form and emotion come together in the volume: Walker infuses herself with the place and the people of "her" South. The first twenty-two lines of "Jackson, Mississippi" present the portrait of a repressive culture "with new white police bullies," as the poem evolves into a testimonial:

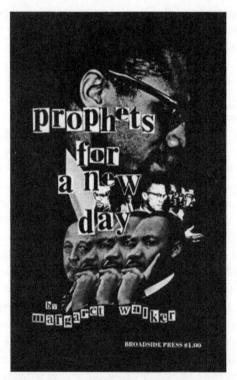

Prophets for a New Day appeared in 1970.

I have planted my seeds of dreams and visions and prophecies
All my fantasies of freedom and of pride,
Here lie three centuries of my eyes and my brains and my hands,
Of my lips and strident demands,
The graves of my dead,
And the birthing stools of nannies long since fled.
Here are echoes of my laughing children
And hungry minds of pupils to be fed.
I give you my brimming heart, Southern City
For my eyes are full and no tears cry
And my throat is dusty and dry.[21]

She had made a remarkable comeback; her twenty-eight years of silence without a book of poetry had ended, and she was celebrated among old and new friends. *Prophets for a New Day* was both soulful inspiration and lived experience.

25

Midwife to a Movement

The Detroit visit introduced another new element into Walker's thinking. She continued to hear and respond to the word "feminist" with unequivocal denunciation. While she was critical of male culture, she was not anti-male, which is what she understood feminism to mean in her initial encounters. But because she was engaging in feminist practices, that is, a recognition of and aggressive response to the oppression she faced as a woman and as a writer, her resistance did not always make sense. Public visibility as a highly sought after speaker and leadership of a major national center justified Walker's belief that she did not need to frame a "new" identity for herself. She was aware of how others might see her and insisted on self-definition to clear up any confusion: "I am fundamentally and contradictorily three things: religious almost to the point of orthodoxy; radical but wishing to see neither the extreme radical left nor the radical right in control; and like the astrological description of a crab, a Cancer—quick to retreat into my shell when hurt or attacked [until] I find another way out when the way I have chosen has been closed to me."[1] Walker confirms the underpinnings of otherworldliness contained in all of her writing. The obstinacy underlying the genteel Southern lady emerges here, an obstinacy that easily transformed into determination and resoluteness on all work-related matters.

The completion of her sixth decade made it important for Walker to assert her own identity and separateness. The confidence she felt in the Institute's work as everything was finally coming together left no room for ambivalence in anything she hoped to do. She allowed neither time nor her age to stand in her way. The contradictions between her public and private lives seemed to subside. At least she had learned how to adjust and navigate them without major confrontation. Publicly, her speeches, theories, and writings continued to set the tone and measure the boundaries for her ideas and applied practice. She still lived according to the values associated with women of her generation, who championed domesticity and the family-centered life. But they demanded as much of themselves in their public and professional roles.

Regardless of the volatile nature of her physical health, Walker had the time, the disposition, and access to do something that was indeed radical for the 1970s, a period during which she had considerable power as a Black woman, albeit within the narrow confines of the academy. The only other woman with whom she could compare herself was Dorothy Porter, another good friend, who had a

The House Where My Soul Lives. Maryemma Graham, Oxford University Press. © Oxford University Press 2022.
DOI: 10.1093/oso/9780195341232.003.0025

Walker with a bust of Phillis Wheatley by Elizabeth Catlett, commissioned for the festival. Courtesy of the Margaret Walker Center

reputation as the visionary leader shaping the future of scholarship by building a powerhouse at the Howard University library, a reputation that spread all the way to libraries in Africa. In the nonacademic world, another key figure was her close friend Margaret Burroughs, head of the DuSable Museum, by that time the first and oldest museum dedicated to the study and preservation of African American culture and heritage. Walker enjoyed the rare prominence and stature that living in the South gave her, and she took great pleasure in her work and her life. Her opinions mattered, and she had learned how to put her words and thoughts into actions.

As long as Walker remained in the South, she felt centered, but the more she traveled outside its borders the more she began to sense dislocation. The reason might well have had to do with getting older, the inability to control the diabetes, and the resulting fatigue from long rides by car, her preferred mode of travel. Her children wanted her to spend more time in Chicago, but she had gotten to the point where having her house occupied only by the two of them, she and Alex, brought great pleasure. But with so much alone time, her search for a more ambitious project intensified.

The search for something entirely new derived from a range of factors. By the 1970's, more Black women writers were emerging on the literary scene. One of them, Alice Walker, had come to Jackson with her husband Melvyn Leventhal as part of the growing community of Civil Rights Movement activists. Alice was from Georgia and a fellow poet, to whom Walker was understandably drawn. Alice had acknowledged Walker's importance in a letter of support and love between women of different generations. "I want to say words of magic," Alice wrote,

> "that would take away all of your illnesses, your tiredness, and give back the years. Words that would soothe your doubts and troubles and wipe away your tears . . . [You] care more for us than we are strong enough to care for ourselves . . . I will cherish the heritage, the courage and the love that made you possible."[2]

But she and Alice were poles apart, given the age differences and Walker's more traditional values. Welcoming the writer when her first novel, *The Third Life of Grange Copeland*, appeared in 1970, was something that Margaret wanted to do and did. She saw Alice's publications as a sign for the future of Black writing, a future associated directly with the South. Walker's decades of classroom experience offered a useful introduction to Alice, who had begun her education at Spelman College. Her opportunities increased following her move to Sarah Lawrence College.

She invited Alice to her classes, an offer that was gladly accepted. There is an often-repeated story of Alice's first learning about Zora Neale Hurston in one of Walker's classes, confirmed by an undated handwritten note. While Hurston had clearly piqued her interest, Alice was eager to get more information about other women writers. Even with years of teaching behind her, Walker had yet to include more discussions of the writing by Black women. Even though Hurston wrote about and documented the South, returning to live in her native Florida for most of her later life, Walker was more likely drawn to the writers she knew well, especially during her Chicago years, like Richard Wright, Ralph Ellison, and Arna Bontemps. Furthermore, not only were Hurston's works out of print, *Their Eyes Were Watching God* would not be reissued until 1978.

The anecdote from Alice Walker highlights a major yet unacknowledged contradiction that persisted for Walker. Despite a lifelong commitment to writing as a woman, she thought that overcoming the difficulties that she and other women had required working harder and demonstrating excellence. "Small minded men," as she called them would always be jealous. Walker considered herself and women like Hurston to be in powerless positions, important but without much recognition. Acceptance of one's position could easily invite dismissiveness, or arrogance, which is what Walker was often accused of. As well read and analytical as she was, Walker had yet to fully comprehend the political dimensions of the Black women's movement. As was her custom, when her understanding of any issue or new ideas lagged behind in any way, she rejected them all except in principle. She may also have held on to a childhood memory of Hurston, whom Marion introduced to her when Hurston was in the earlier stages of her research in Florida. Hurston's rediscovery was something to which Alice Walker would become central. Walker knew the name, but took her cues from her mother, a trained classical musician, who did not recognize the value of Hurston's work at the time the three of them met in Jacksonville. At least in that moment, it was far more important for the students to hear stories about the male writers Walker knew during her time in Chicago, stories that would allow her to relive the excitement of her youth and affirm her importance among major writers.

Whenever Walker spoke about other Black writers, the experience was relational. When she talked about writers she knew personally, she could remember how much work was involved in establishing a career, how much work they had done, and the validation they had received as a result. There was value in hard work, and with it a movement toward individual social responsibility and ethical behavior for every artist. In contrast, Walker was the least familiar with any movement toward advocacy of Black women writers. Yet, she knew more women writers than anyone, especially the poets. Her visits to Chicago always included a gathering of a Chicago group who were part of her friendship circle, many identified with the Black Arts Movement.

More immediately for Walker, the encounters with and parallels between Alice Walker and herself were sufficient to nurture a friendship that she welcomed. Beyond their Southern connection, there were other similarities. Alice's first book of poetry appeared in 1968, when she was twenty-six; Walker was twenty-seven when hers had been published. A book party for the release of *Once* was a sign of Walker's enthusiasm for and acknowledgement of the gifted younger writer. As a young couple living and working in Jackson, Alice Walker and Melvyn Leventhal represented the new South: they had the distinction of being the first interracial marriage in the state to have legal sanction, which was signified by the birth of their daughter Rebekah. They were the most telling example of positive change that was possible in a state known for the most brutal forms of racism and oppression.

Whatever Walker may have imagined in terms of a relationship between them never happened. Alice Walker's success was steady and continuous. A mentor-mentee relationship, whether or not it was desired, does not seem to have developed. Alice had embraced and redefined feminism, becoming increasingly more visible in the mainstream media, as Walker continued to view feminism with suspicion. Alice's decisions to divorce her husband and move to New York created more distance between the two women. For Walker, children and family were central; Alice, Walker told herself, was willing to risk everything for her career.

Walker did not need the acknowledgement of friendship to praise *The Third Life of Grange Copeland* in her journal and publicly. She believed it to be extremely well written, with remarkable and highly convincing characters, and was especially important in affirming the possibility of human, and by implication, social transformation in the South through several generations. It had been Alice's own experience as the child of a sharecropping family from Eatonton, Georgia, Walker concluded, that made for her poignant and evocative depictions of social and economic conditions so convincing.

Besides Alice Walker, Walker was close to SNCC workers, both local and transplanted, who were active in Jackson, where they continued to nurture a thriving literary and arts community in and around the city. Doris Derby, John O'Neal, and Barbara Nayo Watkins were three of those most visible. While some Mississippi writers had migrated, like Sterling Plumpp, Angela Jackson, and Etheridge Knight, as did those from other points South, like Ernest Gaines, John A. Williams, and John O. Killens, all of them claimed the South as a touchstone in their writing. Walker also had begun to draw more students with an interest in the performing arts to her classes and to the Institute, growing closer to Vergia Brock-Shedd, Curtis King, and Tonea (Tommie) Stewart.

Walker was not privy to those networks that saw an astonishing body of new work emerge by Black women in the 1970's, although she was very much aware of Maya Angelou's *I Know Why the Caged Bird Sings* that had appeared in 1969. Another native Southerner, Angelou had drawn on a poem by Paul Laurence Dunbar for the book's title. Tucked away in the back of Walker's mind was the idea that she needed to tell her story as well, with perhaps a question about why Angelou had written an autobiography at forty-one. The separation between the public and the private sphere for women aligned with conventional gender practices. While Frederick Douglass and W. E. B. DuBois had both written multiple autobiographies, it took Walker by surprise every time Angelou would produce another one. Telling a woman's story did not register for her as a marketable item. Nonetheless, a seed of an idea—the relation of Black women to writing more generally—had begun to grow.

After getting an offer from Boston University asking if they might become the repository for her papers, Walker had began to think more intentionally about her legacy and wrote a will. The last thing she wanted was for someone else to make any decisions on her behalf in her absence. The combined activities of women liberationists, the anti-war movement, and student protestors on college campuses South and North may have overshadowed what was happening in the publishing world for Walker. Writing her will brought back feelings—a mix of fear and pride—connected to her early years in Chicago. The United States was still in the throes of the Depression, which made for an exciting literary and cultural scene and her full immersion within it.

And yet, the success of the Institute was still only partially satisfying. It was as if something was staring her in the face, but she could not see it clearly. She escaped from her thoughts temporarily by laying out the themes for her autobiography on Mother's Day 1971. In this early version, she wanted to frame her life as a pilgrimage of the soul, organizing the years between ages twenty-eight and fifty-five, which she turned in 1970. Interestingly, Walker set full maturity to begin at twenty-eight, which meant that any irresponsible actions during earlier years could be attributed to a young, struggling artist. The Chicago period especially she saw as her "years of apostasy." In contrast, by twenty-eight she had begun to prepare for marriage and motherhood, which made her "fully a woman." Following the pattern of traditional religious autobiography, maturity was signified by finding and verifying one's faith, a set of beliefs, and a choice of career, which formed the arc of a responsible life. In this version, Walker could place her life into orderly containers, justifying her early success as a discovery or experimental phase of one life, during which one is allowed to make mistakes, while centering her life on what she had come to value most: love, marriage, and family. What followed were the seven years of "domestic obscurity," with a new phase starting at age thirty-five, corresponding with the year she moved to Jackson State. Between the ages of forty and forty-seven, the theme of "financial insecurity" was appropriate, a time when she also began to experience health issues. Her next organizing theme was the "pinnacle of her success," occurring between the ages forty-seven and fifty-three and leading to the "consolidation of gains." Her prediction for the post-sixty years—five years in the future—was a "return to obscurity."

There would be three more outlines and at least two full drafts of her autobiography, but none as telling as the themes she identified in 1971. It was natural for her to see her career winding down, but the idea of being a "has-been" headed toward obscurity was not something to embrace. She had much more to give, more books unfinished than she had published, and new books to write. Unconsciously, perhaps, she had begun to design a new role for herself that might offset what seemed inevitable.

To go forward meant going backwards, which also meant the review of who she was: first and foremost a poet whose content had always been historical. Even the forms of poetry she selected as her models were public forms like the epic or the ballad, the quintessential narrative derived from the folk. It had a natural sequel in the historical novel since she could draw on the collections of the slave narratives. As Walker began to observe the growing list of publications by women beginning in 1969, her thoughts naturally turned to the most important historical figure in African American poetry, Phillis Wheatley. Wheatley was the first known African American poet to publish a book, whose remark-able achievement was being debated by scholars. Wheatley's poetry was already included in the new group of anthologies of Black literature that were being published. Despite the surge in Black poetry during the Black Arts Movement, there was still little published criticism on Wheatley. The first updated history didn't appear until 1976, when Eugene Redmond published *Drum Voices*. It would be decades before a first book-length study of Wheatley would appear, Vincent Carretta's biography in 2011, marking a renewal of interest in her life and work.

Walker saw no need to compete with a new generation. Her cohort would always be Arna Bontemps, Robert Hayden, Melvin Tolson, and Gwendolyn Brooks. Had she not had a platform unlike anyone else's, Walker may not have been so bold in stepping out in the way she did. Not to use it might have left her open to charges of jealousy or, worse, being classified as a has-been. The critic, the institution builder, and organizer had begun to merge into one as Walker sought a place for herself in a new cultural and literary landscape. As she watched the rise of still younger writers and the mixed response that many of them re-ceived, she knew that Black women themselves would have to form their own networks through the synergy they could create. What she had written in 1963 stayed with her, "this is the tide, now is the time."[3]

If Phillis Wheatley's *Poems on Miscellaneous Subjects, Religious and Moral* marked the beginning of a rich and complex tradition, Walker asked herself, "Where are we now?" Publishing of Black writers was increasing, and the pop-ularity of Black poetry was real, but most of the critical attention continued to center on major male figures. Her assessment was that aside from the Black Arts Movement, most Black women who were writing were doing so in isolation. She was hopeful that these women poets would not only become better known for their work, but that they also would see each other as a powerful literary com-munity. To bring long-overdue attention to something larger than themselves would foreground the long history of Black women's writing. The moment had come and the body of work was abundant, but what was missing was a space to call their own. She understood that their voices needed to be heard in unison. Wheatley could be a lightning rod, but Black women themselves had to take a first step. If ever they needed a reason to come together, it was certainly now. She saw herself as an advocate for women historically and as part of a tradition yet to be recognized:

> The most important reminder for us is that is it indeed a woman who was the best-known black writer of her period, and when today black women writers become as well-known as Toni Morrison or Alice Walker, we are simply contin-uing a tradition begun by Phillis over two hundred years ago.[4]

Was this the thing that was staring her in the face? An even larger undertaking than any of the others? The first major conference on Black women writers? She continued to imagine what might be possible, but the idea gained momentum when she attended the centennial of poet Paul Laurence Dunbar in Dayton, Ohio, in the fall of 1972. She had spent two days in Dayton experiencing a new conference model that gave her fresh ideas. The event showed ways to break down boundaries between audiences and between the different art forms, while maximizing intellectual content in a context created and led by Black women themselves.

Herbert Woodward Martin had been at the University of Dayton only two years when he conceived of the idea to have poets meet and read Dunbar's whole canon at a centennial. He assigned Walker a key role at the conference, one she eagerly accepted. Dunbar, who had died at age thirty-three, was the best-known Black poet at the turn of the twentieth century. Eighty years later, he was known primarily for a body of dialect poems, which most people dismissed. The prevailing view was that by giving white audiences what they wanted, Dunbar produced at best poetry that offered up minstrel characterizations of Black people and diminished Black culture. Walker admired Martin's bravery; he dared to reinsert Dunbar into a conversation about poetry and tradition, and he had invited major figures to speak and read, with an uncertain budget. The conference was so successful that Martin thereafter became the custodian of Dunbar's life and legacy. Although Martin published eight volumes of his own poetry, he became better known for his work in restoring Dunbar's reputation by opening up new ways of understanding his relevance in both communal and public contexts.

Since Walker had cut her performance teeth reading Dunbar's poetry as a child, the Dayton conference found her quickly returning to a world she knew well. Her mother had read Dunbar to her, and through Dunbar, Walker had developed her own performance style, skillfully replicating the intonation, accent, and emphasis appropriate for his folk poems. She was unmatched in her perfect renderings of Dunbar's rich Black speech and the indirect meanings that belie his words. Her performances, later recorded on Folkways records, not only restored Dunbar to his rightful place as a superior composer of poems in dialect and standard English, but they also gave Martin an important lesson in sight-reading as she assumed the character and the voice of the speakers in each poem. Walker made important connections at the conference with the other poets who read: Lorenzo Thomas, Raymond Patterson, Etheridge Knight, Quincy Troupe, Michael Harper, Alvin Aubert, and Martin himself. But it was the presence of women writers there that provided her with the most inspiration: Nikki Giovanni, Sonia Sanchez, Paule Marshall, Gloria Oden, and Paula Giddings.

The Dunbar centennial conference gave Walker her purpose and a design. In contrast to Dunbar, who was in a sense *too Black*, the criticism of Wheatley was that she was *not Black enough*. To celebrate a poet like Wheatley, Walker understood the need to demonstrate a *tradition* of Black women poets, since Black women, for the most part, were invisible. Wheatley and Dunbar were both known and read by white audiences. But in Walker's thinking, Wheatley was the more important of the two. She was the first Black poet to publish a volume of poetry.

On the train ride back to Jackson, she began to map out her thinking about a bi-centennial celebration that marked the two-hundredth anniversary of Wheatley's *Poems on Miscellaneous Subjects*. She took up the pen again, adding the section on Dunbar to an essay she had already composed on Langston Hughes. She entered scattered notes for another essay that eventually became "Rediscovering Black Women Writers in the Mecca of the New Negro." In it she challenged the conception that the Harlem Renaissance "centered on Harlem and a coterie of writers living there and that it was an exclusively male movement. Perhaps the most serious misconception," she added, "is the notion that women were absent from or inconspicuous in the movement. More than a dozen women were an integral part of that decade . . . poets, playwrights, novelists, singers, and dancers, and their successful enterprises were noteworthy."[5] She listed and planned to develop her thoughts on Jessie Redmon Fauset (1882–1961), Georgia Douglas Johnson (1886–1966), Anne Spencer (1882–1976), Zora Neale Hurston (1903–1960), Nella Larsen (1993–1963), Alice Dunbar Nelson (1875–1935), Angelina Weld Grimké (1880–1958), and Gwendolyn Bennett (1902–1981). At the time she was writing, Helene Johnson (1906–1995), Dorothy West (1907–1998), May Miller (1899–1995), and Effie Lee Newsome (1885–1979) were still alive. There had been no scholarly assessments of any of these writers, making Walker's early notes and later essay another of those firsts.

Walker was beginning to pay much more attention to the debates and critiques that had begun surfacing in the Women's Movement. The oppositional nature of the discourse, which is identified in an essay by Gloria Steinem in 1969, "After Black Power, Women's Liberation,"[6] troubled her. Did this mean that women would have to create a political franchise in order to improve their lot? Walker believed that the academy could accomplish that purpose without the kind of divisiveness of partisan politics, no matter how one defined feminism. Coming of age in the leftist movement of the 1930s had taught her what divisive politics did and did not accomplish. For that reason, she had made clear in the mission statement for the Institute that all of its activities would be based on a humanistic approach to knowledge. To move from the ostensible political agenda that characterized Black Power to what she saw as more humanistic concerns seemed a logical goal.

At the time Walker began the new journey, Black women were entering the market as professional writers, scholars, and major stakeholders involved in a process that was both retrospective and forward-looking in its vision, critical and creative in its practice, and filled with a new energy and excitement. They were following a period where volumes like *Black Fire: An Anthology of Afro-American Writing* (1968) and Addison Gayle's *The Black* Aesthetic (1971) had succeeded in codifying an era as unapologetically Black. Together with the smaller independent Black presses, like Third World and Broadside, both of whom she worked with, the publishing industry saw a viable market that lacked neither writers nor readers. The writers freely gave of their time in regular appearances at public events, securing positions at universities where being controversial was lucrative and could lead to a double-sided success.

The new Black Woman's Era, however, saw women in new kinds of interactions that altered the politics of being Black and a woman in the United States. Angela Davis had become a cause célèbre for her dedication to a seventeen-year-old Jonathan Jackson whose life and death symbolized the American penal system at its worst. She had begun drawing us a map of mass incarceration that would redefine America's relationship with Black people. She was in many ways the epitome of the Black woman public intellectual, trained in philosophy, Southern born and bred, radical. Few could resist the call that the actions of this twentieth-century Harriet Tubman represented, a selfless fighter for the masses. As the first of many Black women political prisoners who would experience a higher level of police surveillance and government repression and manage to survive, Davis was fearless in her commitment to speak the truth. That truth, much of which remained untold, became the singular business of Black women in an America in the 1970s. Awareness of a new concept, triple oppression, which Davis and others wrote about, guaranteed that Black women become the subjects of their own stories, not the objects of others. Unlike the more male-centered Black Power Movement, Davis did not represent a political divide among women; her following would continue to be intergenerational. Mari Evans, whose collection of poetry had welcomed the 1970s with its release on January 1, was an early example of the new direction in which Black writing was headed. The volume *I Am a Black Woman*, announced a new era with boldness, confidence, and hope, in the last line of its title poem, "Look on me and be renewed."[7]

In one of the most important publications of the period, *The Black Woman: An Anthology*, by Toni Cade Bambara, the shift from the singular "I" to a more expansive gender dynamic was another sign of the changes occurring. New networks were forming. Black women like Toni Morrison at Random House and Marie Brown at Doubleday became the editorial gurus who helped to stabilize these networks. Random House had already earned its reputation as a publishing powerhouse for Black writers with Langston Hughes, James Baldwin, and Ralph Ellison, adding Maya Angelou to its distinguished list. Morrison, looking through a different lens, saw a new landscape. She played a double role as editor and mentor to a host of new Black women writers by day, and writing at night, ensuring that she would become one of them with her first book, *The Bluest Eye*. Telling many different sides of a Black story, Morrison prompted Davis to re-count her own story in *Angela Davis: Autobiography* in 1974, and brought other popular figures like Muhammad Ali to American readers. Morrison quickly be-came the frontrunner for discovering new writers.

* * *

The Phillis Wheatley Festival was a form of spadework that supported Walker's desire to engage in this larger discourse. She had a year to plan the Festival and map out the conference. One important thing was in her favor: the Mississippi legislature had created in 1972 a Bicentennial Celebration Commission, just as the United States was preparing for its own bicentennial. The commission was charged with designating programs they might fund to mark Mississippi's state-hood. Even if the commission members were not eager to do so, they were obli-gated to include events relevant to Black Mississippians. Her first task was to apply for an official "bicentennial designation," for the festival, which would help guarantee a financial base for the event.

Writing Black people into Mississippi history as a free people in 1973 was an act of metaphorical defiance, made more significant by Walker's selection of Black women writers as an enabling force of change. Mississippi had already earned the reputation as the home of the Civil Rights Movement, and its brave and martyred had left their imprint on everyone in the state, both Black and white. She was thinking of Medgar Evers, Vernon Dahmer, Rev. Herbert Lee, and Ditney Smith and a host of others, like playwright Endesha Mae Holland, whose mother was killed in a firebombing of her home as punishment for the daughter's civil rights activism. Walker was optimistic. She cited the election of a record number of Black public officials, the huge success in voter registration, which was superior to any other state, as well as school integration that was better than most states.

Even if her goal of reframing the view of Mississippi in the public imagina-tion was ambitious, it is doubtful that anyone else could have made the politi-cally savvy move she did with the Phillis Wheatley Festival in 1973. Everyone she invited came, except for Gwendolyn Brooks, who had a previous commit-ment in Nebraska. The twenty-five women who participated came to honor the life and work of Wheatley, but coming to Mississippi caused some trepidation. In her interview with Charlayne Hunter-Gault, who covered the event for the *New York Times*, Carolyn Rodgers, admitted to thinking only of Mississippi as a place "where the Klan ran wild and you were brutalized and afraid."[8] Rodgers had grown up in Chicago, and added, "I expected to come to a place where if you go home you see blood flowing in the streets."[9] Like the other women, she was struck by the reimagining of Mississippi and its history of violence as a place of creative, constructive engagement, a place to discover these hidden "gems of beauty." Through this cultural and ideological transformation, Walker was convinced that "Mississippi could contribute to the richness that has kept Phillis Wheatley's spirit alive."[10]

Her major goal for the festival was to make the connection between Wheatley, who represented Black women enslaved by law and custom, and contemporary Black women writers, who were enslaved by a history of invisibility. "Phillis Wheatley took from her New England culture a very muted sense of the slavery that enveloped her and of her own oppression as a woman who died sick and destitute,"[11] Walker wrote. Even with the immense public access, when looking for the list of "firsts" among women, Wheatley had remained absent. Anne Bradstreet's book of poems *The Tenth Muse Lately Sprung Up in America*, published in 1760, was the first book published by an American woman writer. Mary Katherine Goddard and her mother, in 1766, were the first women publishers. The next name that appears on most of these lists is Susanna Rowson, whose novel *Charlotte: A Tale of Truth* was published in 1791. Surprisingly, despite Walker's assessment in 1973 that "black women writers were in vogue . . . the Jackson, Mississippi festival was only the beginning of things to come,"[12] her exclusion would remain the most difficult factor to overcome.

Targeting this exclusion was a highly personal matter for Walker within the context of the 1970s. Why would she not lead such a battle, as a senior Black woman writer who had established a career for herself, who was among those *firsts*? The significance of Mississippi as a "site for this nurturing . . . a historically black institution, in a state where black people had for a long time been the majority of the population,"[13] increased her sense of duty and commitment, just as the bond she felt to Wheatley as the first of the firsts compelled her. Even with the increase in publishing activity by Black women, how would this translate into an increase in knowledge if the textbooks continued to ignore them? Walker made this concern the focus for one full day of the festival, just as she made a public statement in the *New York Times*.[14]

While the official label "Phillis Wheatley Festival" suggested the celebratory nature of the event, Walker's ethnographic imagination prevailed. She saw the arts as multimodal with fluid boundaries and therefore designed a collaborative project where many parts fit into a whole. The result was a state-of-the-art conference and festival, a place to view the highest level of development among Black women literary and cultural artists, their engagement with each other and with the audience. Performative and interactive elements were crucial.

Not only did she plan for poets to read their original poetry, but this festival also included performances of music, theater, and the unveiling of Elizabeth

Catlett's famous bust of Wheatley in an elaborate ceremony on the opening day. Her reliance on Black ritual guaranteed that the conference would not only reaffirm the past but also establish new traditions. The festival began with the traditional group singing of "Lift Every Voice and Sing," the Negro national anthem, and it ended, as all of the Institute's events did, with the sharing of food.

The sophistication of Walker's thinking is noteworthy, since she was forward-looking in the overall design. As much as she was a shaper of words, she understood intuitively their limitations, what Dwight Conquergood would make explicit years later. "What every ethnographer understands . . . is that the mode of 'discussion,' . . . not always and exclusively verbal: issues and attitudes are expressed and contested in dance, music, gesture, food, ritual, artifact, symbolic action, as well as words."[15] The value and use of performance, instilled since her childhood, followed her development and became embedded in her humanistic philosophy, all of which informed her activism. Performance was, for Walker, reciprocal engagement. With so many poets and artists scheduled to present, the opportunity was ideal for creating a shared experience between and among poets, musicians, lecturers, actors, dancers, visual artists, and the audience.

She had claimed a literary space for herself, first with her signature poem "For My People." Now she claimed a space for Black women writers and made it highly public. After more than three decades, she was generating a different kind of conversation, and it began with these words:

> It was the still, small voice of Phillis Wheatley, as constrained as it was, that enabled us to remember how important it is to write out of our own cultural and historical moment and to tell the truth as we see it. Fortunately for black women in the 1970s, some powerful new truths had forced a new space to accommodate the very telling of them.[16]

With five years of organizing symposia and workshops at the Institute behind her, only Walker's execution could exceed her planning. The women who came, varying widely in age and career paths, were all important in terms of poetry as a larger public discourse. Walker understood how important it was to name a new movement and give it a privileged place, but seeing Margaret Danner at Dayton reminded her of the need to embrace more her own generation. The Wheatley Festival was in that sense a homecoming for Margaret Burroughs, Gloria Oden, and Naomi Long Madgett just as it was a united effort to recenter the future of Black poetry and the arts without dividing lines. Likewise, Vinie Burrows wrote, produced, and performed "Gentle Poet, Child of Africa," a portrait of Wheatley in nine scenes, with a dance sequence performed and choreographed by world-famous dancer Pearl Primus, highlighting important diasporic connections.

Walker's vision had a sense of timelessness that refused to honor any perceived boundaries.

Knowing how to build on the tradition that Wheatley had initiated did distinguish Walker's generation. They were women who had helped to break down barriers that were social and institutional. Seen from this perspective, Walker was and remained a race woman, seeking to advance the work of women and Blacks in general. If Wheatley had established a tradition of Black women's writing against such terrible odds, Walker believed that she and women like her had ensured the survival of that tradition, some of them becoming poets themselves, but others creating those independent infrastructures that would sustain the tradition of women's writing in the twentieth century. Their climb may not have been as steep as Wheatley's, but the odds they did face earned them special recognition. For that reason, this conference was an important place for women like Dorothy Porter and Margaret Burroughs, and also for Doris Saunders, who had created single-handedly John H. Johnson's in-house publishing operation that made Lerone Bennett a household name in America after his initial appearance in the pages of *Ebony* magazine.

There would probably be no other occasion where these pioneering figures would share the stage with their slightly younger counterparts:, Lucille Clifton, Julia Fields, Audre Lorde, June Jordan, Sarah Webster Fabio, Linda Brown Bragg, Johari Amini, Marion Alexander, Carole Gregory Clemmons, and Alice Walker. Or with those poets most associated with the Black Arts Movement: Nikki Giovanni, Carolyn M. Rodgers, Sonia Sanchez, Mari Evans, and Malaika Ayo Wangara.

An analysis of the public space in which poetry existed was one of the unique elements for the gathering. That poets would read from their work was to be expected. But Walker understood that having such conversations was as important as documenting and preserving them. Among the most memorable sessions was a key panel on access and opportunity, challenging the idea of Black women as tokens. The intergenerational group of participants included public figures who were already well known and others who would become cultural and intellectual icons. *Encore*'s founder and editor Ida Lewis, Howard University librarian Dorothy Porter, and its University Press editor Paula Giddings exchanged ideas with civic activist Etta Moten Barnett and artist Vinie Burrows.

If the Black Arts Movement held that poets, critics, theorists, and activists were one, Walker cast an even wider net. She wanted to emphasize the connections and affiliations that were public and private: early career individuals and those more widely acclaimed all were bound to a single tradition. Nor did she ignore the talented artists at Jackson State, Tougaloo College, or in the city of Jackson who provided performances of Black classical and choral music, jazz,

The Phillis Wheatley Festival artists and writers. All photographs courtesy of
Roy Lewis

Videotaping the keynote panel on the future of Black women writers. Left to
right: Vinie Burrows, Ida Lewis, Dorothy Porter Wesley, Walker, Etta Moten Barnet,
Doris Saunders, Paula Giddings.

and blues. Nikki Giovanni's performance accompanied by Tougaloo College's Gospel Choir was a packed-house event that garnered respect and jubilation, and as many remembered, three standing ovations. Walker was never more confident in what she had accomplished. Coverage in both *Jet* magazine and Hunter-Gault's report in the November 9 edition of the *New York Times* gave her the confirmation that she needed.

Although Walker identified the tradition of Black Arts Movement poets as a group by having them read as a cluster, as a barometer for the rise of Black women's writing, the festival was but one node that signaled the break in the major threads that held the Black Arts Movement together. A Black publishing market expanded as more mainstream publishers met the high demands for Black books for school curricula, a demand that smaller independent presses could not meet. Many arts organizations and institutions continued to operate, gaining increased visibility. The decentering that occurred had more to do with the Black political culture, a culture that had enabled and given coherence to the Black Arts Movement, but one that by the mid-1970s had become splintered and fractured through deliberate government intervention, subversion, and repression. The greatest loss was in the visibility of Black poetry, marked by a decline in its production and circulation, the underpinning of any movement.

Books by Black Women poets in demand at Wheatley Festival

One of the first essays Walker wrote after the Wheatley Festival was "My Creative Adventure." The essay affirms the personal pleasure that she derived from her total immersion in the world of art and creativity, and an opportunity to bring the best part of her vision to her experience as an artist. The sounds, rhythms, and images, not only in poetry, but also in an infinite variety of music, dance, theater, and the visual arts, enable a full grasp of the wholeness of Black creativity, she believed. The essay concludes with her reflections on William Blake, who was both a poet and a visual artist interested in imparting his own vision of the world recreated through art. The driving force of all art is the imagination. Blake saw creative energies as forces that combine with raw materials. The transformation occurs through a process that breaks the elements down, which are then "hammered into shape . . . and driven with a flaming touch of creative fire . . . that brings forth beauty."[17] Even if Walker could not live in the world of the imagination as much as she would have hoped, it was enough to feel its fire.

The Phillis Wheatley Festival was a call that demanded a response, one that Walker had heard. Its significance went far beyond what she had imagined. She was learning to adapt to new contexts, nurturing and advancing the work of a new generation that was reclaiming a literary and cultural space for Black women. In doing so she could finally see herself as she now was, the midwife of a new movement. It would satisfy her need for relevance and lead to fulfilling relationships. Whether or not it ensured the legacy remained to be seen.

Audience scene at the Wheatley Festival.

PART VI
UNHOLY WARS
1974–1986

(Mississippi)

26

On Being Female, Black, and Free

When art and resistance came together for Walker, it pushed her beyond her conventional boundaries. She operated through language, words were her choice of weapons, and the Wheatley Festival had been the opening that could lead to a new understanding of where she was in mid-life and what remaining work she needed to do. She had spent a week facing a new generation of women head-on, but any thoughts about what it might signify beyond its immediate impact had yet to materialize. While she recognized the generational differences among women, especially regarding sexual freedom, she ultimately accepted the differences as a matter of fact, not something she could argue or change. The Wheatley Festival might have been the subject of far more revelatory insights that signalled a *real* new awakening were it not for an established pattern of behavior. She would to push through a long period of intense activity as her body disguised the tell-tale signs of a health crisis; following the activity the crisis became immediately visible, forcing her to go to the hospital. The days after the Wheatley Festival were no different. She submitted to the confinement, perhaps more to get rest, always with a journal in tow, where she would remain until Robert Smith released her. The prompt was almost always a high level of sugar, her diabetes spinning out of control due to her lack of attention. She had no one to blame but herself, which made these hospital stays important moments for contemplation.

At fifty-eight, in Southern terms, she was old. She was thinking and writing more about her personal history, life's transformations, and especially those of her children. Rarely after the 1970s did the journal entries fail to include important family updates. Alongside planning for the Wheatley Festival, she had prepared for the marriage of her two sons, one year apart. Sigis had completed his tour of duty in Vietnam and returned to Tougaloo, where he met and fell in love with Norma Jean Grice, whom he married in 1974. James, her oldest son, had married Patricia Patterson in 1973. The early 1970s had bound art, work, and life together in a way that was self-affirming. At no time had she been so emotionally and intellectually alive. Yet, neither had she felt such a need for a greater degree of internal control. The hospital stay was exactly the place to exercise that control because it gave her the space to write.

During the hospital stay in January 1974, completely drained of energy, she chastised herself for any day passing when "nothing [is] written."[1] True, she had not written a line for a poem or an idea for an article or a scheduled

The House Where My Soul Lives. Maryemma Graham, Oxford University Press. © Oxford University Press 2022.
DOI: 10.1093/oso/9780195341232.003.0026

*A Poetic Equation: Conversations between Margaret
Walker and Nikki Giovanni* took Walker on a major
national tour in 1974

speech, but she was, as always, writing on other matters. She overcompen-
sated for her slow writing progress with profuse notes on her medical progress, family visits, and those critical transitions in her adult children's lives.
After her recap of events associated with Sigis and Norma's wedding and a
quick recovery from the self-flagellation, Walker began outlining an essay
"For Freedom, Peace, and Human Dignity." She wanted to look at world revolutions in the twentieth century, in contrast to the incompleteness of the
revolution in the United States. Her notes suggest that she was planning to
examine Adolf Hitler, Joseph Stalin, Benito Mussolini, Winston Churchill,

Fidel Castro, and Mao Tse-tung, concluding with Franklin D. Roosevelt. She intended to link these revolutions to social progress, railroads, diesel engines, automobiles, airplanes, submarines, guided missiles, radio, television, and America's first venture into space.

The political thinking showed Walker's adeptness as much as it provided a private venue for saying what she was unable to say publicly, in part because she had as yet no recognized public platform. If the opportunity presented itself and the occasion was suitable for more political speak, she would be ready. But since such venues were rare, these commentaries became a warm-up session for her imagination when it shifted to more creative possibilities. She outlined a new catalogue poem, focusing on key Black figures, Frederick Douglass and the period of slavery, W. E. B. Du Bois and the period of segregation, as well as Marcus Garvey, Martin Luther King Jr., and Malcolm X, each of whom had a parallel period affiliation. Years later the completed poem appeared in her final collection *This Is My Century* as "Five Black Men . . . and ten will save the city." It was modeled after "For My People," as her long poems so often were. Despite her expanding interest in Black women, an unevenness in the development of her ideas about gender and sexuality was increasingly apparent. She could participate in the recovery of Black women on one level and lose sight of them quickly on another. Yet there was a process whereby thoughts emerged in phrases, as topics, or scattered notes. The birth of a new volume during a period of recovery and recuperation provided the productive tension that pushed her forward.

Darker thoughts also came from hospital stays, encouraging her to make illness, including the possibility of imminent death, the reason for working even harder. As she grew older, illness became directly associated with her multiple recurring periods of enormous productivity: a time for retreat, the time away from burdensome pressures and clarity about the next steps of a carefully orchestrated life. She restored herself emotionally and spiritually even as she began a new round of philosophical questioning.

The productivity she was enjoying was not always focused on more publications, however. She would soon have her third book out in less than ten years after *Jubilee*'s phenomenal success, leaving no question about the status of her career. The Institute was secure and, because she wanted to leave that part of her life in a blaze of glory, she was looking ahead to a succession plan that would allow her to retire before the end of the decade. She had crossed an important threshold in terms of what she had hoped to achieve. Well respected in Mississippi and still in high demand as a speaker in the United States, she felt a new sense of authority that she knew would need an outlet. The interest in Walker the writer often led to an interest in hearing what else she might say. This transformation seemed to take place in real time as she continued her lecture circuit and speaking engagements.

The mid-1970s for Walker was a time when she would become more vocal about state politics and more openly critical of national political scene.

Jacqueline Trescott remembers going to hear Walker regularly after joining the *Washington Post*. She knew her as an iconic figure who could draw a large audience. She saw this at Howard on several occasions, years before she did an official interview. "The women who began writing in the early 1970s adored Walker for her groundbreaking work. She was on everybody's list of people to listen to, to meet and greet." At the time, "Walker was regarded as a modest soft-spoken woman who put her strong views mainly on paper rather than speaking out,"[2] Trescott observed. But Walker became "the woman we thought we knew," says Trescott, as she watched Walker bring her ideas from the page to the stage beginning in the 1970s. She was more open in her autobiographical references to the political education and activism of her Chicago years which found a connection with the political intensity of that decade. But her knowledge and experience went much deeper. She could rely on her knowledge of the Southern Negro Youth Congress, for example, the group she had encountered during her 1943 tour of HBCUs. Approaching her seventh decade, Walker was one of the few Black women who could command attention within the national African American community as well as among Blacks and whites in Mississippi. That, too, might have been one of the reasons that a shift in her thinking about women came slowly.

Cora Norman, founding director of the Mississippi Humanities Council, was one of Mississippi's powerful white women who worked closely with Walker, remembered her as someone who never minced her words. Were these two images of Walker, modest and soft-spoken, yet a woman who never minced her words, a sign of a woman's dissemblance, living in a state known for its repression? While Walker never held office, she had begun to challenge the state politicians and ultimately became close friends with the progressive state leadership, especially William Winter, who would be elected governor in 1980. The ability to speak her mind without fear of consequences, once considered one of her greatest weaknesses, she and others now saw as one of her greatest strengths. In many ways, Walker had become the logical successor to the race women she admired, women who believed that the South could change and that the leadership of any change was dependent upon the education of its Black population. Like them, she remained grounded in a belief in the transformative potential of education of the masses of Black people, which for her was in the South and at HBCUs.

What Walker had, then, as she began to conceive of a new phase of her life was her voice. An inspirational speaker with a world-class education, an inveterate reader and a respected educator, she began to tap into her experiences as a witness to and advocate for social change. In a politically conservative climate, she leveraged her freedom to speak the truth:

> In 1949, when I came to live in Jackson, Mississippi, segregation had a stranglehold on the nation, the state, and the city. I have seen eleven governors in forty years. Five of them demagogues, racists, segregationists, all Democrats or Dixiecrats or boll weevils, and six of them moderates, intelligent and recognizing the need for change in the racial climate in Mississippi.[3]

The speeches that emerged during the period combined didacticism with urgency. She saw herself speaking back to America about a not-too-distant racial history in a style that resonated with every audience. Because she believed that had she been born male she would have been called to the ministry, no matter what speech or lecture she gave, her delivery borrowed the biblical cadence of her poetry. More and more, she was inclined not to speak in broad futuristic metaphors like Martin Luther King Jr., whose iconic speeches remained so familiar, but with the rich imagery drawn from Mississippi history. Her style acknowledged the verbal repetition common in African American oratory:

> The Mississippi mud and clay are red with the blood of black men and women. *Nobody paid for* the death of Emmett Till, a fourteen-year-old black boy who was killed and weighted down in the river. *Nobody paid for* the murder of Mack Charles Parker who was taken from jail and lynched. His body was also later found in the Tallahatchie River. Both of these black males died right after the Supreme Court decision. Certainly *nobody paid for* the deaths of Medgar Evers, Vernon Dahmer, Robert Herbert Lee and Ditney Smith.[4]

If Walker's poetry had made her a household name in the 1940s, by the mid-1970s, she was enjoying the status of a trusted public intellectual who could bring an incisive analysis to a range of contemporary issues with a strong sense of the public good. The attention she gave to the shifting social and political landscape was more than that of the ordinary Mississippian and most of its political leaders. She saw Mississippi as a litmus test for the nation's ability to adapt to changing times. For her, fascism was a clear and present danger when she began to assess the US presidents, especially Richard Nixon, Ronald Reagan, and George Bush. Her preoccupation with the twin enemies of racism and fascism, then, locked her in a generation that saw little value in delving into the "woman question" beyond a recognition of its overall importance. Black women and white women could march together for civil and voting rights, but most Black women who came of age during the New Deal could not join white women in a focus on what seemed a benefit for them only.

She remained one of those women who found, and therefore defined, their liberation in ways not necessarily associated with gender. What mattered was one's ability to compete in the marketplace of ideas, which generally meant achieving the highest level of education. It also meant having important positions of leadership, especially as agents of social change. In recounting Civil Rights Movement history, she would give the roll call of the most well-known women like Rosa Parks, Daisy Bates, and Ella Baker. But she would emphasize Mississippi women, Fannie Lou Hamer, Victoria Gray, and Unita Blackwell, all of whom were younger than she was and who had been major forces in civil rights in the state and nation. She more likely saw herself as a potential Dorothy Height, three years older that Walker, who combined civil and women's rights to become an ideal race woman and national leader. This political side of Walker gave her a new way to use her skillful oratory in arguing for social change:

Do you know that government is the master of our lives? Do you know that without a change, a far reaching and radical change, none of us can be saved?[5]

Armed with this different vision of herself, Walker quickly began making plans to go on her first tour since *Jubilee*. In 1975 for the first time in her career, she had published three books in five years, including two books of poetry, which readers would have expected. *A Poetic Equation: Conversations between Nikki Giovanni and Margaret Walker* was an entirely different kind of book, and it received an extraordinary reception. The project, suggested by Nikki Giovanni, was engineered by Paula Giddings, who was in her early years as editor at Howard University Press. The three women—each from a different generation—were eager to work with one another. She saw Giddings as the next important women's historian, although Paula was hesitant to acknowledge such predictions. Giovanni, for Walker, was still "the princess of Black poetry." Giddings believed that a series of conversations between the two women would require readers to look more closely at and less likely to dismiss the developments in Black women's writing during the period.

Walker and Giovanni represented extreme ends of a pole, which became clearer in the course of the interviews. Giovanni's militant, strident voice and fiery persona alternated with Walker's firm resolve, maternal warmth, and righteous indignation. The women equaled one another in intensity and the desire for change, and their connection to one another was not necessarily the poetry: it was the fierceness and directness that they shared in their beliefs about women. It was, therefore, not a book about poetry, despite its title, but a book about coming into being as a Black woman in the last quarter of the twentieth century. Some early taping had been done in spring 1973 as Walker was preparing for the Phillis Wheatley Festival. The sessions had been finished later at Giddings's apartment

in Washington. These two continuous dialogues focused on history and literature, the role of women during the Civil War, the Vietnam War, post-traumatic
stress, motherhood, and raising children. In these rapid-fire conversations,
Giddings allowed the two women to flow in and out of discord, alternating with
moments of unity. The organization and marketing of the book took full advantage of this discord, with the opening chapter titled "Two Views: One Destiny."
The book became a sensation. The passionate and confrontational style, their impatience with one another, interrupting and opposing each other at every turn,
showed a new way to communicate. As a rhetorical event, it owed much to the
oral discourse it privileged, a seemingly contentiousness among women that be-
lies mutual respect and admiration. Complete with images of the women in different moods and gestures, readers could follow the intensity of the argument
visually. Giddings and her publisher elected to keep the profanity in, a decision
that made readers feel the cutting edge of a sword at times. Walker sometimes felt
that her generation was under attack. She needed to defend those who had no
voice. Compulsion drove her:

> I think people misunderstand this whole business of what my generation felt
> and feels about hatred and violence and love and nonviolence. My integrity is
> violated by my own hate, by my own bitterness, and by my own violence. It isn't
> what I do to the other fellow that hurts me so much as what I do to myself when
> I do something to the other fellow. . . . I think when all the fighting and killing
> are done there's got to be some kind of reconciliation on some kind of basis
> other than a gun. I think there's got to be some kind of understanding.[6]

Giovanni's terse response, "I am existential enough to say we cannot have reconciliation until all the killing is done,"[7] led to Walker's conclusion in an early
part of the book that their differences were grounded in their contrasting belief
systems: one believed in resistance without violence and the other believed in
self-defense. One subscribed to the passive resistance of Martin Luther King Jr.;
the other held to a view of progress "by any means necessary," the slogan identified with Malcolm X.

Giddings had her first encounter with Walker as a student at Howard in 1969
when Walker made one of her visits there. Part of that visit included meeting
students who were part of a poetry circle. Giddings remembered Walker's slow
and deliberate response to a poem that, realizing later, "was influenced by, if
not a poor imitation of "For My People."[8] In time Giddings would find Walker's
name evoked in a different way. Mary Helen Washington, whom many consider the dean of Black women's writing, and who was well into her research by
the 1970s, observed the parallel between Walker and Ida B. Wells, whose biography Giddings had begun working on. That Walker was already on the radar

of women critics became clear in Giddings's conversation with Washington. Giddings remembered responding to Washington's prompt:

> [She] set off a burst of light in my head. Both women [Wells and Walker], born in July, born or lived in Mississippi, were politically courageous Victorians with mercurial tempers, sharp judgments (that got them in trouble with others), brilliant writing abilities, were preoccupied with money matters, and really close to few people other than their families. With that image in my head, it really helped me envision Ida.[9]

Poetic Equation was for Giddings an initial encounter and practice with intergenerational comparisons at a time when Black women were writing more openly about their unique experiences. Walker and Giovanni, precisely because of their differences, signaled the growth of the movement that challenged exclusionary practices. The tension between them was a realistic depiction of what was occurring. Their unity around the view that any form of social progress would be incomplete without radical changes in Black women's lives was consistent with discussions of chauvinist oppression within the Civil Rights and Black Power movements.

The book itself personalized for a larger audience the emerging dialogue on Black women's oppression, one that allowed anyone to participate on her own terms. Walker and Giovanni brought the issues directly to the forefront of many women's lives, pinpointing those concerns that pit mothers against daughters, especially when they share a vision but take different approaches for realizing it. Resisting the view that women were not independent thinkers in their own right, a quote on the dust cover referred to Walker and Giovanni as "always highly opinionated, on a number of topics."[10] *Poetic Equation* was part of a new trend introducing a genre that allowed Black women to express themselves without apology. Formats other than autobiographies adopted the trend as well, which meant that the essay would become an increasingly more popular genre for Black women (with notable works like those by Angela Davis, bell hooks, the Delaney sisters, and Brittney Cooper). Although Walker had always used the name Margaret Walker in her professional life, which is how she began her career, in this one case she elected to identify herself as author "Mrs. Margaret Walker Alexander."[11] She did so in order to take a firm position for the readers and the public at large. Concerned that there would be those who might associate her with either of two major factions, which were either anti-male or antimarriage, she wanted to make sure that the world saw her as neither.

The key question for Walker as she thought about women, herself included, was about the meaning of freedom, who had it and who did not. She began by confirming her belief in existential freedom as a modern writer and a particular brand of Modernism that bore the signs of a deep religious faith and traditional moral values. "What about freedom?" she asked, thinking especially in terms of the artist:

> [F]reedom is an essential subject for any writer. Without freedom, personal and social, to write as one pleases and to express the will of the people, the writer is in bondage. This bondage may seem to be to others outside oneself but closely related by blood or kinship in some human fashion; or this bondage may appear to be to the inimical forces of the society that so impress or repress that individual.[12]

The experience with *Poetic Equation* set off an internal dialogue that Walker could not get out of her head. She had become keenly aware of new developments by younger writers, and knew that Audre Lorde, who had been at the Wheatley Festival, had recently formed the Combahee Collective, a Black Feminist lesbian organization. Their manifesto identified the group as "the logical political movement to combat the manifold and simultaneous oppressions that all women of color face."[13] Later, Walker admitted that the Wheatley Festival had provided a meeting place that helped to give shape to the formation of this early Black feminist group. That they were lesbian was something that Walker opposed, which quickly turned into resistance because it made no sense to her. *Poetic Equation* seemed to be exactly what Walker needed to move more consciously toward her own womanist analysis.

The results of her thinking would not make its formal appearance until Janet Sternberg asked for an essay to include in a new book series, *The Writer on Her Work*. The finished essay shows the evolution of a highly deliberate, systematic approach toward a set of conclusions that expected to put to rest any conflict she had about her relationship to issues of gender and the oppression of women. She began the essay by acknowledging the existence of historical and social factors that made the writer's work difficult, focusing on a racially restrictive environment at the top of her list. She may have been raised as a New Negro, but she now recognized herself as a New Woman, determined to claim her identity and sense of purpose. Unable to reconcile the word "feminist," she named the piece "On Being Female, Black, and Free," parsing out each component in logical fashion. After its original appearance in *The Writer on Her Work*, the essay found an extended life as the title for the last book, a collection of her essays that appeared a year before she died. She began with the triple axes of womanhood:

> My birth certificate reads female, Negro, date of birth and place. Call it fate or circumstance, this is my human condition. I have no wish to change it from being female, black, and free. I like being a woman. I have a proud African

American heritage, and I have learned from the difficult exigencies of life that freedom is a philosophical state of mind and existence. The mind is the only place where I can exist and feel free. In my mind, I am absolutely free.[14]

Looking back at her life, Walker put freedom and womanhood into a single frame. As a young woman, she believed that the fulfillment of womanhood developed in stages: first, one had a romantic attraction to a partner, which was expected to lead to marriage, equated with a nurturing, maternal love. Once romantic love settled into married love, it was sustainable and durable, having reached its fullest evolution. She was comfortable with this narrow and ordered progression, which placed a woman's identity in direct correspondence to a man's and dependent upon the act of marriage. But had the ordered progression always worked smoothly for her? Had she recognized visible cracks in her otherwise smooth surface? Her first marriage proposal had come from James Russell Brown, a most acceptable partner according to the conventions of the day. He was a minister, with an advanced degree from the University of Chicago, an ambitious race man, and had a bright future in the African Methodist Church hierarchy as an educator and leader.[15] Her parents had asked her to wait before accepting his proposal because it would have disrupted her education. By the time he had visited her at Iowa, she knew intuitively, however, that marriage to Brown would have required the complete suppression if not elimination of her career that was on the rise. In that instance, whatever feelings she had for him were in conflict with her sense of freedom. The relationship with Richard Wright, which appeared to symbolize the equality she imagined was possible in a heterosexual relationship, was aborted on his end. It was only after her career was well underway that she had let her guard down, fallen in love, become pregnant, and ultimately married the person who respected her and would not represent any competition for her professional ambitions. Her parents' opposition to Firnist Alexander ultimately mattered little, even if their reasoned disapproval, and his lack of social mobility and education, became causes for some setbacks over time.

Thinking retroactively should have prompted a need to see a more complex picture of Black womanhood and certainly her identity. Her parents had always supported her sense of independence and the need to pursue it. They relied on their own experiences in advising their daughter to leave marriage out of her equation until she completed a requisite amount of education. As a young woman, her mother had given up college for love, and her father had to leave a young family to complete his education. It was easy for Marion to see marriage as a disruption of the freedom she wanted her daughters to have. Walker's decision to remain married to Firnist, no matter how difficult her situation, also caused her to change her ideas about womanhood. If marriage gave a woman respectability, which clearly had been one of the reasons why she married, did it also increase the possibilities for utilizing one's freedom? She sustained a belief that nothing should interfere with her success, and that the obstacles were put in her path to test her faith. Her parents had set boundaries for their children, but they also encouraged her to transfer any constraints she had felt as a child to her imagination, which she gave expression to within the pages of her journal.

Walker had necessarily internalized competing notions of womanhood. An obligation to nineteenth-century ideals of domesticity was channeled through early twentieth-century ideas of racial uplift and social change. Following the example of her mother Marion, a music educator committed to the cultural advancement of the Negro race, Walker desired and had a full career over which she had a certain degree of control. And even though obligations to her family were primary, she followed her own path in creating and then reinventing herself as a major public figure. Throughout her life, her most vehement debates came about when any control she had was challenged.

But she was also entering a transitional moment by the mid-1970s. She understood how important it was to recognize Black women writers and the unheralded intellectual productivity of Black women in general. Her operating premises still formed a single frame: an undifferentiated sense of womanhood and freedom. She was, however, very far away from anything but the most conventional ideas about gender and sexuality, as were most women of her age, race and experience. Her life and work as a woman shaped her understanding of what Brittney Cooper refers to as the "*intellectual genealogy* of the ideas that race women produce about racial identity, gender and leadership . . . and an *intellectual geography* that maps the deliberate ways that they chose to take up and transform intellectual and physical spaces in service of their racial uplift projects."[16] Born into the era of race womanhood, Walker viewed transformation through the prisms of intellectual, social, and cultural history.

Leadership meant that she should remain an independent thinking woman who formed a larger cohort of active women leaders. In the public arena, first on that list for Walker was Shirley Chisholm, whose victory as the first Black woman elected to US Congress she celebrated. The Black women writers want to be themselves, "inviolate and whole," Walker wrote, like "Shirley Chisholm, who is black and female . . . *unbossed and unbought*,"[17] referring to the title of Chisholm's 1970 autobiography. To her list of published Black writers she added good friend and journalist Era Bell Thompson, who had published her autobiography, *An American Daughter*, in 1946; and Pauli Murray who had published *States Rights on Race and Color* in 1950, and her first memoir, *Proud Shoes: The Story of American Family*, in 1956. That Walker mentions so many of these women whom she knew suggests that she, too, saw herself with an active career that brought national attention. While she was among a significant cohort of Black women educators widely revered for their work at HBCUs, Walker differed from most of them who, if they were married, had chosen husbands in the same class and with the same level of education. Her cloak of womanhood, therefore, was composed of multiple threads.

Because of her background and circumstances, Walker was driven by conviction and necessity: by conviction because she believed in the exercise of her independence, and by necessity because of her deepening sense of authorial agency. It was up to the woman to choose a partner who would be neither jealous nor discouraging when it came to her ambitions, rather than one who needed her to primarily support his. She knew that she had the capacity to imagine possibilities where none existed and that as a result, her voice, one through which others could speak, would never belong to her alone. She was, in effect, carrying out her mission as a race woman, to forge a singular discourse from the multiple dialogues she engaged.

Part of the cloak that Walker wore was linked directly to her view of Southern Black womanhood. She believed that she was an *emancipated* rather than *liberated* woman. Emancipated had the most obvious meaning of being free from the physical slavery into which her grandmother had been born. Psychologically, it meant that one was freed from the shackles of mind and body that typified the Victorian woman.

> But never would I call myself the liberated woman in today's vernacular; never the bohemian; never the completely free spirit living in free love; never the lesbian sister; always believing in moderation and nothing to excess; never defying convention, never radical enough to defy tradition; never wanting to be called conservative but never moving beyond the bounds of what I consider the greatest liberty within law, the greatest means of freedom within control. I have lived out my female destiny within the bonds of married love.[18]

A liberated woman was, for Walker, an explicitly sexual construct, someone with a disregard for socially accepted rules and fixed behaviors. The difference was a significant one for her. She had grown up with family conversations that were always about what they could do, not what they could not do. She upheld the beliefs that her parents had given her: to pursue her passions with confidence and pride, to develop the best of herself, and to resist those who thought otherwise. It followed that Walker had also identified the struggles she encountered in her early days at Jackson State with something other than systematic oppression. Seeing men as a less-evolved species, women the more evolved meant, therefore, that women could be superior, something that too many men despised.

And yet feminist discourse in the 1970s began to disturb the clarity she thought she had achieved with regard to the position of women. It was not uncommon for men and women who considered themselves politically and socially aware to name the oppression of women as part of the same system that oppressed Blacks generally. Why she had missed what seemed so obvious did surprise her. But her distaste for the tone and tenor of mainstream feminists made it easier to dismiss out of hand almost everything they said. Trusting in her own explanations of the harmony and dissension between men and women meant that she need not look any further.

One factor always stood uppermost in her mind whenever Walker considered a related topic: divorcing Alex. She was certain that the social criticism would be directed more toward her than him, and that the courts would not be sympathetic toward a woman who had abandoned her husband. Even with the strong support of her parents, she could only see herself as the cause of a broken family, something she believed others would hold against her. The self-censuring that she had done brought the pendulum back to the importance of family and the need to preserve it at all costs. But she now found herself listening to what women were saying in a different way.

> I think it took the women's movement to call my attention to the cases of overt discrimination harking back to my WPA days on the Writers Project. It did not occur to me that Richard Wright as a supervisor on the project made $125 per month and that he claimed no formal education, but that I had just graduated from Northwestern University and I was a junior writer making $85 per month. I had no ambition to be an administrator; I was too glad to have a job; I did not think about it. Now I remember the intense antagonism on the project toward the hiring of a black woman as a supervisor, none other than the famous Katherine Dunham, the dancer, but it never occurred to me that she was undergoing double discrimination.[19]

The unique role of writing as a conduit for mapping the development of one's consciousness and the nature of one's existence remained a key idea. The "writer is no more than his personality endures in the crucible of his times." As a Black woman writer, then, one expects to "come through the fires of hell," especially if one is "poor and live in America," adding, "because I am determined to be both a creative artist and maintain my inner integrity and my instinctive need to be free."[20] The need for a more aggressive ideology allows for a deeper understanding of the conditions that prevent one's existential freedom from reaching fulfillment.

For most of her life as someone who wanted to write, she believed that her books would be her legacy. *For My People* and *Jubilee* had secured for her a solid reputation. The list of books she had planned to write continued to expand. In addition to the mapping she had done for "Mother Beulah," she identified a new book project, "My Black-Eyed Susan School," which would explore the rich history of Black educational institutions."[21] "Minna and Jim" was to be the sequel to *Jubilee*. Most of these she recited endlessly out of a need to remind herself that she was a writer.

The emergence of Walker's activism regarding women had an intensely personal side, providing an opportunity to redirect some of her overt resistance for which she was criticized. In an environment that acknowledged feminism, being a strong-willed woman who liked to be in control no longer made Walker stand out. If she became angry and bitter, her actions seemed more acceptable. She was free to keep dreaming of doing the impossible, even with expenses mounting, as Alex's health declined, preventing him from working as much as he had. So much of who she was had derived from her dreams, an interiority was necessarily the second validating voice. What she was accustomed to doing alone and for personal reasons now had more public affirmation. She need no longer risk losing that which she'd spent so much of her life becoming. Walker was old enough to be the mother of many of the women who were becoming famous, but she could hold her own among the best of them.

She had come late to the body of feminist literature that had begun to circulate widely, but Simone de Beauvoir's *Second Sex* was one of the books she read shortly after its publication in 1949 during the difficult early years of her marriage. The book drew her interest as much as did the author's celebrated relationship with Jean-Paul Sartre. De Beauvoir's analysis appealed to Walker's understanding of social injustice and critique of capitalism, and she saw a literary couple who had competed with each other but managed to maintain a lifelong relationship. What she may well have imagined, but dared not express even to herself, was the parallel in a relationship between Wright and her. Her reality, however, was that she was a Black woman who married and struggled hard to remain married, and there had been no models for what she wanted to do. The kind of feminist model she was looking for was not represented by the examples of urban and suburban women she found in Betty Friedan's *The Feminine Mystique*. Friedan offers a scenario of someone leaving school at nineteen, marrying, and beginning a family, then staying home while her husband builds a successful career. Walker had felt trapped in the early years of her marriage, just as these women did, but the women who dominated the feminist movement were white, Jewish, and middle class. Differences of race, class, and religion were barriers impossible for her to cross.

Signs of a more conscious shift in Walker's thinking had begun to surface as early as 1972 in a speech she gave at a meeting of the National Association of Black Behavioral Scientists in Atlanta. She worked on several revisions of the speech, but when the moment came to deliver it, she looked out at the predominantly Black and male audience and spoke from her heart. For the first time, she was open about her difficulties as a woman in the Academy. She told the audience what she'd only confessed in her journal: she was the single source of income for her family and was working harder for less money than all the men with whom she worked; she had reached a very low point in her life, feeling the walls caving in. She told them she needed to take action: to ask the president of her college at the time for a raise in salary, which she expected him to refuse. He did that twice, but she had come up with a suitable alternative, promising to remain at Jackson State for life, if he would agree to support her return to school to complete her terminal degree.

Her situation might not have been recognizable to many other Black women; she was educated, she had choices. Far too many would have said, "you made your bed; you lie in it." Furthermore, what she had proposed to Jacob Reddix was not new; it was common practice for HBCUs to support faculty returning for advanced degrees, obligating them to these institutions for a longer period, which in most cases meant for life. Because those schools often had difficulty attracting and keeping faculty with PhDs, who found it easier to move, the support of an individual faculty member's professional development bolstered the college's chances of maintaining standards necessary for national accreditation. A further advantage for these schools lay in the prominence of their veteran faculty, many with distinguished, scholarly careers; and the sense of continuity and traditions of excellence that ensured a high-quality education for many generations of Black students during the era of segregation. With so many making these leave requests, Walker simply had to wait her turn, many would have thought.

Never had Walker seen the problem as a form of sexism. Personal jealousy, and control, perhaps, but not sexism. She initially believed her encounters with Reddix had taught an important personal lesson, but until she gave that speech, she had not seen her experience as connected to those of other women since most of them rarely talked about it. At that moment, she began to understand the importance of sharing women's stories and of using hers to educate others. Her conference speech, "Black Women in Academia," revealed the lingering bitterness that she had buried for more than a decade. This clarifying moment in the context of the growing Feminist Movement gave her the cultural capital she needed to claim a new authority. What she remembered most about her experiences with Reddix was not the fear she had to conquer to approach him, but his response. The words had stung, and she carried his insults like a torch. In retelling the story to an audience, she eased the pain his words had caused by creating an identity with others. He had wanted to belittle her:

> He informed me that I wasn't going to get any more money. I was doing well enough. I had a house and a car, and he was sure I was doing better than I ever had done in my life. Besides, he said, you are too old to go back to school and you have been so sick you are not even a good risk for a loan. I got into my

car and went out to the edge of the town. I got out where nobody could see or hear me, and I screamed at the top of my voice. Then I went back to plan my strategy.[22]

His response had infuriated her, and yet it had made her more determined, just as it would give greater meaning to any future success she would achieve. She no longer needed to view his response as mere pettiness and the insecurity of a man who was not as smart as she was. This way of humiliating someone and the need to do so had deeper roots that she could now see as part of the systematic oppression of women.

Walker's refusal to acknowledge a connection to the prevailing women-centered theories has not prevented scholars from identifying its strands in her work. Minrose Gwin reads *Jubilee*, as she does other novels, as an example of a "peculiar sisterhood" among Black and white women during slavery, both of whom resented patriarchal control. Blurring of lines between an enslaved woman and her mistress could occur if the need to confront a common enemy were great enough. Gwin's main point is that Walker had imbued Vyry with this sense of sisterhood that obligates her to find a path for healing through humanism, the organizing principle in Walker's work. Yet, Walker would not have made a distinction between feminism and humanism in practice. Thus, in *Jubilee*, says Gwin, Vyry's assertiveness has two sides: she can show compassion to her former slave mistress Lillian, who has treated her badly, and in the process redefine herself and her reality in a post–Civil War South.[23]

For Gwin, Vyry's most consistent form of feminist remaking, however, is her language, a point that subsequent scholars have actively pursued, often without mentioning Walker's work. Harryette Mullen explores the language and rhetorical practices of enslaved women in "Runaway Tongue: Resistant Orality in *Uncle Tom's Cabin, Incidents in the Life of a Slave Girl, Our Nig*, and *Beloved*."[24] Doveanna Fulton's *Speaking Power: Black Feminist Orality in Narratives of Slavery*, which examines the persistence of Black women's language practices in Black women's literature, brings Vyry's characterization to mind as well. Fulton views these practices as the underpinning of a Black feminist orality, "the progeny of a cultural tradition of verbally articulating the self and experience."[25]

By taking her models from personal experience and family history and applying them to *Jubilee*, Walker critiques conventional notions of feminism, prefiguring the work of a subsequent generation of writers. In a sense, she is in agreement with the Combahee River Collective's primer *All the Women Are White, All the Blacks Are Men, But Some of Us Are Brave: Black Women's Studies*, which situates Black women in a set of discourses related to, but different from, feminism as people understood it in the 1970s. One of them, "Womanism," as popularized by Alice Walker, draws heavily on spiritualism and activism in defining Black women's practices. Margaret Walker's statement that *Jubilee* was a book she lived with and through appropriately identifies the connection she made between life and art. In expressing these connections through her major women characters, however, she became a transitional figure still steeped in religious optimism.

In some ways, Walker's ideas were not less, but rather more, encompassing than those that would gain popularity in Black feminism, ideas with which she appeared not to have affinity. Generational and regional factors account for this since Walker was not looking for legitimacy within a hierarchical academic culture. When she looked backward, she saw models like Paul Laurence Dunbar, Langston Hughes, and Zora Neale Hurston. When she looked forward, she was always in "pursuit of love and justice, truth and beauty, freedom and human dignity."[26] What she added was her 1930s activism, which gave shape and form to an imaginative practice as intent upon remaining true to the Black experience as it was to wedding craft and art.

Approaching Black women's intellectual legacies this way opens up a productive dialogue about the origins of Walker's particular brand of feminism. Locating commonalities among and between generations of women who followed Zora Neale Hurston's model of cultural immersion and engaged art seems important to consider. Like Hurston, Walker was concerned about the responsibility of the artist to remain faithful to the values of the people whose lives she was reimagining. Like Hurston, too, she was grappling with the tenuous nature of life narrated as art. If her claims about humanism shifted attention away from the appropriateness of *Jubilee* as a representative feminist text for a generation after the 1960s, her preoccupation with spirituality and ethics, ritual, and redress are the features of humanism that gave *Jubilee* a large audience. Its chorus of supporting critics talked admiringly of the book, for the most part, concluding that Walker's contribution was to bring Black women into the discussion of literature as subjects rather than objects, to reprise the genre of historical fiction about slavery, and to foreshadow a host of Black women novelists to come.

Delores Williams pursues the relationship between Hurston and Walker further in a discussion of two Hurston novels, *Their Eyes Were Watching God* and *Jonah's Gourd Vine*, and *Jubilee*. These texts serve as a bridge between religion or spiritualism and feminism by showing us what Williams calls "lifeline politics," those strategies that "help women maintain continuity with the past . . . [and] hold on to the traditionally supportive alliances while they struggle to create new relational forms of independence for themselves in the present." In effect, these are all religious narratives that offer a theologically and culturally distinct feminist perspective that traditional feminism does not accommodate. The result is to contextualize the oppression Black women face in more multidimensional terms. For Williams, lifeline politics are "informed by women's experience of transcendence, of faith, of ritual, and of God."[27] While Vyry's life does not mirror Walker's, she is a conduit for her ideas and the embodiment of her Christian beliefs and prayerful practice. Vyry remains committed to her family and her faith while redefining her relationship with those who have oppressed her. Similarly, Walker engaged in a constant struggle to redefine her relationship with the Jackson State community.

There may be some truth to the view that Walker's shift to fiction stems from her belief that she could say in fiction—a form more suitable for narrative sequencing and multiple plotting—what she could not say in poetry. If *Jubilee* is a book driven by an unconscious female legacy, it affirms her maternal lineage. It distinguishes itself from any other narratives, including those testimonies by former slaves recorded as part of a WPA initiative, because of its intimate familial delivery. As the author, she had a keen sense of the story's historical and intellectual importance that added to its personal value. Its theological foundation provides a more nuanced understanding of feminism as expressed through female-to-female relationships, where "there is a recognition of women's oppression, of women exchanging and merging cultural patterns so that new redemptive possibilities emerge for all women."[28] Hetta shows us the brutality of slavery as the continuing sexual assault on Black women. When she dies, the motherless Vyry finds herself in a complementary and supportive relationship with the other Black women on the Dutton plantation and within the household. The kitchen, traditionally a place for the transmission of folk wisdom and domestic skills among women, enables Vyry to receive the nurturing that contrasts with her profoundly negative relationship with her former mistress Lillian. They were all "poets in the kitchen,"[29] as Paule Marshall called this experience among young women during her own formative years.

Because she did not have this experience with her mother, but rather with her grandmother, the kitchen became a physical and emotional site of memory, just as it is the educational, cultural, and moral center of Vyry's childhood. Marshall's words are as true for Walker as they are for Vyry: "The woman stands a better chance of being exposed, while growing up, to the kind of talk that goes on among women, more often than not in the kitchen; and this experience gives her an edge over her male counterpart by instilling in her an appreciation for ordinary speech."[30] Vyry has not only mastered her role as a good female slave, but she has also developed the language for an interior voice and her thought process through important decisions noted in several key monologues. Walker recognized Vyry in herself.

Vyry's lifeline politics are those strategies that are intended to advance her own liberation rather than her oppression. Although her only runaway attempt is unsuccesful, she is highly resourceful and uses her skills and her wisdom to map her independence as a free woman. Vyry's relationship with Lillian is an example of the oppressive relationship between Black and white women that Vyry is ethically bound to transform as she generates actions that help mediate and heal the conflicts. Vyry's empowerment through these actions extends into her new relational forms, not only with her husband Innis Brown as they make a new life in freedom, but also in the various communities she and her family enter and the role she plays as a midwife. She is in a continuous process of remaking herself and her reality in a post–Civil War South.[31]

The novel's conclusion hinges on Vyry's own growth within the context of her faith and her relational identity. She must pray over the decision to allow her son Jim to leave with his father, who has promised him an education, but she does not do so without setting the record straight. She makes clear her ideological differences with Randall Ware but emphasizes her emotional independence from him as well, despite the important role he has played in her life, as a man she has loved, the father of her children, and the first person to teach her the word "freedom." Her relationship with Ware is as much a part of her enslaved past as anything else, a past that she must put behind her to transform as a free woman. She looks to the future that her son represents, not only for her family, but also for an entire Black community. This future is not guaranteed; indeed, it involves great risk, one she is willing to take because of her faith.

Lifeline politics are ways in which women hold on to "traditional supportive alliances while they struggle to create new relational forms of independence for themselves in the present."[32] This explains in part the turn toward more overt forms of activism that Walker had embraced after the 1970s. This turn also had to do with timing. She had spent much of her early life developing her craft: writing was the activism for which she believed she was best suited. As much as *Jubilee* gave voice to women, Walker's conscious awareness came in stages. Crucial to her expanded thinking was the idea of a women's community of writers. In her 1950 essay "New Poets," she listed only Brooks and herself among eight other men. In her 1973 essay "Phillis Wheatley and Black Women Writers," she gave focused attention to twenty-five women who formed the nucleus of the Wheatley Festival.

Eleanor Traylor has suggested that the more overt stage of Walker's feminist activism was part of a natural process of her evolution. Walker became a poet in an intensely radical period of US history. Her signature poem "For My People" measured that radicalism in distinct ways. But as Walker became increasingly more conscious of investing time and historical events with political and symbolic significance, she found herself stepping back and then reemerging at periodic and critical moments. By stepping in and out of public attention as she did, and by maintaining a stable home and family life, she had the confidence to speak and take actions without fear of reprisal from the popular establishment. When read biographically, as Traylor does, each of Walker's published volumes "signaled a major poetic event. . . . *For My People* sounded the second phase of modern poetry written in the United States. . . . *Prophets for a New Day* is a poetic memorial to the Civil Rights movement." And yet these "keyboard exercises through which the poet explores tradition remain only that unless a bolder measure crashes through."[33] By the 1970s, Walker's bolder measure was crashing through as she redefined herself in relationship to tradition and form. Poetry had been that primary form, but the period demanded something more, a new kind of synthesis of her creative, intellectual, and newly realized political powers.

That 1972 Atlanta talk "Black Women in Academe" brings into clearer view a distinction between the public and private Margaret Walker. All of her higher education had been by male writers—at least those that seemed important to discuss—just as those most responsible for her career success were all men. This may have made it difficult for her to see the commonalities she had with other women. She had struggled not only with men but also frequently with women. Her experiences with women in her early days at Jackson State disguised the roots and causes of many issues. But these women had been able to keep their positions because they agreed to support and execute policies that caused them to consent to their own oppression. She remembered that one of the women deans who wanted to return to graduate school was discouraged when she was told that her position would not be held while she was away. To make matters worse, she was told that another degree would not endear her to the men in the department. Walker knew she needed to overcome this when she made her decision to return to graduate school.

Nevertheless, Walker was part of a community of Black women writers and scholars, even if the trajectory of her life did not prepare her to be *like* them. She grew up expecting to work and to support herself and others. As difficult as it was, and as much as she complained about it, she still believed it was her obligation. How could she name it as part of any oppression since she had made the choice to do so? Despite being a member of that community, it was this sense of independence and her underlying Christian humanism that made it difficult for a work like *Jubilee* to gain much traction in the way that Hurston's work did after it was reprinted in the 1970s. *Jubilee* remained in print, while *Their Eyes Were Watching God*, relegated to obscurity long before Hurston's death, required an act of recovery.

Young Janie, the main charter in the novel, contrasted sharply with Vyry, whose coming of age was dictated by a culture of slavery. Janie defied societal norms, providing a break-through vision of modern Black womanhood that was ahead of its time. After her death, Hurston had found a champion in younger writers and emerging Black women critics, while Walker was the epitome of Southern Black womanhood during her lifetime in many ways. Her retirement years were devoted to a different kind of intellectual work.

The foremother role seemed to belong to Walker, while the preferred titles of "critic" and "scholar" were claimed by a new generation who emerged to curate and track the exponential growth of Black women's writing. This began with the work of Mary Helen Washington in 1975, in a lengthy introduction to a collection of stories *Black-Eyed Susan: Classic Stories by and about Black Women*. Walker remained part of the historical narrative and is included in Barbara Christian's *Black Women's Novelists: The Development of a Tradition*, which appeared in 1980.

Ironically, her relationship with many of the new writers and critics was similar to the one that developed between Richard Wright and James Baldwin. Just as Wright and Baldwin had fundamentally different views on the Black experience, Walker's views on Black women and feminism were different from those of later writers and critics. While it is often noted that it was she who introduced Zora Neale Hurston to her students and protégés long before courses or critical works on Black women appeared, Walker was not necessarily among those women writers who received subsequent critical attention. Hurston's earlier fate seemed to have become Walker's.

The movement toward critical invisibility might also be due to Walker's selective ideological borrowings, which makes it difficult to attach a particular label to her. She fully supported women and their right to exercise their freedoms. But what if a woman, using herself as an example, chose to put family first and found her highest pleasure in the home that she saw as her domain? Does that lessen her position of advocacy? Does it make her less free? As a woman accustomed to having her way, Walker easily resisted the control by men, including her husband. And as the family's primary source of support, she resented their financial dependence because it required a constant need for money that caused her feelings of frustration, anger, and impotence.

And yet, she enjoyed the control that being the breadwinner gave her, which was heightened by knowing that her support made the lives of others possible. She was, therefore, dedicated to ensuring that her earnings could sustain them. If an outstanding bill became due, which was often the case, she thought nothing of accepting double engagements—speaking in the morning at a local high school, going to teach classes, going home to cook the family dinner, then heading out in the afternoon to meet with a group of a community college students. The $200 that she might collect on such occasions was worth it, since having the bill paid was an achievement that she could claim. She grew accustomed to putting out these fires, sometimes with extensive traveling for long hours by train to give readings and lectures in exchange for funds to pay an anticipated or overdue bill. On more than one occasion, when things became tough, she would let the phone bill go unpaid, complain in her journal, swear that she couldn't take anymore, only to repeat the cycle again and again. These dynamics were part of her life. Not many women could have a loving husband and full family life, she told herself, which only increased her willingness to work hard. In the public space, Walker understood that she had generational and philosophical differences that distinguished her from the younger women. She was not *like* them, and, therefore, need not compare herself to them.

But Walker's criticisms of practices in the communist movement in the 1930s seemed most appropriate for the feminist movement in the 1970s. White feminists needed Black women to give legitimacy to their movement, just as white communists embraced Black people to gain access to a larger community and affirm their work. She remembered their most successful campaign for increasing Black membership in the Communist Party, organized around the Black Belt thesis. Owing to the particular historical development and experience with oppression of Black people, this view held that the South constituted an oppressed nation. But when the party had accomplished its purpose, Walker, like Richard Wright and others, believed that it abandoned Blacks. She saw a similar splintering in the Women's Movement. Those feminists who began to see the class bias operating within their ranks challenged the view that liberation meant the right to work. But what about those women who had always worked?

Some of the tensions she observed in the Women's Movement began to lessen as Black women turned their gaze toward a more decidedly Black feminism with different origins and ends. For Walker, Black women's literature was central to these new dialogues. Lorraine Hansberry's posthumously published collection, *To Be Young, Gifted, and Black*, struck her as especially powerful, so powerful in fact that it had informed the title of her parallel work "On Being Female, Black, and Free." She agreed with those younger writers who also challenged the Black nationalist thinking that had dominated the Black Power Movement. Toni Cade Bambara's story "My Man Bovanne" and Alice Walker's "Everyday Use" questioned the basic principles of Black nationalist ideology, which put people in boxes and utilized empty rhetoric. In both stories, older women, who seem to be apolitical, are wiser than their more political daughters. Walker was from that older, wiser generation of women, who questioned new ideas openly.

While Walker added literary critic to her practice, her main intellectual production took the form of talks and speeches: "Critical Approaches to the Study of African American Literature" (1968), "Humanities with a Black Focus" (1972), and "Symbol, Myth, and Legend: Folk Elements in African American Literature" (1976) . When published as essays, they align with the literary and cultural research that became a central feature of Black Studies scholarship in the 1970s. The overlay of Christian humanism tempers many of her views, allowing her to operate on multiple registers, sometimes operating at extremes, without feeling a sense of contradiction. "Our destiny is a spiritual destiny. We must rise above the limitations of [class] and circumstance to the rarefied air of gods. . . The spirit of man is truly invincible and immortal. Freedom of the spirit is what we hope to release in all human beings," she concluded in 1976.[34] She held firm to her idea that freedom was in the mind, not in the material world.

Being on the Left, as she had been in the 1930s, together with a strong belief in the precepts of Christianity and a devout religious practice gave Walker a certain advantage. She could honor and respect the divinity in everyone, while reminding us of our need to create the world that we want to see and in which we want to live. This creative function is deeply tied to knowledge, a new kind of knowledge, re-education if you will, that guides us to understand the inextricable nature of personal and social freedom. Ultimately, For Walker humanism linked to "Left" and "Right" positions. Humanism foregrounded the belief in choice, and it existed on a continuum that moved between two poles: toward human and social perfectibility, in the enlightenment sense, or toward hell and damnation. The role of education is to aid one in making the better of these choices.

While she could not fully agree with some versions of radical feminism, she continued to be supportive of Black women writers. Yet Walker never acquired an advocate outside of a few writers, mainly poets and her HBCU network. Her difficulty working with agents—to whom most of the newer generation was committed—and her regional isolation meant that she was not central to the dialogues that were occurring in several key places. New York was clearly one of them as the major center of publishing. Predominately white institutions was another site, actively cultivating a new cadre of Black women scholars. Jacqueline Trescott saw her as an icon, but a figure whose career had temporal and spatial limitations. The generational shift that was occurring may not have prevented her sense of connection to younger Black women poets. But it did disconnect her from the social networks that had emerged in what Derik Smith called the post-movement era. She had the education and professional profile of women writers in the era after her, but became further and further alienated from the white critical establishment that became so central to the careers of those same women. Walker was content with making unmediated choices based on her principles for the last twenty years of her life.

She had given herself a way of being in the world, based on the idea that poets are different, both alike and unlike other human beings. She contended that poets "in [their] capacity to evoke the recurring image . . . are more sensitive and intense. They see the same daffodils, the same waterfall, the same lark on the wing, the same red clover bloom as the poet, yet non-poetic people would not make a poem." If poets are makers, "to make, create, or fabricate . . . the poets' special concern," they are "cooperating with the creative energies of the universe and using [their] total personalities to accomplish this fact."[35] In practical terms, if Black speech and music were references for literature, as Stephen Henderson argues in *Understanding the New Black Poetry*, for Walker, Black poets were part of the process that included a larger community of art makers. Poets "see, hear, think and believe" and their "handiwork . . . is an imprint of the self, seen in style, language, image, music and meaning." As the poet is "transferring an image or concept to a spoken or written word," he becomes a "juggler of words, a dreamer of spoken dreams."[36] But the special conditions that produced what we know as African American culture—being brought from Africa to the New World and the subsequent loss of an indigenous language—did not strip those who were enslaved of their ability to create. They formed new systems of communication and made music infused with "pathos, poignancy, and artistic purity": the spirituals that "form a collective expression of faith culture," and varieties of folk music from which blues and jazz derived. If the "spirituals were hammered out of the creativity of black slaves on a forge of suffering and with a flame of beauty, religious faith and truth together with their indomitable will and integrity," then "all artistic creation and productivity must be understood as developing in this same way."[37]

Walker's continued exploration of the creative process extended her adventure into autobiography and personal history, both of which inform "The Writer and Her Craft." It was one of several prose pieces she prepared for a creative writing conference in 1974, intended to address Black concerns specifically. In this short, topical, highly opinionated essay, she enters new areas, the research on which she was as yet unfamiliar, in this case Black English. Black English was a form of American English and not a language of its own, she argued, showing passion for a subject without familiarizing herself with the accompanying debates. The spiritualism that had begun to preoccupy much of her thinking is evident in the essay, written during a time when she wrote more but had less energy for editing and fine-tuning. As she grew older, managing those publishing tasks less and less allowed for fissures and cracks in her otherwise tightly constructed walls.

Walker's contribution to increasing the visibility of Black women writers with the Wheatley Festival seemed to have a short-lived impact. By 1975, the record of publications by Black women writers had begun to skyrocket. Between 1969, when Maya Angelou's *I Know Why the Caged Bird Sings* appeared, and 1975, more than a dozen Black women writers had emerged, mostly with debut novels. Unlike the previous era, an accompanying critical apparatus grew up alongside it. The Black Women's Literary Renaissance had begun in earnest with the writers we would know best in years to come.

While the essays that explored creativity kept her busy and functioned to allay any fears about being a "has-been," another development began to trouble her. She'd finally read and digested Michel Fabre's new biography, *The Unfinished Quest of Richard Wright*. The reviewing media gave the book its full attention, and the book quickly invalidated an earlier somewhat uneven biography by Constance Webb. Webb had come to know both Wright and his wife when she and her husband C. L. R. James lived in France and were active in the socialist movement. Although some questioned the author's ability to tell Wright's story—Fabre was not only white, he was also French—the book was praised and ultimately became the definitive biography, and Fabre, the leading scholar on Richard Wright.

Since Wright was still the most famous African American writer worldwide, Baldwin and Ellison were close seconds, and Fabre subsequently became one of the most respected scholars of African American literature until his death in 2007. He extended his work to include the experiences of Black expatriates in Europe, inspiring a new era of transatlantic research and collaboration, literary and cultural exchanges, and translation projects. The connection with France and African American culture became further consolidated through these exchanges. Musicians, artists, and later writers who left to live abroad were able to gain the respect for their work that was impossible in the United States. Wright had been one of those artists, and with Fabre's biography, renewed interest in Wright drew a new generation of scholarship. Moreover, seeing the Black experience as a global one, rather than US-based, provided more context for what was already trending as a result of Black student activism within the United States. The contributions of Fabre, along with his wife Genevieve who was also a scholar, and their frequent and lengthy stays at US universities, bolstered the work of many other US scholars. Their work created an upscale momentum, if not a similar validation that brought more attention and international visibility to the work of a generation who were entering the academy in the 1970s. If Black Studies had become the great equalizer to US higher education, parallel centers in France and elsewhere in Europe became important outposts that scholars could claim as reputational capital.

Fabre was wildly popular in US literary circles, making it difficult for anyone to criticize him. But Walker elected to do just that. She knew that several Black scholars had attempted to write a biography of Wright, but without access to much of the Wright materials, the kind of thoroughgoing work Fabre was able to do was impossible. Although a few books had emerged that focused on Wright's emergence as a writer, Fabre's was the first to provide a complete portrait, with the benefit of all new material. Timing was a critical factor, according to French scholar Claudine Raynaud, who knew and worked with Michel and Genevieve Fabre early in her professional career. Wright's death in 1960 had naturally sparked interest in him, and Fabre, who had begun his studies at the Sorbonne in 1961, "had become acquainted with the Wright family in Paris and was searching for a dissertation topic."[38] The thesis was completed in 1968, and once gaining exclusive access to Wright's papers in France, Fabre reworked the biography for publication first in French and then with a translation in English.

Walker had little time to read the book thoroughly until 1975 and became infuriated at his references to her. Although her comments did not go very far beyond a small circle of friends and her journal entry at first, she felt compelled to defend herself against what she perceived as a personal attack. Her attention was diverted away from further developments in the Black Women's Literary Renaissance as her interest in telling her own Wright story began to grow. Her major complaint—that there was as yet no biography of Wright that spoke to the psychological dimensions of his lived experiences in the South in the early decades of the twentieth century—meant that she was the only person at the time who knew Wright and could tell that story. She became preoccupied with the possibility of writing her own biography of Richard Wright.

The idea merged with her ongoing interest in creativity. What is genius, what is creativity, what is the value of craft? These became important questions for discussing the life of a man who had a seventh-grade education and whose literary brilliance was undeniable. Moreover, she had begun to see these essays as part of the new voice through which she was speaking. Taken together, they provide a

Walker and Michel Fabre meeting at the Center for the Study of Southern Culture, Ole Miss. Courtesy of William R. Ferris

Chicago Women Writers with Walker in the 1970s

critical starting point for assessing the breadth and depth of Walker's vision and capacity to integrate multiple levels of knowledge to adapt and readjust in one of the most tumultuous decades in US history. Even though the Wheatley Festival was still a marker for the Black Women's Literary Renaissance of the 1970s, she was embarking on a new mission that might add to its productive lineage. Black women writing biography was indeed rare. But Walker could not have imagined the challenges she would face as a Black woman writing about a Black man she knew and knew well.

It is likely that Walker would have held a secure place in literary history with five books to her credit had she not begun this new journey. She wanted and believed that she needed more visibility, and she was known for doing "firsts" as a literary figure. While she still had the energy and public recognition, she hoped that others would put trust in her to set a new trend in writing by Black women in the future. She was confident that what she was planning was as bold and radical as she believed herself to be. She had theorized women as a distinct species of humankind. For the moment, however, it would be the essay "On Being Female, Black, and Free" that would serve as the personal imprint as she translated herself to others.

27

Fame and Infamy

Walker could not plan a way forward for herself as a writer without giving studied attention to the Institute. When she did, she returned to an early manifesto: "I BELIEVE THAT THE NOVELIST'S VISION MUST ENABLE HIM TO SEE THROUGH HIS AGE. TRANSCEND ITS CHAOS IN HIS ARTISTIC CREATION AND THEREBY HELP MANKIND TO UNDERSTAND THE ULTIMATE MEANING OF THE WORLD AROUND HIM."[1] Was she providing the leadership that the period demanded? She continued to see "the death struggle for freedom, for peace, and for human dignity,"[2] one that Black artists and scholars needed to reflect in their art and actions. Even with the Institute as her platform, she was under no illusions that its success was hers and hers alone. She may have been its engine, but were her literary interests holding back progress? Should the primary objective extend to the affairs of the nation and of the world? Although more writers were writing, she was not certain that their individual achievements combined could sustain a movement.

Because the Institute was based at an educational institution, she held firm to her belief that education must manifest a liberation agenda. "We must begin to use the Black mind as a tool for Black liberation not as yoga to liberate a single individual."[3] This mandate gathered strength from her sense of place, that the South had taken the most blows in the struggle for social change. The longer she remained in the South, the more wedded to it she became. Concerned that even those considered to be *Southern writers* had gained recognition writing *outside* the South, she emphasized what could and should be done *within the* South.

Personal ambitions merged with her ideological orientation once again. The positive responses she received from the *Poetic Equation* book tour convinced her to see the Richard Wright biography as a way to refocus attention on the South and on her as one of its writers. She would repeat a sequence of reasons that always led her to the same conclusion: Wright helped us to understand the contradictory nature of the South and she was the only person who could explain its impact on a writer like him. She had not responded to an early communication from Michel Fabre, asking to exchange the letters she'd received from Wright for the ones Wright had received from her, letters that were in Ellen Wright's possession. Yet she had responded quickly to an invitation from Charles Davis to give a talk on Wright at the University of Iowa in the summer of 1971. The talk she gave was the scaffolding for the biography-in-progress and an opportunity

The House Where My Soul Lives. Maryemma Graham, Oxford University Press. © Oxford University Press 2022. DOI: 10.1093/oso/9780195341232.003.0027

to give public notice of her decision. Finally, she did a timeline, summarizing the work on Wright that she wanted to engage. James Baldwin had called Wright to mind in his essay "Everybody's Protest Novel" in 1955, followed by a more direct attack on Wright in 1961, "Alas, Poor Richard." The interest in Wright continued to increase as Robert Bone, Edward Margolies, and Russell Brignano all published books before Fabre's. What was missing, she believed, was an analysis of the psychological complexity that drove Wright's art. His striving for success had been shaped by his life in the Black Belt South, which accounted for literary genius as much as it demanded a kind of ruthlessness. She had the vision and the talent, but as usual, the project required a process over which she had very little control. For the next two years, the Wright book remained an idea, but long gestation periods were nothing new to Walker.

In terms of her personal life, Walker was probably in the best situation she had ever been as she neared retirement. With four adult children, none of them living at home, and with Alex fully retired and spending time playing golf, she had more time to herself than ever. The possibility seemed to exist that she could devote herself fully to writing again but if she believed this was to be a turning point in her life, she was sadly mistaken. The more time she had, the more Walker allowed into her world. Her interests were simply too broad, and she was too much the public intellectual. Writing "full-time" could not mean closing the rest of the world out. If anything, it allowed her to pay more attention to world and current events that dictated what she wrote when she did put pen to paper. Energized, she wrote furiously as if she were preparing for a debate with a seasoned politician or an appearance before Congress. That no one asked her opinion on matters of national importance made no difference. She was obsessed with her own ideas and thoughts. Writing them down made her feel alive and connected in a way that satisfied her sense of importance. She was accustomed to bearing witness to what she saw and explaining it even if the words never saw the light of day. The Nixon presidency was difficult to ignore, and it drew draw sharp criticism from her:

> Everything in this country is in a mess. Money-fever-obsession has driven the country insane. Racial disturbance—animosity—hostility everywhere. No deficiencies to be seen in Big Business—organized crime and government. The way is horrendous, our schools in turmoil. Nixon is a fathead.[4]

Crippled by the aftermath of the Watergate scandal that forced Richard Nixon's resignation, the country had been further drained of its resources after a lengthy Vietnam War. Civil rights activism was the steady undercurrent, with its wings ever expanding. Black Power had moved from the streets to a more sustainable resting place on college and university campuses, and second-wave feminism was in high gear. Certainly, one of the most heated debates of the period was the attempt to ratify the Equal Rights Amendment, spurred on by the 1973 Supreme Court decision in *Roe v. Wade* that protected a woman's right to have an abortion. Her gaze captured these events as if she were preparing testimony for a public hearing.

Walker's interest in and writing about the Women's Movement, however, proceeded from a distance. The shift from protest signs, bra burnings, and mass mobilization efforts by white middle-class women gave way to a new focus introduced by Black women who were as critical of the white version of feminism as they were of sexism and male chauvinism. While some considered there to be six degrees of separation between these parallel movements, groups like the Combahee River Collective made explicit their difference in ideology and practice from mainstream white feminists. The refusal to lock hands with their white sisters without question placed them on the front lines of a new battle. Narrow definitions of feminism were exposed, and more and more women were foregrounding the legacy of socioeconomic and gender concerns peculiar to Black women. The feminist train would begin to run on at least two tracks, as Black women took center stage demanding that the truth had to be told and the private needed to be made public.

Walker's third poetry collection, *October Journey*, paid homage to a number of Black women, including Phillis Wheatley, Harriet Tubman, Mary McLeod Bethune, and Gwendolyn Brooks. With such vast differences among these women, it's difficult to say where Walker was on the feminist ideological continuum. Racism and its institutional and societal manifestations formed the basis of a united struggle against a common enemy. Concerns expressed by Black women complicated that picture, giving a new understanding of whiteness and maleness as complicit in maintaining oppression. It seemed that Walker, as an established poet, novelist, and public figure, was in the right place at the right time. But almost as soon as the Wheatley Festival concluded, she had begun to feel out of step with the times and with the women who had come to Jackson. With a few exceptions, there had been no further communication.

She had written that all Black women lived in a "male oriented and male dominated white world,"[5] and felt strongly about the need for greater recognition of women. But philosophical and personal reasons removed her from the radical Black feminism that she saw emerging. The inability to insert herself into these conversations could have been lack of interest or being out of touch at best. While Walker saw herself at tackling thorny issues and continuing to do important institution building with the Institute, it was easy to dismiss this behind-the-scenes work. Most of the women who were the most vocal were part of a new generation, and nearly all of them, including Alice Walker, Angela Davis, Audre Lorde, Michele Wallace, Ntozake Shange, and Toni Morrison were sometimes as much as three decades her junior. Although there were those writers who transitioned from the Black Arts Movement, like Nikki Giovanni and Sonia Sanchez, a new map was being created that gave more attention to writing as well as to the interiority of Black women's lives. The new cohort had a conspicuous and consistent presence in print and in the larger public sphere. Their careers multiplied quickly, accompanied by critical support networks and enviable forms of access. To the extent that they had secondary careers in academia, the majority were writers first and foremost.

The playbook had changed. Walker was not affiliated with any of the major publishing houses, and her personal and professional networks, though extensive, were rooted in the South. She was a well-known quantity with a deep connection to HBCU's. Feeling older and less competitive may well have been the case, but she also had a strong belief in the durability of her exceptionality. Given her early fame, an award-winning poet at twenty-seven, making a remarkable comeback in late career with a well-received first novel, and now venturing into a new direction with biography justified her belief. What was harder to notice was that for someone who was once a literary insider, in the new landscape for the Black writers after the 1970s she was rapidly becoming an outsider. Despite her role in bringing increased attention to Black women writers, she lacked the ability to turn an event into something larger or to attract the interest of other writers in doing so.

Whether she understood the impact of the changes in the publishing landscape is not clear. Since her explanation for everything was typically self-incrimination, rarely does evidence of any jealousy surface. She worried too much about her adult children, her finances, and her health (all distractions from her ability to focus on the writing), but she consistently proclaimed that "writing is my only hope of escaping real bondage." If the writing were not for publication, then it filled up the pages in her journal. After the Wheatley Festival, however, she wrote, "I won't ask Gwen [Brooks] again . . . a letter and a ticket and she didn't show,"[6] obviously feeling snubbed by the well-known poet and her peer. She encountered some of the writers at the Amherst Festival of Women poets in 1974, where she conducted a workshop. Her appearance was directly related to the release of *Poetic Equation*. The two poetry collections, *Prophets for a New Day* and *October Journey* served as add-ons.

What did become clear is the extent to which Walker's moralistic views separated her from the new generation. Even at the Wheatley Festival, she expressed her dismay with Sarah Webster Fabio, calling her performance "disgraceful, lewd, coarse, vulgar and crude."[7] Such ideas often colored her judgments about the work of writers who were gaining popularity or being celebrated. Reading through her morality lens, she would comment that the genius that Alice Walker displayed in her 1970 novel, *The Third Life of Grange Copeland*, was not as apparent in *The Color Purple*, published in 1982. She chastised American readers for wanting "soft porn" and Alice Walker for pandering to them with a "filthy book about incest, murder, rape, sodomy, blasphemy. This is her version of Black family life," she wrote. "Truly Alice is daemonic."[8] "Daemonic" was becoming her code word for describing gifted writers with complex personalities. She meant it as a complement, even if it was rarely taken as such. Some of the memoirs from the 1960s, she found equally disturbing. Books like H. Rap Brown's *Die Nigger Die* mixed too much sensationalism with distorted ideas about sexuality under the guise of telling of one's life story. The explicit nature of the groundbreaking work *for colored girls who have considered suicide when the rainbow is enuf*, which made its New York debut in 1975, was important but a necessary evil, she believed.

Walker's literary code was one that she carefully guarded, believing that it was the source of her achievements. She had pushed literary tradition in *Jubilee*, and "For My People" was the near equivalent of the Black national anthem. But the three books published in the 1970s were by small Black presses. She was, therefore, not a central player but a fellow traveler among the newer writers. Operating from premises different from theirs, she was the pioneer and foremother, a breakthrough writer who had paved the way. There was only one example where she had trusted a woman with her career. Dorothy de Santillana was revered in the industry and known for getting first books from prize-winning authors. Walker's world was shaped, her education guided, her career nurtured, her ideas influenced by male mentors, from E. B. Hungerford, Paul Engle, to Richard Wright. In her mind, this was proof of her exceptionalism. Was it only her unwillingness to sacrifice more for her career? The opportunities had come. Despite de Santillana's constantly urging for a second novel after *Jubilee* and her extraordinary personal investment, *Jubilee* was all that Walker was able to give. She had no lack of ambition but did not understand the enormity of the larger mission she had hoped to accomplish. By that time, life had already taken a different turn for her.

Preserving the well-rehearsed life of Southern Black womanhood, complete with its doctrinaire religious beliefs, offered her advantages, one of which was the skillful balancing of her family responsibilities and a career as an educator. Walker knew that her writerly ambitions, if not properly managed, could easily have destroyed such a well-balanced life. She had learned to manage the psychotic ruptures that followed her through her twenties so well that whenever she battled with herself, making decisions that led to her undoing, she could always bring everything back in alignment through her internal reserves. The cost of giving in, as she did when she was younger, was too great. Now she had learned to resolve the persistant tension between ambition and her reality through transference: her ideas, energy, and her talent she folded into the Institute. Because her personal situation had finally reached the stability she needed, she had begun to measure success in those things she had actually accomplished, not the things that she had not. Seen from this perspective, her careful plotting and planning through her career, especially the return to Iowa, had yielded remarkable results. Aside from the books she had published, she had made a marriage work that appeared to be doomed from the start. Secondly, her sense of pleasure and worth came from the continued dependence of her children and her husband on her. The end, therefore, justified the means.

Living in the South had also given her a unique understanding of Southern racism, some of the most vicious examples of which were in Mississippi, making it evident daily the fragile nature of Black manhood. With a husband and two sons, she knew that fragility was the ghost knocking at any door. It seemed only natural that she believed she had a relentless command of knowledge and the ability to imagine some versions of the experience Richard Wright might have had as a young Mississippi boy wanting desperately to claim a different destiny for himself. After all, Alex had about the same formal education as Richard Wright and, she believed, certainly more potential than he was able to realize. The Wright book had the ability to return her to the status of an insider: she alone knew and could describe a world where systemic racism, soaring ambitions, and human potential collide and intersect. She was clearest when responding to the practical and cultural imperatives that drove her. Just as *Jubilee* had been a book that coexisted with and at times mirrored her own life, she began to imagine the Wright book through a reality she saw if she did not encounter daily as a mother, a wife, and Wright's close friend.

Ideology and identity formed an inseparable bond for Walker. "As a daughter, a sister, a sweetheart, a wife, a mother, a grandmother," she wrote, sexual identity was not only important but "almost entirely deterministic. . . . All nature reflects this rhythmic and creative principle."[9] Walker's understanding had not evolved to the point that she could separate biological identity from a social or personal identity and gender. She had no aversion to anyone's personal choice but, when taken to the logical conclusion, an identity that did not recognize itself as male or female was a disruption in the normal cycle of life. That part of her understanding was inclusive, humanistic, and forward-looking. She considered women important to any framework, since human history could not exist without the individual and collective experiences of women throughout the ages.[10] Unfortunately, her view remained grounded in fixed, socially accepted ideas about female identity at a time when those views were being challenged. Although accustomed to extensive self-interrogation about any idea she encountered, she came to a fuller acceptance and understanding of changing gender dynamics. The extent to which she was disengaged, however, could just as easily lead to self-isolation.

In some ways, *Poetic Equation* had been Walker's transition book. Her views were different from those of the younger generation, and the book was the first time she gave public voice to what might have been considered her philosophy of life. Established writers were expected to speak on matters of general significance, and Walker believed that the book did that. If she became aesthetically restless, it suggested to her that she had more to say and needed to find a way to say it. She was comfortable going back and forth between her leftist analysis as it applied to race, class, and politics and still maintain her traditional ideas about morality and womanhood. Moreover, Walker actually enjoyed being the kind of Southern woman who knew when to break her silence. Fortunately, what she never lost was her intellectual curiosity. So while striving toward higher levels of publishing success was always interrupted, the belief in her vision and her talent never wavered. This ambitious idealism is what kept her stable in the most difficult times.

The Wright biography was a big project, the biggest one she had ever attempted. If Mississippi had been the "culture from which I sprang . . . the terror from which I fled,"[11] Wright had said in *Black Boy*, explaining that culture and the impact of that terror was her job. What she might not have realized was that she was beginning to participate in her own critique of men, Black men in particular. She saw the importance of exploring an increasingly important subject— Wright's treatment of Black women—both in his fiction and in his personal life, an undercurrent that had yet to be fleshed out. She was very much connected to the kinds of critiques that Black women were raising, but she would be threading her argument through a biography of the world's best-known Black male writer. Thus, while she remained an outsider within a certain cohort of Black women writers, because she was accustomed to being the first at so many things, her isolation did not seem unusual. She followed her own mind, she had something to say that no one else could say, and she knew that if she worked at it long and hard enough, it would be yet another landmark moment.

What seemed like a new path for Walker was also the one less traveled. Writing biography had always been primarily a male enterprise. She would have relished the idea of being the first Black woman to write a biography of a major author since it was appropriate for someone of her reputation. In addition, she would be bearing witness against a backdrop that drew on her rich knowledge of the political and economic landscape and her understanding of social and institutional imperatives. But it also followed the trajectory of her other work she had begun to do. Even though she had sent an old short story, "Depression Christmas," to *Essence* in 1973, she continued to build a small archive of critical essays for both academic and more popular audiences.

In reality, she did not pay attention to some important shifts that were occurring outside of her immediate domain. The political landscape was always second nature, but the larger cultural landscape was something she could easily miss. Even with five published books, she was a well-known writer, but not widely written about. The scholarship of the period, most of it produced by a new generation of scholars, was moving in new and different directions. Even the popularity of "For My People" did not always survive what was partly generational but mostly an intellectual and institutional divide.

The repeated inclusion of "For My People" in anthologies gave her a presence, but the introduction to literature for the overwhelming number of students and general readers was fiction. Excerpts from the novel were not preferable, which meant the exclusion of *Jubilee* from most anthologies, save one or two that were perceived as "alternative." Exceptions were made for novelists, if they had a certain reputation or were more canonical, like Ralph Ellison. One could count on Ellison's short stories in nearly every anthology, but the added benefit was the easy selection of either the "Prologue" and/or "Epilogue" from *Invisible Man*. By the time the *Norton Anthology of African American Literature* appeared in 1997, one year before her death, Walker's literary value and placement had become fixed. As the definitive map of the tradition and the canon, the *Norton* included four poems, two from her 1942 volume and two from the 1970s, placing her between Ralph Ellison and Gwendolyn Brooks. Comparisons were inevitable with a poet who had won a Pulitzer Prize and a novelist who had given America a much needed modern epic. What Walker became was the author of the most recited poem in the African American poetry canon, earning the title that Nikki Giovanni famously gave her, "the most famous person nobody knows." Giovanni hints at the overall impact of being popular and accessible, rather than elusive and remote, often believed to be an indispensable part of a writer's image. Margaret Walker was, in other words, too normal, which disguised the complicated person that she was.

One feature of that normalcy was her predictability. The depth of her intellectual curiosity, her way of analyzing the world with surgical delicacy, her routine questioning of received opinion were from another place and time. Most of the people who knew or interviewed Walker could quickly discern these qualities about her; she always knew more than one expected and had opinions that were often oppositional. She was direct, rather than manipulative, harsh in her criticisms rather than cautious. What she shared with all writers was a desire for fame, which had come early. It was the kind of fame that was based on the integrity of the work one produced; it was the code she lived by.

What some might call old-fashioned values kept her grounded, but they brought neither the younger editors from the larger commercial houses nor interested scholars to her door. It is true that a second novel, which she had planned, or a collection of short stories, that she ultimately gave up, would have reminded people of what a talented writer she was. She abhorred the cultural imperative to confess, by working through one's troubles in public, which she identified with the memoir boom in American writing.

These factors—her intellectualism, her leftist politics, her personality, and her location—combined to keep her at a distance from those things that did matter to her. She was not included in two groundbreaking volumes, Toni Cade Bambara's *The Black Woman* (1970) and Mary Helen Washington, *Black-Eyed Susans* (1975). The two exceptions where she did appear are worth noting: *Sturdy Black Bridges* by Beverly Guy Sheftall, Bettye J. Parker [Smith], and Roseann Pope Bell that appeared in 1979, and *Black Women Writers: 1950–1980: A Critical Evaluation* by Mari Evans, in 1984. Critical histories of the African American novel written during the period paid cursory attention to her work, and it was not until 1998 that a full-length study of *Jubilee* appeared: Jacqueline Miller Carmichael's *Trumpeting a Fiery Sound, History and Folklore in Jubilee.* Theses and dissertations within the United States and Europe did give more attention. *This Is Her Century: A Study of Margaret Walker's Work* by Doaa Abdelhafez Hamada, based on her dissertation at the University of Leicester, looks specifically at Walker's poetry in relationship to three twentieth-century movements: communism, the Civil Rights Movement, and the Women's Movement.

Eugene Redmond's *Drum Voices: A Critical History* that appeared in 1976 is a notable exception. After admonishing that "More critical assessment of Walker's work is needed," he offers a clue as to why criticism on Walker's work was so slow to come. Her uniqueness and accessibility, which endeared her to readers, had the opposite effect on critics, according to Redmond:

> There are few volumes of poetry published since *For My People* that can get any *blacker*—in the most complex sense of the word. From the red clay of the children's playgrounds to the teaming treachery of urban fuselages; from the quiet fear to the piercing cry of the hungry; from the deeply (unquestioningly) religious to the iconoclastic and the heretic; from the healthy racial to the good dose of modesty and naïveté—it is all there: a wonderful sensitivity and a rich bank of poetry for all times.[12]

Was it possible for a work to be too Black? Had Walker become the late 20th century parallel to Paul Laurence Dunbar, whose reputation also suffered because he was "too black." Toni Morrison concluded in 1981 that the moment for Black writing was quickly fading. Speaking at a forum held at Columbia University, she told the audience that we should no longer expect, "First novels, poetry, combined forms and experimental forms from established publishers. It's not profitable. That situation is devastating to all writers, so you can imagine its practical annihilation of third world writers."[13] These comments seemed surprising coming from someone who had phenomenal success as a writer, but it calls to mind the story Morrison often told about the sixty or so rejections she had received before finding a publisher for her first novel, *The Bluest Eye*. Morrison's extraordinary success notwithstanding, Walker's experience was far more representative of what was really happening on the ground for the majority of Black writers, a reality that needed to be demystified. Walker's career became the classic example of someone whose emergence in one period did not lead to sustained interest by scholars or publishers in another.

The charge that Walker might have been "too Black" is worth exploring. She elected not to pursue the MFA when she went to Iowa, taking instead a traditional literature curriculum—for both degrees—while training herself to be a poet. She had also resisted the more elite forms of Modernism, which she demonstrated in her first volume, half of which are folk ballads. Unwilling to discard her intergenerational lineage, partly from a grandmother who told "old-timey" stories from slavery, Walker elected a blended approach that brought the multiple components of a Black literary tradition, especially sound and orality, together with the Modernist techniques she employed. This refusal to disrupt or replace what she valued for literary effect allowed her to demonstrate that an embedded oral culture could comfortably coexist with a learned literary one. Neither could Walker's audiences be confined to a single type. There were those who heard her at numerous readings, those who studied her work in school, and those who came to know her through the Folkways records, where she read her own work and that of her favorite poets. The lineage question is often a complicated one that does not fit into contemporary ideas about literary value.

Derik Smith evokes Walker in his examination of fellow poet Robert Hayden, suggesting that she might have been affected by her in-between-ness: she did not become a "poet professor" who embraced her formal training and abandoned the earlier models preserved in the Black Arts Movement. Instead, she married Modernism with "a vernacular, saturated, performance poetics."[14]

One footnote to the Walker insider/outsider scenario is the invitation she accepted from Scott Foresman to do a series of anthologies on Black literature. No other comparable series has been identified. She started on the project, but ultimately realized that she was not in a position to do the kind of foundational work that was needed. It became one of the projects that Walker was fond of talking about: she was attracted to it initially precisely because it was different. Rather than a single anthology, she was expected to produce three: one each in poetry, fiction, and drama. Her excitement in doing the project derived from knowing all the writers who would be included.

If Walker was not completing work that was promised, not producing any new work, she told herself that she was working on the Wright book. But in fact, she was her own best promoter, a total package. Based on the reputation she had earned, she accepted invitations to read for enough money to make ends meet.

Her itinerary and notes in her journal and travel schedule for speaking engagements in 1975 indicate that she took the opportunity to become more expressly
philosophical and to make her public commentaries more pronounced. She had
accepted her role as the writer-outsider. In other words, she could be provocative, insisting that Black artists and scholars be accountable to the people and
responsible in their art and actions.

At the same time, Walker felt some uneasiness when Ernest Gaines, whose
Autobiography of Miss Jane Pittman she welcomed, was adapted to a television
movie in 1974. The success of the film made Gaines, who had written several
previous novels, suddenly the South's best-known novelist. He had given readers
a bridge to the twentieth century, dramatized by a most effective portrayal by
Cicely Tyson, as Miss Jane Pittman, walking away from the past and into the future. The film captivated an international audience confirming the commercial
power of Southern Black storytelling.

Aside from her cohorts on the faculty and staff at Jackson State and in the
community, Walker contented herself with friendships—and protégés—whose
views might at times resemble her own. Clinging to her ideas about the South
and Mississippi as the crucible of a new world order had not made it easy to
find any artists or even scholars who matched or appreciated her creative intensity. When she did, they were typically younger, like Jerry Ward who had begun
teaching at Tougaloo, who like Eugene Redmond, was consistent in reviewing
Walker's work.

While the long held tradition of social separations made it more difficult to
maintain close friends across the color line, especially in the South, Walker had
more than cordial relationships with Eudora Welty, Willie Morris, and Ellen
Douglas, Mississippi's best known white authors. William R. Ferris, who began
his teaching career at Jackson State, made a point of befriending and learning
from Walker and would become one of most consistent photographers. Walker
typically saw white Southerners as kindred spirits, with whom she felt a connection. Any separation was more in degree than kind.

Walker's thinking was evolving, however, and her conflicting attitudes were
coming into greater alignment, especially with those of other Black women
writers of the period. She gained renewed confidence in her voice as a spokesperson for a world outside the medium of poetry, resisting the idea that she was
out of step with the times or had little to offer a new generation. In a lengthy
interview published for the Black Women's Oral History Project at Radcliffe's
Schlesinger Library, a more detailed picture of Walker's thinking emerges as it
intersects with the Women's Movement. In the interview, the skills of the literary critic combine with her ideological orientation. The later represented her
"radical" side, where her focus was on the active advancement of and organizing
around social and economic concerns related to women.

Eugene Redmond and Jerry Ward were strong supporters of Walker's work.
Courtesy of Roy Lewis

Walker with William Ferris and Kathy Mosley at a JSU event in the early 1970s

Opera/South produced *Jubilee* as a folk opera in 1976. Courtesy H. T. Sampson Library, University Archives & Special Collections

Alferdteen Harrison and Ruby Dee at opening night reception; Ossie Davis in background. Courtesy of Roland Freeman

What came out of her continued effort to understand the cultural and ideological shifts of the period led to an expanded view of gender. An important recognition was that she could not in principle oppose same-sex relationships because her humanism required her acceptance. Contextualizing sexual preference and sexual difference within the many strands in the human family, she learned to be respectful rather than disdainful of those whose positions on such questions differed from hers. But womanhood, motherhood, and heterosexual relationships were thoroughly intertwined in her mind. At times, her thinking might have linked her to those who believed homosexuality led to the destruction of family life. Pulling back from this extreme view, she found a middle ground in humanism, embracing an equalitarian sensibility. She learned to explain and contain her positions within its parameters. Clarifying her position enabled her to tease out the distinctive threads of humanism as a philosophy. She was prepared to engage the issues of her time with a clear understanding of her evolving framework:

> Ever since I have been an adult, I considered myself a humanist, I suppose various kinds of humanists, in this sense. I grew up in the Judeo-Christian heritage with a minister for a father. My early years were largely influenced by this Christian philosophy. I have not ever gotten completely away from that, and I remember once that I did speak of myself as a Christian humanist. Then, of course, I went through a period of reading a great deal of materialist philosophy, but I never could become a materialist. Today, when we speak of academic humanists, I classify myself in that sense. I am a working humanist. I live, teach, work, write purely in what I consider the humanist and humanistic tradition. My concepts of humanism have broadened greatly in the past 20–25 years. . . . In my speeches, I do not emphasize Christian humanism because Christianity in America has taken such a terrible beating. The institutionalized church . . . has become a tool of a very vicious racist society and system—a system crumbling in front of our eyes. I think it is more important now to emphasize humanism in a technological age than ever before, because . . . the society can redeem itself. I think . . . that mankind is only one race—the human race. The world has many strands in the family of man—many races.[15]

A spate of honorary degrees, including one from Northwestern, did not slow her down. The Northwestern degree was especially noteworthy, since the second awardee was John H. Johnson, the *Ebony* and *Jet* magazine magnate. Even though she was not well, Alex could not talk her out of the trip. As she approached the stadium for the ceremony and was about to reach for Northwestern's president Robert Strotz's hand, she collapsed. She left the stage in a wheelchair and was taken directly to the Evanston hospital. She would never forget the irony of the situation. She'd come all that distance to receive an award, but a commencement photograph shows the awardees and lists her name, without her image.

Walker always knew her physical state better than any doctor. She assumed her kidneys were failing and her diabetes was again out of control, but she had never been in any hospital away from home—except for the birth of her youngest daughter— since her arrival in Jackson in 1949. She wanted to go home now, but the Evanston attending physicians had been ordered to provide her with the best medical care possible—death was not an option. At first, none of them knew who she was or why she was in Evanston. When they did find out, they were more determined to keep her alive.

Her diagnosis this time was wrong. A tumor on her parathyroid gland was causing the dysfunction in her liver, and she needed to have one surgery to remove the tumor before having a second surgery on her liver. The medical team members were especially concerned about the first surgery, a highly specialized procedure, most often done at teaching hospitals like Northwestern. Her condition was life threatening, they told her. Despite their insistence, she refused. She wanted and needed to go home, and she didn't need to know what might be available to her there. The confidence that she had in the care she would receive in Mississippi and the need she felt to *be home* reveal the extent to which she fully comprehended and privileged her interiority over other matters in the material world. They were thinking about the surgery; she was thinking about being a human being.

Although her regular doctors would have preferred that she remain under the care of an experienced surgeon, Jackson did have one doctor who had conducted the surgery before. Walker was more than satisfied with his credentials, just as she was with the success of the surgery. Her recovery was remarkable, and within a month she was planning Marion's wedding. A family wedding of her firstborn child was a milestone that mattered. The ceremony would be in the backyard garden of the familiar residence. It served as the last gathering of the two families, the Walkers and the Alexanders.

The surgery left her feeling as healthy as she'd ever been, especially once she had gained better control over her diabetes. She accepted no engagements for the fall, took a semi-leave from her office work, and made a sincere effort to find more time to write. What she needed most, however, was a vacation. She and Alex had purchased a new car, and since she had a meeting in San Antonio in November, she contacted friends about giving a lecture at Texas Southern University in Houston. Her plan was to go to Cuernavaca, where Elizabeth Catlett and her husband, Francisco Mora, were building a new house. Elizabeth had recently lost her mother, and her trips to New York were growing less frequent. The two had remained in touch, but they had not seen each other in a very long time.

Marion's wedding was a rare reunion for the Walker and Alexander families. Standing: Alex, Margaret, Mercedes, Marion, Emmett, and Brother; Firnist, Jr., wife Patricia and son Barry; daughter Margaret, Sigis and wife Norma. Seated in front are Gwen and Marion Walker. Courtesy of the Walker family

In early November, Margaret, Alex, Norma, and Sigis left for Mexico by way of Houston and San Antonio. They stopped at hotels along the way, some not always the best, and had frequent, wearisome stops by policemen, but their visit to Cuernavaca was uplifting and physically exhilarating. Walker didn't realize the high altitude would be good for her health. They did the usual tourist attractions, visiting the museums and climbing the pyramids. She went shopping daily and drank her first beer. Elizabeth's friends entertained them, and the friendliness of the people matched the beauty of the countryside and the murals. Between the mountains and the desert, Walker delighted in abundant flowers with shades of color that she had never known to exist. Her only regret was her inability to speak Spanish, although it did not prevent their full enjoyment with meeting new friends. Walker never wearied of the activities, nor did she have a single bad day. She wondered why she had taken so long to visit, and Alex indicated that he wouldn't mind another one soon. It was one of the few times that she relished their evenings quietly alone together, when she had no urgent matter to attend to.

She returned to Jackson fully rested, stimulated by the drive from Mexico up through Texas, across Louisiana, Alabama, and finally to Jackson. She was never clearer about why the Southern landscapes mattered so much to her. If living in the South meant that she would not be as successful as other, younger writers, she could accept it. She was different not only from them, just as her point of view distinguished herself from other Southern writers as well. She summed it up in a 1986 interview:

> I feel that I express a different part of the South, a different sensibility, and a different imagination. For me, it is a positive, religious, maybe sentimental but more optimistic, not necessarily Pollyanna, but it is rooted in that other fea-ture of the South. . . . I'm a believer, and for me, faith, family and community are keystones of my life. I don't have that Gothic imagination. . . . Nothing to me is hopeless. Everything has possibilities. I believe in the goodness of the future. No matter how hard things may seem at the moment . . . the political clouds may gather, the racial problems, poverty, even sickness and death. . . . No matter how horrible he may seem or what terrible crimes he may commit, every person has within him the possibilities of good. There is a sacred inner self. Whether it's developed, or whether it has a chance or not, it's there.[16]

The South had restorative value for Walker, and it needed its champions. When she found herself at the end of her tether, her determined optimism would draw her back. That same optimism gave her a sense of satisfaction that always returned her to writing. But the ease of distractions was an ever-present danger. One distraction was more than justified—the decision by the Jackson-based Opera/South to produce *Jubilee* as an opera. The premiere was scheduled for 1976 to coincide with the tenth anniversary of the novel's publication.

Opera/South was the brainchild of a retired Catholic nun, Sister M. Elise, SBS, and an experiment in interracial collaboration among three institu-tions: Tougaloo College, Utica Junior College, and Jackson State. She supported the organization from the beginning because it revised the view of a back-ward, unsophisticated South. Its reputation within the operatic community grew quickly with traditional productions like Giuseppe Verdi's *Aida*, in May 1971. After its initial seasons of doing Black-themed operas—daring to cast Black performers in white roles and white performers in Black ones—the com-pany took another bold step by focusing its efforts on the work of Black com-posers. Their success with William Grant Still's *Bayou Legend*, which ran for two seasons—the aging Still well enough to attend the premiere—helped make *Jubilee* the unanimous choice for the 1976 season. It was timed to premiere for the final year of the United States Bicentennial celebration in Mississippi to give an extra boost, if it needed any. Although her detailed treatments for the movie adaptation of *Jubilee* had yet to bring any options, Walker had practically willed this production into being.

The opening night was as close to a Hollywood premiere as it could get. A full weekend of events was planned, with many out-of-town guests, including Ruby Dee and Ossie Davis, and those high on Mississippi's political and social register. The production, along with the elaborate reception afterward, was the star-studded event she wanted. The message they delivered loudly and clearly: Mississippi was moving toward an agenda of racial reconciliation. Opera/South's adaptation of *Jubilee* gave Mississippi the face it was eager to show to the world.

The cast featured some of the most-established opera performers: Hilda Harris, Marcia Baldwin, Clyde Walker, and Vinson Cole. Ulysses Kay was asked to write the music, and Donald Door, the libretto. The story covered the period 1859–1870 with settings on the Dutton Plantation, Dawson, Georgia and Greenville, Alabama. It drew on the talents of local Jacksonians, as well as students at the institutions in the area for the chorus of slaves, planters, soldiers, and townspeople.

Reveling in the success of the production made it easier to accept Ernest Gaines's success. And it almost pushed the release of Alex Haley's *Roots* in 1976 out of her mind. It, too, would soon be followed by a miniseries based on his novel scheduled to air early in 1977. She was pleased for Haley and with her own success with Opera/South—it was not something to be taken lightly. Opera/South had broken the color barrier. The performance attracted national and international conductors and performers and created a community of art patrons in Mississippi with shared interests. All of Jackson believed they owned Opera/South, according to Ben Bailey's report. "It involved the people: the college students as dancers and set builders, the community people as fund raisers and participants in educational ventures, and children in its productions and through its educational efforts and matinees."[17]

Opera/South had done exactly what she believed was possible: fill a cultural void while also raising a biracial social consciousness in pursuit of art. As a "writer for the people," she knew that opera was a "high" art form, but the company had pushed beyond traditional boundaries in its commitment to access and inclusion. Its performances would feature the Black ballet troupe from Utica Junior College, or a combined choir that brought all-white Millsaps College together with the all-Black choirs from Tougaloo and Jackson State. The cast would offer Saturday matinees for elementary school children. As if she needed it, the production did more to reaffirm her sense of place. Mississippi was indeed her epicenter, the place "with the promise of a brand new tomorrow."[18]

Nineteen seventy-six was one of those extraordinary years for Walker. In addition to the foreign translations for *Jubilee*, Opera/South gave her the "satisfaction from something else," just as she was beginning to feel "passed over," her daughter Marion had told her. She had moved around the country, helping to awaken the national consciousness with her ideas about religion, family, race, and the role of women. She had demonstrated that she was willing to pay the price by committing her time and energy to creating an intellectual center for debate and dialogue in the most unlikely of places, her beloved South. She gained acceptance as an important voice of her generation. She seemed to believe that the more she did, the more she needed to do. She was compulsive, but deliriously happy, seeing this as a form of fame, if not fortune.

At sixty-one, Walker had become a settled woman, a matron who welcomed a new generation of her progeny. Although her health was not the best, she retreated to the hospital only to emerge stronger and better with new ideas that were as vital and relevant as if she had emerged from a gathering of the world's greatest leaders and thinkers. Living by the truth of her convictions, she reassured others that she was a woman of power and significance, a force to be reckoned with. The interviews that she gave painted a portrait of a more-than-satisfied woman, who may have found her voice in Chicago, but who had claimed her independence in the South. The South was her place, and she felt unchallenged in her belief that she had finally come into her own.

By 1977, Walker began to slow down her pace at the Institute. In addition to the annual Martin Luther King Jr. convocation in January, she planned to host three more conferences, train a successor, and retire. It was clear that the Wright book was not going to get written until she did so. The first conference was somewhat scaled down, but no less powerful than the Wheatley Festival. The Conference on Africa and African Affairs (CAAA) was one of the most undeservedly unpublicized neglected projects that the Institute implemented during her tenure. While the Festival of African Culture (FESTAC) was convening on the other side of the huge learning community on Africa, she knew that she could not attend, but she encouraged Alleane Currie to go instead. She concentrated on making CAAA's focus an exploration of economic underdevelopment and political uncertainty while also showing the richness of African history and its legacy in the Black South. She had taken many of the threads of Pan-Africanism from W. E. B. Du Bois, and like him, she saw the promise of a united Black world as nation after nation gained their independence in Africa. Freedom and independence did not make the world free from conflict and turmoil, however, and the conference teased out these complexities.

Always good at making connections, Walker built the event as "a centennial celebration of Jackson State University, a predominantly Black university deep in the heart of Black culture [that] has rendered educational service to the local community, the State, the nation, and the world at large since 1877."[19] Jackson State's founding in the nineteenth century and Africa's historical and cultural importance in the twentieth century were part of the same message. Most of the audience would not have gone to or have heard about FESTAC, and yet they found themselves understanding the ties between peoples of Africa and America that had too often been dismissed.

While the CAAA highlighted her interest in the Black diaspora and the need to dispel myths about Africa and the African heritage, for the next event, Conference on the Plight of the Cities, she expanded her thinking about what she had begun to call the "human encounter." Some of her ideas she used for organizing the conference, but most of them became part of a speech she gave that summer. "Our world is made up of various segments or races of humankind all belonging to the human race or a common family of mankind" with "color and race . . . facts of the modern world," she told the American Association of University Women members who met in Jackson. But, she continued, "we become distressed and confused and unable to understand the ulterior motives for money and power and ascendancy over the lives of others, which [is the] very nature of our political and economic system."[20] One of the results, Walker pointed out, was the unhealthy pattern of urban life. "We are almost into the eye of the storm of the crisis of an old order. The modern stress, which affects our physical selves and our psyche, we must have release from. The chocolate cities ringed with vanilla suburbs are symptomatic of new patterns of living. The subcultures of the society are threatened."[21]

Every event allowed Walker to deliver her strongest message. "I [see] new and encouraging signs for the southern city, and new patterns of living developing in our inner cities of the South."[22] But the particular always proceeded to her more general point: if there was any hope for survival in the next century, we would need to develop "respect for the divinity in every living human being," and a "new concept of education based on the realities of the universe which the Einsteinian revolution brought to the twentieth century." She had the utmost faith in the potential of technology to give form and shape to "a world community developed out of cultural pluralism."[23] The Institute issued its national and global appeals in a distinctly local context, but it was the basis for power, guided by ideas that provided the foundation for her authority. While Walker relied heavily on her writer and artist friends and fellow educators to present at many of her programs, she was equally as successful in hosting major national and international figures and political leaders who debated current topics and policies, both foreign and domestic. For ten years, she made Jackson the site of regular pilgrimages for ambassadors to Africa, the country's ministers of culture and education, members of the United Nations General Assembly, and a host of state senators and US Congress members.

Three things would nonetheless unsettle her in the last years of the decade. During what may have appeared a smooth, comfortable period of her life, the dichotomy of her personality often exerted itself. For all the pleasure she took from her achievements and her pride in those of others, news from the world outside the South could draw bitterness and rage. The awarding of the Nobel Prize to her Northwestern classmate Saul Bellow was one of them. They were the same age and had studied at Northwestern together under Hungerford, who often called them both his best students. The difference between them as Marion was quick to point out was this: he was white, male, and Jewish, while she was Black, female, and poor.[24]

The second development began as a rumor within her household, after her children had read a copy of Alex Haley's new book *Roots*. Haley seemed to have relied heavily upon *Jubilee*, her children contended. But she had put the book aside, promising to read it when time became available. A bout with bronchitis turned into pneumonia, and Dr. Smith demanded that she go to the hospital. While there, she learned that Fannie Lou Hamer had died. Two years her junior, Hamer was diabetic just as she was, but her condition was complicated by breast cancer, a serious heart condition, and the intensity of her civil rights activism.

Hamer's passing tightened the grip that the reality of death had over Walker's thinking and actions, as was apparent in her journal entries. As the face of the Civil Rights Movement in Mississippi, a survivor of racial violence and trauma, a sharecropper who lost her job when she registered to vote, Hamer was a model for Walker. Hamer continued to put her life on the line in the fight for human justice. Her passion and brilliance gained her national attention, but her character was synonymous with fearlessness, a refusal to allow anyone to dissuade her from taking a stand against injustice, even at risk to herself. Walker was especially drawn to Hamer's deep religious faith, a faith inextricably linked to actions, beliefs, and drive in fighting every kind of injustice.

Partly to take her mind off Hamer's death, she turned to Haley's *Roots* and began reading it in earnest. Her response was immediate: she saw "plagiarism . . . blatant, flagrant, rampant . . . complex and cunning."[25] Even though she went about her routine tasks once she recovered from pneumonia, she returned nightly to her tedious cataloguing and enumerating of similarities between *Roots* and *Jubilee*. One evening, she began reading at 10 P.M. and continued nonstop until 5 A.M., identifying thirty-five examples of direct plagiarism. Each time she picked up the book, she saw more. Her knowledge of the literature of the Civil War, especially its fiction, made it easy for her to recognize unacknowledged borrowings from other sources in Haley's novel. She felt that the success of *Roots* had been a manipulation and as such, was a violation of the principles of intellectual honesty and dedication to the art and craft of writing. As she told and retold the story, not only had her children noticed the similarities, but colleagues and friends confirmed that what they read felt as if it were lifted out of *Jubilee*.

She was relentless in gathering her evidence for what she believed to be plagiarism. First, she turned to her son James, a practicing attorney, to prepare the suit asking for an injunction against *Roots*, based on copyright infringement. As her children began to see the toll it was taking on their mother and father, they begged her to let it go, knowing that she would never win. Instead, the more investigation she did, the more she began to unravel a massive complicated plot that included many characters, the publishing industry, literary agencies, the American Broadcasting Corporation (ABC), private foundations, and educational institutions, all connected through money and power. In her thinking, all had conspired to ensure that *Roots* provided a return on their investments, and it did. Aside from the thirty-seven languages that the book was translated into, the television miniseries attracted 130 million viewers for ABC. It was the most widely watched series up to that point, earning nine Emmy awards out of the twenty-six nominations it received. The book drew instant praise and support from an international literary community by winning the National Book Award and a Pulitzer Prize for Haley. *Roots* was a phenomenon.

Walker was under severe distress but framing her discoveries and the actions that followed had most to do with her integrity and the integrity of historical writing, the value and importance of research and scholarship, and the role of American literature as a medium for communicating America's unique history, especially regarding the Civil War. She was clear about these issues in her own mind. "The period is rich enough for any miner to find gold and express his original ideas,"[26] she wrote. But Haley had not used his imagination; he had not been original. "*Roots* bears too many similarities to *Jubilee* to be coincidental,"[27] she concluded. She saw Haley as a writer without integrity or ethics, the most important thing a writer needed. In an instant, her feelings of isolation from a generation of new writers, and her need to be her own advocate, transformed into a manic energy. She felt obligated to defend her work and to use the legal system to do it, even it if meant accusing another Black writer of stealing her words. Suddenly Walker became the woman violated by a Black man, with no one to rescue her.

What happened to Walker's reputation as a result of this decision is as revealing as it is disturbing. The fame *Jubilee* brought her quickly dissipated into infamy. She was tried in the court of public opinion even before the case went before a judge. What was in it for her?, people asked. Was she expecting to get money by challenging the most famous Black man in America in 1977? Did she think she was the only person who could write a story about slavery? Was she not violating her own principle of Black solidarity? As difficult as it was for Blacks to gain this level of visibility and achievement, why would she want to challenge that achievement? Surely we have enough battles to fight against our larger enemy. Her critics said it boiled down to one simple thing, jealousy.

She was troubled by the obligation she felt, but it was as if an unnamed power had taken control and was guiding her. She could not bring herself to put race above principle and literary integrity. Nothing mattered and the truth, she believed, would win out. Her own publisher pulled away. When "Houghton Mifflin left me out there to fight City Hall alone,"[28] refusing to join her in the suit and waiving all rights to the results, she was insulted and frightened. That left God "alive and in charge. . . . I do not enter this trusting in my own righteousness alone but trusting the unfailing mercy, protection, love and justice of God. Whatever happens, I shall accept His will."[29] Her voice was God's voice, and she operated entirely inside of herself. In lengthy journal deliberations summing up her innermost thoughts, she gave a second reason, "Furthermore all ethical principles are violated. I cannot allow this to pass without a challenge."[30] She could not decide which crime was the worst. Selling people a myth about Black history, with an entire establishment knowingly participating? Making money off unsuspecting readers? The devaluing of the scholarly enterprise that she and so many people had made their career, insisting on painstaking work and study to validate narratives of history, whether factually presented or creatively reimagined? The case was as intensely personal as it was moral and ethical. "It would have cost me my sanity if I had been unable to take any action about it though all the odds be against me."[31]

By the time Walker had finished her notes, she catalogued every instance of plagiarism—150 in all—and never wavered from her position. She described in detail Haley's use of the characters, incidents, language, and especially the folklore. She also found that the structure she had described in "How I Wrote *Jubilee*" had been generously used, and she detailed that as well. She agreed to have her son's law firm, Everett, Sanders and Alexander, represent her. The suit filed on April 20, 1977, noted extensive similarities between *Roots* and *Jubilee* beginning on page 200—after the Africa section—and continuing through page 772. Haley appears to have "read, studied, ingested and digested and regurgitated *Jubilee*,"[32] she wrote.

She was thoroughly disgusted when she watched him on television interviews. He took advantage of people without compunction, using their stories to make his sound more convincing. What she saw made her question his credibility further. On an ABC talk show in 1977, she listened to Haley discuss one of the book's fans. She recorded what she called his "pitiable story":

A very elderly Black woman stood in a long line of people waiting for him to autograph his book. This old lady had several of his $12.50 books in her arms . . . he could see her shoes were ragged, her toes peeking out. Proudly she said, "I'm not just buying a book, I'm buying our history!" And with that he began to cry . . . sobs came up from his feet to his head and sobs went down from his head to his feet. And I turned off the TV thinking, "Oh my God, that's a phony nigger! Why would he let her buy his books instead of buying her some shoes!"[33]

Looking at the entire *Roots* controversy from a distance offers the benefit of hindsight, although it won't change the effect on Walker's reputation and career. She subjected herself to venomous public criticism when she elected to sue Haley, and the damage to her reputation was irreparable. Arguably, it affected the reception of her next book, *Richard Wright: Daemonic Genius*, published ten years later. Her conclusions about the method in which *Roots* came together suggested that the entire project rested on a lie. Such exposure is not easily forgiven. The person who does the exposing becomes the enemy, is singled out as a target, and may lose credibility. This is precisely what happened.

At the time Walker filed the suit, with only her family supporting her, she put all of her faith in lawyers who had not handled a case of this type or one with so many powerful people. Judge Marvin Frankel's written opinion showed his bias against her legal team. Identifying their missteps, that they were late in filing their objections, for example, he even suggested that it was only because of his generosity that he considered the case at all, especially when the defense called for ruling it out. The larger misstep was that Walker, as the plaintiff, elected not to testify at the evidentiary hearing. Neither did she ask for an adjournment or a rescheduling. She simply did not appear. Frankel took a hard line. Reading between the lines of his opinion indicates that he was irritated at her lawyers, who were not playing by the rules or, in his words, "deviated more often than they should from fundamental rules of evidence and procedure."[34] He saw sloppy legal work, after he had given them every opportunity to prove their case. Second, the comparison between the Jackson lawyers and the more-prepared and well-paid team of Haley's lawyers tilted the balance toward Haley, whom Frankel found "wholly credible in his denials of copying." Ultimately for Frankel, the case had moved "comfortably past any speculation as to substantial similarities" between *Roots* and *Jubilee*.[35]

Frankel proved himself to be a strict interpreter of the law, unforgiving of any deviations from the legal process. It might have been possible to tilt the balance toward her favor had her lawyers presented more evidence beyond her catalogue of comparisons. But each piece of evidence had failed them. The discovery of a *New West* article on *Playboy* editor Murray Fisher could have certainly served them well. Fisher, who had collaborated with Haley earlier on the *Autobiography of Malcolm X*, had claimed co-authorship of *Roots* and demanded a cash settlement or the addition of his name to the novel. It was Haley's decision, according to the article, to have Doubleday pay Fisher his asking price along with 10 percent of the net proceeds. He did not want Fisher's name on the novel. As Walker quickly understood, the odds were stacked against her. When asked, Fisher confirmed that he had received a settlement, but he was unwilling to testify on Walker's behalf. He would never admit that he'd read *Jubilee*, he told them.[36] Had he done so, he would have pulled the string that would have brought the whole case tumbling down.

The need to protect the truth and Walker's need to tell it were in constant battle; it became her unholy war. The acts that were being committed allowed the media, the large corporations, the literary establishment, and well-placed individuals to become complicit in their entanglements. She summed it up as "Big Money, Business, Big Government, and Big Mafia."[37] The network of collaborators was so huge that it created its own reason for existence. Whether she saw it in terms of the North vs. the South, the rich and powerful vs. the poor and powerless, or the war between the sexes—white and Black men vs. a Black woman— Walker was so consumed by it all that she could talk about nothing else. Her charges of plagiarism, as the first of three suits against Haley, were assumed to be malicious. Neither was the Black media on her side, including *Jet* and *Ebony*.

Moving ahead without support was not uncommon for Walker. She followed her mind, her hunches, her intuition, and surrendered herself to prayer, calling on *Silent Unity*. The case became legendary precisely because it could not be stopped. On a Sunday in early May 1977 after they'd filed the suit, Walker wrote that she had felt God's presence "and the knowledge that God is with me," after a long, dry spell. "This I need, for I have been quite depressed and down spirited. I read the paper and magazines and letters and hear the awful things people have been saying about me," she wrote.[38]

A few months after Walker filed her suit, Harold Courlander sued Haley for copyright infringement of his novel *The African*, published in 1967, a year after *Jubilee*. Haley began his story with the departure from the Gambia and allegedly relied on Courlander's narrative for the first 200 pages of *Roots*. Courlander asserted that Haley relied on Walker, as she identified, for the section of the novel that began just before the Civil War for 400 pages. Walker's 150 instances of plagiarism compare to Courlander's 80. The media speculated that Courlander would undoubtedly lose, basing their projections on the Walker outcome. *New York Magazine* reported, "it is not unlikely that some of the alleged similarities between the two books will fall into the same categories of non-protected expression that were cited in *Alexander v Haley*."[39] The media, however, was wrong. Haley was adamant in his denial in the Walker case. But he admitted to plagiarizing *The African*, after being presented with only half the number of examples that Walker had identified.

One explanation for this turn of events might be that Haley had simply had enough. In March 1977, British journalist Mark Ottaway, in a brief but much-publicized piece in the *London Sunday Times*, claimed that "the man who provided Haley with the vital link to [his African ancestor] Kunta Kinte was a man of notorious unreliability who probably knew beforehand what Haley wanted to hear."[40] Walker filed suit in April, while Courlander filed in May. Walker was discovering information all the time, but her legal team met road-blocks that prevented them from presenting the evidence they needed. Hadn't the admission that *Roots* had a team of writers and was not a single-authored text cast enough doubt about Haley's credibility in both cases? Had Courlander suc-ceeded in proving that Haley had lifted texts from *The African* when Walker did not? Since Haley conceded before a decision, the case was settled out of court. Nothing had to be proved. Had the tide of public opinion changed that quickly? Did one judge have a revelation that another did not?

First World opened the dialogue for an entirely new interpretation in 1979. In his article, Herb Boyd compared the two cases, raising further questions about what actually happened. Boyd's conclusion is that Frankel's ruling in *Margaret Walker v. Alex Haley* seemed as valid for Walker as it was for Courlander, refer-ring to Frankel's summary judgment:

> Many of the claimed similarities are based on matters of historical or contempo-rary fact. No claim of copyright protection can arise from the fact that plaintiff has written about such historical and factual items, even if we were to assume that Haley was alerted to the facts in question by reading *Jubilee*. A number of copyright infringements of the cultural history of black Americans, or of both black and white Americans play out the cruel tragedy of white-imposed slavery. Where common sources exist for the alleged similarities, or the material that is similar is otherwise not original with the plaintiff, there is no infringement.[41]

Judge Frankel dismissed Walker's charge that Haley had copied *Jubilee* alto-gether, on the grounds that she had not proven her case. Furthermore, in each category where Walker claimed infringement, with her extensive list of similari-ties, Frankel ruled in favor of Haley, staying squarely within the laws, using as his reasons "public domain," "standard treatment of a given topic," or that "words or phrases are not subject to copyright." Similarly, Frankel argued that *Jubilee* and *Roots* are different, because *Jubilee* covers childhood and adulthood in slavery through the Civil War years and Reconstruction, while "*Roots* covers a broader canvas, commencing its narrative in Africa and continuing through multiple generations of a single family, described as the ancestors of the author."[42]

Courlander's *The African* is likewise different from *Roots*, since it is "only half the length of *Roots*, and only covers the first two parts of it . . . the voyage to the new world and the plantation experience,"[43] according to Herb Boyd. In both cases, Walker and Courlander cited numerous similarities, but one case was determined to be stronger that the other. Boyd locates the shift in Haley's change of heart. He was being challenged for the third time in a single year, and the suits were filed one month apart. The Courlander case lasted eight days, and Haley observed that Judge Ward's responses were markedly different from Judge Frankel's. Haley did the only thing he could do to save face, according to Boyd, "assign such an error to one of the many folks who were kind enough to give him materials they thought would improve his work."[44]

Courlander was a widely known white folklorist and novelist who had significantly more cultural capital than Walker. She was a teacher at a Negro college in the South. At least one other person saw significance in this fact. Jacqueline Trescott's article "Respected Scholar" appeared in the *Washington Post* the same day that Christopher Dickey reported on the three cases against Haley. Her insight into the complicated nature of race, gender, and regional perceptions introduced a much-needed perspective. Beginning with the familiar connection to Haley, Trescott quickly described Margaret Walker as "a quiet force in American letters for more than three decades." She dismissed the view that Walker was bitter and jealous of Haley's success, noting that such resentment surfaced only on rare, private occasions. Taking readers back to 1973 and the Phillis Wheatley Festival, Trescott noted that Walker's voice at this gathering of women writers spoke loudly on the question of race and gender and the sexism that existed in a publishing industry that historically excluded and critically neglected women writers. To make her case, Trescott referenced male writers in Walker's cohort who had become famous, including Saul Bellow and Richard Wright. The portrait of Walker as a genteel Southern lady, who can "in an hour, cook from scratch, collard greens bar-b-qued chicken, biscuits and strawberry shortcake," contrasts with the Walker whom Trescott quotes in the article's conclusion. "If you're going to be a revolutionary in the arts or elsewhere, please have something to say," was Walker's advice to students. The timely piece, possibly the only one by a woman journalist written during the entire controversy, casts Walker in a new and different light. Yet, as Trescott noted, Walker's world was an "outpost in the nonliterary center of Jackson, Mississippi."[45]

As much as Walker has championed the South, Trescott's term "nonliterary outpost" raises an important question. No part of the United States is more identified with its own literary tradition than the South. Modern American literature has more well-known Southern writers than from any other region of the country. In her journal, Walker explained what Trescott seemed to be getting at, "I am 61, relatively poor and obscure and must either be rash to take on such powerful rich opponents or desperately courageous."[46] If a "literary outpost" in the 1970s was a tightly controlled system of publishers, agents, the reviewing media, and finance capital who form a consensus of validation and protection to ensure maximum benefits, then, yes, Walker had nothing of the kind. For the

South's white writers, America's romance with the South assured their legacy through books and films. Walker was a *nobody* who was attacking a *somebody* who was within that network. Walker and Trescott dared to connect race and gender, exposing a national narrative of deception and in a period that appeared to be making progress on both ends. While she found support among a number of her women friends, especially Sonia Sanchez, whose visits and lengthy phone calls Walker had come to rely on, many others tried to get her to cease and desist. Mari Evans, who considered herself a good friend, believed she was offering good advice and remembered saying to her: "This is a private matter that should never have been made a public affair." [47].

For Margaret Walker, nothing could have been more public, especially when it came to her religion and her ethics. She had accepted defeat, as she had told herself she would. She also knew that she would refuse to capitalize on the controversy in any way. Daphne Ehrlich, an editor at Houghton Mifflin, called to ask for permission to insert a line on the cover of a new edition of *Jubilee* to boost sales. Walker could only think about their refusal to support the suit, but now they were eager to release 150,000 copies of a new edition with the tag line "the million copy best seller before the *Roots* Controversy." She could no more see herself trading on the *Roots* controversy than she could see Houghton Mifflin trading on her. The controversy also brought a call from an executive at Universal Pictures interested in turning *Jubilee* into a television movie. As much as she had desired this, again she stood on principle. She saw the offer as another way to capitalize on the publicity and refused to return the call.

Throughout the two-year battle, Walker talked more publicly about the case than she should have, despite the admonition of her family and others to keep her lips sealed. Curtis King tried to get her to see that "Every time she talked about Haley, she was selling his books for him, and I think it might have finally gotten through," he remembered.[48] The controversy had struck at her core, and because she was so vocal, during the subsequent lectures she gave, she came to expect the inevitable question about the *Roots* controversy. Her last and perhaps most important engagement with the topic was in 1988, when, at the invitation of Detroit heart surgeon Walter Evans, she did a book tour in Michigan on the eve of the publication of *Richard Wright: Daemonic Genius*. Evans arranged multiple talks, honored her with a lavish reception at his home, and paid her handsomely. The event was a homecoming of sorts, where she spent time with fellow poets Alvin Aubert and Dudley Randall and numerous friends. She had planned to talk about the Wright biography in the address at Wayne State University, but she spoke almost exclusively about the *Roots* affair. She was comfortable "Setting the Record Straight," the title of her speech to a large audience of admirers, students, and faculty. Publishing the monograph provided an opportunity to "get it out of her system," many people felt. She had finally taken Curtis King's advice.

The public declaration offered a certain closure. The past was contained, and the space made available for a new phase of her life to begin.

In 1993, Haley's cultural halo was removed with the revelations from the painstaking research conducted after his death by Philip Nobile. Fifteen years after Walker's suit, her allegations were proven correct—*Roots* was a carefully recreated narrative from multiple published sources, including *Jubilee*. Nobile could verify none of Haley's work in the Gambia: dates, location, events, and interviews did not match nor could any sources be identified. Haley had not only plagiarized, but he had also fabricated his research process. No vindication was necessary for Walker. She knew the truth from the beginning and did not

Cover page, *Setting the Record Straight*

require any new supporting information. Haley was dead, and her strong beliefs would not allow her to speak ill of him. Nobile's concluding observation is telling: "white guilt and the sense of Black solidarity had conspired to protect Haley, making victims of us all."[49] Racism is never a one-way street.

In 1996, Dr. Evans had Walker's Detroit speech privately printed as a broadside. Except for her copious journal entries, *Setting the Record Straight* remains the only published record of the story. The publication was also a triumph for her in another way. On the inside cover, the image of Elizabeth Catlett's sculpture "Homage to Black Women Poets" faces Walker's dedication line, "to young, Black women poets." Walker held no grudges against those who stood silent during the entire *Roots* controversy. *Roots* had taught Walker the awful pain a Black woman feels when she tries to penetrate the shield that carefully protects Black men of importance. She needed only the satisfaction that she'd done the right thing and watched it run its full course.

Eight years after she'd given the speech to a large and enthusiastic crowd, two years before her death, Margaret Walker was the woman we thought we knew, the woman who spoke not for herself but for her people. She concluded her talk with familiar words:

> What I have to say is important not just for me but for all my people and for folk in the United States of America and that is why I write; that is why I have written. That is why I shall keep on until I die.[50]

28

Making Peace with My Soul

Walker had many sleepless nights and panic attacks over the two years that the *Roots* controversy dragged on. At some moments she thought she was on the verge of another psychotic break. At other times she was deeply philosophical, engaged in more interior dialogue than usual, asking assorted questions that she felt she needed to answer. What does modern man believe? To what extent are race and religion challenges to morality and ethical behavior? Of what value is the inner life? Are things worth more than people; machines and property more than humanity? How can we balance contemplation and activism? Though her answers were uneven and rarely complete, what mattered most was her belief that she had the power within to find them at all. This sense of power and authority could keep her going through the ruptures in her life. She had evidence of that.

She'd already come to the conclusion that *Jubilee* was indeed her most important book and that it was more than an historical novel: "my blood, sweat and tears and because of the length of time it took to do this book, it took on increasing value as not only a book, but a life force."[1] When she saw that life force being threatened—as *Roots* did—she fought back. By that time, her novel had become a moral symbol for her. She therefore rejected the idea that what had happened was just another lesson to pass through, as James and Marion suggested. It was more like "a coming out of hell, climbing the mountain of prayer, penitence and purgatory into that place of beatific vision of union and communion with God."[2] At some point in her reflections, she concluded that her part in the *Roots* matter was driven by a cardinal sin—excessive pride. She'd become too self-righteous, overly concerned with worldly matters, believing herself to be immune from or above sin. This breach of a religious contract with her God was a serious matter that required a recommitment of her faith. She prayed in church, to *Silent Unity*, and privately, asking to be forgiven. She even promised to evangelize and preach God's word.

Beyond her acknowledgment of corporate greed and the support that Haley had, Walker did not, and never would entertain a more thorough discussion of the *Roots* affair in relationship to larger questions of gender and the prevailing sexist, racist attitudes toward Black women, despite the immensity of these public conversations at the time. She acknowledged that there were differences between Haley and herself—a Black man and a Black woman—but her analysis

The House Where My Soul Lives. Maryemma Graham, Oxford University Press. © Oxford University Press 2022. DOI: 10.1093/oso/9780195341232.003.0028

Retirement meant renewal and reaffirmation of Alex and Margaret's love

remained rooted in corporate class dynamics. Just as her conscience had been the driving force behind her actions in the first place, it was her conscience—her sense of personal responsibility—that drove her to reexamine her actions at the end of the process.

Another factor may have accounted for the lack of broad-based support from other women, especially Black feminists. Whether she was conscious of it or not, because she had stayed as far away as possible from what she and many others saw as a radical lesbian faction, she may have closed herself off from the possibility of broader support. Coalescing around race and gender brought its own

Louis Farrakhan speaking at the Institute's tenth anniversary

problems during the period that acknowledged "interlocking systems" of oppression, as memorialized in the Combahee River Collective Statement of 1977.
It does seem odd that so few Black women who otherwise fought actively against
sexist oppression and long-standing stereotypes of Black women were willing to
speak out publicly. Since Walker was the only Black woman who had spoken out
against a successful Black man, she was either indefensible or she'd given up her
"race card." Her last resort was a tactical retreat: if she internalized the issue, she
could claim ownership on her terms.

Her method of working through this difficult period included a review of earlier periods when she had challenged someone based on principle. When she
challenged the president of Jackson State who had refused to give her permission for a leave, she realized he was her superior. His attitude may have been
sexist, but she attributed his response to personal failings, which in her mind
was simply jealousy. When the tables were turned a decade later, and others accused her of jealousy over Haley's success, she was forced to take back control
of her narrative. In Walker's understanding, jealousy was an outer expression of
self-doubt, often brought on when someone is less intelligent or accomplished
than another. Men, who were often less accomplished than women, she believed,
could only claim their authority over such a person through control. How could
she have been driven by jealousy if she never doubted her ability or who she was?

She was willing to be wrong, but she correctly determined that her pride could spin out of control. Thus, standing up for truth was the right thing to do, but it was excessive pride in doing so that had caused the failure. Only the deepest form of soul-searching could offer the understanding that brought her soul peace.

An unexpected outcome of the whole affair and her associated interior dialogue was the impact on the Institute's public activities. In late 1977, for example, as part of the Jackson State centennial, she organized the Conference on the Teaching of Creative Writing, based on one she had attended at the Library of Congress some years earlier and a short essay she had contributed to the conference proceedings. She was of the opinion, to which the *Roots* controversy no doubt contributed, that academic institutions should be more deliberate in teaching the craft and the integrity of the writing process. She wanted to make this a central topic for a shared conversation between writers and educators. Using her experience at Iowa, in two separate periods, when she was twenty-four and forty-nine, she began to isolate what specific tools could be taught, and what must come from one's research and thorough investigations. What she confronted was the disparity between her thirty-year learning apprenticeship that had led to the publication of *Jubilee* and what she saw happening in MFA programs that had begun to flourish. She concluded correctly that standards in the creative writing field were not easily discernible and, therefore, that higher education needed to be more systematic in its method of instruction. Even though there were no universals, teaching and learning did matter.

For this conference, she seemed to have surpassed her earlier example, the seventy-fifth anniversary of Jackson State's founding. Twenty-five years earlier, she had invited the leading writers of the period. Langston Hughes, Arna Bontemps, and Melvin Tolson had died. Sterling Brown was alive but ailing and unable to travel. Only Owen Dodson and Robert Hayden would appear. Her planning notes did not indicate any of the younger writers although her intent was to recognize a new generation to show the growth of African American literature. Like the Wheatley Festival, she wanted to expand the dialogue among writers, scholars, and publishers. This time, however, she was casting an even wider net to test her expanding ideas about the relationship between literary and cultural expression and education, including for the first time, for example, a children's theater group.

As was typical for Walker, such events resulted from a convergence of many things. She had been paying attention to the public dialogues, intellectual shifts, and academic trends as Black Studies programs began to proliferate. She wanted to reinforce the importance of the Institute as a think tank and showcase for Black excellence. Her essay "The Writer and Her Craft" was enough to begin the conversation. The Haley controversy was the most talked-about topic in Black circles, and she was eager to score a win that could redirect the conversation.

While "The Writer and Her Craft" shows appreciation for the lessons learned over the course of her career, it quickly outlines deeper concerns. Walker resumed her role as critic, looking beneath the surface of things. Without naming the person involved, she shared a personal experience to convey her point.

> I had a shocking experience at Yale when a professor, whom I greatly admired, told me that black people were acceptable as long as they remained primitive and did not imitate white people. I was aghast. Then I realized that what African Americans have experienced in this country is an insidious form of institutional racism that we still feel. . . . the history is overladen with racist implications.[3]

At a time when more Black writers were producing work than ever before, many of them trained in MFA programs, Walker's cautionary tale was a reminder that important work remained to be done. Ignorance of the Black cultural heritage prevented whites from seeing those unlike themselves as human beings. At the same time, there is a failure to accept Black writing "unless it [is] imitative, servile, or compromising . . . never intellectually honest." [4] Institutional racism was responsible for them both. She posed the question: how can creative writing programs assist writers in arriving at the common ground of humanity? She modeled these words with the mix of Black and white writers: Michael Harper, Lance Jeffers, Margaret Danner, Mari Evans, Sam Greenlee, Amiri Baraka, Ernest Gaines, Al Young, Eudora Welty, Ellen Douglas, Mignon Holland, Doris Saunders, Barney McKee, Linda Bragg, Nancy Staub, Christian Garrison, Sybil Hannah, Larice Gross, Ted Shine, Beah Richards, Davis Roberts, Carlton Molette, Vivian Romans, and Peter Zapletal. The surprise guests were Daphne Ehrlich, her editor at Houghton Mifflin, and Harold Courlander, who had won his suit against Alex Haley.

Far less publicity accompanied this festival, but the discussions and readings renewed her desire to write a biography about Richard Wright, which had been put on hiatus during the *Roots* controversy. She applied for a sabbatical as her lecture engagements picked up again, reminding herself that the Wright book would be a scholarly work that would reconfirm her credentials. When she gained clarity about this, new possibilities emerged, like an invitation to serve as the Langston Hughes Visiting Professor at the University of Kansas, which could provide valuable writing time. She still found it difficult to see the "Haley effect" as positive, but it seemed to speed up her transformation from a poet or novelist to a decidedly more public life as a scholar. The adjustment was minor since she had always considered herself as a scholar, a fact that her intensive analytical approach to every aspect of her life confirmed. What she now questioned was her long-held belief that what validates human beings is what lies within. Almost no one had seen what was inside of her when she went against public opinion. Her new assessment that Courlander's success was primarily because of his reputation as a scholar, highly revered as an Africanist—and not because he was white—marked a major shift in her thinking. It was the push she needed to take on a book project that stretched her in new ways. If the conference on creative writing had clarified the relationship between academic training and creative practice, then the path toward *Richard Wright: Daemonic Genius* demanded the kind of critical thinking she had always done. As her private and public worlds began to collide, she saw the benefits of making the fusion public.

Walker had thought and talked about the Wright book for some time since she learned about a project by Horace Cayton, a friend of Wright's during the Chicago years. After Cayton's death, Sue Cayton Woodson, a member of Walker's circle of Chicago friends, followed her brother's instructions to give Walker all of his files. Sue was in agreement with her brother that no one else could do the book but Walker. The talk she had given on Wright at Iowa was published in 1973,[5] but it could not compete with Michel Fabre's *The Unfinished Quest of Richard Wright*. Her essay identified her with a Richard Wright renaissance in the early 1970s, but it was her association with Wright and having possession of Cayton's early research that could be the trump card. Was she ready to open up old wounds? Her answer was an unqualified yes because she would do so on her terms, not someone else's. Wright had made Paris his home, was beloved by the French people, and even though Fabre had gained the confidence of Ellen Wright and produced a well-researched authorized biography, the real Wright, Walker believed, remained hidden.

She was well aware of the times in which she was writing. Black writers during the 1960s and 1970s were questioning the value of work by earlier writers whom they believed were engaged in a futile battle writing about Black people, but to and for a white audience rather than a Black one. Many saw Richard Wright's work as the best example of what a new kind of Black writing should not be. While he was considered to be the most influential African American writer in the twentieth century at that point, his particular brand of fiction set off a round of debates among different groups of writers. The box into which his writing was put, with the term "protest novel," was now outdated. She had her issues with Wright, but did not see herself aligning with those whom he considered his protégés, namely Ralph Ellison and James Baldwin, who were quick to point out his flaws and critique the entire genre with which he had become associated. "Bigger's tragedy is not that he is cold or black or hungry," Baldwin wrote, "not even that he is American, black; but that he has accepted a theology that denies him life, that he admits the possibility of his being subhuman and feels constrained. . . . The failure of the protest novel lies in its rejection of life, the human being, the denial of his beauty, dread, power, in its insistence that it is his categorization alone which is real and which cannot be transcended."[6]

The combined effect of these assessments was to discredit Wright's work and to silence that of others, especially those who were quickly dubbed the Wright school of social protest, or anyone whose approach to narrating the Black experience was comparable. These writers, William Attaway, Ann Petry, Lloyd L. Brown, Chester Himes, and even later writers like John A. Williams, had difficulty gaining critical acceptance because of their association with the protest tradition after it had lost its appeal.

If members of his generation had believed that Wright had failed to understand Black humanity, reinforcing negative conceptions of Black people, many in the next generation believed that his writing remained trapped in limiting ideological paradigms that prevented him from seeing and using the tremendous reservoir of Black culture. The factor that distinguished Wright from those younger writers who criticized him was their ability to tap into this reservoir, whether they did so working through Modernist techniques or the Black aesthetic. Black women critics found little salvageable in Wright as well for personal and ideological reasons. The castigation of Wright came from all sides, but charges against his exploitation of women characters, both Black and white, seemed to be the harshest, at least after the 1970s.

Walker saw her intervention as necessary, especially after she read Fabre's biography thoroughly. She wondered too if her failure to respond to him explained his lack of generosity toward her in the book's discussion of her relationship with Wright. She was "a new talent . . . who had become the most active member of the South Side Group," whom Wright had "introduced to meaningful and committed writing, and [who] proved a devoted friend doing research for him and occasionally comforting him during their frequent correspondence,"[7] Fabre wrote. His conclusion was that "she had committed indiscretions which almost lost Wright some of his friends . . . in fact marked the date when Wright withdrew from her."[8] Fabre correctly identified the end of their correspondence and suggested that Walker expected Wright to marry her.

She had explained the relationship to herself and decided to maintain her silence as she moved on with her life. The less people actually knew, the more persistent were questions about their relationship. A shroud of mystery surrounded their relationship, and her choice of silence was like stoking a fire. To be called out by someone who knew neither Wright nor her, and to be included in Fabre's list of "well-educated, pretty, intelligent black girls, who corresponded to the type of woman he could have married,"[9] was insulting to Wright as much as it objectified her. Wright had his pick of women, and all of them, both Black and white, were part of the franchise. Reading Fabre's passage in the context of the 1970s suggests that Fabre was searching for an explanation for Wright's rejection of the Black middle class, especially its women. Because he had never been able to find all that he wanted in a Black woman, Fabre believed, Wright eventually found a great deal of satisfaction in adulterous affairs with white women, two of whom he ultimately married. Fabre provides further support for his explanation with the forbidden fruit analysis. "This was his revenge for the years of sexual and emotional frustration; he certainly felt additional pleasure in flouting the taboos that, for a black man in Mississippi, were the equivalent of a castration....To possess a white woman was a way of eradicating painful memories."[10]

Racial explanations like these have become far more nuanced, but have not disappeared. Fabre acknowledged the limitations of his point of view in his preface to the second edition of the biography in 1993. Reading his 1973 edition, seeing herself diminished and objectified heightened Walker's desire to write a very different kind of biography of a man that nobody really seemed to know. From her experience, she could point to Wright's negative treatment of and attitudes toward women generally. If he seemed ruthless and manipulative, these characteristics were required, or so it seemed, to gain the success that he desired, a pattern common to many male writers. On this, she and Fabre agreed, but she was convinced that it had more to do with being uncomfortable in his own skin, ambivalent sexuality, and the need to reject the very thing that made him who he was, more than the intellectual and emotional growth Fabre attributed to him.

Walker had expected questions when she agreed to do interviews discussing her relationship to Wright. In most cases, she gave a standard response: she and Wright were never lovers, nor were they romantically involved. Because she held firmly to her Victorian moral principles, her version of the story was appropriate. Denying it as she did only encouraged people to conclude quite the opposite: that she was in love with him, a love that was unrequited.

Her reasons for writing the book were all that mattered. She never saw herself as writing a tell-all biography. She did, however, believe that Fabre had misled the public. No, Wright did not help her with her writing, as Fabre intimated. It was she who had the college degree, she who had been encouraged to write since she was a child, and it was she who had benefited from creative writing classes from her professors at Northwestern. Wright's influence was on her "social perspective," as she called it: "Marxism and the problems of black people in this country." She was adamant: "I helped Wright. He couldn't spell straight. He couldn't write. I had just graduated from Northwestern with a major in English literature. Do you believe that I was just being introduced to literature by Wright?"[11] she told Claudia Tate in an interview.

She was correct, of course. Sexist overtones exist in Fabre's book that harked back to another time. The most famous literary couple in the twentieth century had been French. Simone de Beauvoir and Jean-Paul Sartre had maintained a long-term relationship, and Beauvoir, an outspoken feminist. Her role was significant and her influence lasting. *The Second Sex* put Beauvior in the vanguard of what became an international movement. She was also Sartre's editor, his nurse, his constant companion, *and* lover; she helped to develop his ideas, spending much of her time keeping him from excessive drinking. In short, he could not function without her. If, as her biographer Dierdre Baer says, Beauvoir gave "precedence to public activity over private relationship,"[12] the pattern seemed in no way unusual. Sartre and Beauvoir were intellectual equals, but her importance could not develop alongside his.

Walker never called what may have complicated her relationship with Wright sexism. Rather, she saw it as a learning experience. He was ambitious, and she believed that their friendship meant that she should support him to the fullest extent of that ambition. But she firmly believed that he had committed theft. Passages from *Goose Island,* the manuscript she was working on while they were at the Federal Writers' Project, bears some resemblance to *Native Son.* That thinking may also have fueled the intensity with which she pursued her suit against Haley. The thought of two men stealing her work was unbearable.

Fabre admitted that she provided materials for *Native Son,* using her access to get the books and documents he needed. Walker's assessment was that once Wright got what he needed he had no further use for their relationship. Admitting that she was used enabled her to move beyond the experience. Writing the biography of Richard Wright was her way of "making peace with my soul," she later confessed. "I felt Wright wanted me to write his biography because nobody is going to be more sympathetic and understanding than I am."[13]

Since she had published three books with Black-owned presses, she responded positively when Howard University Press director Charles Harris approached her. She liked what they had done with *Poetic Equation* and felt she was making the right choice. She had mapped out her life so that the Wright book would lead her into retirement. When she signed the contract for the biography in 1976, she planned to finish the manuscript within three years. Having a new book released as she brought her academic career to a close would start the next phase of her life on a high note.

Since this had all occurred before the *Roots* controversy, one wonders why Walker was not more aggressive in pursuing a commercial publisher. She might have been concerned that her motives would be questioned, given the insinuations by Fabre in his book and the widespread rumors that she was in love with Wright. But such a topic would have appealed to readers. Gaining an audience through controversy offered no appeal to her. It would not have been much different from capitalizing on a new edition of *Jubilee* after the *Roots* controversy. Only one woman had written about Wright up to that point, and she was white, but Constance Webb's biography had been quickly displaced.

Her entry into the publishing world had been academic, facilitated by white men. Working with Charles Harris at Howard University Press fulfilled two important requirements for Walker: it honored her commitment to HBCUs and allowed her to remain with an academic press. Harris was a pioneer executive, among the first to make his way in the publishing world after he had begun his career at Doubleday in the 1950s. She trusted his experience and his relationships with writers she knew, like John A. Williams. He and Williams had also produced the two-volume *Amistad* series, appearing in 1970 and 1971, which helped to convince white publishers that Black books had crossover appeal and would boost sales. Most important, she shared a kinship with someone, a Southerner and an HBCU graduate who was now sharing his success and his knowledge with those to whom it mattered the most.

At this late stage in her career, Walker did not need a Stephen Vincent Benét, who had endorsed "For My People." She did not need a Dorothy de Santillana or her successor Daphne Ehrlich at Houghton Mifflin, who had withdrawn support completely during the *Roots* controversy. She felt safe with Harris, confident that he was someone who would not back away should something go awry. There is no indication that Walker reached out to or received any invitations from any of the other publishers who were the most hospitable to Black writers in the 1970s, Random House, Simon & Schuster, or William Morrow. Ultimately, Harris's long association with Doubleday brought the best of two worlds, or so Walker believed, and she felt the Wright book would allow for a relative smooth entrance into a new publishing community. She was satisfied with her decision since, once again, she was driven by principle. Walker after the *Roots* controversy had greater clarity about purpose and intent and a more measured sense of possibilities. She did not want to repeat the mistake she had made earlier in surrendering to excessive pride. That clarity dictated her actions when she set her official retirement date for the end of the spring semester 1979 and began counting down the days.

Her retirement was more than the end of a successful career. By 1979, Walker was well aware that the most important rupture in her life would soon occur. For the first time, she had to consider what it might mean to remap her life in the deliberate manner that had become her custom, without the most vital element that sustained her. Alex had been experiencing health problems, which she referred to in general terms at first, problems that increased during the *Roots* controversy. He was tired, more irritable than usual, and seemed less interested in eating. The latter was a major sign to her that something was wrong, since he always enjoyed and raved about her cooking. She suspected it was cancer without saying it openly. Once the cancer diagnosis was confirmed, she could not be certain how much time he had, but she would make sure they would spend it together.

She knew that she would have to be very deliberate. Her retirement budget was slim, and she did not want to supplement it with a host of speaking engagements.

She had written a letter to Benjamin Payton at the Ford Foundation and enclosed her Wright proposal, something they had discussed. A fellowship would eliminate the need to take on any engagements and allow her to divide her time between writing and Alex. During the summer and early fall of 1978, she got a head start on her research for the Wright book with support from the Ford Foundation.

As part of her pre-retirement planning, Walker convinced Alex to do the one thing she had always wanted to do—visit her father's birthplace, Jamaica. Though reluctant, he eventually consented to join their old friends Bill and Alberta Evans on a weeklong cruise. To have her best traveling companion show reluctance was another sign that he was more ill than he would admit. But their relationship seemed stronger than ever.

In early January 1979, she had her first glimpse of the island of Jamaica. The ship docked at Port Antonio, a place that she only knew from her father's animated descriptions. As important as family was to her, she was surprised how little she knew about her father's side beyond the stories he told. Returning to his native Jamaica had been a dream for him always, but the death of each close relative there, one by one, lessened his desire. Soon Jamaica disappeared from his conversation. Because he grew more silent as he became older, she always thought that his longing for Jamaica had taken his voice. She would be making that symbolic return on his behalf, going to the place he had left seventy years ago. She would hold on to the vivid images of the place of such beauty, paying homage to her father and to Jamaica in her poetry. The cruise was short, and she made no attempt to meet relatives, for she knew of none. But she had made his dream come true.

When she returned, she had one thing left to do at the Institute, a final Martin Luther King, Jr. celebration, her signature event. For the 1979 celebration, Walker invited Louis Farrakhan, Kelly Miller, and Rev. Fred Shuttlesworth to mark her decade as the Institute's director. She sought to shed new light on King to move the dialogue of history and activism in new directions. The event would focus on a much-underdiscussed topic, King's relationship with other religious movements. Few people knew that King and Malcolm X had a brief but significant encounter when Malcolm X was still in good standing within the Nation of Islam. Farrakhan, one of Malcolm's early trainees, was the perfect choice.

Alferdteen Harrison, one of the most active members of the Institute's board, was her choice as the next director of the Institute. They had already begun to work together, their families knew each other, and Harrison was the mother of two sons. Thus, Walker saw a trained historian, an experienced fundraiser, and, importantly, a mother who obviously knew how to multi-task. The relationship between the two women from the very beginning was based on their shared family values and work ethic.

Walker recognized at JSU's commencement in 1979, beginning her official
retirement

In her annual report on the Institute, she made her preference known and proceeded as if the appointment would go through. She knew that Harrison shared
her vision and understood how to operate among people with whom Walker was
frequently at odds. Harrison would make sure to preserve Walker's identity with
the Institute, as its founder and chief architect.

In rapid succession in May and June, Sigis completed his requirements for
his degree from Jackson State, Walker officially retired, and Margaret married
Vernon Williams in a large church wedding. The marriage of her youngest child
and her retirement signaled a critical transition for Walker with mixed feelings,
trepidation, and a sense of excitement. She was not certain she was ready to enter
into this new stage of her life—the confirmation of old age.

She preferred to see her retirement as a journey of renewal. She would turn
sixty-three in July and looked for opportunities that would be meaningful to
both herself and Alex, knowing that it meant curbing her desires at times. She
had not accepted the invitation to go to the University of Kansas when she received it at first, but finally agreed to do so in the summer after retirement. She
had ulterior motives, however, since Lawrence, the home of the university, was
also near Lee's Summit, Missouri, where she could visit *Silent Unity*. Going to
her prayer partner as she faced the possibility of the end of her life with Alex was

Walker considered Sonia Sanchez her literary daughter. Gene Young standing

important. A West Coast tour was also shaping up, but not finalized, and she preferred to take only one trip so as not to be away from Alex or her writing for an extended period.

Retirement energized her for the new beginning. An invitation came from President and Mrs. Jimmy Carter to attend the reception as a recipient of the Living Legacy Awards, created by the National Caucus and Center on Black Aging. The honor contributed to a new certainty about her location in time and place. Bad weather combined with a nagging illness and Alex's declining heath prevented her from attending the White House reception, but her new certitude showed itself in active writing. She drafted new poems, in the longer style that she enjoyed the most, and allowed this poetic interlude to become one way of looking back at her life. She was preparing her final poetry volume, *This Is My Century*, gathering those poems written sporadically over the years. She wrote nearly at the pace of her younger self.

"On Youth and Age" is the journal poem that brought her ideas into focus. She used the title for two different poems: the first is written in four parts; the second, which she titled "On Youth and Age II," had three. Designated as an autobiographical project, she foregrounds her identity within the context of major events in the twentieth century. The poems expressed the theme that would preoccupy her for the rest of her life. The spirit of the two poems cast the long view she was taking as she entered retirement.

The original "On Youth and Age" suggests that Walker would proceed chronologically. "When I was a little girl," she began, "the little girl on Morton Salt was white; / She still is." To extend this self-reflective mode, she eventually added two additional sections. The first lines of stanzas one and two of the published poem read, "The year I was born was a nodal year;" and "I was twelve when Lindbergh crossed the ocean." But the mode quickly gives way to a different kind of narrative journey, a kaleidoscope through which she presents her familiar catalogue of images and events. The call of history forces responses to rhetorical questions or other commentary as social critique. She is a woman entering her last active writing decade convinced of her influence, knowing that what she had to say would be deeply appreciated. No longer seeing her powers in decline, she confirms her role as a witness to experience and purveyor of special knowledge that age confers. Despite the forward movement of history, she insisted that we look beneath the surface of things and consider what this progress really means.

In her journal entry of the first version of the poem "On Youth and Age," she paints a full picture of "age" in symbolic references, individual characters, and the obvious signs of technological and social progress. The words are descriptive, intended to evoke the sounds, images, and the feeling of a period that brings radical changes to people's daily lives and equally radical shifts in our human relationships. This was the "unconscious" and "automatic" process she had mastered, what she had learned to do as a poet, to "conceive in pictures learning different kinds of rhythm, whether patterns of the line or emotional meanings of words."[14] In her revision of the poem, she rearranged sections to improve the flow and ultimate impact of the poem, making her language more precise and collapsing phrases, highly conscious of fleshing out ideas. As a poet who always pointed to the sharp contrasts in the natural, physical, and social worlds, Walker knew that such "ideas come later." But she was also conscious of overburdening the poem, which may account for her decision to write a second poem to complete her thoughts as they evolved.

Two insertions she made were crucial: she linked the advances in transportation with a clearer, more pointed statement about "Jim-crow cars" and she made an explicit distinction between "liberation" and "emancipation," two of her favorite terms. The success of the poem lies in its delicate balance between the specific insights about the twentieth century, *her century*, and the aesthetic requirement that the poem maintain its integrity as visual memory. The contrast between the journal poem and its revision illustrates how well Walker had learned her lessons in craft and the poetic maturity of her art. As published, the stanza reads:

> Streetcar trolleys were everywhere
> With their hairline to the juice above them
> And their feet firmly on the rails below them.
> They had Jim crow and seven cents fare

The following stanza evolved from further thinking:

> Transportation by train was another thing.
> The Jim-crow cars were full of soot and cinders
> the seats were hard
> and the toilets were stinking holes
> but white bankers rode at special rates
> in special cars with kitchens and dining rooms
> and beds and clean toilet facilities;
> they had barbers and hairdressers
> and colored maids.
> They chose the trains and not the planes.
> Why did transportation change with integration?[15]

"On Youth and Age II" is more openly rhetorical and satirical than the first poem and considers the entire meaning of her life in summary fashion. Since she wrote the title poem later, this earlier poem marks the beginning of a process, providing clues to her thinking as her understanding deepens. She knew that she would need to say more, and these periodic snapshots of her process show a fertile creative mind at work:

> This is my century:
> Radio and picture-show;
> Hot-rod, computer, video
> Ancient, rusty, slow auto:
> *Ah—ooga, ooga, ooga*

This poem is shorter and more elusive, with a marked change in tone before she begins the final stanza:

> Call the doctor; call the ambulance.
> Get the fire department.
> Put our feeble century in intensive care.
> See if the old man can't last till tomorrow.
> Everybody's getting burned up in this fire.

In her conclusion, Walker imparts a sharp social critique:

> I guess there's something called Energy
> plaguing the world
> with not enough to eat
> and no clean water to drink
> nothing but oil and coal and gas
> from our fossilized world.
> Now that there's nothing called electricity
> In an electronic world full of space-time continuum
> I guess there's something called Energy
> making big problems for mankind
> womankind and childrenkind too
> only I don't know why.
> Didn't Galileo and Newton, Archimedes and Boyle,
> Mr. "Con" Edison and Einstein know how?
> Where did all the wizards go with our world?[16]

The playfulness should not be confused with the intentional shift here: symbols become fact, and images pull us away from a respectable narrative of progress into the reality of the world of the twentieth century, a world able but unwilling to solve those problems that would signify true progress.

Returning to poetry restored her optimism. When anyone asked what she was working on, she reported the four books on her agenda: "The Vision Splendid" ["Call Me Cassandra"], her autobiography; "Minna and Jim," the sequel to *Jubilee*; "My Black-Eyed Susan School," the history of Black education in Mississippi; and "Mother Beulah," the unfinished book still under contract with Houghton Mifflin. She would explain that these would be completed after the Wright biography. This display of ambition filled the void that she thought she now had. Having had so little time to write since the publication of *Jubilee*, Walker believed that her desire would make up for any ability that she lacked. In the meantime, work on the Wright book proceeded. She could expect $100,000 for the Wright book, half on delivery of the manuscript, the other half on publication. It would be the most money she'd ever made for a manuscript.

For the first time, Walker and Alex, when he was well enough, began to travel without the pressure of returning home, either to work or to family obligations, all of which made for a pleasurable East Coast lecture tour. She accepted invitations from old friends, including Sonia Sanchez. Now on the faculty at Temple University, Sanchez secured a substantial honorarium to bring her to speak. She used her platform to support Walker in numerous ways, urging fellow poets to call Walker's name and to read her "For My People" whenever they were invited to speak. The friendship between them had weathered all assaults. Sanchez had respected Walker's poetic gift from the time they met, had become the major champion of her poetry, and was the literary daughter that Walker wanted and needed at this critical moment in her life.

Their friendship was not simply that between poet and poet. Sanchez took to heart the crushing nature of Walker's reputational slippage. She knew and believed that Walker had "almost died" from the negative energy that had begun to surround her. She remembered fans coming up to Walker to confess how her poems had kept them alive. At one of the readings where they shared a stage, one woman turned to Walker with great emotion, thanking her for "sustaining me in my black skin."[17] Since they continued to talk regularly, Sanchez was determined to support Walker as she returned to writing full time and to protect against her

Walker meeting with Donald Gallup during research trip to Yale's Beinecke Library. Courtesy of William R. Ferris

literary and social isolation as much as possible, an isolation that retirement could quickly increase.

The visit to Temple felt very much like successful reclamation of a literary status, which Walker herself might not have been willing to admit. She and Alex spent a week with Sanchez, where she saw more friends, many of them who came to the party Sanchez hosted in her honor including Kristin Hunter, Muriel Feelings, James Spady, and Askia Toure, with whom she spoke at length. Over the next few years, she made frequent trips back to the East Coast, always to Temple and staying with Sanchez.

That visit was long enough for Sanchez to notice that something else was disturbing Walker. Alex was more reclusive than usual, staying in their bedroom and refusing to come down to meet the guests who attended the party. She knew him as a gracious man, full of pride for the woman he loved and adored, a pride he enjoyed being able to display. She did not discuss with Walker what they both knew: that Alex was not well and his inability to confront his cancer diagnosis made his wife a target. As the closest person to him and the most vulnerable, she had to endure Alex's extreme moods, which might include excessive drinking and lashing out at her unnecessarily, problems that she found difficult to conceal. She was, nevertheless, conscientious about completing the Wright book, and the personal and professional support from Sanchez assured her that she would be putting her retirement years to good use.

She took as a sign of change the successful visit she had at Yale in 1980. She met with Donald Gallup, then a curator and later head of the Beinecke Library, and was able to access Wright's journals from 1945 to 1947 for the first time. She could see more clearly those ways in which she and Wright were alike, confirming her belief that she could tell his story in a way that no one else could. Knowing that her association with Wright was bringing her name back in the news, she was determined to master any situation that confronted her, even redirecting a conversation, especially if she had negative feelings about it.

Another request had come from Michel Fabre, who, in 1980, was spending a semester teaching at Ole Miss, his first visit to the state or the Deep South. Fabre had proposed an exhibit focused on Wright for Ole Miss; William R. Ferris, founding director of the newly created Center for the Study of Southern Culture, conveyed Walker's message that she was on a tight schedule and simply could not make the time just now. She found it difficult to be generous with him, and she bristled every time someone mentioned his name. It would not be until 1985 that Walker and Fabre would actually meet at the first international conference on Richard Wright hosted by the Black Studies Program at Ole Miss.

By the time she returned from her 1980 East Coast visit, she had already learned that Ellen Wright was unhappy about her ongoing research. Ellen would have known that Walker was reviewing the Beinecke holdings on Wright since the collection was open for viewing, even though there could be no quoting without her permission. This would be a growing source of bitterness between the women that gave further credence to the belief that Walker had remained in love with Wright and that her biography was her vendetta. This perspective was not easily discarded, in view of the lingering effects of the Haley lawsuit. Once again, she was being seen as a Black woman who hated to see the success of a Black man.

In the meantime, she spoke to St. Clair Drake, who was then at Stanford, to deepen her understanding of Wright's attitude toward the racial situation in the United States, an attitude that eventually influenced his decision to move permanently to Paris. From Drake she learned that Wright, though happy in his second marriage to Ellen, had felt the need to go through psychological analysis. As she began to sketch out the book, she used the divisions in *Native Son*—Fear, Flight, and Fate—to mark the divisions in Wright's own life. The *fear* came from the early part of his life, from the violent, explosive racism. In his search for balance between a life relatively free of racism and one that supported his art, he *fled* to Chicago and later to New York. Neither city provided what he needed. But this was his *fate*, which he accepted by moving to Paris where he continued his work in relative harmony.

She had no further need to distinguish between Wright's beliefs and hers and elected not to make Wright's Marxism the central argument of her book. Instead, she proceeded to identify the psychological threads that she would use to frame her analysis of a man she characterized as "daemonic." A firm believer in developmental psychology, she believed that Wright's early years growing up in the South had marked him for life, influencing his behavior and attitudes. White racism was his psychic wound, she would argue, one from which he could never heal. No subsequent experience could erase this early influence. Whether she was thinking as a Christian moralist, a cultural nationalist, a quasi-feminist, or a member of the radical Left, the Richard Wright that Walker knew and would write about was a man profoundly impacted by an early life of emotional and physical deprivation. What was missing from his childhood, he more than made up for in aptitude and motivation. But that, too, did not proceed along a consistent path since Wright, who was far in advance of his classmates intellectually, would go no further than the seventh grade, for reasons beyond his control. He was driven to success, not in spite of, but because of these odds against him.

As Walker prepared for her sixty-fifth birthday in July 1980, she was confident that the world would rediscover her with the Wright biography, just as it had with *Jubilee* in 1966. Governor and Mrs. William Winter organized a luncheon as part of the five-day celebration that began July 7, the day the governor proclaimed Margaret Walker Alexander Day. Following a visit to her mother, Walker prepared for the five months she would spend writing. Her plan was to complete the

Wright manuscript by New Year's Day, 1981. She took Jean Blackwell Hutson at the Schomburg Center into her confidence, in an effort to secure permission to use the restricted Wright materials. Knowing that the process would be difficult, she had no intention of slowing down.

Each day, writing late nights and early mornings, she left handwritten pages in spiral notebooks in her study. Mrs. Currie, also now retired, had agreed to assist and maintained the same strict schedule that Walker did. She came in at a scheduled time, finding whatever Walker had written, and without discussion transferred them to the IBM Selectric. Their routine did not stop, even as Alex's health declined. He became her human clock, a "bulwark of emotional strength,"[18] she wrote, pushing her to finish.

Walker and Alex both knew time was not on their side. With every chapter she finished, he grew more ill. He refused to go to the hospital, preferring instead to remain home to provide the support she needed to write more each day. She was in a race, not knowing when it would end, only that it would. The completion of the book kept both of them going. He knew that finishing the book was the one thing left for her to do, and he wanted her to finish it. It would close the door on that part of her life. It had not affected their lives together, but he knew that it was buried deep inside her, that bringing it out in the open would give her the peace that she needed. More important, he knew that he had to be there to help her finish moving it from the inside to the outside. She wanted him to get well and each day having him beside her gave her reason to cling to hope.

In late August, Alex consented to go to St. Dominic's Hospital. After a week of tests, they learned that he had developed a large gastric ulcer, but he refused to have surgery. Walker appealed to *Silent Unity*, reading passages aloud from the *Daily Word* and writing them in her journal to emphasize their power. She accepted his decision not to have surgery, and when he agreed to medication that would relieve some of the discomfort, she brought him home where he wanted to be, where she needed him to be.

With Alex at home, she returned to her grueling writing schedule, and she completed the section on Wright's Paris years. By the end of September, she had finished the analysis of Wright's relationship with Africa and Pan Africanism, including discussions of George Padmore, Kwame Nkrumah, Nnamdi Azikiwe, and Frantz Fanon. On October 13, well ahead of her schedule, she entered a note in her journal that the book was completed. Six days later, Alex finally consented to surgery and entered the hospital. After eight hours of surgery on October 19, he remained in intensive care. She never left his side but wrote praise poems thanking God for bringing him through.

On October 26, 1980, Firnist James Alexander died at St. Dominic's Hospital. The cause of death was heart failure, kidney failure, and cancer. They had been together three years shy of four decades. The book was finished, and so was their life together. On the morning before he died, she told him how much she loved him and thanked him for staying with her until the end of the most difficult book of them all. He had always known what she wanted and had given her the time she needed to do it. That had never changed. She accepted his death with conviction. "Alex died with dignity and pride. He was prepared to die and he tried to prepare me,"[19] she wrote. None of their turbulent times came to her mind. She could only remember the good times they had together.

"Now a new phase of my life begins," she wrote in her journal three days after Alex's funeral. "I am a widow, a senior citizen, sixty-five years old, retired, with four adult married children and five grandchildren. Thank you, dear God, for Alex, for our life together, for all the years, and for our love you gave us to last for a lifetime."[20]

Nationally, this new period of her life was marked by the election of Ronald Reagan. The world was changing in ways that she struggled to understand, and again, she turned to her journal for self-clarification as much as she did for consolation. But it was the Wright manuscript that offered her the most joy. The manuscript was finally finished, her mission impossible, the last book that Alex had wanted her to complete. Without him, she felt an urge to accept engagements right away because that, too, was something that she and Alex had done together. She needed something from that former life to make this new one bearable.

To relieve some of the loneliness they knew she was feeling, Norma and Sigis moved into her home with their son Khari. A second child was on the way, and

Walker with her grandchildren after Alex's death

they wanted Walker to feel pride in, as much as ownership of, this new grandchild, as if it might be possible to replace such a great loss. One other major adjustment had to be made, however, one that Alex had orchestrated. Sigis would replace his father as her companion on the road; he would drive and accompany her wherever she wanted to go. Like his father, Sigis had made a promise, one he would keep until the end of his mother's life. Assured of the necessary support, Walker began to plot her return to her professional life and to some degree of normalcy.

In private, she was a grieving widow. In public, she maintained her local visibility and sought comfort in the invitations that began to pick up as interest in the Wright book grew. Her life had changed, but she needed the Jackson community to remember both of her identities: a nationally recognized writer and now the widow, Mrs. Firnist James Alexander. She did not submit to an older tradition of wearing black for a year; instead, she began to believe that Alex had "sacrificed his life for her career," a career that was far from finished.[21] With this muchdiscussed Wright book forthcoming, she was still in her prime. Life after Alex for Walker was a renewed commitment to the person she believed he had helped her become, the person who could do anything she set out to do. He did not allow himself to die until he was certain of her success at the next stage, a symbol of the covenant they had made as part of their marriage vows, she believed. Continuing to pursue her career with a passion meant even more to her now than it did when Alex was alive.

Shortly before Christmas, she received word that the Jackson City Council had approved renaming Guynes Street in her honor. That it was to become Margaret Walker Alexander Drive pleased her as she thought of Alex. More good news came when she received her first copy of the paperback edition of *Poetic Equation: Conversations between Nikki Giovanni and Margaret Walker*. The book documented discussions that were even more relevant six years after its original release. In addition, Charlotte Momon, then head of one of the city's libraries, led a campaign for the Jackson Library Board to rename the Hinds County Library the Margaret Walker Alexander branch in her honor. She was grateful when it occurred. Remembering her own days as a child at Dryades Library in New Orleans, she saw this development not only as a memorial to her but also to the "adams and eves and their countless generations"[22] announced so powerfully in "For My People."

She could have continued to enjoy the fruits of her earlier labors, graciously accepting the awards and accolades that were rapidly coming her way, but that would never have been enough. She could not believe that the best part of her life was over. One sign of this was the invitation she extended to Eudora Welty to join her for tea. The two often met together publicly. They were the "sister act," as Welty called them. By the 1980s, both women (one Black, one white) had become the South's best-known and most-accessible writers. Because they both lived in Jackson, they could claim a unique position among the growing number of Southern writers who had been born after Faulkner. Both had left the South and returned to it, vowing never to live any other place. Even though some years would pass before many Southern Black writers could see themselves living in and/or reclaiming the South, Walker had embraced it fully. Knowing that she and Welty were the reigning women in Southern letters, Walker intended to remain as connected as possible to a tradition that had given her a secure and rewarding life as a writer. She also relished the idea of an identity that allowed her earlier radicalism to find an affinity with the new activism among a younger generation of women writers. In an era of growing conservatism, with Reaganomics in control, when others were muting their voices, hers would remain strong and forceful. She need not, therefore, let go of any part of herself as she entered the official period of old age.

29

The Outlaw Spirit Prevails

The days and months following Alex's death demanded faith of a different sort to face a new set of challenges. For the moment, however, completing the Wright manuscript offered Walker the most joy. Realizing that much of the joy in her personal life had derived from being needed by her husband and her children, and responding to that need, its absence could easily have negatively affected her confidence. Establishing a new rhythm would counter any negativity.

Thinking about her life as a writer helped to establish that rhythm. In each decade she had published, she had brought something new to the literary table. She was an award-winning Black writer early in her life, and even an extended literary silence had not prevented a second best-selling book. When historical fiction was still struggling for acceptance as a literary genre in American letters, she brought the credibility it needed. She trusted exemplars of the genre like Tolstoy, Dickens, and Balzac to teach her how to explore the tension between historical representation and aesthetic re-creation. Similarly, in her poetry published in the 1970s, she created new metaphors through images, symbols, and themes that derive from religion, nature, and history. Her interest in the natural landscape and spirituality as sources of the imagination found a home in the burgeoning field of Environmental Studies.

The Wright book was her project for the 1980s. She saw herself experimenting again, this time using a genre with which she was much less familiar, biography. Driven more by vision and a desire to create a new dialogue through her creative work, she brought to biography the same compelling need to give attention to Southern Black reality in a new way. She did not hesitate to use language that was artful and complex, seeing biography as a kind of case study. It was necessary to push beyond the genre's own assumptions and conventions. Rather than present a single narrator, accepting the traditional notion of an authoritative voice, she saw a wider framework, one pointing to a social process and a culture of contradictions, consistent with Black life in the South where the natural and social worlds collide.

By the 1980s the process of writing and publishing a book had been demystified. Even though her experience with Alex Haley had taught her that an author's success was not always the result of writing a good book, she had come of age in a different era, without the support of publicists, agents, and accepted strategies for maximizing visibility and profits. With the Wright book, she agreed to try a

The House Where My Soul Lives. Maryemma Graham, Oxford University Press. © Oxford University Press 2022.
DOI: 10.1093/oso/9780195341232.003.0029

Daughters of Margaret Performing Arts Ensemble

new approach. She met and signed a contract with Charlotte Sheedy to serve as her agent, an arrangement that was short-lived. Convinced that her old method would continue to work for her, she found it difficult to put her trust in someone with whom she did not share a strong relationship that went beyond a business arrangement. Sheedy understood that Walker was not always at ease in the relationship, and their association ended almost as quickly as it began, at Walker's insistence. In a conversation years after Walker's death, Sheedy was still uncertain that she had done anything wrong.[1] The truth was that Walker didn't believe anyone could negotiate and secure a book contract as successfully as she could do it herself.

This self-sufficiency was part of her vision of art as engagement, transformation, and change. Walker was accustomed to defining her own place in a changing literary industry and unprepared for having others do it for her. This endeared her to those for whom she served as a model. Others dismissed her approach entirely. As academic critics began to exercise more control over what was important to teach, and publishers made decisions based on what readers would buy, Walker, by refusing any professional support, found herself at a crossroads. She could wait for people to rediscover her whenever she resurfaced. Or she could transform herself into the critic and scholar, creating her own brand. It took her no time to find an answer: because she had always stood on faith alone, allowing nothing to slow her down, Walker's journey throughout the 1980s resembled every other one she had taken.

She failed to see some significant differences between the new and the old Walker, even with two award-winning books. She brought to the 1980s a somewhat tarnished reputation and the choice of a subject that would invite another lengthy legal battle, the warning signs for which began early. Neither of these would she be able to control. What she could control were the interactions she had with people, and she intended to have as many as possible. Following the official street renaming ceremony in January 1981, she and Sigis prepared for a trip to Jacksonville to speak at Florida Agricultural and Mechanical University, with additional engagements at Bethune-Cookman College, the University of South Florida, Miami Dade Community College, and the University of Miami.

Ostensibly, the trip served another purpose. Marion Walker was ailing and as the oldest child, Walker felt an urgency to fill the missing pieces of her mother's paternal family history. She had told her maternal grandmother's story in *Jubilee*, but the story of Reverend Edward Lane Dozier, her grandfather, remained a mystery. She knew little more than what Marion and Aunt Abbie reported. Dozier was a charismatic Baptist minister, and when his calling took him to a church in Jacksonville, his wife elected to remain behind. Rev. Dozier came home often to a marriage that eventually produced twelve children, many of whom barely made it to adulthood. Walker knew more about the female children than the male, since the male children were the first to leave home. The older female siblings were also long gone by the time Marion was born; only Abigail remained at home. Being her aunt's namesake, and living with her for a time in Boston, had made it easier for the maternal narrative to dominate the story while her connections to the paternal side suffered a greater loss.

Elvira Dozier did not have much to say about her husband, Rev. Dozier, the man from whom she was, for the most part, separated. Elvira's story would always begin with the great-grandmother, making the full reconstruction of Dozier family history difficult. The trip ultimately turned up very little to add to what Walker already knew. The church in Jacksonville that he had gone to pastor revered him. The membership continued to grow following his death. She and Sigis would make a return trip to Jacksonville to attend a service dedicated to his memory. No other family members were present.

The Florida trip was the break she had expected to take before her scheduled conversations with Howard University Press. Their receipt of the Wright manuscript had yet to generate a contract. She had completed the bibliographical essay for the book as she was asked, explaining her sources in detail. Then the first bad news arrived: Howard University Press's board of directors had refused to honor the agreement that she and Charles Harris had made. As the press's director, Harris seemed to have little power to do anything. Instead of $100,000 that had been promised, they offered $35,000. The next news she received was that a new editor, Rene Mayfield, had been hired to guide the book through to publication. Walker weighed her options, but because the press seemed serious about getting the book out, she conceded, followed her intuition, signed, and mailed the contract in July 1981.

The relationship between Mayfield and Walker was rocky from the start. Mayfield had agreed to make several visits to Jackson, eliminating Walker's need to travel and speeding up the manuscript revisions. During her first visit in fall 1981, the two women struggled over boundaries of the editor and the author. Walker's two previous encounters with editors had come after a long process of rewriting under the supervision of her professors at Iowa. In that case, *For My People* was published exactly as she had submitted it. The dialect she had used in *Jubilee* required some adjusting to make it easier to read, but none of the changes resulted in a major transformation of the book. Walker did not view Mayfield as equal to her Iowa professors. In fact, she considered Mayfield her inferior, someone who was not qualified to judge her work. Resistance turned to anger, mostly directed toward Mayfield whom she verbally attacked, without Mayfield responding. She confided in her journals that Mayfield had a "certain distaste for the manuscript," and that she detected "hostility and rancor."[2] She wrote letters to both Harris and Mayfield, complaining that the book had passed through the hands of three women editors, and that the level of revision and requested modifications made clear that the press anticipated a suit by Ellen Wright. The idea of a suit fueled her anger, especially when she saw herself, just as she did in the *Roots* case, standing alone.

Howard University Press was relatively new, a rare experiment at an HBCU at the time. Its board of directors would have been fearful of an impending suit by the wife of a major literary figure. Because Charles Harris never mentioned any legal entanglements, Walker could only speculate on the refusal to honor the terms of the original agreement, the lengthy delays, and the editorial wrangling. He apologized profusely and assured her in response to each of her inflammatory letters that the process, although slow, was going forward.

The resulting manuscript, after its reorganization and close editing, met the approval of Howard's editorial board, but not hers. The alterations, she believed, oversimplified her argument. Without the extensive psychological analysis, sociological facts, and historical background, she saw a book that could hardly count as scholarship. In a second set of letters to Harris and Mayfield, she pointed out that her reputation was at stake. "I shall try to revive, resuscitate, or resurrect my manuscript. If I cannot please you then, I am resigned to the fact that we give up this book."[3] Production, nevertheless, seemed to proceed. Attendees at the annual meeting of the American Booksellers Association in May 1982 saw the first advertisements of *The Daemonic Genius of Richard Wright* by Margaret Walker, scheduled for a fall 1982 publication, listed at $15.95.

Because she had the freedom to write without constraint in her journals, seeing herself as both the ideal writer and reader, Walker had grown accustomed to extensive explanatory information, the kind of exposition that a curious mind such as hers demanded. She needed everything to make sense, and she had the knowledge base to locate the answers that reflected the logic of her ideas. She wrote until an idea was clear to *her*. For the Wright book, she sought empirical evidence that supported her view of his genius. She did not set out to attack anyone else's view, but her sense of divine and natural phenomena now merged with her search for scientific and objective truth to explain the human experience. That Wright was a complicated individual was without question, and his genius, when subjected to the most negative extremes of the Southern social landscape, became a powerful creative force. Wright became the vehicle for the transmission of that force, and that was his genius. This fact was not sufficiently clear in the final edited manuscript, "the naked statements that reduced the text to absurdity by throwing out the baby with the bathwater."[4]

Howard University Press was still searching for its audience and had to opt for the broadest possible readership. They chose books that they believed would sell, high-interest subject matter that invited the readers' attention without necessarily challenging their intelligence. They had done well with Walker and Giovanni's *Poetic Equation*, and they were banking on Walker's friendship with Wright, and even her negative reputation from the *Roots* controversy, to be major marketing factors in attracting book sales. They knew, and rightly so, that they had to create a particular kind of book, while preserving much of its integrity. Had Howard been a larger press with several different imprints, it might well have taken a different position on the need to edit the manuscript to meet certain expectations. Walker, in contrast, was not thinking about the audience. She was passionately committed to a book that was different from anything else she had written. "I am known as a poet, novelist, educator, but this last big book, the

Richard Wright book is a scholar's book. My father gave me my first lesson as a scholar. I have become what my father wanted me to be."[5]

What she did not say was that if her father had taught her to be scholar, Richard Wright had given her a reason to make active use of the scholar's mind. He had introduced her to more tools that she would have at her disposal. She was a highly skilled writer and reader long before she met him. Having been formally trained in the structures of poetry as an art, she knew what he did not. She had mastered the craft at a certain level and was determined to continue. Writing about Wright had unleashed her intellectual compass in a new way. When anyone dared to question what she was doing, she took offense. Years of training and practice had taught her the distillation process that was necessary for writing and revising her poetry. *Jubilee* had gone through multiple revisions, again because she was learning how to craft a historical novel. And even when some of its reviewers had complained about the wealth of historical information that was not sufficiently compressed in *Jubilee*, she believed they had simply missed the point. Her tendency was to produce thick narrative prose, and she presented complex ideas that were not easily digested. But her underlying argument was correct: the absence of publicly disseminated history that looked inside the culture of slavery and its aftermath told from the African American perspective required a richly textured historical narrative, the kind that Walker saw herself giving. If her transition from her familiar journal prose to biographical narrative was not smooth, if she lacked the necessary comparative perspective, then it was due to the intellectual design of the book that she had carefully outlined years before she began writing it. The Wright biography was the book that took her the least amount of time to write, but its subject was the most complicated. *Jubilee* had been a book *waiting for her to write. Daemonic Genius* was a book that *she dared to write.* She believed in what she was doing, and, therefore, never saw writing that book as a problem.

Walker put her editorial problems aside to accept a three-week writing residency at Texas Christian University. The break was a return to the familiar. She prepared focused lectures on poetry, the creative process, along with a comparison of different poetry movements from the classical to contemporary, including her own ideas about metaphysical and revolutionary poetry. She gave a final lecture on the contrasts between Black and white poetry. The visit was another form of renewal, and spending time in a different natural environment marked by such beauty provided much satisfaction. She used her free time to visit close friends, most importantly, Curtis King in Dallas. She had become more dependent on Curtis after the *Roots* controversy, and his home, like Sonia Sanchez's in Philadelphia, was one of her favorite places she enjoyed spending time away from home. Although their conversations never replaced her journal entries, they spilled over into the entries that increased after Alex's death. Writing was her one activity that could make each day complete.

Besides Curtis and Sonia, she had grown even closer to Alleane Currie, who remained her faithful collaborator, making sure that her ideas found their way onto the typed page. Each of these people communicated with her different sides. Sonia was the poet most like her who could cut through the protective veneer that she used to shield herself from pain and disappointment. Alleane was her daily barometer who could read her moods and translate her to others who too often made impossible demands.

On the Texas trip, Walker became more acutely aware of the bond she shared with Curtis King. They both refused to conceive of the mind as an ideological fortress, separate and distinct from all other forms of comprehending reality. They both accepted their religious faith as a given, believed in divine inspiration, and had no use for doubt in their lives. They were zealous in their desire to show the strength of their convictions, comfortable stepping out on a limb because failure was never an option. Because of the boldness of their actions in creating and building institutions, both continued to trust in the science of the universe, and their astrology sessions became legendary. Their visits over the years had also reversed their relationship. When they had first met, he was a student willing to be taught, but by the 1980s, Walker found herself easily deferring to his professional expertise, taking his advice as she encountered hurdles time and time again.

During her visit she shared an idea with King and on the phone with Tommie Stewart, who had also been one of Curtis's teachers. She wanted to create a Black Broadway review, using her work. Stewart had a successful television and film career, but, like Walker, was a fulltime faculty member at an HBCU, Alabama State University. For the planned production, Stewart would be the lead performer, and King, the producer. There is no evidence that this ever materialized, but a group of Jackson women did create a professional performing arts ensemble, taking the name Daughters of Margaret. Their formation dated back to 1984 when Ruth Campbell, an executive producer and public relations director at Mississippi Educational Television Network, asked Rosia Wade-Crisler, a local actress-educator, to develop a dramatic performance as part of a special series for her television show *Faces*. Campbell played a critical role in helping the young public television station gain the trust of the local Black community. Though Mississippi was a bit later than most in authorizing a statewide educational television mandate, Campbell was major force in its success. The *Faces* series aired in 1985, and Walker was so impressed that she asked Wade-Crisler to take it on tour. The timing was right. Still grieving over Alex and uncertain of the status of the Wright book, Walker was able to console herself with the new meaning and value she would now have. While the project that she had conceived with Stewart and King would have had her direct involvement, it was easier to accept the Daughters of Margaret as a welcome opportunity. Art was not for art's sake; it was for the people, for *her* people.

Crisler enlisted local poet and friend of Walker's, Virgia Brocks-Shedd, who shared the vision. The group grew quickly as singer and actress Gloria Jackson Winters and Janice K. Neal, another actress-educator, agreed to join them. All members of the ensemble were working women, as were the musicians, Jerry Calvin, Larry Addison, Charles Chiplin, Hugh Davis, and Philip Welch. Word spread quickly throughout Mississippi and the region, as Daughters of Margaret performed with and without Walker, at colleges and universities, as well as for political, social, and religious events. In short order, they began to create productions for major occasions. "When Medgar Was" saluted the slain civil rights leader, and "What Price Freedom" honored the life and work of Fannie Lou Hamer. A number of their productions, like "No Crystal Stair . . . Yet Still Climbing" that celebrated the work of Elizabeth Catlett and Francisco Mora, began as a singular event but would reach an even larger audience when it appeared on Mississippi's public television station. Walker would continue to serve as their patron saint long after her death.

The visit with King helped Walker to look outward rather than inward. She could see more clearly her impact, especially on the people of Mississippi. The three weeks in Texas and the conversations with King were restorative. When she returned to Jackson, she felt like her old self, looking forward to a return to her regular level of activity.

Several joint appearances with Eudora Welty at local and state events attracted a lot of attention. Walker was grateful for this display of support, but she was also aware of perceived differences in their reputations. She knew that they lived in two very different worlds, still sharing a sense of their Southern heritage and an appreciation for what it meant for their work. Welty had popularized the phrase "a sense of place," just as Walker had added "feeling tone." The pride in the South shared an equal place with a hatred of the South's social landscape, creating the tension that was a central element in Walker's poetry. Welty and Walker had used the professional boost that their WPA apprenticeships offered to enhance their powers of observation, which alongside their immersion into the local, storied worlds of the South, was put to good use.

Welty was someone who took the path that Walker had not taken. She had earned Walker's respect by proving what was possible when a writer devoted her life to writing, even in an environment hostile to women. And while the Southern Agrarians were quick to claim Welty as Faulkner's highly capable and most logical successor, Walker was among those who questioned why Welty would "be labeled as a member of the Faulkner school when she is so unlike him."[6] She admired this independence, the ability to carve her own place in American literature as a Southern woman writer. Welty's 1973 Pulitzer Prize for her novel *The Optimist's Daughter* was a shared victory for the state of Mississippi, confirming the Magnolia State as a high-volume producer of the highest achievements in American letters.

While Mississippi honored both women for their accomplishments, Walker understood their differences as being not so much racial, but financial. Had she not had to struggle financially, she might have been able to reap a larger share of the rewards that such dedication to one's art can bring. A full life as a mother, wife, grandmother, and educator had taken her in other directions, reducing her productivity, even as the choice had brought much meaning to her life. On the personal level, she felt fulfilled. She may have questioned, but never regretted her choice.

On the professional level, she felt a continuous need for fulfillment. Her role as an educator and institution builder had been her mission, and she had executed it well. That she was finally able to devote her life to her art as a widow was a major revelation for Walker during the 1980s. She saw signs of this revelation everywhere. In September she joined Shelby Foote, Willie Morris, Walker Percy, and Welty for a special dinner at the Mississippi governor's mansion, one of many occasions where the state would honor her with others. She was grateful for the recognition but saw it as less about what she had done than a sign of what she hoped to do. While most saw her getting long-overdue recognition, Walker tied this directly to her own future expectations.

In late fall 1982, Walker took her first long tour of the United States since Alex's death. Before she left, she delivered a provocative speech at Ole Miss for the twentieth anniversary of the desegregation of the university by James Meredith. The speech, "Integration, Elimination, Amalgamation or Re-segregation," included a poem she had first written in 1962, when Meredith confronted Ross Barnett. "Oxford Is a Legend" ties the threads of Mississippi history and human history together:

> OXFORD is a legend
> Where battlements were placed
> One flaming night
> And they fought the civil war all over again
> With a rebel yell, and rebel flag, and scholars yelling "nigger,"
> A Confederate general,
> And the Union army;
> Where innocent bystanders
> Were killed.

She was going into the mouth of the lion, so to speak, to Faulkner country, to the state's intellectual center. The time had come to speak frankly, the time to let go of old idols:

> Too bad the old man from Jefferson County
> Died before he saw the fighting in his streets
> Before he had to bear arms for Mississippi
> And shoots the Negroes in the streets
> OXFORD is a legend
> Out of time more than battle place, or a name
> With the figure of one brave and smiling little man
> Smiling that courageous, ironic, bright, grim smile.[7]

The dig at Faulkner, the "old man from Jefferson County," shows a simultaneous embrace of the new order in Mississippi and a forthright admission that change had inserted itself into the preserve of white culture. Walker transfers the physical Meredith to the historical Meredith, "the figure of one brave smiling little man / Smiling that courageous, ironic grim smile." The poem recalls in tone and intensity the struggle to integrate the campus, reminding the listeners to see and imagine a different future even as they memorialize the past.

The tension between imagining a different future and memorializing a past gave her tremendous leverage for her many talks and readings during the three-week tour. She relied as always on Sonia Sanchez and her resourceful network that supported her return engagement at Temple, and new ones at the University of Pennsylvania, Delaware State, and Lincoln University in Pennsylvania, Haverford College, and Columbia. While visiting family in Cleveland, she gave talks at Kent State, Cleveland State, the University of Cincinnati, made a return visit to the University of Dayton, and concluded with a longer stay at the Indiana University, Bloomington. Sanchez and Nikki Giovanni paid a surprise visit during her stay. The tour was somewhat bittersweet, a memorial journey that brought a flood of joyful tears and sad thoughts as she returned to familiar places without Alex, beginning with the customary overnight stop with his family at High Point before heading northward.

The journey ended in Chicago, surrounded by her two daughters and grandchildren: Marion, her twins Karen and Katherine, and Margaret. Their hope that their mother would move closer to them became the elephant in the room. She would entertain no such thought, first because she had promised Alex she would remain in their home, where she had the support of Sigis, Norma and their family. A second reason made it impossible to abandon her Jackson home. As her mother's health continued to deteriorate, she made frequent trips to New Orleans. Each return from New Orleans confirmed what

James Meredith surrounded by supporters. Courtesy of the Ernest Withers
Collection

Jackson had become, her refuge, a special province, the place that had given
her life for three and a half decades. Now, especially, it represented the kind
of release she needed. Walker would also have recognized that moving to
Chicago near her two daughters could encourage a dependency that living
with or near her sons did not.

The Margaret Walker that students encountered on these tours was a renowned poet, an innovative writer of fiction, and widely regarded as a human
rights advocate. Some were discovering her for the first time, and for these students, she left a lasting impression. Accustomed to placing current problems
within their historical context, she encouraged students to bring greater analysis
to their impassioned assertions. She spoke to them with ease because she had
read everything she talked about and had lived through most of the events she
mentioned. This was especially the case when she spoke on issues concerning
women, where her expertise on the subject was readily apparent. She generally singled out Zora Neale Hurston as "our greatest forerunner and my favorite
mentor." She explained what she believed, the fire from her experience with
Haley still burning. Few in the audience would have recognized the similarity
between the speaker and the woman about whom she was speaking:

The problem of the black woman novelist is perhaps best illustrated in Zora. Her marriage failed chiefly because of her career. Being a black female of great brilliance and talent, she felt the sting of racism and prejudice even among her own. She was criticized and belittled by her male peers who certainly were not one whit smarter nor more talented. The Langston Hughes feud is well known, and Arna Bontemps's opinion was not much better. Personally I think they were more than jealous of her; they hated her.[8]

She had completed an essay, "Reflections on Black Women Writers," by 1983, but it never appeared in *The Black Scholar* for which it had been written. The essay gives an overview of Black women novelists beginning with Frances Ellen Watkins Harper, whose 1892 novel *Iola Leroy* was still believed to be the first by a Black woman.[9] She discussed Ann Petry, another neglected writer, and other mid-twentieth-century Black women novelists, giving attention to the work of younger writers who had emerged since the 1973 Wheatley Festival. Walker was aware of the growing body of criticism, naming Thadious Davis, Deborah McDowell, and Cheryl Wall as scholars engaged in critical recovery work. In Trudier Harris, she saw a rare understanding of the South and its debt to Black folk expression, refuting conventional interpretations of high and low culture. Her comments on Toni Morrison were telling. She believed that Morrison's National Book Award was for *Song of Solomon*, rather than for *The Bluest Eye* or *Sula*, precisely because it did not highlight the experience of Black women. Moreover, Walker argued, its use of fantasy allowed for a certain "ambiguity [that] relieves it of the stigma of race."[10]

"Reflections" spoke the truth as Walker knew and had experienced it, which most critics would have enthusiastically endorsed. But it is likely that the reviewers of the essay were less enthusiastic because of Walker's tendency to step in and out of her role as writer and critic. Of its eleven pages, she devoted three paragraphs to a discussion of *Jubilee*, confronting the literary establishment directly. A new generation of writers had emerged and their acceptance or rejection was left to the control of publishing houses, the networking of agents, and reviewing media. She had made no pretense regarding her concerns about the critical reception of *Jubilee* as one of thirty novels she discussed in the essay. Her argument that Black women novelists suffered at the hands of male critics, both Black and white, included her own experience. *Jubilee*, she wrote, was not embraced by mainstream critics, with three notable exceptions, Sterling Brown, Richard Barksdale, and Nick Aaron Ford. She gave her standard response as to the reasons why: "... first, I am black; second I am a woman; third, I am southern; and fourth, I am not rich."[11]

Seeing herself as an extreme case, she found that her direct approach and quick wit won over her student audiences, but it did little to raise her status among a new generation of writers and critics. Her thinking was grounded in secular humanism, closely tied to old-fashioned moral values, while continuing to engage in an openly acknowledged battle for social justice and equality. She was no longer working actively with a trade press, hers a voice in the wilderness. She represented a type of intellectual and literary honesty that made those who encountered her uncomfortable. As far as most Black writers were concerned, Margaret Walker no longer had any currency.

When she remained in her comfort zone, where she was a well-known quantity, she was far more effective. Because she was often doing what no one else had tried or even dared to do and was successful, especially during her years as director of the Institute at Jackson State, she was praised and admired. This fact, along with the changing social environment within Mississippi, affirmed her newly productive self. She had always known that her place in Mississippi was not accidental. She charted the state's progress in her speeches and her published essays and earned the love and respect of the state's people. She believed, like others, that Mississippi was the microcosm of the South, if not the human experience as a whole. When Mississippians began to take themselves seriously in the changing landscape of the post–civil rights South, they wanted desperately to rid themselves of the image of backward Southerners, a people dwelling in the world of the past and resistant to change. To do so meant finding a way to express the vitality and subtlety of a complex culture. One could not read Shelby Foote's description of Jefferson Davis,[12] champion of the Confederacy, without reading the reminiscences of John Roy Lynch,[13] the thirteen-year-old house slave at the advent of the Civil War who became the first Black member of the United States House of Representatives and helped to engineer the passage of the 1875 Civil Rights Act. Paul Conklin's *Choctaw Boy* and Ann Moody's *Coming of Age in Mississippi* were as important for Mississippians as Wright's *Black Boy*, even if less well-known.

Her newfound freedom came at a time when Mississippians were becoming more introspective. She was a figure to whom people turned again and again. The massive four-volume *Mississippi Writers: Reflections of Childhood and Youth*[14] was packed with these untold narratives that helped to define much of the state's twentieth-century reality. Walker's work was included in the series, and the editor Dorothy Abbott, had sought her advice in planning the volumes. Walker was also included in the six-segment series *Climate for Genius*, which Robert Phillips created for Mississippi's public television network. Ruth Campbell continued to actively promote Walker's work, featuring her as a guest on *Faces*.

Aside from a few reviews and introductions, Walker also turned her attention to local politics. She wanted to make good on her belief that Mississippi was not only a climate for genius but also endorsed a climate of political change. One of those signs had been the 1980 election of William Winter as governor, which she endorsed. She was invited to give a speech at his inaugural symposium, where she renewed her commitment and belief in the state of Mississippi as being "on the threshold of a decade of destiny." She brought the speech to a prophetic close:

> We must be prepared to deal with world revolution and sinister war threats, to cope with ideological conflict and culture shock, to deal with a shifting economic order and, not least of all, with multiracial, multicultural diversity. We must test our spiritual endurance and our religious faith if we are to survive, not only as a state and a nation, but as a people, as humanity on the planet earth.[15]

Walker stepped into the limelight on these occasions because she knew she was the voice of the people, a role she performed without a hint of pretentiousness. Her truth was a shared truth. Especially in the 1980s, she wanted to help the state of Mississippi reclaim its birthright as a center for culture and art. When Carolyn Vance Smith launched the Natchez Literary and Cinema Celebration, announcing an annual literary award named after Natchez native Richard Wright, Walker went to show her strong support, making numerous return appearances. In return for her support, Mississippians treated her as a favorite daughter.

There was another important element in Walker's transformation in the 1980s. Marion Dozier Walker, died on Easter Sunday, April 3, 1983. Though the death was expected, Walker's own reaction surprised her:

> Slowly it dawned on me that I never shed a tear. I wondered why and years later I decided that mama and I did everything we could for each other, but I wondered if she ever loved me—she never said she did and then I wondered if I ever loved her. I kept trying to remember a kindness, a caress or a bit of affection from her and I couldn't. When I was sick or needy she was there and she was anxious to see me finish school and get a job, but she was never an affectionate parent—at least not to me.[16]

This admission suggests unresolved emotions that often exist between a demanding mother whom a strong-willed daughter used as a yardstick for what not to become. Marion gloated in her negative predictions about her daughter who was in a marriage that derailed her career and constrained her financially. Walker, in turn, showered her mother with gifts when she could, since Marion believed that her professionally successful daughter had an obligation to provide substantial support in return for her parents' early sacrifices.

Telling herself repeatedly "I am my father's daughter" was not a rejection of her mother. Rather, it was a realization that her mother had given her all that she

Walker and Charles Harris, Founding Director, Howard
University Press. Photograph courtesy Robert Townsend Jones

could give, and that she was free to draw from elsewhere in forming her unique
identity. If she had unpleasant memories of her mother, she had already let them
go. The ties between Walker and her parents were both open and flexible, and she
borrowed and exchanged those qualities as needed.

If she did not feel the release and letting -go of her mother to be a good thing
for herself, she felt that it was for her siblings, especially Gwen and Brother, who
had never left their mother, caring for her during her illness and final days. Did
their emotional subjection to Marion rob them of a different kind of life? The answer could only be yes.

After a brief break to travel and to mourn, she returned home with a new determination to publish the Wright biography. She had no need to prove anything to anyone. The *Roots* controversy became her most important lesson. She had refused to walk away, and she had lost. She would do it differently with the Wright book. She believed she had learned when to enter battle, when to let go, and when to engage in strategic realignments. Faith was her imperative, belief in herself primary. Rereading Wright had a strongly personal dimension, stirring up emotions that made it impossible for her to back away. She would not surrender, even in the presence of overwhelming odds. At these times, the rational side of her became so disturbed that it pushed against and eventually gave way to its opposite.

If her refusal to surrender during the *Roots* controversy had been the cause of much emotional pain, that experience prepared her for a second battle over the publication of the Wright biography, a battle she refused to lose. The acrimony that had greeted her manuscript when it arrived at Howard University Press ended only when Walker and her book parted company with that publisher. She was determined to see the process through to the end because she had a story to tell and a right to tell it. The resistance to her telling Wright's story in her own way added strength to her convictions.

Tensions continued to develop between Howard University Press and Ellen Wright, which caused further publication delays. What made it worse was the press's decision not to communicate to Walker its failure to make progress with permissions. She quickly concluded the delays in communication and the announced delay in the production schedule had less to do with what typically occurs in publishing than with other intervening factors, despite knowing no specifics. Her distrust of Rene Mayfield began to extend to Charles Harris more and more. She kept her own counsel, chaffed at the replies she got regarding the manuscript itself, made frantic phone calls, and continued to write angry, accusatory letters to both of them. Because the press staff did not begin the process of securing permission from Ellen Wright before they had announced the book's first publication date in 1983, she surmised that they were never seriously considering publication at all, or that they were incompetent. But she did what she said she would not do: when requested, she sent copies of her letters from Richard Wright to Ellen Wright. She was quoting from what was technically part of the Wright estate, and Ellen held on to the permissions like they were her sword. She knew that the book would not go forward without Ellen Wright's permission. After the *Roots* controversy, Walker had become an expert in the art of war.

Bound galleys of the uncorrected proofs arrived in early October 1983. Despite being told that the press had not received official permission to proceed by its legal advisor, the press called production to a halt at the end of October. In short order, Walker received a copy of a memorandum from Cohn and Marks, the law firm that represented the press, requesting that a publication date be set following the resolution of concerns about the book. The concerns were answered according to Mayfield, who turned everything over to Charles Harris. Harris's sudden resignation before the December holiday in 1985 seemed to suggest that matters had gone beyond a simple resolution. Immediately after Harris's departure, Ellen Wright's lawyers, Lubell and Lubell, threatened to sue Howard University Press, Charles Harris, and Margaret Walker Alexander with "injunctive action for copyright infringement by January 3, 1986."[17]

Harris's resignation from Howard University Press had released him from further involvement, but when Mayfield was ordered to cease communication with her, the only conclusion Walker could draw was that both Harris and Mayfield had been concealing information all along. When the whole matter came to a head, they had both jumped ship, in her mind. Based on an anonymous tip, she assumed that Howard University Press had acceded to Ellen Wright's demands and agreed not to publish the book. Outraged, she instructed her legal team to write to the press and to Howard University president James Cheek, asking to be released from the book contract, a request they refused. As more details emerged, Walker began to map the journey from what she called "if not great, at least a credible book, and of scholarly proportions . . . [to a] disaster."[18] Methodically, she traced the events by year and month, with detailed notes on the nature of every exchange. Given the number of errors of fact and judgment she saw, Walker wrote that the book was "dead from over-kill of copyediting."[19] Further, she did not believe that they would ever get any permissions from Ellen Wright, and since that process, too, had been delayed, Ellen found it easier to argue against the request. Walker copied Ellen's response in her journal:

> I'd been aware of the Margaret Walker projected book on Richard Wright since I saw your announcement in *Publisher's Weekly* some two years ago. Hence it is somewhat surprising that you make your request for the various permissions so close to publication date.[20]

Having heard nothing from Harris, Ellen Wright wrote again, included a photocopy of her original letter, and asked about the intended publishing date since "Time was running short of the clearing of these permissions. It goes without saying that it has diminished still further,"[21] Walker continued to record Ellen's satirical remarks.

In light of the delay and certainty that she would not get permission, Walker proposed several strategies: publish without permission and invite an injunction; take all quotes out and lose the authenticity, but paraphrase and allude to everything, or pay Ellen Wright off to avoid embarrassing accusations about obstruction of Black literary activity. She believed that Ellen's basis for resistance was simply prejudice. Ellen had granted permission for all white authors who had written about Wright, including Constance Webb, Michel Fabre, and Kenneth Kinnamon, but had refused all Black scholars, Horace Cayton, John A. Williams, and Margaret Walker.

The meaning of *Daemonic Genius* changed significantly over the seven-year period between her initial contract in 1981 and the book's publication in 1988. Because of the extensive editorial intervention and constant questioning, Walker's responses were elaborate defenses written with a sense of entitlement. In her journal notes, where she drafted several letters to Charles and Rene, always allowing her anger to settle before she mailed them, Walker frequently mentioned scholars and editors who had read and commented positively on the manuscript. A larger question, one that remained with the critics long after the book's release, was whether Walker was too subjective to write about Wright and whether the book itself said more about her than it did about Wright. She resisted the notion that she was writing a book about herself, regardless of whether those perceptions came from Howard's editors or the reviewers. She strongly made this point in a letter:

> I am utterly disgusted with the monstrous notion that I seem to have created an illusion of a mistreated, abused, rejected and un-appreciated woman who never got what she wanted from this man. We can forget the whole thing if this is what anybody thinks is happening here. Maybe, some would like to think that. I am tired of saying it just ain't so. At my age and after forty years, I refuse to believe that I am a sexually frustrated or unfulfilled woman. I loved my husband and he loved me. It is an insult to his memory; to our children, and our grandchildren to create that impression either on my doing or anybody else's. God knows, I would rather be dead first.[22]

That impression was foremost in her mind when she agreed to give the keynote address at an international conference on Richard Wright at the University of Mississippi in 1985. By that time, her surprisingly open interview with Claudia Tate had circulated widely. In responding to Tate's questions about writing the book, she explained her intellectual and moral obligation—in the form of a confession:

> I was in love with him, and he knew it. He could not marry me. I was not what he could marry. That's the whole truth of it. You can't say he didn't love me; I know he did.[23]

Although she had initially told the Ole Miss organizers that she would "not say a word if she did not have a book," Walker welcomed the opportunity, knowing that every major Wright scholar would be in attendance, including Michel Fabre. She wanted vindication on her terms, another opportunity to set the record straight. A reading from the forthcoming book could also offset rumors about continuous delays of the book's appearance.

As if talking directly to Fabre, who was in the audience, she discussed what she was doing that made the book different from what had come before:

> I wrote this biography because I could not find any comprehensive study about him in which I could read these major factors: his personality, his genius, his political significance, his literary achievement.

Establishing Wright's importance as she saw it was her major objective. In Wright's work, she said:

> Questions of racism, anti-Semitism, imperialism, whether in colonialism or neocolonialism are constantly raised and scrutinized. And this must be for all posterity; for our children's children and all their future generations. Wright is as timely and as universal as tomorrow morning's newspaper. Whether we think of Marxist revolutions in Russia and China or Chile, Cuba, Africa or San Salvador Nicaragua and Argentina, the religious wars of Ireland and the Middle East, or the economics and politics of Europe and the United States with the continuing struggles in the Islands of the Seas, Wright's global and geopolitical significance becomes evident. His predictions are on target with an uncanny accuracy.[24]

Although Walker had difficulty admitting it, in writing about Richard Wright, she was writing about herself. Rather than reciting familiar autobiographical facts or refuting the image of a scorned woman, her concern with the nature of the creative mind pointed both to Wright and herself. She argued that the greatest challenge Wright offered his readers was an intellectual one. She saw him as a "creative worker [who] challenges all areas of human experience . . . for it is the framework as a Marxist and a Black radical that he sees the role of the imaginative worker at its best." She went on to peel back the layers of his thinking, which, in her mind, centered on the areas of psychology and philosophy. "This lone black man seeks to break through the twentieth century with a synthesis of all those pertinent ideas that have marked this century. Five great thinkers are his mentors: Karl Marx, Sigmund Freud, Soren Kierkegaard, Albert Einstein, and William Edward Burghardt Du Bois."[25]

These were all familiar references for her, and while framing the Oxford, Mississippi, speech as an overview of the Wright book, Walker simultaneously provided the scaffolding for her next book, *This Is My Century*. Her analysis allows us to witness her working imagination first-hand. This final collection of verse would be an imaginative recreation of the ideas she presented in this speech. The title poem, "This Is My Century: Black Synthesis of Time," goes further back into history utilizing Greek mythology to reflect the breadth and depth of the synthesis. The second poem in the collection, "Giants of My Century," is familiar:

> Five men shaped this century
> With their thinking, breathing, loving lives.
> They measured out the land of all our years
> And blew the trumpets of the decades in our ears.[26]

The poem devotes a stanza to each of the "giants" and concludes with "Make me a monument for five men / and build no more."[27] Immediately following is the poem "Five Black Men . . . And ten will save the city," a parallel poem that focuses on "Douglass, DuBois, Garvey, King and Malcolm X / Five Black men whose leadership we cherish / in the history books / from Slavery to Segregation and the Age of Integration / down the primrose path to face oblivion/."[28] Again, the connection to Wright is evident.

Her second point in the speech framed Wright: "He was a black radical in the oldest tradition of the radical leaders in America. Wright inherited Black Humanism and a Black Radical tradition which he could not escape."[29] "Five Black Men" is a lyrical history of this tradition, narrating the lives of each of the men who "made revolutions. / They fought wars. / They drew battle lines / and never once with loaded guns."/ Her concluding two lines "Their words were their weapons. / Their deeds were their monuments."/[30] had been frequently said about both Wright and Walker. She knew that she could never have the impact that Wright did, but writing about his life allowed her to relive her literary success as well.

In her explication of Wright's creative projects and his psychological complexity, her exposition is at its best. She was able to tease out the various elements of Wright as an intellectual who was part of multiple traditions, and because he had little formal education and yet an unlimited intellectual capacity, he held on to whatever he learned, translating these experiences into literature. "He could not help himself," she argued, "he had natural feelings [that] became a natural philosophy."[31] Her primary area of concern was Wright's psychological makeup. What she called the "keys to his psyche: anger, ambivalence, alienation and aberration" defined his genius, becoming the demons that drove him "to become a god maker, a fabricator, the maker of dreams and nightmares, monsters and grotesque demi-gods. He was daemonic in the highest, most artistic sense."[32]

The speech was a big hit and Walker was well aware that she had earned the respect of a new community. Prior to the Wright Symposium, she had made infrequent visits to Ole Miss. But she had remembered the highly favorable reviews of *Jubilee* by one of its most distinguished literary scholars and long-time faculty member Louis Dollahide. In fact, some of the worst reviews had come from presumed "liberals" in the North. But Walker had long ago come to the conclusion that the literary establishment was primarily an East Coast elite who viewed the South as generally backwards and unsophisticated intellectually, making exceptions only for a few who would help satisfy a certain taste. Walker had not expected to have such a warm reception, especially in the presence of Michel Fabre. The level of acceptance made Ole Miss more important, where she did return visits and held book signings at Oxford's well-known Square Books. She began to see Ole Miss as a distinct part of her new network, a place that respected her work and the kind of writer she was. She saw a civilized community and a university trying to heal from its deep wounds, even if it didn't always know how. The best part of this realization was that she did not have to compromise her values by appearing to "forgive" Ole Miss for its actions regarding James Meredith, and for upholding segregationist ideals. Rather, she could accept Mississippi for what and who the state was, all of its ugly truths open for the world to see. She had proven herself not only to be outspoken on matters of race and injustice but a dedicated Mississippian as well. Because she was obsessive about her need to speak her truth, she felt more comfortable about going forward with her work.

The Truth-telling always has the potential to backfire, which had been Walker's reality. The result was a practiced exclusion of her unless she had a certain currency at the time. While Mississippi embraced her, Walker's relationship with the white critical establishment in the South overall was quite uneven. Perhaps because many of the South's literary critics were dependent upon Northern approval of the Southern writers, Walker was not often in agreement with their assessments of Southern literature. Yes, the South was about place and family and tradition, but the approaches were not the same, depending upon whose South one was talking about. But she could not deny that she was a Southern writer, and as the author of *Daemonic Genius*, a book about the most famous Black American writer who was also Southern, she added to her status as writer of poetry and fiction, the title critic. An odd situation indeed, one that made it difficult for anyone to ignore her.

The History of Southern Literature that appeared in 1985 was probably one of the projects that gave Walker a sense of things changing. When Blyden Jackson joined the faculty at the University of North Carolina, he added to his reputation as the foremost Black critic of Southern literature. He signed on as a general editor for the *History of Southern Literature*, joining Louis Rubin, Lewis Simpson, Rayburn Moore, and Thomas Daniel Young, big names in the field, who were

Walker and Margaret Burroughs with Richard Howorth (far left) and Ronald Bailey (second from left) at Square Books, Oxford, MS. Photograph courtesy William R. Ferris

at the most respected institutions at the time: Louisiana State, Vanderbilt, and the University of North Carolina, Chapel Hill. Together they were committed to casting a wider net for Southern literature in the volume. Walker probably agreed to a photo shoot because of Jackson's involvement, knowing that her work was discussed, notably in the essay by Trudier Harris.

There were five Black-authored essays in *The History*. The year 1985 was too soon for this particular group of critics to see the larger South that Walker was accustomed to referencing in her talks and in at least two essays she would later publish. Mississippi was the "home to the four races of mankind . . . . . . the Chickasaw and Choctaw, the Creek and the Natchez, . . . " she wrote, ". . . for more than a hundred years, the Delta has been home to Asian Americans."[33] Walker often spoke about the multicultural nature of Mississippi, although major critics were not yet willing to acknowledge any accompanying literary tradition. Nevertheless, Walker was comfortably welcomed into the mostly male tradition. What mattered most to her was that Jackson had not only opened the door for other, younger scholars, but he had also added an essay of his own on the role of HBCU's in nurturing a Black literary tradition, the writers who had produced it, and a culture of reading. His mention of CLA and other Black professional

Walker with the editors of *History of Southern Literature*

organizations that provided a critical apparatus otherwise unavailable to Black writers was unusual in a volume of this type.

Jackson had chosen to write the essay on Richard Wright for the volume, which made the appearance of *Daemonic Genius* important, since it was the first full-length book on Wright by a Southerner. Walker saw *Daemonic Genius* as collective in its intent, a search to explain what drove a person like Wright and others in his generation to succeed against all odds. She believed that that she alone had brought an understanding of Black social and intellectual history to the project, as a much-needed filter for grasping the significance of Wright in his own time. Wright had rejected the South, but Walker gave it back to him in no uncertain terms. She preferred Rousseau's approach to life writing, one that emphasized the shaping influences of childhood. Wright himself, like Benjamin Franklin and Frederick Douglass before him, had opted for a different model, just as their subsequent biographers had done. What may have seemed a disadvantage for Walker, her lack of familiarity with the longer critical tradition in American autobiography, became her advantage, precisely because she was not following accepted convention but rather borrowing from a deeper and richer tradition of humanistic practice.

In the end, despite Ellen Wright's injunction and her repeated objections, *Daemonic Genius* was moving toward production. Charles Harris succeeded in regaining Walker's trust as well. He had given her the impression that he was no longer committed to the book, but in fact, he remained determined to publish it. After leaving Howard, he accepted a position first at Dodd, Mead and took the manuscript with him. The pressure from the Wright estate was equally overwhelming for Dodd, Mead, whose board decided against publication after the bound galleys were in hand. Harris then negotiated a deal with Warner Books where he started his own imprint, Amistad Books. *Daemonic Genius* was the first book published by Warner. After the book appeared, on behalf of Ellen Wright, Lubell and Lubell sued Warner Books and Margaret Walker Alexander for copyright infringement, demanding a jury trial and damages in excess of $10,000, a permanent injunction, false designation of origin, breach of contract, and libel.[34]

The entire ordeal was stressful because she was the target of much attention in a much-publicized court dispute for the second time in her life. Circuit Judge Ellsworth A. Van Graafeiland in his concurring opinion noted that Walker had made the same arguments against Alex Haley that Ellen Wright was now making against her. He continued, "It would be ironic indeed, if in this instance where Alexander's role is reversed, she lost again."[35] But as Walker told Jacqueline Trescott in an interview for the *Washington Post*, she was fully prepared. "Now, Lord I know why . . . I had to go through all that stuff. . . . I had to know everything about copyright infringement, fair use."[36]

She was correct. *Roots* had forced her to study the law carefully; she stayed strictly within the fair-use provisions in quoting from Wright's material. She had also carefully researched where Wright's work had appeared with Ellen Wright's permission. With no distractions to lure her away from her cause, she grew more motivated throughout the protracted disputes, in all three of the turns they took: at Howard University Press from 1982 to 1985, Dodd, Mead in 1986, and finally, with Warner in 1987 and 1988. She gave up on obtaining consent, rewriting portions of the earlier manuscript using less of Wright's published and unpublished works, and relying more heavily on paraphrasing. When Ellen Wright requested bound galleys, the press did not send them. Warner Books and Walker were so confident that this expurgated version could not be challenged that they published the book without further hesitation.

Ellen Wright's charges did not hold up in court. The final statement in the Plaintiff-Appellant argued in Walker's favor: "The court's grant of summary judgment on the Plaintiff's breach of contract claim was unfounded and should be reversed."[37] Each of Ellen Wright's assertions was dismissed. Satterlee, Stephens, Burke, and Burke had written in their defense statement that the "plaintiff [Ellen Wright] stubbornly refuses or ignores the rulings of the Supreme Court." The case hinged on their well-proven fact:

> All or virtually all of the works at issue in this case have been previously published or at the very least widely and publicly disseminated, which favors an expanded availability of the fair use doctrine.[38]

Although Walker organized her own case against Ellen Wright, charging racial discrimination, she wisely elected not to file a countersuit. Had she done so, she would not have been able to say convincingly that she was operating on principle and not her emotions, as she believed Ellen had been. In the end, the case stood on its own merits. Her lawyers presented conclusive evidence that those letters that Wright wrote to Walker from which she quoted, in the words of the reply memorandum, had "been voluntarily disseminated, publicly displayed and (in many instances) extensively quoted with the permission of copyright holder."[39] The summary judgment decision in her favor was, moreover, affirmed by Van Graafeiland, in a separate six-page opinion. "I am in wholehearted agreement with my colleagues' decision to affirm," he wrote. "I have written only to emphasize the strength of my conviction."[40]

Walker had won in the courts, but the biography had other challenges. In making her case in the book, she singled out Wright's previous biographers; she argued that they had each written a biography of concealment under the watchful eye of his widow. Michel Fabre, Wright's authorized biographer, replied in an essay: "Margaret Walker's Richard Wright: A Wrong Righted or Wright Wronged." Its appearance in the *Mississippi Quarterly* ensured its broad circulation in her home state. She did not respond to Fabre, but Jerry Ward did. In his "Open Letter to Michel Fabre,"[41] Ward was outraged that Fabre used Mississippi to launch his counterattack, an action that caused others to question not only his ethics, but also his intent.

Milton Moskowitz asserted that "Margaret Walker was smitten . . . there are plenty of signs here that she loved Richard Wright." He summarily dismissed the book with his assessment, "Margaret Walker's biography crackles with emotion, passion, and fury, spilled out in a chaotic fashion. It has a certain raw quality. Above all it is personal and prone to endless psychological analysis of its subject.

Daemonic Genius appeared in 1988

Walker is never far from the couch."[42] As late as 1998, Hazel Rowley accepted the Wright biographer's mantle from Fabre, whose illness prevented him from further engagement, publishing her own biography in 2001.[43] In an article for the *Yale Library Gazette*, she addressed Walker's book directly: "The trite, sensationalist title, *Richard Wright: Daemonic Genius* . . . It quickly becomes apparent to the reader that Walker was in love with Wright, a passion that was not reciprocated and that she has not forgiven him his preference for white women."[44]

Walker had little to say about any of this. The reviews were all by white writers, making them easier to dismiss. She expected no more than what she got because she had done the ungenerous thing of speaking her mind, as she always did. *Publishers' Weekly*, however, named *Daemonic Genius* as one of the fifteen most significant books of 1988.

Walker had won a major victory. She had proved to herself that her scholarly work was highly credible, and she had been vindicated in the courts. She took her literary comeback as a precious gift. She had waged two major battles and had won the war.

PART VII
THIS IS MY CENTURY
1986–1998

(Mississippi)

30

Politics and Possibilities

Once she had stored the memory of Alex in that part of her mind that no longer needed to grieve, Walker discovered a void bigger than she had imagined. The personal and professional rollercoaster that she rode with the Wright book had filled the void for a while, but she needed a different kind of project moving forward. The only thing she had not done was to engage more directly in politics, about which she always had a lot to say in her journals. The more she watched the unfolding of Ronald Reagan's political agenda, the more strongly she felt a sense of imminent danger for the country and for its people. Reagan was determined to carry out the Republican's goals: "Kill the New Deal, including Social Security, destroy the Civil Rights Movement, including Affirmative Action [appoint] a conservative Supreme Court, and above all avoid Southernness,"[1] she wrote.

Her first opportunity to express her sentiments publicly came at a rally in support of Lesley McLemore's US Senate bid. She proved her acumen for the political arena with masterful oratory:

> I am neither a politician nor a money expert. I come as a layman in the field, as your average American citizen, an everyday consumer of goods; a registered voter; a concerned person for the quality of life for all black people, and especially for black Mississippians in this crucial decade of the eighties. I speak to you today as a woman, mother and grandmother, a daughter and sister. I am that person who shops every week for groceries to feed her family, who finds the market basket costing more and more dollars to fill. I am the black woman who is insulted daily by the clerks and underlings who take my hundreds of dollars for escalating utility bills: telephone, electricity, water, and natural gas. We live on a fixed income. What happens if we are stricken by catastrophic illness and we need expensive health care and must pay exorbitant drug bills? When we are dead how much does it cost for a decent funeral and standard burial? Will the prices double next year or when will they reach a ceiling or bottom out?[2]

She was not only one of the people: she was the people's voice in a new way. She easily adopted the homespun style that Mississippians had grown accustomed to, mindful of Fannie Lou Hamer. Walker called her concerns "the practical business of living":[3]

The House Where My Soul Lives. Maryemma Graham, Oxford University Press. © Oxford University Press 2022. DOI: 10.1093/oso/9780195341232.003.0030

Book cover, *This Is My Century*

I know you and I don't give a tinker's damn about the theories and scientific ideas. We want to know what is going to be done about this *mess* we are in *now*. Who is going to help us get out of this jam, and how long are we going to be the victims of an evil system that works against us while it feeds upon us?[4]

In the crescendo of her final "Send a message, Black Mississippians," Walker showed her dedication to 1980s politics, making clear her point that "We need a *black voice* in Washington for the people of Mississippi."[5]

Her ability to connect with people had earned her success in another way: election as a delegate-at-large for the Democratic National Convention in 1984. The delegation included Rose Wilson, Janet Self, Joyce Johnson, Lesley McLemore, and Senator Henry Kirksey. Bennie Thompson was selected as the Democratic National Committeeman. The time to do this, she felt, was right. She would give unyielding support to Jessie Jackson's bid as the presidential nominee and travel to California by train for the convention. The opportunity was not one she could turn down, and for once, she was not constrained by money. Both the political and practical side of her had encouraged her to invest in a Black-owned radio station. When the station was sold, she received $270,000, the largest amount of money she had ever received at one time. It relieved her immediate financial problems, but her admitted lack of financial literacy made her incapable of seeing the money as anything other than something she could spend. She was guided by Luke 12:48, "Everyone to whom much was given, of him much will be required."[6] Alex had tried to balance her Christian piety with more practical concerns about financial security, but in his absence, she was often more extravagant than she should have been. His absence also made more visible her family's dependence upon her, and she extended her practice of supplying their needs or her wishes for them. Family now mattered to her more than ever before. If her emotions guided her entry into politics, it also guided her actions toward her family.

The money from the sale of the radio station made her feel especially generous. She decided to pay for her entire family to go to California: Sigis, Norma and their two boys, Khari and Little Sigis; James, Pat, and their children Joy Dale, and Barry; Marion, Emmett, and the twins Karen and Katherine; and Margaret, Vernon, and their son, Jarrett. Although Walker invited her siblings, Mercedes, Gwen, and Brother, only Mercedes joined them. Walker saw it as a journey of a lifetime. In contrast to her usual careful attention to planning a trip, she engaged a travel agent and prepared for the first trip in her life without any financial concerns.

Walker rarely let go of her identity as a New Deal Democrat. She was too young to vote in 1932, when she and Mercedes had just arrived at Northwestern, but as a beneficiary of Roosevelt's premier program, the WPA, she voted for his reelection in 1936. She had learned to vote for those she believed in even when it meant, as it did in 1944, "creeping to the polls with trepidation to vote for Truman despite the fact that most newspapers said he wouldn't win, that Thomas Dewey, the Republican candidate had already won, according to the *Chicago Tribune*."[7] Living in Mississippi, she had witnessed profound changes. In the absence of someone like Fannie Lou Hamer, she believed she had been called into service.

Jesse Jackson had campaigned throughout Mississippi and the South and had earned her respect. Hopeful that the climate would change, she committed herself to making that change happen. She had followed Jackson's rise to prominence, especially his work through the Chicago-based Operation PUSH. When asked to serve as co-chair of the new Rainbow Coalition, she willingly accepted.

When she was notified of her election as a delegate-at-large, she said to herself, "I could not get over the 69 year old Black woman delegate from Mississippi for Jesse Jackson."[8] This new direction was evidence for her and everyone else that she had become a master of reinvention.

The Alexander family boarded the train in Jackson, changing in New Orleans and Dallas with side trips to Los Angeles and San Diego before arriving in San Francisco. Their seventeen-member caravan with thirty-eight pieces of luggage drew attention right away, a fact they used to their advantage. Walker celebrated her sixty-ninth birthday on the train, complete with a birthday cake, and the size of their party secured for them the use of the entire club car for the celebration. They arrived in Los Angeles as typical tourists and visited the major attractions, including Disneyland. They stayed at the Biltmore, greeted Hollywood actors, including Davis Roberts, her old friend from the Chicago days, and stumbled into Sidney Poitier, a pleasant surprise. San Diego and Mexico were on their itinerary, and they shopped lavishly the week before the start of the San Francisco convention.

Jesse Jackson was at the beginning of what he hoped would be a longer journey in 1984. If he did his work well, by 1988 he could have a solid chance at the nomination, she concluded. As she and others predicted, his appearance at the Democratic National Convention in 1984 was important. On the other hand, Jackson's failure in the 1988 campaign stemmed from what he did not understand about coalition building. Walker was neither an experienced politician, nor had she followed campaign politics, but she was accustomed to teasing out political issues, examining the political, social, and economic landscape. Her analysis of the 1980s came directly from what she understood to be the keys to Roosevelt's success. If Jackson's failure four years later resulted from his antagonizing the Jewish community, "who have always been our friends," then Roosevelt's success was due to the exact opposite. Walker concluded that Roosevelt had relied on a "coalition of Labor, Jewish intellectuals, Negroes and old time Democrats which not only served him well for umpteen years but also delivered the Democratic party."[9] She was perhaps overly optimistic about what Jackson could achieve as compared to others in 1988.

Walker would have been thinking about her relationship to the nation's political history, which began before her first job with the WPA. She recalled the popular jingles as far back as Calvin Coolidge when she was nine. She could almost hear her mother's voice in the daily ritual of reading the newspaper before rising in the morning, reporting aloud to her father important events like the election of a new president. Yet, she had no memory of her parents' actual involvement in the election process; there was no discussion of voting. If they did vote, they would have had to pay a poll tax, since Louisiana laws, like those throughout the South, had imposed new qualifications at the end of the nineteenth century that led to the disenfranchisement of the Black population and a segment of the white population. Thus, while her father "listened between snores"[10] to her mother's daily news recaps, Walker's curiosity and trained critical eye easily lent themselves to robust discussions, usually with herself in the pages of her journals. With no opportunity for dialogue, she developed strong opinions and gave herself long historical summaries of Black disenfranchisement.

The 1984 convention experience was a look toward the future as much as the past, while still remaining extremely personal for Walker. She had grown up at a time when civics class required a verbatim reciting of America's elected presidents, despite a contradictory reality: Black people as a whole had no direct participation in that history. They might as well be "listening between snores," as her father did. Her first voting experience in Chicago during an intensely political period of her life did not change when she moved to Mississippi. It became even more important as she witnessed the transformation in Mississippi. In that state, the right to vote and the exercise of that right became a life-and-death issue. How could she take lightly any bold actions in the last decades of her life? She was not just any sixty-nine-year-old woman making a public political commitment, but someone with a desperate need to become part of history in the making. She felt a certain ownership over the process of historical change, and taking everyone to the convention symbolized her desire to transmit to the younger members of her family that same sense of ownership. The "race of men [who would] rise and take control" would be her grandchildren, not her.[11] Had she not accepted her delegate status, had she not gone to the convention, seeing herself as too old, she would not have completed the cycle of her very full life, one that her parents' sacrifices had enabled; she would not have been able to pass the torch on, as she believed she was doing now. She was a living witness, returning to the kind of engagement that characterized her early days as a writer. The older she became, the more becoming a model for her family converged with the need to ensure her legacy. "I wish I could live to see my grandchildren grown as my mother and her mother and my grandmother did," she wrote in a journal entry that year. "*Then I might finish my work* as a *writer as well as a woman, mother, grandmother, etc.*"[12]

The part of her statement, "My work as a writer," precedes her identity as "a woman, mother, grandmother, etc." For Walker, "my work" was variable since she always had a list of unfinished book projects. "Work" referred to her writing, which was necessary for her to live. Her ability to compartmentalize permitted the distinction between a project in its planning stages and "finishing," which meant completion through publication.

Entry into politics was a new type of "work," one that symbolized the progress of her life from the segregated South to the urban North and then back South again. After she adopted Mississippi as her home, she followed and advocated for its growth. Through a painful and decidedly uneven process, the state went from the Old South to a New South, a more visibly democratic state, yet one with deep wounds that would be slow to heal. Over time, she believed the practice of democracy on a larger scale was sometimes more visible in Mississippi than in other parts of the country that had more progressive reputations. Walker was eager to see that slice of democracy get bigger, as one way of leaving a small imprint in the most obvious of public spaces, politics.

What she hadn't realized was that her reputation as a writer and educator made her stand out in the eyes of Mississippians more than many others who may have been better known outside the state. While political sensibilities and activism of her Chicago days were no longer on display, she remained a fierce advocate for a socially just society, feared no one when speaking her mind, and followed political developments very closely. Her actions were driven by those political sensibilities of long standing. Testifying before the Mississippi Commission on Campus Unrest after the Jackson State killings had been one of the opportunities that brought her an even larger audience. Another had been her testimony as the first witness for the Ayers case, a pivotal event in the pathway to desegregation in the state of Mississippi. Such actions confirmed her political mindedness: she was operating in the public arena as the people's champion. Being identified with the landmark case gave Walker some leverage, which she hoped she might be able to use in the future. The Ayers case divided the old Mississippi from the new Mississippi, making Jackson the "crossroads of the South," the city's new moniker.

In 1975, more than a decade after the Brown Decision, one Jake Ayers filed a suit that challenged the governor and the state for its failure to comply with school desegregation. The three public institutions that served its Black population—Jackson State, Alcorn State, and Mississippi Valley—were underfunded and unequal, according to custom. The differential allocation of resources was undeniably an effort to deter the progress of Black people, which, given their majority status in the state, had been a constant source of fear among ruling whites. What Blacks lacked in terms of access and opportunity, they more than made up for in determination to make full use of those few resources they did have. As the income and education gap widened, especially after the the state's reign of violence during the 1960s, Mississippi's Black population became even more vigilant and determined to use the court system to get their just due. Despite the desegregation of Ole Miss by James Meredith, admission to the state's formerly white institutions was impossible. Ayers, therefore, did for higher education what the Brown family had done for public education generally, which made racially segregated schools illegal. Ayers challenged Mississippi's extended noncompliance. Again the Supreme Court was called in to make a ruling. The case hung in the balance for twenty-five years, for although the Supreme Court had ruled in favor of the plaintiffs and ordered the full desegregation of the state's higher education system, it left the matter of implementation to the state. By the time an agreement was reached, Ayers had died, and Mississippi had gone through three governors. In stating the case, the shapers created a definition in the class action suit that was was iconic, leaving no doubts about those affected by enforced segregation, namely:

> All black citizens residing in Mississippi, whether students, former students, parents, employees or taxpayers, who have been, are, or will be discriminated against on account of race in receiving equal educational opportunity and/or equal employment opportunities in the universities operated by [the] Board of Trustees [of State Institutions of Higher Learning].[13]

The bold move, in Walker's mind, reflected both the destiny and the humanity of the people of Mississippi. When she spoke, she argued strongly in favor of an aggressive settlement that would do right by its Black citizens, maintaining that the state had a unique opportunity and "the indomitable will and the stamina . . . to meet the challenges of a new decade." looking in her vision, she was characteristically optimistic: "we are already living in another age, and the next century is already upon us. . . . We must test our spiritual endurance and our religious faith if we are to survive, not only as a state and a nation, but as a people, as humanity on the planet earth."[14]

Walker saw no conflict between her role as a writer and educator and her sense of duty that centered a distinct form of political activism. Ultimately, the $70 million settlement secured by Bennie Thompson addressed many of the basic inequities in Mississippi's educational system. And it was left to Thompson, who would become a Mississippi legend for his lengthy service as a congressional representative in the nation's capital, to ensure that Governor Ronnie Musgrove executed the plan that called not only for complete desegregation, but also upgrades in the state's Black institutions. As a result, Jackson State would be designated as Mississippi's Comprehensive University, which essentially meant a transformed campus, with new schools and greater capacity to accommodate a steadily increasing enrollment. While many saw an ulterior motive behind this physical growth—the need to have a campus attractive to white students—it also meant that the state's Black student population would not as easily rush to the formerly all-white schools. Dedicated Mississippians now had a choice, as did students they attracted from the surrounding states. The Ayers settlement offered further support for Walker's belief in Mississippi's potential for progressive change. The state provided a new model for desegregation that did not result in the decline of historically Black institutions, which was increasingly the case throughout the South.

Once Walker had performed her civic duty, she quickly returned to her writing projects, one in particular that related to the legacy of Black education in Mississippi and the South. She was thinking more about "Minna and Jim" as a way to follow Vyry's children, who would be Walker's immediate ancestors. She also began to see the book as the prequel to her autobiography by providing the essential family history. The focus would be on Minna, Vyry's daughter and the subject of much criticism among *Jubilee*'s reviewers, because that novel ended with Jim leaving with his father Randall Ware to pursue his education, while Minna remained behind. Walker had to finally admit that she was wedded to an older paradigm when she worked on *Jubilee*, believing in a messianic, male-centered tradition. Contextually, this worked for *Jubilee*, but she was eager to explore new possibilities from the perspective of Black womanhood.

When asked to speak at the newly organized National Conference on Women and the Arts (NCWA), she met women with whom she could connect and an organization whose causes she shared. Walker saw that these women cared about art, scholarship, and publishing as much as she did. But she also wanted and needed to be read, to be published again, and to be remembered. She began to feel the kind of support that women often talked about, and for Walker, the connection was insurance for her future. The second NCWA conference was held at the University of Wisconsin, Madison, in 1985 where she met, for the first time, Nellie McKay, who was earning a reputation as a scholar of Black women's literature. She also met Elizabeth Juneway, Rhoda Lerman, and Genevieve Whitford, white women in whom she saw generational if not literary parallels. It was her first meeting with Florence Howe, who had established the Feminist Press, and who made clear that she would welcome something from Walker. The press has already produced an impressive line of books by women. Howe would become a good friend and supporter, the first white woman in the publishing world to earn Walker's trust since Dorothy de Santillana, a major accomplishment in itself.

These encounters and the distinguished alumna award from Northwestern at her fiftieth reunion boosted her ego as much as they facilitated her second return to the literary world. The next decade would bring her renewed attention. While she was not a widely reviewed author, Walker had her own publishing boom that was consistent with her goals. She had begun talking with Dorothy Abbott at the University of Mississippi about compiling a volume of recorded conversations she had done over the years. Similarly, Myriam Diaz-Diocaretz, a European scholar, was the first to mention the need for a collection of critical essays on her work. Even though both projects would pass to other hands before they were completed, they presented Walker with an increased desire to leave more books as part of her legacy.

The NCWA had a much larger impact on Walker, however. She did more than think about the new novel. It took only a short while for a four-page outline with fifty-eight episodes to appear for "Minna and Jim." It is likely that thinking about Black education in the Deep South and the active dialogues during the two hearings remained uppermost in her mind. The result was a focus on the period spanning the years 1876 to 1915, an intensely political period for Black America from the end of Reconstruction to the beginning years of the migration North. She organized "Minna and Jim" in a three-part novel, the same template she had used for *Jubilee*. Historical context is established as the characters take center stage. The novel relies on the natural progression of the characters' personal histories as they connect with the history of African Americans who enter the twentieth century during a period of major domestic and global developments. Geographically, the multiple settings in Alabama, Mississippi, Florida, and Louisiana give it the full scope of a historical novel while centering that movement on personal moments, beginning with Minna's marriage and ending with Vyry's death.

Part I establishes the context of segregation as a substitute system for slavery through its use of the crop-lien system. Against the background of Jim Crow legislation, the Ku Klux Klan, and lynching, Walker places the growth of Negro educational institutions and the Negro church, a distinct community in social, economic, and political terms, while emphasizing the role of Black expressive culture, especially music, as a mechanism for cohesion and continuity. Part II belongs to Minna, the fictional name for Walker's grandmother. Minna marries Edward Lane Dozier and gives birth to nine, rather than the twelve children the real Elvira Dozier did have, thus keeping the story from any dependency upon biographical facts. The couple moves first to Mississippi, and then to Pensacola, Florida, following Dozier's ministry. The narrative moves through each of the children's lives and records the death of Rev. Dozier. Most of the section is the coming of age of the last of the Dozier children, including Walker's mother Marion, and continues through the early days of her marriage to Walker's father.

The thread of a family chronicle then shifts to Minna's brother Jim for Part III. Creating Jim's story fulfilled Walker's need for a concrete example about Black education in the South and would replace "My Black-Eyed Susan School," a book that never materialized. She planned to include significant elements of Jackson State's history and its founding as Natchez Seminary by the American Baptist Home Mission Society of New York. With little history to go on, Jim's story would necessarily rely more heavily on her imagination. She had traced the real Jim to a courthouse in Greenville, Alabama, and remembered writing letters to him for her grandmother. Jim had one living nephew, she learned, but the only thing that came from the memories of others was Jim's attendance at the funeral of his father, Randall Ware. He had seen both his sister and his mother and given them fifty dollars. Even though rumor outstripped the facts about the life of James (Jim) Ware, Walker was clear that his presence in the novel provided a dramatic counterpoint to Minna's story. His life does not have the richness or the depth of meaning we see in the lives of Minna and her children.

Telling her mother's story was a major motivation for the new novel. While she believed whatever emotional connection to her mother had been loosened when Marion died, her emotional memory was binding. Memory was also elemental for her, and she could only grasp the significance of her mother's life through her actual recovery of it. The retrospective telling of her Marion's life was essential to her own going forward. That story, about the life and times of an unusually gifted daughter of a washerwoman and a folk preacher, became the primary framework for cultural and racial memory. The facts were well known—a young woman leaves her home in the rural South, takes the train alone at fifteen, and enters the care of a Black woman educator in Washington. This was not uncommon for the period. The recording and reimagining of that story, however, was. Walker understood that she had more than enough plot for a single novel, enough twists and turns for the story to match several of those that gained appeal in the 1980s. But her desire to write another historical novel at seventy exceeded her ability to do so. It had taken her three decades to write *Jubilee*. Now, neither time nor her physical health was on her side.

Walker may not have realized that just as *Jubilee* had elements of her own life as a mother, "Minna and Jim" actually created a symbolic, unacknowledged connection between her life and her mother's. Her resistance to exploring the connection is suggested in her outline for this book. Of the nine siblings in the Dozier family, Marion's name is the only one that is never mentioned. Several speaking voices serve as chapter or episode titles for Marion's history. "A Scholarship to College," "I want to go home," and "My Mamma Is a Washerwoman" are taken from the stories Walker remembered hearing about Marion's time at the Nannie Burroughs school. A second episode that begins with "Mama, when we eat our lunch—give this man a piece of fried chicken, please. He hasn't got any lunch," may or may not be Marion's voice. Walker is intentionally setting up the tension between the two sisters who are vying for Sigismund's attention. Marion is the object in numerous episodes, since Part II of the novel is about her. But with no speaking voice for a Marion-type figure, these variations suggest Walker's own uncertainty about where her mother fits in the narrative, and how much control she, as the author, was willing to give to her mother. Could she allow art to follow life? The woman who tried unsuccessfully to control her daughter in real life could not be allowed such permission in the fictional equivalent.

What she had planned to do, which would have been another important first, was to use the marriage of Marion to Sigismund Constantine Walker to explore conflicts between American-born and Caribbean-born Blacks. She called one episode "If Your Daddy was Alive He wouldn't let you marry A Monkey-chaser," shifting the narrative away from its emphasis on the competition between the two sisters, Abigail and Marion, which was the family lore. The new telling reflects the insights Walker gained as a daughter of a bicultural marriage, insights that were available to her only as an adult. Employing this derogatory term used for West Indian Blacks, "monkey-chaser," could help her draw this picture more sharply. There is no indication anywhere in her journals that she was aware of any negative treatment or insults toward her father as a child, but she would have observed her father's difference from the people with whom the family associated, especially because she was so sensitive to language. Her reference to his silence on several occasions suggests self-consciousness on his part, as much as his distinct personality traits. Now, as an adult, it would be easier for her to describe what she saw around her and those qualities she noticed in others.

She was not yet ready to contemplate those qualities that she possessed and their relationship to parental influence. The role that outlining her novel did play was to give her access to those parts of her family history that she needed to prioritize. The process was critical to her understanding of the way her mind worked. Like much of her journal writing, it was outlining a process that led to a certain outcome, but not necessarily the outcome that might take shape in the real world.

The background research for "Minna and Jim" shows that Walker was still operating with broad strokes and with a narrative sense grounded in the traditional historical novel. Her notes include the names Kelly Miller, William Pickens, Theodore Roosevelt, Booker T. Washington, George Washington Carver, Emmett Scott, and W. E. B. Du Bois. She also listed topics she needed to consider: the race riots, particular lynchings, the founding of the NAACP, the establishment of Black churches, African secret societies, the death of President McKinley, and three global wars: the Spanish-American, Mexican, and Boer wars. Her historical framing gave attention to the story of American Indians, cowboys, and the move westward, the building of railroads, the growth of oil wealth, and the rise of cities in the Middle and Far West. It was an era of American life that had fascinated her since it corresponded with the birth of her writing career at a time she was learning about the Rockefellers, the Rosenwalds, and the Harrimans. Planting the story in the midst of a major growth period of American culture made for exciting research and realistic content for her narrative.

Jubilee had been a journey of discovery, enabling the characters to come alive. "Minna and Jim," however, would be fiction that entered deeply into memory, a way for her to reclaim the voices of Black women in the story. For this second novel, she may have been drawing upon what she was reading associated with the rise of memory studies. Toni Morrison would make the French term introduced by Pierre Nora, *les lieux de mémoire*, more familiar to American readers in her 1987 essay "The Site of Memory," but Houston Baker's definition of "critical memory" might explain Walker's process more directly: "a type of looking that judges severely, censures righteously, that renders hard ethical decisions of the past."[15] In "Minna and Jim," Walker looked at the past while judging it doubly: selecting a significant moment in time in order to examine certain practices. Minna was not only the fictional equivalent of Walker's grandmother, but she was also a symbolic descendant for a generation of Black grandmothers who had to shepherd their children (especially their daughters) into a new century, a new era, and a radically changing world. She relied on Vyry's Christian values in *Jubilee* and had ended the novel with the potential of male success. In her new thinking, rather than embracing Jim's success, Walker addresses what she had begun to see as the experiences of women in her own generation as well as those of her mother and her grandmother.

Walker's instincts were correct: "Minna and Jim" could help secure her reputation during a period when Black women were filling gaps in the literary landscape with numerous books, many of them focused on the subject of slavery, and its aftermath with the rural South as one of the settings. A few years after *Jubilee*, novels would appear in rapid succession: Ernest Gaines's *The Autobiography of Miss Jane Pittman* (1971), Charles Johnson's *Faith and the Good Thing* (1974), and Gayl Jones's *Corregidora* (1975), all of which alerted the reading public to a growing interest in the subject of slavery and the rural South that expanded with the 1974 television adaptation of Gaines's novel. Walker and Gaines had both paved the way for the celebrated attention that Alex Haley brought in 1976 with *Roots* as novel and film, which somewhat overshadowed Sherley Anne Williams's *Dessa Rose* (1976) that appeared the same year. Were it not for Ishmael Reed's steady output and his reputation for experimental fiction, *Flight to Canada*, published that same year, might have been easier to ignore. The critical apparatus necessary to bring these works to the public's attention in a consistent way was slow and uneven at best. For example, earlier critics like Sandra Govan had paid attention to Octavia Butler's work in an effort to extract her from that end of the literary continuum into which science fiction had become stuck, but the critical consensus was rather resistant. It was only later when scholars began to rescue Butler, especially *Kindred* (1979), placing her within a newly evolving tradition. Further, the second novel published that year, Barbara Chase Riboud's *Sally Hemings* (1979), benefited from the controversial validation of Thomas Jefferson's bloodline resulting from his extended relationship with an enslaved woman, before, during and after his presidency. When the critical consensus did catch up, drawing attention to this development in Black writing, Walker's output was too slim and too removed in time and critical distance. While few critics offered assessments during this period, Angelyn Mitchell foregrounds Walker's relationship to the new work on slavery by Black women writers. "Mitchell observed that " . . . the proliferation of contemporary texts that revisit slavery begins with *Jubilee* . . . [recuperating] the Black woman's history by situating the enslaved Black woman as central." Mitchell also noted a critical shift that made it easy to overlook Walker " . . . in revealing the social and material conditions

of enslavement in the Black woman's life." Walker's commitment to realistic depictions of that life, she continued, "function to recover . . . not interrogate that
life."[16] It was exactly what Walker had hoped to expand in her sequel.

   Instinct alone was insufficient for Walker to follow through with her detailed
plan. Her writing pace was slow, her commercial publishing network invisible,
and it is doubtful if she would have garnered the energy to do more work on
"Minna and Jim" after two major developments. As Mitchell suggests, Walker
was wedded to the historical novel genre, so that by the time Toni Morrison's
Beloved hit the publishing world by storm, historical fiction of a certain type
had lost its value. Perhaps more influential in her decision to abandon the project was the appearance of *Queen* in 1993, Alex Haley's novel turned television
mini-series, based on his own family history. Both Walker and Haley seemed
to have learned important lessons. Haley was sticking to the personal family
chronicle genre, basing *Queen* on his paternal grandmother, which had an odd
resemblance to *Jubilee*, based on Walker's maternal great-grandmother. Again,
the mini-series followed quickly after the novel, even though Haley died a year
before the release. Walker had no words to offer on the appearance of the book
or film. Ironically, had she pursued "Minna and Jim" after Haley's second success, she might have found herself in a reverse position, inviting accompanying
criticism. *Jubilee* had come first. Now Haley's sequel would come first. Both were
using family chronicles about a similar period. Would readers see hers as a copy-
cat? She would have taken careful note of the ways in which the world of academia, publishing, and eventually Hollywood had become consolidated. With
no indication that Walker thought or wrote consciously about any of these developments, it seems that she was content to accept her status offered by Bernard
Bell. In his 1987 history of the Afro-American novel, Bell popularized the term
"neo-slave narrative," including her in his discussion. While Angelyn Mitchell's
term "liberatory narratives" would have served the entire genre in more precise
ways, the publishing industry embraced the term "neo-slave narrative." With it,
came a highly successful market of readers and writers.

   Since Walker's brand of historical fiction was no longer in vogue, and she was
not like another member of her cohort, Frank Yerby, who had built a successful
empire on the genre, the desire to complete another novel lost its appeal. She was
content to be at the front end of this new era. Had "Minna and Jim" been published, it might have resembled a version of Southern Black manhood that she
had found unacceptable in Alice Walker's *The Color Purple*. Jim was not the kind
of man Walker would not have taken pride in. Family lore had confirmed that
Jim lost his first wife, because he was too mean, and married a second one, whom
he treated as his slave.[17]

   While a keen interest in women's lives was something Walker shared with
younger women writers, she believed women were stronger and ultimately too

powerful to allow themselves to be humiliated or even to succumb to trauma. There were practical matters that grew out of her experience. She used her marriage as an example of how to turn a bad thing into a good thing whenever she counseled younger women. Living in the South, Walker found that her inability to accept defeat and a belief that women really were generally more intelligent than men endeared her to many women. In those discussions about the difficulties one encounters at certain points in marriage, she had a favorite response. "Don't you know how to make love to your man's mind?" she had once asked Tommie Stewart. As Stewart remembered, "Walker would go on to help you map out a workable strategy that had several layers over time. She reminded you that as a woman you were in control."[18]

The real reason that "Minna and Jim" or any of the other writing projects remained incomplete had as much to do with Walker's new preoccupation: managing the way people would see her after she died. That had to be the focus of the time she had left. Thus, in the *Jackson Advocate*'s full-page tribute for her seventieth birthday in 1985, she announced three new books—a collection of her essays, her collected and new poems, and a collection of critical essays on her work—but excluded "Minna and Jim." She was intentional in the design she gave to her ongoing career as she approached her final decade. Although being a poet had always mattered the most to her, she saw herself as well-rounded, someone who operated in several domains. By shaping her legacy in this way, she did not run the risk of needing others to rediscover her. The Wright book might have proven her to be a scholar, but *Daemonic Genius* alone was not sufficient to anchor her broader literary reputation.

New invitations demanded her attention as well. Some she gladly accepted because they reconfirmed her core identity as a poet, which meant reading her poetry before audiences, something she never ceased to enjoy. Accepting a commission to write a group of poems called *Farish Street*, to honor the Farish Street Redevelopment Project, allowed Walker to link memory, history, and home. The seven poems celebrated the historic commercial district in Jackson, a vibrant area where Black businesses once thrived, providing a social, economic, and cultural base during an era of segregation. In the first poem "The African Village," Walker discussed Farish Street as a reconstruction in the new world, "this separate place" created when "our blackness was not thought so beautiful."

African Americans' ability to adapt to restrictive conditions required them to "[make] our village here . . . our gifts with singing, dancing, giving." Walker's nostalgia is evident as she proclaims Farish Street "this place of yesteryears, forgotten stream of dreams."[19] In the remaining poems, she explored the sights and sounds of a community that met its needs as a culture of contradiction. "The Crystal Palace," where elegance conjoins with the finest dance hall music, exists on the one end of the block, while "The House of Prayer" and funeral homes sit

The dedication of Farish Street Green, designated as the area bounded by Farish, Hamilton, and Bloom Streets, is the culmination of a six-year effort by city and community leaders. The significance of this area of Jackson is further recognized with a commemorative sculpture located in the new community park.

The sculpture, designed by Linda S. Trobaugh, is the result of a statewide competition sponsored by the Arts Alliance of Jackson/Hinds County. Trobaugh's _Farish Quilt_ is an artist's reflection on the color, vitality, and strength of the remarkable community it honors. Trobaugh drew on Romare Bearden's celebrated painting _Patchwork Quilt_ as inspiration for her design.

Poet Margaret Walker was commissioned to compose a literary tribute to complement the sculpture. "A Poem for Farish Street," which appears complete in this volume, is a celebration of the past as well as the future of the street and lauds the people, places, and events the street has known.

Funding for the sculpture was provided by the Arts Alliance of Jackson/Hinds County with a Community Development Block Grant and assistance from the Farish Street Management Corporation and David Hegwood.

Cover and introduction, *For Farish Street*

on the other, symbolizing the fluid coexistence of the secular and sacred as essential features of Black humanity. In the poem "Black Magic," there is the "Root doctor, hoodoo man," images of people "playing checkers in the twilight / Before the barber shop / Before the beauty parlor / Before the store."[20] *Farish Street* as a memorial act recounts the "Small Black World," confirming that "All our history is here / All our yearning, dreaming, hoping, loving, dying / All our lives are buried here." As she concludes the poem, her tone shifts from the nostalgic to the critical:

> I have walked these streets all over the world
> Black Streets, Farish Streets Black
> where all the black people all over the world
> have set up their shops
> in the markets of the world
> where we sell our souls daily to every passerby
> and our children come to play in emptiness
> and softly night falls suddenly.[21]

The poems were completely new, and they demonstrate Walker's engagement with visual memory as an extension of her historical project. Without sacrificing the specificity of Farish Street, she takes the reader on a spatial journey through African American history, Jackson, Mississippi, in particular. Reminding the reader that individual sites coalesce into a collective whole, she shows us how crucial the parts are for understanding the nature of Black humanity. "All of our history is here / All our yearning, dreaming, hoping, loving, dying / All our lives are buried here."[22]

Her daughter Margaret was due to give birth to her second child, but Walker went to Chicago by way of New York. In 1986, Raymond Patterson organized the inaugural Langston Hughes Festival at the City College of New York. It was her first visit to New York in some time. Seeing old friends renewed her sense of connection, but meeting new ones made clear the world had changed. The conference honored a group of writers and actors who had made major contributions to African American culture. A photograph from the occasion shows Walker surrounded by Toni Cade Bambara, James Baldwin, Toni Morrison, Ruby Dee, Ossie Davis, Paule Marshall, Michael Harper, Raymond Patterson and actor Roscoe Lee Brown. John Oliver Killens was the only person present who was not in the photograph. It would be the last time she would see Killens or Baldwin, both of whom would die the next year. And it was her first and only time meeting Toni Morrison. She confronted her own mortality as this was the beginning of a series of losses in short order.

The arrival in Chicago pushed back those feelings, since it turned out to be one of her most pleasurable visits. She spent more time than usual, but for good cause. This second child, her daughter vowed, would be her last. For Walker, it was the end of another cycle. The birth of this eighth and last grandchild pleased her immensely especially since it was a daughter. The naming practice was crucial. Just as Margaret had been her namesake, they decided that the new baby would be named after the youngest member of the Walker family, her sister Gwendolyn. The baby's given name was Gwendolyn Gail, who quickly became Gigi, the grandchild who would help bring back some of the joy she shared with Alex. She had enjoyed Sigis's boys who lived with her, but a girl would give her someone she could continue to dote on, since Marion's twin girls, Karen and Katherine, were growing up and too quickly, she had concluded. The pleasure she derived from the fulfillment of motherhood never ceased. The new boost of energy became the fuel she used to dive into an old manuscript, "Mother Beulah," and a new essay with thoughts that had coalesced during the 1980s. Like many of her unfinished essays, "Philosophy, Poetry, and Politics" was written more for self-clarification than publication.

By the time Walker returned to Jackson, she had a packed schedule. She did another television appearance on *Faces*, completed the blurbs for a series of

Langston Hughes Festival participants at the City College of New York, 1986

books that had been waiting, and received potentially good news from Charlotte Sheedy and Dorothy Gilbert, who were hoping to negotiate a mini-series for *Jubilee*. Venturing into the world of Hollywood and television no longer seemed to hold any attraction, and she refused to get her hopes up about it. She seemed to be running a race with time, setting an impossible schedule for herself so much so that when Julia Wright wrote to set up a meeting with her, she was unable to commit. Wright's daughter was coming from Paris to accept a posthumous award at the University of Mississippi on behalf of her father. Lingering feelings about Ellen Wright's efforts to stop the publication of *Daemonic Genius*, and assuming that Julia was in agreement with her mother's actions, were likely the reasons Walker did not make a more concerted effort to find time to meet.

The loss of important people in her life over the next several years was inevitable: close friends, mentors, and those she had long admired. The list was long and they were all men—John O. Killens, Frank Marshall Davis, Harold Washington, James Baldwin, J. Saunders Redding, St. Clair Drake, Paul Engle, and Darwin Turner. She marked each passing with an anecdote. Thus, when Alferdteen Harrison proposed changing the Institute's name to the Margaret Walker Alexander National Research Center, she sensed the beginning of a new

Despite her open criticism of Ray Mabus's administration, Walker graciously accepts the governor's proclamation from Lieutenant Governor Brad at the state capital, 1990.

life. It wasn't about ego so much as it was the need to have something to hold on to, something with which she could associate a concrete plan. Harrison had her own goals for the Institute, but she also recognized that its founder was her biggest asset and advocate. Walker had also grown accustomed to planning and executing her life for so long, not directing the Institute had left a huge void. To put it simply, she needed a new cause. The list of books she had hoped to write were expanding, but they were simply placeholders.

Having the center as the official repository for her papers would maintain her tradition of firsts, which was something else Walker was accustomed to. Tuskegee, Howard, and Fisk universities had important collections, but the Institute, with her official name, would be the only complete collection by any African American writer housed at an HBCU. Thus began a protracted process of getting the collection appraised, drawing up the contract, and stating the terms and amount in order to make the acquisition legal and binding.

Her investment in the idea of becoming a national repository—a center bearing her name—was total. The Martin Luther King Center had become widely known for its focus on the historical documentation of civil rights activism, but Walker was not certain that the Mississippi movement would be given the attention it deserved. Jackson State was the most appropriate site for preserving twentieth-century history, with the added advantage of allowing the university to develop the expertise in and have some control over the Mississippi story. Since she had refused to sell her papers to Boston University, it is very unlikely that she would have been proprietary about anything associated with the state. The era of collecting Black archival materials had begun in earnest, and she saw herself as the home-grown protector of the state's legacy and predictor of its future. Jackson State, in her mind, could be a model for the rest of America in its investment in historical preservation and ensuring the future value of HBCUs. Moreover, Mississippi, once atypical of the United States, had become not only central to "the pluralistic fabric of the nation" but the place where "the same hard realistic facts of American life prevail as elsewhere, . . .[its] problems . . .are the nation's dilemmas." Her idealism led to the conclusion that Mississippi was one place where one might search and find "a common ground of humanity."[23]

The Institute and Mississippi had already become wedded to one destiny for Walker. In the back of her mind was a belief that the successes of a new generation would erase her legacy. She knew how easy it was to paint Mississippi with one broad, undifferentiated stroke, unchanging and unredeemable. Margaret Walker in that scenario was a woman of her time, and while she had no desire to be someone different from that, Mississippi was key to that image. She understood further that if she did not plan and orchestrate her ideas, she would fall victim to an even longer history of conspicuous absenteeism from a history to which she had contributed so much.

If "Minna and Jim" had been too ambitious, given her diminishing publishing opportunities, Walker felt some confirmation that the named Institute was the only way to ensure a sustainable public legacy, and to invite further expansion. Her participation in the Black Women's Oral History Project at the Schlesinger Library brought even more public attention added to that legacy, as one of the ten women Judith Sedgwick had photographed for *Women of Courage*. The opening of the exhibit in Washington DC was an elaborate gala, with a reception for the honorees and a stunning media blitz. The exhibit would tour for the next two decades. This recognition affirmed Walker's importance, brought even more public attention, and was most influential in placing her within a distinct cohort of distinguished women whose accomplishments were undeniable. Five years later, she would appear in *I Dream a World: Portraits of Black Women Who Changed America*, by Brian Lanker. The photograph was not as striking as Sedgwick's, but the biographical statement was by far the most important. Along with *For My People* and *Jubilee*, she could claim by then authorship of a biography, *Richard Wright: Daemonic Genius*. Out of her conversation with another honoree, Rosa Parks, came the idea for authoring Parks's biography. She returned home and immediately began outlining the three-part story, proposing to spend at least six hours taping Parks to begin the project. Replacing "Minna and Jim" with a biography was appealing since such a project would have much broader audience. It was also Walker's way of narrating a story that blended history and politics, focusing on the women of her time.

The Parks biography brought Walker back to her autobiography and the need to tell her own story rather than relegate the task to others. She elected to call it "The Vision Splendid," organizing her thoughts around the visions she had as a child, visions that continued to present themselves to her as dreams. She made note of the day of her decision and asked for spiritual guidance:

> I am about to begin writing my greatest work and I guess must have a period of prayer and meditation of careful fasting and prayer that I may be able to be an instrument of God's will and medium for his message. My life story is a story of vision of hope and prayer and a triumph of faith.[24]

Organizing her life in cycles of seven moved through the astrological houses. She wanted to unpack the various layers of her experience and to explore their meaning. It was here where Walker moved beyond writing as compulsion. Now the writing was far more purposeful and public. In thinking about her life, she'd have to ask what drove her to do what she did and how she managed the consequences. For someone who did not believe in *blind* faith, she knew that as she got older, she looked for more signs to serve as confirmation for her decisions, with further verification drawn from her astrological readings.

Going forward, Walker seemed to have a clear vision for every action, one connected to a different lived reality as it interacted with the political moment. She had wanted to write something on Jesse Jackson and did complete an essay, "Jessie Jackson, the Man and His Message," which was later included in her collection *On Being Female, Black, and Free*. It was originally planned for a volume entitled *Jessie Jackson's Role in Mississippi's Black Politics*. The book remained on Wayne State's prospective book lists, but there is no evidence that a contract was ever signed, even though a note in her journal indicated her plan to finish the book and deliver the manuscript in one year.

Walker was about to enter her last decade. In a journal entry in April 1990, she described a troubling dream that had awakened her. A prayerful response followed:

> If I trust God to fight my battles, to give me my heart's desires and remain at peace, I know none mean any harm to me. More important that [this] is the health and welfare of all my family—my children, grandchildren and myself as well as the peace and health of my sisters and brother. . . .
>
> The fact remains that whether I live or die soon three major things carry the name of Margaret Walker Alexander—a street, a library, and a research center.

What more can I ask or desire? I never anticipated any of this. God alone is responsible and to God be the glory. He has promised to make our enemies a footstool—and I know his promises are pure.[25]

Several developments prompted the reflections. *This Is My Century: New and Collected Poems* had been published by the University of Georgia Press in 1989, allowing her to bring her poetry career to an official close. With all of the volumes together, *For My People, Prophets for a New Day, October Journey*, the commissioned volume *For Farish Street*, and a selection of new poems, she hoped to join the community of poets who were actively publishing. There had been no further awards for her poetry, but the award system had become the primary means for measuring the worth and importance of contemporary poets. Whether or not the new volume would be viewed as more than warmed-over milk would be left for others to decide.

Another matter tugged at her conscience more deeply. The Natchez Cinema and Literary Celebration had been in the planning stages for some time. The key organizer, Carolyn Vance Smith, was counting on Walker to give a keynote address for the inaugural celebration in late June. An historic marker of Richard Wright would be dedicated, and the stretch of highway between Roxie and Natchez leading to his birthplace on Rucker's Plantation would be renamed in his honor. Attention to Wright necessarily meant attention to her biography, whose negative reviews created some uneasiness. Walker nonetheless gave a spirited talk on "The Historic South, the Mythic South, the Violent South" dedicated to Wright, but she quickly returned to Jackson, avoiding any dialogue about the book. She gave as her reason two upcoming events, final planning for her seventy-fifth birthday party and the congressional hearing for the establishment of the Margaret Walker Alexander National Research Center, both held in Jackson within days of each other.

Two years after the publication of *Daemonic Genius*, any thought of Wright still brought up bitter feelings about the lengthy legal battle and Ellen Wright's attempt to stop publication. Although she succeeded with delaying tactics, Walker understood that the controversy over *Roots* had affected the book's critical reception. Though she was beloved in Mississippi, she could never be sure that at such a major public event, which the Natchez Celebration was, some journalist would not try to press her with a question. How might she respond to the charge of jealousy as her motivation for the Haley suit or her bitterness over the failed relationship with Wright as the motivation behind the biography?

Such a "troubled dream" was, therefore, both a meditation and a mediation. In these routine devotionals, she did not have to be explicit in her journals, seeing God as all-knowing. She would have been worried both about her reputation with two new books out, and hopeful that the negative reviews of *Daemonic*

Genius might be offset by more positive reviews of *This Is My Century.* That she had finally stopped talking about the Haley suit publicly did not mean that it was not on her mind. The entry references "battles," which were real and those she waged internally. Aware of her tendency—a decided weakness—to succumb to excessive pride, Walker is intentionally understated, even humble in her choice of words. Referring to her achievements, she says, "I never anticipated any of this. God alone is responsible and to God be the glory." However, as if to remind God of her expectation, the tone quickly shifts. One might have anticipated Walker to ask to be forgiving of her enemies. Instead, she reminds God of his promise "to make our enemies a footstool." The troubled dream anticipated what was ahead in the event of any new battles. With her confidence restored, she concludes, "Now I pray to finish my writing—my work—until I die as God wills."[26]

The ability to operate in and shift between multiple and extreme registers, often blending the political, the personal, and the religious, seemed to become more visible as she grew older. They simply merged into a calculated decision to which she would commit. With more time on her hands, she not only wrote longer and more intensely in her journals, but she also came up with new projects, associated with either her experiences, her vision of society and the world, or what might be called Black intellectual history. It was almost as if she was starting her career all over again in the 1990s, but more focused on Mississippi itself. Even if time were not on her side, she was identifying notable voids in the written record and imagining her capacity to fill them with her work.

This Is My Century, for example, while mostly a compilation with some new poems, made a statement with its organization. It had a forward and a backward gaze, symbolizing both an intellectual and poetic vision. The plan was for each volume to appear in chronological order. Had she done so, the volume would have ended with "Fanfare, Coda, and Finale," one of the newer, unpublished poems. But its connection to death and dying seemed too final. While preparing the volume, she looked at her life as a whole, and because Jackson, Mississippi, had been so central, she wanted to make a point with the book's ending. Thus, *Farish Street*, a commissioned work, rather than the last poems she had been writing, served as the bookend. The decision allowed her to take the reader on a journey through the seven poems that began with "The African Village." The journey is a kaleidoscope where colorful scenes and images jump out at the reader. Rather than evoking the horror of segregation, Walker depicts what people made out of that life in its fullness. Since neither she nor the reader knows what the future might hold, the ending poem offers a sense of being in the present moment, pondering what is gained through the process of living:

> I have come through the maze and the mystery of living
> to this miraculous place of meaning

finding all things less than vanity
all values overlaid and blessed with truth and love and peace
knowing magic of reconciliation and hope . . .
I lift my voice above a rising wind . . .
Because I now declare
this place called Farish Street in sacred memory . . .
one wheel of fortune a-turning in the wind
as I go
a traveler through this labyrinth . . .
and I look to the glory of the morning of all life.[27]

As she often did, Walker had turned to Greek mythology, borrowing the word "labyrinth," when she named the final poem "The Labyrinth of Life." The poem signaled life not as a straight line, from beginning to end, but rather a circular movement, more akin to the cycles of nature. Memories of place, time, and experience become sacred just as the constant renewal of life.

After the release of *This Is My Century*, Walker embarked on a major book tour. Although there was not a promise of much money, she had other reasons that compelled her. Even though some bittersweet memories of her time in Boston as a distraught single mother nearly forty years earlier followed her, the years since had cultivated relationships of long standing. She drew on her connections for the trip, which the new director of Northeastern University's African American Studies Program, Ronald Bailey, understood. He had just arrived from the University of Mississippi, and they had become friends during his years in the state. Her readings and other programs were scattered between lunches with reunions. One of them was with Adelaide Cromwell, who was Walker's counterpart in New England. Although they were not in the same fields, one a poet, the other a social scientist, they shared the same vision of institutional refashioning and were known and widely respected in their communities. Cromwell's work at Boston University—in creating early programs for the study of Africa and the Black diaspora there—provided a model long before it became popular elsewhere. Walker and Cromwell were now both retired, after spending more than three decades in two radically different institutions, one Black and one white, who now served as driving forces in the transformation of higher education. Yet by accident of birth and socialization, both women seemed to be at a comfortable distance from the generation that succeeded them.

Walker's visit with Dorothy West, on the other hand, was a first meeting between two women who had both worked with Richard Wright, one before, the other after he left Chicago for New York. They recounted the story of *New Challenge*, West revealing how Wright had "taken over" the journal she had founded in an effort to move it to a more radical posture as one of the few journals founded by Blacks during the period. West willingly agreed to publish "Blueprint for Negro Writing" in *New Challenge* in 1937, which had introduced the Chicago-based South Side Writers Group to New York, regarded as the center of literary activity. The controversy between West and Wright over leadership of *New Challenge* had caused the journal to fold, but the years between 1937 and this 1989 encounter with a friend of Wright's had resolved any bitterness on West's part. More important was their recognition that they that were part of an important, even radical legacy, something that neither of them knew at the time. After a fair amount of gossip, some lunch and laughter, they found themselves expressing their deep sadness at the demonizing of Zora Neale Hurston, whom West knew fairly well. They were both overjoyed that her work was finally getting the attention it deserved.

Time spent with Elma Lewis, who was Boston's leading figure in the Black Arts community, gave Walker a chance to see an institution builder in action. Lewis had founded her School of Fine Arts for Black youth in 1950, which expanded into the National Center for Afro-American Artists in 1968, the major venue for performances and outdoor festivals for the greater Boston area. It became famously known for annual productions of *Black Nativity*, based on a play by Langston Hughes, whom both of them knew. The Boston trip gave Walker further confirmation that she was on the right path. What Elma Lewis and Adelaide Hill had done in Boston, Walker could do in Jackson. Touring the Center made Walker curious about how Elma had managed all of this. What connections did she have? Walker assumed that Lewis had drawn on the Boston political machine to sustain the work despite all the changes over the decades in the city's leadership.

As it turned out, by the time Walker returned to Jackson, Alferdteen Harrison had garnered the necessary support to introduce a bill for national designation of the Margaret Walker Alexander Center, which if approved, would bring a Senate appropriation of funds. Once that had been done, Walker felt comfortable accepting another project, a publishing opportunity that displayed that blend of personal, political, and religious action. Harper & Row reached out to her at the request of Sister Thea Bowman, who wanted Walker to write her autobiography. A Mississippi native and professionally trained concert vocalist, Bowman was best known for her influence in establishing the legitimacy of an African American Catholic ritual practice. Diagnosed with cancer, she returned to her birth home in Canton, Mississippi, to live out her final days. Sister Thea's request was unusual, asking Walker, someone outside the Catholic Church, to write her story. Because it appeared to her as a form of ghostwriting, Walker at first declined, anticipating a difficult and bureaucratic project with a contract with the Franciscan Sisters of Perpetual Adoration in addition to Sister Thea and herself. Given the state of Bowman's health, with only a short time remaining for the project to be done, Walker also felt a strong spiritual connection to the project. She believed that Sister Thea had selected a non-Catholic for a reason. She concluded that her role was an intervention on behalf of a woman who needed to say something. She felt she could bring the kind of honesty that Sister Thea wanted; at the same time, there was a sense of joy at being able to write a religious story, something she had always wanted to do. Father Joe Dyer, the priest at Sacred Heart, Thea's home church, agreed to provide transportation to facilitate the interviews. Walker's excitement ultimately grew as she saw the melding of different worlds: the rural South and the Urban North, the Catholic and the Protestant worlds, and the ultimate return to one's roots. What the two women shared was the trust between them as Black women, known for their public, rather than their private lives.

The eight tapes that were completed covered Thea's early life in the Baptist Church in Canton, her decision to convert to Catholicism, and the journey from Canton to St. Rose Convent in Wisconsin, where she joined the Franciscan Sisters of Perpetual Adoration. Sister Thea completed her MA and PhD, and began to actively wed Black culture to the Catholic faith. Carving out a vision for her life in the church, she became influential in the transformation of Black Catholic ministries, work that would eventually put her on the path to sainthood. Walker's last visit took place one day before Sister Thea's death in March 1990, when she was too weak to interview. Composing from her notes, Walker started the life story at the end, describing Sister Thea on that last visit until her death, and the elaborate funeral in the largest church in Jackson. In keeping with Thea's interest in African culture, the funeral blended African American motifs and music together with the Catholic eucharist. Much to her surprise, in organizing her notes, Walker found a connection to her unfinished novel, "Mother Beulah," the story of the faith healer that, by then, was only a distant memory. The funeral scene was the beginning of both the novel and life of a real person. The project began to take on a much larger meaning; Bowman was a vehicle for the transfer of a fictional narrative to a real life story.

Throwing herself into finishing "Sister Thea: God Touched My Life" after the funeral gave Walker a sense of satisfaction she'd not felt before. Here was the opportunity to talk about the impact of deeply religious faith and political activism in the life of another that had meaning for hers as well. Sister Thea saw organizing and evangelizing as a call from God; she was an advocate for young Black Catholic women and succeeded in creating an organization for their support. The twenty-three-chapter outline—much larger than the book Walker had agreed to write—appears in her journals.[28] No further written communication exists in Walker's papers, except for the contract that specified the Franciscan Sisters of Perpetual Adoration and Sister Thea Bowman were "individually and collectively 'the Owner.'" That the contract also included an option granted to

Harbel Productions, a company owned by Harry Belafonte, "to acquire the motion picture, television rights and customary ancillary rights to her life story,"[29] suggests the interest in Sister Thea's life beyond the Catholic Church. Like "Mother Beulah," Sister Thea's story disappeared from view. The story of a life given to God was no longer Walker's to tell.

An inquiry to the head of the St. Rose Convent after Walker's death revealed that the archives were closed and no update could be shared. Walker believed that they had never intended the book to be published but consented to her authorship as the last wish of a beloved nun, knowing they could void the contract since Sister Thea's death was imminent. In any case, her hunch had been correct: the Catholic Church preferred that any interpretation of Sister Thea's life remain under the control of the Catholic Church. She wondered if Sister Thea had become too ill to say all that she wanted. Was there a "tell-all" story waiting to be shared that Walker simply didn't get? In 1991, a collection of Thea's speeches appeared, edited by Christina Koontz, RSM. In 2009, Father Maurice Nutt, active in the Black Catholic Clergy Movement, published a collection of Thea's writing, *In My Own Words*. Although no autobiography appeared, a biography *Thea's Song: The Life of Sister Thea Bowman* finally did.[30] The part of the story that Sister Thea was able to transmit remains in Walker's papers, just as the story that Sister Thea may have wanted to tell she took with her to the grave. Walker felt an obligation to share what she had learned. In her eighth decade, however, she was not prepared for another lengthy court battle. She had experienced enough in her publishing life to realize that while Sister Thea had given her the authority to tell the story, the law did not.

Writing the biographies of two women, Rosa Parks and Sister Thea Bowman, was directly related to Walker's views about the way women's lives, no matter how well received or acclaimed, remained hidden. Their public selves were simply taken for granted. Despite an expanding market for Black women writers, autobiographies and biographies of Black women were rare. She told herself that if she'd completed one biography, and having learned from the difficulties, she could certainly do more. She understood the need to honor the larger roles that women played in society, roles that could be too easily lost. These projects were further testaments to Walker's radicalism, which surfaced at critical moments to guide her. She always held views that were ahead of her time, even if she did not have the ability or level of access to make them visible. What mattered was laying a seed for important work to come.

Interest in Rosa Parks grew as the Civil Rights Movement became part of both the symbolic and written history of the United States. Parks, regarded as the "Mother of the Civil Rights Movement," became more popular in death than she was in life when books and biographies about her began to appear. Sister Thea, in the hands of the Catholic Church, was given saint-like status, even if certain truths about her life were never revealed. Another side of this equation

Walker only referred to indirectly: that women of historical or literary significance, if they were remembered at all, were known more for their personality
than their work. The well-known example of Zora Neale Hurston, which Walker
used often, would also apply to Walker herself in time.

By late spring, Walker had nearly completed the preparations for her seventy-
fifth birthday celebration. Not only had she done all the planning for the event
herself, she also oversaw the landscaping of her backyard. Of the 300 invitations
sent to people all over the United States, more than half would attend. The media
was already alerted in anticipation of the large number of out-of-town guests.
Whatever Walker lacked in public recognition in those areas where she had no
control, she made sure to make up for in areas where she did. Her children responded in kind with a plan to give her a gift that fit their mother's stature: a
diamond ring. Her wish list was to have, by the end of the party, the plan for the
golden anniversary celebration of *For My People*, two years away. She had already
spoken to Doris O. Ginn about coordinating an international conference on
Black Women Writers, the last event she planned to co-host at Jackson State. Her
career as a poet had seen its last publication; now she needed a fitting close to her
academic career. She was not surprised, even if she appeared to be, when invited
to the state capital to receive the Margaret Walker Alexander Day proclamation
from Governor Ray Mabus and his wife.

Walker lobbying with lawmakers on Capitol Hill . From left to right: JSU President
James A. Hefner, Mike Parker (MS), Joseph P. Kennedy, II (MA), Walker, David
Dreier (CA). Photograph by Roy Lewis

But one event Walker did have a major hand in planning. By late spring, Walker had gotten word that the request for a hearing before the Committee on the Appropriations Bill for the Research Center to be held in Jackson had been granted. The parts of a much larger agenda were coming together. Thus, while the seventy-fifth birthday was a celebration, it would come following the scheduled hearing. The energy that seemed to be self-generating for Walker. She made every event to which she was invited between Easter and her birthday, July 7. But nothing could compare to her excitement about the forthcoming hearing.

Mike Parker, at the time a Democrat, and Thad Cochran, long-serving Republican US Senator, had introduced HR 3252 and S 1678 respectively as sponsors for legislation to "provide for the establishment of the Margaret Walker Alexander National African American Research Center." The pressure to get action on the bill had been building for some time, and Walker was determined to move it forward. She had welcomed Harrison's proposal for a national research center, seeing it as reward for all of her work and a vindication of all of those who ignored or scorned her. Having two principal supporters was the strategy they hoped would ensure the passage of the legislation. The meeting would be held at Jackson State University, Jackson, MS on June 29, 1990, one week before her seventy-fifth birthday, giving enough time to prepare an announcement, if there were a positive one, and to thank those who had worked so diligently.

Lobbying for the hearing to be held in Jackson gave Walker what she believed was the home court advantage. The bill had been forwarded to the Subcommittee on Postsecondary Education, chaired by Pat Williams of Montana, who consented on behalf of the committee. Walker was convinced that a foremost exquisite display of her Southern hospitality could go a long way in persuading the committee toward approval. Since it was the weekend before the July 4 holiday, most of the subcommittee members were absent, but Chairman Williams gave his full attention to the hearing. Walker's extensive preparations were not wasted. Parker, who had served as the state's official host, said as the hearing began, "We want the testimony to be somewhat lively because we are about to go to sleep we have eaten so much for lunch."[31]

What she considered a major political event for the state was also a teachable moment for the Jackson community, who provided a full audience of attendees. The protocol for the hearing recognized all public officials who were present, which gave Mike Espy, in his third term as US Representative for Mississippi's Second Congressional District, a chance to provide more context for the occasion. He contrasted the huge amounts of funding on defense with the amount spent on education in an appeal that emphasized the need to preserve history for all Mississippians, not just African Americans. Espy drew on global events to support his argument, reminding those gathered that "so much of the history that reshaped our region and our nation and which inspires the people currently in Eastern Europe, South Africa and all around the world, remains unpreserved, and that is exactly why we are here today."[32] Chairman Williams detailed the long history of civil rights in the United States in his opening statement, citing the Declaration of Independence, Abraham Lincoln, Emancipation, and legislation from 1948 through 1967. Referencing the murders of civil rights workers, and especially Medgar Evers, he reminded those convened that "the eyes of the Nation turned here to this city. That tragedy . . . a turning point in the march across America . . . brought both white and black into the civil rights effort."[33]

Walker had identified fifteen individuals who submitted written statements, six of whom were present to give their testimonies. Each referred to her singular importance. "The twentieth century is her century, her peer and her protégé," Ruby Dee said as the first to speak, bringing a rousing applause following her reading of "For My People." The succession of accolades to Walker and the rhetorical excellence of those speaking generated such a response from the audience that Chairman Williams, realizing how little control he would have going forward, suspended the rules of the House, allowing people to continue their public displays of enthusiasm. The hearing was intended to persuade, but it was also a form of witnessing as each person spoke passionately about a world they knew intimately. In addition to Ruby Dee, prepared statements came from the historian Lerone Bennet, NAACP state president Aaron Henry, arts educator Curtis King, Morehouse College President Emeritus Hugh Gloster, Jackson State University student government former president Marcus Dilworth, and Alcorn State University president Walter Washington. Walker had also gathered statements from the state's leading officials, Arts Commissioner Jane Hiatt and State Archives and History Director Elbert Hilliard, along with the Center's board chair Dr. Robert Smith and Director Harrison. Jackson State's president James Hefner joined other notables from the state: Humanities Council Director Cora Norman, Higher Education Commissioner Ray Cleere, and former Governor William Winter.

Harrison provided the strongest appeal for the uniqueness of the proposed Center, by contrasting the idea of history of famous individuals with the history of everyday people. Records pertaining to the lives of African Americans in Mississippi and the South were endangered, and Harrison, well known for her oral history work, emphasized that an important untold story was from "those who stayed." She pointed to the value of modern technology in the interpretation of the African American experience, the need to computerize everything for ease of retrieval, and the importance of historic preservation at the time. Cora Norman cited hard facts: Mississippi as the state with the largest Black population, the state's contribution to United States culture, and the economic incentive that a research center would bring.

As expected, the request for $8 million, which was the price tag affixed to the bill, was a huge ask, which the presentations repeatedly addressed. As important was the need to argue for efficacy of Jackson State over the Martin Luther King Center in Atlanta. Chairman Williams channeled these and other questions to all of the presenters. In response, Walker referred to Mississippi as the "bedrock of African American culture . . . its 'climate for genius,'" along with the contrast between its image as the worst racist state in the union and the significant political advances that outstripped any other state in the union. Consistent with her earlier comments, Harrison emphasized the difference between looking at the age of segregation and civil rights as a whole, rather than looking at individual pieces of history, as was possible with the Mississippi legacy. Both Governor Winter and Ray Cleere pledged their support to the Center, commenting on the national and international significance and the collaborative work that was already in process in an effort to direct attention away from the $8 million request.

Cleere tackled the most difficult question, the elephant in the room: whether or not Jackson State was strong enough to complement the establishment of such a center. His two-fold strategy allowed him to compare Jackson State with Kent State as an example of the unknown and known. He then quickly pivoted to Jackson State's transformation as the state's major urban university, which implied an appeal beyond its status as an all-Black institution and the state's commitment. Referring to Jackson as the crucible of history, he focused on its centrality to the Civil Rights Movement, 1963, the killing of Medgar Evers, and the Freedom Summer Voters Registration Project. He presented Jackson as a "city deeply committed to fostering solutions for those problems facing its community as a whole." Jackson, was indeed, he said, "the crossroads of the South."[34]

The hearing had done its job and done it well. There was enthusiasm, even with all the expressed doubts. Walker was confident that the legislation would pass, but she was new to the political process, and the passage of the bill, if it were to happen, would require much more time and effort. She quickly went into lobbying mode and made at least one trip to Washington following the Jackson hearing. As reported in her journal, she went to the Senate building three days in a row. On the third day, clad in a dazzling brocade dress, matching hat, purse, and gloves, she met with Jackson State's president James Hefner; Mike Parker; Representative Joe Kennedy, Democrat from Massachusetts; and Representative David Brier, Republican from California. The photograph from that meeting tells the story. Walker is in the middle, giving instructions to the four men who are listening intently. Huddled together, Walker, pencil in hand, is going over the strategy, her presence one that cannot be ignored. Parker, who appears more confident in the picture, would introduce the bill four times, every other year between 1989 and 1995, shuttling it through the subcommittees to which it was referred in each case. Cochran would also introduce the bill before the Senate on three occasions, 1989, 1991, and 1995.

Reading the transcript of the hearing years later reveals its larger importance. The effort to get it passed had become a ritual that demanded allegiance. Walker never admitted failure. Her success was in constructing the map and following the path wherever it took her. While the Center had mushroomed into a living testimonial, its existence had never depended upon the congressional appropriation. Like many of her projects, her ideas were ahead of the times, which meant, in this case, that funding from the government to position Black people in advance of the rest of the nation stood little chance of succeeding. What she had succeeded in doing was perhaps more valuable: putting Mississippi on the political map in a new way. The Senate and the House of Representatives were confronted with testimony about a place in the South that looked to the future, one that had risen like a phoenix from the ashes of an old South and was determined to serve as the foundation for a new South. What the hearing had done was to lay the groundwork for what could happen to ensure that the twentieth century was Walker's century, and the city of Jackson, the crossroads of the South.

31

Reaping the Whirlwind

Not acknowledging failure Walker saw as one of her greatest strengths. She remained optimistic about the Center and Mississippi's future, even if the nation seemed to be headed toward a reckoning. What she would acknowledge were her many successes. And even though she refused to allow Mississippi to forget its past, the state and its people saw her as one of its three most important women, especially in the arts. Eudora Welty, Thalia Mara, and Margaret Walker all held firmly to a belief in the state's ability to right horrible wrongs as it continued to display the full measure of its genius. That belief drove Walker's need for more direct ways to have an impact.

She observed three things. First, a civil rights agenda sustained a powerful presence in the state and in the nation, but had become more decentralized and dispersed. Second, civil rights was connected directly to equal rights, reflected, for example, in the passage of the American Disabilities Act in 1990, one year before the passage of the Civil Rights Act, which solidified provisions of the 1964 legislation. Third was the election of William Jefferson "Bill" Clinton as president in 1992, which brought renewed interest in the South. Clinton seemed to give the perception of unity between the Black and white South. At least, racial differences appeared to be minimized, making it easier to forget the high human cost of real progress.

Clinton had been in office only one month before the bombing of the World Trade Center by Islamic extremists, a sign of more trouble to come. But the major difference for Walker was her heightened awareness of major changes in higher education. She felt even closer to Jackson State, in part because she watched too many HBCUs enter a state of decline as the enrollments of Black students increased at PWIs, just as a new generation of Black faculty would choose careers there. Even if she had predicted and helped to orchestrate a new world being born, it was a world in which she did not always feel welcome.

She was getting older, continuing to travel by car, convinced that air travel was inconvenient and unreliable. Leaving home was only offset by the joy of returning. What changed during the early 1990s was her relationship to those beyond Mississippi. Those who sought her advice no longer saw a distinction between HBCUs and PWIs. Walker's knowledge and experience were what they were after.

The House Where My Soul Lives. Maryemma Graham, Oxford University Press. © Oxford University Press 2022.
DOI: 10.1093/oso/9780195341232.003.0031

Acklyn Lynch, a specialist in African American Studies, and photographer Roland Freeman meet at Walker's home. Courtesy of Roland Freeman

Walker elected to do a press conference in front of the City Hall, built by enslaved people. Courtesy of Robert Townsend Jones

Infrequent visits to New York kept Walker from making any traction in a continually changing publishing industry. She talked about and prayed over the books she hoped to finish as the number kept growing. A list from the early 1990s that appeared in her journal restored all of the unfinished projects and included new ones:

> To finish writing—
>> Sister Thea: God touched my life
>> Jesse Jackson—Black Man of Destiny
>> My Black-Eyed Susan School
>> Sistah Mamah, the story of sex and black religion
>> Minna and Jim—a sequel to *Jubilee*
>> I am Cassandra—My Life and Times
> Minor works are—
>> Southern Cooking—Black Cuisine, Creole, Cajun and Native American
>> Vietnam, Black Nationalism, and 3 decades: "My Knees in the Rice Paddies"
>> Rip-off *Roots* Style—My Big Black Brother
>> The Personality of Jesus—History in our world today[1]

Sometimes she'd add two more, "Mother Beulah" and "Anthology of African American literature." The wish list was Walker's way of countering her "dry" spell with desired productivity, not actual practice. Nevertheless, the list shows how wide-ranging her interests were at a time when she was no longer actively working, and without any domestic responsibilities. There was no room in her world for someone without ambition, and she would assert that to herself and others. In reality, she was drained of energy, regaining enough to give another lecture, only to discover that her body took more and more time to restore.

None of these books materialized, except for several manuscript versions of her unfinished autobiography. Instead, she agreed that a collection of her essays and talks given over the years would familiarize a younger generation with her work. The manuscript was easily compiled since Mrs. Currie had typed all of them and a few had previously appeared in print. Two projects were planned as she identified four theme essays: "How I Wrote *Jubilee*," "On Being, Female, Black and Free," "Mississippi and the Nation," and "Revolution and the University." While these themes did not define all she had talked and written about, they provided the scaffolding for two more books that were published during her lifetime. Since "How I Wrote *Jubilee*" had appeared as a pamphlet, it became the title essay for the first collection of her selected writings.

What really preoccupied Walker was watching the future of the Margaret Walker Alexander Center—the name it officially claimed—unfold, and talking with Harrison about her vision. Important to these discussions was the Center's placement within the larger network of repositories. Walker could boast that Howard University's Moorland Spingarn Collection had more money and prestige and was in the nation's capital. She admitted that the most important component of its success was Dorothy Porter Wesley, whose four decades as the librarian at Howard had resulted in the major transformations of its collection. There was New York's Schomburg Center for Research in Black Culture, part of the New York Public Library System, in the middle of the Negro capital of the world, which guaranteed its success. She knew the Schomburg legacy, from Lawrence Reddick, Jean Blackwell Hudson, Ernest Kaiser, to Howard Dotson. What Howard University, the Schomburg Center, and Margaret Walker Alexander Center had in common were their foundational collections. Arturo Schomburg was a bibliophile whose personal collection had been transferred to the New York Public Library, just as Howard had acquired the private libraries of Jesse Edward Moorland and Arthur Spingarn. She wanted to see Jackson State, with her papers, become the only Southern Black institution with such a distinction. Regular conversations with Doris Saunders helped her to see legacy in terms of an extended life in print.

The Center became an expanded image in Walker's mind. It would be her way of conquering her inside world, the one spelled out in her journals, where she bared her soul. The more she wrote, the more as she saw the Center as belonging to others. The Center was the public version of her autobiography, even if she didn't finish the personal version. Everything she'd written and all that remained unpublished would be in the repository, thoughts of which were uppermost in her mind. She thought about herself and her generation of writers, many of them poets, and felt an even stronger obligation to share the world that had made them, and that they had in turn remade. What would happen to Frank Marshall Davis, Melvin Tolson, Owen Dodson, Dudley Randall, Margaret Danner, Robert Hayden, Bruce McMarion Wright, Myron O'Higgins, and others whose careers were established after 1935 and before 1960, she did not know. They were all poets "between worlds," as R. Baxter Miller called them, emerging after the Harlem Renaissance and before the Black Arts Movement, whose lives were directly impacted by World War I, World War II, and the Korean War. There was only one publication that treated the cohort as a whole, and it was her essay that had appeared in *Phylon* in 1950. She felt the burden of preservation not only for herself but for others. The average person looking at the period could call up only a few names, Richard Wright, Ralph Ellison, James Baldwin, and Gwendolyn Brooks. If Wright had become the most recognized Black writer before 1945, Gwendolyn Brooks took up that mantle for Black poetry by 1950. Ellison and Baldwin were the only other names that might come up. Too many saw that generation's identity with a sense of indeterminacy. In contrast, she was determined that it not be lost.

Once Walker completed the agreement concerning the transfer of her papers to Jackson State, they waited on the federal appropriations, trying different angles. If legislation were approved, it would be icing on the cake. Her success lay in the vision she provided, one that continued to guide the process. She made specific stipulations, which were included in the transfer memorandum: the new center would develop goals and aims, maintain a professional archivist, and meet all the standard preservation requirements. Ayer Hall was the oldest, most historic building on campus. As the campus landmark, it was centrally located. A redesign of the three floors would make possible space for a repository for current and future collections and a museum that would showcase exhibits. Eventually it would display Walker's writing desk, her typewriter, and some of her apparel, especially her hats. Areas for offices, visitor reception, and a full reading room completed the renovation. Jackson State was committed to the continued growth of the Margaret Walker Alexander Center as part of its research initiative as a public university.

She was satisfied with the arrangement, which freed her up to read more for pleasure and watching television. Keeping incredibly detailed journal entries served her well, especially as she watched the developments leading up to and following the Anita Hill–Clarence Thomas hearings. A certain amount of transference would have been hard to deny, whether Walker admitted it or not, since Thomas was married to a white woman, and was publicly denouncing the Black woman who worked for him and had accused him of sexual harassment. The proceedings provided Walker with an opportunity to make a larger point about the state of late twentieth-century America. While she had been very deliberate in cultivating an analysis of gender relations that worked for her, she found a meaningful convergence in what she believed was America's descent into fascism. The result was a fuller understanding of the complementarity of race, gender, and class.

> Fascist means forced government by the strong, powerful, big money, and big guns. Sexist means a disregard for the rights of women's labor and sex for male purposes, placing women on a lower salary scale than men for the same work, and most of all, male chauvinists exploiting or using sex to dominate the lives of women.[2]

Watching the television spectacle demanded written commentary. A sense of moral outrage combined with her distaste for "not-so-subtle pornography. Family, church, and school kit-and-caboodle seem nastily exposed in the whole spectrum to our appalled viewing."[3] For Walker, the display of America's new buppie culture (Black, upwardly mobile, and conservative) confirmed the ultra-corrupt nature society, one based on a drug empire, drug-related crime within a fascist state, and, she added, "the world plague of sexually transmitted AIDS."[4]

She began writing one of her strongest critiques of America's political culture during the Hill-Thomas hearings. The essay would be included in *African American Women Speak Out on Anita Hill–Clarence Thomas,* edited by Geneva Smitherman and published by Wayne State University in 1995. Written in the wake of the reviews of *Daemonic Genius,* Walker could easily transfer anger that came from those reviews on to her analysis in "Whose 'Boy' Is This?"

She initially framed Clarence Thomas and Anita Hill as two people impacted by America's corrupt society, its "sexual and monetary reality." Her explanation was consistent with her Judeo-Christian sensibility:

> In our biblical morality lies are as big a sin as adultery—if not as big as blasphemy—against the Holy Spirit. Who is as pure as the driven snow in this case? Do they know what they are saying about each other, and about themselves? Psychologically, is he really a sadist and she a masochist? Is he mad . . . because he is black and both white and black men have abused him because of color? Does she look around her and see herself mirrored in all the dozens of black women whom black men have used and then married white women? What's going on here? Whether they are telling the truth or lying, they have allowed themselves to be trashed on television before the nation, and the mark of Cain is on their heads.[5]

She was expressing views held by many, especially as she presented both Thomas and Hill as complicit in a process driven by sexist and racist standards.

Finding this a useful way to respond to some of the critics of the Wright book may have contributed to the clarity of her analysis of Hill and Thomas. The charge by Thomas's wife that Hill was in love with her husband and wanted to marry him, for example, would have struck a familiar enough chord. Thinking of the accusations of those who called her Wright biography the work of a scorned woman, she wrote, "Why would a woman like Anita Hill—good-looking well educated, holding a substantial position—want to marry that man?" Walker considered the snide remark as punishment for Hill's speaking out and noted, that if the remark were true, then Hill would have been out of her "cotton-picking (or wool gathering) mind to marry any such creature, snail, worm, caterpillar, or crocodile! Then perhaps you say it is all sexual and racial jealousy of a scorned woman,"[6] she concluded. In the end, the "two buppies," as she referred to them, conservative Republicans, were both tainted by their relationship to the changing culture. Unlike most of the criticism during the period, Walker did not take sides. She identified Thomas and Hill in clear ways: Thomas had placed himself on the side of a system that abused and misused Black people, while Hill became a victim by playing into the system and getting burned. In short, she should have known better. The same could have been said of Walker, who knowing the system, should have had no illusions when she challenged it. And yet, in both the Alex Haley and Ellen Wright cases, she had come out with her integrity intact, or so she believed.

In retrospect, Walker's essay seems to be an effort to regain the public's trust. She might not convince people that her decisions had been correct regarding her suit against Alex Haley and writing a book about Richard Wright, but people could believe her analysis of the various ingredients of racism as they became compounded in an increasingly conservative political era. She was also working out in her mind a way to understand a new generation, where black and white lines were not so easily drawn. Coming at the end of her publishing life, Walker took on a distinctive voice of a twentieth-century thinker, as many would refer to her later. While she might not have had the level of access as many others, her loyalty was to the masses of people, not the elite leadership, regardless of whether they were Black or white. The essay demonstrated her ability to bring together what often seemed opposite poles, religion and politics in a purposeful language, something she had a great deal of experience doing. With her old-fashioned moralizing, and her sophisticated knowledge of race, class, and power dynamics, she could expose the architecture that was now holding America together. "Whose 'Boy' Is This?" was her vehicle, with its startling example of Clarence Thomas and Anita Hill, in an effort to explain "How we got to this place."

The essay offered an understanding of political history, not widely known outside of those for whom it was a formal study. She considered a critical moment to be 1946, for example, with Richard Nixon's defeat of Helen Gahagan Douglas, in one of the nastiest displays of sexist campaign rhetoric. Walker had followed Douglas's career, a former actress, who had become politicized. Once becoming a New Deal Democrat, Douglas had served on the advisory committee for the WPA and the National Youth Administration and was a familiar name to Walker. Mapping the path toward fascism, Walker identified early what she calls the "fringe of extremist hate groups such as the John Birch Society, the Ku Klux Klan, the neo-Nazis, the Americans for the Preservation of the White Race, the military-paramilitary American First, and the Skin Heads [who] began to rear their ugly racist and fascist heads in the Republican Party."[7] Linking together Richard Nixon, Ronald Reagan, and George Bush, she drew this conclusion:

> In these minds, black liberal, and leftist Democrats are dirty words. . . . Nixon had the "plan," Reagan had the revolution, and George Bush brought his

operation as head of the CIA to form the basis of his foreign policy. All of the scandals of Watergate, the Iran-contra affair, the sale of American land and industry to Japan, the breaking of the back of American unionized labor with the aid of the Mafia and the stockpile building of armaments while downgrading education, health, welfare, and the domestic infrastructure. This is how we got to this place.[8]

Since the essay was written before the 1992 presidential election, her views of American politics represent more than a tongue-in-check foreshadowing, especially her conclusion that "what the society has been breeding for twenty-eight years. . . . We have sown the wind. How can we escape reaping the whirlwind?"[9]

Walker was probably more obsessive in her writing than usual following this essay, as if recognizing that time was running out. In rapid succession, she completed a sixteen-page essay "Life and Legacy of Horace Cayton," although there is no indication of its publication. It paralleled "How I Wrote *Jubilee*," except the focus was on the birth and writing of *Daemonic Genius*. She recounts Cayton's life as a research scholar who wrote labor and social history, and was a community leader, race relations expert, and journalist. She then discussed Cayton's work on Wright's biography and the conditions that gave rise to her taking over the project after Cayton's untimely death. The death of St. Clair Drake may have prompted the essay, since it had been he who had asked her to write a brief statement for Cayton's memorial service more than a decade earlier. With the publication of the Wright book, one door in her life was closing. She would have felt indebted to Cayton and wanted to leave a longer public statement about their relationship and the evolution of the Wright biography. She remembered the two words she used in her earlier memorial piece, "passion" and "ambition." She concluded her tribute with a statement of respect for Cayton:

> I hope the Richard Wright book is a symbol of Horace Cayton's legacy. He felt that Richard Wright made a profound impact on his life. I used the Cayton file for information, for notes and/or documentation. Cayton's sociological research was a prime basis not only for Richard Wright's *12 Million Black Voices* and for *Daemonic Genius*. It is the sociological backbone of the Chicago School of Social Protest of the 1930s. . . . Horace Cayton had an insatiable passion for living and an overwhelming ambition to succeed.[10]

The essay confirmed Walker's particular method of engagement with biographical writing. While the ostensible reason for the essay was Cayton, the narrative is a kind of quilt whose pieces derive from history, her own experience, primary sources, and scholarly texts. The result is an embedded narrative with Walker's experience as the visible, acknowledged thread that holds all the parts together. She had used the approach in the Wright book, one that few under-stood and therefore criticized.

In 1992, Walker showed no indication of slowing down, and had it not been for the change in her journal handwriting, it would have been impossible for an-yone to recognize signs of her declining health. Because no one saw her journal, any accompanying changes to her body went unnoticed. Even if they had, 1992 was too important an anniversary year for her to allow any distractions, medical or otherwise. She began the year looking forward to Mardi Gras in New Orleans and visiting with her siblings. In June, she packed for a Nashville trip, agreeing to it only because the invitation had come from James Hefner, Jackson State's former president. She gave a master class in poetry at Tennessee State University, spoke on *Jubilee* at Vanderbilt and Fisk Universities, and even had time for a bridge game with her former bridge partner, Mrs. Hefner.

Returning home from Nashville, she had what appeared to be a stroke that required her to spend twenty-four days in the hospital. She described it as a "slight stroke in the cerebellum,"[11] and it left her nearly incapacitated once she was home. Her speedy recovery—in time for her seventy-seventh birthday in a few weeks—did not suggest that she made any real adjustments to her life. It was not the first time, however. She had noted in her journal that she may have had an earlier episode that April when she lost equilibrium and could not walk un-assisted. Because the Governor's Excellence in the Arts Award was to take place on the next day, and the lifetime achievement award from the College Language Association soon after, she ignored any preliminary warnings. On that night in April, she spoke with *Silent Unity* and surrendered to God, reminding him, "Every time I think I'm going to get some serious writing done, I get sick. Please God help me."[12] Whether she had to rely on theological or metaphysical princi-ples, she found the justification and the strength she needed to keep going.

Generally speaking, Walker was in a good place as she felt herself slowing down. She had the freedom to accept or decline invitations to speak and a host of other reasons to keep going. One of the invitations she did accept several weeks after her birthday was speaking at the Biennial Boule of the Alpha Kappa Alpha sorority in Washington DC. Although she had not always been among its most active members, she was one of its most distinguished. She appreciated the Golden Soror Award for Excellence, but reading "For My People" before 10,000 Black women followed by a standing ovation represented the greater symbol of her importance, an experience rare for any poet.

The experience doubled her excitement as she left Washington and traveled to New York for a round of festivities. The planning for the golden anniversary of *For My People* was accompanied by a new book project in honor of the milestone event. The title poem had enjoyed a lengthy history, both inside and outside the collection in which it first appeared. Five decades later, the iconic status that the poem had reached was symbolized by its elevation as a material object. Elizabeth Catlett provided five lithographs to illustrate the poem's ten stanzas.

The project had symbolism beyond the publication itself. The two women who had met each other as graduate students became artists whose bond was both generational and aesthetic. The project reflected the coalescing of their successful careers, as much as it was a model for the production of art in a highly revered space. Limited Editions Club published 400 copies of the oversized volume that measured 18 × 22½", each autographed by both authors and listed at $1,500. The catalog described the "beautiful and striking" images that borrow "from the African American tradition of using form to communicate spirit and purpose." Walker is referred to as "one of the most powerful voices of America." The expert craftsmanship is then detailed, along with the process and the materials used to create the aesthetical powerful work:

> Each of the poem's ten stanzas was hand-set in thirty-point Albertus type, a sans-serif face that looks as if chiseled from granite and printed letterpress on French-made Arches cover paper, the same paper upon which were printed the Elizabeth Catlett lithographs. The book is bound in imported red Japanese line over heavy board, the box is covered in black cotton.[13]

The price was not intended to attract a large consumer audience. But Walker and others understood that no price could have been placed on the value of the poem or its status as a symbol of cultural memory. An invitation-only book party followed the release of the book in New York that September. Florence Howe had helped to organize the event, giving her a chance to secure a commitment from Walker for her second essay collection bearing the title *On Being Female, Black, and Free.* The effort to bring that manuscript to completion was more than Walker could handle, and the book eventually appeared the year before her death. There was a certain irony for the woman who had found it difficult to digest feminism as it was emerging, who refused to call herself a feminist, now to have the Feminist Press publish what would become one of her most widely circulating works. The difference between the early and late Walker was context. She was impressed with Florence Howe, founding editor of Feminist Press, and with the anniversary celebration, both of which resolved any contradictory feelings. The time had come when she no longer felt undervalued. Those who reached out to her were honoring her as the woman who had honored her people. She could now see the power in what she had done and take pride in the legacy that it had inspired.

The Washington and New York events were important, but for Walker, it was the Jackson community celebration she considered most amazing. Roland Freeman had published a volume in her honor with a collection of

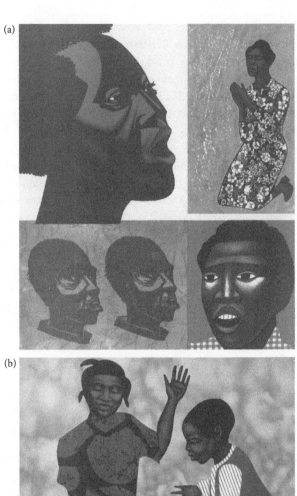

(a)

(b)

Selected lithographs by Elizabeth Catlett, *For My People* by
Limited Editions Club

his photographs. *Margaret Walker's "For My People": A Tribute* was part of the Jackson celebration, complete with a book-release party and exhibit.

Just as she had always done, Walker wanted to mark this event with a conference, one she had begun planning several years earlier. The visionary idea that emerged, "An International Conference on Black Women of Magic Realism" was again the first conference of its kind that centered women in a discourse that had largely excluded them. Walker was preparing to start a different kind of critical conversation about the nature of Black women's writing. Doris O. Ginn, who had joined the JSU's English Department, served the conference director. While the conference did not have the energy or the large attendance of the Wheatley Festival two decades earlier, Ginn was determined to make it a fitting conclusion to the professional career for a woman who could be difficult to please if she were not in charge. The five-day event was packed with presenters, themed discussion panels, performances, musical events, art exhibits, film showings and communal gatherings with food. The Phillis Wheatley conference had told America "this is who we are." But "Black Women Writers of Magic Realism," was a referendum on Black women that said "this is where we are now." It was the ultimate opportunity to see the larger house that had served as a metaphor for her life. She was indeed in the last room where her soul would continue to live. Her professional "family" was in attendance as expected: Howard Dodson, Margaret

Celebrating the golden anniversary of *For My People* ("International Conference on Black Women Writers of Magic Realism") and Exhibit Tribute, 1992. Courtesy of Roland Freeman

Burroughs, Jessie Carney Smith, Florence Howe, Ida Lewis, Doris Saunders, Haki Madhubuti, Eugene Redmond, Mari Evans, Ruby Dee, Ossie Davis, Ed Bullins, Roland Freeman, Maya Angelou, Eleanor Traylor, Ruthe Sheffey, Joyce Ann Joyce, Beverly Guy Sheftall, Ann Julia Cooper, Bettye Parker Smith, Alma Freeman, Acklyn Lynch, Jerry Ward, Floyd Coleman, Dilla Buckner, Regine La Torture and Ester Rolle were joined by newer friends Buchi Emecheta and Tess Onwueme. These were her people whose worlds she had shaped as much as they had shaped hers, who represented the best of "the African American tradition of using form to communicate spirit and purpose."[14] The Jackson event was a chance for Walker to unwind, even though the negative publicity from the Wright book followed her. Ginn saw the woman who had been her mentor in rare form. She knew that the event had been successful because it showed us "one of Walker's best qualities . . . [the] ability to laugh at herself."[15]

Both exhilarated and fatigued, Walker finally consented to spending more time in Chicago, although she was determined not to move from her Jackson home. On one of her return visits to Chicago, Margaret Burroughs invited Walker and Gwendolyn Brooks to share a dialogue during a symposium on the Black Chicago Renaissance at the DuSable Museum. Those who may have believed Walker to be envious of Brooks's literary career and fame following Brooks's receipt of the Pulitzer Prize noticed no tension between them. The conversation between the two poets was open and honest. Both women recalled their early careers and the importance of Chicago, praising the younger writers who had made the city such a visible place. Carol Adams, DuSable's former CEO, believed that the event was a special moment for both women, who felt at home with each other and with the audience. It was 1993, and whatever differences they might have had, if they existed at all, were behind them. The importance of that event seems even clearer from a distance, since it was the last time the two women who had given as much to the City as it had given them, would share a stage together.

She ended the year in New Orleans, where she received a special tribute from the Modern Language Association during its annual meeting there. Walker, the woman who was so accustomed to planning events, found herself at an event organized in her honor without her knowledge. Arrangements were made for Brother, who had continued to pursue his musical interests after his retirement, to give a surprise piano performance, which Walker had been told was a reception for someone else. She was stunned when she saw him walk in and begin playing. It was her first and only time hearing him playing the music that their parents had forbidden in the household, jazz. The siblings united in the absence of parents, acknowledged each other, recognizing perhaps that they found something more important than Marion's approval: a time to take what she had given them and make it their own.

For My People, Golden Anniversary Program, 1992

32

Call Me Cassandra

The Alexander family could no longer ignore the signs of decline. They had become concerned for their mother's health, combining their observations in late 1992. Whether or not Walker was aware that she had not fully recovered from the stroke in Nashville, she continued her usual practice. Her steady and well-formed cursive handwriting, however, was becoming less legible, and for the compulsive writer that she was, the task became more onerous each day. Her journal entries were uneven, often shorter, and more frequently out of chronological order. She was not yet ready to lay down her pen and seemed to gain renewed interest as she began a new journal, one that she'd been saving, as if to realize it would be her last. She had received it on her seventy-fifth birthday and taken care to label it, "given to Margaret Walker Alexander by Bettye Parker Smith July 7, 1990."[1] The new journal helped to finally convince her to focus on the autobiography in earnest. The early writing in the journal shows a feeble hand, but quickly transitions into recurring periods of steady, lengthy sections of prose. On these occasions, the writing is clear and her thoughts showed their characteristic distinctiveness.

A renewal of energy from the *For My People* celebrations, and the thought of a second essay collection, "On Being Female, Black, and Free," now under contract with Feminist Press, led Walker to believe she was never stronger. Near Christmas in 1992, when she was feeling as if she were back to her old self, in an entry following the news about Bosnia, Walker provided one of her classic mini-essays. Her thesis is the spread of segregation throughout the world, using the examples of Bosnia, the Middle East, and Africa. She concludes that "A people's democracy all over the world is dying to be born."[2]

That appeared to have been the last real infusion of energy that she would experience for an extended period. Changes in her habits caused more alarm. That Christmas was the first time she decided not to have her annual Christmas party. She gave as her reason the recent heart attack by Mr. Washington, who had helped her prepare for every dinner party she had given over the years. She started the tedious cutting-up of ingredients for the dozens of fruitcakes she always made but had to put that aside as well. The decision seems also to have been influenced by the diminishing royalty checks. The June check from sales of *Jubilee*, which she usually set aside for the holiday purchases, had been only $200. Nor was she as prompt in responding to invitations. The one to attend the inauguration of Bill Clinton that came at the end of December received no response

The House Where My Soul Lives. Maryemma Graham, Oxford University Press. © Oxford University Press 2022.
DOI: 10.1093/oso/9780195341232.003.0032

MARGARET WALKER ALEXANDER

THIS
IS MY
CENTURY

100
years
—— of ——
Margaret
Walker
Alexander
1915 - 2015

Artist, Brandon Thompson

at all. It was simply easier to stay in Chicago through the holidays, splitting her time between Marion and Margaret.

A discussion with Charles Harris had ended with her promise to send him 100 pages of the autobiography. She was excited, but knew that she needed to save her energy in order to write as much and as often as possible. News of the auctioning off of Alex Haley's farm brought several calls from friends and journalists, the latter asking for comments. She refused all but two major conversations with people she had not spoken with earlier. Dick Gregory was one, and Barbara Reynolds was the other, one of few journalists she felt she could trust. Reynolds had published the biography of Jesse Jackson in 1975, one of the books Walker looked at for her model of the form. She and Reynolds had met during the Jackson campaign and were in touch now and again.

The autobiography was uppermost in her mind and as always proceeded with a plan and a protocol. She was preparing her talk, which would be her last published essay, "Race, Gender and the Law," but if indeed she were going to complete an autobiography, it had to be of lasting significance. If *For My People* and *Jubilee* had allowed her to turn history into art, this was a new challenge: how to turn one's lived experience into a compelling narrative. Having seen herself as a plain, ordinary woman, she was fond of saying, she knew that her life was anything but ordinary. The autobiography, therefore, had to be a book to stand for the ages.

For the first few months of 1993, she outlined what she knew, starting with the question, "What is Autobiography?" Her approach was methodical, moving from the particular to the general. "Is all black writing autobiography?" she asked. Her answer listed in order Frederick Douglass as author of the classic slave narrative; three autobiographies of W. E. B. Du Bois, the two published and one unpublished by Langston Hughes; and the autobiographies of Zora Neale Hurston, Maya Angelou, James Weldon Johnson, Richard Wright, Piri Thomas, Claude Brown, and Katherine Dunham. She included criticism on Black autobiography written by James Olney before moving to the longer history. To her list of well-known English autobiographies, those from the Middle Ages and Renaissance, she added Benjamin Franklin's as her only white male American autobiography. The point of the exercise was not only to create the models to review, but also to create a vision to guide her process. She ended the exercise with her reading list of books by and about historical figures she considered important for giving her a range of perspectives: Catherine Peare, Helen Keller's well-known biographer; St. Teresa of Avila; St. Catherine of Siena, *Lives of the Saints*, *The Confessions of St. Augustine*; and Gwendolyn Brooks's *Report from Part One*. The list had to be both inspirational and aspirational in order to feed her ambition and sense of mission. The women who provided the most immediate life models were educators, activists, and national and international figures. Mary

Church Terrell's 1940 autobiography, *A Colored Woman in a White World*, provided Walker with a specific example to follow as she began writing.

She had promised to spend two weeks with Gwen, while Brother was on tour in Europe, but the two weeks without the necessary help with bathing and dressing led to the conclusion, "don't think [I] will go to New Orleans again."[3] When Walker returned to Jackson, she did something she was reluctant but needed to do—turn over to her daughter-in-law Norma most of the responsibility for the meal preparations. It would give her time to work closely with Mrs. Currie, who had agreed to prepare the typed manuscript for the autobiography. Both women were equally clear that this was a last book, just as they knew that working as a team was the only way to get it done.

Alex's birthday, which she continued to celebrate, gave Walker an unusual burst of energy. She took it as a sign that it was the day to commit fully to writing the autobiography. Having his spirit guide the process gave her the assurance she needed. The pre-thinking and pre-writing continued. Her first task was to frame her story and identify its themes. Early notes show what she considered the psychological condition of Black women in America: oppression, stress, anxiety, sexism, racism, and fascism. Five other approaches emerged as a way to frame her thoughts: Greek mythology, twentieth-century American history, war and world revolution, sociology, geography and the physical environment, and a more purely aesthetic approach. She eventually settled on "Call Me Cassandra" after abandoning "The Vision Splendid" as a first title. The preference for mythology was tactical, and the choice of Cassandra rhetorical. Greek mythology was a favorite class she taught at Jackson State, but her firm belief in the African origins of civilization always gave her an opportunity to make her point:

> Before Greek myths were invented, the African myths of creation, death, and the resurrection races of mankind, languages, supergods and their lesser divinities lived in the dust, air, fire, and water of black Egypt, and flourished along the banks of the Nile River some five thousand or more years ago. Since the seed of all literature as well as religion may be found in myth and since such symbols continue to exist through legend, we must look for the beginnings of African American literature in our African past.[4]

That the autobiography of a Black writer could not be divorced from the history of the African American literary tradition made sense. The choice of Cassandra makes clear Walker's understanding of cultural synthesis that produced an African American culture, formed out of European, African, and Indigenous elements in the Americas. It was the kind of story that could draw readers into a web of facts and good storytelling.

"Call Me Cassandra," or "I Am Cassandra" both show up as working titles in her journals, as she tried to tease out the who, what, where, and why of her story. Cassandra, according to Greek mythology, was pursued by Apollo but then rejected him. Whether she had divine powers or were given them by Apollo, his anger over the rejection resulted in a curse. She could see the future and speak the truth, but no one would believe her. It was a perfect fit for Walker, who was a twentieth-century Cassandra, someone with extraordinary abilities and foresight, but whose ideas people often questioned. Her truth telling—especially the Haley suit and the Wright biography—singled her out for ridicule, even when she was later proven to be correct. The strategy allowed for the incorporation of fantastic elements; love, romance, and sex; faith, religion, and loss; those action-packed events that produce all the complexities of womanhood. In other words, Walker understood that the success of the book was based on her truth expressed through skilled storytelling. The anchors of the story soon emerged. She'd begin with herself in an innocent, fantasy world of childhood, surrounded by nature, myth, religion, and poetry. What came next in this version were ongoing encounters with various systems of belief that were often in conflict and the reason for her frequent attacks of anxiety:

The Woods Beyond—
     God above us—angels watching over me, my lewd
          My Mythopoeic World—
          Greeks, Romans, Christian, Myth of Redemption,
          Black Religion of Liberation, My Grandmother's superstitions

Calvinism
     Age of Anxiety—I belong to the Age of Anxiety
Neurosis and Situational Psychosis
Myth—The Seedbed of Religion & Literature

Painful Adolescence—Age 10–20
     Conflict—Nourished by Poetry, Religion,
     History and Music, 1925–1935

On My Own—20–30
     1936–1945
     Finding my way in the world
     Goals, Methods and Results

Love and Marriage—28–65—1943–1980—Early maturity
     Discipline—Work—Family—Church & Commitment

Old Age and the Mortal Sense
        Senior Citizen—Widow (Mortality) 1980 + beyond
        Grandmother—and Creativity
        The Vision Splendid—
        and by the vision splendid is on (her) way attended[5]

While a more detailed typed outline and handwritten, spiralbound notebook version of "Call Me Cassandra" exists, the last lines that she had initially used for the autobiography, "The Vision Splendid," invited ongoing consideration. Her decision to settle on "Call Me Cassandra" provides a useful window into Walker's thinking process. The "Vision Splendid" is a line taken from *Intimations of Immortality* by William Wordsworth, the first poetry learned from her father. He had been trained in the British system in Jamaica, and his library was filled with British writers, which he encouraged her to read. If she wanted to signal that her autobiography was a more formal attempt to connect to an Anglo-American literary tradition, "The Vision Splendid" would have served the purpose. But Walker saw a more diverse range of traditions that informed Black culture, just as they had informed her work and the woman she had become. She was struck by the idea of having power that could not be put to use, a life controlled by others, especially a man. A strong identification with a woman figure who maintained her independence and did not allow her fate to deter her from speaking the truth impressed Walker as exactly the message she wanted to give readers. She had come to the realization that what she shared with other women was not dependent upon ideology. A first attempt at this was the essay "On Being, Female, Black, and Free," but now she would have to dig deeper.

The writing was painstakingly slow, interrupted by the engagements she continued to schedule. The slow pace caused her concern, since the longer she took, the more likely it was that she might become incapacitated, either mentally or physically. She rewrote the outline over and over again, and Mrs. Currie retyped each new version without comment. The repeated outlines suggest that she was still uncertain about the direction that her autobiography would take and how it might fit with the current boom in memoir writing. By June 1993, she had written the first five pages, still a long way from what she had promised Harris.

Fearful of what impact the delay might have, she made a radical move, writing a letter to the William Morris Agency seeking a literary agent. Although Charles Harris had proven himself to be a valuable ally during her ordeal with the Wright book, memories of her experience with Rene Mayfield caused her to pause. And she thought that having someone do the legwork that she might need would be enormously helpful. She knew that she was no longer in a position to do what an agent located in New York could do. There is no evidence of follow-up, and Walker allowed herself to feel grateful with a second Amistad imprint that Harris had negotiated at Warner Books. She also hoped that her autobiography would be a best-seller for Warner, with none of the contentiousness associated with the Wright book. The search for an agent came out of fear, but when she calmed herself, her first priority was loyalty, and at seventy-eight, although money was still a concern, she gave it short shrift.

In the spring, she had been contacted about three major film projects. Mississippi Educational Television was producing a film biography on Richard Wright and had hired filmmaker Madison Davis Lacy to direct it. Lacy, Art Cromwell, and the film crew for *Richard Wright: Black Boy* transformed Walker's home into a set and taped her at length over several days. Walker's appearance on film is strong and forceful. Indeed, it is her powerful testimony that drives the narrative, and she looks larger than life. Although a host of critics appeared in the film, including Constance Webb and Michel Fabre, Walker is the centerpiece. The Wright film crew required three visits and found Walker's capacities diminishing, making a last visit in November 1993. Because they had shot so much footage, they could select the best of Walker to show, allowing her commanding presence to come through. She was eager to have another moment of vindication through the film, establishing herself once and for all as a major Wright critic, which viewers would find difficult to dispute.

Keeping her promise to her children, Walker spent one month in Chicago, but it was the joy she felt in being around four children of various ages that made her eager to return to writing. By the time she returned, Judith McCray of Juneteenth Productions had requested a meeting to explore the possibility of a full-length film biography about her. Finding Walker so frail, she decided to push ahead quickly to produce a shorter thirty-minute introductory film, *For My People: The Life and Writing of Margaret Walker*. McCray, like so many others, was struck by Walker's long-overdue recognition, especially since her work, at least "For My People," was so well known. McCray's visits to Jackson were not as intense as the Wright film project since she could use materials that did not require lengthy interviews. Walker, nevertheless, enjoyed meeting and working with this young Black filmmaker. McCray had made a wise decision, and it remains the only film ever done on Margaret Walker.

The last person who brought a film crew to interview was Walker's longtime friend Mari Evans. Evans had received initial funding to do a film on Black women, which she saw as complementary to her early book, *Black Women Writers*. She was not new to the medium of film, having served as writer, producer, and director of the five-year-long series *The Black Experience* for WTTV Television in Indianapolis. Evans, like McCray, recognized that shooting film footage on Walker needed to be done sooner than later. She moved up their shooting schedule to do Walker first in the series. Ultimately, the project was abandoned for lack of money, but extensive footage on Walker is preserved with Evans's papers in Emory University's archives.

Meanwhile, Harris continued to press for the initial pages of the autobiography, and Walker tried her best to comply. Mrs. Currie reinstituted her system of coming in daily for the few pages that Walker had written and return them quickly, as an inducement for producing more. But Walker couldn't manage to slow down her engagements, either because she needed the money or wanted the recognition, more than likely the former. Every time the writing gathered some steam, she had to stop for an engagement. One from Johnnetta Cole, she accepted, an honorary degree from Spelman awarded on Founders Day in April 1994.

The appearance of a few poems during this period suggests Walker elected to use the little energy she had in writing the autobiography, but that poetry remained her most comfortable form. The poems look over a past life and seem to meander a bit. The longer poem "I know I have lived before" is a collection of sentences all starting with "I." "There were bizarre beginnings" is much stronger, although the "I" lines are still more frequent. The sonnet form gives her more control, however, and the images are at times compelling as she relies on her familiar catalog technique. The past is recalled in the sonnet's first two quatrains, while the response in the final quatrain points to new possibilities, with a sense of uncertainty. Even more uncertain is the speaker of the poem:

> There were bizarre beginnings in old lands for the making of me
> There were sugar sands and island of fern and peal
> Palm jungles and stretches of a never ending sea
> There were wooing nights of tropical lands
> And the cool discretion of flowering plains
> Between two stalwart hills
> They nurtured my coming with wanderlust
> I sucked fevers of adventure through the veins of my mothers' milk
> Someday I shall go to the tropical lands of my birth
> To the coast of continent and the tiny wharves of island shores
> I shall roam the Balkans and the hot lanes of Africa and Asia
> I shall stand on mountain tops and gaze on fertile lands below
> And when I return to Mobile I shall by way of Panama and Bocas del Toro
> The littered streets and the one room shacks of my old poverty
> And blazing suns may struggle then to reconcile
> The pride and the pain in me.[6]

Giving speeches was something Walker could do easily, so accustomed was she to the routine. But the coming and going she found incredibly tiring. Despite her popularity and her age, she refused to give "warmed-over" talks even though it would have been more than acceptable to do so. She wrote and gave entirely new speeches focused on current topics. She had ideas for the last speeches she would give as early as 1992, including a rousing speech at the Mississippi University for Women on "Education and the Global Village," and one on "Race, Gender, and the Law" at the American University Law Symposium in Washington DC. She prepared a seven-page address dated September 1996 for a National Conversation on American Pluralism and Identity, which appeared to have been an NEH-sponsored event. It is uncertain whether she gave the speech since it was never published.

If Walker ever wanted attention, she was getting it during the 1990s. Longtime friend and native Mississippian Roy Lewis presented her with his idea for a planned documentary *Come and Go with Me*, the story of her life in pictures. Jacqueline Miller Carmichael was even more eager to interview her for the dissertation she was completing, the only full-length study of *Jubilee*, which appeared as a book in 1998, the year Walker died. Carmichael had hoped to bring increased attention to the connection between Walker's historical fiction and the growing popularity of the neo-slave narrative. Her book *Trumpeting a Fiery Sound: History and Folklore in Margaret Walker's Jubilee* was published five years after Toni Morrison had won the Nobel Prize, which shifted literary attention toward newer work by Morrison herself and subsequent Black women writers.

Other interviews she gave during the 1990s did not necessarily focus on the work for which she was best known, although it brought her into valuable conversations on emerging issues, like spirituality, the focus of Dilla Buckner's 1995 interview. She agreed to an interview with Studs Terkel for his book *Coming of Age: The Story of Our Century by Those Who Have Lived It*, but it was not included in the final version of the book, which profiled other better-known senior celebrities.

Another unpublished, but revealing, interview was the one she did with Bettye Parker Smith, who had asked her to comment on the *Black Man's Guide to Understanding the Black Woman* by Shahrazad Ali. The book had enraged Black women, including those who did not call themselves feminists. Although the interview was never published, Walker spoke with her usual bluntness, calling it "dangerous [with an] unintelligent premise." She believed, however, that "It is important for us to dialogue about the book, talk about where it is coming from and try to understand why a book like this has surfaced and how sad this whole thing is."[7] She was referring to the sudden popularity that the book had gained as its author appeared on talk shows. That Walker was asked at seventy-eight to comment on a contemporary issue was a clear indication that her beliefs still mattered, and that even as she neared the end of her life, her ideas resonated with people and with contemporary movements. While she realized that others had come to similar conclusions about the book, her words remind us how entrenched Walker's thinking was long after her involvement with the leftist politics of the 1930s. She was no fellow traveler for traveler's sake. Rather she had a

sustained understanding of political systems and power relations as they operated within the United States and the world. And even though her practice and
some of her personal ideas as a woman seemed traditional, when she stepped
outside of that, she drew comfortably on a body of knowledge that brought great
clarity to any subject that she broached. About the Ali book, she concluded:

> This book is a very good example of the enemies we face. In fact, this book
> is one of the best examples I know of reminding us who the enemy is: how it
> lurks around and among us, and why a woman like this would allow herself
> to become the tool of a system and the voice of our own enemy. When I heard
> her talk, I said this sounds like the worst form of fundamentalist Moslem belief
> I have known . . . but I realized and accepted the fact that this is not funda-
> mental Moslem teaching, because true Moslem persons respect their women.
> This book demonstrates that women are not to be respected at all. I do not want
> to use the term which is generally reserved for men, but the word "castration"
> comes to mind when I think of her.[8]

It seems odd that interest in Walker was declining generally, even as poetry
continued to experience a major resurgence after the 1990s. The younger poets
were reaching levels of recognition beyond anything Walker could imagine. The
awarding of the first Pulitzer Prize to a Black poet, Gwendolyn Brooks, in 1950
appeared to be an anomaly. The next Pulitzer was not awarded to an African
American poet until 1987 for Rita Dove's *Thomas and Beulah*. In those thirty-
seven years, Walker was a mainstay in American poetry and enjoyed a successful, if not lucrative, career. Dove's achievement set a new trend, with more
Pulitzers and National Book Awards coming quickly to other Black poets. The
legacy of Black poetry became more identified with these highly visible prestigious awards. The poets from Walker's generation who were seen as influencers
were Brooks and increasingly Robert Hayden, but Walker much less often.

That she was not able to attend the first of a series of poetry events organized
by Joanne Gabbin in 1994 at James Madison University may have been one of the
reasons for Walker's seeming separation from the contemporary poetry movement. Even though the event and those that followed had been inspired by and
bore a striking resemblance to the 1973 Phillis Wheatley Festival, Walker had
hit a major slump that year. Journaling was rare and she seemed to be preoccupied with family and financial matters. Gabbin had become guardian of the
Black poetry legacy by creating the Furious Flower Poetry Center and generating large crowds for poetry. For the first event, she identified a generation of
the "pioneers" and expected Walker to join Brooks and a host of their peers at the
star-studded event that November. Walker's absence was noteworthy and ironic
since she had paid such careful attention to looking at the past and present of
Black poetry. While Walker's Wheatley Festival had identified fewer than thirty

Black women poets in 1973, Furious Flower would organize its celebrations over the next two decades showcasing multiple generations of Black poets and demonstrating the exponential growth of the genre. Yet Gabbin saw Walker often, importantly in 1996, moderating a final interview at the Atlanta Arts Festival. Thus, while Walker had been absent from the conferences, Gabbin made sure her voice was not missing from the subsequent publication, the first volume of *The Furious Flowering of African American Poetry*. In contrast, by the time Cave Canem, a retreat for Black poets to engage in the intense study of poetry was founded, Margaret Walker was a poet of the past, not one that current and future generations of poets would consider a significant influence on their careers. She was, for them, an important legacy.

Following her eightieth birthday in 1995, Margaret Walker threw herself back into writing, even as general public interest in her diminished. She was not particularly concerned about the critical void into which she had fallen. On the contrary, she saw an opportunity; it brought her back to who she was. She enjoyed longer trips to Chicago to visit her children and grandchildren, watched a bit more television, and worked consistently on "Call Me Cassandra." Walker embraced the priestess who had been given the gift of prophecy. In taking the name, she had the framework for connecting her contradictory parts that had always existed: an ancient and modern world, religious and secular views, spiritual and the material realities, and the need to create beauty when surrounded by ugliness. She was at once a rebel and the epitome of tradition.

Walker followed her initial plan of organizing "Call Me Cassandra" around a series of visions that she considered central to her life: literary, religious, and political. She returned to those dreams that had haunted her youth—a blazing white cross in the sky, being left alone by her parents as a child, and grappling with an evil spirit— powerful presence, she believed, calling her to Christian service that was in conflict with the equally strong call she felt to become a writer. These dreams had eventually fulfilled her, because in struggling to contain them, they had been transformed into her life's work. What artist could live without visions and dreams? she wondered. They had made her the artist who she was, someone who learned that hope and courage were necessary to fight pain and suffering.

As her physical dependencies on others increased, Walker enjoyed less and less of the privacy she had grown accustomed to, the time to write alone and uninterrupted. In the last few years of her life, the act of writing something for the public, and shifting away from the privacy of her journals, became increasingly more important. She showed no signs of dementia, however, which made the exercise of her memory more important. With her papers permanently housed at the Margaret Walker Alexander Center, she also understood herself to be an active participant in reconstructing her own life, even as others extracted it from her archives.

Walker did not want to languish in either the relative obscurity or the notoriety that had characterized too much of her life. If *This Is My Century* had been her way of envisioning her life as a symbolic act, "Call Me Cassandra" was a way of translating and naming herself for others while showing her ultimate faith in the process of art. Giving an account of her own life was itself a demonstration of the creative process.

Most people who visited Walker in the final two years of her life saw the autobiography, an incomplete but typed draft that Mrs. Currie had prepared. While her family primarily took responsibility for her personal care, Mrs. Currie kept to the routine they had always followed. She came in more often but for shorter periods, since Walker tired easily. Currie produced freshly typed material, taking anything she saw in spiral notebooks. Her goal was to have Walker see something finished as often as possible, no matter how little she had actually written. Thus, when friends came calling, there was always a fresh copy of the autobiography as a subject of discussion.

Walker's energy level declined rapidly, and the reason why was soon clear. Diagnosed with breast cancer in late 1996, she decided against surgery but agreed to a round of radiation treatments, each one leaving her tired and listless. She was convinced that she would recover, however, because she had confronted so many bleak conditions in her life, from childhood through adulthood; this was just the latest one. She did her best to remain true to her own words:

> I will not darken all my days with bitterness and fear, but lift my heart with faith and hope and dream, as always, of a brighter place.[9]

The radiation burned her skin and eased the discomfort only slightly since it would not eliminate her cancer, which was spreading. She managed the pain with an assortment of medications.

By 1997, however, Walker appeared to be feeling some relief from the radiation treatments. It was probably the invitation she received from Trudier Harris at the University of North Carolina to be a featured guest at a conference that boosted her spirits since there had been no change in her diagnosis. The conference, scheduled for April 1998 and hosted by the George Moses Horton Society for the Study of African American Poetry, was smaller and more focused than the Furious Flower event she had missed. It obviously appealed to her since she did not hesitate to accept the invitation. The three poets who headlined the conference—Rita Dove, Yusef Komunyakaa, and Walker—and its seeming intimacy were big attractions. Moreover, having grown accustomed to the travel route between Jackson and North Carolina, she likely saw an opportunity to visit family, perhaps for the last time. She also had fond memories of Chapel Hill, whose Southern Historical Collection had been so important to *Jubilee*. There was no disagreement among her family members who recognized how important it was for Walker to get the recognition that she deserved.

The Society had been named for an enslaved poet who resided in the Chapel Hill area, and who was reported to have earned extra money by writing poems for students who passed them on as their own. The University of North Carolina Press had also published Joan Sherman's edited collection *The Black Board of North Carolina: George Moses Horton and His Poetry* a year earlier. The opening lecture of the two-day conference was on Horton's significance as a poet, and Walker knew many of the people who would be speaking. The conference also fit Walker's interest in historical excavation.

Although it was an academic conference, the gathering was also a community of scholar-friends, including Jerry Ward, Sally Ann Ferguson, Joyce Pettis, and Joanne Gabbin, who all gave presentations on Walker. Their papers would help to inspire the collection *Fields Watered with Blood: Critical Essays on Margaret Walker*, the first volume of criticism on her work, but which did not appear during her lifetime. Short of that, hearing others dig beneath the surface of her works and find such novel readings, she found exhilarating. Having had to operate from her internal reserves for so much of her life—from that house where her soul lived—she had an urgent need for feedback that did not question her integrity or secondary motives but focused on nothing more than her intellectual and aesthetic achievement. Over the two days, as she met and dined with seasoned and emerging scholars, Walker must have had a glimpse of what might be possible in the future as people continually read her work or were just discovering it for the first time. She felt as if the people for whom she had written were now writing back to her.

It was especially significant for Walker to be in the company of two Pulitzer Prize–winning poets, for although she had not acquired that level of acclaim, she had the longest biography in the conference booklet, "one of the most formidable literary voices to emerge in the 20th century," it read, "[who] remains one of the foremost transcribers of African American heritage."[10] The program biographies were listed alphabetically, which meant that Walker came after Dove and Komunyakaa, but she was featured first. This acknowledgment of status and the longevity of her career within the community mattered. Harris, who chaired the planning committee, remembered the event well:

> Margaret Walker, revered and esteemed elder, was assigned an escort, Lovalerie King, for the duration of her stay. She strutted around the conference in beautiful outfits that often included matching purses, shoes, and hats, including a

vibrant purple. The highlight of her participation in the conference came when she read to a packed house in a theater-style auditorium. As was her custom, just before her reading of "For My People," she stood up in an almost gleeful—though reverential—manner and performed her signature poem. We audience members let her know how thoroughly we appreciated her customary reading as well as her bringing that panoramic portrayal to our hearing.[11]

It would be the last event Walker attended where she was in full control of her faculties. The Internet Poetry Archive includes the panel session and the full concert of readings that she gave. She was at that moment who she had always been—cerebral but accessible and relentlessly Southern. However, the event itself and the drive there and back to Jackson must have taken all she had left. No further journal entries followed and friends who visited Walker in the summer and fall found that she tired easily, but enjoyed entertaining. She did some reading for pleasure and made revisions to her autobiography. Joanne Gabbin remembered her visit to Walker in August that year:

> She was preoccupied with showing me her autobiography which she had almost finished. As ill as she was, she raised herself from the brown leather easy chair that was the focal point of the room and started toward the den where the walls were lined with books and boxes of manuscripts. Knowing that she could not make it there unassisted, Sigis guided her back to the chair. Her will to finish this work was so strong because of her belief in the prophetic role of the writer: to write about that future that you do not see, but that is evident in everything you do and hear. You know what's going to happen tomorrow because the seeds of it are happening today.[12]

Walker had agreed that once she completed the final round of radiation treatments, she would spend some time with Marion and her family in Chicago. As the pain in her breast and shoulder became more acute, she required more medication and grew increasingly more incapacitated. She stopped writing, answering letters, or making phone calls.

While she was in Chicago, Walker did make an unexpected appearance on October 17, 1998, as a special guest at the Gwendolyn Brooks Center for Black Literature and Creative Writing at Chicago State University. Unaware of the extent of her illness, Haki Madhubuti, the Center's director, expected the lively woman he had always known. She was lifted to the stage in her wheelchair, showing signs of limited cognition. Her words were uncertain, slurred, and although a document had been prepared to assist her memory, she was unable to read from it. The moderator began to read on her behalf when Walker suddenly seemed startled when hearing her own words read by another. In an instant, she reclaimed everyone's attention, recited her signature poem with total recall, her voice never more powerful. When she finished, an exuberant crowd gave her a last standing ovation. The significance of this final Chicago reading would not be missed. Margaret Walker had returned to say goodbye to the city that had made her a poet, the city that knew her voice, the city that had given the author of "For My People" to the world.

In the next month, Walker hardly recognized any of those who visited her. Marion and Emmett turned the upstairs of their Berkeley Street house into a home-care unit, where Walker could be comfortable. Sonia Sanchez and Joanne Gabbin came for one last visit and weren't sure if she recognized or heard them. The once strong, commanding voice grew weaker until there was nothing but silence. For Thanksgiving 1998, James, Sigis, Margaret, and the grandchildren drove up from Jackson so that they could spend what they knew was a last holiday together. Under heavy sedation, Walker remained surrounded by family throughout the holiday. A few sounds, barely audible, emerged from her throat. The family was intent on making her last days quiet. Expecting the worst and confident that they had done everything they could, her Jackson family returned home following the holiday.

On Saturday, November 27, Walker was rushed to Trinity Hospital, but not to stay. It had been two months since her last radiation treatment and the pain was unbearable. She was losing strength fast and the physician who knew her best, Robert Smith, flew to Chicago to be with her. The diagnosis was severe; the cancer had spread to her brain. In the early morning, November 30, Marion called her siblings to tell them their mother had passed. Although it is not clear when exactly she took her last breath, at 1:58 A.M., the doctor, having checked her vital signs, pronounced her dead. She was eighty-three years old, her body worn out from diabetes and cancer. One ailment kept her wounds from healing, making it easier for the other to take control.

In death, as in life, Walker would not allow the sadness to disrupt this final rite of passage. Leaving explicit instructions concerning her burial service, she requested few rituals on this last occasion. She had prepared the outline for her memorial service requests: two favorite songs, "Amazing Grace" and "Come, Ye Disconsolate"; a biblical passage; and a brief eulogy by her favorite pastor, Rev. Hickman Johnson, who returned to Jackson to honor her wishes. She wanted no celebration in death that she had not earned in life. The passage she chose, Revelations 21:4, served as a reminder of the deep religious faith that had guided her throughout life.

> And God shall wipe away all tears from their eyes; and there shall be no more death, neither sorrow, nor crying, neither shall there be any more pain; for the former things are passed away.

After her body was flown back to Jackson, the instructions were followed to the letter. The memorial was her last visit to Farish Street for services that were held at the Central United Methodist Church on December 4, 1998. Friends from all parts of her life, locally and nationally, came to pay homage. The closing words of her obituary read: "She leaves a legacy of abiding faith, spirituality, humanism, excellence and self-determination,"[13] an accurate summation, to be sure.

As for the Margaret Walker Alexander National Research Center, Walker's cherished legacy, success did come, in three major waves. Alferdteen Harrison succeeded in getting state appropriation for the restoration of Ayer Hall, based on its approval as an historic state site, which Walker had welcomed. Following her death, the state assisted in getting national historic status, enabling two rounds of funding for historic preservation from the National Park Service, Department of the Interior. Phase II, Restoration of Ayer Hall, was a five-year project be-tween 2001–2006, while the remaining floors of Ayer Hall were restored with a three-year grant, 2002–2005, in final Phase III. Two years after Walker's death, the Center officially opened the Margaret Walker papers to the public, with the support of a National Endowment for the Humanities Manuscript Preservation grant. As per her instructions, Walker's papers were secured in a vault on the ground floor of the building.

Eleanor Traylor asserts that the canon of Walker's work is a literary montage of Africa, America, the South, and the North, that the thematic strand that runs through it speaks of and to the historical complexities and transformations of twentieth-century America.[14] This is a bold assessment about someone whom critics tended to ignore and writers too easily forgot. Although Walker wanted recognition for her achievements, a recognition that she received early but di-minished as she aged, she found true redemption in the art that she created. She was a purist and most saw her as a perfectionist, the one thing "She didn't compromise on,"[15] remarked Bill Ferris. Nevertheless, she was comfortable with the multiple lives that she had lived, even as they competed with her art. She regretted none of her choices and never apologized for her aggressiveness when she took the moral high ground, especially concerning ethical standards in lit-erary and scholarly practice.

Margaret Walker created her own kind of power, both as a literary insider and outsider, who, as a radical thinker, offered masterful observations about social, economic, and political developments in the United States and the world. She believed in convention—that of a Southern lady—but she hated pretentiousness and could quickly discern the masks of hypocrisy, whether in friend or foe. Over the years, she learned to apply her creative, intellectual—and many would add, psychic—powers to institutional changes and innovations that have endured. She was, above all, a woman whose capacity to connect to others was deeply human and spiritual. It would have been enough for her to be remembered for giving audiences a sustained appreciation for form and meaning in poetry as it becomes part of our historical memory. Because she dared not mute her voice, she became our moral compass as well.

In 1989 as the preface to *This Is My Century*, Walker wrote her own epitaph, one that recalls her wit, her intelligence, vision, and ambition. Anyone who knew Margaret Walker saw a woman of passion and purpose. And yes, she would always have the last word:

> Here lies Margaret Walker
> Poet and Dreamer
> She tried to make her life
> a Poem.[16]

Afterword

The violence that erupted at Jackson State University in 1970 was state-sanctioned. The target was a peaceful protest by JSU students who stood against racism and war. The event inspired one of Walker's most powerful poems. The words recount experiences etched in the memory of families who lost sons and fathers as well as those who survived:

> Shotguns, high powered rifles crackling in the night
>   splattering glass and blood; screams cutting air with
>   death and fright; ambulances and sirens wailing;
>   streets covered with casings from their guns-highway
>   patrolmen's guns. . . .

That terrible tragedy at Jackson State went mostly unnoticed by the outside world while the Jackson community remained committed to protecting the living and the unborn.

In the years since Walker's death, we have seen far too much evidence of the world she warned us against, one perhaps more deadly than even she had imagined, one that makes it impossible to find that "common ground of humanity." Instead, we keep daily count of each defenseless Black child, woman, or man taken from us as her words remind us:

> Death came and took our frozen young, our
>   flowers, our black-eyed susan boys and men, and
>   wounded dozens more: women crouching in vain
>   behind the broken window panes, lying along
>   stairs, faces caricatured into spams of despair

Yet Margaret Walker was a woman who refused to allow the flame of hope for a better world to be born to be extinguished. The desire for that world became the driving force for her life's work. She had one code: do what you believe and believe what you do without fear. By the end of her life, the poet, scholar, and educator, the woman who turned ideas into action time and time again had reshaped each era of American life by producing transformative models that others could follow.

Many knew her—never understanding when she might be singling one of us out for some unknown task. Through the Institute she founded—today the Margaret Walker Center—she built her house of humanity. As a lasting achievement, it has inspired a global community who share her sense of mission and her foundational ideas about acquiring and producing knowledge for social change. Her legacy is its mission: to create a better world.

Opera/South's adaptation of *Jubilee* and the Daughters of Margaret brought Walker new audiences. Randy Klein, a New York composer, who discovered her years after her death, has begun to widen that audience even more. He put one poem to music, then another and another. The "Margaret Walker Song Cycle" was born and began its own journey. Klein and the JSU choral celebrated the Walker Centennial in 2015 among friends and admirers in Mississippi, the place she came during one of the most turbulent periods in American life. . . and said she'd never leave. The Jackson Symphony Orchestra has continued to put her words to music, just as the Mississippi Museum of Art keeps her vision alive through a range of exhibits. Both honor Walker's gift to the state, its people, and to the world.

Still, the debt we owe Margaret Walker is not so easily identified or measured. Her place in the literary canon remains less than secure. The critical void that exists makes it difficult to get the kind of ringing endorsements that elevate a writer's status. Walker has yet to find her Renaissance moment like Zora Neale Hurston. Retracing her journey took me in many different directions, introduced me to communities I did not know existed, and uncovered archives that

The Jackson State University Chorale performs the "Margaret Walker Song Cycle"; Dr. Willenham C. Castilla, director, Aurelia Williams, guest soloist, and Randy Klein, composer. Courtesy of C. B. Claiborne

are too valuable to be as underutilized as they are. This book is that necessary beginning that raises more questions even as it answers others, a reminder that the best discoveries about a person's life – especially if that person is a writer – come through repeated engagement with the new questions that surface. This first full accounting nearly twenty-five years after Walker's death can only be seen as an invitation if not a challenge to go beyond the limits of the journals that have been a major source material for this biography. After more than 100 years of Margaret Walker, there are most assuredly the other Margaret Walkers that remain for us to know. That indeed is the Margaret Walker effect: starting a journey and leveling the path that makes it absolutely necessary for others to complete.

Notes

Introduction: The Woman We Thought We Knew

1. "Jackson State, May 15, 1970," *This Is My Century: New and Collected Poems* (Athens: University of Georgia Press, 1989), 178.
2. Charlayne Hunter-Gault, "Poets Extol a Sister's Unfettered Soul," *New York Times*, November 9, 1973.
3. Maryemma Graham, ed., "Preface," *Fields Watered with Blood: Critical Essays on Margaret Walker* (Athens: University of Georgia Press, 2001), xi.
4. "Preface," *This Is My Century: New and Collected Poems* (Athens: University of Georgia Press, 1989), xvii.
5. Trudier Harris, "Black Writers in a Changed Landscape, Since 1950," in *The History of Southern Literature*, ed. Louis D. Rubin et al. (Baton Rouge: LSU Press, 1985), 367.
6. "On Being Female, Black, and Free," *On Being Female, Black, and Free: Essays by Margaret Walker, 1932–1992*, ed. Maryemma Graham (Knoxville: University of Tennessee Press, 1997), 3.

Chapter 1

1. Margaret Walker, unpublished manuscript, n.p.
2. Ibid., n.p.
3. Ibid., 13.
4. Ibid., n.p.
5. Ibid., 15.
6. Margaret Walker, "Growing out of Shadow," in *How I Wrote Jubilee* (New York: Feminist Press, 1990), 3–9; 3.
7. Margaret Walker, "The Vision Splendid," unpublished manuscript, 4.
8. Ibid., 5.
9. Margaret Walker, typescript, n.p.
10. "The Vision Splendid," 7.
11. Ibid., 7.
12. Census records different spellings for several of the siblings: According to th 1900 census, the Walker siblings included Charlie born in 1882, Bedo born in 1888; the eldest daughter, born 1879, is listed as "Adriel," and an older brother named "Abbey" who was born in 1877. (In the 1880 census he is spelled "Abie" with an older sister Euphemia who may have died young.) "Adriel" is spelled "E. Abelgale" in the 1910 enumeration. It is likely that the family history transposed the names since the

brothers left home early and died early, without clear documentation of their death. Marion was too young to remember her bothers. Neither did Walker's Aunt Abbie divulge much of the brothers' history. In addition, early Census records frequently misspelled names of those whose information they were recording or spelled them phonetically. I have reported the information using Walker's journal notes.

13. Ibid., 8.
14. Ibid., 8.
15. Ibid., 9.
16. Ibid., 9.
17. Margaret Walker, typescript, n.p.
18. "The Vision Splendid," 10.
19. Ibid., 5.
20. Ibid., 10.
21. Ibid., 11.
22. Ibid., 11.
23. Unpublished typescript, 41.
24. Ibid.
25. Margaret Walker, "How I Wrote *Jubilee*," *HIWJ*, 51.
26. Ibid.
27. Ibid.
28. Unpublished typescript, n.p.
29. Ibid.
30. "Growing out of Shadow," *HIWJ*, 3. Variations of this appear in numerous personal essays and in her unpublished autobiography.
31. Journal #2, June 5, 1932.

Chapter 2

1. "Childhood," in *This Is My Century: New and Collected Poems by Margaret Walker* (Athens: University of Georgia Press, 2014 [1989]), 46. Hereafter, *TIMC*.
2. "Birmingham," *TIMC*, 65.
3. "Growing Out of Shadow," in *How I Wrote Jubilee and Other Essays on Life and Literature by Margaret Walker*, ed. Maryemma Graham (New York: Feminist Press, 1990), 4. Hereafter, *HIWJ*.
4. Ibid., 4–5.
5. Journal #1, January 29, 1930.
6. "Growing Out of Shadow," *HIWJ*, 4.
7. Interview with Antoinette Handy, Jackson, MS, July 10, 2001.
8. Unpublished typescript, n.p.
9. Ibid.
10. Journal #2, June 5, 1932.
11. Unpublished typescript, 37.
12. "The Vision Splendid," 31.

13. Ibid., 32.

14. Gilbert Academy was the premier institution for New Orleans' Black community until 1949. In 2000, Gilbert was given new life as the location for a summer enrichment program for college-bound students.

15. "My Creative Adventure," in *On Being Female, Black, and Free*, ed. Maryemma Graham (Knoxville: University of Tennessee Press, 1997), 12. Hereafter, *OBFBF*.

16. "The Vision Splendid," 32.

17. "Daydream," *The Crisis* 41, no. 5 (1934): 129. This poem was reprinted under the title "I Want to Write" in *This Is My Century*, 113.

Chapter 3

1. "The Vision Splendid," unpublished ms, 28.

2. UM, n.d.

3. UA, 31, 33.

4. Interview with Gwendolyn Walker, July 11, 2001.

5. Notebook, 1931.

6. "My Creative Adventure," *On Being Female, Black, and Free: Essays by Margaret Walker*, ed. Maryemma Graham (Knoxville: University of Tennessee Press, 1997), 12. Hereafter, *OBFBF*

7. "On Being Female, Black, and Free," *OBFBF*, 4.

8. Ibid., 4.

9. Ibid., 5.

10. "My Creative Adventure," *OBFBF*, 13–14.

11. "On Being Female, Black, and Free," *OBFBF*, 3.

12. Ibid., 3–4.

13. Journal #2, June 7, 1934.

14. Journal #2, June 6, 1932.

15. Unpublished autobiography, 32.

16. "My Creative Adventure," *OBFBF*, 13.

17. Unpublished autobiography, 32.

18. Typescript, n.p.

19. Interview with Dr. Robert Smith, July 26, 2006.

20. Journal #3, August 13, 1934.

21. Ibid.

22. Typescript, n.d.

23. "Preface," in Margaret Walker, *This Is My Century: New and Collection Poems* (Athens: University of Georgia Press: 1989), xi. Hereafter, *TIMC*.

24. Journal #3, August 13, 1934.

25. Ibid.

26. Unpublished autobiography, 32.

27. Journal #3, July 8, 1934.

28. Journal #1, Inscription.
29. Ibid., December 25, 1929.
30. Typescript, n.p.
31. Ibid.
32. Journal #2, June 6, 1932.
33. Ibid., June 12, 1932.
34. Ibid., June 12, 1932.
35. Journal # , January 29, 1930
36. "Dear Are the Names That Charmed Me in My Youth," *TIMC*, 112.
37. *TIMC*, 11.

Chapter 4

1. Journal # , June 5, 1932.
2. Typescript, n.p.
3. Ibid.
4. "Introduction," in *Four Lincoln University Poets, Lincoln University Herald*, Vol. XXXIII (Lincoln University, PA: Lincoln University, March 1930), 4.
5. Ibid., 16.
6. Arnold Rampersad, *The Life of Langston Hughes*, Vol. I: 1902–1941, *I, Too, Sing America* (New York: Oxford University Press, 2002), 231.
7. Typescript, n.p.
8. "Preface," in *I Wonder as I Wander: An Autobiographical Journey* by Langston Hughes (New York: Persea Books, 1986), vi.
9. "What Is to Become of Us?," *Our Youth Magazine* 1, no. 5 (August 1932), 10. Reprinted in *On Being Female, Black, and Free: Essays by Margaret Walker, 1921–1992*, ed. Maryemma Graham (Knoxville: University of Tennessee Press, 1997), 176. Hereafter, *OBFBF*.
10. Ibid., 9–10.
11. Ibid., 10.
12. Ibid.
13. *TIMC*, 137.
14. "What Is to Become of Us?," 10.
15. Ibid.
16. Ibid.
17. "Tribute to Black Teachers," *OBFBF*, 193–95.
18. Journal #2, June 5, 1932.
19. Ibid.
20. Journal #2, June 6, 1932.
21. Ibid.
22. Journal #2, June 5, 1932.
23. Ibid., June 12, 1932.

24. Ibid., June 28, 1932.
25. Ibid., June 6, 1932.

Chapter 5

1. "My Creative Adventure," in *On Being Female, Black, and Free*, ed. Maryemma Graham (Knoxville: University of Tennessee Press, 1997), 14. Hereafter, *OBFBF*.
2. MW Papers, 6.31 Subseries IIIA: Box 1.
3. Journal #2, June 19, 1932.
4. Ibid.
5. "Growing Out of Shadow," in *How I Wrote "Jubilee,"* ed. Maryemma Graham (New York: Feminist Press, 1990), 6. Hereafter, *HIWJ*
6. Ibid., 6.
7. Ibid., 5.
8. Ibid., 5.
9. Ibid., 6.
10. UA, n.p.
11. Ibid.
12. Ibid.
13. Ibid.
14. Ibid.

Chapter 6

1. Journal #3, August 4, 1934.
2. Ibid., June 7, 1934.
3. Ibid., July 12, 1934.
4. Ibid., July 12, 1934.
5. Ibid., July 12, 1934.
6. *Crisis* 41, no. 5 (1934): 129. The poem was retitled "I Want to Write" in the volume *October Journey* (Detroit: Broadside Press, 1973) and finally in *This Is My Century: New and Collected Poems* (Athens: University of Georgia Press, 1989), 113.
7. Eleanor Traylor, "'Bolder Measures Crashing Through,' Margaret Walker's Poem of the Century," in *Fields Watered with Blood: Critical Essays on Margaret Walker*, ed. Maryemma Graham (Athens: University of Georgia Press, 2001) 110–38; 111.
8. Journal #6, November 1935.
9. *Modern American Poetry—1932*, ed. Gerta Aison (New York: The Galleon Press, 1932), 242.
10. *American States Anthology—1936*, vol. I, ed. Gerta Aison (New York: The Galleon Press, 1936), xxiv.
11. Margaret Walker Papers, 6:31 subseries IIIA: Box 1.

12. Ibid.
13. Georgia Douglas Johnson, *The Heart of a Woman and Other Poems* and *Bronze: A Book of Verse* (Charleston, SC: Nabu Press, 2010).
14. Journal #3, January–June 1934.
15. Alicia Ostriker, *Stealing the Language: The Emergence of Women's Poetry in America* (Boston: Beacon Press, 1987).
16. Ibid., 2–3.
17. Journal #4, September 16, 1934.
18. Ibid.
19. Ibid.
20. "Yet Do I Marvel," in *My Soul's High Song: The Collected Writings of Countee Cullen,* ed. Gerald Early (New York: Anchor Books, 1991),79..
21. "Growing Out of Shadow," *HIWJ*, 7–8.
22. Journal #4, May 20, 1935.
23. Ibid., August 11, 1935.
24. Ibid., June 3, 1935.

Chapter 7

1. "My Chicago Years," unpublished ms, 68.
2. Ibid., 68.
3. Ibid., 68.
4. Ibid, 69.
5. Journal #5, September 3, 1932
6. "My Chicago Years," 69.
7. "Growing Out of Shadow," in *How I Wrote Jubilee and Other Essays on Literature*, ed. Maryemma Graham (New York: Feminist Press), 7. Hereafter, *HIWJ*.
8. "People of Unrest and Hunger," in *New Challenge* Fall 1937, p. 49.
9. Journal #9, January 31, 1937.
10. Margaret Walker, "Richard Wright," *HIWJ*, 35.
11. Ibid.
12. Maryemma Graham, "Frank Yerby, King of the Costume Novel," *Essence* (October 1975), 70.
13. Walker, *Richard Wright: Daemonic Genius* (New York: Warner Books, 1988), 69.
14. Walker, "Growing Out of Shadow," *HIWJ*, 6.
15. *A Poetic Equation: Conversations between Nikki Giovanni and Margaret Walker* (Washington, DC: Howard University Press, 1974), 90.
16. German scholar Kathi King conducted an extensive search in all of the WPA archives and confirmed that Walker made her fiction debut "Red Satin Dress" in *New Anvil,* but consistently listed it as *Creative Writing*, where she continued to publish poems only.
17. Typescript, n.p.
18. Ibid.
19. Ibid.
20. Journal #9, January 31, 1937.

Chapter 8

1. "Richard Wright," in *How I Wrote Jubilee and Other Essays on Life and Literature*, ed. Maryemma Graham (New York: Feminist Press, 1990), 35. Hereafter, *HIWJ*.

2. Ibid.

3. *Challenge: A Literary Quarterly* (April 1937), 41.

4. Allison Davis, Mary R. Gardner, and Burleigh B. Gardner, *Deep South: A Social Anthropological Study of Caste and Class* (Columbia: University of South Carolina Press, 2009 [1941]).

5. Arna Bontemps, *The Harlem Renaissance Remembered: Essays Edited with a Memoir* (New York: Dodd, Mead and Company, 1972).

6. *This Is My Century: New and Collected Poems* (Athens: University of Georgia Press, 1989), 11. Hereafter, *TIMC*.

7. Ibid.

8. "Richard Wright," *HIWJ*, 36.

9. Ibid., 36.

10. Ibid., 37.

11. Ibid., 39.

12. According to George Hutchinson, it was not until the 1930s that the term "Negro writing" was associated with African American authors, rather than Black subject matter by any author. The shift in designation, therefore, emphasizes the extent to which there is "growing acknowledgment of black writers' authority over the literary representation of African American experience." "The Novel and the Negro Renaissance," in *The Cambridge Companion to the African American Novel*, ed. Maryemma Graham (Cambridge, UK: Cambridge University Press, 2004), 51.

13. The first issue appeared in 1934. West, who had been identified with the Harlem Renaissance, wanted to revive the spirit of a movement that had all but disappeared. Having Marian so strategically placed made it easier for Wright to convince West that the Chicago group deserved attention. Walker reported that Wright was also in love with Minus, and he was disappointed to discover that she was a lesbian.

14. Interview with Dorothy West, Oak Bluffs, MA, 1989.

15. *New Challenge* II, no. 2 (fall 1937).

16. Journal #9, February 5, 1937.

17. Margaret Walker, *Richard Wright: Daemonic Genius: A Portrait of the Man, a Critical Look at His Work* (New York: Warner Books, 1988).

18. *HIWJ*, 41.

19. Journal #10, April 8, 1937.

20. Interview with Walker and Gayden, Oxford, MS, November 3, 1985.

21. George Kent, *A Life of Gwendolyn Brooks* (Lexington: University Press of Kentucky 1990), 77.

22. Alain Locke, "Towards a Critique of Negro Music," *Opportunity* 12 (November 1934): 328.

Chapter 9

1. Journal #6, March 15, 1935.
2. Ibid., July 12, 1936.
3. Ibid., July 12, 1936.
4. Journal #9, February 1, 1937.
5. Ibid., March 10, 1937.
6. Ibid., February 1, 1937.
7. Ibid., February 5, 1937.
8. Ibid., February 5, 1937.
9. Ibid., February 5, 1937.
10. Ibid., March 1, 1937.
11. Ibid., March 4, 1937.
12. Ibid., March 7, 1937.
13. Ibid., March 1, 1937.
14. Ibid., April 8, 1937.
15. Ibid., April 8, 1937.
16. Ibid., April 8, 1937. Walker referred to Wright as Dick.
17. Journal #11, May 28, 1937.
18. Journal #9, March 7, 1937.
19. Journal #11, May 31, 1937.
20. Journal #9, March 16, 1937.
21. Ibid.
22. Ibid.
23. Ibid.
24. "The Vision Splendid," UA, 123.
25. Ibid.
26. Journal #11, May 28, 1937.
27. Ibid.
28. Ibid.
29. Ibid.
30. Ibid.

Chapter 10

1. Wright's review "Between Laughter and Tears" appeared in *New Masses*, October 5, 1937.
2. Walker letter to Richard Wright, July 1, 1937, Richard Wright Papers, Yale University, Beinecke Library.
3. Journal #11, May 28, 1937.
4. Ibid.

5. Walker believed that Wright was in love with Minus until he discovered she was a lesbian. Walker, *Richard Wright: Daemonic Genius* (New York: Warner Books, 1988), 91.

6. Hazel Rowley, *Richard Wright: The Life and Times* (New York: Henry Holt, 2001), 138.

7. Walker letter to Wright, July 1, 1937, RWP, Yale University, Beinecke Library.

8. Ibid.

9. Ibid.

10. Walker letter to Wright, September 29, 1937, RWP, Yale University, Beinecke Library.

11. Rowley, 137.

12. Walker letter to Wright, November 24, 1937, RWP, Yale University, Beinecke Library.

13. Author interview with Dorothy West and Margaret Walker, September 15, 1990.

14. "Foreword," *Challenge* 1, no. 1 (1934).

15. Walker letter to Wright, October 9, 1937, RWP, Yale University, Beinecke Library.

16. Walker letter to Wright, August 28, 1937, RWP, Yale University, Beinecke Library.

17. Walker letter to Wright, July 1, 1937, RWP, Yale University, Beinecke Library.

18. Ibid.

19. Ibid.

20. Ibid.

21. Walker letter to Wright, December 21, 1937, RWP, Yale University, Beinecke Library.

22. Walker letter to Richard Wright, ND, RWP, Yale University, Beinecke Library.

23. Ibid.

24. Ibid.

25. Journal #11, July 15, 1937.

26. Walker letter to Wright, November 24, 1937, RWP, Yale University, Beinecke Library.

27. John Griffin Jones, "A Mississippi Writer Talks," in *Conversations with Margaret Walker*, ed. Maryemma Graham (Jackson: University Press of Mississippi, 2002), 82.

28. Journal #12, June 2, 1938.

29. "My Creative Adventure," in *On Being Female, Black, and Free: Essays by Margaret Walker*, ed. Maryemma Graham (Knoxville: University of Tennessee Press, 1997), 16. Hereafter, *OBFBF*.

30. Walker letter to Wright, December 21, 1937, RWP, Yale University, Beinecke Library.

31. "For My People," in *This Is My Century: New and Collected Poems* (Athens: University of Georgia Press, 1989), 6.

32. Ibid., 6.

33. Ibid., 6.

34. Ibid., 6.

35. Ibid., 7.

36. Ibid., 7.

37. Ibid., 7.

38. Ibid., 7.

39. Mary Kinzie, *A Poet's Guide to Poetry* (Chicago: University of Chicago Press, 1999), 15.

40. Journal #12, June 2, 1938.

41. Jerry W. Ward, "Everybody's Protest Novel: The Era of Richard Wright," in *The Cambridge Companion to the African American Novel*, ed. Maryemma Graham (Cambridge, UK: Cambridge University Press, 2004), 173.

42. Eugenia Collier, "Fields Watered with Blood: Myth and Ritual in the Poetry of Margaret Walker," in *Black Women Writers 1950–1980: A Critical Evaluation*, ed. Mari Evans (New York: Doubleday, 1983), 500.

Chapter 11

1. Walker, "Richard Wright," manuscript, n.p.

2. Walker, "The Writer and Her Craft," in *On Being Female, Black, and Free: Essays by Margaret Walker, 1932–1992*, ed. Maryemma Graham (Knoxville: University of Tennessee Press, 1997), 23. Hereafter, *OBFBF*.

3. Walker, "What Is to Become of Us," *OBFBF*, 176.

4. Walker, "Willing to Pay the Price," in *How I Wrote "Jubilee" and Other Essays on Life and Literature*, ed. Maryemma Graham (New York: Feminist Press, 1990), 19. Hereafter, *HIWJ*.

5. Preface, in *This Is My Century: New and Collected Poems* (Athens: University of Georgia Press, 1989), xi. Hereafter, *TIMC*.

6. Interview with Margaret Taylor Goss Burroughs, June 28, 2007.

7. Journal #11, July 17, 1937.

8. Walker letter to Wright, June 10, 1938, RWP, Yale University, Beinecke Library.

9. Ibid.

10. Walker letter to Wright, May 9, 1938, RWP, Yale University, Beinecke Library.

11. Walker letter to Wright, July 5, 1938, RWP, Yale University, Beinecke Library.

12. Walker letter to Wright, June 30, 1938, RWP, Yale University, Beinecke Library.

13. Journal #12, May 18, 1938.

14. Ibid., May 22, 1938.

15. Ibid., May 22, 1938.

16. MWP, unpublished poem, September 4, 1938.

17. *HIWJ*, 41.

18. Journal #14, November 27, 1938.

19. Walker letter to Wright, November 24, 1937, RWP, Yale University, Beinecke Library.

20. Ibid.

    Dialectial materialism, a core concept in Marxist thought, is the view that historical change results from the conflict between social forces in the world, and that the actions of people are inevitability shaped by the conditions of their existence. Walker understood the scientific view of societal change, but her religious training brought the presence of the spiritual together with the need for social progress, both inspired by a belief in a common, shared humanity.

21. Walker letter to Wright, December 21, 1937, RWP, Yale University, Beinecke Library.

22. Journal #14, June 11, 1939. This may have been Dhimah Meidman, whom Wright was seeing regularly and whom he would secretly marry that August, or possibly Jane Newton, whom Walker indicated she met on this trip to New York.

23. Ibid.

24. Ibid.

25. Ibid.

26. Ibid.

27. Ibid.

28. Ibid.

29. Ibid.

30. Walker letter to Wright, June 7, 1939, RWP, Yale University, Beinecke Library.

31. Hazel Rowley, *Richard Wright, The Life and Times* (New York: Henry Hold, 2001), 118.

32. Walker letter to Wright, June 7, 1939, RWP, Yale University, Beinecke Library

33. "Richard Wright," *HIWJ*, 33.

Chapter 12

1. "The Situation of New Masses Is *Critical!*" (italics in original), *New Masses* 24 (1937), editorial statement.

2. Ibid.

3. Journal #33, September 4, 1938.

4. Walker letter to Wright, November 24, 1937, RWP, Yale University, Beinecke Library.

5. Journal #13, September 4, 1938.

6. Ibid.

7. Ibid.

8. Walker letter to Wright, April 4, 1938, RWP, Yale University, Beinecke Library.

9. Journal #12, June 2, 1938.

10. Walker letter to Wright, August 30, 1938, RWP, Yale University, Beinecke Library.

11. Daniel Patrick Moynihan, *Secrecy: The American Experience* (New Haven: Yale University Press, 1998), 159.

12. Undated letter from Walker to Wright in 1938, RWP, Yale University, Beinecke Library.

13. *New Masses* 29, no. 9 (November 22, 1938): 5.

14. Undated letter from Walker to Wright in 1938, RWP, Yale University, Beinecke Library.

15. Journal #13, October 10, 1938.

16. "Proletarian Short Stories," *New Masses* 30, no. 1 (January 3, 1939): 21.

17. Bonner's daughter, Joyce O. Striklin, who kept the stories, collaborated with Joyce Flynn for the 1987 publication. Bonner has been the subject of significant recovery work and is included in Cheryl Wall's 1995 study *Women of the Harlem Renaissance* (Indiana University Press) and the expansive collection of literary biographies by Lorraine Elena Roses and Ruth Elizabeth Randolph, *The Harlem Renaissance and Beyond* (G. K. Hall), first published in 1989.

18. James Nagel in *The Contemporary American Short-Story Cycle* (Louisiana State Univesity, 1991), refers to the "composite novel," noting its popularity among ethnic writers in particular.
19. Jacqueline Miller Carmichael, "Margaret Walker's Reflections and Celebrations: An Interview," in *Conversations with Margaret Walker*, ed. Maryemma Graham (Jackson: University Press of Mississippi, 2002), 165.
20. Walker letter to Wright, July 1, 1937, RWP, Yale University, Beinecke Library.

Chapter 13

1. Journal #5, March–July 1936
2. "My Creative Adventure," 13–17, *OBFBF*. Originally written as a speech for the annual meeting of the National Association for Teachers of English, the essay was not published until 1997
3. Ibid., 14.
4. Ibid., 15.
5. Ibid., 18.
6. Journal #28, May 28, 1937.
7. Journal #16, August 21, 1939.
8. Ibid.
9. Ibid.
10. Journal #14, November 27, 1938.
11. Journal #16, September 4, 1939.
12. Ibid.
13. Interview with Elizabeth Catlett Mora, January 24, 2000.
14. Catlett indicates that an African American woman from Texas moved to Iowa and opened a house for Black girls, which became the unofficial off-campus dormitory for those women restricted from Iowa campus housing.
15. Journal #17, October 18, 1939.
16. Walker, unpublished manuscript, n.d.
17. Ibid.
18. Ibid.
19. Ibid.
20. Journal #18, June 14, 1940.
21. Ibid., July 2, 1940.
22. Ibid., July 2, 1940.
23. "My Chicago Years," chapter from unpublished ms, 103.
24. Margaret Walker, unpublished ms, n.p.
25. Interview with Margaret Walker, January 19, 1992.

Chapter 14

1. Margaret Walker, "Black Women in Academia," *HIWJ*, 29.
2. Margaret Walker papers, AF012, Series III-C Biography. Box 19. F06. P.3
3. Marie H. Buncombe, "Legacy from the Past, Agenda for the Future: The College Language Association, 1937–1987," *CLA Journal* 57, no. 1 (September 2013): 43–50)
4. Ibid., 43.
5. "Introduction," in *The Negro Caravan*, ed. Sterling Brown, Arthur P. Davis, Ulysses K. Lee (New York: Dryden Press, 1943), 7.
6. The original name of the organization, founded by Hugh Gloster and Gladstone Lewis Chandler at LeMoyne Owen College in 1937. Eight men and women were present at the inaugural meeting.
7. The term HBCU, was probably used as early as 1944 with the founding of the United Negro College Fund by Mary McCleod Bethune and Frederick Patterson. It became popularized especially after the 1950s during the era of desegregation as away of highlighting the historical significance of these institutions, their graduates, and their contribution to America. The two parallel terms, PWI (predominately white institution) and HBCU, are often used together.
8. Yale University Library Manuscript & Archives, Yale Press Collection: Box 6, Folder 246.
9. Journal #20, 1942, undated entry.
10. Ibid.
11. *Book Review Digest* 1942
12. Journal #20: October 1942.
13. MWA, interview, June 28, 1996.

Chapter 15

1. Journal #20, October 15, 1943.
2. Ibid., October 17, 1943.
3. Ibid., October 17, 1943.
4. Ibid., October 17, 1943.
5. Ibid., November 19, 1943
6. Ibid., October 22, 1943.
7. Ibid., October 25, 1943
8. Ibid., October 25, 1943.
9. Ibid., October 25, 1943.
10. UM, Margaret Walker, "Autobiography," 1–2.
11. Journal #20, October 28, 1943
12. Ibid., October 1942

Chapter 16

1. Margaret Walker Papers. Box 19. F06. Series IIIC
2. See the foundational work of Paula Giddings, *When and Where I Enter: The Impact of Black Women on Race and Sex in America* (New York: Perennial, 2001); Darlene Clark Hine, *Hine Sight: Black Women and the Re-Construction of American History* (Bloomington: Indiana University Press, 1998); and Evelyn Brooks Higgenbotham. "The Politics of Respectability," in *Righteous Indignation: The Women's Movement in the Black Baptist Church, 1880–1920* (Cambridge, MA: Harvard University Press, 1993)
3. Journal #20; 1943. Undated.
4. Ibid.
5. Ibid.
6. Ibid.
7. Ibid.
8. Ibid., November 10, 1943.
9. Ibid., November 10, 1943. [are all repetitions necessary here?]
10. Ibid., November 10, 1943.
11. Ibid., November 10, 1943.
12. Ibid., November 10, 1943.
13. Ibid., November 10, 1943.
14. Ibid., November 10, 1943.
15. Ibid., November 10, 1943.
16. Ibid., November 24, 1943.
17. Ibid., November 24, 1943. [are these reptitions necessary]
18. Ibid., November 24, 1943
19. Ibid., November 24, 1943.
20. Interview with Mrs. Josephine Rogers and Mrs. Dorothy Williams (Walker's cousins-in-law), High Point, NC, June 19, 1999.
21. Ibid.
22. Alicia Ostriker, *Stealing the Language: The Emergence of Women's Poetry in America* (Boston: Beacon Press, 1987), 60.
23. Walker, "On Being Female, Black, and Free," *OBFBF*, 3.
24. Journal #20, December 15, 1943.
25. Journal #21, March 1, 1944.
26. Ibid., April 13, 1944.
27. Conversation with Catlett, January 24, 2001.
28. Ibid.
29. Journal #23: November 25, 1944.
30. Journal #2, June 10, 1932.
31. Psalm27,*TheHolyBible*,KingJamesVersion(NewYork:TheWorldPublishingCompany), 603.
32. Ibid.

Chapter 17

1. "Growing Out of Shadow," in *How I Wrote Jubilee*, ed. Maryemma Graham (New York: Feminist Press, 1990), 3. Hereafter, *HIWJ*.
2. Ibid, 8.
3. Ibid., 9.
4. Mike Pride, "One Who Got Away," The Pulitzer Prize Archives.
5. "How I Wrote *Jubilee*," *HIWJ*, 50.
6. Ibid., 51–52.
7. Ibid., 52.
8. Ibid., 52.
9. Mary Kelley, *Private Woman, Public Stage: Literary Domesticity in Nineteenth-Century America* (New York: Oxford University Press, 1984), viii.
10. Walker, 1940–1942, handwritten pages.
11. Interview with Josephine Rogers and Dorothy Williams, ibid.
12. Ibid.
13. Ibid.
14. Alex had learned carpentry from working in the furniture mills around High Point from the time he was ten years old. When he returned from the army at thirty-three, he was a skilled craftsman in great demand.
15. Walker, "How I Wrote *Jubilee*," *HIWJ*, 56.
16. See Hazel Rowley's article on Paul Green and Richard Wright in *Mississippi Quarterly* 52, no. 2 (Spring 1999): 215–37, for a perspective of African American visitors to the University of North Carolina, Chapel Hill, under the sponsorship of Paul Green during the 1940s and '950s.
17. Walker, "How I Wrote *Jubilee*," 56.

Chapter 18

1. Journal #26, January 21, 1946.
2. Journal #27, February 1, 1947.
3. Journal #26, January 21, 1946.
4. Journal #27, February 1, 1947.
5. Ibid., February 1, 1947.
6. Ibid., February 1, 1947.
7. Ibid., February 1, 1947.
8. Ibid., January 1, 1947.
9. Ibid., January 1, 1947.
10. Ibid., January 1, 1947.
11. Ibid., January 1, 1947.
12. Ibid., January 1, 1947.
13. Journal #31, May 31, 1948.

14. Ibid.
15. Marcus Christian (1900–1976) was a New Orleans poet whose work Walker came to know after she'd left the city college.
16. Journal #31, June 30, 1948.
17. Ibid., June 4, 1948.
18. Journal #32, September 29, 1948.
19. Ibid., October 3, 1948.
20. Ibid., October 3, 1948.
21. Ibid., October 3, 1948.
22. Ibid., October 6, 1948.
23. Ibid., October 8, 1948.
24. Ibid., October 8, 1948.
25. Ibid., October 9, 1948.
26. Ibid., October 9, 1948.
27. Silent Unity is a collaborative prayer network offered by Unity Village as a part of Unity Church ministry. While Walker did not become a convert to the Church, her outreach to Silent Unity became a regular practice for the remainder of her life.
28. Ibid., October 9, 1948.
29. Ibid., October 11, 1948.
30. Ibid., October 11, 1948.
31. Ibid., October 17, 1948.
32. Journal #33, May 1, 1949.
33. Ibid.

Chapter 19

1. Journal #36, September 28, 1949.
2. Eleanor Traylor, "Bolder Measures Crashing Through, Margaret Walker's Poem of the Century," in *Fields Watered with Blood: Critical Essays on Margaret Walker*, ed. Maryemma Graham (Athens: University of Georgia Press, 2001), 111.
3. Journal #36, September 27, 1949.
4. Ibid.
5. Ibid.
6. Journal #58, August 13, 1960.
7. Jerry Ward Jr., "A Writer for Her People," *Mississippi Quarterly* 41 (Fall 1988): 515–27; reprinted in *Conversations with Margaret Walker*, 114.
8. *This Is My Century: New and Collected Poems* (Athens: University of Georgia Press, 1989), 62. Hereafter, *TIMC*.
9. Journal #41, June 8, 11, 1951.
10. *TIMC*, 125–26.
11. Journal #48, July 4, 1954.
12. Ibid.

13. Journal #58, August 8, 1960.
14. Journal #48, July 5, 1954.
15. Journal #51, October 9, 1955.
16. Ibid., October 9, 1955.
17. Ibid., October 9, 1955.
18. Ibid., October 9, 1955.
19. Ibid., October 25, 1955.
20. Ibid., October 25, 1955.
21. Ibid., October 25, 1955.

Chapter 20

1. Journal #59, August 28, 1960.
2. Journal #55, October 16, 1958.
3. Ibid.
4. Journal #58, August 8, 1960.
5. Journal #61, July 9, 1961.
6. Ibid., July 9, 1961.
7. Ibid., July 1, 1961.

Chapter 21

1. Margaret Walker Papers. AF012 Series III C: Biography, Box 19 F06.
2. "New Poets," *Phylon* 11, no. 4 (1950): 145–54.
3. Ibid.
4. "How I Wrote *Jubilee*," in *How I Wrote "Jubilee" and Other Essays on Life and Literature*, ed. Maryemma Graham (New York: Feminist Press, 1990), 50. Hereafter *HIWJ*.
5. "On Being Female, Black, and Free," in *On Being Female, Black, and Free: Essays by Margaret Walker, 1932–1992*, ed. Maryemma Graham (Knoxville: University of Tennessee Press, 1997), 21. Hereafter *OBFBF*.
6. Journal #61, July 9, 1961.
7. Journal #68, June 13, 1963.
8. Ibid., no date.
9. Ibid., no date.
10. Journal #70, November 24, 1963.
11. Ibid.
12. *This Is My Century: New and Collected Poems* (Athens: University of Georgia Press, 1989), 100–7. Hereafter *TIMC*.
13. Journal #70, November 26, 1963.
14. Ibid., January 20, 1964.

15. Ibid., January 20, 1964.
16. Ibid., February 1, 1964.
17. "Street Demonstration," *TIMC*, 55.
18. Journal #74, April 9, 1965.
19. Journal #76, May 25, 1965.
20. Ibid.
21. Journal #74, April 9, 1965.
22. Ibid.
23. Ibid.
24. "On Being Female, Black, and Free," *OBFBF*, 3.
25. "Black Writers in a Changed Landscape since 1950," in *The History of Southern Literature*, eds. Louis D. Rubin, Blyden Jackson, Rayburn S. Moore, Lewis P. Simpson, and Thomas Daniel Young (Baton Rouge: Louisiana State University Press, 1985), 567.
26. "A Hateful Passion, a Lost Love," in *Feminist Issues in Literary Scholarship*, ed. Shari Benstock (Bloomington: Indiana University Press, 1987), 186–205.

Chapter 22

1. Journal #56, February 1, 1959.
2. Martha Biondi, *The Black Revolution on Campus* (Berkeley: University of California Press, 2012), 142–73.
3. Ibid., 167.
4. Ibid., 160.
5. "Religion, Poetry, History: Foundations for a New Educational System" (1968), in *On Being Female, Black, and Free: Essays by Margaret Walker 1932–1992*, ed. Maryemma Graham (Knoxville: University of Tennessee Press, 1997), 209. Hereafter, *OBFBF*.
6. *This Is My Century: New and Collected Poems* (Athens: University of Georgia Press, 1989), 7. Hereafter, *TIMC*.
7. *OBFBF*, ibid, 209
8. "The Challenge of the 1970s to the Black Scholar," *OBFBF*, 183–84.
9. Howard Rambsy, *The Black Arts Enterprise and the Production of African American Art* (Ann Arbor: University of Michigan Press, 2011), 2.
10. Lawrence P. Jackson, *The Indignant Generation: A Narrative History of African American Writers and Critics 1934–1960* (Princeton, NJ: Princeton University Press, 2010).
11. "Agenda for Action," *OBFBF*, 95.
12. *TIMC*, 187.
13. Journal #82, April 15, 1968.
14. "The Education of a Seminal Mind, W. E. B. Du Bois," in *How I Wrote Jubilee and Other Essays, by Margaret Walker*, ed. Maryemma Graham (New York: Feminist Press, 1990), 86. Hereafter, *HIWJ*.
15. Ibid.

16. See J. Saunders Redding, "The Black Revolution in American Studies," and Imamu Amiri Baraka, "Reply," in *American Studies International* 17, no. 4 (1970): 8–21.

17. "Revolution and the University," *OBFBF*, 220.

18. Ibid., 220.

19. Ibid, 221.

20. Ibid., 221–22.

21. Ibid., 222.

22. "Publisher's Note," in *For My People* (New Haven: Yale University Press, 1969 [1942]), 5.

23. *OBFBF*, 222.

24. Ibid., 223.

25. Ibid., 221.

26. "Willing to Pay the Price," *HIWJ*, 23.

27. Ibid., 22.

Chapter 23

1. Journal #84, July 30, 1969.

2. Jerry W. Ward, unpublished review, May 16, 2014.

3. Ibid. translation: "the poet and the thinker."

4. Ibid.

5. Ibid.

6. Ibid.

7. Journal #85, September 28, 1969.

8. Interview, John A. Peoples, July 8, 2005.

9. *This Is My Century: New and Collection Poems* (Athens: University of Georgia Press, 1989), 108. Hereafter, *TIMC*.

10. Ibid., 7.

11. Ibid., 111.

12. Ibid., 111.

13. Interview with Peoples.

14. Ibid.

15. Ibid.

16. Journal #85, October 4, 1969.

17. Ibid., October 5, 1969.

18. Ibid., October 6, 1969.

19. Ibid., October 16, 1969.

20. An informal poll showed that no Negro women scholars at Morgan State, Stillman, Fisk, Hampton, Howard, and Spelman colleges left for positions at PWIs during the 1960s, years that showed the largest increase in Black student college enrollment.

21. Alex Poinsett, "Brain Drain at Negro Colleges," *Ebony* 25, no. 12 (October 1970): 76.

22. Journal #85, January 1, 1970.

23. Ibid.

24. Ibid.

25. "How I Told My Child about Race," in *How I Wrote "Jubilee" and Other Essays on Life and Literature*, ed. Maryemma Graham (New York: Feminist Press, 1990), 13, 14. Hereafter, *HIWJ*.

26. "My Creative Adventure," *OBFBF*, 13–14.

27. Journal #84, July 30, 1969.

28. Alfred North Whitehead, *The Aims of Education and Other Essays* (New York: The Free Press, 1967), 93.

29. Journal #83, September 3, 1968.

30. Journal #86, May 17, 1970.

31. Ibid.

32. Ibid.

33. Ibid.

34. Ibid.

35. Interview with Curtis King, April 1, 2014.

36. "Agenda for Action," *OBFBF*, 86–87.

37. Ibid.

38. King interview.

39. Ibid.

40. "Agenda for Action."

41. Ibid.

Chapter 24

1. Walker, quoted in *The Storied South: Voices of Artists and Writers*, ed. William R. Ferris (Chapel Hill: University of North Carolina Press, 2013), 102.

2. "Religion, Poetry, and History: Foundations for a New Educational System," *OBFBF*, 208–17; 208.

3. Quoted in "Revolution and the University," *OBFBF*, 218–25; 224.

4. *OBFBF*, 224–25.

5. Journal #85: September 28, 1969; emphasis mine.

6. Doris Kearns Goodwin provides an important overview of Eleanor Roosevelt's enormous influence during her husband's presidency in the sphere of race relations in *No Ordinary Time* (New York: Simon & Schuster: 1994).

7. John Shelton Reed, *My Tears Spoiled My Aim and Other Reflections of Southern Culture* (New York: Harcourt Brace:1993), 43.

8. Reed, 55.

9. Journal #83, September 15, 1968.

10. "Humanities with a Black Focus," *OBFBF*, 99–100.

11. Ibid., 103.

12. Ibid., 101–2.

13. Ibid., 103. Nobel prize-winning Stanford physicist William Shockely and his University of Berkeley colleague Arthur Jensen were known for their controversial research on a race-based theory of intelligence, and for their association with social control. Daniel Patrick Moynihan, as assistant secretary of labor in the Johnson Administration, authored the equally controversial 1965 study, *The Negro Family: The Case for National Action*, which popularized the view that linked the lack of Black economic and political progress to the persistence of Black female headed households emerging after slavery. Such theories were used to guide educational and social policy and advance popular racial stereotypes. Many viewed these developments as extensions of late 19th century ideas and cautioned against the use of science and technology to perpetuate racism and justify genocide.

14. Interview with Doris Derby, March 28, 2020.

15. Conference brochure.

16. Thadious Davis, *Southscapes: Geographics of Race, Religion, & Literature* (Chapel Hill: University of North Carolina Press, 2011), 23, 39, 57, 93–94.

17. Proposal to the National Endowment for the Humanities, MWA papers.

18. Ibid.

19. Abdul Alkalimat and Associates, *Introduction to Afro-American Studies: A Peoples College Primer* (Fund for the Improvement of Post-Secondary Education [FIPSE], n.d.), 1.

20. *This Is My Century: New and Collected Poems* (Athens: University of Georgia Press, 1987), 66. Hereafter, *TIMC*.

21. "Jackson, Mississippi," *TIMC*, 62–63.

Chapter 25

1. Margaret Walker, "On Being, Female, Black, and Free," in *On Being Female, Black, and Free: Essays by Margaret Walker*, ed. Maryemma Graham (Knoxville: University of Tennessee Press, 1997), 8–9. Hereafter, *OBFBF*.

2. Letter from Alice Walker to Margaret Walker, August 11, 1972, Margaret Walker Papers

3. Journal #68, June 13, 1963.

4. "Phillis Wheatley and Black Women Writers, 1773–1973," *OBFBF*, 37.

5. "Rediscovering Black Women in the Mecca of the New Negro," in *How I Wrote "Jubilee" and Other Essays on Life and Literature*, ed. Maryemma Graham (New York: Feminist Press, 1990), 91. Hereafter, *HIWJ*.

6. Gloria Steinem, "After Black Power, Women's Liberation," *New York Magazine*, April 4, 1969.

7. Mari Evans, *I Am a Black Woman* (New York: William Morrow, 1970).

8. Charlayne Hunter-Gault, "Poets Extol a Sister's Unfettered Soul," *New York Times*, November 9, 1973, p 1.

9. Ibid.

10. "Phillis Wheatley and Black Women Writers, 1773–1983," *OBFBF*, 39–40.
11. Ibid.
12. Ibid.
13. Ibid., 39.
14. Hunter-Gault, "Poets Extol a Sister's Unfettered Soul."
15. Dwight Conquergood, "Rethinking Ethnography: Towards a Critical Cultural Politics," in *The Sage Handbook of Performance Studies*, eds. D S. Madison and J. Hamera (Thousand Oaks, CA: Sage, 2006), 351–65, 360.
16. "Phillis Wheatley and Black Women Writers, 1773–1973," *OBFBF*, 39–40.
17. "My Creative Adventure," *OBFBF*, 21.

Chapter 26

1. Journal #93, January 18, 1974.
2. Jacqueline Trescott, telephone interview, December 30, 2019.
3. "The Civil Rights Movement in Mississippi," in *On Being Female, Black, and Free: Essays by Margaret Walker, 1932–1992*, ed. Maryemma Graham (Knoxville: University of Tennessee Press, 1997), 139–144; 139. Hereafter, *OBFBF*.
4. Ibid., 142.
5. "On Money, Race, and Politics," *OBFBF*, 135–139; 136.
6. *A Poetic Equation: Conversations between Nikki Giovanni and Margaret Walker*, ed. Paula Giddings (Washington, DC: Howard University Press, 1974), 29, 33. Hereafter, *Poetic Equation*.
7. Ibid., 33.
8. Interview with Giddings, May 27, 2014.
9. Ibid.
10. *A Poetic Equation*, inside dust jacket cover.
11. Ibid.
12. "On Being Female, Black, and Free," *OBFBF*, 9.
13. The Combahee River Collective Statement, 1974
14. *OBFBF*, 3.
15. In 1944, Brown became the first Black commissioned officer in the Navy Chaplain's Corps. After a number of teaching and ministerial duties in Kansas, Missouri, and Colorado, Brown returned to Chicago as the General Secretary of the AME Church denomination.
16. Brittney C. Cooper, *Beyond Respectability: The Intellectual Thought of Race Women* (Urbana: University of Illinois, 2017), 12.
17. "On Being Female, Black and Free," *OBFBF*, 8.
18. Ibid., 8.
19. Ibid., 5.
20. Ibid., 5.

21. Years later when asked about the name of the book, Walker explained that Negro schools were like the "daisy with a black center and yellow petals, [they] grow wild all over the Southland." Journal #129, August 24, 1990.

22. "Black Women in Academia," in *How I Wrote "Jubilee" and Other Essays on Life and Literature*, ed. Maryemma Graham (New York: Feminist Press, 1990), 31–32. Hereafter, *HIWJ*.

23. Minrose Gwin, *Black and White Women of the Old South: A Peculiar Sisterhood* (Knoxville: University of Tennessee Press, 1985), 47.

24. *The Culture of Sentiment: Race, Gender and Sentimentality in the 19th Century*, ed. Shirley Samuels (New York: Oxford University Press, 1992), 244–64.

25. DoVeanna S. Fulton, *Speaking Power: Black Feminist Orality in Narratives of Slavery* (Albany: State University of New York Press, 2006), 3.

26. Margaret Walker, "Reflections on Black Women Writers," *OBFBF*, 42.

27. Delores S. Williams, "Women's Oppression and Lifeline Politics in Black Women's Religious Narratives," *Journal of Feminist Studies in Religion* 1, no. 2 (fall 1985): 59–71; 68.

28. Ibid., 70.

29. Paule Marshall, "From the Poets in the Kitchen," *New York Times*, January 9, 1983.

30. Ibid.

31. Gwin, *Black and White Women of the Old South*.

32. Ibid., 68.

33. Eleanor Traylor, "'Bolder Measures Crashing Through,' Margaret Walker's Poem of the Century," in *Fields Watered with Blood: Critical Essays on Margaret Walker*, ed. Maryemma Graham (Athens: University of Georgia Press, 2001), 110–38; 111–14.

34. "World Pluralism: The Human Encounter," *OBFBF*, 230–31.

35. "My Creative Adventure," *OBFBF*, 15.

36. Ibid., 16.

37. Ibid., 21.

38. Claudine Raynaud, "Richard Wright's Many Lives and the Travails of Literary Biography," Ms. viewed April 6, 2020.

Chapter 27

1. Journal #93, January 4, 1974.

2. "Agenda for Action," in *On Being Female, Black, and Free, Essays by Margaret Walker 1932–1992*, ed. Maryemma Graham (Knoxville: University of Tennessee Press, 1997), 87. Hereafter, *OBFBF*.

3. Ibid.

4. Journal #88, April 18, 1971.

5. *OBFBF*, 10.

6. Journal #93, November 11, 1973.

7. Journal #93, November 11, 1973.

8. Journal #113, July 7, 1983.

9. "On Being Female, Black, and Free," *OBFBF*, 3.

10. Ibid.

11. Wright, *Black Boy*, 257

12. Eugene Redmond, *Drumvoices: A Critical History* (New York: Anchor Books, 1976), 269–70.

13. Mel Watkins, "Hard Times for Black Writers," *New York Times*, February 22, 1981.

14. Derek Smith, *Robert Hayden in Verse* (Ann Arbor: University of Michigan, 2018), 15.

15. Charles Rowell, "Poetry, History and Humanism: An Interview with Margaret Walker," *Black World* 25, no. 2 (1975): 4–17; 9.

16. Jerry W. Ward Jr., "A Writer for Her People," in *Conversations with Margaret Walker*, ed. Maryemma Graham (Jackson: University Press of Mississippi, 2002), 115.

17. Ben E. Bailey, "Opera/South: A Brief History," *The Black Perspective in Music* 13, no. 1 (spring 1985): 48–78, 79.

18. Ward, "A Writer for Her People," 114.

19. Institute materials, Margaret Walker papers, JSU.

20. "World Pluralism: The Human Encounter," *OBFBF*, 226.

21. Ibid., 229.

22. "World Pluralism," *OBFBF*, 229.

23. Ibid., 230.

24. Journal #100, October 21, 1976.

25. Journal #101, April 3, 1977.

26. Ibid.

27. Ibid.

28. Walker, Margaret Walker Alexander Center, JSU, unpublished MS, 69.

29. Journal #101, April 3, 1977.

30. Ibid.

31. Ibid.

32. Ibid.

33. Unpublished ms, Margaret Walker papers.

34. Margaret Walker Alexander, *Plaintiff v. Alex Haley, Doubleday & Company, Inc. and Doubleday Publishing Company*, Defendants; Nos. 77 Civ 1907 (M.E.F.), 77 Civ. 1908 (M.E.F.). United States District Court for the Southern District of New York. September 20, 1978.

35. Ibid.

36. Walker had intended to include the full story of the *Roots* controversy in her autobiography, in addition to writing an essay "Roots Rip Off Style," but was persuaded by friends and her family to discard the article. Her reputation had suffered enough, and whatever she said would support the media's vilification of her, they believed.

37. Journal #101, April 27, 1977.

38. Journal #101, May 6, 1977.

39. *New York Magazine*, 11, no. 47 (November 20, 1978).

40. Quoted by Christopher Dickey, "Roots Author Facing Accusations: Novelist Suit Charges Haley's Book Is Largely Copied," *Washington Post*, April 28, 1977.

41. *Margaret Walker Alexander, Plaintiff v. Alex Haley.*

42. Ibid.

43. Herb Boyd, "Plagiarism and the Roots Suits," *First World* 2, no. 3 (1979): 31–33, 32.

44. Ibid.

45. Jacqueline Trescott, "Respected Scholar: Margaret Walker Has Intense Feelings on Black Writers' Spiritual Alliance," *Washington Post*, April 28, 1977.

46. Journal #101, May 15, 1977.

47. Interview with Mari Evans, April 20, 2013.

48. Interview with Curtis King, April 1, 2014.

49. Quoted in Tony Burton, "Roots of a Great Lie," *The Daily Mail*, February 19, 1993.

50. *Setting the Record Straight* (Detroit: Walter O. Evans, 1996), 12.

Chapter 28

1. Journal #102, August 20, 1977.

2. Ibid.

3. "The Writer and Her Craft," in *On Being Female, Black, and Free: Essays by Margaret Walker, 1932–1992*, ed. Maryemma Graham (Knoxville: University of Tennessee Press), 23–24. Hereafter, *OBFBF*.

4. Ibid., 23

5. "Richard Wright," in *Richard Wright: Impressions and Perspectives*, ed. David Ray and Richard M. Farnsworth (Ann Arbor: University of Michigan Press, 1973), 47–67.

6. James Baldwin, "Everybody's Protest Novel," *Notes of a Native Son* (Boston: Beacon Press, 1955), 22–23.

7. Michel Fabre, *The Unfinished Quest of Richard Wright* (Urbana: University of Illinois Press, 1973), 145.

8. Ibid., 195.

9. Ibid., 195.

10. Ibid., 197.

11. Claudia Tate, "Interview with Margaret Walker," *Black Women Writers at Work* (New York: Continuum, 1983), 62.

12. Dierdre Baer, *Simone de Beauvoir: A Biography* (New York: Simon & Schuster, 1990), 479.

13. Tate, "Interview with Margaret Walker."

14. "My Creative Process," *OBFBF*, 13–14.

15. *This Is My Century: New and Collected Poems* (Athens: University of Georgia Press, 1989), 152. Hereafter, *TIMC*.

16. Ibid., 164–66.

17. Conversation with Sonia Sanchez, July 20, 2014.

18. Journal #107, September 5, 1980.

19. Ibid., October 26, 1980.

20. Ibid., November 2, 1980.

21. Journal #108, December 31, 1980.
22. *TIMC*, 7.

Chapter 29

1. Conversation with Charlotte Sheedy, August 4, 2014.
2. Journal # 112, October 19, 1982.
3. Ibid.
4. Ibid.
5. Margaret Walker, unpublished autobiography, 103.
6. "A Brief Introduction to Southern Literature," in *How I Wrote "Jubilee" and Other Essays on Life and Literature* (New York: Feminist Press, 1990), 140. Hereafter, *HIWJ*.
7. "Oxford Is a Legend," in *This Is My Century: New and Collected Poems* (Athens: University of Georgia Press, 1989), 64. Hereafter, *TIMC*.
8. "Reflections on Black Women Writers," in *On Being Female, Black, and Free: Essays by Margaret Walker, 1932--1992*) (TennesseeKnoxville: University of Tennessee Press, 1997), 45–46. Hereafter, *OBFBF*.
9. In 1982, *Our Nig*, by Harriett E. Wilson: *Sketches from the Life of a Free Black*, was confirmed as the first known novel by an African American woman, published in 1859. The manuscript of *The Bondwoman's Narrative* by Hannah Craft, believed to have been written between 1853 and 1861, surfaced in the estate sale of well-known Howard University librarian Dorothy Porter Wesley in 2001. Henry Louis Gates, Jr is responsible for the recovery of both books.
10. Ibid., 48.
11. Ibid., 48.
12. Foote published a three-volume series, *The Civil War: A Narrative*, ending with the death of Jefferson Davis.
13. Lynch was a Natchez politician, the last surviving Black congressman of the Reconstruction era, and he became an author and historian.
14. *Mississippi Writers: Reflections of Childhood and Youth: Volumes I--IV*, Center for the Study of Southern Culture. Eed. Dorothy Abbott (Jackson: University Press of Mississippi, 1985, 1986, 1988, 1991).
15. "Mississippi and the Nation," *OBFBF*, 145.
16. MWA, unpublished MSms, 101.
17. "Chronology of Events Concerning the Richard Wright Book," Margaret Walker papers.
18. Journal #114, November 24, 1982.
19. Ibid., November 24, 1982.
20. Ibid.Journal # 114, June 21, 1984.
21. Ibid., September 20, 1984.
22. Ibid., September 20, 1984.

23. Claudia Tate, "Interview with Margaret Walker," in *Black Women Writers at Work* (New York: Continuum, 1983), 62.

24. Margaret Walker, " 'The Daemonic Genius of Richard Wright,' " by Margaret Walker," speech given at the Mississippi's Native Son: An International Symposium on Richard Wright, University of Mississippi, November 1985, 5, Unpublished.

25. Ibid.

26. *TIMC*, 135.

27. Ibid., 139.

28. Ibid., 139.

29. University of Mississippi, unpublished speech, ibid, 5. ovelrical workkcame athould be the sentence before given the war theme in this part.eas she had been expression in her journals [is this supposed to be here]

30. *TIMC*,Ibid., 144.

31. University of Mississippi, unpublished speech, ibid., 10.

32. Ibid., 11.

33. *OBFBF*, "Mississippi and the Nation," *OBFBF*, 146.

34. *Ellen Wright against Warner Books, Inc., and Margaret Walker*, 90-9054 Brief for Plaintiff-Appellant, 7.

35. *Ellen Wright v. Warner Books, Inc., and Margaret Walker a/k/a. United States District Court Summons in a Civil Action.* Decided November 21, 1991.

36. Jacqueline Trescott, "Margaret Walker and the Ghost of a Friendship," *Washington Post*, November 20, 1988, K 1.

37. Brief for Plaintiff-Appellant, 34.

38. *Ellen Wright v. Warner Books, Inc., and Margaret Walker Alexander*, Defendants' Reply Memorandum in Further Support of Cross-Motion for Summary Judgment. 89 CIV-3075, 2.

39. Ibid., 7.

40. Summons in a Civil Action, ibid., 6.

41. Jerry Ward, "An Open Letter to Michele Fabre," *Mississippi Quarterly* 43., no. 2 (1990): 235.

42. Milton Moskowitz, "Bizarre Conclusions: *Richard Wright, Daemonic Genius*, by Margaret Walker," *Threepenny Review* # 39 (autumn 1989):, 19–20.

43. Hazel Rowley, *Richard Wright: The Life and Times* (New York: Henry Holt, 2001).

44. Hazel Rowley, "Framing Richard Wright," *Yale University Library Gazette*, 73: (October 1998):, 56–63; 61.

Chapter 30

1. Margaret Walker, unpublished autobiography, Margaret Walker papers, Margaret Walker Center, JSU, 109.

2. "On Money, Race, and Politics," in *On Being Female, Black, and Free: Essays by Margaret Walker, 1932–1992*, ed. Maryemma Graham (Knoxville: University of Tennessee, 1997), 135–39, 136. Hereafter, *OBFBF*.

3. Ibid., 136.

4. Ibid., 135–36.

5. Ibid., 139.

6. English Standard Version, Biblehub.com/luke12-48.htm. Accessed August 16, 2014.

7. UB, 106.

8. Ibid., 108.

9. Ibid., 109.

10. Ibid., 105.

11. "For My People," in *This Is My Century: New and Collected Poems* (Athens: University of Georgia Press, 1989), 7. Hereafter, *TIMC*.

12. Journal #115, January 11, 1984.

13. *In the United States District Court for the Northern District of Mississippi Greenville Division, Settlement Agreement, Jake Ayers, Jr., et al., and United States of America v. Ronnie Musgrove, Governor, State of Mississippi, et al.. and United States of America*, 1990, 2.

14. "Mississippi and the Nation," *OBFBF*, 147; 150.

15. Houston A. Baker. "Critical Memory and the Black Public Sphere," *Public Culture* 7, no. 1 (October 1994): 3–33; 3.

16. Angelyn Mitchell, *The Freedom to Remember: Narrative, Slavery, and Gender in Contemporary Women's Fiction* (New Brunswick, NJ: Rutgers University Press, 2002), 6–10.

17. Journal #118, May 4, 1985.

18. Interview with Tommie Stewart, August 6, 2014.

19. *TIMC*, 200.

20. Ibid., 207.

21. Ibid., 206.

22. "Small Black World," *TIMC*, 205.

23. OBFBF, "Mississippi and the Nation," 146–49.

24. Journal #118, October 3, 1985.

25. Journal #128, April 28, 1990.

26. Ibid.

27. *TIMC*, 209.

28. Journal #129, July 15, 1990.

29. Unsigned contract between Franciscan Sisters of Perpetual Adoration, Inc., Sister Thea Bowman, Margaret Walker Alexander, and Harper & Row, Publishers, 1989.

30. All the books about Bowman were published by Catholic presses (St. Mary's, Sheed and Ward, Liquori). Orbis, a leading religious publisher, published a children's book and in 2010, her biography.

31. House of Representatives, Subcommittee on Postsecondary Education, Committee on Education and Labor. "Hearing on H.R. 3252, the Margaret Walker Alexander National African American Research Center, June 29, 1990," 2

32. Ibid., 3.
33. Ibid., 5.
34. Ibid., 40–42.

Chapter 31

1. Journal #128, 1990s undated
2. "Whose 'Boy' Is This?," in *On Being Female, Black, and Free: Essays by Margaret Walker, 1932–1992*, ed. Maryemma Graham (Knoxville: University of Tennessee, 1997), 162. Hereafter, *OBFBF.*
3. Ibid., 162.
4. Ibid., 162.
5. Ibid., 164.
6. Ibid., 165.
7. Ibid., 165.
8. Ibid., 166.
9. Ibid., 166.
10. Unpublished essay, Margaret Walker Papers, JSU.
11. Journal #121, June 19, 1992.
12. Ibid., April 7, 1992.
13. Limitededitionsclub.com/for-my-people. Accessed August 18, 2014.
14. Ibid, Limitededitionsclp`
15. Conversation with Doris O.Ginn, May 20, 2021

Chapter 32

1. Journal #131, February 4, 1992.
2. Ibid., December 16, 1992.
3. Ibid., April 18, 1993.
4. "Symbol, Myth, and Legend: Folks Elements in African American Literature," in *On Being Female, Black, and Free: Essays by Margaret Walker, 1932–1992*, ed. Maryemma Graham (Knoxville: University of Tennessee, 1997), 57.
5. Journal #127, 1990s
6. Journal #132, July 1995
7. Bettye Parker Smith, Unpublished interview with Margaret Walker, March 16, 1993, 4.
8. Ibid., 5.
9. "Solace," in *This Is My Century: New and Collected Poems* (Athens: University of Georgia Press, 1989), 193.
10. The George Moses Horton Society Conference Program, April 3–5, 1998, Chapel Hill, North Carolina.

11. Trudier Harris, interview August 18, 2020.

12. Joanne Gabbin, "In Memoriam: Margaret Walker Alexander (1915–1998), *Callaloo* 22, no. 1 (1999): v-vii; vi.

13. Memorial Service Program, December 4, 1998.

14. Eleanor Traylor, "'Bolder Measure Crashing Through': Margaret Walker's Poem of the Century," in *Fields Watered with Blood: Critical Essays on Margaret Walker*, ed. Maryemma Graham (Athens: University of Georgia Press, 2014 [2001]), 110–38.

15. Interview with Bill Ferris, April 1, 2014.

16. "Preface," in *This Is My Century: New and Collected Poems*, xi.

Recommended Reading

Alkalimat, Abdul. *The History of Black Studies*. London: Pluto Press, 2021

Berke, Nancy. *Women Poets on the Left: Lola Ridge, Genevieve Taggard, Margaret Walker* Gainsville: University Press of Florida, 2001

Brown, Carolyn J. *Song Of My Life: A Biography of Margaret Walker*. Jackson: University Press of Mississippi, 2014

Brown, Fahamisha Patricia. *Performing the Word: African American Poetry as Vernacular Culture*. New Brunswick: Rutgers University Press, 1999

Carmichael, Jacqueline Miller. *Trumpeting a Fiery Sound: History and Folklore in Margaret Walker's Jubilee*. Athens: University of Georgia Press, 1998

Cataliotti, Robert H. *The Music in African American Fiction*. New York: Routledge, 2018

Cook, Mercer and Stephen E. Henderson. *The Militant Black Writer in Africa and the United States*. Madison: University of Wisconsin Press, 1969

Davis, Arthur Paul. *From the Dark Tower: Afro-American Writers 1900-1960*. London: Howard University Press, 1981

Dolinar, Brian. *The Black Cultural Front: Black Writers and Artists of the Depression Generation*. Jackson: University of Press of Mississippi, 2012

Dunbar, Eve and Ayesha K. Hardison, eds. *African American Literature in Traditions 1930-1940*. Cambridge: Cambridge University Press, 2022

Eubanks, W. Ralph. *A Place Like Mississippi: A Journey Through a Real and Imagined Literary Landscape*. Portland: Timber Press, 2021

Ferris, William R., ed. "My Idol was Langston Hughes: The Poet, the Renaissance and Their Enduring Influence" (from a talk delivered by Margaret Walker), *Southern Cultures*, Summer 2010, 53–72

Freedman, Eden Wales. *Reading Testimony, Witnessing Trauma, Confronting Race*. Jackson: University Press of Mississippi, 2020

Hamada, Doaa Abdelhafez. *This Is Her Century: A Study of Margaret Walker's Work*. Newcastle upon Tyne: Cambridge Scholars Publishing, 2013

Harris, Trudier. *Depictions of Home in African American Literature*. Lexington Books, 2021

US. Congress. Committee on Education and Labor. Subcommittee on Postsecondary Education. *Hearing on H.R. 3252 the Margaret Walker Alexander National Research Center*, 1990

Gwin, Minrose C. *Remembering Medgar Evers: Writing the Long Civil Rights Movement*. Athens: University of Georgia Press, 2013

Hill, Ruth Edmonds, ed. *The Black Women Oral History Project: From the Arthur and Elizabeth Schlesinger Library on the History of Women in America, Radcliffe College*. Washington, D.C.: University Publications of America, 1991

Hine, Darlene Clark and John McCluskey, Jr., eds. *The Black Chicago Renaissance*. Champaign: University of Illinois Press, 2012

Miller, R. Baxter, Jr. *Black American Poets Between Worlds, 1940-1960*. Tennessee Studies in Literature, Volume 30. Knoxville: University of Tennessee Press, 1986

Morris, Tiyi. *Womanpower Unlimited and the Black Freedom Struggle in Mississippi.* Athens: University of Georgia Press, 2015

Muller, Timo. *The African American Sonnet: A Literary History.* Jackson: University Press of Mississippi, 2018

Nunes, A. *African American Women Writers' Historical Fiction.* London: Palgrave Macmillan, 2011

Parry, Tyler D. "The Politics of Plagiarism: *Roots*, Margaret Walker, and Alex Haley, in *Reconsidering Roots: Race, Politics, and Memory* edited by Erica L. Ball and Kellie Carter Jackson. Athens: University of Georgia Press, 2017, 47–62

Rambsy, Howard II. *The Black Arts Enterprise and the Production of African American Poetry.* Ann Arbor: University of Michigan Press, 2011

Rutkowski, Sarah. Literary *Legacies of the Federal Writers Project: Voices of the Depression in the American Postwar Era.* London: Palgrave Macmillan, 2017

Sievers, Stefanie. *Liberating Narratives: The Authorization of Black Female Voices in African American Women Writers' Novels of Slavery.* Wien: Lit Verlag, 1999

Smith, Charlene and John Felster. *Thea's Song: The Life of Thea Bowman.* Orbis Books, 2009

Sorett, Josef. *Spirit in the Dark: A Religious History of Racial Aesthetics.* Oxford: Oxford University Press, 2016.

Spillers, Hortense J. *Black, White, and in Color: Essays on American Literature and Culture.* Chicago: University of Chicago Press, 2003

Till-Mobley, Mamie. *Death of Innocence: The Story of the Hate Crime that Changed America.* London: Random House, 2003.

Thompson, Julius. *Dudley Randall, Broadside Press and the Black Arts Movement.* Jefferson: McFarland Publishing, 1998

Tracy, Steven C. *Writers of the Black Chicago Renaissance.* University of Illinois Press, 2011

Walker, Melissa. *Down from the Mountaintop: Black Women's Novels in the Wake of the Civil Rights Movement, 1966-1989.* New Haven: Yale University Press, 1991.

Williams, Delores S. *Sisters in the Wilderness: The Challenge of Womanist God-Talk.* London: Orbis Books, 1993

Williams, Seretha D. "Mother of us poets": Margaret Walker and the Black Arts Movement," in *With Fists Raised: Radical Art, Contemporary Activism, and Iconoclasm of the Black Arts Movement* edited by True Leverette. Liverpool: Liverpool University Press, 2021, 21–40.

Index

For the benefit of digital users, indexed terms that span two pages (e.g., 52–53) may, on occasion, appear on only one of those pages.

16th Street Baptist Church, 354

Abbott, Dorothy, 533, 556
Adams, Carol, 592
Aison, Gerta, see *Modern American Poetry*
Alabama State Normal School, 254–55
Alabama State Teachers College, 247, 255–56
Alcorn State University, 554–55, 577
Alexander, Margaret Walker, essays of
  "The Challenge of the 1970s to the Black Scholar", 371–72
  "Chief Worshippers at All World Altars", 365
  "Critical Approaches to the Study of African American Literature", 462–63
  "Curriculum Changes in Black Colleges III", 411
  "Humanities with a Black Focus", xvii–xviii, 327–28, 462–63
  "The Nausea of Sartre: A Review of *Nausea* by Jean Paul Sartre", 346–47
  "One Hundred Years Since Appomattox", 360
  "Reflections on Black Women Writers", 532
  "Religion, Poetry, and History: Foundations for a New Educational System", xvii, 327–28, 369, 407–8
  "Symbol, Myth, and Legend: Folk Elements in African American Literature", 462–63
  "What is to Become of Us?", xv, 75–80, 186, 357
  "Whose 'Boy' Is This?", xx
  "Willing to Pay the Price", 381–82
Alexander, Margaret Walker, family of
  Alexander Brown, Daisy, 194–95, 279–85, 292–97, 303, 308
  Alexander Williams, Margaret Elvira, xvii
  Alexander, Ella, 303
  Alexander, Firnist James, xv, 49, 274–77, 285, 308, 350, 517–19
  Alexander, Norma Grice, 441, 483, 518–19, 551
  Alexander, Patricia Patterson 441
  Alexander, Sigismund, 310, 312, 320, 335–36, 348–49, 367, 377, 391–93, 418, 441, 483, 509, 518–19, 523, 530–31, 551, 607–8

Coleman, Emmet, 551
Coleman, Marion Elizabeth Alexander, xvi, 283–84, 293
Dozier, Abigail, 7–8, 12
Dozier, Edward Lane, 7, 79, 523, 557
Dozier, Elvira Ware, xv, 7–9, 17, 283–84, 293
Rogers, Josephine, 278, 292
Walker, Gwendolyn Stewart, 15, 20, 45
Walker, Marion Dozier, xv, 3–13, 15–16, 19–21, 26–37, 39–62, 65, 67, 73–74, 79, 83–87, 95, 103, 157, 205, 226–28, 246, 257, 330–34, 534
Walker, Mercedes Elvira, 19–20, 32, 34, 42, 67, 85–89, 99, 109, 118–19, 196, 203, 218, 222, 225–28, 260, 322, 551
Walker, Rev. Sigismund Constantine, xvi, 25*f*
Williams, Dorothy, 278
Williams, Vernon, 509
Alexander, Margaret Walker, interviews and speeches of
  "Agenda for Action", xvii–xviii, 402
  "Black Women in Academe", 365, 460
  "Education and the Global Village", 596–97
  "Growing out of Shadow", xvi, 106, 286, 289, 344–45, 396
  "The Historic South, the Mythic South, the Violent South", 569
  "How I Told My Children About Race", 344–45, 396
  "My Creative Adventure", 215–16, 396
  "Race, Gender, and the Law", xx, 601–2
  "Revolution and the University", xxxiii, 327–28, 381–82, 408, 582
Alexander, Margaret Walker, poems and prose of
  "The African Village", 562, 570
  "The Aquarium", 384, 386–87
  "Birmingham", 419–20
  "Dear Are the Names that Charmed Me in My Youth", 61, 344–45
  "Epitaph for My Father", 69, 354

Alexander, Margaret Walker, poems and prose
    of (*cont.*)
  "Five Black Men . . . and ten will save the
    city", 443, 540
  "For Mary McCloud Bethune", 344–45
  "For My People" (poem), xxiii, 63, 78, 139,
    148, 171–76, 177–78, 179–81, 192–94,
    201–5, 216, 228–29, 237, 316–17, 322, 354,
    405, 410, 447–48, 459–60, 475
  "Harriet Tubman", 344–46
  "I know I have lived before", 601
  "Jackson, Mississippi," 316, 420
  "A Litany for Dark People", 344–45
  "On Police Brutality", 374
  "On Youth and Age", 511
  "People of Unrest and Hunger", 112–13, 167
  "Red Satin Dress," 125–26
  "Street Demonstration", 358–59
  "The Writer and Her Craft", 464, 501
Alexander, Margaret Walker, unfinished
    works of
  "Call me Cassandra", 513–14, 597, 599, 604–5
  "Goose Island", xxxv, 125, 147, 166, 170,
    190, 192, 210–13, 215, 288–91, 322–23,
    347, 506
  "Minna and Jim," 453–54, 513–14, 555–62,
    567–68, 582
  "Mother Beulah," 305, 307, 379–80, 387, 453–
    54, 513–14, 564, 573, 582
  "The Vision Splendid", *see* Alexander,
    Margaret Walker, unfinished works of,
    "Call Me Cassandra"
Algren, Nelson, 117–19, 164, 171, 177–78
Alpha Kappa Alpha Sorority (AKA), xvi, 313–
    14, 588
AME Church, 31, 158
American Book Award, xx
Amherst Festival of Women Writers, 471
Anderson, Marian, 35, 52–53, 85, 233, 257–60
Angelou, Maya, 426, 431, 464, 596–97
Annie Allen, 151–52
Assassinations, 354, 356, 376, 377, 407
Association for the Study of Negro Life and
    History, 233–34, 380
Astrology, 49–50, 314–15, 374, 392, 405, 527
Atlanta Arts Festival, 604
Atlanta University, 7, 77–78, 98, 247, 260, 345, 393
Attaway, William, 114–15, 144, 504
Autobiography, 161, 225, 279, 464, 513–14,
    555–56, 568, 572–73, 583, 594–97, 599–
    601, 605
Ayer Hall, xx–xxi, 584, 609
Ayers case, 554

Azikiwe, Nnamdi, 71, 517

Baker, Houston, 559–60
Baldwin, James, xix, 347, 362, 461, 468–69,
    503–4, 583
Bambara, Toni Cade, 431, 564
Baraka, Amiri, *see* Jones, LeRoi
Barber-Scotia College, 264
Barnett, Etta Moten, 435
Bell, Bernice, 394
Bellow, Saul, 117–18, 487–88, 494
Benet, Stephen Vincent, 105, 224, 237–45,
    255–56, 507
Bennett, Gwendolyn, 104, 201
Bennett, Lerone, see *Ebony Magazine*
Bethune, Mary McCleod, 11, 69–70, 235–36,
    267–68, 329–30, 344–45, 444, 470
Bethune-Cookman College, 329–30, 523
Billingsley, Andrew, 415
Black Academy of Letters, 401
Black Arts Movement, xvii, 143, 372–73, 419,
    477, 583
Black Belt, 4–5, 24–25, 128–29, 130, 254, 415,
    462, 468–69
Black Chicago Renaissance, 114–15, 120–
    21, 592
Black colleges, *see* Negro college
Black education, 10, 83–84, 155, 254, 324, 327,
    411, 513–14, 555–56
Black educational institutions, *see* Negro college
Black middle class, 11, 232, 249–50, 261–62,
    291, 395, 504–5
Black Panther Party, 395, 399
Black Power, 368, 377, 381, 391, 418,
    448, 469–70
Black students, 72–73, 220, 250–51, 368–69,
    378, 388–89, 455, 580
Black Studies, 371, 391, 411, 415–18, 462–
    63, 515
Black Women's Oral History Project,
    478, 567–68
Black writers, xxviii, 98, 109–10, 118, 138,
    186, 201, 235, 345, 413–14, 451–52, 502,
    507, 519–20
Blacks in the South, 22–23, 31
Bogan, Louise, 194, 202, 309
Bond, Horace Mann, 249–50, 255
Bonner, Marita, 120–21, 212
Bontemps, Arna, 73, 114–21, 134–35, 138, 150,
    228–29, 241–42, 281–82, 300, 318, 346–47,
    362, 388, 501
Botkin, Benjamin P., 210
Bourgeois, 112, 132, 169, 195, 367

Bowen, G.W.E., 7, 57
Bowman, Sister Thea, 572–74
Boyd, Herb, 493–94
Bragg, Linda Brown, 435
Braithwaite, William Stanley, 260
Brocks-Shedd, Virgia, 528
Bronzeville, 130, 151–52
Brooks, Gwendolyn, *see* Black Chicago
    Renaissance
Brooks, Nathaniel, 28–29
Brown vs. Topeka Board of Education,
    87, 405–6
Brown, Innis, 362–63, 458–59
Brown, James Russell, 155, 158, 171–72, 187–
    88, 199, 227–28
Brown, Lloyd L., 504
Brown, Marie, 431
Brown, Roscoe Lee, 564
Brown, Sterling, 114, 167, 228–29, 235, 241,
    297, 318, 345–47, 360, 501, 532
Buncombe, Marie, 234
Burroughs, Margaret Taylor Goss, 154, 419, 592
Burroughs, Nannie Helen, 11, 86, 89, 330–
    32, 365
Burrows, Vinie, 431, 435

Campbell, Ruth, 394, 527–28, 533
Cardinal Newman, 398, 408
Carmichael, Jacqueline Miller, 212, 476, 602
Carmichael, Stokely, 371
Carnival/Mardi Gras, 93–94, 588
Carter, Jimmy, 510–11
Cartey, Wilfred, 415
Carver, George Washington, 52, 559
Cassill, Verlin, 336, 351, 360–61
Catlett, Elizabeth, xvi, 220, 423*f*, 433–34, 482,
    497, 528, 588–89, 590*f*
Cayton, Horace, 132–33, 137, 146, 215, 503,
    537–38, 587
Central Alabama Institute, 16, 24–25, 28–29
Central Jurisdiction, *see* Methodist Church
Central United Methodist Church, 313–14, 609
Cheek, James, 537
Chicago Defender, 118, 144–45, 227–28,
    242, 303
Christian, Marcus, 303–4,
Civil Rights Movement, 37, 210–11, 228–29,
    269, 327–28, 358, 373, 377, 398–99, 405,
    418, 446, 476, 549, 574–75, 611
Clarke, John Henrik, 413, 415
Clayton, Jean, 313–14
Cleere, Ray, 577–78
Clemmons, Carole Gregory, 435

Clifton, Lucille, 435
Clinton, Bill [William], 580, 594–96
Cochran, Thad, 576
Cole, Johnnetta B., xx, 601
Cole, Vinson, 485
College Language Association (CLA), xvi,
    233–34, 588
Colored Juvenile Delinquent Rescue
    Association, 75
Coltrane, John, 291
Combahee River Collective, 449, 470
Common Ground, xvi, 116, 286, 305, 308, 396
Communist Party-USA (CP-USA), 115–16,
    132, 142–50, 186–97, 205–10, 261–62, 462
Conference on Africa and African Affairs
    (CAAA), 486
Conference on the Plight of the Cities, 487
Conference on the Teaching of Creative
    Writing, 501
Conroy, Jack, *see* Federal Writers' Project
Conyers, John, 415
Cook, Marvel, 196
Cooper, Brittney, 448, 451
Courlander, Harold, 492–94, 502
Crogman, William H., 7
Cromwell, Adelaide, 571
Culbertson, Frances, 220
Cullen, Countee, 252
Cunningham, Inez, 151–52
Currie, Alleane, xxxi, 391, 486, 527

Daily Word, 302–3, 373–74, 517
Danner, Margaret, xxxviii, 114–15, 151–53,
    418–19, 502, 583
Daughters of Margaret, xix, 527–28, 533
Daughters of the American Revolution, 256–57
Davis, Angela, 399, 448, 470–71, 540
Davis, Arthur P., 228–29, 235, 345
Davis, Ossie, 485, 564
Davis, Robert, 130, 143
Davis, Thadious, 415, 532
Dawson, GA, 294–95, 308, 365, 485
de Beauvoir, Simone, 388, 454, 505–6
de Santillana, Dorothy, 153, 360–62, 379–80,
    397, 472, 507
Dee, Ruby, 485, 564, 577
Delaware State University, 530
Dent, Albert Warner, 255
Derby, Doris, 406*f*, 413
Diaz-Diocaretz, Myriam, 556
Dillon, George, xvi, 122, 180, 202–3
Dodson, Owen, xxxviii, 143, 152–53, 167, 237,
    243, 318, 345–46, 501, 583

Douglas, Alta Sawyer, 245–46
Douglas, Ellen, 478, 502
Dove, Rita, 603, 605–6
Drake, Joseph Fanning, 254–55
Drake, St. Clair, 115, 131*f*, 132–33, 137, 146,
    215, 249–50, 388, 516, 565–66, 587
Dryades Library, 47, 96, 99, 519
DuBois, W.E.B., *see* Pan-Africanism
Dunbar, Paul Laurence, xvii–xviii, 36, 85, 105,
    241–42, 251–52, 457
Dunham, Katherine, 114–15, 118–19, 138–39,
    165, 245–46, 453, 596–97
Dunlap, Nadene, xxxii
DuSable Museum, 119, 154, 592

Ebony Magazine, xx, 401
Elections, 90, 207, 405–6, 408, 518, 533–34,
    550–51, 580, 587
Ellison, Ralph, xx, 83–84, 143, 194–95, 201–2,
    347, 362, 411, 475, 503–4, 583
Emecheta, Buchi, 591–92
Emotional health, *see* Illness
Engle, Paul, 150–51, 217–18, 222, 224, 238–39,
    337, 351, 472, 565–66
Espy, Mike, 576–77
Evans, Mari, 431, 476, 494–95, 502, 600
Evans, Walter, 495–96, 497
Evers, Medgar, xvii, 352, 376, 445, 576–78

Fabio, Sarah Webster, 435, 471–72
Fabre, Michel, 464–65, 466*f*, 468–69, 503, 515,
    537–39, 541, 545, 600
Fascism, 207–8, 253, 405, 445, 584, 597
Faulkner, William, xxviii, 174, 185, 234,
    307, 318
Fayetteville State College, 264
Federal Writers' Project, xvi, 113–15, 192, 210,
    215–16, 218, 240, 337, 506
Feminism, 26, 364–66, 456–63, 469–71, 589
Ferris, William Reynolds, 405, 478, 515
Festival of African Culture (FESTAC), 486
Finney, Nikky, xxi, 394
Fisk University, 53–54, 73, 245–46, 417
Flight to Canada, see Reed, Ishmael
Florida Agricultural and Mechanical University
    (FAMU), 523
Fluke, Ella, 69, 87
Foerster, Norman, 152–53, 217–18, 239
Folklore, 165, 185–86, 194–95, 210, 219,
    297, 490
For Farish Street, xix, 562–64, 569, 609
For My People (poetry collection), 105, 161,
    169, 239–44, 267, 290, 303, 329, 337–38,

344–45, 367, 379–80, 459–60, 476, 524,
    569, 588–89, 596
For My People: A Tribute Book and Exhibit,
    xx, 589–91
*For My People: The Life and Writing of Margaret
    Walker, see* McCray, Judith
Ford Foundation, 319–20, 329, 397, 418, 507–8
Fort Valley State College, 247, 249–53
Franklin, John Hope, 296–97
Freedmen's Bureau, 34–35
Freeman, Roland, xx, 581*f*, 589–91
Frost, Robert, 103, 237–38, 287–88
Furious Flower Poetry Center, 603–4, 605–6

Gabbin, Joanne, 394, 603–4, 606–8
Gaines, Ernest, 426, 478, 485, 502, 560–61
Gallagher, Buell, 255–56
Gammon Theological Seminary, 6–7, 29, 77–78
Gayden, Fern, 136, 170, 198
George Cleveland Hall Branch of the Chicago
    Public Library, *see* Harsch, Vivian
Giddings, Paula, 267–68, 394, 446
Gilbert Academy, 34–35, 42, 47, 53–54, 57, 61,
    62–63, 66, 86
Ginn, Doris, 575, 591–92
Giovanni, Nikki, xxi, 124, 382, 394, 419, 442*f*,
    446, 470–71, 519, 530
Gloster, Hugh, 360, 577
Govan, Sandra, 560–61
Great Depression, 67, 94, 112, 120, 141,
    150, 294–95
Green, Paul, 185, 297
Greenville, AL, 12, 297–98, 365, 485, 557
Guynes Street, xix, 313–14, 519
Guy-Sheftall, Beverly, 476
Gwin, Minrose, 456

Haley, Alex, xviii, 392, 415, 485, 488, 493, 502,
    521–22, 544, 561, 586, 596
Hamer, Fannie Lou, xxvi–xxvii, 358–59, 418,
    445, 488, 528, 549, 551
Harlem Renaissance, xxxiii–xxxiv, 120–21, 134,
    150, 201, 278, 294–95, 583
Harper, Michael, 429, 502, 564
Harris, Charles, 506–7, 524, 536–37, 544, 549,
    596, 599–600
Harris, Hilda, 485
Harris, Trudier, xxxvii–xxxviii, 365–66, 394,
    532, 541–42, 605–6
Harrison, Alferdteen, 508, 565–66, 572–73
Harsh, Vivian, 164, 210–11
Hayden, Robert, 152–53, 318, 345–46, 477, 501,
    583, 603

Hayes, Roland, 35, 52–53, 85
Health, *see* Illness
Hefner, James, 409, 588
Henderson, Stephen, 415, 463–64
Henry, Aaron, 358–59, 577
Henry, John, 125–26, 398
Hiatt, Jane, 577
High Point, NC, 277–81, 291–96, 302–6, 312,
    318–21, 530
Hill, Anita, 584–86
Hilliard, Elbert, 577
Himes, Chester, 504
Historically Black Colleges and Universities
    (HBCU), 236, 246, 368, 373, 388–89, 394,
    399, 411–18, 444, 451–52, 455, 463, 471,
    507, 580
Horton, George Moses, xxi, 605–6
House on UnAmerican Activities Committee
    (HUAC), 207
Hovey, Alma, xvii, 351,
How I Wrote Jubilee and Other Essays on
    Life and Literature, 288–89, 397, 490,
    582, 587
Howard University Press, xviii, 11–12, 220, 237,
    370–71, 380, 412–13, 416, 446, 506, 524–
    26, 536–37, 544–45, 582–83
Howe, Florence, xxxiii, 556, 589
Hughes, Langston, xviii, 36, 69–71, 85, 100, 116,
    134, 143, 174, 194–95, 201, 228–29, 233,
    246–47, 252, 294–95, 303–8, 318, 501, 532,
    564, 572, 596–97
Humanism, 109, 306–7, 412, 456, 460, 481,
    532–33, 609
Hungerford, Edward Buell (E.B.), 99–108, 117–
    18, 124, 152–53, 174, 186, 318, 329, 351,
    362, 382, 472
Hurston, Zora Neale, 52–53, 69–70, 164, 212,
    228–29, 235, 256–57, 287, 457, 461, 571,
    574–75, 596–97
Hutson, Jean Blackwell, 516–17

Illness, 39, 49, 85, 443, 510–11, 535, 545–46,
    549, 607–8
Indiana University, 304, 530
Institute for Juvenile Research, 113, 124, 137,
    211, 212
Institute for the Study of the Life, History, and
    Culture of Black People, *see* Margaret
    Walker Alexander Center
Institute of the Black World, 397, 407
International Conference on Black Women
    Writers and Magic Realism, xx,
    575, 591–92

International Symposium on Richard
    Wright, xix
Iowa Writers' Workshop, 152–53, 217–18, 337

Jackson State Massacre, *see* Jackson State
    University
Jackson State University, xviii, 319*f*, 486–87,
    576–77, 611
Jackson, Angela, 419
Jackson, MS, 90, 203, 224, 312, 363, 445,
    564, 570
Jacobs, Harriet, 363
Jeffries, Leonard, 415
Jet Magazine, 437, 481–82
Jim Crow, xxxvii, 20, 26, 84–85, 94, 203, 231,
    244, 274, 313, 512, 557
John Reed Club, 131–35
Johnson, Georgia Douglas, 104
Johnson, Grace Nail, 245–46
Johnson, Helene, 104, 430
Johnson, J. Rosamond, 53
Johnson, James Weldon, xv, 52–53, 73, 85, 120–
    21, 228–29, 241, 596–97
Johnson, John H., 401, 481–82
Johnson, Lyndon B., 376
Jones, Lawrence, 414
Jones, LeRoi, 375, 377–78, 382
Jones, Lois Mailou, 220
Jordan, June, 435
Jubilee, xxvi–xxxi, 18, 22–23, 90, 124, 153,
    166, 210, 227, 249, 280–81, 288–95, 297,
    298–300, 304–8, 316–17, 320, 322, 328–
    32, 336–38, 344–54, 357–58, 360–66,
    367, 375–76, 379, 382, 389, 396, 400–1,
    443–44, 446, 453–60, 472–75, 484–97,
    498–501, 506, 513–14, 516–17, 523–26,
    532, 541, 555–68, 588, 594–96, 602,
    605–6, 612
Judge Marvin Frankel, 493

Kay, Ulysses, 485
Kennedy, John F., 353–54, 376
Kennedy, Robert F., 377
Kent State University, 369, 530, 578
Killens, Grace, 413
Killens, John Oliver, xxxviii, 413, 564, 565–66
Killings, *see* Assassinations
King, Curtis, 394, 400–1, 402*f*, 495–96, 526–
    27, 577
King, Jr., Martin Luther, 130, 178, 333, 376, 407,
    443–47, 486, 508, 566–67, 578
Klein, Randy, xxi, 612
Knoxville College, 247

Kriege, Otto E., 57
Ku Klux Klan (KKK), 323, 358, 400, 557, 586

Lacy, Madison Davis, 600
Lamb, Clifford, 221–22
Laney, Lucy Craft, 99, 329–30, 444
Langston Hughes Festival, 564
Lawrence, Jacob, 230–31
Lawsuits, xxxi–xxxii, 515–16
League of Struggle for Negro Rights, 116, 207–8
Lee, Don, 397, 419, 607–8
Lee, Ulysses, 228–29, 345
The Left, 101–2, 114–18, 131–32, 137, 144–48,
   164–65, 180, 186, 201, 463
Lewis, Ida, 592
Lewis, Roy, 602
Libraries, 70–71, 72–73, 164, 210–11, 292–93
Library of Congress, xviii, 501
Lifeline politics, 457–59
Lincoln University, PA, 70–73, 530
Lincoln, C. Eric, 415
Lipscomb, Ernestine, 313–14, 314f, 394
Living Legacy Award, 510–11
Livingstone College, 230, 284–85, 299–300
Locke, Alain, 87, 120–21, 143, 194–95, 228–
   29, 346–47
Lorde, Audre, 435, 449, 470–71
Lyceum, 53–54, 74, 249–50
Lynching, 84, 147–48, 262, 389, 557

Madgett, Naomi Long, 418–19
Madhubuti, Haki, see Lee, Don
Margaret Walker Alexander Center, 572–73,
   582–83, 604–5
Margaret Walker Alexander Day, xviii–xix,
   516–17, 575
Margaret Walker Song Cycle, see Klein, Randy
Marshall, Paule, 429, 458, 564
Marshall, Russell, 136, 150, 170, 219
Marshall, Thurgood, 71
Mayfield, Rene, 524–25, 536–37, 599–600
McCarthyism, 150
McCray, Judith, see For My People: The Life and
   Writing
McDowell, Deborah, 532
McLemore, Lesley, 550–51
Mental health, see Illness
Methodist Church, 13, 19, 31, 47, 88–
   89, 254–55
Methodist Episcopal, see Methodist Church
Miami Dade Community College, 523
Middle Class, 11, 16–17, 26, 62, 232, 249–50,
   278, 411, 454, 470

Miles College, 13, 254–55
Miller, Ron Baxter, 152–53, 583
Minus, Marian, 136, 165
Mississippi's Native Son, see International
   Symposium on Richard Wright
Mitchell, Angelyn, 560–61
Modern American Poetry, 101–3
Modern Language Association, xx, 234
Modernism, 104, 105–6, 141–42, 153, 174,
   448–49, 477
Moir, Phyllis, 245, 246–47, 251, 270, 280–
   81, 295–96
Momon, Charlotte, xix
Monroe, Harriet, xv, 101, 122, 174
Moody, Ann, 377, 533
Moon, Henry Lee, 143, 245–46
Morgan State University, 251, 418
Morris, Willie, 478, 529
Morrison, Toni, xxvii, 363, 470–71, 532, 559–
   60, 564, 602
Motley, Willard, 114–15, 118, 144, 318

Nannie Burroughs School for Girls, 10, 11, 86,
   89, 332
National Association for the Advancement of
   Colored People (NAACP), xv, 11, 35–36,
   115, 133–34, 323, 352, 559, 577
National Association of Black Behavioral
   Scientists, 454–55
National Concert and Arts Commission, see
   Moir, Phyllis
National Council for Teachers of English, see
   Black Chicago Renaissance
National Council of Negro Women, 235–36
National Council on Women and the Arts
   (NCWA), 556–57
National Endowment for the Humanities
   (NEH), xvii–xviii, xx, 415, 609
National Evaluative Conference, 415, 416
National Negro Congress, xxxv, 115, 125–26,
   141, 207–8, 261–62
Neal, Janice K., 528
Negro art, 107–8, 216
Negro college, 57, 71, 134–35, 209, 232, 233,
   236, 251–52, 254, 258, 330–32, 335, 354,
   368, 371, 388–89, 453–54, 494, 557
Negro Digest, xvi, 344–45
Negro folklore, 165, 194–95, 219
Negro History Week, see Association for the
   Study of Negro Life and History
Negro literature, 136, 142–43,
   180, 234, 360
Negro music, 330–32

Negro spirituals, 257
Negroes and the Communist Party, 116, 132–33, 144, 187, 207–8
Neo-Slave Narrative, 561, 602
New Challenge, xvi, 112, 143–44, 166–68, 194–95, 198, 571
New Deal Democrat, 405, 551, 586
New Negro, xxxvi, 21, 35, 62, 120–21, 133, 166, 243, 345, 449
New Orleans University (NOU), 28–29, 34–35, 42, 65, 155, 209
New Orleans, 4–5, 27–37, 42–53, 61, 65–78, 82–83, 93–94, 100, 104, 110, 119, 152–53, 186, 203–9, 224–29, 233, 246, 254, 280–81, 290, 292–93, 302–4, 312–15, 330–35, 348–49, 387, 530–31, 592
Nixon, Richard, 376, 408, 445, 586
Nkrumah, Kwame, 71, 517
Nobel Prize, 487–88, 602
Norman, Cora, 444, 577
North Carolina Agricultural and Technical State University, 37, 264, 273
North Carolina College, 296
Northwestern University, xxiii–xxiv, 453
Norton Anthology, The, 304

O'Daniel, Therman, 251
Oakwood College, 73, 134–35
October Journey, xviii, 61, 69, 249, 263, 270, 320–21, 470, 569
Oden, Gloria, 429, 434
On Being Female, Black and Free: Essays by Margaret Walker, 1932-1992, 344–45, 449, 462, 467, 568, 582, 594, 599
Opera/South, 484–86
Orangeburg Massacre, 368–69, 375
Ostriker, Alicia, 105, 278
Our Youth magazine, *see* Colored Juvenile Delinquent Rescue Association

Pan-Africanism, 377–78, 484, 540
Park, Robert, 124
Parker, Mike, 576, 578–79
Peoples College, 417
Peoples, John Arthur, 388–91, 399, 403*f*
Perry, Bernard, 304
Petry, Ann, 318, 504, 532
Phillis Wheatley Festival, 432, 441–49, 464, 468–72, 494, 532, 603–4
Plagiarism, xviii, 488–92
Plantation, 34–35, 67–68, 297–98, 362–64, 458, 485, 569

A Poetic Equation: Conversations between Nikki Giovanni and Margaret Walker, 446, 448, 506, 519, 525–26
Police brutality, 368–69, 374, 395
Porter, Dorothy (Wesley), xxvii, 435, 436*f*, 582–83
Porter, James, 220
Predominately White Institution (PWI), 393–94, 405, 418, 580
Proletarian literature, 117–25, 132–33
Prophets for a New Day, xvii, 46, 358, 419–20, 421, 459–60, 569
Protest novel, 144, 503–4
Pulitzer Prize, 120, 150–51, 240–41, 287–88, 345, 414–15, 475, 528–29, 592, 603, 606
Pullman porters, 269–70

Race woman, xxxvii, 79, 267–68, 405, 452
Radcliffe College, 478
Randall, Dudley, 152–53, 418–19, 583
Raynaud, Claudine, 465–66
Reagan, Ronald, 376, 445, 518, 549, 586
Reddick, Lawrence, 244–45, 249–50, 297, 308, 582–83
Redding, J. Saunders, 244, 252, 318, 346–47, 378, 565–66
Reddix, Jacob, 310, 312–13, 388, 455
Redmond, Eugene, 428, 463, 478
Reed, Ishmael, 560–61
Reynolds, Barbara, 596
Richard Wright: Black Boy (film): 474, 533, 600
Richard Wright: Daemonic Genius, xxxi–xxxv, 146, 185–86, 491, 495–96, 502–3, 525, 538, 543–46, 549, 562, 567–68, 569, 587
Rodgers, Carolyn M., 432
Roosevelt, Franklin Delano, 90, 206, 408–9, 549
Rosenwald Fellowship, xvi, 135, 137, 230–31, 280, 297, 321

Sanchez, Sonia, 417, 419, 470–71, 494, 514, 530, 608
Saunders, Doris, 394, 502
Schomburg Center for Research in Black Culture, 280–81, 305, 516–17, 582–83
Segregation, 24, 63, 67, 114, 132, 203–4, 220, 231, 254, 270, 313, 323–24, 371, 415, 445, 540, 554–55, 557, 570, 578
Seventy-fifth anniversary of Jackson State, 501
Sheedy, Charlotte, 521–22, 564–65
Shukotoff, Arnold, 211
Silent Unity, 306, 367, 492, 498, 509–10, 517, 588
Smith, Bettye Parker, xxvii, 594, 602–3

Smith, Derek, 477
Smith, Dr. Robert, 49, 577, 608
South Carolina State College, *see* Orangeburg
    Massacre
South Side Writers Group (SSWG), xvi, 131–32,
    141, 252, 345–46, 571
Southern Black writers, 235, 519–20
Southern Historical Collection, xvi, 295, 297–
    98, 304, 319–20
Southern Negro Youth Congress (SNYC), 261–62
Southern Tenants Farmers Labor Union, 235–36
Spelman College, xx, 260, 601
St Elmo, *see* Williams, Augusta Evans
Stewart, Tommie, 394, 478, 527–28, 561–62
Stone, Chuck, 415
Strickland, William, 415

Talladega College, 53–54, 57, 225
Temple University, 514, 515, 530
Tennessee State University, 588
Terkel , Studs, 117–18, 602
Texas Christian University, 526–27
Third World Press, 397
*This Is My Century: New and Collected Poems by
    Margaret Walker*, 569
Thomas, Clarence, 584, 585
Thompson, Bennie (Congressman), 550–51
Tift, Nelson, 298–99
Till, Emmett, 324, 333, 353–54, 445
Tougaloo College, 367, 377, 413, 441,
    478, 484–85
Traylor, Eleanor, 98, 459–60, 609
Trent, William, 233, 236
Trescott, Jacqueline, 444, 544
Tulane University, 53–54
Tuskegee Institute, 6–7, 76–77, 259–60

University of Iowa, xxxiv–xxxv, 138, 199–200,
    217, 334, 468–69
University of Kansas, 502–3, 509–10
University of Miami, 523
University of Mississippi, 601–2
University of North Carolina, xvi, 295, 297,
    541–42, 605–6
University of South Florida, 523

Van Vechten, Carl, 275, 308
Voting rights, 254, 354, 368, 445
Vyry, see *Jubilee*

Wade-Crisler, Rosia, 527–28
Walker, Alice, xxvii, 424–26, 435, 456–57, 462,
    470–71, 531, 561

Wall, Cheryl, 532
Wangara, Malaika Ayo, 435
Ward, Jerry, 179–80, 316, 385–86, 463, 478,
    545, 606
Ward, Theodore (Ted), 114–15, 117
Ware, Randall, 17, 90, 280–81, 293, 297–98, 307,
    362–63, 459, 555–56, 557
Washington, Booker T., xxxiii–xxxiv, 6–7, 64,
    75–78, 186, 259–60, 330, 377–78
Washington, Mary Helen, 447–48, 461, 476
Washington, Walter, 577
Webb, Constance, 464–65, 537–38, 600
Welty, Eudora, xxviii, 234, 318, 360, 414–15,
    478, 502, 519–20, 528, 580
West, Dorothy, 136, 166, 571
Western College for
    Women, 348–49, 360
Wheatley, Phillis, xvii–xviii, xxvi–xxviii, 105,
    446–47, 459, 470, 494, 603–4
Whitehead, Alfred North, 398, 408
Williams, Augusta Evans, 307
Williams, John A., 426, 504, 507, 537–38
Williams, John Bell, 405–6
Winston-Salem Teachers College, 264
Winter, William, xviii–xix, 444, 516–17, 533–
    34, 577
Winters, Gloria Jackson, 528
Wirth, Louis, 117, 132–33
Wolfe, Thomas, 307, 360
Women's Liberation, xxxviii–xxxix, 430
Women's poetry, *see* Ostriker, Alicia
Wood, Grant, 220
Woodson, Carter, 186, 233–34
Woodson, Sue Cayton, 503
Works Projects Administration (WPA), xxxiv–
    xxxv, 114, 134, 144, 155–56, 170, 185,
    205–12, 215–16, 287, 296, 313, 414, 453,
    528, 551, 586
Wright, Ellen see *Richard Wright:
    Daemonic Genius*
Wright, Julia, 564–65
Wright, Luella Margaret, 221–22
Wright, Richard, xxxi–xxxii, xxxvi–xxxvii,
    83–84, 109, 114–15, 116–19, 127, 130–36,
    144–48, 159, 179–80, 185, 193, 211, 218–
    19, 223, 227–29, 282, 307, 345–46, 450,
    453, 461, 462, 464–65, 466, 468–73, 494,
    502–6, 515, 516, 525–26, 534, 536, 538,
    539, 543–46, 569, 571, 586, 596–97, 600

Yerby, Frank, 118–19, 144, 318, 561
Yette, Sam, 412–13
Young Communist League, 148–49